INDEX.

A.

Abbey, Buildwas, *App.* 6
——, Hales Owen, *ditto*, 13
——, Haughmond, *ditto*, 4
——, Lilleshull, *ditto*, 20
——, of St. Peter and St. Paul, 63
Abbots of ditto, 70
——, Principal of England, 68, n.
Abbot, Explanation of the Office of, 67
Adams, Dr. William, 224
Allatt's Schools, 273
Alkmund's (St.) Old Church, 94
—— New Church, 97 ; Vicars and Parish, 101, n.
Alkmund (St.) 97, n.
Anecdote of Rev. T. Stedman, 243, n.
Anderson, Thomas, shot, 257
Austin's (St.) Friars, 24, 103

B.

Bage, Charles, 248
Bagley, George, 237
Bailiffs and Mayors, 177
Bannister, Humphry, betrays the Duke of Buckingham, 27
Burges and Owners, 6
Battle of Shrewsbury, 22
Battlefield, Bullfield or Oldfield, 22
—— Church, 26. *App.* 5
Bellstone, 146
Benbow, Colonel John, 44, 208, n.
——, Admiral, 208
Benedictines, Account of, 63
Blase's (St.) Chapel, 106
Bowdler's, or Blue School, 117
Blakeway, Rev. J. B., 244
Brocas, Thomas, 218
Burney, Dr. Charles, 223
Burton, Edward, Esq. buried at Longner, 204
—— Family of, 204, n.
Bryan, Rev. John, 218
Butler, Rev. Archdeacon, 130, n.

C

Cadogan's (St.) Chapel & Fort, 36, 112
Cadman, Robert, fatal exploits of, 92
Catherine's, (St) Chapel, 106
Castle, Shrewsbury, 17, 139
——, Acton Burnell, *App.* page 21
——, Bridgnorth, *ditto*, 7
——, Cause, *ditto*, 12
——, Chun, *ditto*, 14
——, Ellesmere, *ditto*, 12
——, Knockin, *ditto*, 16
——, Ludlow, *ditto*, 8
——, Middle, *ditto*, 22
——, Moreton Corbet, *ditto*, 21
——, Oswestry, *ditto*, 19
——, Tong, *ditto*, 17
——, Watle-burgh, *ditto*, 18
——, Whittington, *ditto*, 13
Chad (St.) 78, n.
Chad's (St.) Old Church of, 79
——, Fall of, 79, n.

Chad's (St.) Alms Houses, 120
——, College, 120
Challoner, Thomas, 208
Chapel, Roman Catholic, 109
Charles I. visits the town, and borrows from the Free School, 34
—— Speech to the Freeholders, 35
Chester, Image of the Virgin at, 75
Cheshire Knights and Gentlemen slain, 24
Chirbury, 95
Churchyard, Thomas, 207
Chronological Account of Remarkable Occurrences, 259
Clive, family of, 187, n.
Clothworker's Hall, 139
Cole Hall, 148
College of Newport, *App.* 23
—— of Tong, *ditto*, 23
Corbet, Peter, commissioned to destroy Wolves, 20
Corbet and Corbett, families of, 11, 14, 20, 24, 36, 82
Corporation, List of, in 1775, 189
—— 1828, 190
—— 1836, *App.* 28
Courts of King's Bench and Exchequer removed to the town, 20
County Gaol, 143
—— Bridewell, 145
Council House, 148

D.

Davies, Dr. Sneyd, 224
De Courcy, John, 232, n.
——, Rev. Richard, 232
Derby, Earl of, beheaded at Bolton, 43
Dogpole, 49
Dominican Friars, 105
Domville, Silas, 218
Doomsday Book, Survey of Shrewsbury, 12
Draper's Hall, 136

E.

Earls of Shrewsbury, List of, 209
——, Roger de Montgomery, 11, 64
——, Hugh de Montgomery, 13 ; Robt. de Belesme, 14
East, Stone or English Bridge, 150
Edric Streon murdered, 10
Edmund, son of Ethelred, punishes the inhabitants for revolt, 10
Edward the Confessor, coinage of, 11
——, Prince, afterwards Edward I., appointed Governor, 19
—— 2nd's Parliament at Shrewsbury and Acton Burnell, 22
Elections & Members of Parliament, 193
Epidemical Distempers, 4
Ethelfleda, foundress of St. Alkmund's Church, 95, n.

Ethelred, King, holds his Court, 10
Ermley, Sir M. taken prisoner, 40

F.

Fairs, 173
Firman, Thomas, 240, n.
Franciscan, or Grey Friars, 104
Free Grammar Schools, Speeches of the Boys to Sir H. Sidney, 32
——, Loan to Charles I., 34
——, Account of, 120, 128, n.

G.

George's (St.) Chapel, 113
Giles's (St.) Church, 76
—— Hospital, 113
Glendwyr, Owen, and his Oak, 25,
—— brief memoir of, 167, e.
Grants and Charters, 162
Glover, William, 206, n.

H.

Haughmond Hill & Earl Douglas, 24
Henry IV. at Battle of Shrewsbury, 22
—— VII. enters the town, 28
—— entertainment on revisiting the town, 29
Hide of Land explained, 158, n.
Hill's Lane, 156
Hill's, Lord, Column, 277
Hospital of St. John the Baptist, 110
House of Industry, 120, n.
Howard, John, Bust of, 273
Howell, Thomas, 248

I.

Infirmary, Old, 132 ; New, 278
Inundation, Extraordinary, 274

J.

James II. entertained at Shrewsbury, 45
Jeffries, Judge, 46, n.
Jones, Sir Thomas, family of, 93
Jones's Mansion, 154
Jones, Henry, 248
Julian's (St.) Church, 101
Juliana (St.), 102, n.

K.

Kingsland, 254
Knights of the Shire, List of, *App.* 28

L.

Lancasterian School, 276
Leighton, Rev. Francis, 238
Lee, Rev. Professor, 117, n.
Leybourne's Monument, 25, n.
Liberties of the Town, 158
Llewellyn, Prince of Wales, 18, 21
Lyster, family of, 79, 90, 148

M.

Mackworth, Colonel, 43
Magdalen's, St. Mary, Chapel, 106
March, Earl of, leagued with Piercy, 23,—at Shrewsbury, 27

Marches of Wales, Earls of, and Court, 15
Mardol, 48
Mary's (St.) Church, 84 ; jurisdiction, 84, n.
———— Almshouses, 123
Matthews, Rev. James, M. A. 131, n.
Market House, 134
———— Cross, 135
Mayors of the Borough, since 1830, *App.* 28
Mason, James, Esq. 218
Meeting House, Presbyterian, High Street, 107
————, Independent, Swan Hill, 108
————, Baptist, High Street, 108
———— Ditto, Dog Lane, 109
————, Quakers, 109
————, Wesleyan, 109
Men at Arms, term explained, 25
Merival, 52
Mercer's Hall, 138
Michael's (St.) Chapel in the Castle, 106
———— New Chapel, 280
Millington's Hospital, 114, 116, n.
Minshull, Thomas, 248
Monastery, Wenlock, *App.* 10
————, Bromfield, *ditto*, 18
Monasteries, dissolved, and value, in Cheshire, *App.* ii.
———— Herefordshire, *ditto*, ii.
———— North and South Wales, *ditto*, iii.
———— Shropshire, *ditto*, 3
———— Staffordshire, *ditto*, ii.
———— Various parts of the Kingdom, *ditto*, i.
———— Worcestershire, *do*, iii.
Mortimer, John, slain in a tournament, 22
Mottershead, Rev. Joseph, 226, n.
Mysteries, or Religious Plays, 252, n.
Mytton, John, 27, n.—Maister, 28,
————, General, 36, 37
N.
Navigation of the Severn, 6
Nicholas's (St.) Chapel, 106
O,
Odericus Vitalis, 215
Offa's Dyke, 9
Okey, John, tombstone of, 43, n.
Oldest Timber House, 154
Onslow, Richard, tomb of, 80
Orders of the Corporation, 174
Oriel, 148
Orton, Rev. Job, 224
Ouseley, or Oseley, family of, 52, n.

Outeley, Sir Gore—Sir Wm. 53, n.
Owen, Rev. Hugh, 246
———— Gwynnedd lays siege to the town, the siege raised by Wm. I. 11
P.
Palmer, Rev. John, 240
Pantulph, Hugh de, 67
Parliament, origin of at Shrewsbury, 15
————, held again, and at Acton Burnell, 20 ; and under Rich. II. 22
———— Representatives in, 1836, *App.* 28
Parry, Joseph, 239
Phillips, Ambrose, 217
Phipps, T. and his son, executed, 271
Picture of Christ, poetical controversy about, 74
Piercy, Henry, slain at Battlefield, 23
Plague at Shrewsbury, 4
Plantagenet, Richard, Duke of York, 26, 203
———— George, 203
Plinlimmon Mountain, 5
Police, 162
Population and Bills of Mortality, 59
Powis, Princes of, 1, 9
Powisland, or Powysia, 1, 9, 145, n.
Powys, family of, 73, 104
Preston Gubballs, tragical occurrence at, 41
Price, Dr. Sampson, 207
Priory, Chirbury, *App.* 18
————, Alberbury, *ditto*, 17
————, Ludlow, *ditto*, 23
Pulpit in the Abbey Garden, 72
Pulteney, Sir William, 197, 237
Q.
Quarry Walk, 251
R.
Ralph of Shrewsbury, Bishop of Bangor, 204
Richard II. visits the town, 22
Robert of Shrewsbury, Bishop of Bath and Wells, 203
R. de Montgomery, memoir of, 65, n.
Rowland, Rev. John, 132, n.
Rowland, Rev. W. Gorsuch, 77 n.
Religious Houses, Catalogue of, *App.* 3
————, Suppression of, *do.* 1
S.
Sandford, Alice, exploit of, 100, n.
Sessions, Quarter, 173
Sextry, 48
Schools, Free, and Masters, 131, n.
Severn River, rise, progress, floods, fish, origin of name, 7
Scott, Dr. Jonathan, 247
Siege of the town by Owen Gwynnedd, 11

Siege of the Town by King Stephen, 18 ; taken by Gen. Mytton, 37
Sidney, Sir H. visits Shrewsbury, 30
————, death and burial of, 33
Shelton Oak, 25
Sheriffs, List of, *App.* 24
Shinewood, 27
Show, the Annual, 255
Shrewsbury, origin of the name, 1
————, situation, climate, epidemical distempers, soil, river, 3
Stedman, Rev. Thomas, 241
Street Act, Old, 57 ; New, 58
Streets and Passages, names of, 47
Studley, Peter, 217
Subscription Charity or Brown School, 117
Suffragan Bishops, 260, n.
Sutton Mill, 67
Sweating sickness prevalent, 4
T.
Tailors' Hall, 139
Talbot, Sir Gilbert, 204
————, family of, 210, n.
Tallents, Rev. Francis, 219
Taylor, Dr. John, 221
Theatre, 148
Thorpe, William, 215
Thomas, Dr. John, Bishop of Salisbury, 220
Thomas, Evan, 248
Town Hall, 133
———— Walls, 142
———— Bridewell, 145.
U.
Uriconium, or Wroxeter, 249
V.
Vaud, Switzerland, comparative salubrity of, 62
Vaughan's Place, 147 and n.
W.
Waring, Dr. Edward, 222
Wesley's, Rev. John, last visit to Shrewsbury, 243, n.
Weavers' Hall, 139
Welsh Bridge, 149
Webb's, Mr. Charities, 276.
White Hall, 153
Williams, Thomas Clio, 233
Whitchurch, Account of, 210, n.
Winefred (St.) account of, her bones removed to the Abbey, guild of, 16
Worcester, Earl of, beheaded, 26
Wood, Thomas, 228
————, Joseph, 234
Wolley, Dr. Edward, 207
Wrekin Hill, 8
Wroxeter, 2, 8, 249
Wyle Cop, 48

ERRATA, IN THE ORIGINAL AND PRESENT EDITIONS.

Page 17, l. 22, for *convoca* read *convoco.*—P. 48, l. 8, for *Cucumen* read *Cacumen.*—P. 49, l. 22, for *Aulum* read *Aulam.*—P. 90, l. 8, for *possuit* read *posuit.*—P. 130, for *Rev.* read *Judwine, Esq.*—P. 132, l. 35, after *trustee* add *or n subscriber of one guinea at least.*—P. 146, l. 29, for *Aulum* read *Aulam.*—P. 169, l. 29, for *suburbs* read *suburb.*—P. 193, l. 27, for *infra* read *intra.*—P. 204, l. 23, for *Longnar* read *Langner.*—P. 222, new edition, l. 29, for *Miscellaneous* read *Miscellanea* ; also l. 32, for *Bononia* read *Bologna.*—P. 44, stating that *no traces of Captain Benbow's grave-stone now exist,* is corrected p. 208.

The History And Antiquities Of Shrewsbury: From Its First Foundation To The Present Time, Comprising A Recital Of Occurrences And Remarkable Events, For Above Twelve Hundred Years, Volume 1

Thomas Phillips, James Bowen, Charles Hulbert

Gay

South View of Shrewsbury taken (From Hermitage Coffee-House) 1778

Engraved from the Original, for Hulberts' new edition of Phillips' History of Shrewsbury, by Cha. Askey 1828.

THE
HISTORY AND ANTIQUITIES
OF
SHREWSBURY,

FROM

ITS FIRST FOUNDATION TO THE PRESENT TIME, COMPRISING A RECITAL OF OCCURRENCES
AND REMARKABLE EVENTS, FOR ABOVE TWELVE HUNDRED YEARS;

WITH

AN APPENDIX,

CONTAINING

SEVERAL PARTICULARS RELATIVE TO CASTLES, MONASTERIES, &c. IN SHROPSHIRE.

BY THOMAS PHILLIPS:

THE SECOND EDITION,

WITH A CONTINUATION OF THE HISTORY,

NUMEROUS NOTES, AND ADDITIONAL PARTICULARS;

INCLUDING ALSO, THE

HISTORY AND DESCRIPTION OF THE COUNTY OF SALOP,

THE COURSE OF THE RIVER SEVERN, &c.

BY CHARLES HULBERT,

AUTHOR OF THE MUSEUM OF THE WORLD; RELIGIONS OF BRITAIN; ROYAL BIOGRAPHY;
CHRISTIAN MEMOIRS; SELECT ANTIQUITIES, &c.

Acquaintance with the History of our own country, furnishes the mind for conversation; and affords entertainment
to men of sense and reflection.—ESSAY ON HISTORY.
———————————— tactusque soli natalis amore.—OVID.

IN TWO VOLUMES.
VOL. I.

PROVIDENCE GROVE, NEAR SHREWSBURY:
PRINTED AND PUBLISHED BY THE EDITOR.
AND SOLD BY H. WASHBOURNE, LONDON.

1837.

70.333

TO THE

ILLUSTRIOUS NOBLEMEN;

TO THE

RIGHT HONOURABLE, AND THE HONOURABLE,

THE

REPRESENTATIVES IN PARLIAMENT

OF

THE COUNTY, AND BOROUGHS OF SHROPSHIRE;

TO

THE HIGH AND DISTINGUISHED COMMONERS;

TO THE

REVEREND AND VENERABLE THE CLERGY;

AND TO

EVERY LADY AND GENTLEMAN,

WHOSE NAME IS RECORDED IN THE APPENDED LIST OF SUBSCRIBERS;

THIS ENLARGED EDITION

OF THE LATE

MR. PHILLIPS'S HISTORY OF SHREWSBURY:

AND ALSO,

THE ORIGINAL HISTORY AND DESCRIPTION OF THE COUNTY OF SALOP,

INCLUDING

PORTIONS OF COUNTIES ADJOINING,

IS

WITH EVERY SENTIMENT OF GRATITUDE AND ESTEEM,

MOST RESPECTFULLY AND MOST DUTIFULLY INSCRIBED,

BY THEIR MOST OBEDIENT

AND OBLIGED SERVANT,

C. HULBERT.

Jan. 1, 1837

DEDICATION TO THE ORIGINAL EDITION.

TO

THE RIGHT WORSHIPFUL

NOEL HILL, Esq. MAYOR,

AND THE REST OF THE

ALDERMEN AND BURGESSES OF SHREWSBURY,

THIS

HISTORY OF SHREWSBURY,

IS (BY PERMISSION)

WITH THE GREATEST RESPECT DEDICATED,

BY THEIR

MOST OBEDIENT HUMBLE SERVANT,

THE EDITOR, (T. P.)

MR. PHILLIPS'S ADDRESS TO THE INHABITANTS OF SHREWSBURY, AND THE PUBLIC.

AN ardent affection for the place of my nativity, induced me in early life, to collect together all the particulars I could, relative to its first rise, with the various incidents and occurrences of succeeding centuries. In the course of twenty years, I had ranged together a considerable chronological list, which lately, by the favour of several gentlemen (to whom I acknowledge myself under great obligations) has much increased.

My own satisfaction, and the pleasure I participated in a retrospection to a variety of particulars, were the only incentives I had thus to employ myself; nor had I the most distant thought of publishing, until urged to it by several persons, to whom I had at different times communicated some of the historical passages I had before met with.

The importance of such an undertaking, together with a sense of my inability, and engagements I had on hand, of my own, and others for whom I am concerned, prevented my compliance with the requests of my friends; and moreover, understanding that several gentlemen had been collecting materials for a general History of Shropshire, I imagined anything of mine would, by a publication from some or other of them, be superseded.

Nothing of the sort appearing as yet, I have ventured to publish this short History, which (notwithstanding it may have many defects) has cost me much pains, and not a little expence. I trust this humble attempt will meet with your candour and approbation, being confident I have aimed at your entertainment, more than my own emolument; and flatter myself, you will meet with something calculated both to inform and amuse you.

> *I am,*
> *with hearty good wishes for the prosperity of*
> *the Town and Inhabitants of Shrewsbury,*
> *Your devoted humble Servant,*
> *THE EDITOR.*

Shrewsbury, July 1st, 1779.

PREFACE TO THE SECOND EDITION.

PRIOR to the year 1808, when that valuable little volume, "Some Account of the Ancient and Present State of Shrewsbury," by the Rev. H. Owen, made its appearance,—Mr. Phillips's History was the only separately published record of the Town extant. The *originality* of the undertaking, and the ability with which the work was edited, aided also by the active and valuable exertions of my late venerated father-in-law, Mr. Wood, obtained for it immediate patronage.

The work was announced for publication in the Shrewsbury Chronicle, of Sept. 19th, 1778: and March 6th, 1779, in a very lively advertisement, Mr. Phillips introduces the often quoted lines from Leland—

> " Built on a hill, fair Salop greets the eye,
> While Severn forms a crescent gliding by ;
> Two Bridges cross the navigable stream,
> And British alders gave the town a name."

On the 10th of April, he again advertises, and says—"The task is now undertaken, and I persuade myself, every one who reads the performance will meet with information and amusement. No private view or emolument has hitherto prompted me, and if that had been the case, I should be disappointed, as the *price* was *fixed* when it was intended to complete the publication in little more than *half* the number of sheets it will now extend to. The publication being for the most part local, it was natural to expect most encouragement from the inhabitants of Shrewsbury and its environs; notwithstanding which, the present respectable List of Subscribers, amounting to 400,* more than half that number are inhabitants of other towns, and many of them at a great distance."

On the 10th of May, he announced, his History would be ready to deliver to Subscribers, by the 1st of the ensuing month.

The price of the publication being fixed so extremely low—8s. with Plates, the whole impression did not pay its expences, and the Author was indebted to the liberality of his Printer for entire liberation from responsibility. The Plates, fourteen in number, were engraved by Hollingworth, who then resided next house to the Sun Tavern, Milk Street. These Plates, on the late proprietor of the Shrewsbury Chronicle coming of age, in 1807, were made the property of the present Editor, who, at *that* period, contemplated publishing a second edition of the work, with additions, in the manner he has *now* done. These Copper Plates were never delivered to him, and where they are he cannot say : and though of little value to any one else, they would have saved the expence of copies, and they *were his lawful property.*

In 1825, the valuable History of Shrewsbury, in 2 vols. Quarto, by the Rev. Messrs. Owen and Blakeway, was completed. The testimony these Reverend and learned Authors bear to Mr. Phillips's diligence, is concise, but to the purpose.—" The work," they say, " is creditable to the researches of Mr. Phillips, and we have never wantonly deviated from his statements, when we have had to travel over the same ground." In later times, the value which the public set upon Mr. Phillips's labours, may be estimated, from the fact, that copies, prior to the commencement of this new edition, sold at from two to three pounds. The copy purchased by the Editor, for the purpose of reprinting, was bought at the sale of the late Mr. Charles Llewellyn's Books, for £2 8s. The present edition contains every word of the original, except the List of Subscribers (never given in reprints); copies of all the Plates in outline, numerous interesting and illustrative Notes, very extensive additions, continuations, and index, superior paper and type, with other improvements, which, without enumeration, will be instantly cognizable, and acknowledged by the discerning reader.

Of the AUTHOR of the original work, the editor of the present edition regrets to state, there are no published particulars. He was a native of Shrewsbury, and at the time he published his History, was a Grocer, conducting his business on the premises now Mr. Hackney's China Establishment, Pride Hill. He was a Member of the Society of Baptists, a Deacon of their church, and always considered a conscientious, intelligent man. In the later period of his life, through the interest and influence of Sir Wm. Pulteney, of whom he was an *honest political opponent*, he obtained the situation of Tide Waiter, at Chatham.—Messrs. Owen and Blakeway say, Mr. Phillips died at *Shrewsbury*, in March, 1815 ;—the information of the venerated Authors,

---

*Out of which number, the present Rev. Sir Edward Kynaston, Bart., then a Student at Cambridge University, appears to be the principal, if not, the only survivor.—C. H.

happens, in this particular, to be a little inaccurate,—he died in LONDON, Jan. 9th, the year named. Mr. Phillips most respectably reared and educated a numerous family, including sons and daughters; of the latter, one is now the wife of the Rev. W. Gurney, of St. Clement Danes, London; another was the second wife of the late Mr. Henry Parry, formerly Draper on St. John's Hill, Shrewsbury, and which lady, it is said, resides in London; and a third married Mr. Jackson, Commander of a Merchant Vessel of the Port of Liverpool, whom she survives.

Of the delay in completing the volume, it is only necessary to remark, it has waited the completion of the County History; its value will not, however, be lessened by the circumstance, —various portions of the work having been enlarged, and have also received considerably more attention than was originally designed. The Appendix, though not *necessarily* connected with the volume, by binding therewith, will render *this* and the County History of similar dimensions, in which case it may be considered either a first volume, in connection with that work, or a separate one of the Town only, as may best accord with the taste and wishes of the proprietors.

C. H.

CONTENTS.

CHAP. I. SHREWSBURY—its Name, its Etymology, and Orthography . . . . . p. 1
CHAP. II. Situation, Climate, Epidemical Distempers, Soil, River, &c. . . . p. 3
CHAP. III. Ancient History . . . . . p. 8
CHAP. IV. Names of Streets and Passages . . . . p. 47
CHAP. V. Number of Inhabitants, and Bills of Mortality . . . . . p. 59
CHAP. VI. Public Structures, viz.—The Abbey, p. 63. St. Giles's Church, p. 76. St. Chad's Ditto, p. 77. St. Mary's Ditto, p. 84. St. Alkmund's Ditto, p. 94. St. Julian's Ditto, p. 101. Austin's Friary, p. 103. Franciscan ditto, p. 104. Dominican Ditto, p. 105. St. Michael's Chapel, p. 106. St. Nicholas's Ditto, ibid. St. Catharine's Ditto, ibid. St. Blase's ditto, ibid. St. Mary Magdalen's Ditto, ibid. Dissenting Meeting Houses, p. 107. St. John's Hospital, p. 110. St. Giles's Ditto, p. 113. Millington's Ditto, p. 114. Bowdler's Charity School, p. 117. Subscription Ditto, ibid. Orphan Hospital, p. 119. St. Chad's Almshouses, p. 120. St. Mary's Ditto, p. 123. Free Schools, p. 124. Infirmary, p. 132. Town Hall, p. 133. Market House, p. 134. Market Cross, p. 135. Drapers Hall, p. 136. Mercers Ditto, p. 138. Taylors Ditto, p. 139. Weavers Ditto, ibid. Clothworkers Ditto, ibid. The Castle, ibid. Town Walls, p. 142. County Gaol, p. 143. County Bridewell, p. 145. Town Ditto, ibid. Chorlton Hall, ibid. Bell Stone, p. 146. Vaughan's Place, p. 147. Cole Hall, p. 148. Council House, ibid. The Theatre, ibid. The Oriel, ibid. Welsh Bridge, p. 149. New Bridge, p. 150.
CHAP. VII. Extent of the Town Liberties . . . . . p. 158
CHAP. VIII. Internal Police . . . . . p. 162
CHAP. IX. Elections . . . . . p. 193
CHAP. X. Anecdotes of eminent and learned Men, who were born or inhabited in the Town or its neighbourhood, &c. . . . . . p. 203
CHAP. XI. The Environs . . . . . p. 249
CHAP. XII. A Chronological Account of Occurrences not reducible to, or omitted under the former heads . . . . . p. 269
APPENDIX. Account of Castles and Monasteries in Shropshire; Lists of Sheriffs, Knights of the Shire, &c.

DIRECTIONS to the BINDER for PLACING the PLATES.

View of Shrewsbury to face the Title-page.
The Abbey . . . . . p. 63
St. Giles's Church 76
St. Chad's ditto 77
St. Mary's ditto 84
St. Alkmund's ditto 94
St. Julian's ditto 101
Orphan Hospital 119

Free Schools . . . . p. 124
Infirmary 132
General State of ditto 133
Market-House, and Cross 135
The Castle 139
Welsh Bridge 149
New Bridge 150

SHROPSHIRE PAROCHIAL VALUATION, JANUARY, 1837.

On the eve of this volume being entirely completed, the following New Valuation of the Parishes, Chapelries, and Townships in the County, was published by the Treasurer, J. J. PEELE, Esq.—Its insertion at so late a period, and also of the Table, containing the Value of the Benefices in Shropshire, will not, the Publisher humbly hopes, be useless to, or unobserved by that respectable class of readers, for whose advantage they are designed. The County Rate for this year will be One Halfpenny in the Pound.

After the name of each place, the letter *t* means Township ; *c* means Chapelry ; *p* means Parish ; H. means Hundred.

Name of Place	Ann. Value £
ALBRIGHTON NEW DIVISION.	
Astley, c	1357
Albrighton, c	934
Battlefield, p	1133
Broughton, p	1541
Clive, c	2080
Fitz, p	2693
*Hadnal, c	2654
Haughmond, extra parochial	1227
Grinshill, p	1694
Preston Gobalds, p	2759
St. Alkmond, Shrewsbury, p	4278
St. Mary, ditto, p	5990
Uffington, p	1997
BRADFORD H.	
Drayton Division.	
Adderley, p	3540
Cheswardine, p	6937
Drayton, p	16920
Ercall parva, p	3760
Hinstock, p	2665
Hodnet, p	13638
Moreton Sea, p	4916
Mucclestone, p	4785
Norton, p	2446
Stoke-upon-Tern, p	6744
Newport Division.	
Cherrington, t	1287
Chetwynd, p	5363
Chetwynd Aston, t	2383
Church Aston, c	3157
Edgmond, p	5700
Great Bolas, p	2910
Kinnersley, p	2520
Lilleshall, p	10028
Longford, p	3011
Newport, p	7171
Preston-on-the-Wild Moors, p	1466
Sherif Hales, p	2178
Tibberton, c	1819
Woodcote, c	1667
Wellington Division.	
Atcham, p	7602
Buildwas, p	2153
Eaton Constantine, p	1274
Ercall Magna, p	13391
Eyton-on-the-Wild Moors, p	1623
Great Dawley, p	10125
Leighton, p	2739
Longden-upon-Tern, p	951
Rodington, p	2344
Stirchley, p	2187
Uppington, p	897
Upton Magna, p	4663
Waters Upton, p	1162
Wellington, p	24571

Name of Place	Ann. Value £
Withington, p	1825
Wombridge, p	2290
Wrockwardine, p	11691
Wroxeter, p	6803
Whitchurch Division.	
Ightfield, p	1843
Lee Brockhurst, p	1797
Prees, p	16193
Stanton, p	4492
Whitchurch, p	29409
Wem New Division.	
Moreton Corbet, p	2306
Shawbury, p	7018
Wem, p	22605
Weston, c	2583
BRIMSTREE H.	
Bridgnorth Division.	
Claverley, p	12000
Worfield, p	13711
Shiffnal Division.	
Albrighton, p	6192
Badger, p	1047
Beckbury, p	1880
Bonningale, p	1694
Boscobel	600
Donnington, p	3743
Kemberton, p	1835
Ryton, p	1998
Shiffnal, p	25097
Stockton, p	4865
Sutton Maddock, p	4752
Tonge, p	5438
Hales Owen Division.	
Cakemore, t	1181
Hales Owen, t	3466
Hasbury, t	2164
Hawn, t	1044
Hill, t	2355
Hunnington, t	1709
Illey, t	488
Langley, t	1317
Lapal, t	1658
Oldbury, t	15868
Ridgacre, t	1232
Romsley, t	1936
Warley, t	1509
CHIRBURY H.	
Upper Division.	
Brompton and Rhistou, t	2239
Chirbury, p	11272
Lower Division.	
Muckelwick, t	241
Shelve, p	454
Worthen, p	10643
CLUN H.	
Mainstone Division.	
Bettus, p	2540
Llanvair, p	3546
Mainstone, p	2166
Clun Division.	
Clun, p	

Name of Place	Ann. Value £
CONDOVER H.	
Cound Division.	
Acton Burnell, p.	2453
Berrington, p	5660
Church Preen, p	1155
Cressage, c	1785
Cound, p	5189
Harley, p	2357
Kenley, p	1400
Pitchford, p	2072
Ruckley & Langley, c	917
Condover Division.	
Church Pulverbatch, p	4112
Condover, p	9933
Frodesley, p	2275
Leebotwood, p	1391
Longnor, p	1195
Smethcott, p	2076
Stapleton, p	3693
Sutton, p	1016
Meole Brace, p, part of	6169
Woolstaston, p	951
St. Julian, Shrewsbury, p	1822
FORD H.	
Ford Division.	
Alberbury, Lower, p	8315
Cardiston, p	2651
Ford, p	1701
Minsterley, c	2776
Westbury, p	10203
Wollaston, c	3421
St. Chad, Shrewsbury, p	11605
Great Hanwood, p	992
Pontesbury Division.	
Habberley, p	995
Pontesbury, p	16073
MUNSLOW H.	
Upper Division.	
Acton Scott, p	1591
Cardington, p	4645
Church Stretton, p	5202
Eaton, p	3722
Hope Bowdler, p	1129
Rushbury, p	2822
Shipton, p	2313
Lower Division.	
Abdon, p	759
Ashford Bowdler, p	1243
Ashford Carbonel, p	1940
Clee St. Margaret, p	748
Bromfield, p	7509
Cold Weston, p	241
Culmington, p	4687
Diddlebury, p	9668
Easthope, p	802
Halford & Dinchop, c	1434
Heath, c	470
Holdgate, p	1359

Name of Place	Ann. Value £
Hopton, p	312
Long Stanton, p	2148
Ludford, Salop, p.	2066
Munslow, p	3500
Onibury, p	2124
Richard's Castle, p	2949
Stanton Lacy, p	11171
Stokesay, p	3542
Tugford, p	1622
OSWESTRY H.	
Upper Division.	
Llanyblodwell, p	5380
Llanymynech, p	2811
The out-liberties of Oswestry	16316
Saint Martin, p	7211
Selattyn, p	6088
Soughton, t	1414
Whittington, p	14154
Lower Division.	
Kynnerley, p	7780
Knockin, p	2032
Melverley, p	2271
Ruyton, p	5648
West Felton, p	8276
Town of Oswestry	14244
OVERS H.	
Bitterley, p	5350
Burford, p	6275
Greet, p	971
Milson, p	996
Neen Sollers, p	1258
Silvington, p	364
Whitton, t	692
PIMHILL H.	
Ellesmere Division.	
Ellesmere, p	26767
Hordley, p	2753
Loppington, p	4308
Middle, p	5056
Welshampton, p	1925
Baschurch Division.	
Baschurch, p	9647
Great Ness, p	4722
Little Ness, c	1451
Montford, p	4340
Petton, p	1075
Shrawardine, p	2663
PURSLOW H.	
Bishop's Castle Division.	
Borough of Bishop's Castle	4715
Liberties of ditto	4264
Dinmore, extra parochial	150
Lydbury North, p	8009
Lydham, p	2325
Mindtown, p	506
More, p	2223
Norbury, p	2980
Ratlinghope, p	2111
Wentnor, p	3152

Name of Place	Ann. Value £
Stow Division.	
Bedstone, p	
Bucknell, p	2009
Clunbury, p	7779
Clungunford, p	3968
Edgton, p	1300
Hopesay, p	4512
Hopton Castle, p.	1696
Sibdon, p	824
Stow, p	1495
Wistanstow, p	6008
STOTTESDEN H.	
Aston Botterell, p	1749
Burwarton, p	1018
Cainham, p	3326
Cleobury Mortimer, p	8980
Coreley, p	2943
Hope Baggot, p	497
Hopton Wafers, p	1669
Kinlet, p	5659
Loughton, c	513
Neen Savage, p	3774
Stottesden, p	7810
Wheathill, p	1286
Chelmarsh Division.	
Acton Round, p	1183
Alveley, p	4716
Astley Abbotts, p	3256
Aston Ayres, t	1196
Billingsley, p	1003
Chelmarsh, p	3294
Chetton, p	3563
Cleobury North, p	1015
Deuxhill, p	530
Eardington, t	1765
Glazeley, p	639
Higley, p	1341
Middleton Scriven, p	740
Morvil, p	3558
Neenton, p	828
Oldbury, p	2120
Quat Malvern, t	1500
Shineton, p	1384
Rudge, t	1417
Sidbury, p	1220
Romsley	1300
Tasley, p	1319
Upton Cressett, p	910
Borough of Wenlock.	
Barrow, p	2323
Benthall, p	1668
Broseley, p	6178
Ditton Priors, p	2807
Hughley, p	930
Linley, p	865
Little Wenlock, p	3932
Madeley, p	11636
Monk Hopton, p	1463
Much Wenlock, p	10378
Posenhall	409
Willey, p	1331

* Since printing the account of Hadnal Chapel of Ease, page 249, the want of due accommodation in Pews and Free Sittings, there expressed, has been honoured with unexampled attention, and the humblest of efforts received a thousand-fold reward, in the prompt and liberal contributions of noble-minded individuals, for the erection of a Gallery, &c.—exceeding even the estimated expence of the undertaking.—This circumstance has contributed greatly to cheer the author's wearied spirits.—C. H.

LIST OF ENGRAVINGS, WITH DIRECTIONS TO THE BINDER.

FRONTISPECE, containing FIFTEEN SUBJECTS, viz.—the *Source of the Severn, on Plinlimmon Hill; Newtown Church; the *Wrekin Hill; the Iron Bridge; King Road, near Bristol; the *County Hall, and the Infirmary, Shrewsbury; the new *Longner Hall; Ellesmere Church, from a beautiful lithographic print, just published by Mr. Baugh, of Ellesmere; *Boscobel House and Royal Oak; *Bolas Church and part of Rectory; Powis Castle; Ludlow Castle; St. Alkmund's, or the Old Church of Whitchurch; *Battlefield Church.

BODHILIN, Seat of J. Humphreys, Esq.—to face page 6
†MAP OF THE COUNTY . . ———— 9
VALE CRUCIS ABBEY . . ———— 72

PORTRAIT OF GEN. LORD HILL—to face page 121
————— ARCHDEACON GORBETT ———— 184
————— OF JAMES II. . ———— 208
PROVIDENCE GROVE . . ———— 252
MILITARY & NAVAL HEROES . ———— 254
VIEW OF SHREWSBURY . . ———— 289
PLAN OF SHREWSBURY . . ———— 295
ST. CHAD'S CHURCH, SHREWSBURY ———— 296
PULPIT IN THE ABBEY GARDEN ———— 304
LORD HILL'S COLUMN . . ———— 305
SHREWSBURY CASTLE . . ———— 311
PORTRAIT of Rev. JOHN FLETCHER ———— 346
WENLOCK ABBEY . . ———— 355

Those marked thus (*) are from original drawings, made expressly for this work.
† The Map was executed under the entire direction of the late Mr. D. Parkes.

CORRECTIONS.

The following may be considered as errors of the press, chiefly occasional oversights, and many of them exist only in a few impressions of the sheets,—having been observed and corrected while in printing.

Page 25, last line but 2, for Gamen Junciodes, read Gramen Juncoides

26 for Rosmerjnum, read Rosmarinum; for Clubmass, read Club moss; for Alchymilla, read Alchemilla; for Pinquicula, read Pinguicula; for Caryophillus, read Caryophyllus; for Palystre, read Palustre; for Helleborine, read Helleborus; for Canda, read Cauda; for Fraximus, read Fraxinus; for Vaccina, read Vaccinia; line 41, for Mendip, read Stretton

27 for odorato, read odorata; for Echium, read Echinum; for Campantla, read Campanula; for Hair Bell, read Hare-bell; for Ohrysosplinium, read Chrysosplenium

28 for hyderaceus, read hederaceus; for Galepsis galeybdolon, read Galeopsis galeobdolon; for Schrophularia, read Scrophularia; for tennifolium, read tenuifolium; for Geranuium, read Geranium

29, line 16, for lispidus, read hispidus
50 — 27, for were, read was
56 — 29, for legitimacy, read illegitimacy
62 — 31, the Monument of Richard Herbert, see Concluding Observations, page 357
71 — 2, for Jones, Robinson, read Robinson Jones
— 3, for Thomas, read Edward
— 5, for Whittal, read Whitehall
73 — 4, for latter, read former
75 — 1, for one, read four
108 — 9, for is, read are
115 — 25, for Donnington, read Dorrington
116 — 7, for Balleport, read Bellaport
127 — 17, for whom, read who
129 — 42, for vicarage, read rectory, the residence of the Rev. J. M. Long, present rector
130 — , for the Townships of Whitchurch, as there arranged, read Alkington, Ash Parva, Ash Magna, Black Park, Broughall, Dodington, Edgeley, Hinton, Hollyhurst, and Chinnel; Tilstock, Old Woodhouses, New Woodhouses, and Whitchurch
132 — 13, in a very few copies, for 1745, read 1785
145 — 1, for have, read give
168 in a few copies, for Anuca, read Amica; for tantœ, read tantæ; for firmæ, read firmæ; for retilyerunt, read restituerunt

Page 153, line 8, for Bull Inn, read Bull's Head Inn
171 — 21, for elegant tomb, read a plain flat stone, surrounded with iron pallisading
180 — 6, for seat, read residence
184 — 7, read R. S. instead of J. R.
192 — 3, for Frances, read Francis
194 — 11, for John, read William
195 — 16, for Norton Lodge, read Horton Lodge
199 — 16, for are upwards, read is upwards
200 — 20, read M. Y. instead of N. G.
211 — 15, for Broughton, read Boughton
— 28, read Rev. C. and omit the R.
— 40, for conical, read pyramidical
213 — 38, for vulgularly, read vulgarly
215 where Middleton occurs, read Myddelton
226 — 11, dele of the Lords
228 the notice respecting the monument appeared in a Shrewsbury Paper: for Tettensor, read Titteratone
232 — 25, for have, read has
246 — 14, for has been and is, read have been and are
254 47, note, for oversteps and propagates, read overstep and propagate
265 — 32, for Edward, read Edmund; 10 lines below, for White, read Wight
275 — 36, note, for restudo, read testudo
276 — 34, for Chapels, read Chapelries
282 — 27, for devised, read alienated
292 — 4, for Trenecatus, read Truncatus
301 — 9, omit the comma after breathes
— 10, for by, read with; L 19, for view, read vein
302 — 16, omit the first the, and read, But oh lovely the sunset, &c.
310 — 17, for was, read were
312 — 37, for stands, read stand
313 — 26, read five sycamore trees; for Powis, read Powys
314 — 6, after plan, read on which
316 — 15 and 28, for stands, read stand
336 — 37, for Acton Dalburgh, read Dalburgh Acton
343 — 2, in 43 copies, for local bank, Messrs. Pritchard, read the local bank of Messrs. Pritchard
347 — 25, for there are no places, read there is no place
348 — 19, for whence, read which
352 — 30, for Hon. G. C. Forester, read G. C. W., and for Miles, read Milnes

The Liber Ecclesiasticus gives the following as present Patrons of the several Livings named.

Page 106—Adderley, H. C. Cotton, Esq.
107—Cheswardine, G. S. Harding, Esq.
107—Drayton, Trustees of Sir C. Corbet
116—Stoke-upon-Terne, R. Corbet, Esq.
117—Lee Brockhurst, John Walford, Esq.
139—Longdon-upon-Terne, is corrected page 194
145—Buildwas is of exempt jurisdiction
146—Dawley and Stirchley, are corrected page 194

Page 147—Ercall Magna, the Earl of Darlington
159—Kemberton, R. Slaney, Esq.
164—Donnington, Duke of Sutherland
181—Harley, the Duke of Cleveland
208—Longford, Thomas Leeke, Esq.
226—Melverley, the Bishop of St. Asaph
151—Upton Magna, St. Lucia as the Patron Saint.

TO THE

ILLUSTRIOUS NOBLEMEN;

TO THE

RIGHT HONOURABLE, AND THE HONOURABLE,

THE

REPRESENTATIVES IN PARLIAMENT

OF

THE COUNTY, AND BOROUGHS OF SHROPSHIRE;

TO

THE HIGH AND DISTINGUISHED COMMONERS;

TO THE

REVEREND AND VENERABLE THE CLERGY;

AND TO

EVERY LADY AND GENTLEMAN,

WHOSE NAME IS RECORDED IN THE APPENDED LIST OF SUBSCRIBERS;

THIS

ORIGINAL HISTORY AND DESCRIPTION OF THE COUNTY OF SALOP,

INCLUDING

PORTIONS OF COUNTIES ADJOINING,

IS

WITH EVERY SENTIMENT OF GRATITUDE AND ESTEEM,

MOST RESPECTFULLY AND MOST DUTIFULLY INSCRIBED,

BY THEIR MOST OBEDIENT
AND OBLIGED SERVANT,

C. HULBERT.

Jan. 1, 1837.

LIST OF SUBSCRIBERS.

Royal Paper.
(Only Sixty copies printed.)

His Grace the Duke of Newcastle
The Most Noble the Marquis of Anglesey
Right Hon. the Earl of Darlington
Right Hon. the Earl of Shrewsbury
Right Hon. the Earl of Tankerville
Right Hon. the Earl Spencer
Right Hon. the Earl of Powis
Right Hon. the Earl Kilmorey
Right Hon. Lord Viscount Clive
Hon. and Right Rev. the Lord Bishop of Lichfield and Coventry, *deceased*
Right Hon. Lord Forester
Right Hon. Sir Gore Ouseley, Bart.
Sir. W. Ouseley, Knt. LL.D.
Sir G. Naylor, Knt. King-at-Arms, *dec.*
Amott, John, Esq. Gloucester
Betteley, Joseph, Esq. Liverpool
Bright, Rev. J. B. Totterton Hall, Salop
Bucknall, Jas. Esq. Ketley Bank, Salop
Cartwright, Mr. Admaston, Salop
Cooper, Wm. Esq. Solicitor, Shrewsbury
Corbett, the Venerable and Rev. Archdeacon, Longnor Hall, Salop
Corbett, Panton, Esq. late M.P. for Shrewsbury, Leighton Hall, Montgomeryshire
Corfield, Rev. Richard, M. A. Pitchford
Darby, Richard, Esq. Coalbrookdale
Darby, Francis, Esq. Ditto
Ford, Rich. Esq. Solicitor, Shrewsbury
Harley, Wm. Esq. Shrewsbury
Howell, Mr. St. John's Hill, Shrewsbury
Iliffe, Rev. F. M. A. Liverpool
Jackson, T. Esq. the Grove, Wrexham
Jones, Mr. John, Wyle Cop, Shrewsbury
Jones, Mr. Newtown, Baschurch
Kough, T. H. Esq. Solicitor, Shrewsbury
Kynnersly, T. Esq. Leighton Hall
Lawrence, Mr. John, Shiffnal
Leighton, W. A. Esq. Leightonville, Shrewsbury
Nightingale, Mr. J. C. Shrewsbury
Parry, Edward, Esq. Liverpool
Payne, H. Esq. the Newark, Leicester
Perry, W. H. Esq. Surgeon, Shrewsbury
Pidgeon, Mr. H. High-street, ditto
Phillips, Lieutenant-General, ditto
Pool, Mr. B. Mardol, ditto
Pritchard, the Misses, Aberystwith
Richards, Mr. David, Shrewsbury
Sandford, Rev. H., M. A. the Isle
Shakeshaft, Mrs. Wellington, *deceased*
Shepperd, Levi, Esq. Dawley Bank
Slaney, R. A. Esq. late M. P. Walford House
Tomkies, Mr. John, Abbey Foregate, Shrewsbury
Wakefield, Rev. J. M., M.A. Shrewsbury
Watson, J. W. Esq. Solicitor, ditto
Williams, J. B. Esq. LL.D. Mayor, ditto
Wood, Rev. Theodosius, M. A. Leysdown, Kent, *deceased*
Woodall, Mr. John, Shrewsbury
Woodward, Mr. Thomas, ditto
Woodward, Mr. John, ditto, *deceased*
Wyley, Wm. Esq. Admaston
Yevily, Mr. W. Shrewsbury, *deceased*

Demy Paper.
His Grace the Duke of Sutherland
Right Hon. Lord Viscount Combermere
Right Hon. the Earl of Liverpool
Right Hon. the Earl Grosvenor
Right Hon. Lord Rodney

Right Hon. Lord Kenyon
Right Hon. Lord Berwick
Right Hon. Gen. Lord Hill, Commander-in-Chief
Hon. R. H. Clive, M. P.
Hon. Thomas Kenyon
Sir Rowland Hill, Bart. M. P.
Sir John Hanmer, Bart. M. P.
Rev. Sir Edward Kynaston, Bart.
Lady Tyrwhitt Jones
Sir Edward Bayton Sandys, Bt. D. C. L.
Sir Andrew Corbet, Bart. *deceased*
Sir Salisbury Humphreys, K.C.H. & C.B.
Sir Robert C. Hill, Knt. C.B. &c.
Sir Francis Bryan Hill, Knt.
Sir S. Rush Meyrick, Knt. LL.D. F.S.A.

SHREWSBURY.

Asterley, Mr. S. Frankwell
Astley, Rev. R. Claremont Hill.
Bennet, Mrs. National School
Bertenshaw, Mr. High Street
Billington, Mr. John, Castle Foregate
Binnal, Mr. Henry, Old Heath
Bishop, Mr. W. Millington's School
Blakemore, Mr. R. B. Mardol
Blount, Mr. Abbey Foregate
Bloxam, H. Esq. Solicitor, Howard St.
Bowen, R. Esq. Solicitor, St. Mary's Place
Boyce, J. Esq. Paymaster of the Shropshire Militia
Brayne, Wm. Esq. Mardol Head
Burton, Robert, Esq. Banker
Case, Rev. G. *deceased*
Clayton, Mr. Thomas, Printer
Cole, Mr. John, Coal Wharf
Cooke, Mr. Thurstan, Grocer, Mardol
Davies, Mr. George, College Hill
Davies, Mr. H. V. Printer
Davies, Mr. John, Artist
Dodd, Mr. William, Glass Stainer
Drinkwater, R. Esq. Frankwell
Driver, John, Esq. *deceased*
Du Gard, T. Esq. M. D., F. G. S., &c.
Eddowes, Miss, St. John's Hill
Evans, Mr. James, Taylor, Mardol
Ford, Mr. John, Painter, Barker Street
Gittins, Mr. W. Mardol
Goodwin, George, Esq. *deceased*
Green, Mr. Thomas, Claremont Street
Griffithes, Wm. Henry, Esq. Salop Gaol
Hams, Mr. Builder, Abbey Foregate
Hanley, Mr. Thomas, High Street
Hanmer, Mr. C. J. Castle Street
Harley, Samuel, Esq. Mardol
Hazledine, Wm. Esq. late Mayor, Dogpole House
Hicks, Chris. Esq. Solicitor, Wyle Cop
Higgins, Thomas, Esq. Mount Fields
Jacob, Mr. James, Kingsland
Jaffray, Mr. P. St. Alkmond's Square
Jobson, Mr. Talbot Hotel
Johnson, Mr. Samuel, Belmont
Jones, Mr. T. E. Howard Street
Jones, John, Esq. Liquor Merchant
Jones, Mr. John, Mardol Head
Jones, Mr. Lewis, Salop Brewery
Jones, Mr. John, Hatter, High Street
Keate, Mr. Robert, High Street
Knowles, Mr. C. St. John's Hill
Leach, Mr. Thomas, Castle Foregate
Legh, Mr. John, Pride Hill
Legh, Mr. Robert, Pride Hill
Lloyd, Mr. Charles, Plough Inn
Locke, Edward, Esq. Belmont
Loxdale, Joseph, Esq. Sen.

Maddox, John, Esq. Frankwell
Mansel, Mr. Edward, College Hill
Martin, Mr. W. Artist
Mason, Mr. Francis, *deceased*
Meredith, Mr. Lewis, Wyle Cop
Moody, Mr. Samuel, High Street
Morris, Mr. W. *deceased*
Mottram, Mr. Thomas, Jun. Mardol
Mottram, Mr. E. Claremont Bank
Mottram, Mr. William, *deceased*
Muckleston, Edward, Esq. Quarry Place
Muckleston, Mr. R. J. Pride Hill
Newton, Mr. Henry, Wharfinger
Nightingale, Mr. Samuel, Coleham
Oliver, Mr. Fox Inn, *deceased*
Olney, Mrs the Crescent, 2 copies
Onions, Mr. Mardol and Royal Baths
Owen, Mr. W. Coach Maker
Palmer, Joseph, Esq. Abbey Foregate
Parkes, Mr. D. *deceased*
Parkes, Mr. James, *ditto*
Parkes, Mr. John, *ditto*
Parry, Miss, near the Crescent
Parry, Scarlett Lloyd, Esq. Solicitor
Parsons, Mr. John, Octagon Cottage
Pickin, Mr. W. Iron Founder, Castle Foregate
Pickstock, Mrs. High Street
Pidduck, Mr. Thomas, Castle Gates
Pidduck, Mr. W. *deceased*
Pierce, Mr. Painter, Welsh Bridge
Price, Mr. Richard, Castle Street
Pritchard, Mr. Daniel, Dogpole
Pyefinch, Mr. John, High Street
Pugh, Mr. Gilder, *deceased*
Richards, Rev. J. St. Alkmond's Vicarage
Richards, Mr. Henry, Dogpole, *deceased*
Ridding, Wm. Esq. *deceased*
Roberts, Mr. Thomas, Castle Foregate
Rogers, Mr. John, Coleham
Sancto, Mr. William
Sayer, Mr. James, Mardol Head
Schofield, Mr. G. Castle Foregate
Scoltock, Mr. Richard, Market Place
Shaw, Mr. Mardol Head
Slade, Mr. John
Smith, W. Esq. senior Alderman, *dec.*
Smith, Mr. Samuel, Timber Merchant
Smith, Wm. Esq. Sion Villa
Strange, Mr. John, St. Mary's Street
Sutton, Thomas, Esq. Castle Street
Tanner, Mr. John, High Street
Taylor, Mr. Maltster, Abbey Foregate
Teece, Josiah, Esq. *deceased*
Thomas, Rev. W. Hill's Lane
Tipton, Mr. R. Cross Hill
Tisdale, Mr. J. Quarry Buildings
Towers, T. Esq. Post Master, Dogpole
Travis, Mr. Thomas, Spring Gardens
Tudor, Mr. John, late of Calcot
Wardley, Wm. Esq. Collector of Excise, Kingsland
Watkis, Price, Esq. *deceased*
Webster, Mr. James, Belmont Street
Whitehurst, John, Esq. the Mount
Wildblood, Mr. St. Alkmond's Square
Wilding, Mr. Robert, Market Square
Wilding, Mr. James, Fish Street
Wilkinson, Mr. Robert, Jun. Hill's Lane
Williams, Mr. John, Builder
Woodall, Mr. William, Brazier
Wynne, Rice, Esq. the College
Yates, Mr. Francis, College Hill
Yearsley, Mr. Joseph, *deceased*

VICINITY OF SHREWSBURY, Within 8 or 10 Miles.

Alcock, Mr. Moreton Corbet, *deceased*
Barber, S. Esq. Walcot, *deceased*
Barkley, R. Esq. Grinshill
Barrett, Mr. William, Ford
Bather, T. J. Esq. Great Ness
Bayley, Thomas, Esq. Black Birches
Beaumont, John, Esq. Mount Hermon
Bickerton, W. Esq. Newton-on-the-Hill
Blantern, G. Esq. Haston
Brown, Rev. Corbet, Withington
Bunn, Mr. Longner Hall
Burd, Rev. John, Cound Lodge
Burton, Rt. Esq. Longner Hall, 10 copies
Burton, Rev. Henry, Atcham
Burton, Mrs. Vicarage, Atcham
Calcott, Mrs. Abbots Betton
Cartwright, Mr. Preston Brockhurst
Charlton, Philip, Esq. Wytheford Hall
Corbett, Rev. Waties, Longnor
Corbett, Miss Falconer, Arscott House
Cullis, Mr. William, late of Meole Brace
Dathan, Lieut. Royal Navy, Kingsland Cottage
Davies, Mr. Henry, late of Cardiston
Davies, Mr. Thomas, Astley
Deighton, Thomas, Esq. Rose Hill
Drury, Rev. Charles, M. A. Pontesbury
Durnell, John, Esq. Surgeon, Pitchford
Egremont, Rev. E., Wroxeter
Evans, Mr. Roden
Gardner, Rev. L., D.D. Sansaw Hall
Goodman, Mr. Hotel, Atcham
Griffiths, Mrs. Bicton Cottage
Groome, Wm. Esq. Clive
Groome, T. Esq. Sen. Smethcott
Groome, Edward, Esq. ditto
Hampton, Mr. Wm. Great Wytheford
Harding, G. Esq. Clive Hall
Harnage, Mrs. Belswardine Park
Harries, Edward, Esq. Cruckton Hall
Harrison, Rev. H., B.D. Pontesbury
Heath, Mr. Thomas, Hadnal
Highway, Miss, Pontesford House
Hitchin, Mr. Sundorne Wharf
Home, Mr. Richard, Hadnal
Hope, T. H. Esq. Netley Hall
Horsman, Rev. J., M. A. Middle
Howells, Thomas, Esq. Fox Farm
Jackson, Mrs. Great Betton, *deceased*
Jenkins, R. Esq. late M. P. Bicton House
Jones, Mr. John, Preston Boats
Jones, W. Esq. Jun. Shelton House
Jones, Mr. Thomas, Hadnal Wood
Lacon, Frederick, Esq. Yorton Villa
Lee, Mr. George, Wroxeter
Lee, Mr. Francis, New House
Lee, Mr. John, Hope's Farm, Sansaw
Lee, Mrs. Leaton
Legh, Mrs. Corbet, Sutton
Leighton, Rev. B., M. A. Ford
Lloyd, Miss, Cruckton Hall
Maddock, Mr. C. Alderton Hall
Marvin, Rev. W. S. M. A. Shawbury
Massey, Mr. Cross Houses Inn
Matthews, Mr. Elephant Inn, Grinshill
Matthews, Mr. Stephen, the Isle
Matthews, Mr. T. Lea Hall
Matthews, W. Esq. Preston Boats
Minor, J. Esq. Shawbury
Minor, Mrs. ditto
Minor, Mrs. Astley House
Minton, Mr. Thomas, Downton
Minton, Mr. Samuel, Woodstile
Minton, Mr. John, Albright Lee
Moreton, Miss, Albright Hussey
Nevett, Mr. Samuel, Upton Magna
Oakley, Mrs. Horson
Ogle, Mr. J. R. Harlescott

Parr, Mr. Richard, Yorton Farm
Payne, Mr. James, Adcott Hall
Pearce, Mr. Thomas, Cruckton Hall
Peele, Miss, Ryton, near Condover
Pescal, Mr. Thomas, Hadnal
Pickering, Mr. Cruck Meole Mill
Pickstock, Seth, Esq. Balderton Hall
Pigott, the Misses, Upton Magna Villa
Pitchford, Mr. W. Shawbury Park
Price, Wm. Birch, Esq. Banker, Mitton Hall
Price, Mr. John, Rodington
Puleston, W. Esq. Clive
Reynolds, Mr. J. late of Pontesbury
Shepherd, J. Esq. Horton Lodge
Smith, Mr. Robert, Shawbury, *deceased*
Stanier, Edward, Esq. Wroxeter
Swann, John, Esq. Redbrook Cottage
Taylor, Rev. M. D., M. A. Moreton Corbet
Thompson, Mr. Shawwell Cottage
Thornton, Mr. W. Sundorne Castle
Vaughan, John, Esq. Chilton Grove
Vaughan, Mr. Fitz Mill
Walford, James, Esq. Cronkhill
Walmsley, Mr. John, Battlefield
Watkins, W. Esq. Shotton Hall
Watters, John, Esq. Longnor Villa
Wellings, Mr. Elephant Inn, Shawbury
Wilde, Mrs. Young, Alderton
Wilkinson, Mrs. Yeaton Villa
Williams, Mr. Tern Bridge
Wingfield, Colonel, Onslow Hall
Wood, John, Esq. Grinshill
Wood, Mr. J. E. late of Shrewsbury

BISHOP'S CASTLE & VICINITY.

Beddoes, J. Esq. H. Bailiff, Bishop's Castle
Bryan, Roger, Esq. Little Hall
Bebb, Mr. E. Chandler
Prowd, Rev. I. Bishop's Castle, *deceased*
George, Robert, Esq. Lydbury
Griffiths, John, Esq. Bishop's Castle
Griffiths, Mr. E. Stationer, ditto
Harding, Rev. John, Hopesay, *deceased*
Morgan, Rev. John, late of Clun
Norton, Mr. Robert, Bishop's Castle
Neville, Mr. John, Banker, ditto
Playfair, Mr. John, Castle Inn, ditto

BRIDGNORTH & VICINITY.

Browne, T. Wylde, Esq. Woodlands
Bangham, Joseph, Esq. Bridgnorth
Gatacre, Colonel, Gatacre Hall
Gitton, Mr. G. R. Postmaster, ditto
Griffiths, Mr. J. Chauntrey, Quatford
Hardwick, J. Bell, Esq. Bridgnorth
Homfrey, Frederick, Esq. ditto
Nicholas, Mr. Grocer, ditto
Nock, Mr. Castle Inn, ditto
Pilkington, Rev. M., M. A. ditto
Sing, Joshua, Esq. late Mayor of ditto
Smallman, John, Esq. Quatford Castle

BROSELEY & VICINITY.

Davies, Mr. W. Brick Works, Jackfield
Guest, Mr. Charles, Broseley
Harries, F. B. Esq. Benthall Hall
Jones and Bathurst, Messrs. Posenhall
Myatt, Mr. John, Pottery, Jackfield
Oare, Mr. J. B. Willey Park
Price, Mr. Calcot Iron Works
Pitt, Mr. Thomas, Posenhall
Pritchard, G. Esq. Banker and Solicitor, Broseley
Roden, Mr. T. Brick Works, Jackfield
Scale, Mr. S. National School, Barrow

CHURCH STRETTON & VICINITY.

Belton, John, Esq. Church Stretton
Phillips, Mr. A. Draper, ditto
Robinson, Mr. Draper, ditto
Wilding, W. Esq. Surgeon, ditto
Wilding, Henry, Esq. All Stretton, *dec.*
Wilding, Samuel, Esq. ditto, *dec.*.

CLEOBURY MORTIMER AND VICINITY.

Bancks, C. Esq. Holly-west Cottage
Davison, Mr. John, Cleobury Mortimer
Dorell, Mr. W. Talbot Hotel, ditto
Downes, Mr. John, Grocer, ditto
Harding, Mr. Thomas, Draper, ditto
Nicholls, W. Esq. Paper Mills, Hopton Wafers
Southam, S. P. Esq. Coroner, Solicitor, Cleobury Mortimer
Weaver, W. Jones, Esq. Surgeon, ditto
Whitcomb, Edward, Esq. Surgeon, ditto
Williams, Mr. Thomas, Butcher, ditto
Woodward, J. W. Esq. Solicitor, ditto
Woodward, Rev. Thomas, M.A. Hopton Wafers

MARKET DRAYTON & VICINITY

Adlington, Mr. E. Market Drayton
Arden, James, Esq. M. D. Betton Villa
Bratton, John, Esq. Drayton
Cholmondeley, Mrs. Hodnet Hall
Davison, D. W. Esq. Brand Hall, *dec.*
Dicken, Joseph, Esq. Coroner, Wollerton
Foden, Joseph, Esq. Oak Cottage
Grant, Mrs. Phœnix Inn, Drayton
Leycester, Rev. Oswald, M. A. Stoke-upon-Terne
Morris, John, Esq. Hawkestone
Noneley, R. Marigold, Esq. Drayton
Norcop, W. C. Esq. Betton Hall
Pace, Mr. Sandford, Hodnet
Silvester, Mr. Bookseller, Drayton
Skitt, Mr. G. Veterinary Surgeon, Hodnet, *deceased*
Tagg, Mr. A. Wistanwick
Tayler, Rev. C. B., M. A. Hodnet

ELLESMERE & VICINITY.

Baugh, Mr. Bookseller, Ellesmere
Cotton, Rev. J. A., M. A. ditto
Crain, Mr. Henry, Brook Cottage, near Emrall Hall
Dicken, Edward, Esq. Plas Thomas
Dymock, Edward, Esq. Ellesmere
Dymock, Rev. E. H., B. A. ditto
Edwards, Edward, Esq. Cross Lanes
Ferral, Lovett, Esq. Hardwick Lodge
Fonnereau, Philip, Esq. Overton
Frumston, Mr. John, Ellesmere
Hawkins, Mrs. ditto, *deceased*
Hignett, Mr. ditto
Hughes, Charles, Esq. ditto
Jenkins, Mr. Auctioneer, ditto
Jones, Mr. Thomas, ditto
Lack, Mr. Francis, ditto
Menlove, Richard, Esq. Pentreheylin
Menlove, Joseph, Esq. Ellesmere
Oakley, John, Esq. English Frankton
Pay, Mr. W. Red Lion Inn, Ellesmere
Phillips, Rev. John, M. A. ditto
Phillips, Mrs. T. Wackley Lodge
Price, Mr. R. Ellesmere, *deceased*
Pritchard, Peter, Esq. Solicitor, ditto
Roaf, Rev. W. ditto
Sandland, Mr. John, ditto
Tonks, Mr. Thomas, ditto
Thompson, Mr. T. Bookseller, ditto
Tylston, John, Esq. ditto
Weston, Mr. W. Cabinet Maker, ditto
Wynn, Richard, Esq. Crickett
Wynn, Mrs. New Crickett

LUDLOW & VICINITY.

Evans, Mr. Edward, Ludlow
Glaze, Mr. James, ditto
Harding, Mr. W. ditto
Hutchings, John, Esq. ditto
Jennings, Mr. J. National School, ditto
Nicholls, Thomas, Esq. 'Aston Hall
Price, R. Bell, Esq. Bitterly Hall, dec.
Sankey, R. Esq. late High Bailiff, Ludlow
Smalley, Mr. John,   ditto
Smith, Mr. R. B. Stanton Lacy
Turner, Edward, Esq. Coston Hall
Whittall, Mr. H. Ludlow

MADELEY, PARISH, & VICINITY.

Anstice, W. Esq. Madeley
Bartlett, Rev. J., M. A. Marnwood
Baylis, Mr. W. Coalport
Beckwith, Rev. H. Eaton Constantine
Blocksidge, Mr. John, Coalport
Borroughs, Mr. J. Watch-maker, Iron-
 bridge
Bycott, Mr. Thomas, Coalbrookdale
Clinton, Mr. J. Ironbridge
Cooper, Thomas, Esq. Madeley
Court, M. Esq. Solicitor, Ironbridge
Edmonds, Rev. G. Madeley
Edwards, Mr. Draper, &c. Ironbridge
Glazebrook, Mr. John, Draper, ditto
Griffiths, Mr. G. Timber Merchant,
 Coalport
Jenkins, R. Esq. Charlton Hill, dec.
Lloyd, Mr. B. Swan Inn, Ironbridge
Lloyd, Mr. Cabinet Maker, ditto
Rose, John, Esq. the Hay, Madeley
Smith, Mr. Henry, Grocer, Ironbridge
Smith, Mr. Thomas, Builder, Madeley
Thompson, Jas. Esq. Lightmoor
Tranter, Mr. Buildwas Bridge Inn
Williams, Mr. Richard, Ironbridge
Walter, Mr. S. E.   ditto
Ward, John, Esq. Madeley
Wright, Mr. B. Draper, Coalbrookdale
Yates, Edward, Esq. Madeley

OSWESTRY AND VICINITY.

Bickerton, Mr. S. Druggist, Oswestry
Cooper, Mr. Banker, ditto
Dovaston, J. F. M. Esq. West Felton
Frank, John, Esq. Maesbury Hall
Gore, W. O. Esq. M. P. Porkington Hall
Hughes, Mr. Draper, Oswestry
Jones, Mr. Thomas, Grocer, ditto
Knight, Mr. Wynnstay Arms, ditto
Minshull, Mr. Salop Road, Oswestry
Montgomery, Rev. R. late of Whittington
Mytton, John, Esq. Halston, deceased
Parker, Thos. N. Esq. Sweeney Hall
Parker, Rev. J. ditto
Penson, T. Esq. Architect, Oswestry
Piercy, Mr. Land Surveyor
Povey, John, Esq. Derwen y Pandy
Roberts, Mr. Gas Proprietor, Oswestry
Stevens, H. Esq. late of Maesbrook
Symmonds, — Esq. Oswestry
Whitehurst, Rev. E., M. A. Moreton

RUYTON OF THE 11 TOWNS AND VICINITY.

Bather, E. P. Esq. Ruyton
Bickerton, Joseph, Esq. Shotatton
Broughton, R. Esq. Surgeon, Ruyton
Burroughs, Mr. Cross Keys Inn, Knockin
Cumberbach, Mr. Draper, &c. Ruyton
Edwards, J. Esq. Ness Strange Hall
Edwards, Robert, Esq. Baschurch
Evans, Rev. George, M. A. Ruyton
Evans, John, Esq. M. D. Llwyn-y-groes
Hughes, Mr. Edward, Baschurch

Jones, Mr. T. Auctioneer, Knockin
Kempster, W. Esq. Solicitor, Llanymynech
Luxmore, Rev. J., M. A.
Tompson, Rev. F. H., Knockin
Ward, Mr. W. National School, ditto

SHIFFNAL AND VICINITY.

Bradburn, W. Esq. Priors Lee
Brown, Gilbert, Esq. Solicitor, Shiffnal
Cameron, Rev. Charles, Priors Lee
Corbett, Mr. Edward, Shiffnal
Garbett, Mr. Richard, ditto
Halley, Mr. Francis, Builder, ditto
Harding, Mr. Grocer, ditto
Matthews, Rev. J. T., ditto
Montford, Richard, Esq. ditto
Morris, Mr. Jerningham Arms, ditto
Ombersley, Wm. Esq. Priors Lee
Plowden, Edmund, Esq. Haughton Hall
Roden, Mr. W. Druggist, Shiffnal
Smythe, Miss, Rock Terrace
Turner, Mr. Haughton Hall
Venables, Mr. R. Shiffnal
Whitmore, J. C. Esq. M.P. Cotsbrook

WELLINGTON AND VICINITY.

Adney, Edward, Esq. Wellington
Anslow, S. Esq. Eyton
Ball, Mr. Samuel, Draper, Wellington
Barney, Mr. John,   ditto, deceased
Belliss, Wm. Phillips, Esq. near Eyton
Belton, John, Esq. Long Hall
Bickerton, R. Esq. Longdon-upon-Terne
Blandford, Mr. Samuel, Eyton Hall
Buffery, Mr. William, Wellington
Charlton, Wm. Esq. Apley Castle
Clarke, Mr. Thomas, Admaston Spa
Clarke, Mr. G. Buck's Head Inn, Long
 Lane
Cludde, Edward, Esq. Orelton Hall
Danby, Mr. W. Draper, Wellington
Davies, Mr. W. Draper, ditto
Edwards, Mr. Gas Proprietor, ditto
Ellis, Mr. Maurice,   ditto, dec.
Evans, Rev. T., Longdon-upon-Terne
Eyton, Thomas, Esq. Eyton Hall
Fox, Mr. Apley Castle
Garbett, E. Esq. Solicitor, Wellington
Griffiths, Mr. Talbot Inn,   ditto
Gough, Mr. Shoe Maker,   ditto
Hodgkiss, Mrs. Cock Inn, Watling Street
Houlston and Son, Messrs. Wellington
Icke, Mr. Aston, deceased
Jones, Mr. Thomas, Draper, Wellington
Jones, — Esq. Surgeon,   ditto
Jones, Mr. Thomas, Dawley Green
Juckes, Thomas, Esq. Terne
Keey, Rev. W. Wellington
Lawley, W. Esq. Leegomery
Leese, W. Esq. Wellington, deceased
Mackay, Mr. James, Ketley Grange
Mark, Mr. Engraver, Watling Street
Nock, W. Esq. Solicitor, Wellington
Oliver, James, Esq.   ditto
Pearce, T. Esq. Hadley Lodge
Pearson, Rev. C. High Ercall
Phillips, A. Esq. Wellington
Pickin, W. Esq. Solicitor, Wellington
Pierce, Mr. Richard, Grocer, ditto
Pocock, Mr. S. J. Ketley
Ravenshaw, John, Esq. Uckington
Roberts, Mr. Thomas, Wellington
Robinson, C. M. Esq. Solicitor, ditto
Seagur, C. Esq. Surgeon, Wellington
Smith, Mr. W. Long Waste
Steedman, E. Esq. High Ercall Hall
Sumner, Mr. R. Wellington
Tarbitt, Mr. Draper, Watling Street
Taylor, Richard, Esq. Crudgington
Taylor, Mr. W. Wellington

Tranter, Mr. Bramlee
Turner, Mr. Thos. Sun Inn, Wellington
Webster, Mr. Walton
Whitfield, Mr. John, Ironmonger, Wel-
 lington
Yardley, Mr. Free School, ditto

WEM AND VICINITY.

Boughey, Mr. Corn Mills, Wem
Braxenor, Mr. Richard, Saddler, ditto
Dicken, Thos. Esq. Loppington House
Franklin, Mr. Bookseller, Wem
Hassal, Stephen, Esq. Aston Park
Ireland, Thomas, Esq. Wem
Jeffreys, Mr. R. National School, ditto
Vaughan, R. C. Esq. Buriton Hall
Williams, Mr. John, Loppington
Worrall, Mr. E. Free School, Loppington

WHITCHURCH AND VICINITY.

Evans, Rev. John, M. A. Whitchurch
Evanson, Mr. J. H.   ditto
Groome, Thomas, Esq. Surgeon, ditto
Harper, George, Esq. Solicitor, ditto
Hawkesworth, Rev. John, Moore
Jones, Mr. late of the National School,
 Whitchurch
Lakin, Mr. W. Auctioneer, ditto
Lowe, John, Esq. Banker, ditto
Neville, Rev. E., M. A. Prees
Potter, Rev. Thomas, late of Whitchurch
Saxton, Mr. Charles,   ditto
Shirley, John, Esq. Prees
Skidmore, Mr. James, Whitchurch
Tudman, Edward, Esq. ditto
Woodward, S. W. Esq. Surgeon, Prees

WENLOCK AND VICINITY.

Adney, George, Esq. Wenlock
Belcher, Mr. Grocer, ditto
Bowyer, Abraham, Esq. Surgeon
Bowyer, Mr. Atterley
Brookes, W. P. Esq. Surgeon, Wenlock
Collins, Richard, Esq.   ditto
Cooper, John, Esq. Burton Hall
Cotton, Mr. Thomas, Wenlock
Davies, Mrs. Wenlock Abbey
Griffiths, Mr. William, Wenlock
Hinton, Henry, Esq. Solicitor, ditto
Horton, Mr. John, Plough Inn, ditto
Mason, Mr. John,   ditto
More, Rev. R. H. G. Larden Hall
Mytton, Miss, Horley Grange
Smith, Mr. W. Grocer, Wenlock
Vaughan, Miss Sarah, ditto

VARIOUS PARTS of SHROPSHIRE.

Corbet, Mr. R. Bromlow
Crompton, R. Esq. Surgeon, Munslow
Davies, Mr. Aaron, Brockton
Edwards, John, Esq. Hampton Hall
Fenessey, Mr. Peter, late of Quatford
Haughton, Mrs. Windmill Inn, near
 Rowton
Huntly, Rev. R. W., M. A. Alberbury
Lloyd, Thomas, Esq. Osbaston
Lyster, Henry, Esq. Rowton Castle
Meredith, Rev. E., M. A. Head Master
 of the Grammar School, Newport
Naylor, Mr. S. Santley, near Minsterley
Nevett, Wm. Esq. Marton Villa
Parry, John, Esq. Stoney Stretton
Pugh, Mr. H. Chirbury School
Rogers, Mr. J. Innkeeper, Alberbury
Silvester, Mr. H. P. Bookseller, Newport
Wall, Mr. Thomas, Brockton, deceased
Ward, Mr. J. Raven & Bell Inn, Newport
Webb, Mr. James, Cold Hatton Inn
Williams, Mr. G. Auctioneer, Chirbury

Wales.

ABERYSTWITH AND VICINITY.
Cox, Mr. J. Bookseller, Aberystwith
Davies, Mr. W. Cambrian Foundry, ditto
Davies, Mr. A. P. Goggerddan Arms Hotel, ditto
Edwards, Mr. R. Silk Mercer, ditto
Evans, Mr. E. Belle Vue Hotel, ditto
Hughes, Mr. E. late of Plinlimmon Hotel
James, Rev. J. near Aberystwith
Jenkins, Mr. W. Clarence Place
Powell, Colonel, M.P. Nanteos Hall
Roberts, Mr. W. Tymaer, Llanbadarn Vawr
Smith, Mr. John, Marine Terrace
Stephenson, James, Esq. deceased
Williams, Mr. R. late of the Talbot Hotel

MONTGOMERY AND VICINITY.
Bagley, Mr. A. Free School, Montgomery
Baxter, R. Esq. Surgeon, ditto
Davies, Colonel, late of Nantcribba Hall
Downes, Middleton, Esq. View House
Edye, E. Esq. Solicitor, Montgomery
Towns, G. Esq. Surgeon, Montgomery
Woollaston, Mrs. Ivy House

NEWTOWN AND VICINITY.
Bickerton, Mr. Draper, Newtown
Brandstrom, F. Esq. Solicitor, deceased
Cowdal, Mr. Thomas, Tymawr
Cross, Mr. James, late of Newtown
Davies, Rev. R. J. Aberhafesp Rectory
Davies, Mr. David, Newtown
Edge, Mr. John, Gas Works, ditto
Evans, Rev. G. A. Newtown Hall
Gittins, Mr. Grapes Inn, Newtown
Herbert, Mr. Mark, ditto
Horton, Mr. ditto
Humphreys, C. M. D. Esq. Surgeon and County Coroner, Glanhafren
James, Rev. D. Llanwnnog Vicarage
James, Mr. Half-way House Inn
Jones, W. Esq. Rock House
Jones, Mrs. Rock Cottage
Jones, Mr. R. Angel Inn, Newtown
Jones, William, Esq. Solicitor, ditto
Kinsey, Mr. Buck Inn, ditto
Lloyd, Mr. Edward, Canal Bason
Lloyd, Mrs. the Court
Lutener, William, Esq. Dolerw
Matthews, G. Esq. Solicitor, Newtown
Morgan, Mr. T. Newtown, deceased
Morris, Miss, Pengelly
Morris, Mrs. Kilgogan
Nokes, Mr. Taylor, Newtown
Parry, Mr. A. Mochtre
Price, Rev. J. Dolforwyn Hall, deceased
Pugh, W. Esq. late of Brynllwarch
Pugh, Mr. R. P. Caersws
Rowlands, Mr. R. T. Red Lion Inn, Newtown
Salter, Mr. Jackson, Bookseller, ditto
Slyman, W. Esq. Surgeon, ditto
Smout, Mr. G. Aberminle, two copies
Stephens, Edward, Esq. jun. late of Glansevern, deceased
Thomas, Mr. D. Bookseller, Newtown
Watkins, Mr. E. Wool Merchant, ditto
Williams, J. Buckley, Esq. Pennant
Williams, Mr. E. Printer, Newtown
Williams, Mr. T. Machine Maker, ditto
Williams, Mr. R. Manufacturer, ditto
Williams, Mrs. Kerry
Wingfield, Rev. C., M.A. the Gro

WELSHPOOL AND VICINITY.
Allen, F. Esq. Solicitor, Welshpool
Davies, Mr. Edward, Bear Inn, ditto
Davies, Mr. Druggist, late of Welshpool
Davies, Mr. Lime Works, Garthmill
Davies, Mrs. Lime Works, Garthmill
Ellis, Mr. Innkeeper, Coidway
Gilder, W. Esq. Welshpool
Goldsbro, Rev. Thomas, ditto

Griffiths, W. Esq. Solicitor, Welshpool
Howell, Mr. A. ditto
Humphreys, John, Esq. Bodhilin
Johnes, — Esq. M.D. Lower Garthmill
Johnes, William, Esq. Welshpool
Johnson, James Proud, Esq. M. D. High Sheriff of Montgomeryshire
Jones, J. Esq. Solicitor, Welshpool
Jones, John, Esq. Crosswood Hall
Kempster, Mr. Thomas, Welshpool
Lloyd, R. Esq. Llanerbrochwell, dec.
Owen, William, Esq. Glansevern Hall
Pugh, D. Esq. late M.P. Llanerchydol Hall
Pugh, E. Esq. Alderman, Welshpool
Pugh, D. Esq. late of Park Place, ditto
Russell, Rev. J. Llandrinio Rectory
Waidson, Mr. John, Welshpool
Whitehall, Mrs. Oak Hotel, ditto
Williams, Rev. C. ditto, deceased
Yates, Thomas, Esq. Solicitor, Welshpool
Yearsley, W. Esq. Solicitor, ditto

VARIOUS PARTS OF WALES.
Barrett, Miss, Mallwyd
Davies, Rev. Walter, Manafon
Dickenson, James H. Esq. Solicitor, Highfield Cottage, Wrexham
Davies, Mr. R. Llangollen
Davies, Rev. Richard, Court y Gollen
Edwards, Rev. W. Llanymwddy Rectory
Ellis, Mr. J. P. Wynnstay Arms Hotel, Machynlleth
Evans, Mr. D. late of the New Inn, Llanidloes
Hotchkiss, John, Esq. Llanwrst Villa, Crickhowel
Jarman, Mr. W. Builder, Llanidloes
Johnson, Mr. Hand Inn, Chirk
Jones, Mr. Bookseller, Dolgelly
Lewis, Mr. Edward, Llanidloes
Lloyd, Mr. King's Head Hotel, Llangollen
Lloyd, T. Esq. Glangwnna Hall, dec.
Owen, Mr. John, Flannel Manufacturer, Llanidloes
Payne, the Ven. Archdeacon, Crickhowel
Powell, Mr. Dolobran, near Myfod
Price, Rev. Thomas, Crickhowel
Rogers, E. Esq. late M.P. Stannage Park, Radnorshire
Skyce, Rev. George, Wrexham
Williams, Rev. D. Llanfair, deceased
Williams, Mr. John, Wrexham, deceased

CHESHIRE, generally.
Brown, E. Esq. Henton Lane, Stockport
Clementson, Rev E.M, Church Minshull
Dereijuer, Mrs. Nantwich
Griffiths, Mr. Bookseller, ditto
Hemmingway, Mr. J. Chester
Hislop, Mr. Alexander, Stockport
Levason, L. Esq. late of Chester
Morris, Mr. late of Middlewich
Riley, Mr. J. China Merchant, Chester
Robinson, Mr. Head Master of the Free Grammar School, Nantwich
Stocks, S. Esq. Heaton, near Stockport
Tomlinson, Henry, Esq. Nantwich

LANCASHIRE, generally.
Alsop, Mr. W. Bookseller, Southport
Barrett and Ridgway, Messrs. Solicitors, Manchester
Cathrall, Mr. W. Manchester
Clayton, Mr. Edward, Liverpool
Cuppage, Rev. A. Middleton
Harrisson, Mrs. Manchester
Hulbert, Mr. Samuel, Moston Green
Hulbert, Mr. Samuel, Swinton
Lloyd, E. Esq. Banker, Manchester
Loxdale, Rev. E. Liverpool
Marston, Mr. W. Liverpool
Moody, Mr. Charles, Manchester
Taylor, John, Esq. Solicitor, Manchester

Taylor, Mr. R. Bookseller, Liverpool
Thomas, J. S. Esq. Police, Manchester
Williams, Mr. John, Draper, Liverpool
Winstanley, W. Esq. Solicitor, Manchester
Woodcock, Mr. Manchester

LONDON.
Cowie, Mr. Newcastle Street; Strand
Davies, Mr. T. Rosamond Street
Hughes, Mr. Hugh, Bookseller
Hulbert, Rev. C. A., M. A. Islington
Hulbert, John F. Esq. Surgeon
Jones, Thomas, Esq. Strand
Knox, Mr. Mordan House, Greenwich
Ludlow, Ebenezer, Esq. Barrister-at-law
Mason, Rev. Robert
Meredith, R. C. Esq. Lombard Street
Moreton, John, Esq. Islington, deceased
Ouseley, William Gore, Esq.
Peate, Mr. Ratcliff Highway
Powis, Wm. Esq. Wilmington Square
Pratt, John, Esq. Nelson Square
Price, Mr. Thomas
Rees, O. Esq. Messrs. Longman & Co's
Smith, Mr. Thomas Charles
Sturgeon, Mr. Woolwich
Thomas, Mr. C. S. Doctor's Commons
Watson, C. Esq. Barrister-at-law, Temple
Weeks, Henry, Esq. Solicitor
Wright, Mr. Charles, Coleman Street

SUBSCRIBERS in VARIOUS PARTS of the KINGDOM, and ABROAD.
Alcott, Mr. T. Wheatsheaf Inn, Bewdley
Benyon, Henry, Esq. Leeds
Brown, Mr. H. Amesbury, Wilts
Charlet, Col. N. Henley Court, Worcester
Danks, Mr. I. Lickhill, Stourport
Davies, R. Esq. Kingston, Jamaica
Dearsly, Rev. W., B.A. Abbots Bromley
Dowling, Edward, Esq. B. A. Monmouth
Eyton, R. Esq. Ch. Ch. College, Oxford
Fallows, John, Esq. Birmingham
Fereday, Mr. John, Birmingham
Gaskell, J. Milnes, Esq. Thornes House, Wakefield
Gibson, Rev. J. late of Cambridge
Gough, Rev. Walter, Worcester
Hamel, Etienne Bruno, Esq. Tamworth
Hardy, J. S. Esq. F. S. A. Leicester
Hill, John, Esq. Clifton, near Bristol
Horlick, C. Esq. Painswick, Gloucestershire
Law, Wm. Esq. Gawcott, Bucks
Lee, Rev. Samuel, D. D. Vicar of Banwell, Somersetshire
Lloyd, Mr. W. Soho, near Birmingham
Newling, Rev. John, Canon of Lichfield
Ouseley, Rev. J. Blaston, Leicestershire
Ouseley, Captain J. W. Jasper, Calcutta, East Indies
Pierce, Mr. late of Wolverhampton
Pope, Mr. F. Iron Founder, Wolverhampton
Potts, R. Esq. M.A. Trin.Col. Cambridge
Price, Wm. Esq. Solicitor, Abergavenny
Rabett, Rev. Reginald, M. A. Rector of Thornton, Leicestershire
Rawson, John, Esq. Kegworth, ditto
Salmon, Rev. F. Rector of Culworth, Northamptonshire
Sainsbury, W. Esq. M.D. Corsham, Wilts
Scott, Rev. T. Rector of Wappenham, dec.
Sillitoe, Mr. John, Stafford
Simpson, Rev. John, Methodist Minister, late of Wellington
Simpson, John, Esq. LL.D. Worcester
Strutt, Joseph, Esq. Derby
Tart, Mr. James, Bewdley
Walsh, Mrs. Sheffield, deceased
Wooding, Mr. Thomas, Leominster

ADDITIONAL SUBSCRIBERS.

Corbet, Mrs. Sundorne Castle.
Downes, Mr. John, Auctioneer, 15, Howard Street, Shrewsbury.
Fowler, Mr. Acton Reynald.
Mytton, Thomas, Esq. Shipton Hall, near Wenlock.
Nicholas, Mr. R. 19, Howard Street, Shrewsbury.

ADDITIONAL CORRECTIONS AND NOTICES.

Page 193, line 18, in a few copies, *for* devised, *read* disposed of.
— 308, — 2, *for* Longden and Meole Coleham, *read* Longden Coleham and Meole Coleham.
— 320, — 29, *for* T. *read* J. Corne.
— 351, last line of note, *after* P. B. Thompson, add the word *late*.
— iv. line 1, Prefatory Observations, *for* delate, *read* dilate.
— xiii.—in the List of Subscribers, line 2, *for* Most Noble, *read* Most Honourable.
— — Lord Viscount Combermere should follow the Earl Grosvenor.
— — line 11, column 2, *for* Bayton, *read* Baynton.
— xvi.—M. P. should be added to the name of J. Milnes Gaskell, Esq.

☞ James Usher, in the year 1598, afterwards Archbishop, had a controversy with the Catholics, and is the Divine referred to by Mr. Cox, page 335, line 2; and not the Archbishop Usher, supposed, in the note at foot of the same page, to have been buried at Dudliston. James was only 18 years of age, when he wrote the Answer to the "Challenge;" consequently might easily be mistaken for his Uncle, who, at that time, occupied the Archiepiscopal See of Armagh. The Arch-Primate, James, died at Ryegate, in Surrey, 1656, and is buried in Westminster Abbey.

Page x.—in the LIST OF ENGRAVINGS AND DIRECTIONS TO THE BINDER, *after* BODHILIN, *read* to face page 65; *after* Portrait of James II., *read* to face page 205.

N. B.—The Binder will also take care to place the single leaf, page 281, to follow page 280 in vol. 1; and THIS LEAF in THIS volume, after the List of Subscribers.

The FIVE VIEWS in the centre of the Plate, intended for the Frontispiece of this volume, are designed to convey the idea of the Course of the River Severn, from its source to its termination. The Side Views and Objects have each also their peculiar intention, as representing scenes and places eventful in History, viz.—Boscobel and the Royal Oak, connected with the Providential Escape of Charles II.; Bolas Church and part of the Rectory, eminent for events pertaining to the interesting History of the late Earl and Countess of Exeter; Battlefield Church, commemorating the Battle of Shrewsbury; Ellesmere Church, as a venerable structure; Whitchurch Church, as a spacious and delightful edifice; Ludlow Castle, as the most magnificent ruin in the County of Salop; and Powis Castle, the most perfect and original structure of the kind within the districts embraced by our History. To Longuer Hall, the word NEW should be prefixed.—The Tomb of the Protestant, Edward Burton, Esq. is still an object of great veneration. To the County Hall, the word NEW should also have been prefixed, as is to the Infirmary:—these two latter splendid erections display the regard for justice, and the feelings of benevolence, by which the inhabitants of Shropshire are unceasingly actuated. It will be observed that this plate is the size of the Map, and may very properly be placed with it; and the plate in Honour of Naval and Military Heroes, or the View of Shrewsbury in 1830, adopted instead, as the Frontispiece.

The Plate not mentioned in the List, and accompanying the work, is a very humble present to the Subscribers by the Publisher, and may or may not be bound up with the volume.

The View of Bodhilin was engraved at the expence of the worthy owner of the delightful residence it represents, and is the only engraving of any kind not supplied at the Publisher's own cost.—In many publications of a similar nature, a great portion of the Plates are gifts to the author; this is especially the case in Baker's History of the County of Northampton.

While engaged in preparing a List of the various Translators of the Scriptures into English, for an intended new publication, the attention of the Author of this work was directed to a great, good, and learned Divine, born at Owlbury, near Bishop's Castle, in 1549, died 1612, viz.—HUGH BROUGHTON; descended from an ancient family of rank, worth and estate. On his armorial bearings, Mr. Broughton, it appears, displayed three Owls, probably referring to some tradition from which the place of his birth derived its name—OWLBURY. It is remarked, that in some editions of the genealogies set before our Bibles, two Owls are pictured, holding each of them a burning torch, intimating the wisdom and light Mr. Broughton had exhibited in his Translation of several portions of the Holy Bible, particularly the Books of Daniel, Ecclesiastes, and Job. He was tutor to Sir Rowland Cotton, of Cotton, Alkington, and Bellaport, Sheriff of Shropshire in 1647, and instructed his pupil perfectly in the Hebrew Language, by the time he was 7 years of age.—This Sir Rowland is noticed by Fuller, among the worthies of Shropshire. The Rev. J. B. Blakeway says—" the Cottons, Baronets of Combermere, now raised to the Peerage, are supposed by some genealogists to be of the same family;" and which opinion has been adopted by the author of this publication, (*vide page* 359, *this vol.*)—but who, without presuming to give a decided judgment in the case, is now most strongly inclined to believe, that the ancestors of the Combermere Cottons were seated at Coton, or Cotton, in the Parish of Hodnet, from which place Sir G. Cotton, Steward of the Household to Henry VIII., removed to Combermere Abbey.— This family, it is said, was resident at the above Coton or Cotton, before the Norman Conquest, and is of Saxon extraction.

In the Preface to Vol. 1, the Author has stated that Mr. Phillips was a Tide Waiter at Chatham,—it is probable that information may not be correct, as in looking over some volumes of the Shrewsbury Chronicle, he observed that Mrs. Phillips, the wife of Mr. P. died in London, October 1792; he might therefore be an officer of the Port of London. At the same time, the Author likewise observed the following notice—" Nov. 16, 1772, died in Skyddy's Alms-houses, Cork, Catharine Parr, aged 103, Great Grand-daughter of old Thomas Parr, of Alberbury."

On the 21st February, 1837, died Stephen Davies of Leighton, of whom mention is made (*vide page* 149), in his 103rd year—retaining the use of all his faculties and limbs, to the last hour.

Among recent deaths of individuals connected with Shropshire, we have to regret those of the beloved Sir Richard Ferdinand Dalbergh Acton, of Aldenham Hall; and the talented J. Marshall, Jun. Esq., M. P., one of the proprietors of the Linen Mills, Shrewsbury.—The former died in Paris, and the latter in London.

THE

HISTORY AND ANTIQUITIES OF SHREWSBURY.

CHAPTER I.

THE NAME, ITS ETYMOLOGY, AND ORTHOGRAPHY.

IT may give pleasure to some, especially those who have a partiality for their native place, to ascertain its true name, and the etymology of it; and indeed this necessarily enters into, and should constitute the first part of every local description, and so far as we can obtain help, merits a distinct enquiry.

Various conjectures are generally formed concerning the derivation of names, but the orthography of our ancestors is so extremely defective, that after the most minute enquiry, we arrive only at a state of uncertainty and conjecture.

Concerning Shrewsbury, we find it was called by the Saxons Scrobesburie, or Scrobbesbyri, and by the Britons who were the founders, (as generally supposed), Pengwerne, both which names signify the same, viz. a hill of shrubs or alders; before the Norman conquest, it was called Pengwerne Powis, probably because the princes of Powis, or Powis-land, had their palace and residence here.

When the Normans became possessed of this island, the names of places were very much altered; either owing to a partiality for their own language, or from an inability, or unwillingness, to frame their mouths to pronounce some of the harsh names used by the Saxons; hence they called this town Slopesbury, from whence say some, the name Salop, in Latin Salopiæ, is formed; others say, from two Saxon words *Sel*, pleasant, great, or advantageous, and *hope*, a side of a hill; which name answers very well to its situation, especially to that part which probably was first built upon to stop the pass over the ford, near the Stone Bridge, viz. the Wyle-Cop, which is a steep ascent.

In some old records and charters, we find it spelt various ways; about the time of the Norman conquest, it was written Sciropesberie, Scropesbery, Scroburiæ; in the reign of Henry II. it is spelt Salopesberie; in King John's reign in sundry grants and charters, we find it written Salopesbirie, Salopes-

B

beri, Salopesbiri, and Salopesbyriæ: Leland, in his itinerary, giving a description of Bridgnorth castle, founded by Robert de Belesmo, says, he also founded a chapel at Quatford, and stiles him Robert de Belesmo, Earl of Schrobbesbury.

Mr. Cambden declares himself quite ignorant, how the Normans, upon their first settlement here, came to give this town the names of Slopesbury, and Salop, unless they took those names from the old Scrobbesburi, awkwardly wrested.

Leland the poet and antiquary, thus describes Shrewsbury:

Edita Pinguerni late vestigia splendent,
Urbs sita lunato veluti mediamnis in orbe,
Colle tumet modica, duplici quoque ponte superbit,
Accipiens patria sibi lingua nomen ab alnis*.

In English,

Built on a hill, fair Salop greets the eye,
While Severn forms a crescent gliding by;
Two bridges cross the navigable stream,
And British alders gave the town a name.

Notwithstanding it may fairly be concluded from the above account that the derivation of the names of Shrewsbury and Salop, are from the names by which the place appears to have been called in the times of the Saxons and Normans, yet some plausible conjectures have been made relative to their derivation from some fabulous traditions or accidental circumstances; with one of these perhaps may rank a tradition, that before the foundation of Shrewsbury, the public road or highway from Wroxeter (then called Uriconium) to Chester, was through the ford near the place where the bridge was afterwards built, up the hill now called the Wyle-Cop, and so on for the turning for Chester, near where the cross now stands; and that at that time there stood only two houses, one an inn for the accommodation of travellers, on the side of the road near the place where the Bull's-Head inn now stands, and the other a sort of religious house, on the spot where Mr. Partridge's† house now stands, below the Cross; it is further said that in this house, a number of prostitutes were kept in private, who after their untimely or else natural deaths, were buried in a vault underneath the building, which being discovered in after times, occasioned the calling of the place by some Shrewsbury, i. e. the place where the shrews were buried; hence the town was called by some for the reasons before noticed, Salop, and by others on the above account Shrewsbury: what favours the above report, is the great number of human bones that have been dug up in the aforesaid vault (now Mr. Flint's† wine cellar) in the memory of several persons yet living.

* Cambden's Brit. vol. i. page 655.

---

† † 1828, occupied by Mr. Tomlins, Liquor Merchant.—ED.

CHAPTER. II.

SITUATION, CLIMATE, EPIDEMICAL DISTEMPERS, SOIL, RIVER.

SHREWSBURY is situate nearly in the centre of Shropshire, or the county of Salop, of which it is the principal town ; it stands for the most part upon two gently rising hills, on the banks of the river Severn, and the country for ten miles round is nearly upon a level, so that from many parts of the town the inhabitants have an extensive and delightful prospect of the country, and the meandrings of the Severn. It is in the hundred to which it gives name, commonly called the liberties of Shrewsbury, which liberties are bounded on the east, by the hundred of South Bradford ; on the south by the hundreds of Condover and Ford ; and on the north, by North Bradford hundred ; and is distant from*

MILES.		MILES.		MILES.
London, - - 156	Chester, - - 40	Ludlow, - - 28
Bristol, - - 114	Worcester, - 48	Bridgnorth, - 20
Liverpool, - 55	Litchfield, - 40	Whitchurch, - 20
York, - - - 136	Birmingham, - 44	Newport, - - 20

Shrewsbury is 20 deg. and 37 min. distant from the Azores, and 52 deg. and 53 min. from the Equator.

Few places enjoy a more healthful climate, or happy temperature of air than Shrewsbury ; its elevated situation, laying it open to a perpetual current of air ; and though upon this account, on the north side of this town is exposed to severe blasts, especially in the winter season ; yet it is free from those disagreeable and injurious effects that are frequently produced, where the situation of a town is low, owing to a perpetual damp and a moist air.

The variations of the weather are not more common here, than in other places ; nor are transitions from heat to cold, or from cold to heat, frequent or sudden.

The continual resort of strangers to Shrewsbury, and the number of genteel families, who frequently come and settle here, are indisputable proofs of the opinion such entertain, of the beauty and healthfulness of the situation, together with common observation and experience.

---

* From London (*by* Coventry) only 153 miles, from Welshpool 18 miles, from Oswestry 18 miles, from Holyhead 107 miles.—ED.

Epidemical disorders, have at several times visited this town, but seldom for a long duration ; the most remarkable we meet with any account of, were the following, viz.

In the year 1525, when the plague swept away great numbers, and was followed by a dearth, so that many died for want of bread.

The next time this most dreadful disorder made its appearance here, was in 1575, when it may be supposed, numbers were infected, and the carrying on trade and business, attended with hazard ; the fairs and markets during its continuance, being held at distant places; St. Matthew's fair (the 21st. September) was kept in Kingsland.

After a short interval of 29 years, in the year 1604, we find the plague again raged with great violence, so that from the 2nd day of June when it first began, to the 6th of April in the following year, when it ceased, 667 persons died in the five parishes ; so little were the streets frequented at this time, that they were mostly covered with grass.

Once more, in the year 1630, the plague was in Shrewsbury, only in St. Chad's parish; it begun in Frankwell, on the 24th day of May: the inhabitants of that street, being denied the liberty of coming into the town, lest the infection should spread, at length made an attempt to force a passage over the bridge, but were repulsed, and beaten back, by the bailiffs and townsmen. The pesthouse was in Kingsland ; Saturday's market was kept at the Claypits, on the Old-Heath, and Wednesday's market at Kingsland.

The sweating sickness, which spread towards the north, and over the greatest part of the kingdom, first began here, in the year 1551, on the 15th of April, and did not cease till October following, in which time near a thousand died*. This distemper raged with great violence, carrying off most that were seized with it in twenty-four hours; the patients when seized were thrown into a prodigious sweat, first affecting some particular part ; with unquenchable thirst, restlessness, sickness at stomach and heart, (though seldom vomiting), head ache, delirium, then faintings, and excessive drowsiness ; the pulse quick and vehement, and the breath short and labouring. If the patients took cold, they died within three hours; if they slept within six hours after seizure, they died raving ; if they lived twenty-four hours, they were almost sure to recover. The method of cure, was, to keep the patient in a moderate sweat, and to give him temperate cordials, which without much increasing the heat, helped nature to expel the humours that caused such violent sweats. It raged chiefly among young men of strong constitutions. From this disorder being peculiar to the English nation, it was called the English sweat. It did not seize foreigners who were here in England, and in other countries only Englishmen were afflicted with it.

One remedy in this disorder was, those who were taken ill in the day time, were immediately put to bed in their clothes ; and those who sickened

* Friend's History of Physic, vol. ii. page 335.

in the night, were ordered to lie there twenty-four hours, but were not to sleep at all. The most eminent physicians were puzzled about the cause of this distemper; some ascribed it to the chalky grounds in England, (but these are not to be found about Shrewsbury, where it first began) supposing that the steam from that sort of soil infected the animal spirits, or the blood; but this is uncertain conjecture, though undoubtedly the subtle parts of the blood were infected in this disease, which occasioned the expiration of the patient, or removal of the disorder in so short a time. This disorder first appeared in England in 1483, in Henry VII's army, upon his landing at Milford Haven; and spread itself in London from the 21st Sept. to the end of October.—It returned five times, and always in summer; first in 1485, then in 1506, afterwards in 1517, when it was so violent that it killed in three hours: it appeared again in 1528, and proved mortal then in the space of six hours; many courtiers died of it, and Henry VIII. himself was in danger. In 1529, and only then, it infested the Netherlands and Germany, and the last return of it was in 1551, the time above mentioned*.

The soil in and near Shrewsbury is in general dry, and a reddish kind of earth; little or nothing of rock appears in the hills on which it is built, though it is probable some stone was formerly got on the south side of the town.

The river Severn, which nearly encompasses Shrewsbury, has its rise at the foot of Plinlimmon Hill†, in Montgomeryshire, and after being joined by the Verneyw, and some other small rivers, passes on by Shrewsbury, Bridgnorth, Worcester, and Gloucester, and empties itself into the sea near Bristol, having run nearly two hundred miles, and is navigable for vessels of considerable burthen;

* Friend's History of Physic, vol. ii. page 336.

---

† This mountain is partly in Montgomeryshire, and partly in Cardiganshire; forming, as it were, one of the boundaries of North Wales. Its height is 2463 feet; consequently, in comparison with its neighbour, Cader Idris, whose height is 2914 feet, its altitude is not great. It is one of those eminences, however, which powerfully aided the ancient inhabitants of the island in resisting the successive inroads of the Romans, the Saxons, and the Normans. Of later date, the famous Glyndwr —the man who could " call spirits from the vasty deep"—proved it a strong hold. In the first year of his insurrection, finding himself unable to meet the formidable force which had been dispatched against him, he, with a chosen band of adherents, formed an advantageous encampment on Plynlimmon. Thus he was enabled to receive succours from the north as well as from the south; and subsequently, to alarm and ravage the country, by sacking Montgomery, burning Poole, and destroying the Abbey of Cwm Hir, in Radnorshire.

Plynlimmon is supposed, by some, to derive its name from the circumstance of its giving birth to five rivers; three of which, the Severn, the Rheidiol, and the Wye, are of considerable note. Others, however, contend that in ancient times, on five of its most conspicuous heights it had so many beacons; whence it acquired the appellation of Pumlumon, or Five Beacons.

Ireland's Picturesque Views on the Severn.

fourteen vessels* of from 30 to 50 tons burthen, are in constant employ between Shrewsbury and Gloucester, and numbers more lower down in the river. By reason of the mountainous country adjoining, the river is frequently subject to floods, through the rapid descent of rain down their declivities, and the sudden melting of snow; the most material that have happened, are inserted in the following table.

Anno 1338, a great flood, occasioned by a continual rain from the beginning of October to December.

Anno 1348, through a violent rain, from Midsummer to Christmas, a constant swell of the river was occasioned; during that period there was not one day or night dry together.

Anno 1545, a great flood, when through the violence of its passage under the stone bridge, the gate thereupon fell down.

Anno 1673, during a great flood, a small whale came up the river Severn, and was taken.

Anno 1729, a great flood.

Anno 1740, in December, was the greatest flood that had been known in the memory of man; the water rose to the greatest height on the 10th day of the month; it flowed into the chancel of the Abbey church, and greatly damaged the floor and pews.

---

* The following is a List of the present owners in Shrewsbury, the names and tonnage of their respective vessels:—

The Eliza,	50 Tons,		Mr. Thomas Bratton.
The Nelly,	30 Tons,		Ditto
The John,	6 Tons,		Ditto
The Welcome,	30 Tons,		Mr. James Harwood.
The William,	40 Tons,		Mr. Thomas Harwood,
The Mary,	40 Tons,		Ditto
The Flora,	12 Tons,		Ditto
The Hero,	8 Tons,		Ditto
The Black Boat,	6 Tons,		Ditto
The Perseverance,	50 Tons,		Mr. John Jones
The Union,	45 Tons,		Ditto
The Wonder,	40 Tons,		Ditto
The Utility,	8 Tons,		Ditto
The Success,	40 Tons,		Mr. John Rees.
The Betsey,	40 Tons,		Ditto
The Prudence,	35 Tons,		Ditto
Two Boats, one 10 Tons, the other 6 Tons, but no name to them.			Ditto
The Prosper,	35 Tons,		Mr. Thomas Wilcox.
The Happy Return,	6 Tons,		Ditto

It will appear extraordinary to some, that after the advance of half a century, the navigation of the River Severn, by Shrewsbury Owners, should have so little increased. The reason may probably be found in the ready communication with Liverpool, through the medium of the Ellesmere Canal.—ED.

Anno 1748, in the time of a flood, a dolphin, one yard, four inches in length, came up the river, and was taken in the wear.

Anno 1770, a great flood, near a foot higher than the marks placed in several places at the height of the flood in 1740.

Anno, 1772*, in November, was a great flood; the river rose to such a height, that many poor families were exceedingly distressed,

Various conjectures are formed relative to the etymology of the name of this river; some say it is derived from Abren, the beautiful base daughter of Locrinus, begotten out of wedlock upon Estrildis, the daughter of Humber, the Scythian king, who invaded this island; both of them were drowned in this river by Guendolena, King Locrinus's surviving widow; agreeable to this notion are the following lines of Geoffrey†, an ancient poet.

> Into this stream, fair Abren's body cast,
> Gave name of Abren to the waters vast,
> Corruptly called SABRINA, now at last.

Henry, in his History of England, says, Sœfirne, Saxon, signifies sea-flowing, called in English, Severn.

SABRINA in Latin, and Severn in English, is no other than the British word Savr or Havr, (for S and H are often changed in the dialect of that language) which word we suppose had anciently violence in its meaning‡.

The Britains call this river Hafren, from Aber a cataract or fall of waters, or rather by way of excellence, it imports the same as Æstuarium, an arm of the sea; for places where salt and fresh water meet have the addition of Aber, as Abergavenny, Abertivi, &c.

Excellent fish are found in this river, particularly salmon, pike, shad, trout, flounders, eels, chubs, gudgeons, roach, dace, and others of the smaller sort, with some carp and lampreys.

‡ Britain Antiq. et Nov. page 119.

---

* For subsequent floods see Continuation.—ED.

† Camden ridicules this account of Geoffrey, as a mere legendary fiction; but, at the same time, he acknowledges his own ignorance as to the derivation of the river's name. Neither Lloyd nor Pennant have thrown any new light upon the subject.

The conversion of *Hafren*, or *Havren*, into the English appellation *Severn*, appears easy. At Llanidloes, the Hafren is joined by a rivulet, formed of three mountain streams, bearing the name of *Si*, or *Se*, on account of the hissing sound of its waters; thus a junction of names, as well as of rivers, is formed; as, from *Se-havren*, the passage is natural to *Seavren*, as it is termed in the old maps, and thence to *Severn*.—*Ireland's Picturesque Views on the Severn*.

CHAPTER III.

ANCIENT HISTORY.

SHREWSBURY cannot boast of having derived its name from the Romans; no monuments of their greatness are here visible; it is true indeed, some writers have mentioned it, as existing in a very early period; but their assertions, or conjectures, want sufficient support; among these, in a copy of a manuscript, at the end of Hearne's History of Glastonbury, Shrewsbury is said to have been built by Diffenwall Moel Myd, about 669 years after Brutus's first entrance into this island, anno mundi 3525, before Christ 438.

But as it would be disagreeable to the reader, to be detained with uncertainties, or puzzled with doubtful facts; we shall proceed to mention the first certain account we have, and in a regular course, take notice of various historical occurrences down to the present time.

The town is supposed to have been built by the Britons*, between the

---

* We conceive that our town was built *after the Saxon invasion;* but that it owed its foundation *to the Britons.* We cannot claim for it any pretensions to the dignity of a Roman station. No vestige of that imperial people has ever been discovered within its circuit. But a few miles lower down the river, at the present village of Wroxeter, was the flourishing town of Uriconium: and here doubtless, after the Romans had finally withdrawn their forces from the island, the Britons continued to occupy the seats deserted by their ancient masters, until they were driven from them by superior force; to the time of which we may approximate within no very wide range of years. We are in possession of the valuable poems of Llywarc Hèn: valuable, notwithstanding their great obscurity, for the few rays of light which they scatter over the darkest period of our history. He was a prince of the Cumbrian Britons; who, pressed by the Northumbrian Saxons, retired, towards the end of the sixth century, to his countrymen in Powis, among whom he is said to have protracted his life to the unusual extent of 145 years, driving thence the epithet of *hèn*, or *the old.* His writings contain several proofs of his acquaintance with the district now called Shropshire. Its streams, Severn, and Morlas, and Tern; its mountains, Digoll, Ness Cliff or Clegyr, and Digon; its towns, Baschurch, Earcall, Hodnet, all appear in his poems: and when he speaks also of Pengwern, and when it is known that this was the Welsh name of Shrewsbury, we need not doubt that he designed by that appellation to mark our town, and consequently that it had then arisen.—*Owen and Blakeway's History of Shrewsbury.*

The ancient Uriconium, now Wroxeter, in Shropshire, was the capital of the Cornavii. In the catalogues of Bishop Usher and T. Williams, it is called Caer Wrygion, and no doubt, to be indentified with Caer Gwrgon in the Triads of the Isle of Britain. Llywarch Hèn, who spent a portion of his life in Powys, has the following allusion to this ancient city under the Saxon name of Wrecon.

> Neu'r syllais o ddinlle *Vrecon,*
> Freuer werydre;
> Hiraeth am daminhorth broadyrdde?

> Have I not gazed from the high city of Wrecon,
> The region of Freuer;
> With longing for the guardian of the commonwealth?—*Elegy on Cynddylan.*

This name of Wrecon is still retained in the Wrekin Hill in the vicinity.—*Cambro-Briton, June* 1822, *page* 461.

years 520 and 594, as a refuge from the Saxons, who levelled their ancient fortress of Wroxeter with the ground, and forced them to retreat beyond the Severn; which river then became the boundary of the kingdom of Mercia, the finest and most considerable of all the kingdoms of the Heptarchy, and was bounded on the north by the Humber, on the west by the river Severn, on the south by the Thames, and on the east by the kingdoms of Essex, and East Anglia; its length was 160 miles, breadth about 100; derivation from Mer, Saxon, signifying a bound.

In 617, the town was called Pengwerne Powis; Brockwel* Yisithroe, Prince of Powis, and Earl of Chester, then dwelt here; his palace stood on the same spot, where the church of St. Chad now stands, but was afterwards burnt down, in some of the wars with the Saxons; notwithstanding, this continued the place of their residence; for we find in the reign of Offa, about the year 777, that the seat of the Princes of Powis was translated from hence to Matraval, in Montgomeryshire; the Britons who were then in possession of this town, having made incursions into the kingdom of Mercia, were forced not only to abandon all their conquests there, but also that part of their country which lay between Severn and Offa's dyke, or ditch, which that king threw up as a new boundary between them and Mercia, instead of Severn their former boundary. The Britons, or Welsh had made their incursions into Offa's territories, while he was employed in subduing the Saxon kings, and having no opposition, they were very successful, till at length Offa being obliged to conclude a peace with the English, that he might dispossess them of their new acquisitions, he proved so successful as to force their retreat; and to prevent their ever returning, threw up the before-mentioned ditch, or rampart, on the side of which, next to his dominions, no Welshman durst ever afterwards appear with arms. King Harold afterwards aggravated this oppression, by a law, enacting, that if any Welshman was found with weapons in his hands, on this side that ditch, he should forthwith have his right hand cut off†.

"This dyke, or ditch, may be seen on Brachy Hill, and near Rhydor, "Helig, and Lanterden, in Herefordshire, and is continued northwards from

† Speed.

---

* This Brochwel is called of the Latine writers *Brecinallus* and *Brochmaelus*, of whom it is thus written *in Historia divæ monacellæ.*

Fuit olim in POWYSIA *quidam Princeps illustrissimus nomine* Brochwel Ysgithrog, *consul* Legecestriæ, *qui in urbe tunc temporis,* Pengwern Powys, *nunc vero* Salopia *dicta est habitabat; cujus domicilium seu Habitaculum ibi Steterat, ubi collegium divi Ceddæ nunc situm est.*

That is, there was sometimes in *Powys* a noble Prince, named *Brochwel Ysgithrog* Consul or Earl of *Chester*, who dwelt in a Town then called *Pengwern Powis,* and now *Salop,* whose dwelling House was in the very same place where the College of *St. Chadd* now standeth.—"*A Display of Herauldry*," *by Mr. John Davies of Llan-Silin-Parish in Denbighshire, Antiquary. Printed by John Roderick, Salop,* 1716.

C

" Knighton, over part of Shropshire, and goes over the long mountain of
" Kevn Digoth, to Harden Castle, across the Severn and Llandrinio common ;
" from whence it passes the Vyrnwy again into Shropshire, not far from
" Oswestry : in Denbighshire it is visible along the road between Rhyabon
" and Wrexham, and being continued through Flintshire, ends a little below
" Holywell." *

In King Alfred's reign, Shrewsbury was numbered among the British
cities, by the name of Caer Pengwerne ; and in the reign of Edward the
Elder, there was a mint for coining money here, the coin having the following
inscription thereon, viz. *Edward Rex Angliæ*, and on the reverse, *Aelmaer
on Scrobe*.

King Ethelred, in the Christmas, 1006, kept his court at Shrewsbury,
about which time the Danes under Swaine, were grown so powerful, and
intolerably insolent, that the king could neither by law or force, redress his
subjects grievances. The Danes had been stirred up to invade this kingdom,
by an edict of Ethelred's, issued in 1002, when, contriving to effect their
destruction by policy, which he found himself unable to do by strength, he
sent a secret commission to all cities and towns, with orders to fall upon the
Danes, and kill them all on St. Brice's day, Nov. 13, which order was executed
with rigour ; the Danes, determined to revenge this massacre of their brethren,
landed in the Isle of Wight ; the king being then here, called a council, to
know what was best to be done ; Edric, Duke of Mercia, and several others
present, advised him to offer the Danes £30,000, to purchase a peace, they
accepted the offer, and departed ; but soon returned, and never left off
destroying, till they so weakened the nation, as to have it in their power to
establish a king of their own here.

The above mentioned Duke, Edric Streon, who was husband to Edgith,
second daughter to King Ethelred, and who had by him been created Duke
of Mercia, murdered Duke Alfhelm, a prince of the blood, near Shrewsbury,
which he effected by the following stratagem ; he invited him to a banquet
in Shrewsbury, afterwards took him out a hunting, and led him into a wood,
where was laid in ambush for that purpose, one Godwin Porthund, a butcher
of the town, who was hired by Edric to kill the Duke, and spying an
opportunity, fell upon him, and murdered him. From whence probably,
came that custom of the city of Salop, recorded in doomsday book, viz.
That twelve of the chief citizens should guard the king's person, during his
stay here, and the same number attend him whenever he went out a hunting.

Edmund, son of King Ethelred, marched with his forces from the north
to Shrewsbury, in the year 1016 ; the town had then revolted to Canute the
Dane ; but Edmund retaking it, with great cruelty punished the inhabitants
for their revolt.

* Cambden, p. 698, v. ii.

In the reign of Edward the Confessor, we are informed by doomsday book, there was a mint for coinage here; also particular mention is therein made of the following churches, viz. St. Almund, St. Julian, Salton church, St. Coed, and the monastery of St. Peter, which is stiled the parish of the city.

Nothing further do we meet with that is material, till after the Norman conquest; when in the year 1067,* the Welsh, under the command of Owen Gwynedd, Prince of Wales, laid siege to Shrewsbury; but the King, (William the Conqueror,) marching thither from York, raised the siege, and took vengeance on the Welsh.

In this and following reigns, the Earls of Shrewsbury kept their court here, this being the capital of the Earldom; they had subordinate Barons under them, who were convened about all affairs of weight or moment, and in their presence the Earls did most solemn acts of donation, investiture, &c. as appears by several charters or grants, made by the Earls of Shrewsbury to that abbey, which recite the same to be confirmed in the presence of their Barons, assembled for that purpose; these Barons probably were such as held land of the Earls in Shropshire. Roger de Montgomery, at this time Earl of Shrewsbury, had almost the whole of the county given him by the King, (William I.) to whom he was nearly related; and under the Earl the following persons held lordships or manors, granted by the king, who was obliged to gratify his commanders with honours and large estates, viz.

William Pantulf, held twenty-nine lordships of Roger de Montgomery, of which Wem was the chief, and head of his barony.

Roger Lacey, the son of Walter Lacey, who came with the Conqueror into England, held of himself and of Roger de Montgomery twenty-three manors.

Ralph de Montgomery, another of his captains, held fifty manors, nineteen of them under Roger de Montgomery.

Guarine, or Warine de Meez, (an ancestor of the family of Waring's, now possessed of considerable estates in this town and county,) a branch of the house of Lorraine, held one manor.

Osborne Fitz Richard, held nine manors.

Roger Fitz Corbett, (an ancestor of the several illustrious families in Shropshire of that name),also held twenty-four manors under the aforesaid Earl†.

Earl Roger, in one of these aforementioned deeds, stiles himself *Rogerius dei gratia Scrodesburiensis Comes.*

* Rapin says 1069.

† ORD VITALIS says, that Earl Corbett, (ancestor of the Shropshire Corbetts,) came over with the Conqueror in 1066, having two sons, Roger and Robert; Roger, the eldest, gave Wentalage to the Benedictine monks of the great abbey in Shrewsbury, finished in 1083, to which gift William and Everard, his sons, were consenting: Robert, the younger son, also gave Nutenne, and several other places. At the compiling of doomsday book, both Roger and Robert held several lordships in Shropshire, of Roger de Montgomery, chief lord of the county. William Corbett, (often called Corbel,) cousin of the abovesaid Roger and Robert, was a monk of Shrewsbury abbey, 1115, afterwards prior of Chirk in Essex, founded in 1120, was made archbishop of Canterbury in 1123, died and was buried there in 1136.

In doomsday survey, taken in the year 1086, Shrewsbury is stiled a city, and the abbey said to be founded where the parish church of the city stood. The following customs and usages are there also recorded, viz.

In the city of Sciropesburie, in King Edward's time, there were 252 houses, and an equal number of burgesses inhabiting these houses, who paid yearly £7. 16s. 8d. de gablo (excise.)

If any person broke the peace, given under the King's own hand, that person was to be outlawed: but if any man committed a breach of the King's peace, signified by the sheriff, he forfeited ten shillings.

He that drew blood in an affray was to pay forty shillings by way of amends.

When the King left the city, the sheriff sent 24 horses to Lenteurde, to conduct him the first stage into Staffordshire.

The King had here three masters of the mint, who were obliged, as the other coiners of the country, to pay the King twenty shillings at the end of fifteen days; while the money was uttered out of the mint, and while it was current.

The city paid in the whole £20 yearly, the King had two-thirds, and the sheriff one.

This city in King Edward's time was rated at 100 hides, of these hides the church of St. Alkmond had two, St. Julian half one, St. Milburg one hide, St. Chad three hides and a half, St. Mary one rood, the Bishop of Chester three hides, Edric three hides, which Ralph de Mortimer afterwards enjoyed.

Whenever the King lay in Shrewsbury, twelve of the best citizens were to sit up and guard him, and the like number to attend him with horse and arms, when he went a hunting.

Every woman marrying, was to pay to the King, if a widow, twenty shillings, if a maid, ten shillings.

Every burgess whose house should be burnt down, must forfeit to the king forty shillings, and to his two next neighbours two shillings each.

Every burgess dying, his executors were to pay ten shillings to the king.

The above-mentioned book, called doomsday book, was collected by order of William I. it contained a description of all England; how much land every one of the Barons possessed; how many Knights fees; how many plough lands; how many cities, villages, monasteries and religious houses; the number of the people, and their names, with what each one might be supposed to spend in the year; also how much ready money every man, from the greatest to the least, possessed; and what rents might be made from every man's possessions. This done, he exacted six shillings for every hide of land, which amounted to a great sum of money. This book of inquisition was called doomsday, because in it the land was judged. It is in two volumes, wrote in a legible hand, still remaining in the Exchequer. Five justices, in each county, were appointed to make the collection, in 1081, and finished it in 1086. Of this collection, Robert, a poet, at Gloucester, wrote as follows, in the language of the time in which he lived :—

The King William, ver to whe the worth of his lond,
Let enqueri stretlich, thorn all Engelond,
How moni plow land, and how moni hiden also,
Were in everich sire, and wat all were wurth yereto,
And the rents of eich toun, and of the waters echone,
The wurth ; and of woods, the were ne lived none :
But that he wist wat he were wurth of all Engelond,
And wite all clene, that wurth thereof eich understond,
And let it write clene inou, and that scrite dude iwis
In the tresorie at Westminster, there it yut is,
So that ure King sith when hii ransome toke,
Yrede what folc might give, hii fond there in yor boke.

In the next reign of William II. in the year 1098, Hugh de Montgomery, second son of Earl Roger, and who succeeded him in the earldom of Shrewsbury, being invited, together with the Eàrl of Chester, into Wales, by Owen, a Welsh Lord, father-in-law to Griffith, and uncle to Cadogan, Kings of Wales, who had disobliged him ; he, (Owen) promising the two Earls a great booty, they raised some troops, and joined him in Wales, where they committed unspeakable cruelties, particularly on one Kenred, a priest, an aged man, on whose counsel the Welsh relied, and who had fled to a church for sanctuary ; when the Earl was informed where he was, orders were given to drag him out, and to cut off his testicles ; and when they had done this, they also put out one of his eyes, and cut his tongue out.

The two Welsh Kings, surprised by this unexpected attack, were forced to fly into Ireland, and leave their country to the mercy of the English. Their flight giving their enemies an opportunity to continue their march, they penetrated to the Isle of Anglesey, where they destroyed all before them with fire and sword. While they were thus exercising their cruelties, Magnus, King of Norway, who had lately made himself master of the Isle of Man, advanced as far as Anglesey ; as he offered to land, the English endeavoured to hinder him, and the Earl of Shrewsbury, was slain in the skirmish ; for in order to prevent their landing, he ran to the sea side, and plunged himself into the water ; Magnus seeing him so resolute, levelled an arrow, and though the Earl was covered with armour, all but his eyes, it pierced his right eye, and reaching his brain, down he fell sprawling in the water, whereupon Magnus, in the Danish language, cried out, " Let him dance*."

His death was looked upon as a just judgment for the horrid cruelties committed by him in that isle ; he was brought to Shrewsbury, and buried in the abbey cloister, with great lamentation, the bishops of Hereford and Chester being present, with the whole body of Monks ; his portraiture was made of stone, with the legs across. This Earl's death caused some disorder among

* Itiner. Cambr. Lib. 2, C. 7.

the English troops, and constrained them to abandon the shore ; when Magnus landed,, and finding the English had left nothing to plunder, he reimbarked, and they retired richly laden with spoil.

In the reign of Henry 1. A. D. 1102, Robert de Belesme, eldest son of Earl Roger, who succeeded his younger brother Hugh, in the Earldom of Shrewsbury, being a rash and discontented young man, was among those who were for bringing in Duke Robert, instead of Henry I. and even after Henry was crowned, he spoke several disrespectful things of him, and afterwards rebelled ; in consequence of which he fortified his castles in Shropshire, and at Shrewsbury built and fortified a flank wall, from each side of the castle, across the Isthmus down to severn side; hereupon the king declared him a traitor, and marched with a considerable force against him. Robert, hearing of the king's arrival at Bridgnorth, and the taking of that town, immediately left Shrewsbury to the care of Roger the son of Corbeth, Roger de Nevil, and Ulger Grosvenor, alias Ulger de Venables, and with them 80 stipendiary soldiers; having made peace with the Welsh, he frequently disturbed the king's forces, but being much harassed by William Pantulf, a great man in Shropshire, whom he had before slighted, he was forced to return again to Shrewsbury, to which place the king marched with 60,000 soldiers, in order to besiege it. Upon his Majesty's approach to the town, he threatened the governors, if the castle was not delivered to him in three days, he would hang all he should take therein ; upon which the Earl implored the king's mercy, acknowledged his crime of treason, and sent the keys by Ralph, Abbot of Seys, afterwards Archbishop of Canterbury, which the King graciously accepted, and banished the Earl to Normandy, to the general joy of all the people, who got rid of so great an oppressor. On the forfeiture of this Earl, the king seized the town of Shrewsbury, and all his other possessions, into his own hands, and granted the town their first charter.

When he was got abroad, he found means to appear again in arms against his prince ; but at length was brought over in chains to England, where he was kept prisoner for life, at Wareham, and died a miserable death, leaving only one son, William, who through the intercession of Maud, the king's daughter, enjoyed part of his father's possessions in Normandy, by the stile of Earl of Ponthiev.

Towards the end of the same year, the king sent several of his council to Shrewsbury; among whom were Richard de Belmersh, Bishop of London, Warden of the Marches*, and Governor of the county of Salop; Rayner, Lieutenant of the said county, and others, to meet there Iorweth ap Blithyn,

---

* The Marches of Wales, are supposed to be settled by the Saxons, to prevent the incursions of the Britons, or Welsh. At the coronation of Queen Eleanor, consort of King Henry III the Lords Marchers claim to provide silver spears and support the canopy of purple silk, and were allowed it
. The Earls held their courts severally in their jurisdictions, till Henry VIII, fixed a court at Ludlow, which was continued till William III. After the death of the Earl of Macclesfield, the last Lord President thought fit to divide the government, between two Peers of the realm, with the titles of Lord Lieutenants of North and South Wales, and dissolved the court, which used to consist of a

on pretence of consulting with him about the king's affairs : but when he came there, contrary to all equity, he was condemned for treason, and committed to prison.

In 1116, the nobility of the realm, did homage, and swore fealty, to William, son of king Henry I. by Queen Maud, at Shrewsbury, March 19. It is said, this act of theirs, was the occasion of first establishing the high court of parliament.

In the next reign, viz. of King Stephen, we meet with an astonishing account, which must by no means be passed over with silence: viz. that in the year 1138, the bones of St. Wenefride were translated from Guitherin, a village in Denbighshire, to the Abbey at Shrewsbury ; Dugdale says, they were brought by the order of Robert, a monk, and afterwards made abbot ; however, on their arrival, we are told they were deposited in St. Giles's church, which is said to be near the gates of the city ; there they rested till an order of procession could be settled, to conduct them with all necessary pomp, to the abbey ; at this ceremony the bishop and convent assisted, a great number of people kneeling on each side the street ; and during the time of procession, it is recorded as a miracle, that notwithstanding abundance of rain fell in all other parts of the city, and in the fields round about, yet not a drop fell where the relics passed.

The advocates for St. Wenefride, and the miracles wrought on her account, relate her story thus :

In the seventh century, there lived a virgin whose name was Wenefride, she was born of noble parents, her father's name was Thewith, a noble and potent Lord in that part of Wales where Holywell stands, her mother's name was Wenlo, descended from a family in Montgomeryshire, and sister to St. Bueno. Bueno assumed the monastic habit, and retired to Clynnog in Caer-

lord president, as many councellors as the Prince pleased, a secretary, an attorney, a solicitor, and four justices of the counties of Wales —The marches extended from Bristol to Chester ; all the country between Offa's dyke and England, was called the marches, or bounds between the Welsh and English : the Lords Marchers had the power of life and death in their respective courts. and in every frontier manor, a gallows was erected, and if any Welshman came over the boundary, between them and the English, (then Saxons), they were taken up and hanged, every town within such marches being furnished with an horseman, armed with sword and spear, maintained on purpose to take them up ; and if any Englishman was catched on the Welsh side, he suffered the same fate, such was their antipathy to each other : for the Welshmen counted all lawful prizes they took from the English : for this reason houses were frequently moated round, and pallisadoes, or stakes, set round the edge of the moat, to make a stronger fence, into which places the inhabitants every night drove their cattle for better security. If a Welshman could get a stolen horse or cow over the bar, he cried out " my own," and further the horsemen durst not follow, or they would have hanged them.

Sir John Bridgman, one of the presidents of the Princes court at Ludlow was a very severe man, frequently committing persons to Porter Lodge, the proper prison of that court, for very small crimes ; on whom Ralph Gittins made the following epitaph :

Here lies Sir John Bridgman, clad in this clay,
God said to the Devil, sirrah, take him away.

narvonshire, where he built a church, and founded a convent; he afterwards visited his relations in Flintshire, and his brother-in-law giving him land, he built a church there, and took under his care his niece Wenefride, who as she grew up, was so wrought upon by the moving discourses of her pious uncle, that she determined to preserve her virginity, and accordingly made a vow of chastity.

A neighbouring Prince, Cradocus, the son of King Allen, was so ena-moured with the beauty of Wenefride, that espying an opportunity when her parents were gone to church, he came to her, made known his passion, and earnestly pressed her to comply with his desires: the blushing virgin made an excuse to go into the next room, when she privately slipt out of the house, and ran towards the church; the impatient Prince finding her gone, pursued, and on the descent of an hill, with a drawn sword in his hand, threatened to separate her head from her body if she did not consent to his will; the virgin still bravely refusing, he gave her a blow that at once separated her head from her body, which falling upon the descent of the hill, rolled down to the church where the congregation were assembled, and at that time kneeling before the altar: Cradocus instantly received the reward of his crime, for he fell down dead, and the earth opening swallowed up his corps. Where Wenefride's head stopt, a spring immediately burst forth, famous in succeeding times for its many virtues, and miraculous cures wrought by it. St. Bueno taking up the head, carried it to the corps, and offering up his devotions, nicely joined it to the body, which instantly reunited; the place was visible only by a slender white line encircling her neck, and she survived her decolation fifteen years. She died at Gwytherin in Denbighshire, (a small village near the river Cluide, which separates that county from Flintshire), where her bones rested till the time of the before-mentioned translation of them to the Abbey at Shrewsbury.*

The Abbot Robert, by whose order her bones were removed, (Dugdale says) was a man equally addicted to integrity of life, and good literature; and equally successful in both, he became renowned for both, and to shew his devotion and learning, he composed an elegant piece of St. Wenefride's life and martyrdom. Capgrave says, he died in 1148.

The 3rd of November, the day of St. Wenefride's death, was appointed by the church, for the celebration of her memory; and the feast of her deco-lation, was on the 22nd of June, which is one of the Abbey Foregate fairs, O. S. as the other is on the feast of St. Peter, *ad vincula.*

A fraternity or guild was established at Shrewsbury, in honour of this saint; it had its common seal of copper†, in which was a representation of her martyrdom; above was a cross in form of a T placed between the letters *T m,* which mark the time when the fraternity was instituted, during the

* Life of St. Wenefride. † Pennant's Tour.

Abbacy of Thomas Mynde, who was elected in 1459, and died in 1499. The T or cross, refers to the church of St. Cross, within the Monastery; beneath are the arms of the house, a sword and a key, and round the margin is the following inscription:

Sigillu coe Ffraternitat beate Wenefride virginis |‾eceia sce cruc‾|: *fra monaster. sci Petri Salopie.*

A bell belonging to the Abbey was christened in honour of St. Wenefride, at which ceremony the gossips laid hold of the rope, bestowed a name on the bell, and the Priest sprinkling it with holy water, baptized it in the name of the Father, Son, and Holy Ghost;[*] the Priest then cloathed the bell with a fine garment, the gossips gave a grand feast, and made great presents, which the Priest received in behalf of the bell; and the bell thus blessed, it was generally believed, that on being rung, it allayed storms, diverted thunder-bolts, and drove away evil spirits. Consecrated bells were always inscribed; the inscription on this was:

Round the outside, a little below the crown, in old English characters,
Sancta Wenefreda, Deo hoc commendare memento,
Ut pietate tua, nos servet ab hoste cruento.
O holy St. Wenefride, recommend us to God—That by thy goodness, he may preserve us from the bloody enemy.

Between the crown and the skirt, in text capitals,
Protege prece piâ, quos convoca virgo Maria.
O Virgin Mary, protect by thy pious prayers, those whom I call together.
Vidi El.

This great bell, commonly called St. Wenefride's bell, was remaining in the year 1673, when the rest of the bells were recast, and made into eight; about the year 1700, it was cracked, and sold to Mr. Rudhal, of Gloucester, and the money applied to the new pewing the church.

The castle of Shrewsbury, which had been built in the year 1068, by Roger de Montgomery, who appointed Warine the Bald the first governor thereof, we find in the year 1139, in possession of Wm. Fitz Allan, the son of Allan, who had married the daughter and heir of the before-mentioned Warine, and in her right became possessed of Warine's baronies.

William Fitz Allen was at this time governor of the town, and sheriff of the county; and several noblemen taking up arms in behalf of the Empress Maud, against King Stephen, he joined with them, leaving the castle, which

---

[*] Staveley's History of Churches.

D

he had strongly fortified, in the hands of a deputy governor, whom he made take an oath not to deliver the castle to the king; but the king besieged, stormed, and took it, and hanged several of the garrison for their obstinacy. Allan was forced to fly, leaving his castle and all his estates in the King's hands, still adhering to Maud; till her son, Henry II. came to the throne, when he was restored to his government, upon Henry's taking the castle, in 1152.

During the siege just now mentioned, by King Stephen, at which he was present in person, he granted a charter of confirmation to the abbey of Buildwas, with this remarkable date, viz. *Apud Salopesbiriam in Obsidione* (at Shrewsbury siege) Anno Dom. 1139.

In the beginning of the next reign, (King John), frequent engagements happened on the borders of Wales, between the King's forces and the Welsh; and the King's council being assembled at Shrewsbury, to determine what course to take with the Welsh, to prevent their ravages and depredations on the borders, Gwenwynwyn, Lord of Powis, coming there to treat with the council, was detained as a prisoner; and soon after this, in the year 1212, the Welsh having entered into a treaty, and given Rees, the son of Maelgon, a boy under seven years of age, as an hostage for performance of covenants; they breaking truce, the boy was hanged in Shrewsbury, by Robert Vepont, a friend of the King's.

Anno 1215 Llewellin, Prince of Wales* had gained considerably upon the King, in frequent incursions along the Marches, and coming to Shrewsbury with a great army, the town and castle were delivered to him without any resistance.

Though no particulars transpire relative to the dispossessing the Welsh, or the repossession of the English, yet it is evident that the Welsh did not remain masters of this town long; for in the year 1220, the King (Henry III.) by letters patent, dated at Shrewsbury, May 5, takes David the son of Llewellin, into his protection† ; and the following year sent for Llewellin, Prince of Wales, to Shrewsbury, and there settled a difference that had subsisted between Llewellin, and Rees, the son of Griffith ap Rees.

In the seventeenth year of this reign, A. D. 1233, in the week after Epiphany, Richard, Earl of Pembroke, and several other noblemen, being much disgusted with the conduct of the King; by the advice of Peter de Rupibus, Bishop of Winchester, they undertook openly to reprove him, representing his doings as pernicious and dangerous to the state, and afterwards broke out into open rebellion, for which they were publicly declared traitors.

† Rymer's Fœdera.

---

* This Prince had in 1195 asserted his just claim to the Sovereignty, which had been wrested from him by his uncle David. In the year 1202 King John gave him in marriage his natural daughter Johanna, and settled upon her the Lordship of Ellesmere; she had by him David, who did homage to Henry III.—*Owen and Blakeway, and Rapin.*

The Earl and his confederates, taking advantage of the animosities and war, almost always subsisting between the Welsh and English fled into Wales, and joined Llewellin. Being thus furnished with an army, they laid waste all the Marches between Wales and Shrewsbury, plundering wherever they came; and marching to Shrewsbury, they found great booty there, and put the inhabitants to the sword. The King being then at Gloucester, and much troubled for the miseries and afflictions of his people, called a council there, to advise him how to remedy their grievances; opinions were various, but at length it was thought expedient to appease the rebels with offers of pardon and mercy, and to banish the Bishop of Winchester, and Peter de Rivalis, by whose counsels public affairs had been managed; also to discard all strangers from his service, and to employ the English only; which conduct of the King had been one occasion of the rebellion. These matters being determined on, the Archbishop of Canterbury, and the Bishops of Chester and Rochester, were sent into Wales, with offers of pardon for all past injuries, and proposals of peace, if they would return to their obedience; which being accepted, all things became quiet, and all persons satisfied; notwithstanding, soon after this, the Earl was treacherously drawn away into Ireland, and there killed, being stabbed in the back with a dagger.

Notwithstanding the treaty just mentioned, peace with the Welsh had but a short continuance; for in the year 1241, about the beginning of August, the King marched with his army from Gloucester to Shrewsbury, and together with many noblemen, remained there fifteen days; he designed from thence to have proceeded against David ap Llewellin, but during his residence here, a submission being made by David, he stopped his march.

In 1256; the castle, during the King's pleasure, was committed to the custody of Hugh de Akor; and in 1260, the army, by command of the King, rendezvoused in Shrewsbury on the 8th of September.

Shortly after, Shrewsbury came into the hands of another master, Simon de Montford*, Earl of Leicester, who through discontent rebelled, and in defiance of the laws of his country, seized the town, and took possession without any material opposition.

About Michaelmas, 1267, Henry again appeared at Shrewsbury, at the head of his army, designing to march against Llewellin, whose restless temper created new disturbances; but by the mediation of the Pope's Legate, and upon Llewellin's submission a peace was concluded.

Anno 1269, the eldest son of the King was appointed governor of the town and castle: the following copy of the appointment is from the original in the Exchequer.

" Henry, by the grace of God, King of England, &c. &c. to the bailiffs, " and their good men of the town of Salop. Health.

---

* This Simon de Montford built a castle at Broadway, near Churchstoke, called Simon's Castle, now demolished.—*Llewellin's Manuscript.*

"Know ye, that we have committed to our very dear son Edward, our "first born, our castle and town of Salop, with the appurtenances, to be "kept during our pleasure. And therefore we command you, that to the "said Edward, or his certain attorney, whom he shall depute, by his letters "patent, for the custody of the same; ye shall be obedient in all things "that appertain to that charge, and shall be responsible as aforesaid. In "testimony whereof, we have caused these our letters to be made patent. "Witness myself, at Winchester, the 23rd day of September, in the 53rd year of our reign."

In the reign of Edward I. anno 1277, we find the disturbances by the Welsh still continued; upon which account the Courts of Exchequer and King's Bench were removed to Shrewsbury, that they (the Welsh) might be awed into submission, and all necessary help be at hand for taming them. The courts were held here for a considerable time, probably for some months, for in the next year Michaelmas term was held here.

The situation of the inhabitants of these parts, in these times, appears peculiarly distressing; they were continually subject to the depredations and incursions of the Welsh, their hostile and unmerciful neighbours; and not only were their sufferings great from brutes in human shape, but the wolves inhabiting the desolate mountains of that country, whose ferocity and disposition probably was near of kin to the ungovernable tribe, with whom they had their residence, would come down in herds, and miserably ravage the country. A commission was given to Peter Corbet*, to destroy all he could find in 1281, and by offering a sum of money to those who killed a certain number and brought their heads to Shrewsbury, they were in a short time considerably reduced in their number; and not long after, as will appear in due course, the Welsh also were subdued and brought under the English government, an event highly beneficial to them, and advantageous to the kingdom of England, especially the parts bordering on their country.

About Michaelmas, 1283, the Parliament met at Shrewsbury, and the King and court removing to Acton Burnell, the seat of Bishop Burnell, his Chancellor, the Lords and Commons assembled there. At this meeting the statute of Acton Burnell was made, so called because the royal assent was given there. The Lords sat in the castle, and the Commons in a barn, then belonging to the Abbot of the monastery of St. Peter and Paul, at Shrewsbury. By the statute above-mentioned it was enacted, or rather an act was renewed for the assurance of debts, and called the statute merchant, by which act, debtors in London, York and Bristol were obliged to appear before the different mayors, and agree upon a certain day for payment, otherwise an execution was issued out against their goods, for imprisonment for debt did not take place till some hundreds of years after this time. The writ to summon this Parliament to meet at Shrewsbury, on the morrow after Michaelmas day,

* Rymer's Fœdera.

recites the occasion of its meeting to be for consulting what course to take with David, Prince of Wales, whom the King therein declares he had received in his banishment, had nursed while an orphan, and enriched out of his own possessions, placing him among the chief persons of his court.

David having fled from his brother Llewellin, Prince of Wales, who had imprisoned his two brothers, Owen and Roderick; the King received him into his service, created him Earl of Denbigh, and gave him land to the yearly value of a thousand marks, in lieu of those possessions he ought to have had in Anglesea, and to attach him to the interests of England, gave him to wife Eleanor, the daughter of Robert de Ferras, a rich English heiress.

What care soever Edward had taken to gain his affections by several favours, David never ceased to excite his brother Llewellin to free himself from subjection; he thought it his own concern, because as Llewellin had no children, he was his presumptive successor. Llewellin took up arms, and penetrated into the territories of the English, where he defeated two of their armies; Edward, in hopes of being more fortunate if he went himself, marched into Wales, at the head of a numerous army; Llewellin retired to Snowdon Hill, where he could not be attacked; but at length, regardless of the inequality of his forces, he descended into the plain to fight the English. The English proved conquerors, Llewellin was slain on the spot, his army entirely routed, and David his brother after some time roving about the country, was taken by the English about Midsummer following, and with his wife, two sons, and seven daughters was sent to Rhyddlan castle in Flintshire, where the King then was. In vain did David beg earnestly to be allowed the favour of casting himself at the King's feet to implore his mercy. As he was the last of the race of Welsh Princes, Edward was inclined to secure his late conquest by his death; accordingly, after having been for some time kept prisoner at Rhyddlan, he was brought to Shrewsbury, where he was tried by the Parliament as before mentioned, assembled for that purpose, and by their advice, on the 30th of September, 1283, he was condemned to die the death of a traitor, viz. to be drawn, hanged, and quartered, which sentence was executed with all the circumstances attending that infamous punishment, for he was first drawn at a horse's tail about the town, then hanged, afterwards beheaded, his body quartered, and his bowels burnt; his head was fixed near that of the Prince his brother, on the Tower of London, and his four quarters were sent to York, Bristol, Northampton, and Winchester.

This was the first execution of the kind, which was afterwards usually inflicted upon traitors.

When Llewellin began this rebellion, it is said he asked counsel of some wizzards, who advised him to go forward boldly, promising him he should be conqueror, and ride along Cheapside, with a crown on his head, reminding him also of an ancient prophecy of Merlin, in which they made him believe it was foretold he should wear the crown of Brutus, king of the whole island. This prophecy, however, had no fulfilment, except in Llewellin's head, being carried in procession through Cheapside, to be fixed upon the Tower, with a crown of silver (some say ivy) upon it.

A. D. 1322, King Edward II. after Epiphany, marched with his army from Worcester to Shrewsbury, where at his coming near the town, he was honourably received by the burgesses, who went out to meet him, clad in armour, and brought him into the town, which was then strongly fenced.

The same year, in a tournament held in this town, John, one of the sons of the famous Roger Mortimer, Earl of March, was slain.

Nov. 17th, 1326, Edmund Fitz Allan, Earl of Arundel, a rebellious nobleman was apprehended by the inhabitants of Shrewsbury, (in consequence of a proclamation issued out for that purpose), somewhere near the town, for which service the King granted to the town by the name of the good men of Salop, for their trouble in apprehending Edmund, Earl of Arundel, and his adherents, in their precincts, all the goods and chattels found upon him.

A Parliament was again held at Shrewsbury on the Monday after the Quinden of Hillary, 1397,* in pursuance of their adjournment from Westminster, which was (as the King† expressed himself) upon account of the great love he bore to the inhabitants of these parts, where he had many friends. On the King's arrival, he held a great feast for all his nobility and commonalty. At this session, the King sat with the crown on his head; and here he created several Peers, who first took their seats in this Parliament; Chester was at this time made a principality, the King stiling himself Prince thereof; during the King's residence here, he had a numerous guard of the militia of Cheshire. On the Thursday following, the Chancellor, by command of the King, thanked the Lords and Commons for their travels, and licensed them to depart.

All the exorbitant acts of this Parliament were repealed in the next reign; though (which is very extraordinary) the Pope's bull had been obtained for their ratification.

The articles of accusation, on which this King was deposed shortly after, charge him among many other things, with procuring the many oppressive acts passed in the parliament at Shrewsbury, with intimidating the judges and other persons, whom he caused to come before him in his chamber there, and with collecting together a great multitude of malefactors out of the county of Chester, who marching about with him, had committed great outrages, such as murders, robberies, ravishing men's wives, and other women, &c.

Speed calls this Parliament, "the great Parliament," on account of the extraordinary number of Peers that attended with their retinues; for besides making himself Prince of Chester, he had not long before created five dukes, one marquis, and four earls, who first took their seats at this adjournment.

The reign of Henry IV. is memorable for a battle fought on St. Magdalen's eve, July 22nd, 1403, at a place then called Oldfield, Bullfield, and

---

* Rapin says, Jan. 29th, 1398.   † Richard II.

Haitlefield, near Shrewsbury, and commonly called the battle of Shrewsbury, between the forces of the King, and the Earls of Worcester and Northumberland; the forces of the rebels being commanded by Henry Lord Piercy, son of the Earl of Northumberland, who for his hot and fiery spirit was nicknamed Hotspur. Some disputes had taken place between the King and the Earl of Northumberland concerning prisoners taken at the battle of Holmedon, and the Earl having dropt some expressions that offended the King, he was forbid coming to court any more, under the pain of being declared a traitor; the soul of Piercy fired at this treatment, and from thence he meditated revenge. As it was chiefly through his assistance Henry came to the crown, he thought it was still in his power to take it from him. It was necessary in order to favour his design, that the Earl should set up some pretender to the crown, and their first scheme was to publish to the people that King Richard was still alive; but that having been disproved, they set up Mortimer, Earl of March, who was descended from the third son of Edward III. and consequently had a better title than Henry, who was the son of John of Gaunt, the fourth son of Edward. Mortimer, however, was in too depressed circumstances to assert his title, and therefore obliged to submit to his more powerful cousin of Lancaster, till the Earl of Northumberland sent to him, and offered to assist him, not only with all the men he could raise in the north, but also to call in the Earl of Douglas from Scotland.

This proposal was readily accepted by Mortimer, and a solemn league was entered into between him and the young Piercy, who was to bring a great army to the Marches, where the Welsh were to join him. The Earl of Worcester, brother of Northumberland was also brought into the scheme, and with many other Lords, he joined the rebel army, whilst Piercy, in order to oblige the Scots, set all their prisoners at liberty.

Henry Piercy, Northumberland's son, marched in company with the Earl of Douglas, and joined his uncle the Earl of Worcester and the Welsh near Shrewsbury, after which they published a manifesto, enumerating all the grievances which the people laboured under from the King's tyranny, declaring they came to force him to put up with the dutchy of Lancaster, and to restore the crown to Mortimer, the true and lawful heir.

Piercy designed to have got into Shrewsbury (which was then a strong town) before the King, but by a speedy march, the King came there first, which Hotspur hearing of, made a stand with his army, consisting of 14,000 choice men, and got an advantage of ground. The morning when the two armies were to engage, and Hotspur was told of the King's approach, he drew up his men in order of battle, telling them, they must either conquer or die an ignominious death, to which they answered with loud shouts of applause. The Abbot of Shrewsbury, and one of the clerks of the privy seal, were sent by the King to offer pardon to Hotspur if he would lay down his arms, but to no purpose.

The King disposed of his army to great advantage, and just before the battle, asked Piercy the cause of his appearing in arms against him; Piercy laid many things to the King's charge, when his Majesty advised him to trust to his favour, but the other replying he would not, the King then said, " I pray God you may answer for the blood that shall be spilt this day, and not me," and then ordered the standard bearer to march, on which the battle ensued.

The battle began with a dreadful discharge of arrows from both the front lines ; the Scots, who were too impatient to fight at a distance, rushed with great fury upon the front line of the royal army, and put them into confusion, so that they would have been totally routed, had not the impetuosity of Hotspur defeated his own intention ; he fought with such undaunted courage, seconded by Douglas, that a way was opened into the centre of the royal army, but his men were unable to follow. In the heat of the battle Hotspur himself and the the Earl of Douglas, with incredible valour, bent all their aim at the person of the King, furiously making towards him with swords and lances ; this being discerned, the King withdrew from his station, and by so doing saved his life, for they slew Sir Walter Blount, his standard-bearer, and those who were with it, but missing the King, charged into the middle of their enemies. Heaps of dead bodies lay on every side, and victory was beginning to declare for the rebels, when the King brought up his reserve, which soon turned the scale. The rebels were put in confusion, but Douglas and Piercy continued to fight with extraordinary courage.

At last the rout became general ; the rebels fled in great confusion, and Douglas having also fled, Hotspur being resolved to sell his life as dear as possible, rushed into the hottest part of the battle and was killed, whose death occasioned an utter rout of his whole party.

The King had a horse killed under him, and it is said slew thirty-six persons with his own hand. The Prince of Wales was wounded with an arrow in the face, and afterwards continued fighting. Of the King's side were slain, besides the Earl of Stafford, ten new knights who had been knighted but that morning, viz. Sir Hugh Shortley, Sir John Clinton, Sir John Cockaine, Sir Nicholas Gausel, Sir Walter Blount, Sir John Calverley, Sir John Massey, Sir Hugh Mortimer, Sir Robert Gausel, and Sir Thomas Wendesley ; sixteen hundred royalists were killed, and three thousand sorely wounded.

On the side of the rebels there were six thousand slain, among whom were Lord Piercy, and most of the esquires and gentlemen of Cheshire.

Most of the slain were buried upon the field of battle, (where Battlefield church now stands), and many persons of note were buried in the Black, and Austin's Friars, in Shrewsbury. There fell on both sides 2291 men of note.

Earl Douglas slew three or four, armed in all respects like the King, and after his flight, it is said, he fell from the crag of a rock on Haughmond Hill, and broke one of his cullions ;* he was taken prisoner, but the King released him for his valour.

* Lately found, and now in the possession of Mr. Corbett.

Speed says the above battle was the most bloody that had been fought in England for above one hundred years, for there was the father against the son, and the son against the father. He adds, " the slaughter must be great, the archers shooting continually, and the men of arms* doing their utmost for the space of three hours."

The old Earl of Northumberland, who had raised an army† to support his son, went and joined the King, telling him it was his design to suppress the rebellion, and although Henry had great reason to question his sincerity, yet he thought it best to take no notice of it, and therefore restored him to his honour and fortune.

On the Monday following the battle, were condemned and beheaded, at the High Cross in Shrewsbury, the Earl of Worcester,‡ Sir Theobald Trussel,

---

* Men of war, or men of arms, as they were termed in these days, were soldiers carrying lances; other soldiers had battle axes, bills, spears, cross bows, and bows and arrows; the archers had their bodies covered all over with armour, especially the horsemen, who carried lances, and rode on barbed horses, covered with iron.

---

† The celebrated Owen Glendwyr, it appears, had also raised an army of twelve thousand men, with which he remained in a state of inactivity at Oswestry. Tradition says that he advanced as far as Shelton, within little more than a mile of Shrewsbury; and that from the summit of a large Oak now called Glendwyr's Observatory, he surveyed the field of battle and there witnessed the defeat of Hotspur; and that, alarmed for his own safety, he with all expedition hastened back into Wales. This Oak is venerated as one of the greatest curiosities in the neighbourhood of Shrewsbury. For particulars of which, see volume 4, " Hulbert's Museum of the World." Near to this venerable Oak is the beautiful residence of William Jones Esq. of the firm of Price, Hughes, Jones and Edwards, Bankers, Shrewsbury.—Ed.

‡ In the chapel on the south side of St. Mary's church, formerly dedicated to the Holy Trinity, was heretofore the monument of a cross-legged knight. Tradition called it the tomb of Hotspur; but the architecture and the fashion of the armour are at least a century antecedent to his time; and Churchyard informs us, that it belonged to one of the Leybournes, formerly lords of Berwick, in the parish of St. Mary. On the 19th of July, 1816, it was removed to a more conspicuous situation on the north side of the chancel. On this occasion an opportunity was afforded of inspecting the remains within. The external appearance of the tomb shewed that it had formerly sustained much violence. The right arm was gone, and the stone slab on which the figure lay was greatly broken at the lower end; that the whole corner of the tomb is defaced in all its ornamental parts, and a large hole is still visible, through which an iron crow may have passed to force the slab upwards. Appearances within exactly corresponded to these without. The remains had evidently been disturbed at some former period. After a few inches of loose rubbish was taken away, a skull and some leg and thigh bones were found lying confusedly. At the bottom of the grave, which was of well-squared stone-work, and entirely filled with rubbish, lay a body which had not been disturbed, and was quite perfect: except that there were not the least traces of a head, and it appeared certain that it never could have been there, as the shoulders lay close up to the upper end of the grave. The body had been wrapped in leather, which was still tolerably perfect, though the wooden coffin had disappeared, having left no vestige but some brown mould in the line of its direction, and a good many large nails reduced to a mass of rust. On the whole it appeared, that three adults and an infant of about six years had been deposited in the grave, which was three feet one inch deep from the level of the course of stones laid upon the floor of the chapel. The thigh bones of one of these adults were nineteen inches long, and his leg bones fifteen inches: of another the thigh bones were eighteen inches, and the leg

E

Baron of Kinderton, and Sir Richard Vernon.   The Earl of Worcester's head was taken and set up over London Bridge.

The body of Henry Lord Piercy being found among the slain, was delivered to the Lord Furnival to be buried, but was afterwards by the King's command taken up again, and placed between two millstones* in Shrewsbury, after which it was there also beheaded and quartered, and the quarters fixed upon the gates in Shrewsbury, and other places.

The King, after having caused public thanks to be given to God, built and endowed a collegiate church upon the spot where the battle was fought, settling upon it £54. 1s. 1d. yearly, and two priests to pray for the souls of the slain.   For a further account of this church, see the Appendix.

Nothing material occurs in the history of this place, until the reign of Henry VI. A. D. 1455.   When Richard Plantaganet, Duke of York, being at his castle in Ludlow, in the month of February, wrote a letter to the bailiffs, burgesses, and commons of Shrewsbury, complaining of the many misdoings of the Duke of Somerset, the King's chief favorite; and acquainting them of his design to raise what force he could, to remove that Duke from the king's person and councils; at the same time exhorting them to come to his assistance, wherever he should draw his forces together, with as many able men as they

---

bones fourteen: of the entire headless skeleton (the whole length of which was five feet three inches) the thigh bones were nineteen inches and a half, and the leg bones sixteen. After these remains (the lowest of which, the headless trunk, was left undisturbed,) had been exposed sufficiently for the gratification of curiosity, those which had been taken out were carefully replaced, and the grave filled up. The absence of a head from the lowermost body gave rise to various conjectures. The tradition respecting Hotspur deserves no attention. His remains were, we are sure, ignominiously quartered and dispersed over the kingdom; and if that had not been the case, it would perhaps have been scarcely possible to reduce the body of a warrior who fell in battle, and which must have lain till it was quite cold in a distorted posture, to the order in which the body in question was placed. But there was another nobleman whose head was severed from his body, but of whose quarters we read nothing; the Earl of Worcester; who, as we have seen, was beheaded at Shrewsbury, and his head sent to London. The family of Leyburne was by this time extinct; and the then Lord Berwick, Sir Roger de Trumpeton, a stranger to their blood, and a resident in a distant county. Henry, after having permitted the interment of Hotspur, had caused the body to be taken up again; and if the Earl's friends, apprehensive of the same indignity in his case, devised the expedient of placing his remains below those of the Leyburnes, there seems to have been nothing to hinder the execution of their purpose. This conjecture would reconcile the tradition rejected by Phillips and the account given by Churchyard, and prove that both of them were in some degree founded in truth.

Owen's and Blakeway's History of Shrewsbury.

* A few years ago a Millstone was dug up near the Tan yard of Mr. Hughes, St. Austin's Friars, which by some was supposed to have been one of those between, which the gallant Hotspur was inclosed.—ED.

In the year 1801, when the the upper part of the Friars was partially levelled, many remains were disinterred. A gentleman was present when a skeleton was dug up seven feet two inches in length, and another saw there five skeletons laid close together, without any appearance of a coffin. These were probably some of those who fell at Battlefield. Our latter informant, an eminent physician, says, what he saw were young subjects, the teeth firm in their heads.

Owen's and Blakeway's History of Shrewsbury.

could bring. With the army raised on this occasion, the King's troops were defeated at St. Albans, and the Duke of Somerset slain; whereupon the Duke of York was made protector of the realm.

A. D. 1460. Edward, Earl of March, son and heir of Richard Duke of York, and afterwards King of England, came to Shrewsbury, where the inhabitants were much attached to him, desiring help to avenge his father's death; he raised an army of 23,000 men in these parts, with which, on Candlemas day, he defeated Henry VI. at Mortimer's Cross, near Hereford, having slain 3800 men, and soon afterwards he was proclaimed King.

Upon a proclamation being issued to apprehend Henry Stafford, Duke of Buckingham, who had taken up arms against King Richard III. A. D. 1484, he was forced to abscond and conceal himself at the house of one Bannister, a servant to his family at Shinewood,* near Wenlock. He had collected together a considerable force, principally consisting of Welshmen, and intended to have crossed the Severn at Gloucester, and to have joined the two Courtneys, who had been raising forces for him in Devonshire and Cornwall; but the river Severn was broke out beyond its bounds, and impossible to be passed, which the Welshmen looking upon as an ill omen, they secretly slipt away, leaving the Duke alone, without either a page or footman. Bannister at whose house the Duke took refuge, having been raised to his present situation in life by the kindness of the Duke† and his father, he never doubted his safety; but the perfidious villain unable to resist the temptation of the offered reward of a thousand pounds, betrayed him to John Mytton, Esq. then sheriff of Shropshire, who with a company of armed men, apprehended him, disguised in an old black cloak, in a grove or orchard adjoining Bannister's house, and conducted him to Shrewsbury, where King Richard then kept his household, and there without any legal process, by the king's bare order, he was beheaded on a scaffold, erected in the market place.

The Duke was very desirous to speak with the King, but was not per-

---

* Some say at Lacon Hall, near Wem.

---

† Humphry Banister was brought up and exalted to promotion by the Duke of Buckingham his master; the Duke being afterwards driven to extremity, by reason of the seperation of his army, which he had mustered against King Richard, the usurper fled to this Banister, as his most trusty friend, not doubting to be kept secret by him, till he could find an opportunity to escape. There was a thousand pounds proposed as a reward to him that could discover the Duke, and this ungrateful traitor, upon the hopes of this sum, betrayed the Duke his benefactor into the hands of John Mytton, sheriff of Shropshire, who conveyed him to the city of *Salisbury*, where King Richard was, and soon after the Duke was put to death. But as for this perfidious monster, the vengeance of God fell upon him to his utter ignominy, in a visible and strange manner, for presently after his eldest son fell mad and died in a boar's sty; his eldest daughter was suddenly stricken with a leprosy; his second son became strangely deformed in his limbs, and lame; his youngest son was drowned in a pool; and he himself arraigned and found guilty of a murder, was saved by his clergy. As for his thousand pounds, King Richard gave him not a farthing, saying, that "he who would be so untrue to so good a master, must needs be false to all others."—*Wanley of Coventry.*

E2

mitted; if he had, it is supposed he intended to have killed him with a dagger, which was found upon him after his death.

He is supposed to buried in St. Alkmond's church.*

The reward offered for apprehending the Duke, is said† to be £1000 sterling, or £100 per annum in Lands; and that King Richard gave Banister, the manor of Earlding, in Kent.

Henry Earl of Richmond, afterwards Henry the VII. landed at Milford Haven, in Wales, about the middle of August, A. D. 1485, after a passage of about seventeen days from Harfleur. From Milford he went to Hereford, where he was well received, and from thence came to Shrewsbury, where he first caused himself to be proclaimed King; he was on his march to give battle to Richard III. and while he was at Shrewsbury, was joined by Sir Gilbert Talbot, Knight, sheriff of Shropshire, with two thousand men, most of them tenants and retainers to his nephew George Earl of Shrewsbury, then in his minority, before which, his forces scarce deserved the name of an army. While the Earl lay at Shrewsbury, he had information given him, that Sir Robert Herbert, and Rice ap Thomas, were preparing with a considerable force to stop his progress; as they had professed great friendship, their revolt gave Henry great uneasiness, but it appeared afterwards, that the report was propagated with a design to force the Earl into a compliance with some proposals they had to offer, for Rice ap Thomas afterwards met him, and offered his service, if Henry, would promise to make him, sole governor of Wales, when he obtained the crown; Henry made him the promise and afterwards performed it.

The following account of the Earl's‡ passing through Shrewsbury, in his way from Milford to Hereford, transcribed from an old manuscript, must not be omitted.

"Thys Yeare, in the monthe of August, 1485, Henry Earle of Rych-
" moond, came out of Bryttane, towards England, wyth a small companye,
" and landyd at Mylford Haven in Wales, nygh Penbrooke, the 7th daye of
" August, having help Inoughe in England, and so marchynge forward,
" beinge stayed at no place, untyll he came to the towne of Shrosberie, where
" the gates where shutt against hym, and the pullys let downe; so the Earle's
" messengers came to the gate to say the Welsh gate, commandynge them
" to open the gates to theyre right Kynge, and Maister Myttoon made answere,
" being head bayley, and a stoute royste gentilman, sayinge that he knew
" no Kynge, but only Kynge Richard, whose lyffetenants he and hys fellows
" were, and before he should entir there, he should goe over hys belly,
" meaninge thereby, that he would be slayne to the grounde, and so to roon

---

† Acta Regia fol. 1733.   ‡ Henry Earl of Richmond.

---

* This must be an erroneous supposition, as the Earl was not beheaded at Shrewsbury, but at Salisbury, as the best authorities testify.—ED.

" over hym before he entird, and that he protestyd vehementlye uppon the
" Othe he had tacken ; so the sayd Erle returnyd wyth hys companye backe
" agayne to a vylledge callyd Forton, 3 Myles and a halfe from Shrosberie,
" where he lay that night, and in the mornynge followynge, there came Em-
" bassadors to speake with the Baylyff, requesting to passe quyetlye, and
" that the Erle theyre master dyd not meane to hurt the towne, nor noue
" therein, but to goe to trye hys right, and that he promysed further, that he
" would save his othe, and hym, and hys fellows harmles ; uppon thys they
" entered, and the sayd Myttoon laye alonge the grounde, and hys belly
" uppwardes, and soe the sayd Erle stepped over hym and saved his othe ;
" and so passing forthe, and marching forwarde, he came to Bosworth, where
" the Battel was fought betwyxt hym and Kynge Richard, in which Kynge
" Richard was slayne."*

Henry never forgot the assistance he received here, in his attempt to get
possession of the crown ; when he had obtained it he frequently visited these
parts, particularly in the year 1488, when he came to Shrewsbury and staid
several days, and again in 1490, the King, Queen, and Prince Arthur were
present at St. George's feast, which was held in St. Chad's church. In 1495
the King again visited Shrewsbury, and was entertained by the corporation
at their expense ; the following account of the various particulars, and the
charge of them are worth notice.

JOHN GITTINS, AND LAWRENCE HOSSYER, Bailiffs, 1495.

CHARGE OF THE ENTERTAINMENT.

	£.	s.	d.		£.	s.	d.
Bread	2	0	0	Wine to make Ipocrass for the			
A tun of wine	8	0	0	Queen	0	4	0
Six hogsheads of ale	2	6	0	Spice and Sugar to make the			
Six empty hogsheads	0	4	0	same	0	13	9
To them that brought the present	0	6	2	Sweet wine given to the Queen	0	2	8
Four oxen	3	6	8	Wine given to the guard	0	14	10
Twenty-four wethers	1	12	0	Wine spent on the King's gen-			
Twenty-four pottles of wine bes-				tlemen	0	13	2
towed on the king and the				Wine given to the minstrels	0	6	2
lords in the castle	0	16	0	Bread for the Queen	0	2	8
Bread then	0	1	4	Rewards to officers	6	18	4

FOR THE PRINCE.

	£.	s.	d.		£.	s.	d.
Bread	0	10	0	To the carriers of it	0	1	5
Half a tun of wine	4	0	0				

* Dr. Taylor's M. S.

REWARDS.

	£.	s.	d.		£.	s.	d.
To the King's children ...	1	0	0	To the King's henkyfmen ...	0	10	0
To the serjeant's at arms ...	1	0	0	To the Queen's footmen ...	0	6	8
To the King's minstrels ...	1	0	0	To the King's mother's footmen	0	6	8
To the Queen's minstrels ...	0	10	0	To the Prince's serjeants at arms	0	6	8
To the clerk of the market ...	0	5	0	To the Earl of Shrewsbury's			
To the Prince's players ...	0	6	8	players	0	10	0
To the Earl of Derby's players	0	3	4				
To the King's footmen ..	0	10	0	Total charge	39	17	6
To the Prince's footmen ...	0	3	4				

The following account of Sir Henry Sidney's visit to Shrewsbury and reception there, seems to merit attention, as a specimen of the humour, style, and orthography of the time.*

"1581, The 24th of April beinge St. George's daye; the right honorable
" Sir Henry Sidney, Lord President of the Marches of Wales, beinge of the
" pryvy counsell, and one of the Knights of the most noble order of the
" garter, kept at St. George's feast in Shrewsbury, most honorably, com-
"mynge the sayd daye, from the Counsell-house there, in hys knightly robes,
" most valiant, wyth hys gentilmen before hym, and hys knights followyng
" hym in brave order, and after them the bayliffes and aldermen, in theire
" scarlet gownes, wyth the companyes of all occupations in the sayde towne,
" in theire best livereys, and before every wardens of every company theire
" two stuardes, with whit roddes in theire handes, evrie company followinge
" in good and seemely order toward St. Chadd's churche, where he was stallid
" upon the right hande in the chancell, neere unto the Queen's Majesties
" place, prepared in the same quire; also with all the nobilities arms that
" were Knightes of the garter, and passinge and repassinge by the Queens
" Majesties place, he dyd as much honour as thoughe the Queen's Majestie
" had been present, where he had there the divine servys sunge by note to
" the gloryfying of God, and the greate honor of the sayd Sir Henry, who
" began the feast upon the eve, and kept open household for the tyme. It
" hys to be notyd, that there was sutch a goodly number of townesmen
" followynge hym to the churche, that when he entired into the churche, the
" last end of the trayne was at my Lord's place, (the Councill-house), which
" is the lengthe of 700 paces at the least. And on the first daye of Maye,
" the masters of the free scoole, whose names were Thomas Larrance, John
" Barker, Rychard Atkys, and Roger Kent, made a brave and costly bancket
" after supper of the same daye, before the scoole, to the number of forty
" dishes, and the masters before them, every scoole presenting 10 dyshes, with
" a shewer before every scoole, pronowncynge these words.

* From Dr. Taylor's Collection of M. S. S.

" Larrance I.

" These are all of Larrauce lore,
" Acompt hys hart above hys store.

" Barker II.

" These ten are all of Barker's bande,
" Good wyll, not welthe, now to be scaude.

" Atkys III.

" These ten are all in Atkys chardge,
" Hys gyffts are small, hys good wyll lardge.

" Kent IV.

" These ten coom last and are the least,
" Yett Kent's good wyll ys wythe the beast.

" These verses followinge were written and heareafter followe about the
" bancketinge dyshes.

" *En mittunt librum, libram non mittere possunt.*
" *Virgam, non vaccam mittere quisq. potest.*

" And the daye followinge, beinge the seconde daye of Maye, all the
" scollars of the sayd free scoole, beinge taught by the foresaid four masters,
" beinge in number 360, with their masters before every of them, marchyng
" braveley from the sayd scoole, in battell order, with their generalls, captens,
" drumms, trumpetts, and ensigns, before them, through the town, towards a
" large filde, called the Geye in the Abbey suburbs of Salop, and there devyd-
" inge theire banndes into 4 partes, met the sayde Lord President, being
" upon a lusty courser, who turned hym about, and came to them, the
" Generall openinge to hys Lordshyp the purpose and assembly of hym and
" the rest, then he wyth the other Captens made theire orations howe valiantly
" they would feight and defend the countrey, at whych the sayd Lord had
" greate pleasure, and mutche rejoisyd, gyvinge greate prayse to the sayde
" Masters for the eloquence thereof ; and on the 13th daye of Maye the sayde
" Sir Henry Sidney departed from Shrewsberie by water, and tooke hys
" Barge under the Cassell Hyll by hys place, and as he passid by there were
" 14 chamber pieces bravely shot off, with a certain shott of Harquebushers,
" and so passing alonge, not the lengthe of a quarter of a myle of by water,
" theire were placid in an Ilet, hard by the water syde, serten appointed scol-
" lars of the free scoole, being apparelyd all in greene, and greene wyllows
" upon theire heads, marching by, and callyng to hym, macking theire lament-
" able orations, sorrowinge hys departure, the which was done so pityfully, and
" of such excellency that truly it made many, both in the bardge upon the
" water, as also the people uppon lande, to weepe, and my Lord hymself to
" change countenance."

(The orations made upon this occasion being too many to insert in this
place, one part shall be quoted as a specimen.)

ONE BOY ALONE.

"Oh stay the barge, rowe not soe fast,
  "Rowe not soe fast, oh stay awhile ;
"Oh stay and hear the playntts at last,
  "Of nymphs that harbour in thys isle.

"Thear woe is greate, greate moan they make,
  "With doleful tunes they due lament,
They howle, they crie, theire leave to tacke,
  "Theire garments greene for woe they rent.

"O Seavern, turn thy stream quite backe,
  "Alas why doyst thou us anoye ?
"Wilt thou cause us this Lord to lacke,
  "Whose presince is our onelie joye ?

"But harke, methinks I heare a sounde,
  "A wofull sounde I plaguly heare,
"Some sorrow greate thear hart dothe wound,
  "Pass on my Lord, to them draw neare.

FOUR BOYS APPEAR IN GREEN, SINGING.

"O woefull wretched tyme, oh doleful day and houre,
"Lament we may the loss we have, and flood of tears out poure,
"Come nymphs of woods and hilles, come help us moane we pray,
"The water nymphes our sisters dear, do take our Lord away.
"Bewayle we may our wrongs, revenge we cannot take,
"Oh that the gods would bring him back, our sorrows for to flake.

ONE ALONE, WITH MUSIC.

"O pinching payne, that gripes my hart, O thrise unhappy wight,
"O sillie soule, what hap have I, to see this woful sight ;
"Shall I now leave my lovinge Lord, shall he now from me goe ?
"Why wyll he Salop nowe forsake, alas why wyll he so ?
"Alas my sorrows doe increase, my hart doth rent in twayne,
"For that my Lord doth hence depart, and will not hear remayne.

ALL.

"And wyll youre honor now depart ?
  "And must it needs be soe ?
"Would God we could like fishes swyme,
  "That we myght with thee goe.

"Or else would God this littil isle,
    " Were stretched out soe lardge,
" That we on foot, myght follow thee,
    " And wayt upon thy bardge.

" But seeing that we cannot swyme,
    " And island's at an end,
" Saffe passage with a short return,
    " The myghty God thee sende.

"And soe the bardge departed, the Bayliffes, and serten of the Aldermen
" accompanyinge hym by water, untill they came to Atcham brydge, and
" theire they dynd all together in the bardge uppon the water; and after
" dyner, tacking theire leave with mourninge countenances departyd."

Shortly after, the town of Shrewsbury was again honoured with a visit
by Sir Henry Sidney and his Lady; if the reader is not tired he shall have
another account of his reception.

" This yeare, 1582, and the 11th daye of Marche, being Moonday, at
" nyght, the right honorable Lady Mary Sidney came to thys towne of Salop
" in her wagon,* and tooke up hyr lodgynge at my Lord's place† theire;
" and the 12th daye ensueing, the most valyant Knyght Sir Harry Sidney, her
" husbannd beinge Lorde President of the Marches, came also from Ludlowe
" to this towne of Salop, in honorable manner, and as he passyd in hys wagon
" by the Condit at the Wyle Coppe, were made too excellent orations, by
" two of the free scoole scollars; he staying in hys wagon to heare the same,
" the which in the end he praysed very well, and soe passed through towards
" hys Lady, wyth hys troompeter, blowynge verey joyfully to behold and see."‡

We do not find Shrewsbury honoured with any royal visits, nor does any
very remarkable occurrence appear that merits a place in this chapter, (many
local occurrences in the intermediate space of time will appear in this history,
arranged under proper heads); until the reign of Charles I. A. D. 1642, on
Tuesday, September 20th, that King came with his army from Nottingham

* Coaches at this time were not used in England, being first introduced in the year 1585.

                † Council House.   *Tablet of Memory*.

‡ Sir Henry Sidney was twenty-six years President of the King's Council for the principality of
Wales, and Lord Lieutenant of Ireland; he died at Bewdley in 1584, his heart was buried at
Shrewsbury, his bowels at Bewdley, and his body* at Ludlow, in his daughter Ambrosia's tomb.

---

* From the intelligent author of the Ludlow Guide we learn, that he died at *Worcester*, where his
entrails were buried; that his body was interred at Penshurst in Kent, and his heart brought to Ludlow,
and deposited in his beloved Ambrosia's tomb. Which tomb I lately had the pleasure of visiting. The
leaden urn which contained the heart was a short time ago in the possession of Mr. Nicholas of Leominster,
and is about six inches deep, and five in diameter at the top, and hath on it the following inscription:—

                HERE LITH THE HEART OF
            SIR HENRY SIDNEY, L. P.
                ANNO. 1586.   ED.

F

to this town, * which was very commodious for him in all respects, being strong in its situation, and by reason of the neighbourhood of North Wales, and the use of the river Severn, yielding excellent provisions of all kinds, so that the King and Court, were for a while very well accommodated. Here he formed an army being joined by Prince Rupert, Prince Charles, the Duke of York, and many other noblemen and gentlemen of the adjacent counties, some of whom raised both horse and foot for him at their own charge, and others brought in their money and plate to be coined for his use, at the mint he had set up in this town.

Among the rest, Thomas Lyster, Esq. of Rowton presented the King with a purse of gold, for which the King conferred on him the honour of knighthood. And graciously condescending to consider the worthy services of Sir Richard Newport, he advanced him to be a baron of England, by the title of Lord Newport, of High Ercall, for which that loyal gentleman presented his Majesty with the sum of £600. The universities of Oxford and Cambridge also sent a quantity of plate.

The King at the same time borrowed £600 out of the Free School chest, for which he gave the following acknowledgement :

" Charles Rex.

" Trusty and well beloved, we greet you well : Whereas you have out " of your good affection to our present service, and towards the supply of " our extraordinary occasions, lent unto us the sum of £600, being a stock " belonging to the school, founded by our royal predecessor, King Edward " VI. in this our town of Shrewsbury ; we do hereby promise, that we shall " cause the same to be truly repaid to you, whenever you shall demand the " same ; and shall always remember the loan of it as a very acceptable service " unto us. Given under our signet, at our court of Shrewsbury, this 11th " October, 1642.

" To our trusty and well beloved Richard
    " Gibbons, late Mayor of Shrewsbury,
    " and Thomas Challoner, scoolmaster
    " of the free school there."

Sometime after, the corporation brought a, bill in chancery, before the commissioners of the great seal against Richard Gibbons, Thomas Challoner, the sons of Robert Betton, deceased, (who was senior alderman) and Richard Berrington, senior common-council-man, who kept the keys of the school chest at the time the money was taken out ; this bill was brought to recover the money, but May 19th, 1653, it was dismissed without any relief.

---

* On September 19th, the day before the King's arrival at Shrewsbury, he mustered his forces at Wellington, that being their first rendezvous. His Majesty caused military orders to be read there at the head of each regiment, and then mounting his horse, and placing himself in the midst, from whence he might be heard by all, he made the following speech to the soldiers.

" Gentlemen—You have heard the orders read."

Before the King's arrival the people had been poisoned with an odious character of him; but when they saw his obliging behaviour, and heard his kind speech,* they laid aside their prejudices, and were greatly enamoured with him; a number of the townsmen enlisted as volunteers, and the Lords Newport and Littleton offered his Majesty to keep the town for him. During his residence here, the King bestowed the honour of knighthood on the following gentlemen, viz. Richard Gibbons, Esq. then Mayor, Thomas Scriven, Thomas Eyton, and Francis Ottley, Esqrs. On the 12th of October, he went from hence with his army to Bridgnorth, and before his departure ordered proclamation to be made through the town, that all soldiers should depart before him, or with him; and that no violence should be offered, or done, to any persons in the town or liberties, on pain of death to common soldiers, and of cashiering to the officers. The King afterwards marched towards London, but was stopped at Edgehill by the Parliament's forces.

When King Charles was in Shrewsbury, in the year before-mentioned, observing it to be a place fortified by nature and art, he soon after sent Lord Capel to place a garrison here.—Upon his coming he repaired the Castle Gates,

---

* A few days after the King's arrival he summoned the gentlemen and freeholders of the county to attend him, and addressed them in the following affectionate terms:—

"Gentlemen,

"It is some benefit to me, from the insolencies and misfortunes which have driven me about, that "they have brought me to so good a part of my Kingdom, and so faithful a part of my people: I hope "neither you nor I shall repent my coming hither; I will do my part that you may not; and of you "I was confident before I came. The residence of an army is not usually pleasant to any place; and "mine may carry more fear with it, since it may be thought (being robb'd and spoiled of all mine own, "and such terror used to fright and keep all men from supplying me) I must only live upon the aid "and relief of my people. But be not afraid; I would to God my poor subjects suffered no more by "the insolence and violence of that army raised against me, (though they have made themselves "wanton even with plenty) than you shall do by mine; and yet I fear I cannot prevent all disorders; "I will do my best: And this I promise you, no man shall be a loser by me, if I can help it. I have "sent hither for a mint; I will melt down all my own plate, and expose all my land to sale or mort- "gage, that if it be possible, I may not bring the least pressure upon you: In the mean time, I have "summoned you hither to do that for me and yourselves, for the maintenance of your Religion, and "the law of the land (by which you enjoy all that you have) which other men do against us. Do not "suffer so good a cause to be lost, for want of supplying me with that, which will be taken from you "by those who pursue me with this violence. And whilst these ill men sacrifice their money, plate, and "utmost industry to destroy the commonwealth, be you no less liberal to preserve it. Assure your- "selves, if it please God to bless me with success, I shall remember the assistance that every particu- "lar man here gives me, to his advantage. However, it will hereafter (how furiously soever the "minds of men are now possessed) be honour and comfort to you, that with some charge and trouble "to yourselves, you did your part to support your King, and preserve the kingdom."

During his residence here the King kept his court at the Council House. The Princes Rupert and Maurice were stationed with the army which exercised in the fields near the Hall. The attendants on the court lodged in the houses of the principal inhabitants. In the family of Mr. Challoner the chief school-master, a gentleman of eminent loyalty, were entertained the Lord Keeper Littleton, Dr. Williams Archbishop of York, Lord Cholmondeley, and Sir Richard Dyas. In that of Mr. Evans the second master, Lord Grey of Ruthin, Lord North and his brother.

Owen's Account of Shrewsbury.

F2

pulled down many houses near the Castle, and brought the water from Severn up to the gate, by means of a deep ditch, over which he placed a draw-bridge; he also built a strong fort at the upper end of Frankwell, to prevent any enemy from planting cannon there (this fort stood in the road leading to Welsh-Pool and Oswestry, within a few yards of the place where the first turnpike is erected; a house is now built on the spot, to this day called the Mount;* it was called Cadogan's Fort, from its Vicinity to St. Cadogan's Chapel, which stood near the Bull in the Barn) in this fort and in the Castle he planted cannon, and made it a strong place.† In 1644 the garrison were under command of Sir Michael Ermley, and at that time Colonel Mytton (an excellent soldier for valour and conduct) was Governor of a small garrison at Wem, and General ‡ of the Parliament's forces in this county; he had a strong desire to reduce Shrewsbury, for which town he was a representative in parliament, and made two unsuccessful attempts; once on a Saturday when the townsmen were busied at their market, he attacked the fort at Frankwell, but was repulsed with some loss;

† Mr. Gough's M. S.

‡ Anecdotes of General Mytton.

Oliver's Parliament made an ordinance that every Irishman found in the King's army, when taken should be hanged; and two of Cornet Collins's men falling into their hands at the time he was shot at Middle, they were hanged. Prince Rupert hearing of this, vowed that the next thirteen prisoners he took of Oliver's men, should suffer death. The next summer, 1644, about the time of the taking Shrewsbury, Prince Rupert and his brother Prince Maurice made their rendezvous at Holloway-hills, Cockshutt, and Ellesmere. Mr. Mytton (the Parliament's General) hearing of this, intended through some bye ways, to entrap them with a troop of horse; but when he came to Oatley Park gate, the Princes, with three or four troops of horse, being at Mr. Kynaston's at Oatley Hall, got between him and home, which Mytton perceiving, shot one of his troop horses against the gate to prevent its opening, but the Princes men soon broke down the park pales, took Mr. Mytton's troop of horse prisoners, and the General himself and one George Higley were pursued by some of the soldiers, who overtook them, and one of them laying his hand upon General Mytton's shoulder, saying "you are my prisoner," Higley with his sword cut the soldier in the face and fell him, upon which he and the General (who had lost his hat in the scuffle) escaped by way of Welsh Franckton to Oswestry, which place was then in the Parliament's hands. The next day the prince caused all the prisoners to cast dice upon the drum head which thirteen of them should be hanged, according to his vow; among the thirteen to whom the lot fell, was one Philip Littleton, formerly a park keeper to Mr. Vincent Corbett of Stanwardine, who observing Sir Vincent Corbett of Moreton Corbett ride by, said, if Mr. Corbett had seen him, he would have saved his life, upon which a charitable soldier ran after Sir Vincent and told him what Littleton had said, he immediately returned, alighted, and falling down upon his knees before Prince Rupert, who sat on horseback to see the executions, he begged Littleton's life, which the Prince granted, upon condition he would never again fight against the King. After this time no more Irish prisoners were executed by the Parliament's forces.

---

* The Scite on which the Chapel and Fort formerly stood is now the property of John Whitehurst, Esq. purchased by his late father from the Berringtons of Moat Hall. In the year 1824, while some workmen in the employment of the present proprietor were sinking foundations for twelve small houses adjoining the Westbury road, about eighteen inches below the surface, they discovered remains of a wall of red stone, five feet in thickness, which wall was traced for several hundred feet, crossing the Mount from the Westbury to the Oswestry roads.—ED.

on the Saturday following, in the night time, he with Major Braine, Captain Shipley, Captain Church, and Captain Sheinton, with their forces, came to the Old Heath, but the night being very dark the horse mistook their way, marching towards Pimley and Atcham, and could not be got together till the opportunity was lost; on the next Friday night General Mytton came with his forces, consisting of 250 foot, and 250 horse, drawn out of the garrisons of Wem, Moreton Corbet, and Stoke, assisted by Sir William Brereton, a friend to the parliament; 250 foot, and 250 horse of the Staffordshire forces, under the command of Colonel Bowyer also joined them; all the foot were put under the command of Lieutenant Colonel Rinking, and the horse were commanded by Colonel Mytton; these marched towards Shrewsbury, where they arrived about three o'clock on Saturday morning, February 22nd.*

---

* The following Extracts will supply a few particulars relative to this extraordinary Assault and taking of the Town by Colonel Mytton, and at the same time afford a specimen of the style and phraseology of writers of the parliament party, and other Historians of the day.

"And about the latter end of this Moneth of February, wee received the most welcome news of the most memorable and suddain surprisall of the strong Town of Shrewsbury by Colonel Mitton, that most active and loyall Commander, and Colonel Bowyer, assisted by Sir William Breretons, and Colonell Mittons forces; together with the eminent prisoners and prizes taken by those Parliament forces, which was certified and ratified by severall letters out of Shropshire, sent to London, with the exact and true relation of the manner of the taking of it, it being a place of great concernment, and one of the most considerable Upland Garrisons which the King then held in the whole Kingdome; I shall therefore give the reader a most true though brief narration thereof, extracted out of the letters written from the committees of Shrewsbury, to the Speaker of the House of Commons, with the list of the prisoners and prizes taken therein, which was as followeth.

"Right Honourable Sir,"

"It hath pleased God miraculously to deliver the strong town of Shrewsbury into our hands, with all the Commanders, Officers, and Souldiers therein; a list of the cheif of whom wee have sent inclosed to you. The manner of taking of it was briefly thus. Upon the 22nd of this Moneth of February, wee drew out of our Garrisons of Wem, Moreton, and Stoke, 250 horse, and the like number of foot, Sir William Brereton having sent us 250 foot, and 350 horse, which party by our order was commanded by Leivtenant Colonel Rincking, (who in the marshalling and managing of this designe deserves much honour) and Captain Willyer, together with Mr. Huson, a minister, who also most valiantly and bravely led on the firelockes, with fifty troopers dismounted under the command of Leivtenant Bendebne, who led on their men with great courage and undaunted resolutions, after whom also followed 360 foot more, which by Severn side stormed the town, neer unto the Castle wall, and marched unto the Market house, and there surprised the Main guard, and then sent a party to secure the Castle-forehead gate, which was effected without much difficulty, and after a quarter of an houre the draw-bridge was let down and the gate opened, where valiant Colonell Mitton, Colonell Bowyer, and all the gentlemen of this Committee, with the horse entered, and immediately became masters of the town, and within four hours after the Castle was surrendered upon quarter, for all but the Irish to march to Ludlow, and then the enemy delivered up a strong out-work in Frankwell, upon bare quarter for their lives.

By twelve of the clock at noon, wee became absolute masters of the Castle and Town, wherein were taken many considerable prisoners, good store of ammunition, and great store of ordnance. The Committee of Wem took as great care as possibly could bee, that the well-affected in the town might not in any measure suffer or bee plundered, and therefore the Officers kept of the Souldiers from plundering the town, that so the committee might see right down, and none but malignants only to suffer. The Committee gave present notice thereof to Sir William Brereton, certifying him what they had

The town was well fortified, and strongly palisaded; eight carpenters were conveyed up the river in a little boat, and landed within the enemy's breast work, under the Castle Hill, on the east side; the centinels after some pause fired upon them, but they soon sawed down so many of the pallisadoes as gave the men free passage.

---

done, who thereupon took care for forces to lye neer them to releive Colonell Mitton if occasion should bee. The whole country, I mean especially the well-affected party, were exceeding glad of this, and desired that Colonell Mitton might bee Governour thereof, being well known unto them all, to be a most honest cordiall, and well-affected gentleman, and of singular and true integrity to the Parliament's Cause, whereof by many reall experiments they had strong and indubitable ground and knowledge. Our horse the day before had a long and weary march, they having been sent to surprize Sir William and Sir Thomas Whitmore a Parliament man, whereof more immediately. Sir, we shall not trouble you any further, but to subscribe ourselves

Your most Humble Servants,

A. LLOYD,
SAMUEL MOORE,
THOMAS HUNT,
ROBERT CLIVE,
ROBERT CARLTON,
LEIGH OWEN.

Salop, February 24th, 1644.

A LIST OF THE PRISONERS TAKEN IN SALOP, AS AFORESAID.

Sir Michael Ernley, Knight, and his Brother; Sir Richard Lee, Baronet; Sir Thomas Harris, Baronet; Sir Henry Frederick-Thyn, Baronet; Sir William Owen, Knight; Sir John Wilde, senior, Knight; Sir John Wilde, junior, Knight; Sir Thomas Lister, Knight, together with eleven Esquires, two Leivtenant Colonels, one Major two Doctors, eight Captains, fifteen Gentlemen, three Ancients, four sargents, nine or ten other Officers, and about fifty other Prisoners, whereof some were Irish; one Captain, and five others slain. Wee also took fifteen pieces of ordnance, many hundreds of arms, divers barrels of gunpowder, all Prince Maurice his Magazine; the Town, the Castle, and all the works, divers carriages, bagge and baggage of the Princes; besides many other prisoners and purchases not discovered when this list was gathered. Wee lost only two men, and was not this a most rare and remarkable mercy and famous victory indeed, and never to bee obliterated out of the tables of eternall memory and gratitude? As accordingly and most worthily it was shortly after ordered by the Parliament, that a solemn day of publike Thanksgiving to God should bee kept; and 20 *li.* was given to the first messenger that brought this most welcome newes, and 10 *li.* to the second.

And heer I must desire the Reader to take notice of the most wise and righteous disposall of this great Mercy unto us by the great and glorious Moderatour of all things in Heaven and Earth, viz. That this so rare and famous defeat, given to the impious enemies of God's Cause and Truth, was upon the very same day that the mock treaty, or rather plot treaty at Uxbridge, was happily dissolved, namely, Saturday, Feb. 22, 1644. A passage of singular divine providence, and not slightly to be pretermitted of us—*Vicars's Parliamentary Chronicle*, 1646.

Burghall, generally called the Puritanical Vicar of Acton, near Nantwich in Cheshire, in his journal of occurrences from 1628 to 1663 gives the following:—

"February 22nd, 1644.—Colonels Mytton and Bowyer, with about 1500 men, took Shrewsbury, and Sir Michael Earnely, then governor, with many hundreds of prisoners; all their magazines, ammunition, and ordnance; some fled into the castle, which was delivered up the same night upon fair terms. Many of great rank were there taken; Sir Nich. Biron, Sir Rich. Lea, Sir Rich. Leveson, Sir J. Wield, senior and junior, Sir Tho. Cecil, Sir H. Frederick Thynne, Sir William Owen, Sir Herbert Vaughan, Sir Tho. Leicester, Mr. Ireland, Mr. Kynaston of Oakley, Mr. Barker, Mr. Pontsbury Owen, Mr. Pelham, and divers more; 2000 arms, 100 barrels of gunpowder, all the cannon,

The first that stormed were forty-two troopers dismounted, with their pistols, and about as many firelocks: they were led on by Mr. Huson, a minister, Captain Willers, and Lieutenant Benbow; after these followed some other musquetteers along Severn side, under the Castle Hill, and near Sir William Owen's House, (now the Council-House), entered the town at the Water Lane Gate; after these marched 350 foot, commanded by Lieutenant Colonel Rinking. Having gained the streets of the town, they marched to the market place, and after exchanging some shot gained the main court of guard there; the rest marched to the Castle-forward Gate, which within a quarter of an hour was gained, the guard having fled; the gates were opened, and the draw-bridge let down, at which the horse, under the command of Colonel Mytton and Colonel Bowyer entered, together with the gentlemen of the committee. It was now about break of day, the town was in the greatest distress, and nothing was heard but shrieks and outcries. The castle, and the strong out-work in Frankwell held out for some time, but by twelve o'clock the castle was delivered up, upon these conditions, viz. that the

---

and great store of money and plate, to the value of £40,000, and much other goods and treasure; which most of the great men had sent thither, as to a place impregnable.

Upon taking Shrewsbury, the enemy quitted and burned Leahall and Tonge-Castle; they quitted, likewise Madeley, Rowton, and Moreton Corbett, which last house was burnt by the Parliament."

Burghall's account of the " Prisoners of rank" contains the names of several not enumerated by Vicars, nor to be found in Phillips's List.—The following various particulars are added from the same authority, as being descriptive of the mode of warfare and of skirmishes which took place in the neighbourhood, a short time preceding the taking of Shrewsbury.

" September, 1643, Thursday.—Captain Bromhall and some others came to Loppington, two miles from Wem, and were assaulted by the enemy, being about 2000; they kept them in play for awhile, but at last were forced to take the church, and before aid could come from Wem, the enemy fired the church, and by that means forced them out, and Captain Bromhall with his company, and some others were taken prisoners; Sir Thomas Middleton's Lieutenant and some few more hurt, and three slain of the enemy; a son of the Lord Killmorry's, a brother of Sir Vincent Corbet's, and divers others were taken prisoners, and some slain. This skirmish lasted about two hours, the King's party being about 2000, the Parliament's not more than 600. Night coming on, the enemy sorely handled and scattered, fled, and Wem forces had the better.

Michaelmas-day.—The Train-bands of Nantwich Hundred marched towards Wem, to aid the forces there; they lodged the first night at Drayton, and the second at Wem in safety, fortifying the town, many times sallying out, they gave alarms to Shrewsbury, provoking the enemy to battle, but they had no mind to it.

St. Luke's-day.—Sir William Brereton hearing the enemy had besieged Wem, drew out the army and townsmen to relieve it; coming to Priest heath, they were informed the enemy had assaulted the town, coming up to the very walls, but were beaten off with great loss; Colonel Wynn, Captain Wynn, Captain Ellis, Captain Jones, and to the number of 100 being slain, the rest marched off to Shrewsbury; the Parliament forces followed and overtook them at Lee-bridge in the evening, for there they had pitched, and taken the ground to their own advantage. It began to grow dark, they then fired one upon the other, three were slain on the Parliament side, and fifteen on the King's, besides Captain Chapman and some others taken prisoners. The Royalists fled to Shrewsbury, and the Parliament forces to Wem, after they had pillaged the field. Next night they came to Whitchurch, and fined the town £300 to save it from plunder; and the next day came to Nantwich, all except some horse which went towards Chester."

English should march to Ludlow, but the Irish to be delivered up to the conquerors. The strong work at Frankwell was delivered up before night, surrendering upon bare quarter, The loss on both sides was only two killed, viz. on the Parliament's side, one Richard Wicherley, born at Clive, and on the King's side, the captain of the main guard, killed at the market-house. Several tradesmen were ruined by plundering their goods, and the plate and goods of gentlemen and strangers, who had brought them into the garrison, were all taken, amounting to a great sum.

Prince Maurice came to town just before it was taken.

For this service Colonel Mytton received public thanks in the House of Commons, and was made Governor of the Castle, it being one of the King's strongest garrisons, for here was taken 8 Knights and Baronets, 40 Colonels, Majors, Captains, and others of quality, besides common men; also 15 pieces of ordnance, several hundred of arms, several barrels of powder, and Prince Maurice's magazine.

A LIST OF PRISONERS TAKEN.

Sir Michael Ermley,* Knight, Governor, and his brother.
Sir Richard Lee, Baronet
Sir Thomas Harris, Baronet

Sir Henry Fred. Thin. Baronet
Sir William Owen, Knight
Sir John Wilde and Son, Knights
Sir Thomas Lyster, Knight

ESQUIRES.

Francis Thornes
Herbert Vaughan
Thomas Owen
Edward Kynaston
Robert Ireland
Richard Trevis

Thomas Morris
Arthur Sandford
Robert Sandford
Pelham Corbett
Thomas Jones

Lieutenant Colonel Edward Owen
Major Francis Ranger

Doctor Lewyn
Doctor Arnwey

CAPTAINS.

T. Raynsford
William Lucas
John Cressey
Thomas Collins

William Long
Pontesbury Owen
Henry Harrison

GENTLEMEN.

John Pay, Feodary
Cassey Benthall

Peter Dorrington
Thomas Barker

---

* September 24th, the same year, according to Burghall, Sir Michael Ermley was again taken prisoner at the Battle of Hooleheath, near Chester, when 2000 fellow countrymen and neighbours fell a sacrifice to the fury of the times.—Sir Michael was Captain of the Queen's troop, so called.—A greatly esteemed scarf which the Queen had taken from her neck and presented to Sir Michael to use as her colours also fell into the hands of the Parliamentarians.—ED.

Edward Talbot	John Witacres
Richard Lee	Joseph Tayler
Edward Stanley	Francis Sandford
Francis Manwaring	Richard Gibbons
John Bradshaw	George Manwaring
Edward Littleton	Charles Smith

ENSIGNS.

Thomas Palmer	Matthew Whitwick

SERJEANTS.

Vincent Tayler	Humphrey Davis
Thomas Dew	Richard Brein

Nicholas Proude, Clerk.

CORPORALS.

James Lacon	Moses Hotchkiss
———— Lendall	George Bucknall

Patrick Lacepaid, and forty-nine others, Irish Prisoners.

The reason why no more commanders were in the garrison was, because Prince Maurice had drawn them out against Chester.*

King Charles soon after his coronation at Scoone, arrived in England, with an army he had raised in Scotland, at which time there was a garrison for the Parliament in Shrewsbury, commanded by Col. Mackworth, youngest son of Judge Mackworth, of Betton. In the Month of August 1651, as the king was on his march to Worcester, when he arrived at Drayton he dispatched messages and invitations to several Governors of towns and castles, requiring them to deliver up to his use, the several places they had in possession, and principally to Sir Thomas Middleton, Governor of Chirk castle, and to Col. Mackworth, Governor of Shrewsbury. To the first of these the Earl of Derby wrote, and sent the letters by one Simkis, whom Sir Thomas caused to be seized, and sent to Wrexham. To the Governor of Shrewsbury, a formal letter and summons was sent by a trumpeter, as follows:

---

* After the town was taken by the Parliament's forces, all the criminal prisoners in the Castle were set at liberty, among them was one Lyth, concerning whom we have the following account :— One Clarke, of Preston Gobbals near Shrewsbury, was in arrears of rent for a tenement in Welsh-Hampton, to Sir Edward Kynaston of Oatley. Sir Edward sent a bailiff and one of his servants to arrest him, but one of Clarke's sons with a peat iron (though the others were well armed) struck the servant on the head, and so cleaved his skull, that his brains dropped out, and then fled from justice; when he had been absent several years, he returned to Welsh-Hampton, and one Hopkin his next neighbour and he quarrelling about their garden fences, each standing in his own garden. Hopkin threw a stone at Clarke, which hit him on the head, and killed him instantly; vengeance followed Hopkin next, for Lyth, his near neighbour quarrelling with him one evening at an ale house in Ellesmere; when Hopkin went home Lyth followed him, and next morning Hopkin was found murdered in Oatley Park, and it appeared that he had been knocked in the head with the foot of a washing block that stood by the side of Ellesmere Mere. Lyth was taken up, and sent to gaol, and was there confined at the time before-mentioned.

G

A COPY OF THE LETTER.

" Colonel Mackworth,

" Having sent you herewith, a summons to render into my hands, my
" town, with the castle of Shrewsbury, I cannot but persuade myself you will
" do it, when I consider you a gentleman of an ancient house, and of very
" different principles (as I am informed) from those with whom your employ-
" ment ranks you at present; if you shall peaceably deliver them unto me, I
" will not only pardon you what is past, and protect you and yours in your
" persons, and all that belongs to you, but reward so eminent and seasonable a
" testimony of your loyalty, with future trust and favour, and do leave it to
" yourself to propose the particular, being upon that condition, ready to grant
" you presently any thing you shall reasonably desire, and to prove myself
" your friend,

"C. R."

The following Summons was sent with the Letter.

" Colonel Mackworth,

" Being desirous to attempt all fair ways, for recovering our own, before
" we proceed to force and extremity, and (where the controversy is with
" subjects) accounting that a double victory, which is gained without effusion
" of blood, and where the hearts that of right belong to us are gained, as well
" as their strengths: We do hereby summon you to surrender unto us our
" town, with the Castle of Shrewsbury, as in duty and allegiance, by the laws
" of God and the land, you are bound to do, thereby preventing the mischiefs
" which you may otherwise draw upon yourself and that place, and also open-
" ing the first door to peace and quietness, and the enjoyment of every one,
" both King and people; that which pertains to them under certain and known
" laws, the end for which we are come.

" Given at our Camp at Tong Norton, this 20th day of August, 1651."

Governor Mackworth's Answer.

" For the Commander in Chief of the Scottish Army.

" Sir,

" By your trumpet I received two papers, the one containing a propo-
" sition, the other a direct summons for the rendition of the town and Castle
" of Shrewsbury, the custody whereof I have received by authority of Par-
" liament, and if you believe me a gentleman, as you say you do) you may
" believe I will be faithful to my trust, to the violation whereof neither allure-
" ments can perswade me, nor threatenings of force (especially when but
" paper ones) compel me ; what principles I am judged to be of I know not,
" but I hope they are such as shall ever declare me honest, and no way differ-
" ing (as I know) from those engaged in the same employment with me, who,

" should they desert that cause they are imbarqued in, I resolve to be found
" as I am, unremovable, the faithful servant of the Commonwealth of England.

" H. Mackworth."

The above, with other summonses from the King's army, being taken no notice of or rejected, the King with his forces passed on to Worcester.

This year also a court-martial was appointed to sit at Chester, wherein Colonel Mackworth was President, Major-General Mytton, and other staunch friends to the Parliament assisting, by whom ten gentlemen of the first families in England were sentenced to death for corresponding with the King, and five of them were executed; Sir Thomas Featherstonhough, the Earl of Derby, and Colonel John Benbow, were at the same time tried for being in the King's service. They were all condemned, and in order to strike the greater terror in different parts of the country, the Earl of Derby was adjudged to suffer death the 15th of October at Bolton,* Sir Thomas to be beheaded the 17th

---

* The following interesting account of the last moments and execution of this loyal, gallant, and amiable nobleman, from Baine's History of the County Palatine of Lancaster, will, I trust, be acceptable to the readers of this Edition of Phillips's History.—ED.

" In the year 1651, after the disastrous battle of Worcester, fought between Cromwell and Prince Charles, afterwards Charles II. the Earl of Derby was made prisoner in Cheshire, by Major Edge, on his way into Lancashire, and being brought to trial before a military tribunal at Chester, upon a charge of treason against the commonwealth, he was sentenced to die at Bolton. The trial took place on Saturday the 11th of October, 1651, and on the Wednesday following being the day appointed for his execution, his lordship arrived in Bolton about mid-day under a military escort of two troops of horse and a company of foot soldiers. The public sympathy was strongly excited in his favour. His lordship alighted near the cross, and going into a room with some of his friends and servants, had time allowed him till three o'clock in the afternoon. This interval he spent principally in prayer, and in relating how he had lived, and how he had prepared to die. The fear of death he said was no trouble to him, and his only care was for his wife and children; but he was satisfied to commit them to God. On the scaffold he preserved the equanimity of his deportment, and having justified himself from the charge of being a man of blood, and professed his unshaken allegiance to his king, he laid his neck upon the block, exclaiming with great energy—" The Lord bless my wife and children, and the Lord bless us all." He then gave the signal, and the executioner struck off his head at a blow, while many of the spectators testified their grief by sobs and prayers. On the following day the remains of his lordship were conveyed from Bolton to Ormskirk and interred in the family vault of the house of Stanley.*

* It is principally to these agitated times that the following singular inscription on a tomb-stone in Bolton church yard refers:—

" 𝔍𝔬𝔥𝔫 𝔒𝔨𝔢𝔭,

" The servant of God, was born in London, 1608, came to this town in 1629, married Mary, the daughter of James Crompton, of Breightmet, 1635, with whom he lived comfortable twenty years, and begot four sons and six daughters. Since this he lived sole till the day of his death. In his time were many great changes, and terrible alterations—eighteen years civil war in England, besides several sea-fights—the crown or command of England changed eight times, Episcopacy laid aside fourteen years. London burnt by the papists, and more stately built again. Germany wasted three hundred miles. Two hundred thousand protestants murdered by the papists. This town thrice stormed—once taken and plundered. He went through many troubles and divers conditions, found rest, joy and happiness only in Holiness—the faith, fear, and love of God in Jesus Christ. He died the 29th of April, 1684. and lieth here buried.

" Holiness is man's happiness."

The inscription is still legible, and has at the foot the arms of Okey.

at Chester, and Colonel John Benbow to be shot the 15th at Shrewsbury; all these sentences were severally put in execution, the Colonel was shot in Shrewsbury, in the Cabbage Garden, afterwards the Bowling Green, near the Castle, and on the 16th buried on the left hand going down the middle walk in St. Chad's Church-yard, and a stone set over him with this inscription:

"Here lieth the body of Colonel* John Benbow,
who was buried October 16th, 1651"

Which stone was new cut in the year 1740, at the expence of ——— Scott, Esq, of Betton, to perpetuate his memory.

The Colonel first joined the King upon his coming to Shrewsbury on the the 20th of September, 1642, at the same time the Lords Newport and Littleton did; the King in his way to Shrewsbury having rendezvoused at Wellington, the order he there published for strict discipline, and the protestation he made that he would defend the established religion, govern by law,

---

* Mr. Phillips appears to have committed an error in giving the unfortunate officer the title of Colonel. The register of St. Chad's Parish, October 16th, 1651, says, "John Benbow, Captaine, who as shot at the Castle."

The reverend, learned, and indefatigable Messrs. Owen and Blakeway have made no less a mistake in stating,* that the stone *still remains* in St. Chad's church yard, and that any reader resident in Shrewsbury may satisfy himself that it bears the following inscription:—

> HERE LIETH THE BODY
> OF CAPTAINE IOHN
> BENBOW WHO WAS
> BURIED OCTOBER Y^E
> 16. 1651.

No traces whatever of Benbow's grave stone now exist, nor can the place of his interment be exactly ascertained. The Sexton informed me, that no stone had been seen for these last thirty years, and that he believed it was broken to pieces by timber being thrown upon it, in clearing away the ruins of the church, after its fall in 1788; but this must also be an error, as Mr. D. Parkes saw and copied the inscription, nearly agreeing with the above, in the year 1800. The letters were then scarcely discernable, and shortly after the *stone itself* totally *disappeared*.—ED.

* See History of Shrewsbury, vol. 1, page 469.

preserve the liberty of the subject, and if he conquered would maintain the privileges of Parliament, and if he failed he desired neither the assistance of heaven nor men ; this protestation animated the army, and drew to him a great number of friends, some of whom suffered severely from the Parliament.

While King Charles was at Calais, in the year 1654, an attempt was made to take Shrewsbury Castle by surprize, in order to favor his restoration ; Lord Newport, and several others in the King's interest, were very active ; but a discovery of the conspiracy being made by Sir Richard Willis, many of the conspirators were apprehended, and punished, and Sir Thomas Harris, the most active person therein, was taken prisoner and sent up to London.

The last royal visit to this town, was by King James II. A. D. 1687, when he was attended by the Mayor, Aldermen, Burgesses, and by all the Nobility and Gentry of the county of Salop ; he kept his Court at the Council-House August 25, and went to Whitchurch the next day,

The following Order was made for the King's Entertainment, *viz.*

" Whereas his Majesty, upon his progress, is to come to this town, It is " unanimously agreed, that £200 be expended in presenting to and entertain- " ing his Majesty, and such further sums as shall be thought reasonable ; the " entertainment to be made as the House shall further consider and agree at " the next meeting.— Agreed, To send to Gloucester and Worcester, to en- " quire at those places, in what manner they entertained his Majesty.—That the " Chamberlain find £200, and the town give security, that the streets shall be " gravell'd just before the King arrives, every inhabitant to throw it before " their own doors.—That all the Companies appear with their drums beating, " colours flying, &c.—That the conduits run with wine, the day his Majesty " comes to town.—And that a Committee be appointed, to consult about his " Majesty's reception,—Agreed to meet on the Morrow in their gowns under " the market-house.

THE EXPENCE OF ENTERTAINING THE KING BY THE MAYOR AND CORPORATION, VIZ.

	£.	s.	d.		£.	s.	d.
Paid Mr. Corbet	10	15	6	Paid to Mr. Scott and Mr. Kynaston for going to Gloucester	5	0	0
Paid for fruit	0	5	0				
Paid to the committee	0	11	6				
Paid to the fidlers	0	7	6	Paid to the yeomen of the guard	1	1	6
Paid expences	0	4	0	Paid to Henry Vernon, for flourishing a flag on St. Mary's steeple	1	1	6
Paid for a ton of coal	0	9	0				
Paid for painting the conduit on the Wyle-Cop	0	1	0				
Paid for a gold purse, making, and gold thread	2	12	6	Paid for ale and bonfires	0	5	0
In the purse	107	10	0	Paid for 54 yards of flannel	5	8	0
Paid for a silk string for the purse	0	1	0	Paid to Mr. Thornton	2	7	10
Paid for ale	0	10	0	Total	138	10	10

The following year Lord Chancellor Jeffries,* by letter dated June 12, acquaints the Mayor, by his Majesty's command, that on the Sunday preceding, (June 10th) about ten o'clock in the morning, it had pleased God to bless his Majesty, and his royal consort the Queen, with the birth of a hopeful son, and his Majesty's kingdoms with a prince.† Desiring the Mayor and Corporation to direct and assist at a thanksgiving to God, for so inestimable a blessing, and in such other public rejoicings as are suitable on so great an occasion.

† The Chevalier de St. George Edward Francis, died at Rome on the 1st of January, 1766, aged 77 years, 6 months, and 20 days; 28th May, 1719, he married Maria Clementina, daughter to Prince James Lewis Sobieski of Poland, by whom he had two sons, Charles Edward Lewis, born 31st December, 1720, and Henry Benoit, born March 6th, 1725.

---

* George Jeffries, or Jeffreys, one of the worst, yet greatest of men, was born at Acton, near Wrexham, in Denbighshire. His father had been a silk weaver, and in that business had acquired an estate of £500 per annum. George himself being intended for the law was sent to Oxford, and thence removed to the inns of court. As soon as he was qualified for the bar, William Williams, Esq. and a certain London attorney were greatly instrumental in introducing him into business
1678. The 30th Charles II. he was grown so eminent in his profession, that the city of London chose him for their Recorder. When the Oxford parliament had been dissolved, Jeffreys appeared with a sword on, as one of the lieutenancy of London, to present an address to the King. About this time he was made the king's sergeant, and as such expressed great zeal and devotion for the court. To encourage and reward him, on the 7th of November he was created a baronet, September 29th, 1678, he was made lord chief justice of the king's bench. In his new station he presided at the state trials, which he managed in so arbitrary and indecent a manner, that he shewed a conscience which disdained scruples, a heart incapable of remorse, and a disposition equally prone to submit to any baseness, or commit any outrage. 1684. As he was setting out on the northern circuit, King James gave him a ring from his finger; and telling him that it was a hot summer, advised him not to drink too much. At last the king grew weary of Sir George, and would probably have removed him, had he lived six months longer. Whilst his Majesty was thinking about a change of measures, Sir George was treating about the purchase of the barony of Wem, and the manors of Wem and Loppington, which on 23rd December were sold unto him; Edward Kynaston, of Oatley, Esq. and William Adams, of Loppington, gentleman, having been nominated to compute the rents, and ascertain the true value thereof.
1685. May 13th, 1st James II. a little before the meeting of the parliament Sir George Jeffreys was created baron Jeffreys of Wem, being the first baron of that place by creation. In August he began his bloody campaign, guarded by troops of soldiers, and marking his progress by the carnage he left behind him. Of those unhappy persons who had been concerned in Monmouth's rebellion, he caused two hundred and fifty-one to be executed. He forced others to purchase their pardons at the expence of half, all, and sometimes more than they were worth. He practised these extortions on the innocent as well as the guilty. Mr. Prideaux was obliged to buy his liberty at the price of £14,760. The lord keeper North dying on the 5th of September, George, lord Jeffreys was made lord high chancellor of England, on the 28th of the same month; and soon after lord high steward for the trial of Lord Delamere. When the prince of Orange's design first began to be talked of, this lord being asked whether he could guess what the heads of his manifesto would be, he jocosely answered, mine will be one. November 1st, when the danger grew nearer, he got a pardon from the king for what he had done. December 11th he disappeared, and not trusting to his pardon, resolved to make his escape. In order thereto, he shaved his eyebrows, put on a seaman's habit, and all alone, Dec. 12th made the best of his way to Wapping, with a design to take shipping for Hamburgh. But while he was looking out at a window, say some, or while he was drinking his pot of ale in a public house, say others, a scrivener whom he had once upon a trial frightened almost into convulsions, got a glimpse of him, and recollecting in a moment all the terrors which had then taken such hold of him, gave the word to the mob, who rushing in upon him like a herd of wolves, and shewed a disposition to

CHAPTER IV.

NAMES OF STREETS AND PASSAGES.

PLACES MENTIONED IN AN OLD RENTAL OF THE TOWN.

30th HENRY III. 1246.

IN Vico de Mardevall
Kundestret
Rumaldesham
Apud Hokerstall
Will de Claremonte
Vico de Candelan
Terra Erwy
In Foro
Gerewaldis castell
Super Wilam
Terra sub Wila
Apud Rorishal
In Claro monte
Juxta furnum in Rumaldisham
Messuagio in Hundredo
De Stallagio Carnificum
Terra versus Sᵗᵃᵐ Werburgum
In Gomestall
Terra in Bailla
Terra ad Portam
In Colenham.   Colham
In Cleremund
Hospitale Stl. Johannis
In Soteplace.   Soetplace
Juxta Wallas.   Juxta Wallias
Doggepole   Dokepoll

Apud Bispestan
In Cotes, Vicum de Cotes
Neudygi
Apud Pilloriam
De Selda
Soppœ Corvisariorum
Capella B. Maria
Eccl. B. Maria
In Foryate
In Frankvill
Retro Castellum, Salop
Terra Juxta, Sanctum Sepulchrum
In Prestefurlong
Cromacre
Ruenhull
Terra St. Michaelis
Bromhull
In Terra Campestri
Fratres Minores
Foricta Monachorum
In libertate Foricta Mon.
In Suburbii Salop, inter ponte de Colebrugge, et pontem Monachorum
Abbathiæ Salop.

tear him to pieces. Every face that he saw was the face of a fury. Every grasp he felt he had reason to believe was that of the demon waiting for him. Every voice that he could distinguish in so wild an uproar. overwhelmed him with reproaches, and his conscience echoed within him, that he deserved them all. In this miserable plight, in these merciless hands, with these distracted thoughts, and with horror and despair in his ghastly face, he was goaded on to the lord mayor, who seeing so great a man whom he had never looked up to without trembling, brought before him as the worst and most abhorred of all malefactors, fell into fits, and was carried off to his bed, from whence he never rose more. Before the government was at leisure to punish him, he died in the Tower on the 18th of April, 1689, having, as it is said, hastened his end by intemperate use of spirituous liquors.

Garbet's History of Wem.

STREETS,† &c.

WYLE COP. In the rental of the town before cited, taken 30th of Henry III. 1246, mention is made of places called *Terru sub Wila*, and *Super Wilam*, which are what we now call under the Wyle, and the Wyle Cop.

As this street is upon a steep bank or declivity, Quere, Whether it is not corruptly stiled the Wyle, for the Hill? and then the bottom is rightly called, from its situation; under the Wyle, or under the Hill.

Or the derivation may be from *Coppe*, Sax. the top of a Hill; the word is often used by Chaucer in that sense, as *Cucumen Montis*, the Coppe of the Mountain.

Wyle may mean the Vill, or Town, for Spelman quotes the word Wila, or Will, as used in that sense, in the names of German towns. Frankwell was anciently written Frankwyle, or Frankville.

BEECHES LANE, (now the Back lane), corruptly so called, for the ancient name Bispestan, or Bushpestanes.

Bispestanes; probably from Bishop's Town, or Bishop's Stone, as being the residence, or in possession of the Bishop of the diocese, who in doomsday survey is said to have been lately possessed of 16 dwelling houses in Shrewsbury, inhabited by so many Burgesses, 10 whereof at that time lay waste, which houses probably lay in this part of the town, from thence called Bispestan, or Bishopston; as Bushwood in Warwickshire, so called corruptly for Bishop's Wood, as being part of the possessions of the Bishop of Worcester.*

In the town roll, 30 Henry III. a place called Bispestan, is mentioned: in a deed dated 5 Edward I. it is written Bushpestanes, where a garden is described as lying under the Wyle, between the King's highway and Bushpestanes Street. It is also called in old deeds, Bispestan, Bipstan, Biston's Lane, and Beeches Lane, and described as leading from the east end of St. Chad's church, down to the walls, behind the Wyle Cop.

The SEXTRY, was the shut or passage from Kiln Lane to the High Street, now called the King's Head Shut. Sextry is corruptly used for Sacristary, being the place where the Sacrist of St. Chad's kept the vessels and ornaments of the church, and also the vestments of the Dean and Prebendaries.

MARDOL, antiently wrote Marlesford, Mardefole, and in the time of Henry VIII. Mardvole. It had the name Marlesford, from the ford through Severn, at the bottom of that street, near the Welsh Bridge; *Mar*, and *Leas* (pastures), that is the ford at the marly pastures.

* Dug. War. p. 588

---

† For the *present* names of the Streets, improvements, &c. see another department of this volume.—ED.

Marlesford, and Mardefole, seem to be the same street, from a grant of one Randolph to the Austin Fryers; where it is called Marlesford, and in the confirmation of that grant by Edward I. it is written Marlefole.

DOGPOLE, formerly Dokepoll, from *Ducken*, Teutonic, to bend or stoop, or *Duick*, in the Cimbric language, used in the same sense we use the word duck, or to duck ones head; hence Duck, to stoop; Poll, the head or summit the bank whereon it stands has a very deep descent down to the river.

IKESLODE, a lane that went from Dogpole to the walls.

The CORNCHEPYNGE; the Corn Market, from the Saxon, *Ceapan*, to buy; or *Ceping*, Saxon, a market; in the above mentioned rental, *In Foro*.

CHEPYNGESTREET, an antient name, probably of the street leading from the Corn Market, to the bottom of Murivance or Swan Hill.

The SHIELDS, sometimes called the Shilds, the Sylds, and the Shelds; now the Plough, near the Market-House; all the different names seem to be derived from the word *Selda*, a shop or a row of shops; it is in the rental before-mentioned, called *Selda*, and in the reign of Henry VI. was called the *Draprye*. There went a thoroughfare here under two houses, from the Corn Market, to the street called the Stalles, near Mardol Head, which was granted by the town in fee-farm, still reserving a passage at all proper times. The passage was four feet wide, and is in some old writings called the Thorghwey. In a manuscript in the Exchequer, mention is made of *"quondam shopam subtus communem Aulum inter shopam Joh. Hordeley & in-troitum ad le Drapyre, vocat; le Seldes,"* viz. a certain shop under the common Hall, between the shop of John Hordley, and the entrance to the Drapyre, called the Seldes.—Seld in Islandic is sold.

After the above grant in fee-farm, the Plough house belonging to Mr. Harding, and those on each side of it to Mr. Owen of Woodhouse, a law suit commenced between them, relative to the right of a passage through the Plough, which was at last accommodated by Mr. Owen's purchasing the same.

The STALLES; the street leading from Mardol Head, to the High Street, now called Lee Stalls.

The HIGH STREET, formerly called Baxter's Row, also Bakers Row; probably it was the Street where the Bakers principally resided.

FRANKWELL; anciently *Frankville*, i. e. the Franks Vill, or Town, probably inhabited by the Franks, for in Doomsday book it is recorded that a part of the town, containing 45 Burgase houses were inhabited by those peo-

H

ple, who are there called *Francigence* ; * this street seems to have been regarded as in some sort unconnected with the other part of the town, they had a strong work erected there for their defence, which at the time Shrewsbury was taken by the Parliament's forces, surrendered upon bare quarter ; and in the year 1640. when the plague begun there, the inhabitants made an attempt to come into the town, but were beaten back by the bailiffs and townsmen.

CHEDDELODE ; the lane that goes to Severn, by Stury's Close : some think from the Saxon, *ladian* to empty or to cleanse ; we use the word lade (which probably is a derivation from the same) to empty out water.

CREPULLODE, from the same; is the place where the town water is discharged, at the bottom of Knucking Street.

BULGERLODE ; probably from the French *Boulever*, a bulwark built for the defence of the town; but more likely from *Bullenger*, an old word for a boat, or barge; it is so used in Cotton's Records of Parliament, 2d of Henry IV. p. 406. The place so called was the way from the bottom of the Wyle Cop to Severn, on the right hand the stone-bridge, latterly called the Gulph, as discharging all the water from that side the town, into Severn, wherein it was ingulphed, or swallowed up.

This place, with the houses over it, was taken down in the year 1766, to make room for building the new bridge.

MURIVANCE, or Muryvaunce ; a name of French extraction, signifying, before the walls, or within the walls ; probably when the town was first fortified it was the parade for the soldiers to be drawn up upon, for the defence of the town, it being a convenient spot, as it is very level, and near the centre of that side of the town, so that from thence the soldiers might be readily dispatched to any part of the walls. In process of time it was built upon, and the streets retain the ancient name of Murivance. These streets are, that leading from the west end of St. Chad's now commonly called St. Chad's Hill ; and that crossing the end of it towards the walls, now called the Swan Hill, from a public house called the Swan, some time since situate at the bottom of it.

Formerly there was a gate, or postern, in the wall, at the end of Murivance-Street, (or Swan Hill) and the wall was continued over it, till in 1743 the Mayor, William Turner, Esq ; got gravel there for his garden, and gave others leave to do the like ; when the workmen digging too close to, and under the wall, about 20 yards of it fell down, and three men narrowly escaped with their lives.

* At Richmond in Yorkshire is a gate and suburb, that goes by the name of the French Gate and Suburb, probably for the same reason.

MURIVANCE LANE, led from the town-wall at the end of Murivance Street, (or Swan Hill) down to the river, at the place where the walk is, now called Gosnel's Slang.

CANDELAN, afterwards called Kellen Lane, from *Canwill* Br. for Candle and *Cannel*, for Candle Coal, now Kiln ·Lane, (as generally supposed) from a kiln or kilns erected there, to burn bricks made upon the spot.

SHETEPLACE, now Shop Latch, in the oldest records written Sotteplace and Soetteplace, which probably was pronounced Shottplace, interpolating an h between the S and o, the like being observed in most words where an S or C precede a vowel, as in Shottesbrook in Berks, anciently written Sottesbrook, &c.

It seems likely to have been the name of a house, or place, belonging to one Soto, and to have stood near the Carrier's Inn, about where the old building, now a warehouse belonging to Messrs. J. and T. Baker stands, which it is probable might be the place.

On the first of Edward II. it was written Sheteplach. Sote by Chaucer, is used for sweet, and then it might have its name sweetplace, from its situation, or conveniences.

RATONYSLONE, now called the School Lane.

BEHIND THE WALLS ; (now the Quarry) so called from its situation behind the walls, as another part of the town was called Murivance, from a French word signifying before, or within the walls.

PRIESTS LANE, led from Murivance, near the west side of the college Garden, and so on by the Tenters to the walls, near the Tower. Another lane led from Murivance into Priests Lane, near the house late Sir Henry Edwards's, now Rev Mr. Leighton's. Both these lanes are now inclosed.

ROMBOLDESHAM, (now Barker or Tanner's Street,) in the town rental Henry III. 1246, it is called Rumaldesham ; also Rombaldi, and Romboldesham, in an Exch. M. S. *viz.* Hen. III. *Posterna sci Romboldi*—Henry IV. *Juxta Capellam de Romboldesham.*

The BAILEY ; that part of the town which lies before the Castle. Many other towns have places in them called by the same name, especially Richmond, which some think to have been once the *extima Area Castelli*, and since built with houses. *

HOUND STREET, in Speed's map appears to be the street leading from the Play House to Barker Street.

* Leland's Itinerary, vol. I. page 75.

CORVISORS ROW, in old writings the same now called Pride Hill, (but why so called uncertain) in the town rental 30th of Henry III. called *Soppæ Corvisariorum.*

SHOEMAKERS ROW, in Speed's map appears to be the same as Corvisors Row, or Pride Hill, rather the lowest part of that street.

HAWMONSTRETE, (uncertain where) probably that part now called Castle Street, and Raven Street.

MERIVAL*, at the east end of the New Bridge ; so called probably from its being dedicated to St. Mary, and so Mary's Ville, or Field; or from its wet situation†. Mary Ville, *Mere* being Saxon for a marsh or low ground ; this

---

† There was a chapel at Salisbury, called St. Mary's Chapel, in a place called Miryfelde ; and a church at Southampton, in a place called Mariefeld.—Also a place called Merrivale near Atherstone in Warwickshire, lying near a river, and probably so called from its situation. *Leland's Itinerary.*

---

* Early in the 16th Century it appears that Merivale was seperated from the jurisdiction of the Corporation, and considered a Hamlet within the *Liberty* of the Town, and that persons residing in Merivale could not, as aforetime, be members of the Body Corporate.

In vol. 1. page 272, of Owen and Blakeway's History, we have the following note :—

" 29 July, 21 H. 8. [1529.] Forasmoche as Richard Oseley, being one of the common counsell, dwelleth in Myryvale by thabbey of Salop, which myryvale by arbitrement is awarded to be oute of the liberty of the towne ; and is not content to inhabite hym self within the towne, by reason whereof, he, perceyvying that by the tenure of the composicon of the said towne, he cannet occupy the rowme of the comen counsell, of his owne assent and consent is content to be discharged of that rowme." &c.

We learn from the same authority, that the Oseleys (Ouseleys or Owsleys, for the name has been variously written, although the arms have always continued the same,) were once " a considerable family in this town : and, as it appears particularly in the Abbeyforegate,"

The will of Thomas Oseley. (who seems to have been a wealthy man,) dated 1556, and preserved in Doctor's Commons, mentions his tenements in " *East Forgate, Salop,*" and " St. John's Hill." He also bequeathes money to repair the churches of Morvill and Stockton, where other members of this family appear from their wills to have possessed lands and houses, as well as at Astley, Abeley, Haughton, Croft, Downwal, &c. In 1632, we find John O. bequeathing five pounds to the poor of Morvill. But of those who more particularly resided in Shrewsbury, were, Thomas O. and Alice his wife, members of the gild of St. Winifred, in 1486. (*Owen and Blakeway's History of Shrewsbury,*) His son Richard O. residing in Miryvale near the Abbey, in 1529. (*ib.*) His son Thomas O. who married Joan, daughter of William Acton, of Aldenham, and in his will dated 1556, mentions his son Richard O. his daughter Elizabeth, (who was married to Christopher Cotes, lineally descended from John Cotes, of Woodcott, 35 of Henry 6,) *See Harl. M. S. No.* 157. Thomas O. also mentions his *base* son, to whom he bequeathes a legacy, and from whom some descendants were living within a few years.

Richard O. son of Thomas O. and Joan Acton, above mentioned, was rewarded for his long services by Queen Elizabeth, with the manor of Courten Hall, in Northamptonshire, where he died in 1598, and was interred under a handsome monument, having an inscription in quaint verses which describes him as " *A Sallop's Oseley.*" By his first wife, the widow of Sir Miles Partridge, he had no children, his second wife was Magdalen Wake, daughter of John Wake, of the illustrious and ancient family of Blissworth, in Northamptonshire ; by her he had several children, John, Richard, Jasper, &c. and was succeeded in his estates both in that County and in Buckinghamshire, by his Son John O.

seems most likely to be the original of Merival, which must have been a very wet situation, before Severn was confined to its present channel, and when Meole river ran on the other side of it, through its old channel, still discernible in the meadow called the Gay, from *Kae*, a field, or from *Kai*, or *Cæg*, Saxon, a key. *Kai*, in the Br. language, signifies to enclose.

---

who for his military services was knighted at White Hall by King James, July 23rd. 1603. *(See Harl. M. S. No. 6063. Lansd. M. S. No. 673, and others.)* Sir John O. married Martha, daughter of Bartholomew Tate of Delapre, in Northamptonshire, died at the Siege of Breda, and was interred in the Church of Williamstadt, in 1624, leaving an only Son Richard O. of Courten Hall, who married Mary, daughter of Mark Parker, of Olney in Buckinghamshire, and by whom he had John, Richard, Jasper, and Charles, *(See Bridge's History of Northampt. p. 352.)* He was the Gentleman mentioned by Owen and Blakeway, *(History of Shrewsbury, Vol.* 1. *p.* 272,) as a major in the service of Charles I. and lineal ancestor through Richard, (his eldest son John dying unmarried.) Jasper, Jasper 2nd, Jasper 3rd, William and Ralph, to Sir William Ouseley, Knt. L. L. D. the Right Honourable Sir Gore Ouseley, Bart. and Jasper Ouseley, captain in the East India Company's military service, and professor of the Oriental Languages in the College of Calcutta, three brothers now living, 1828.

A very able Memoir of SIR GORE OUSELEY, appeared in the European Magazine for July 1810, and of Sir William Ouseley, in June 1811, from which highly respectable publication, the following extracts are selected :—

"SIR GORE OUSELEY, our immediate subject, was born on the 24th of June 1770, and went, when young, in a military capacity to *India*, where he served as *aide-de-camp*, confidential secretary, and commandant of the body guard to his Highness SAUDAH ALI KHAN, the *Navaub Vizir* of OUDE at LUCKNOW, and afterwards received a patent of nobility from SHAH ALLUM, the *Emperor* of HINDOSTAN. He was created a baronet of the united kingdom of GREAT BRITAIN and IRELAND on the 28th of September 1788; and on the 10th of March 1810, was appointed his Majesty's AMBASSADOR *Extraordinary* and *Minister Plenipotentiary* at the Court of his Majesty the *King of Persia.*"

The Editor of the *European Magazine,* speaking of the necessity of some individual of Talent being selected for the important mission to Persia, then in contemplation, remarks :—

"To SIR GORE OUSELEY, Bart. whose talents and integrity, whose perfect *geographical* and *political* knowledge of INDIA, whose intimacy with the courts and various interests of its princes, (some of whom he has personally served,) and whose admirable skill in its *languages*, render him, perhaps of all men living, the fittest for such a charge, this important embassy is entrusted."

Page 403, vol. 59, *(European Magazine,)* previously alluded to, in reference to SIR WILLIAM OUSELEY, the Editor remarks :—"This gentleman has his descent from a family of ancient distinction in Shropshire, and Northamptonshire. He was born in the year 1771. Mr. Ouseley while an Officer in the 8th Regiment of dragoons, sought in literature a resource for amusement during the leisure of country-quarters. The study of antiquities, which presents so many images of grandeur and tenderness, to interest the imagination and the heart, was that for which he first conceived a passionate curiosity. It led him insensibly into the kindred study of the ancient languages of the East; the Hebrew, Arabic, and Persian."

"Early in the spring of the year 1794, the regiment to which he belonged was ordered on foreign service. At Ostend, under the immediate command of General Richard Whyte, they joined the Austrian army. The French, however, with whom they were soon engaged in different skirmishes, prevented their junction with the troops under the Duke of York. On the 8th of May, a general action was fought between the allied army and the French, in which the 8th regiment of dragoons had a conspicuous part. At a village between Wervick and Commines, a squadron of the British cavalry was nearly cut in pieces; and among the losses of the 8th regiment, so many of the superior officers fell, that Mr. Ouseley remained first lieutenant, after the engagement of the day was over. By General Whyte, and by Colonel Hart, who had the command of the regiment, he was warmly recommended to the Commander-in-Chief for appointment to a troop, of which the command was vacant.

ALTUS VICUS, the highway or street, now called the High Pavement, near the Cross, made by direction and at the expence of Mr. Humphrey Onslow, one of the bailiffs, in the year 1570.

But his wishes, and these good offices of his friends, were disappointed. On his return to London, he began to prepare for the press, a curious work, which he made public, under the title of Persian Miscellanies, in the year 1795."

"Soon after this period, Mr. Ouseley, obtaining the rank of Major in the Ayrshire regiment of fencible dragoons, joined that corps at the city of Carlisle. At Carlisle in the beginning of the year 1796, he married a young lady, of great beauty and accomplishments, the daughter of Colonel John Irving, and niece to General Paulus Emilius Irving. In the year 1797, he published from an immense number of manuscripts in his own possession, the first number of *Oriental Collections, &c.* In 1799, he gave to the world under the title of an " Epitome of the Ancient History of Persia:" a work of great utility, though in a form peculiarly modest and unostentatious. His writings were read and admired by men of learning in various countries, who were not backward in public testimonies of their just esteem for the author. He was hence, without solicitation, adopted as an associate by the members of the various academies, and favoured with honorary graduation in different universities. About the same period he had the honour of knighthood conferred upon him."

"In the year 1800, Sir William Ouseley had the honour to present to his Majesty, at St. James's, a copy of a new fruit of his learned labours, a translation of the *"Oriental Geography of* EBN HAU-KAL." His next publication was a translation of a Persian work, named *Bakhtyar Nameh,* or, " Tales of Baktyar and the Ten Viziers," which we have perused with great pleasure.

"In 1801, Sir William, in a paper of learned and ingenious "Observations on some Gems and Medals bearing inscriptions in the Pahlavi or ancient Persick characters," produced a specimen of his diligence to introduce new light even into the deepest obscurities of Persian literature, and an incontestible proof that there was in this province nothing too dark or arduous for the perspicuity of his understanding, and the energies of his genius."

"By the University of Rostock, Sir William Ouseley has been created a doctor in philosophy. He has been elected a fellow of the Royal Society of Edinburgh, a member of the Asiatick Society at Calcutta, a member also of the Royal Academy of Sciences at Gottingen, and of several literary societies. We have hopes that hereafter, when Sir William shall have returned from that splendid embassy, with which he stands so closely connected, as secretary to his brother, the public will receive a most valuable accession of oriental literature, and a picture of Persian manners, taken from actual observation, by which Sir William will justly merit the title of the English Chardin."

The anticipations of the liberal intelligent Editor of the European Magazine have been most eminently realized, in the publication by Sir William, of his " Travels in various countries of the East, more particularly Persia," in three handsome quarto volumes, printed under his own inspection at Brecknock, in the years 1819, 1821, and 1823, illustrated with an immense number of engravings and maps, from actual drawings by Sir William, in several of which, it appears. he had the assistance of two of his own sons, of his brother Sir Gore Ouseley, and of his friend Colonel D'Arcy. These engravings are of the highest value to Travellers in the East, or to students of Oriental Antiquities and Literature. The Typography of the work would not disgrace a London Press; and though not entirely faultless, will perpetuate, with honour, the establishment of *Priscilla Hughes,* in which was employed a most ingenious young artist, *Mr. Evan Prosser,* by whom alone the numerous quotations in Arabic, Persian, and other languages were arranged.

Sir William's Travels are already entirely out of Print, as are all his other Publications. It is now currently rumoured that he has engaged to edit a third volume of the late *Lewis Burckhardt's Travels in Arabia,* for which undertaking no individual in the kingdom can be more ably qualified.

From undoubted authority we learn, that Sir William frequently expresses a desire to become the purchaser of some tract of Land, or Property, originally forming a portion of the possessions of his Shropshire Ancestors, to become a Freeholder, perhaps a resident of the County of Salop, and to revive in himself the ancient appellation of " *A Sallop's Oseley.*" In the wish, that so distin-

GROPE LANE. See account of Austin's Friary,

COLNHAM, now **Coleham.**

CORD LODE, or **CORD LANE.** Uncertain.

SADLERS ROW. Uncertain.

GLOVERS ROW. Uncertain.

The number of streets, and open passages, at present in Shrewsbury, exclusive of shutts* or alleys, is thirty-three; the following is a list of their present names, and the ancient names of those known.

PRESENT NAMES.	ANCIENT NAMES.
Wyle Cop, or Wild Cop.	Terra sub Willa, and Super Wilam.
Back Lane.	Bispestan, Bushpestanes, Beeches Lane
King's Head Shutt.	The Sextry.

* Probably derived from the word shoot, i. e. a passage that shoots from one street or place to another.

---

guished a scholar and gentleman, may accomplish the object of his desire, every reader of this edition of Phillips's Shrewsbury, will, with its Editor, most cordially unite.

Of Captain JASPER OUSELEY, few particulars have yet been published. But to the *pedigree* of the Ouseley's :—

Of the old *Shrewsbury* Branch was Robert Oseley, Principal of Great White Hall, (now Alban Hall) in Oxford, A. D. 1499. (*See Gutch's History of Oxford, Vol.* 1. *p.* 658.) and captain Nicholas Oseley, who for his bravery displayed in Sea Fights with the Spaniards, and various services on shore, was rewarded by Queen Elizabeth, in 1588, with a grant of ground in St. Helen's, London. (*See Purchas's Pilgrims, Vol.* 4, *p.* 1925, *Seymour's History of London,* 1. *p.* 362, *Lansdowne M. S. No.* 59, *Art.* 4, &c.) And we find others of this name, and originally from Shropshire, established some generations ago in Cheshire, Somersetshire, Essex, Dorsetshire, and different parts of England. But these are not to our present purpose. The monument of Richard the "Sallop's Oseley," at Courten Hall, is described by Bridges in his History of Northamptonshire, and in the Gentleman's Magazine, for January 1799, which gives an engraving of it, and offers some remarks on the extraordinary inscription, particularly the word *"ruen"* never yet satisfactorily explained, although it has been the subject of many conjectures. According to *Edmonson's Heraldry, and the Harleian M. S. S. Nos.* 1187, 1467, 1553, *and others,* the arms, of Ouseley (of Courten Hall, Northamptonshire,) are "Or, a chevron, sable between three holly leaves vert, chief sable, crest a wolf's head, erased sable, out of a ducal coronet, holding in his mouth a bleeding hand, gules." The origin of this crest and holly leaf, as a bearing, is assigned to the reign of Edward I. by an old family tradition, which however, the Gentleman's Magazine, above quoted, declares "too romantic and absurd to be given here." Page 19, *The Harleian M. S. S.* that give the arms and the crest, (See their Nos. already quoted,) were compiled in 1618 and 1619. Of the "Sallops Oseley," the monument erected a few years before, still exhibits the holly leaf, although some large scutcheons of Arms which originally ornamented it, were defaced by Cromwell's soldiers, who also tore off the brass plates, representing, Richard O. his wife and children.—*Editor.*

PRESENT NAMES.	ANCIENT NAMES.
Mardol.	Marlesford, Mardefole, Mardvole.
Dogpole.	Dokepoll.
Corn Market.	Cornchepynge.
High Street	Baxter's Row, and Bakers Row.
Pride Hill.	Corvisors Row, and Shoemakers Row.
Kiln Lane.	Candellan, Kellen Lane.
Frankwell.	Frankville, Frankvile.
Doglane.	
Barker Street.	Romboldesham, Rumaldesham.
Clarimond Hill.	Claro Monte.
St. John's Hill.	
Cross Hill.	
Swan Hill.	Murivance.
St. Chad's Hill.	Murivance.
Milk Street.	
Fish Street.	
Berrington's Square.	Old Fish Street.
Grope Lane.	
Butcher Row.	Flesh Stalls.
Rousbill	Rorishall.
Lee Stalls.	The Stalles.
Raven Street.	Castle Street.
Hills Lane.	Knuckin Street.
St. Chad's Water Lane.	Cheddelode.
St. Mary's Water Lane.	Seynt Mary Waterlode.
Shop Latch.	Sheteplace, Sotteplace, and Shottplace.
Ox Lane.	
School Laue.	Ratonyslone.
High Pavement.	Altus Vicus.
Abbey Foregate.	For Yate, and Before Yette.
Castle Foregate.	Ditto. Ditto.

The streets of Shrewsbury in general are wide and open, though it must be owned the buildings for the most part have neither regularity nor elegance. Our ancestors, it is well known, had no regular plan of building; they built in the place and in the form best fitting their own purposes, and their stile of architecture in the present day appears very strange and uncouth. Considerable improvements have been made in the buildings of this town, especially in later years, and here and there a house stands, displaying the taste of the proprietor, and the ingenuity of the architect. The streets of this town were first paved in the reign of Henry III. A. D. 1254, the King granting a lease of the tolls for three years for so doing. Great care has been taken at all times, by the Corporation to issue orders, and by the inhabitants to observe those orders for the cleansing the streets, and removing all nuisances; notwithstanding it was found necessary in the year 1756, to apply for an Act of Parliament, which act was obtained, and entituled "An act for the better paving, "amending, cleansing, enlighting, and watching the streets, highways, lanes, "and passages, within the town of Shrewsbury, in the county of Salop."

The following is an abstract of the act, viz. That from and after the twenty-fourth day of June, 1756, the Mayor, Recorder, and Justices of the peace, of and for the said town and liberties for the time being, should be trustees of and for the interests and purposes of the act, and also all other inhabitants who are in actual possession and enjoyment of the rents and profits of lands, &c. to the clear yearly value of £80, or possessed of, or entituled to a personal estate, or a real and personal estate together, to the amount or value of two thousand pounds.

That persons not qualified, acting as trustees, forfeit £10.

That the trustees are to meet where, and as often as they think proper, giving notice of such meetings.

That they should appoint officers, and order the number of lamps to be put up and lighted, regulate the watch, settle the officers' wages, and make orders.

That the following penalties should be inflicted by this act, viz.

	£.	s.	d.
On officers not observing orders	0	5	0
For every inhabitant neglecting to sweep and cleanse before his door at the time appointed, viz. Wednesdays and Saturdays.	0	1	0
For Scavengers neglecting to sweep and carry away the dirt and soil from the streets, before void houses and walls,	0	1	0
For every inhabitant throwing rubbish, ashes, dung, &c. into the streets,	0	1	0
That the scavenger neglecting to carry away dirt, muck, &c. swept up in the streets, shall forfeit for every neglect,	0	10	0
That rubbish occasioned by buildings shall be carried away by the owners, or forfeit	1	0	0
Every person for carrying away ashes, dust, muck, manure, &c. out of the street, except the scavenger appointed, shall forfeit	1	0	0
All muck, dung, manure, &c. brought out into the streets from back yards, stables, &c. shall be carried away by the owners in the space of 48 hours, or forfeit	0	10	0
That the place called the Green Market, shall be swept up and cleaned every night, by the persons keeping standings there, or forfeit for every offence	0	5	0
For every waggon, cart, and other carriage, bench, tub, or other annoyance left in the streets	0	10	0
For every beast killed by any butcher in an open street	1	0	0
For every swine seen about the streets	0	2	0
For all dung, filth, or night soil, carried out before eleven at night, or after four in the morning.	0	10	0

The above penalties to be levied by distress, on the goods and chattels of the parties offending.

By the said act, assessors and collectors are to be appointed yearly, and an assessment gathered from every inhabitant, who is assessed and pays church and poor rates, not exceeding eight-pence in the pound. Also boarders

I

and lodgers are charged with this assessment, in a sum not exceeding ten shillings yearly, according to their abilities.

The Mayor and Corporation in consideration of the sum of forty-five pounds, annually paid by them for the purposes of this act,* are idemnified from the repair of the streets.

The town is now well paved and lighted, and many of the inhabitants have at their own expence, laid flags before their doors for a footpath, adding thereby much to the beauty of the town, and the convenience of walking.

----

* In the year 1821 the above act was repealed, and a new one granted, appointing the Mayor, Aldermen, and Recorder of the town, for the time being, Trustees for putting the act in execution; granting also the same power to all persons residing within the walls, possessing property, the clear yearly rent of which is eighty pounds, or those who are rated at fifty pounds per annum, or who are possessed of £2000 personal property; or if without the walls, and within any part which the River Severn encompasses; the possession of Hereditaments of the clear yearly value of £100 is required. Nine of the trustees are a committee of management. All the property of former trustees is vested in the present, who have power to take up all pavements, pave, flag, &c.; all streets, lanes, and public passages. Proprietors of new houses, &c. are to pave or flag the foot path before their several erections, as far as the channel, at their own expence. Inhabitants of houses, &c. are required to sweep and keep clean the foot path before their doors, or be subject to a fine of three shillings. Goods not to be exposed to sale in any of the streets, &c. without leave of the committee of management, to cause any annoyance or obstruction whatever, under a penalty of forty shillings for the first offence, and five pounds for the second, &c.; unless according to due order on fair and market days. No carriages or waggons are to be left in the public streets. The committee have power to contract for houses, buildings, &c. and to take down all steps, projections, &c. which may annoy passengers. The act also directs that the streets be named, and the houses numbered. The committee have power to make sewers and fix lamps according to their own discretion; they have also the authority to appoint meetings to elect the watch committee, who regulate the watchmen, and who also appoint two substantial householders, to act as constables of the night for one week.

To enable the said trustees to carry into effect the conditions of the said act, they are empowered to collect from the tenants or occupiers of all tenements, gardens, and land, within the town of Shrewsbury, the sum of one shilling in the pound upon the actual value of rent of such hereditaments and premises.

The present committee of management are, Mr. JOHN MAXON, Mr. EDWARD LAWRENCE, Mr. WILLIAM NICCOLLS, Mr. JOHN MUCKLESTON, Mr. THOMAS HANCORNE, Mr. ALDERMAN SAMUEL HARLEY, Mr. THOMAS LLOYD, Mr. EDWARD JONES, and Mr. WILLIAM SMITH.

The Treasurer and Surveyor of works, Mr. ALDERMAN WILLIAM HARLEY.

EDITOR.

CHAPTER V.

NUMBER OF INHABITANTS, AND BILLS OF MORTALITY.

THE number of inhabitants in cities and large towns, has of late been a considerable object of attention. Dr. Price, the author of a valuable work, entitled "Observations on Reversionary Payments, &c." has taken great pains to collect authentic accounts of different places, and has proved from the materials he has collected, that the number of inhabitants in each house through Great Britain, does not amount to five; it is of importance that this subject should be canvassed, since enquiries of this kind, are not only a pleasing gratification of curiosity, but of real use with respect to particular towns, as they ascertain the increase of trade, and the degree of health in any place.

But an actual calculation will best answer this purpose, and herein a very great deficiency appears in the inhabitants of Shrewsbury, whose proper business it might be supposed to be, to engage in such a work. Making the best use of advantages already offered, we shall briefly attempt to ascertain the past and present state of Shrewsbury, respecting the number of inhabitants.

In Doomsday Survey taken in the year 1086, it is recorded, that in the reign of King Edward the Confessor there were 252 taxable Burgesses, but that then the Castle, built by Roger Earl of Montgomery, &c. took up fifty-one of the Burgesses houses, and that fifty lay waste, besides forty-three held by the Francigence, and thirty-nine annexed to the Abbey, none of which contributed to the taxes with the English, which they complained of as a great grievance.

Nothing appears relative to the number of inhabitants, upon which a probable conjecture may be formed, until the year 1695, when, in the month of June, an account was taken of the number of inhabitants in Shrewsbury, by order of Simon Hanmer, Esq. then Mayor, viz.

In Castle Ward, 1917—In Welch Ward, 2600—In Stone Ward, 2866—Total, 7383.

In December, 1750, the number of houses and inhabitants in Shrewsbury were taken by Mr. John Leigh, as follows, viz.

AGED 21 AND UPWARDS.	UNDER 21 YEARS	TOTAL.	HOUSES.
St. Chad's, - - - - 2,371	1400	3771	837
St. Mary's, - - - - 951	478	1399	315
St. Alkmond's, - - - 668	343	1011	237
St. Julian's, - - - - 688	362	1050	252
Holy Cross, - - - - 539	371	910	243
	In the whole Town,	8141	1884

12

Since the time last mentioned no account has been taken of the number of inhabitants, yet upon the whole it may be supposed the number has increased,* for houses are very seldom void, the rents are increased, and numbers offer as tenants upon every vacancy.

Bills of mortality have never been regularly published, consequently it is difficult to ascertain the increase or decrease of inhabitants. Several general bills for the whole town, have been published by Mr. John Leigh, of which the following are abstracts, viz.

From the first day of January, 1748, to the first day of January, 1749, including one buried in the Quakers burial ground.

	CHRISTENED.			BURIED.		
	MALES.	FEMALES.	TOTAL.	MALES.	FEMALES	TOTAL.
St. Chad's, - - - - - -	58	66	124	46	38	84
St. Mary's, - - - - - -	31	29	60	18	18	36
St. Alkmond's, - - - - -	11	20	31	10	17	27
St. Julian's, - - - - - -	20	22	42	10	9	19
Holy Cross, - - - - - -	16	19	35	8	17	25
In the whole Town, - - -	Christened,		292	Buried,		191

* In the returns to Parliament of 1821, the following are given as the numbers of houses and inhabitants within the borough :—

The parish of Saint Alkmond	308 houses	1712 inhabitants
———————— Saint Chad	1322 ——	7214 ——
———————— Holy Cross and Saint Giles	299 ——	1444 ——
———————— Saint Julian	955 ——	2656 ——
Part of the parish of Saint Mary	955 ——	5328 ——
Total,	3939	18,254

From 1750 to 1821, a period of 71 years, we have the astonishing increase of 10,113 inhabitants, and that, not in consequence of the introduction of large manufacturing establishments, or occasioned by accidental circumstances; but from the best of all causes, good air, good water, good living, and good society.

The subjoined is also from the returns of 1821, and contains the numbers of houses and inhabitants in the parishes and townships within the TOWN LIBERTIES, though not within the borough :—

	HOUSES:	INHTS:		HOUSES.	INHTS.
Meole Brace Parish....	213	1348	Hadnal Chapelry, part in		
Battlefield Parish..........	13	64	Middle Parish........... 61		363
Broughton Parish..........	31	177	Preston Gubbals Parish 38		166
Grinshill Parish..........	40	214	Merrington Township... 41		203
Hanwood Great, & Hanwood Little Parish	31	157	Acton Reynald Township, part in the Parish		
Astley Chapel, Parish of Saint Mary..........	40	204	of Shawbury...... 32		168
Clive Chapelry............	64	306	Sutton Parish............. 15		71

Total in Parishes and Townships not within the Borough, 609   3941
Within the Borough   2939   18,254

Total in the Town and Liberties,   3538   22,195

EDITOR.

From the first day of January, 1750, to the first day of January, 1751.

	CHRISTENED.			BURIED.		
	MALES.	FEMALES.	TOTAL.	MALES.	FEMALES.	TOTAL.
St. Chad's - - - - - -	73	58	131	70	96	166
St. Mary's - - - - - -	22	36	58	20	21	41
St. Alkmond's - - - - -	19	16	35	11	16	27
St. Julian's - - - - - -	25	18	43	14	14	28
Holy Cross - - - - - -	18	21	39	19	15	34
		Total,	306		Total,	296

From January 1, 1754 to January 1, 1755.*

	CHRISTENED.			BURIED.		
	MALES.	FEMALES.	TOTAL.	MALES.	FEMALES.	TOTAL.
St. Chad's - - - - - -	70	65	135	60	63	123
St. Mary's - - - - - -	33	23	56	27	34	61
St. Alkmond's - - - - -	25	16	41	15	22	37
St. Julian's - - - - - -	24	16	40	9	11	20
Holy Cross - - - - - -	27	13	40	15	19	34
In the whole town, - - -	Christened,		312	Buried,		275

An Extract of the Register of the Parish of Holy Cross, from Michaelmas 1751, to Michaelmas 1760, taken by the Rev. Mr. Gorsuch, and communicated to the Royal Society, by R. More, Esq. F. R. S.

		1751	1752	1753	1754	1755	1756	1757	1758	1759	1760	Tot.
Christened,	Males,	19	16	9	22	23	15	14	11	25	14	168 331
	Females,	18	22	18	12	16	17	18	12	15	15	163
Buried,	Males,	19	16	16	15	6	16	11	12	10	10	131 284
	Females,	11	12	14	20	10	11	11	24	23	17	153
											Increase,	47

* From the first day of January to the 31st of December 1827, the following were registered as the Births, Marriages, and Deaths, in the five Parishes of the town :—

	BAPTISMS.	MARRIAGES.	BURIALS.
St. Chad's, - - -	188	90	171
St. Alkmond's, - - -	31	28	46
St. Julian's - - -	82	62	23
Holy Cross, - - -	35	13	32
St. Mary's, - - -	142	60	110
Total,	478	253	382 EDITOR.

An Account of the Number of Christenings, Marriages, and Burials, in the several Parishes within the Town of Shrewsbury, from the Year 1762 to 1768, inclusive.

Years	St. Chad's			St. Mary's			St. Alkd.'s			St. Julian's			Holy Cross			TOTAL IN EACH YEAR.		
	Christenings.	Marriages.	Burials.	Christenings.	Marriages.	Burials.	Christenings.	Marriages.	Burials.	Christenings.	Marriages.	Burials.	Christenings.	Marriages.	Burials.	Christenings.	Marriages.	Burials.
1762	139	38	161	57	18	72	37	8	32	48	14	26	39	10	29	320	88	320
1763	116	54	144	41	14	73	32	17	34	33	13	38	38	19	34	260	117	323
1764	133	62	102	55	40	67	50	13	31	54	14	28	38	21	27	330	150	255
1765	137	46	152	60	20	55	41	7	29	43	9	41	38	23	47	319	105	324
1766	113	45	245	39	18	88	30	10	59	45	17	64	44	8	88	271	98	544
1767	139	41	104	53	21	65	35	10	33	45	11	21	46	10	28	318	93	251
1768	114	45	122	63	28	58	29	15	30	48	10	28	33	18	45	287	116	283
At a medium yearly about	127	47	147	53	23	68	36	11	35	45	13	35	39	16	43	301	110	329

To close this chapter, it may not be unacceptable to subjoin, the proportionable number of inhabitants that die annually in the following places; taken from the History and Antiquities of Cheshire, and Dr. Price's observations, &c.

Vienna, one in ... ... 19½   Breslaw, one in 25
London, one in ... ... 20½   Berlin, one in 26½
Edinburgh, one in ... ... 20½   Shrewsbury, one in, ... 26½
Leeds, one in ... ... 21½   Northampton, one in 26½
Dublin, one in 22   Liverpool, one in 27½
Rome, one in 23   Manchester, one in 28
Amsterdam, one in 24   Chester, one in 40

COUNTRY PARISHES.

Holy Cross near Shrewsbury, one in 33   Parishes in Brandenburgh, one in ... ... 45 to 50
Dukedom of Wirtemburg, town and country together, one in 33   Island of Madeira, one in 50
Pais de Vaud,* in Switzerland, one in 45   A parish in Hampshire, for 90 years, one in 50

---

* In thirty-nine parishes of the district of Vaud in Switzerland, the number of males that died during ten years before 1766 was 8170; of females 8167; of whom the numbers that died under one year of age were 1817 males, and 1305 females; and under ten years of age, 3099 males, and 2598 females. In the beginning of life, therefore, and before any emigrations can take place, the rate of mortality among males appears to be greater than among females. And this is rendered yet more certain by the following accounts. At Vevey, in the district of Vaud, there died in twenty years, ending 1764, in the first month after birth, of males 135 to eighty-nine females; and in the first year 225 to 162. It appears from a table given by Susmilch, in his Gottliche Ordnung, vol. ii. p. 317, that in Berlin 203 males die in the first month, and but 168 females; and in the first year 489 to 395;

CHAPTER VI.

PUBLIC STRUCTURES.

UNDER this head may be ranked, 1st. buildings erected for religious worship, 2nd. for charitable uses, 3rd. for business, and 4th. for defence, confinement, ornament, &c. &c.

In the first class are those that have been or are, devoted to religious worship; and among these the ancient monastry of St. Peter and St. Paul first deserves our notice.

The MONASTRY of St. PETER and St. PAUL, of the Order of Benedictines.*

---

and also, from a table of Struycks, that in Holland 396 males die in the first year to 306 females. But no country in Europe can equal Sweden in respect to exactness in their registers of births, marriages, and burials. At Stockholm a society is established, whose business it is to superintend and regulate the enumerations, and to collect all the information they possibly can, from every part of the kingdom, and to digest the whole, and from thence to draw tables of observation.—*Editor, from various authorities.*

* "The Benedictines were themselves the founders of several Monasteries in England, as also the metropolitan church of Canterbury, and all the cathedrals that were afterwards erected. Pope John XXII. who died in 1354, after an exact enquiry, found that since the first rise of the order, there had been of it twenty-four popes, near 200 cardinals, 7000 archbishops, 15,000 bishops, 15,000 abbots of renown, above 4000 saints, and upwards of 37,000 monasteries. There have been likewise of this order, twenty emperors and ten empresses, forty-seven kings, and above fifty queens, twenty sons of emperors, and forty-eight sons of kings; about 100 princesses, daughters of kings and emperors: besides dukes, marquisses, earls, countesses, &c. innumerable. The order has produced a vast number of eminent authors and other learned men. Their Rabanus set up the school of Germany. Their Alcuinus founded the university of Paris. Their Dionysius Exiguus perfected the ecclesiastical computation. Their Guido invented the scale of music; and their Sylvester the organ. They boast to have produced Anselmus, Ildephonsus, Venerable Bede, &c. There are nuns likewise who follow the order of St. Benedict; among whom those who call themselves mitigated, eat flesh three times a week, on Sundays, Tuesdays, and Thursdays; the others observe the rule of St. Benedict in its rigor, and eat no flesh unless they are sick.

The Benedictines, being those only that are properly called monks, wear a loose black gown, with large wide sleeves, and a capuche, or cowl, on their heads, ending in a point behind. In the canon law, they are styled black friars, from the colour of their habit. The time when this order came into England is well known; for to it the English are said to owe their conversion from idolatry. In 596 Pope Gregory sent hither Augustin, prior of the monastery of St. Andrew at Rome, with several other Benedictin monks. St. Augustin became archbishop of Canterbury.

St. Benedict, the founder of the order, was born in Italy about A. D. 480. He was sent to Rome when very young, and there received the first part of his education. At fourteen he was

Built by Roger de Montgomery Earl of Arundel and Shrewsbury, in the
year 1083. "This Abbey was begun in the year above-mentioned, near the
" East Gate of the City, to the honour of St. Peter, the Prince of the Apos-
" tles, near the River of Meole, where the said River falls into the Severn.
" In the same place stood a Timber Church or Chapel, built by Siward,
'· and dedicated to St. Peter, which at this time was in the possesion of Odili-
" rius, who was a Lover of Justice, and exhorted the Earl to build the Monas-
" tery, therefore upon the 3rd. of March, in the Year aforesaid he called toge-
" ther his Council, consisting of Gaurine or Warine, then Sheriff of Shropshire,
" Picotus de Says, with other great Men, and they all approving of the scheme,
" the Abbey was built and consecrated to the honour of St, Peter and St. Paul,
" many witnesses being present at the ceremony ; at the same time the Earl
" gave the whole suburb which is without the East Gate to the blessed Peter.
" Immediately upon the Earl's determination in Council, several Monks were
" sent for, who, together with Odilirius and Guarinus, begun the building ;
" the first Monks were Sagis, Rinaldis, and Frodias."*

AN ACCOUNT OF THE FOUNDATION AND ENDOWMENT.

" When William Duke of Normandy (by the providence of God, in
" whose hand is the heart and power of Kings) obtained this Kingdom, he
" gave the province or county of Shrewsbury to Roger de Montgomery, who,
" together with his Countess Adelaisa, studying to reform the service of God,
" with the consent of King William, Archbishop Lanfranck, and Bishop Peter,
" put Monks in a certain church built to the honour of St. Peter and St. Paul,
" in the East suburbs of the City of Shrewsbury, who should diligently pray
" for their souls, and for the souls of their ancestors and Heirs."†

* M. S.   † M. S.

removed from thence to Sebiaco, about forty miles distant. Here he lived a most ascetic life, and
shut himself up in a cavern, where nobody knew any thing of him except St. Romanus, who, we are
told, used to descend to him by a rope, and to supply him with provisions. Being afterwards discovered by the monks of a neighbouring monastery, they chose him their abbot. Their manners,
however, not agreeing with his, he returned to his solitude ; whither many persons followed him,
and put themselves under his direction, so that in a short time he built twelve monasteries. In 528,
or 529, he retired to mount Cassina, where idolatry was still prevalent, there being a temple of
Apollo erected on it. He instructed the people in the adjacent country, and having converted them,
broke the image of Apollo, and built two chapels on the mountain. Here he founded a monastery,
and instituted the order of his name, which in time became so famous. Here too he composed his
Regula Monachorum, which Gregory the Great mentions as the most sensible and best written piece
of that kind ever published. The time of his death is uncertain, but is placed between 540 and 550.
He was looked upon as the Elisha of his time, and is reported to have wrought a great number of
miracles, which are recorded in the second book of the dialogues of St. Gregory.

London Encyclopædia.

The Earl and Countess having a very great affection for this church, begun to make it fit for receiving the Monks, but died before they could accomplish their design, nevertheless they liberally endowed it, which endowments were added to, by several other benefactors, as in the following account.

THE ENDOWMENTS.

" Roger de Montgomery* gave to the Abbey, a certain street near the " Church, which is seperated from the City of Shrewsbury only by a River, " which is called Sabrina (Severn.) But this street is called Before Yette, " which in French we call *Ante Portam* ; they likewise added several churches " with all their possessions, viz. the Church of St. Gregory, (or Morsefield) " Stotesden, Dudelcomb, Conedour, Walinton, Recordin, Edmonton, Hode- " not, Arikalon, Tong, Domaton, Basechurch, and Ness, they also gave the

---

* Roger Pictavensia, third son of Roger de Montgomery. was also a benefactor to the Abbey. In Blore's History of the Manor and Manor House of South Winfield in Derbyshire, we meet with the following particulars, relative to this Norman family.—EDITOR.

" Roger de Montgomery, a noble Norman, and a person prudent, skilful, spirited, and valiant, was amongst the counsellors who advised William the Conqueror in the invasion of England, and led the centre of his victorious army at the battle of Hastings ; for which, and for many other services, the King conferred upon him the Earldoms of Arundel and Shrewsbury. His eldest son, Robert de Belesme, succeeded him in his lands and honours in Normandy ; and Hugh, second son of Earl Roger succeeded in the Earldoms of Arundel and Shrewsbury. The latter was killed in the year 1098, near the sea shore, in the Isle of Anglesey, by an arrow, shot from a ship of Magnus, King of Norway ; and, having no issue, his Earldoms descended to Robert, his eldest brother. The third son of Earl Roger, called Roger after his father. and Pictavensis, (i. e. of Poictou) from his having married a wife out of the country of Poictou, being a younger son, enjoyed no part of his father's great inheritance ; but distinguishing himself in arms, received from the Conqueror the Earldom of Lancaster, and all the lands between the rivers of Ribble and Mersey in that county ; and divers manors and lands in the counties of York, Nottingham, Lincoln, Norfolk, Suffolk, and Essex, and four or five manors in Derbyshire.

Being thus a man of great possessions, he became a considerable benefactor to the abbey founded by Earl Roger, his father, at Shrewsbury ; and by his charter, in which he stiles himself *Rogerus comes Pictavensis*, to which Sibilla his daughter is a witness, he gave the church of St. Mary in Lancaster and divers churches and lands to God, and the monastery of St. Martin at Sais, " *Sagiensis,*" in France, (which his father and mother had restored) for the health of his soul, and of the soul of Roger Earl of Shrewsbury his father, the Countess Mabilla his mother, his brethren, and his friends. But in the year 1101, joining with his elder brother, Robert De Belesme Earl of Shrewsbury, who then took up arms against King Henry the First, in the behalf of Robert Curthose, Duke of Normandy, eldest son of that Conqueror, and being vanquished in the contest, he was driven out of the kingdom for his offence, and some of his possessions were given, by King Stephen, or King Henry the Second, or both of them, to Ranulph Earl of Chester. Dugdale says, " *all* his possessions" were given to the Earl of Chester; but in this he must be mistaken ; for, though the Earls of Chester unquestionably enjoyed that part of his lands lying between the Ribble and the Mersey, yet none of them ever had those lands mentioned in Domesday Book to have been enjoyed by him in Derbyshire ; and indeed, the Derbyshire estates appear to have reverted to the Crown long before his unsuccessful enterprise in behalf of Curthose ; and this manor, in some way, became annexed to the barony of William Peverell."

K

" Villages of Aiton and Burton ; likewise gave to the Monks Toll of Wood,
" which was carried in through the East Gate of the City, and granted that
" a Fair should be held in the said Suburbs yearly, to the honour of St. Peter
" and St. Paul on the Festival of St. Peter, which is called *ad Vincula*. This
" was done in the year 1087. ·

" Witnesses,

" Godebaldus, ⎱
" Odilirious, ⎰ Priests.
" Herbert,   Arch Deacon.
" Warinus,   Sheriff.
" Robert Fitz Theobald.
" Roger Fitz Corbett.
" Robert the Butler.   Also

" many other Chiefs and Commonalty, who heard and confirmed these
" things."*

The place in which the abbey was built, belonged to Siward a Knight,
and the Earl being unwilling to build upon his land without making him a
recompence, gave him a village called Langfield, whereupon he consented to
give the land on which the abbey was erected, and the village of Langfield
Siward at his death left to the abbey, to which legacy the following were
witnesses :

Godebald.
Richard de Belmersh.
Richard de Montwarol.

Siward's sons Edward and Alfred consenting to the above grant, Richard
Bishop of London and several others were witnesses to it.

This village of Langfield was afterwards exchanged with the consent of
King Henry and his council, by the Monks, for the village of Brampton, of
Henry de Say.   •

Several Knights and Lords gave large benefactions for the salvation of
their souls, viz. Warine the Sheriff of Shropshire gave two hides of land
in the village of Tugford, and ten in Upton, also the church of Berrington,
with ten hides in that village ; and after his death (her sons consenting) his
widow gave for the salvation of her husband's soul, her house in the city, the
tenant whereof was to find a wax-light every night through the year, to burn
before the altar of the holy innocents in this monastery.

Herbert de Ferches gave a farm.   Reginald the brother of Warine the
Sheriff, gave the village of Leigh.   Gerrard de Tourney gave the village of
Betton.   Helgotus gave one hide of land near Severn, which from the adjoin-

* M. S.

ing wood was called Moor, and likewise a fishery in the said river. Godfrey half a hide in Harley ; to these grants are signed

Witness,
Richard, Bishop of London.

Hugh Pantulf gave his mills at Sutton* to the abbey, the following is a copy of the grant :

" Be it known to all persons, now and for ever, That I Hugh Pantulf, " have given and bequeathed to God, and to the holy church of St. Peter, " and to the Monks serving God therein, in the same holy church of St. " Peter, in Salopesburie, for the salvation of my soul, and the soul of my " wife, and each of our souls), the mill at Sutton, for a pure and perpetual " alms, so that neither I nor my heirs, shall henceforward claim, or attempt to " claim, any thing, save the prayers of the church.

" Hugh Pantulf.

" Witnesses,
" Robert Corbet,
" Robert the son of Robert Corbet.
" Stephen of Francton.
" Stephen de Hocklep. And others."†

Several other benefactions were given by the inhabitants of this county, by which the monastery grew so rich, that the Abbots‡ were mitred, and sat in

† M. S.

---

* From the grant of Hugh Pantulf, it is certain that a corn mill existed at Sutton in the days of the Conqueror, and perhaps centuies prior to that period. Sutton Mill may therefore be considered among the earliest in the kingdom : the present erection bearing that name is the property of Mr. Hiles.—EDITOR.

‡ Abbot, or Abbat, and Archimandrite, were titles at first indifferently assumed by the governors of the primitive monasteries. They were really distinguished from the clergy; though frequently confounded with them, because a degree above laymen. In those early days, the abbots were subject to the bishops and the ordinary pastors. Their monasteries being remote from cities, built in the farthest solitudes, they had no share in ecclesiastical affairs.. They went on Sundays to the parish church with the rest of the people ; or, if they were too remote, a priest was sent them to administer the sacraments ; till at length they were allowed to have priests of their own. The abbot or archimandrite himself was usually the priest; but his function extended no farther than to the spiritual assistance of his monastery ; and he remained still in obedience to the bishop. There being among the abbots several persons of learning, they made a vigorous opposition to the rising heresies of those times ; which first occasioned the bishops to call them out of their deserts, and fix them about the suburbs of cities, and at length in the cities themselves ; from which æra their degeneracy is to be dated. The abbots, now, soon wore off their former plainness and simplicity, and began to be looked on as prelates. They aspired at being independent of the bishops ; and became so insupportable, that some severe laws were made against them at the council of Chalcedon ; notwithstanding this, in time

the upper House of Parliament. The Abbot of Shrewsbury was the 15th in priority, among 29 mitred Abbots permitted to sit there.

The Earl Roger, in the year 1094, having by the hands of Reginald, then Prior of Shrewsbury, obtained from the house of Cluni, in Burgundy, the coat of St. Hugh, sometime Abbot there, for himself to put on; he was shorn a Monk in the abbey he had founded, with the consent of his Countess Adelaisa, and it is observed of him, that three days before his death, he wholly applied himself to divine conference and prayers, with the rest of that convent. He died the 27th day of July, 1094, and was honourably buried in St. Mary's chapel of the abbey; over his tomb was placed the figure of an armed Knight in hard stone, of which we shall give an account when we come to speak of the present state of this church.

When the body of the Earl was brought to be interred, Roger Fitz Corbet being present, gave to the Monks the church of Newton-Basschurch, with ten villages.

Ranulph de Gernon, Earl of Chester, gave two houses in Chindred Wiche, and as much salt as they could make, toll free.

When Hugh the son of Roger, who succeeded him in the earldom, came to visit his father's sepulchre, being (as it is said) divinely inspired and moved with paternal affection, he called Fulcheridus, the first Lord Abbot of the house, and before him and other Barons then present, he said,—" Peace be to this " place.—Therefore I order the abbey, with all its possessions, to be forever " free from taxes, and that the Monks exercise no business, either in building " of castles or bridges, or in mending the highways, &c. but be free from all

---

many of them carried the point of independency, and got the appellation of *lord*, with other badges of the episcopate, particularly the *mitre*. Hence arose a new species of distinction between the abbots. Those were termed *mitred* abbots, who were privileged to wear the mitre, and exercised episcopal authority within their respective precincts, being exempted from the jurisdiction of the bishop. Others were termed *crosiered* abbots, from their bearing the crosier, or pastoral staff. Others were styled *œcumenical* or universal abbots, in imitation of the patriarch of Constantinople; while others were termed *cardinal* abbots, from their superiority over all other abbots. Among us, the mitred abbots were lords of parliament; and called abbots sovereign, and abbots general. And as there were lords abbots, so there were also lords priors, who had exempt jurisdiction, and were likewise lords of parliament. Some reckon 26 of these lords abbots and priors that sat in parliament. Sir Edward Coke says, that there were 27 parliamentary abbots, and two priors. In the parliament, 20 Rich. II. there were but 25 abbots and two priors; but in the summons to parliament, *anno* 4, Ed. III. more are named.

The abbots and priors who statedly and constantly enjoyed this privilege were the abbot of Tewkesbury, the Prior of Coventry, the Abbots of Waltham, Cirencester, St. John's at Colchester, Croyland, SHREWSBURY, Selby, Bardney, St. Bennet's of Holme, Thorney, Hyde at Winchester, Winchelcomb, Battel, Reading, St. Mary's in York, Ramsey, Peterborough, St. Peter's in Gloucester, Glastonbury, St. Edmundsbury, St. Austin in Canterbury, St. Alban's, Westminster, Abingdon, Evesham, Malmsbury, and Tavistock, and the Prior of St. John,s of Jerusalem, who was styled the first baron of England, but it was in respect to the lay barons only, for he was the last of the spiritual barons.—*Editor, from Various Authorities.*

" taxes of the Earls ; but if any difference arises within the liberty of St. Peter,
" it shall be rectified by the then Abbot.

" But if the Abbot of this convent shall be puffed up with pride, and will
" not do the things that are right, it shall be in the power of me, or my heirs,
" to compel him to do justice to his neighbours.

" I do all this for the souls of my father and mother, my own, my brothers,
" and all my relations, for the souls of King William, his Queen Matilda, and
" all their children.

" But if any one while I live, or after my death, shall infringe, take, or
" any ways diminish any thing—may the Most High ! who rules over the earth,
" blot out his name from the book of life, may he be punished with perpetual
" excommunication, and destroyed by worms."*

The Barons who were then present, observing his piety, gave thanks to
God, and added many lordships and villages to the monastery.

King Henry confirmed all the before-mentioned grants in a full and extensive manner, and so did King Stephen afterwards, as appears by the following
grant :

" Whereas my uncle King Henry, by the petition of his Barons confirmed
" their priviledges, and I being a witness heard and saw him consent and verify
" every thing which Earl Hugh had granted, and speak the same words which
" the foresaid Earl did, when he constituted the liberty of the Church of St.
" Peter in so extensive a manner ; therefore I for the salvation of my soul, and
" the peace of my kingdom, grant and confirm all above written, viz. the same
" liberty and ease to the foresaid Church of St. Peter, as EARL HUGH gave,
" and King Henry confirmed. I ALSO GRANT, and confirm the liberties
" of that church in so full a manner, that no one after me can add any thing,
" and whosoever shall dare to diminish any thing let him be for ever accursed.

" I Stephen Rex have assented and signed,.
" Henry Bishop of Winchester.
" Roger Bishop of Salisbury.
" Neal Bishop of Ely.
" Robert Bishop of Hereford.
" Seifrid Bishop of Chichester.
" Gervase Abbot of Westminster:.
" Geof. Abbot of St. Albans.
" Roger Lord Chancellor.
" Randal Earl of Chester."†

Nothing further transpires relative to this monastery, till the reign of
Henry III. 1222, when a dispute arising between the abbot and burgesses of
Salop, concerning mills : it was at length adjudged that the burgesses should

* M. S.　　　† M. S.

not erect mills to the prejudice of the abbot. The King likewise granted the abbot and convent, liberty of free warren in their manor of Abbey Foregate. Notwithstanding the above determination it appears that the burgesses made encroachments on the monastery, for in the year 1267 a suit was commenced between the abbot and burgesses, concerning mills erected in the town by the burgesses, contrary to the charters of the abbey; this controversy was decided by the King in council at Shrewsbury, on the Friday before Michaelmas: The King's council present were,* the Chancellor, Treasurer, Keeper of the Privy Seal, Justices of both Benches, with the Chancellor and Barons of the Exchequer.

In the reign of Edward I. A. D. 1279, the barony of the abbot of this monastery was for a contempt seized into the King's hands, but for a fine of fifty marks the abbot was pardoned, and the barony restored to him by the Sheriff of the county.

Very little further occurs relative to this monastery till the time of its dissolution, excepting a meeting held by the abbot and corporation to settle some differences subsisting about the Abbey Foregate fairs; and their joining together in the reign of Henry VIII. 1513, in a general triumph and grand procession, on account of two victories gained by the King's forces.

At the time of general suppression† in the year 1531, this abbey was suppressed, and the images were taken down and burnt. And in 1539 the Dukes of Richmond, Norfolk and Somerset, who were appointed commissioners, came to Shrewsbury, to enquire into the due performance and execution of the orders, relative to the suppression.

The value of this monastery was, according to Dugdale £132 4s. 10d. to Speed £615 4s. 3d.

A LIST OF THE ABBOTS OF THIS MONASTERY FROM ITS FOUNDATION TO ITS SUPPRESSION.

1. Fulcheridus	Was appointed first Lord Abbot by the founder, he died in March 1113.
2. Godefrid	Died suddenly 1127.
3. Herbert	Usurped and succeeded.
4. Robert	Died 1167.
5. Adam	Deposed 1175.
6. Ralph	Died 1218.
7. William	Succeeded in 1218.
8. Walter	Prior of Leominster 1221.
9. Henry	Abbot in 1223.

* Hale's Pleas, vol. 1. p. 422.   † See an account in the Appendix.

10. Adam	Ditto 1244.
11. Thomas	Elected 1251 and afterwards was sent Embassador to Alonso King of Castile, died 1266.
12. Henry	A Monk of Evesham 1258.
13. William de Upton	Succeeded in 1271.
14. Luke de Wenlocke	Succeeded the same year, to whose election King Henry III. assented, he resigned 1278.
15. John de Drayton	Succeeded 1278, died 1291.
16. William de Mokeley	Succeeded and governed 40 years, died 1332.
17. Adam de Clebury	Died 1334.
18. Henry de Alston	Died 1360.
19. Nicholas Stephens	
20. Thomas Presbury	Who was Chancellor of Oxford 1393, and again 1409.
21. Thomas	Who was falsely accused of felony in 1414, was honourably acquitted, and governed 10 years after.
22. John Hampton	Elected 1425, died 1433.
23. Thomas Ludlow	Died Dec. 8, 1459.
24. Thomas Mynde	Elected 1459, died 1499.
25. Richard Lye	Admitted 1499, died 1512.
26. Richard Baker	Elected 1512.
27. Richard Marshall	Resigned to the next Abbot,
28. Thomas Butler	Who appears to be Abbot in 1533, and again 1539, at the time of dissolution, when he surrendered the Monastery to the King's use January 20, and had a pension of £80 per annum, and when he died Richard Marshall the former Abbot, had a pension of £10 per annum.

The following Pensions were assigned to the Abbot and Convent of Shrewsbury, Jan. 24, 1539, the 31st of Henry VIII. on their surrender of that Monastery.

	per Annum.					per Annum.		
	£	s.	d.			£	s.	d.
To Thomas Butler, Abbot,	80	0	0	— Richard Owen, - -		6	6	8
— Thomas Wenlock, Prior,	10	0	0	— John Colley, - -		6	6	8
— Richard Broughton, Priest,	6	0	0	— John Waryton, Priest, -		6	0	0
— Thomas Howell, Sub-Prior,	6	0	0	— Robert Coventry, Ditto, -		6	0	0
— Thomas Leech, -	6	13	4	— William Creplege, Ditto, -		6	0	0
— John Wall, - -	6	0	0	— Thomas Preston, Ditto -		6	0	0
— John Lane, - -	6	6	8	— John Drayton, - -		1	6	8
— William Litchfield, -	6	6	8	— John Wellyton, - -		1	6	8
— William Malpas, -	6	6	8	— Richard Alleyne, Novice,		1	6	8
						174	6	8

Signed   Walter Kendle,
Thomas Legh,
Richard Bellasis,
Richard Watkins,   } Commissioners.

There is nothing now remaining of this large Abbey Church but the west part from from the cross aisle to the west tower.* The choir, cloyster, and chapter-house being entirely destroyed, as is also the stone roof of the middle aisle of that which is now standing, which probably was, some time after the dissolution stript of its lead, and this might occasion its falling in. The arches of the two side aisles still remain, and between the columns is a wall run up, out of which east windows have been made. It seems thus to have been patched up and made parochial in Queen Elizabeth's time. The great broad tower is still standing, and in it are eight large bells. There is an elegant window at the west end, and in a Gothic niche over it stands the effigy of the founder Roger de Montgomery†, with a mitre and a sword in his hand. The whole of the remaining part of the building is in the Norman Gothic stile.

In a garden on the south side of the Abbey, stands an octagonal building, commonly called St. Wenefride's pulpit; the ascent to it is by a flight of about ten steps, the building is in neat Gothic stile, and at present in good preservation, and looked upon by artists to be a master-piece of its kind; it is thought by some, that this building stood formerly in the centre of the cloysters, and was intended for a light house, or lanthorn, for the benefit of the religious there; it does not seem calculated to answer that end, but whether so or not, let those who esteem themselves competent judges, determine.‡

---

* According to the Rev. H. Owen's "Account of Shrewsbury" "some of the dimensions of the existing remnants of the Abbey are as follows: FEET.

Length of the present parish church from east to west, having been the nave of the conventual church	123
Breadth, including the side aisles	63
Internal breadth of the tower	24
Height thereof	104
Height of the great arch under the tower	52
Circumference of one of the round Norman pillars	16½
Height of ditto...	12
Length of the transept calculated from its ruin	111

The dimensions of the cloyster, which was in all instances nearly square, and, except in the very largest churches, usually determined by the length of the nave to which it stood attached, was from east to west, or from the ruins of the transept to those of the dormitory adjoining the western end of the nave, 104 feet. From the church to the pulpit in the garden is 140 feet, which, after calculating 104 feet for the breadth of the cloyster from north to south, leaves 38 feet for the breadth of the refectory."

† "A Figure like this," armed at all points exactly Cap à pèe, appears on the seals of King Edward III, the only one of our monarchs who wore the pointed helmet; hence we can scarcely doubt that the Statue was intended to represent that warlike prince.—*Owen & Blakeway's History of Shrewsbury.*

‡ The most probable conjecture is that it was the Reader's Pulpit, or Pulpit of the refectory or eating room. In the days of our Catholic fore-fathers, among the Benedictines, it was the custom for one of the junior brethren, while the the monks were at dinner, to read aloud a portion of the scriptures or a subject in divinity. There are several remains of stone pulpits in the kingdom, particularly in Worcester and Chester Cathedrals. But the one on which I have gazed with the most exquisite delight is in the noble parish church of Nantwich, and which remain has hitherto been little, it at all noticed, except in the local History of the Town.—EDITOR.

34th Henry VIII. Thomas Forster, and Elizabeth his wife, account in the Exchequer for the temporalities of the monastery of St. Peter and Paul, at Salop.

"22d July, 38th Hen. VIII. the King grants to Edward Watson, of Rock-
"ingham, in Com. North. Esq; and Henry Herdson, of London, tanner,
"*Domum et Scitum nuper Monasterii de Petri & Pauli Salop;* and all the
"church-yard, and orchard, called the Pole Yard, alias Camecole, with a
"certain close of land, on the south side the said Pole Yard, with all and
"singular their appurtenances, &c. for ever, to hold of the King, as of his
"honor of Grafton in Com. North. by fealty only, in free soccage and not in
"capite, paying yearly 4s. in the Court of Augmentation, for all services."

The 23d July, being the next day, the said Watson and Herdson, grant the same to William Langley, of Salop, taylor, and the 5th of August following, seizen and livery was given to the said William Langley, in which family it continued till about the year 1702, when it was purchased by Edward Baldwin, Esq. who left it by will to Henry Powys, Esq.* his nephew, whose surviving widow now enjoys it.

His Majesty's heralds at arms, in the year 1622, visited this town, and ordered the image belonging to the monument of Roger de Montgomery, which had been buried among the ruins of the Monastery of St. Peter and St. Paul, to be removed into the Abbey Church, and placed there, with the following inscription over it, viz.

The figure underneath, at first placed within the Monastery of St. Peter and St. Paul, and afterwards found in the ruins, was removed hither by the direction of his Majesty's heralds at arms, in the visitation, 1622, to remain as it was originally intended, in perpetual memory of Roger de Montgomery, Earl of Shrewsbury, who was kinsman to the Conqueror, and one of his chief commanders in the victorious battle of Hastings. He erected many useful buildings here, both public and private, not only fortified this town with walls, and built the castle on the isthmus, but also the castles of Ludlow and Bridgnorth, with the monastery of Wenlock: He founded and endowed in an ample manner this large Benedictine Abbey, and when he was advanced in years, by the consent of his Countess Adelisa, he entered into holy orders, and was shorn a Monk of this his own foundation, where he lies interred.

He died the 27th of July, 1094.

---

* Mr. Henry Powys died in July 1774, and was succeeded in this estate (according to the entail created by Mr. Baldwyn) by his nephew Thomas Jelf Powys, Esq. of Berwick, eldest son of his younger brother Edward · but the widow of Mr. Henry Powys continued to reside here to her decease in December 1791. T. J. Powys, Esq. died in January 1805, having directed the abbey estate to be sold ; as accordingly it was, by his trustees, in March 1810, to Mr. John Hiles of Sutton ; who, by his will 30th Dec. 1814, devised it to his sons John and Henry, subject to the chief rent of 18s. 2d. payable to the crown, and also subject to the right of the occupier of the abbey mill, which he devised to his son James, to draw off the water from the abbey pool to the depth of the wash.

Owen and Blakeway's History of Shrewsbury.

L

In the year 1728, Mr. Latham, who had been lately inducted to the vicarage of the Holy Cross,* presented a petition to the Bishop of Litchfield and Coventry, praying that a picture, representing our Lord and Saviour upon the cross, might be removed out of the said church.—A counter petition was also presented, signed by the parishioners, as follows :

" To the Right Rev. Father in God, Edward, Lord Bishop of Litchfield " and Coventry.

" The humble petition of the church-wardens and parishioners, of the " parish of Holy Cross, Shrewsbury :

" Humbly sheweth,

" That your petitioners having had intimation at a parish meeting, of an " order, as from your Lordship, for taking down a picture, representing our " Savour upon the cross, from the chancel of our parish church, do beg leave " in humble manner to remonstrate to your Lordship, that the said picture, " as it was by way of donation set up, with an innocent intention (as we verily " persuade ourselves) by our late minister, who had discharged that trust with " great reputation and esteem among us for the space of 51 years; so it has " not (as we know of) given any offence, nor been abused to any superstitious " use whatever : We do, with the utmost deference and submission to your " Lordship, make it our humble petition, that the said picture may be permit- " ted to continue; or if your Lordship thinks fit to remove it from the place " where it now is fixed, that your Lordship would be pleased to appoint it a " station somewhere within the church, which indulgence of your Lordship's, " will ever be acknowledged a particular favor, by your Lordship's most obe- " dient humble servants."

Orders came from the Bishop to the wardens, to remove the said picture out of the church, and deliver it to the proper owners of it. This dispute between the Vicar and the parish, gave occasion to many severe reflections from both parties ; the parishioners losing their aim, very severely lampooned the Vicar ; the following lines are a specimen of the spirit shewn on that occasion :

" The Parson's the man
" Let him say what he can
" Will for gain leave his God in the lurch ;
" Could Iscariot do more
" Had it been in his power,
" Than to turn his Lord out of the Church.†

* In the Augmentation Office, is an agreement (without date) between Brother John, sometime Abbot of the Monastery of the blessed Peter, in Salop, and the Convent of the same, on the one part ; and Sir William, of Baschurch, Vicar of the Holy Cross, in the same Monastery, on the other part. From which it appears, that the church part now remaining, was called the Holy Cross, by which name it has been called ever since.

---

† These lines bring to my recollection a portion of Cowdroy's Cheshire Directory, published in 1789, which publication was the first Topographical work I had the pleasure to read, being put into

THE REPLY.

" The Lord I adore,
" Is mighty in pow'r,
" The one only living and true,
" But that Lord of yours
" Which was turn'd out of doors,
" Had just as much knowledge as you.

" But since you bemoan
" This God of your own
" Chear up my disconsolate brother,
" Though it seems very odd,
" Yet if this be your God
" Mr. Burley* can make you another.†

* A painter in Shrewsbury.‡

---

my hands at the early age of eight years, and to which circumstance I consider myself primarily indebted for what little taste] I may have for Local History. The portion to which I most particularly allude is the four lines on the stone which covered the grave of the Image of the Virgin Mary.—ED.

" Chester Roodee," says Cowdroy, " is remarkable for being the place of interment of an image of the Virgin Mary, with a very large cross, in the year 946 ;—the place of the residence of this *pious* lady was, in a Christian Temple at Hawarden. in Flintshire, where, in those days of superstition, they used to offer up their orisons to this idol; to her they applied for relief under every affliction; till at last it happened, while they were on their knees invoking her for a few gentle showers to soften their parched land, (the carpenter not having securely fastened her *Goddess-ship*) she very unpolitely fell upon the head of the Governor of the castle's wife, Lady Trawst; the effect of which was immediately fatal. For this offence the Goddess was indicted, and tried by a *special* jury, who, after a wise and solemn trial, found her guilty of *wilful murder*, and she *received sentence of death !* One juror proposed *hanging ;* another *drowning ;* till, from motives of fear, being a Goddess, they agreed not to take her *life* but *banish* her, by leaving her on the sands of the river ; from whence (the waters not paying much respect to her sacred person) she was carried away by the tide and *drowded !*—Her body was the next day found near the place now called the Roodee ; on which it was interred, with all *due pomp*, by the inhabitants of *Chester*, and a large stone erected over the grave (a vestige of which still remains as a memento of the ignorance of those days) whereon appeared the following inscription :

The Jews their God did crucify,
The Hardeners theirs did drown,
'Cause with their wants she'd not supply,
And lies under this cold stone."

I beg it may not be inferred from the insertion of this note, that I disapprove of paintings (Scriptural subjects) being introduced into churches, and places of public worship ; on the contrary, if worthily executed they are most agreeable, and in my opinion, elegantly decorative.—EDITOR.

† The painting celebrated by the above verses has been restored to the parishioners of the Holy Cross, by the kindness of Mrs. Simpson of Hilton, in the county of Derby, and may now be seen in the vestry of the Abbey church. The subject is the Crucifixion, very indifferently executed.—ED.

‡ Mr. Burley, the painter alluded to, it appears, had his workshop at the bottom of the 70 steps, leading from Pride Hill to Roushill, and by some people still recognised as Burley's Shut.—ED.

The King is Patron of the vicarage of Holy Cross, *cum* St. Giles's.

St. GILES'S CHURCH, at the east end of the town, near the upper end of the Abbey Foregate, is by tradition said to be the oldest church in town. Yet it is said by some to have been founded by Roger de Montgomery, and dedicated to St. Gregory or St. Giles, and the following is said to be the condition on which this church was founded, viz. That when the Prebendaries died the Prebends should go to the Monks, and from hence arose no small contest between the Monks and Seculars; for the sons of the Prebendaries immediately went to law with the Monks for their further Prebends, this being at a time when the clergy were not obliged to celibacy, and it was customary for ecclesiastical benefices to descend to the next of blood.

In Doomsday book the Abbey is said to be founded in the parish of the city, from which it may be conjectured St. Giles's was built before it.

In the reign of King Stephen when the bones of St. Wenefrede were translated to the abbey at Shrewsbury, it is said they were deposited for a time in St. Giles's church, near the gate of the city, from which, together with its being called the parish of the city, it is probable the city extended itself at that time considerably more eastward than it now does.

There is nothing remarkable either within or without this church, it is a low and small building, and is now only an appendage to the parish of Holy Cross.

St. Giles, to whom this church is dedicated was a Grecian, born at Athens, and came into France A. D. 715, having first disposed of his patrimony to charitable uses. He lived two years with Cesaria, Bishop of Arles, and afterwards an hermetical life, till he was made Abbot of an Abbey at Nismes, which the King (who had found him in his cell by chance as he was hunting, and was pleased with his sanctity) built for his sake. He died in the year 795.

VICARS OF HOLY CROSS AND ST. GILES'S.

1619 Rev. Francis Gibbons, D. D.
1640 Rev. James Logan.
1647 Rev. John Beale.
1649 Rev. Moses Leigh,   Turn'd out by the Parliament.
1652 Rev. John Bryan,   Removed and afterwards Minister of St. Chad's.
1664 Rev. Timothy Hammond.
1671 Rev. Moses Leigh,   Rechosen.
1676 Rev. Samuel Pearson.
1728 Rev. John Latham,   Died 1750.

St. Giles's Church 1778.

Eng.d from the Original in Hulbert's new Edition of Phillip's History of Shrewsbury

St Chads Church. 1778.

Eng.d from the Original, for Hulbert's new edition of Phillips' History of Shrewsbury. 1830.

1750 Rev. William Gorsuch.*   Died 1781.

___

1782 Rev. William Oakley,   Died 1803.
1804 Rev. Henry Burton.   Resigned 1825.
1825 Rev. Robert Lingen Burton, M.A. the present Vicar.

St. CHAD'S CHURCH. On the spot where this church stands, was a palace belonging to the Princes of Powis, burnt down in the Saxon wars ; after which, about the time of the conquest, a collegiate church was erected, having a Dean and ten Prebendaries, under the patronage of the Bishop of Litchfield and Coventry. In the Lincolnshire taxation, 29th Edward I. it was valued at 28 marks per annum ; and afterwards, in 26th Henry VIII. at £14 14s. 4d. per annum. The seite was granted to John Southcote, and John Chadderton, 3d, Edw. VI. In the register of writs it is said to be of royal foundation. This old church, together with a great part of the town, was burnt, down in the year 1398 ; the fire was occasioned by John Plomer, a workman, leaving his fire carelessly, while mending the leads of the church. Seeing the building in flames, he endeavoured to escape over the ford near the Stone Bridge, but was drowned in the attempt ; an inquisition was taken on his body, 16th Rich. II. before William Longmore and Roger Wycherly, coroners of the town of Shrewsbury. The jury find " That John Plomer, working upon the leads " of St. Chad's church, preceiving the same in flames through his neglect, he " ran to his own house, in the High Street, put 5 marks, 4 shillings, and six- " pence, in his pocket, and fled, and when he came to the ford at the Stone " Gate, endeavouring to make his escape, he was drowned in the river Severn."

King Richard II. in consideration of the damages and losses sustained by this fire, granted to the bailiffs, good men, and commonalty of the town, that for their relief and towards repairing the damages, they should for three years next coming, be quit of their fee-farm, and likewise of their arrears of taxes, lately granted to the King by Parliament. The present fabric was built about that time, and we meet with but little relative to it, until the year 1547, the first year of King Edw. VI. when by the the direction of Sir Adam Mytton, and Roger Pope, Esq. bailiffs, the pictures of Mary Magdalen and St. Chad, were taken down in this church, and burned at the Market House. And in the 26th of Eliz. 1584, Doctor Berkeley, Doctor Merrick, and the Arch-deacon of

___

* The Rev. William Gorsuch Rowland, the present excellent and greatly esteemed Official of St. Mary, and for many years Curate of the Holy Cross, is a grandson of the worthy Vicar, Gorsuch. Mr. Rowland has recently, at very considerable expense to himself, beautified and repaired the venerable and long neglected church of St. Giles. A more particular description of its present state, and of the MODERN CONDITION of ALL the churches in the town will be found in another department of this work.—EDITOR.

Derby, commissioners from the Archbishop of Canterbury, together with the bailiffs, and others, met in this church, and ordered several regulations respecting church service, and order; they pulled down a large stone cross which stood in the church-yard, under which was found a large stone, with the butchers arms engraved on it, and a butcher's knife; from which it may be conjectured, the cross was erected by the butchers company; behind one of the pictures in the cross a wax candle was found, which probably had been offered by some superstitious person. In 1638, the town granted the perpetual advowson of this church to the King.

Cedde, or Chad, to whom this church is dedicated, was obliged by Egfrid, King of Northumberland, to accept of that see, in the absence of Wilfride, then Archbishop of York, who was gone to Paris for consecration, and gave no hopes of a speedy return. Chad had a considerable hand in the conversion of the East Saxons, and was their Bishop, about the middle of the 7th century. He was born in Northumberland, and exercised the greatest part of his ministry in Mercia. It is said that he was very much afraid of thunder and lightning, and never heard thunder but he instantly went to prayer, saying it represented the day of judgment.

When Wilfride returned from Paris, Chad was persuaded by Theodorus Archbishop of Canterbury, to resign the see to him; after which he for some time led a monastic life at Lestingaeg, until by means of the same Theodorus, he was made Bishop of Litchfield, under Wulphere,* King of Mercia, whom he is said to have converted. He died on the 2d of March, 672.

---

* Wulphere, or Wulfer, according to the most ancient church historians, was the son and successor of Penda, the Pagan king of Mercia, who had been a great persecutor of the Christians. But after his father's death he became a Christian himself, and married Ermenilda, a Christian lady, daughter of Egbert, King of Kent, by whom he had those two sons, Wulfad and Rufin, also a daughter named Werburgh. He continued a very zealous convert for a time, and being successful in arms, took the the Isle of Wight, caused the inhabitants to be baptized, and gave the island to his god-son Ethelwald, King of the South Saxons, whom he had also caused to be baptized. At length he again revolted to his Pagan worship, which he embraced with greater zeal than before, and had his children brought up in it.

St. Cedda, or Chad, who was an hermit, had his cell by a spring side at Stow near Lichfield, where he lived, (as the Legend says) only upon the milk of a doe, which being hunted by Wulfad, brought him to that place, and there St. Cedda first converted him to the Christian faith, and afterwards Rufin his brother. This place being too remote from Wulfercester, (Bury bank) the seat of their father, they intreated the holy man to remove nearer them, in order that they might receive further instructions, and perform their devotions with him.

To this request of the young Princes, Cedda readily complied, and came to another cell; whither under pretence of hunting, to avoid their father's anger, they constantly repaired and were instructed accordingly. At length being observed by Werebod, one of their father's evil counsellors, they were accused of Christianity to him, who soon watched them, and finding them at their devotions in this new oratory, in the midst of his wrath slew them both; Wulfad at Stone, and Rufin at Burston, about three miles distant. The sad news being carried to Queen Ermenilda, their mother, she caused stones to be erected, as usual, in memory of the dead; from whence the names of those places are derived. In this juncture Cedda fled from the fury of the Pagan King, to his former cell

The present building is a Norman Gothic structure, in the usual form of a cross, and consisting of a nave, and two side aisles, with a cross aisle, and chancel; the roof is supported by a double row of pillars, in form of a single cylinder, supporting semicircular arches; the ceiling is painted in an antique manner, with celestial devices, the signs of the Zodiac, &c. done in the year 1635, among which appears a label, with the following inscription,

> Samuel Kyrke of Litchfield, hath not left behind,
> The figure of his face, but the image of his mind.

The east window of this church is elegantly painted, with the history of the Kings of Israel, from Jesse, the father of David, who is represented reclined in the sleeping attitude, having a stem arising from his middle which encircles the whole.

The altar is of oak, in the Corinthian stile of architecture, and over it, resting on the pediment, are two figures elegantly carved, one representing the Gospel, and the other Hope.

At the west end of the church is a large, neat organ, erected in the year 1716, on the top of which stands the effigy of St. Chad, to whom the church is dedicated; towards the organ the company of Drapers gave £100, and the Corporation of Shrewsbury settled £20 per ann. upon the organist for ever. This organ was dedicated the 28th July, when a sermon was preached on the occasion by the Rev. Mr. Gregory, of Gloucester, from xcii. Psalm, v. 1 and 2.

The organist is chosen by the corporation.

The walls are ornamented with several monuments, belonging to the families of the Lyster's, Owen's, Edwards's, and Hollings's.

On the south side of the chancel stands a raised tomb*, with the figures

---

near Lichfield, where he had not retired long, when Wulfer, at the instigation of his wounded conscience, and the advice of his Queen, repaired thither in sorrow and lamentations, becoming a sincere penitent was converted, and from that time banished all idolatry out of his dominions; and soon after the death of Jarumanus, rewarded the holy Cedda with the Bishoprick of Lichfield, founded by King Oswy about 656. Wulfer being thus again converted, became very devout and zealous, and gave many proofs of his sincerity by building churches and monasteries, and among others, Peterborough Abbey; and in the places where he slew his sons, Ermenilda founded at Stone a Nunnery, and at Burston a Chapel, which Mr. Erdeswick in his view of Staffordshire asserts was but then lately standing.—*Topographer.*

* Within ten years after the publication of Mr. Phillips's History, the venerable church of St. Chad sank to the earth, and became a ruin; the Lady chapel alone now remains. The raised tomb of Richard Onslow has been consequently removed to the Abbey church, where it has been most piously preserved. The particulars of the disaster to which I allude may be found in almost every publication relative to the town; but that given by Messrs. Owen and Blakeway surpasses all others in pathos and feeling: it is therefore selected under the conviction it will be read with the deepest interest by every pious and intelligent Salopian.—EDITOR.

" Early in the summer of 1778 the north-west pier of the tower exhibited several fissures. These gradually increasing, caused such alarm, that the occupiers of seats in the adjoining gallery of Richard Onslow, Esq. and his wife thereon at full length; on the sides and at the feet of the tomb are two figures of two sons and five daughters, with this inscription:

Richardo Onsloweo, Salopiensi armigero, generosa orto familia, libere educato, et ab incunabulis humanarum literarum studiosissimo, et juris domestici legumque nostrarum peritissimo academiæ Templariæ facile principi oratori, scribæ cancel. duc. Lancastr. pro civitate Londoniensi oratori publico, et judici (quem recordatorem ipsi dicunt) æquissimo, dein regio in regni foro supremo oratori, serenissimæ Ma. regiæ admonitori, in curia parliamenti de rebus arduis primum loquuto, majoris amplitudinis pertæso, Ma. regiæ tutelarum procuratori, tandem febri correpto pestilenti, in patria Hernegia in villa quintum post diem mortuo; summo cum dolore, impensis maximis Katharina Hardinga suavissimo conjugi posuit MDLXXIIII. kal. Aprilis secundo. Natus est a redempto genere humano MDXXVIII. anno, mortuus anno MDLXXI. Vixit annos XLIII. Fuit staturá procerá, fronte gratissimá, voce gravi, linguá facundá, veritatis studiosissimus, virtutum omnium thesaurus, sincerus, liberalis, incorruptus.

Repaired 1742, by the Right Honourable Arthur Onslow, Esq. speaker of the house of commons, lineally descended from this Mr. Onslow, who was speaker of the house of commons in the 8th of Queen Elizabeth, and was lineal ancestor also to the Right Honourable Sir Richard Onslow, Bart. speaker of the house of commons, in the 8th of Queen Anne, afterwards Lord Onslow.

---

ceased to attend divine service. At length, the fears even of the church-wardens were excited, and Mr. Thomas Telford, then resident in the town, was requested by them to survey the fabrick, and report his sentiments of its real state.

That gentleman, since so eminently distinguished as a civil engineer, reported, that in consequence of graves having been heedlessly made adjoining the foot of the north-western pillar beneath the tower, that main support of the steeple had shrunk, and that the whole north side of the nave was in a most dangerous state, which was greatly augmented by the nearly total decay of the chief timbers of the roof; insomuch that the weight was almost entirely supported by the lateral pressure of the walls, in themselves extremely defective; and that the least additional outward spread might bring down the ponderous roof with scarcely a moment's warning. He recommended, therefore, the immediate taking down of the tower, that the shattered pier might be rebuilt, that the decayed timbers of the roof should be renewed, and the north-west wall of the nave secured. A vestry meeting, however, which was summoned on the occasion, decided that this alarming description was a gross exaggeration, and that the suggestion of a stone-mason was fatally listened to, who proposed to cut away the lower parts of the infirm pier, and to underbuild it with free stone, without removing, or even lessening the vast incumbent weight of the tower and bells. This infatuated advice was unanimously approved, the attempt was made, and on the second evening after the workmen had commenced their operations, the sexton, on entering the belfry to ring the knell previous to a funeral, perceived the floor covered with particles of mortar. On his attempting to raise the great bell, the tower shook, a shower of stones descended, and a cloud of dust arose. Trembling and in haste he descended into the church, and carried off the service books, and as much of the furniture as his alarm would allow him to collect. During the same evening, a gentleman while walking in his garden in the college, observed the cross and vane of the tower to be agitated by a constantly tremulous motion. On the following morning, July 9th, 1788, just as

A small stone monument, near the Bishop's Court, is remarkable for the

---

the chimes struck four, the decayed pier gave way, the tower was instantly rent asunder, and the north side of it, with most of the east and west sides, falling on the roofs of the nave and transept, all that part of the venerable fabrick was precipitated with a tremendous crash. The fall was seen by three persons only. A man walking by the Severn side beyond Frankwell suburb, having his eyes accidentally directed to the town, beheld the large mass of the church suddenly vanish from his view, attended by a loud report. Two chimney-sweepers also, who were employed on their occupation in Belmont, witnessed the disaster. They described it as first exciting their notice by the sudden opening of the tower on the playing of the chimes. It stood for a moment, as it were suspended on the balance; as it sunk, a cloud of dust succeeded, which for a while concealed every surrounding object. The crash was heard by persons as far distant as the Old Heath, yet very few of the neighbouring inhabitants were alarmed by it; and their astonishment and dismay when they arose and beheld the desolation can scarcely be conceived. The morning, dark and rainy, added to the awful effect of the sad spectacle. The roof of the nave with the northern range of pillars and arches lay prostrate. That of the north wing of the transept was beaten in, and a great portion of the walls, together with three sides of the tower, lay in total ruin. The whole area was overspread with masses of stone, lead, and timber, in confused heaps, mingled with the shattered remains of pews, monuments, bells, and fragments of the gilded pipes and case of the noble organ. The whole of the south side of the tower hung in air, with portions of its beams, threatening destruction to any who should dare to approach them.* From the altar, where only a spectator might stand with safety, the whole ruin was seen at once, forming a scene of desolation and horror, which will never be effaced from the memory of those who witnessed it, one of whom was the present writer.

Several circumstances concurred to impress on the minds of the parishioners a deep sense of their providential deliverance. About a month before the church fell, it was crowded to excess at the interment of an officer, with military honours, on which occasion three thousand persons were thought to have been assembled. Had the fatal crisis then been hastened by the unusual throng in the north gallery, which rested entirely on the defective pier, no imagination could have pictured the dreadful result. A very few evenings previous to the fall, the members of a ringing society had assembled in the tower to enjoy their favourite pastime, but, as one of the number was wanting, the club, after waiting some time for his arrival, dispersed. An attempt to raise the ten bells would probably have shaken down the tower on their heads, and buried them all in its ruins. Even the slight vibration of the chime barrel appears to have been the immediate cause of the fall. The lives of the workmen were spared by the interval of a very few minutes. They were gone to the house of the sexton, who lived close at hand, for the keys, in order to resume their operations. Had they been at work, nothing could have saved them from destruction. So insensible had the parishioners in general been of their danger, that the large congregations continued to assemble with little diminution, even to the Sunday before. These remarkable instances of providential interference thus arresting, as it were, the progress of gravitation, excited a sense of devout gratitude in the breasts of many whose time on earth was thus prolonged. Thursday in the following week was observed as a day of solemn thanksgiving, not by the parishioners only, but by the inhabitants of the town at large. This pious sentiment was much increased by a sensible and affectionate pastoral letter, which the vicar printed and distributed among his parishioners. The shops were shut, all business was suspended; and a crowded and devout congregation attended him at St. Mary's church, where he delivered an impressive and highly appropriate discourse."

The effigy of St. Chad, in his episcopal vestments, was preserved; and the beautiful stained glass of the west window fortunately escaped destruction, and was afterwards placed in the communion window of St. Mary's church. The Altar Piece of carved oak was removed to the chapel of Bicton. All attempts, however, to repair the old building were deemed unadvisable, and a more eligible site, for the erection of a new church was consequently fixed upon.—ED.

* Messrs. Owen and Blakeway, (in a note) page 246, vol. 2, refer to "a faithful representation by Mr. Sanders, of the scene of ruin which presented itself" when "the whole of the south tower hung in

M

following odd inscription, *viz.* (under the figure of a pheasant, with two hands pointing upwards.)

> At this Signe lived I,
> God Bles the Knight and his Posterity.

> Here lieth the body of a trve penitent
> and beleevinge Sovle.

> This every Man is born to dye
> And leaves this World and so do I.
> Price Vintner.

From the arms adjoining the inscription, and the letters H B over it, it appears likely the landlord of the Vintner, the Knight alluded to, was of the name of Botvylle, an ancient family in this town, one of whom obtained the honour of knighthood.

Under a monument to the memory of Thomas Lyster, Esq. stands an old stone tomb, with the figure of a skeleton painted on the side of it, and over the skeleton are the following lines in gold letters, without any name or date, viz.

> FFleshe and blode as Yow are so was I,
> dust and Asses as I am soe shall Yov be.

On the south side of the chancel are two marble monuments in the form of shields, one to the memory of Vincent Corbet, of Moreton Corbet, Esq. the other to the memory of Anne wife of John Hill, Gent. And on the north side a small stone monument in the same form to the memory of John Ellis, S.T.P.

In the Bishop's Court, on the south wall is a neat monument lately erected, with the following inscription, viz.

> Sacred to the memory of Hugh Owen, M. D. son of Thomas Owen of Llunllo, in the county of Montgomery, Esq. who died June 28th, 1764.
> Aged 56.

> Mewn Daear oer. tan Draed, fel finnaú
> Pwy bynnag wyt, y byddi dithan;
> Crêd yn Ghrist, casí pob Pechod,
> A Dim dan Haul, na char di yn ormond.

The length of this church, inside is, viz.	YDS.	F.	I.
From the chancel to the west end - - - - -	53	1	4
Width of the nave or body - - - - -	17	2	0
Length of the cross aisles - - - - -	30	2	2

air, with portions of its beams threatening destruction." The identical engraved copper-plate alluded to, is now in my possession, having recently had the good fortune to purchase it from a respectable broker in London. The size of the engraving is 15 inches by 10 inches, and is in excellent preservation.
EDITOR.

A musical peal of ten bells are in the tower, the largest of which weighs upwards of 28 cwt.

Underneath this church, on the north side is a vaulted room, called the Dimery; which place probably has been used as a repository for the bones and skulls of the dead, and might receive its name from the Saxon word *Dwimora*, ghosts, which in times of ignorance and superstition, were supposed to haunt such places; or more likely from the common word Dim, dark; a Dimery or dark room, or place. It has been said that there was a subterranean passage from this place to the old building on St. Chad's Hill, formerly called Vaughan's Place, and now a warehouse belonging to Joshua Blakeway, Esq. and a stopt up arch'd door way in this vault, seems to favour the report, but for what end it was made is entirely unknown.

The Sacristry (corruptly called the Sextry) belonging to the church, where the vestments and church utensils were kept, was in the King's-Head Shut; and some manuscripts mention the next shut or passage, commonly called the the Steelyard Shut, as being the place of residence for the Prebendaries and others belonging to this church while collegiate; and also that their usual way was, to go over the street, (Kiln Lane) through a covered way or passage, still remaining, into the church-yard, and from thence down into the Dimery, and so by stairs from thence into the church.

The Parish of St. Chad's is the largest in the town, being nearly one half thereof, and extends a considerable way into the country, including part of Shelton—Up, and down Rossal—The Isle—Bicton, (where there is a chapel) Calcot—Horton—Woodcot—Betton-Strange—Whitley—Welbach—Longnor, &c. The King is Patron of this Living.

A LIST OF THE MINISTERS.

1550 Rev. Henry Stephens,	Ejected May 1, 1553, being a married man.
1553 Rev. John Marshall.	*(Ejected.)*
1606 Rev. Thomas Price,	Resigned May 16, 1622.
1640 Rev. Richard Poole.	*(Died* 1643-4.)
*	
1661 Rev. John Bryan, M. A.	Ejected August 24, 1662.
1662 Rev. Richard Hayward,	Presented Dec. 24, 1662.
1680 Rev. William Bennett,	Presented Feb. 13, 1680.
1721 Rev. Thomas Adams,	Presented Feb. 15, 1721.
1728 Rev. Theophilus Ryder,	Died 1732.
1732 Rev William Adams, D. D.	Resigned 1775.
1775 Rev. Tho. Humphries, A. M.	Presented Nov. 10, 1775, *(Died* 1783.)

1783 Rev. Thos. Stedman, M. A. who died Dec. 5, 1825.
1826 Rev. James Compson, M. A. is the present Vicar.—ED.

---

* It appears that during the interregnum a Mr. Lendall and a Mr. Thomas Paget (omitted by Phillips) were appointed vicars in succession, occupying the period between Mr. Poole and Mr. Bryan.

ED.

St. MARY'S CHURCH, " Was founded* by King Edgar, but in what
" year not known, there was then belonging to it a Dean, and seven Preben-
" daries, and the parish priest's stipend was £6. 6s. 8d. and in the parish were
" 1000 householding persons."†

In Edward the Confessor's time it had a Dean and nine Prebendaries, and
in this state continued till the dissolution, in the reign of Henry VIII. The
King was then the Patron. It is styled in the tower records, *Libera Capella
Regis*.

This church held *unam Virgatam* of the hides geldable in the city, also
Bertune and Pleslie in Baschurch hundred. Melam in Shrewsbury hundred,
Mutone and Bruntelde in the Baschurch hundred. In the Confessor's time the
twelve canons of this church had twenty hides of land, one of them whose name
was Spirtes had ten of those hides to his own share, but afterwards when he
was banished the kingdom, King Edward gave those ten hides to Robert the
son of Wimarch, another of the canons.

6th of Henry III. the Archbishop of Dublin was presented to this Deanry,
which 20th of Edward I. was valued at twenty marks.

King Edward II. in the 11th year of his reign, by his letters declared
that St. Mary's at Shrewsbury was his free chapel, and as such exempt from
all ordinary jurisdiction. It is now parochial, but remains a peculiar, exempt
from the jurisdiction of the Bishop.‡

Before the foundation of the Abbey, St. Mary's was reckoned the chief
church in the town, though no mention is made of it in Doomsday book,
which as it held nothing but tithes was there omitted.

On a survey taken 37th Hen. VIII.§ it appears,

	£.	s.	d.
" The revenue of this church was - - -	32	4	2
" Of which the Dean's part was - - - -	22	6	8

† M. S. dated 3rd of Edward VI. in the Augmentation Office.

§ From Parish Book belonging to St. Mary's.

---

* Messrs. Owen and Blakeway suppose the foundation preceded the reign of Edgar, and that as
it comprises the greatest portion of the town after St. Chad, so it is next to it in point of antiquity.
EDITOR.

‡ The Minister, or Official of St. Mary, is not only *exempt* from the jurisdiction of the Bishop of
the Diocese, but possesses many of the powers and privileges of a prelate. He appoints his own sur-
rogate, holds his court for proving wills, &c. of persons dying within his parish, which is indeed very
extensive, comprising not only about one fourth of the whole town of Shrewsbury, but extending itself
into the country—includes Great and Little Berwick, Newton, Leaton, Bomer Heath, Great and Little
Wolascot, part of Harlescot, and the three Parochial Chapelries of Albrighton, Astley, and Clive.—ED.

St Mary's Church. 1778.

Engᵈ from the Original, for Hulberts new edition of Phillips' History of Shrewsbury. by I Pereday. 1830.

	£.	s.	d.
" By another account, Nov. 20, 2nd, Edw. VI. when }	49	0	0
" Wm. Cureton was Dean, it was - - }			
" At the same time paid to the parish Priest -	4	19	0
" To a stipendiary Clerk" - - - -	4	0	0

King Edward IV. in the year 1460, founded the fraternity of the Holy Trinity in this church, giving certain lands and tenements in Salop to the masters and wardens, with license to purchase £40 per annum for their support, which society remained till 1608, when King James incorporated the masters. wardens, and brotherhood of the Holy Trinity, and the company of Drapers into one body.

Upon the dissolution of this college, the revenues were given by King Edward VI. for founding the free grammar school in Shrewsbury, viz. the tythes of Astley, Sansaw, Clive, Leaton and Almond Park.

The church is now a donative, the nomination by the Mayor of Shrewsbury, and the head schoolmaster ;* the minister who serves the cure, must be one that has been brought up in the said school, being the son of a burgess, or one born in the parish of Chirbury, whose stipend was directed to be paid by the bailiff of the said school, in such sort, and at such times as the schoolmasters receive their stipends or wages ; and in choosing the said minister the chief schoolmaster is to be sworn to give his voice freely to the most worthy person, without reward or bribery.

From among the numerous benefactors to this church, one only shall be selected, (i. e.) " Tho. de la Clive, Town Clerk of Shrewsbury, who by his " will dated A. D. 1336, bequeaths his soul to God, the blessed Mary, and all " the Saints, and his body to be buried in St. Mary's church, directing the " whole choir of the said church to be present at his funeral obsequies, as also " two Chaplains, one Deacon, and two Clerks of every parish church in Shrews- " bury. He also leaves to the fraternity of the said church, 2s. and to the " building Litchfield church 2s. also four pounds of wax to make four tapers " to burn round his corpse at his funeral, two of which tapers are directed to " remain in the said church, also one other taper to be placed on St. Maries " altar in the said church, and the other to go to the chapel of Clive, and also " 12d. to the use of the said chapel. He also directs 20s. to be given to the " poor at his burial, also to the preaching Friars in Shrewsbury 2s. and to the " Friers Minors, and St. Augustine's 12d. each."†

* The Mayor and head master in their choice, the Sheriff and Justices of the county may demand their reasons ; as in Mr. Meighen's case.

† From St. Mary's Parish Book.

THE FOLLOWING ENTERIES ARE SELECTED FROM SOME OLD BOOKS BELONGING TO ST. MARY'S PARISH.

	£	s.	d.
" Paid for 21 quarts of wine at Easter, at 4½ per quart - -	0	4	0

" About this time an order was made for putting up forms* in
" St. Mary's church, said to be for the convenience of God's
" people in attending worship."†

	£	s.	d.
" 1553, Paid for ringing the day Queen Mary was proclaimed -	0	4	0
" Paid for setting up an altar before Sir Adam Mytton's grave -	0	4	0
" Paid for two tapers for the high altar - - - -	0	1	4
" Paid for mending our Lady's chapel, and for a paschal taper -	0	4	0
" Paid for taper, wax-candles, and frankincense at Christmas -	0	1	11
" Paid for a chain and hook to set up the rood - -	0	0	5
" 1554, Paid for a chain for the holy water stoke - -	0	0	2
" Paid for making an altar in our Lady's chapel - -	0	2	6
" Paid for making Trinity altar - - - - -	0	3	5
" Paid for two tapers on Witsunday - - - -	0	0	8
" IV. Eliz. 1562. Paid for taking down the rood - -	0	2	0
" Paid for pulling down the chapels and altars - -	0	1	10
" VIII. Eliz. 1566. Paid for calves heads for the ringers at Easter	0	1	8
" Paid for ringing in honour of the Queen, Nov. 17. -	0	3	9

EXTRACTS FROM A BOOK BELONGING TO THE OFFICIAL OF ST. MARY'S.

" 1583, Jan. 24, Sentence was given against two persons of ill fame for
" cohabitation. Ordered that John Tomkies, M. A. and public preacher, shall
" at his own cost and charges, provide and bestow such garments upon Isabel,
" as unto Mr. Bailiff's of the town of Salop, and said Ordinary shall seem

---

† It is probable before this time there were neither seats nor benches in churches, the floors were commonly strewed with flowers and sweet herbs, especially at midnight masses, and festivals, upon which the people must prostrate themselves. The pride of the clergy, and the bigotry of the laity were such, that both rich and poor were married at the church doors, and new married couples were made to wait till midnight after the marriage day, before they could pronounce a benediction, unless handsomely paid for it, and they durst not undress without it, on pain of excommunication.—*Historical Passages concerning the Clergy.—M. S.*

---

* " St. Mary's church, then, had not as yet been deformed by *pews*, an unfortunate peculiarity of our reformed church, which curtails the fair proportions of the architecture of the sacred edifice, maintains a distinction of ranks in His presence before whom all are equal ; diminishes the accommodation which the building might afford ; precludes the attendance of many, and admits and encourages a carelessness of posture which connects itself too easily with a languor of devotion. How a practice unknown to every church on the continent, except for the magistracy and lords of manors, found admission into that of England, has never, we believe, been ascertained. It was almost unknown with us before the Reformation, and at St. Mary's, as we see, for several years after it. Like other abuses, it probably stole in by degrees : and is now so inveterate as to be incapable of correction."—*Owen and Blakeway's History of Shrewsbury.*

" meet and convenient ; and that she shall depart (after penance) from the
" town and liberties, according to the Bailiff's and Ordinaries order.*

" 1584, May 12, order'd that three superstitious images and inscriptions
" in the north window of St. Mary's, be taken down by the church wardens.

" 1584, Sept. 18, order'd that the stone altar should be removed, having
" been sometimes used to idolatry, and the stones applied to the use of the parish.

" 1595, May 6, a complaint was lodged against the church wardens, for
" not removing from the north window, the feigned miracle of the assumption
" of the blessed virgin.†

" 1685, The inhabitants of Astley were complained against for playing at
" Bowls on a Sunday. Ordered, that they shall adorn and repair their chapel
" at their own expence, as a commutation.

A License granted by the Vicar of St. Alkmond's to the Minister of
St. Mary's, to eat Flesh during his sickness.‡ 1591.

" Whereas John Tomkies, M. A. and public preacher of the word in the
" Town of Salop, is notoriously visited with sickness, insomuch that he is
" desirous to eat Flesh, for the recovery of his former health, during the time
" of his sickness.

" By the Minister of the Parish next adjoining, according to the statutes
" in that behalf provided.

" I, therefore, Andrew Duker, Minister of the Parish of St. Alkmond's,
" do licence the aforesaid John Tomkies, to eat Flesh during his sickness, and
" no longer, according to the true meaning and intent of the aforementioned
" statute. In witness whereof I have subscribed my name, this 15th day of
" February, 1591.

" And. Duker."

Within this parish, at a place called Broughton, was formerly a small
monastery, dedicated to the Virgin Mary, with a church adjoining to it, which
probably was the oldest church near the town, several Popes, and Cardinals,
granting particular privileges to it ; this church was afterwards accounted a
chapel dependant upon St. Mary's. The following indulgence and pardon,
was found among the papers of Mr. William Sukar, Minister there, viz.

" These are statutes, indulgences, and pardons, granted to the holy Chapel
" of our Lady of Broughton in the County of Salop. The which holy Chapel
" was begun by the great revelation and power of God, and by the miracle

---

* Official's Book, p. 25.   † Official's Book, p. 51.

‡ From St. Mary's Parish Book, fo. 131.

" of our Lady; which indulgence and pardon, is granted to every Man.
" Woman, and Child, that is so virtuously disposed for to visit this holy Cha-
" pel, saying there one Pater Noster, and one Ave Mary, before our blessed
" Lady; or else to send any portion of their goods towards the building and
" maintenance of this holy Chapel, as hereafter followeth; which is granted
" by our holy Father Pope Leo the 10th, and also by Pope Julian 2d,
" and lately confirmed by 15 Cardinals of the Court of Rome, with all, or
" most part of the Bishops of this Realm of England, at every one of these
" Feasts following, viz. at the conception of our Lady, the Nativity, the Puri-
" fication, the Annunciation, with the Assumption, and the Octaves of the
" same; this indulgence is granted, to every Brother, and Sister, for the saying
" of one Pater Noster, and one Ave Mary, 1800 Days of Pardon, with clear
" remission. And also all they that be dispos'd to receive a letter of holy in-
" dulgence and pardon, they may choose unto them, once in their Life, and
" at the hour of death, a discreet ghostly father, the which ghostly father hath
" full power by the Authority of their letter, for to absolve, and grant clear
" remission, and absolution, of all their sins, nothing excepted, although
" within the said chapel is yearly kept, 4 times, an Obiter with dirge, and
" mass of requiem, for the souls of all the brethren, and sisters, that be de-
" parted out of this world; besides all other suffrages and prayers which be
" said and done within the holy Chapel, for all good benefactors and good
" doers, which prayers shall endure there for evermore.

" Forma Absolutionis

" Authoritate Domini Nostri Jesu Christi, et beatorum Petri et Pauli
" Apostolorum ejus. Nobis in hac parte Commissâ ego absolvo te ab omnibus
" pænis tuis in purgatorio debitis propter culpas et offensas, qus contra Deum
" et hominem commisisti In quantum mihi admittitur. restituo te illi honori in
" quo Baptizatus fuisti, vivas cum Christo in sæculo seculorum.   Amen."*

The monastery before mentioned, stood upon a bank, about the middle
way between Broughton and Yorton; when it was dissolved, or destroyed, is
not known.

St. Mary's Church, is a neat Gothic structure, in the form of a cross, consisting of a nave, and two aisles, with a cross aisle, and chancel; the nave is
supported by neat Gothic pillars, and in the chancel is a neat altar piece of the
Corinthian order, the gift of the Rev. Mr. Richard Tiesdale, in the year 1706;
on the pedestal of which, appear the names of

Christopher Coney,	- - -	Projector and Carver.
Robert Fosbrooke,	- - -	Joyner.
Isaac Richardson,	- - -	Painter, 1708.

* From Mr. Gough's M. S. p. 153.

On the north side of the chancel is a vestry, and on the south side a large and lofty chapel, where before stood several chantries and small chapels, there being several adjoining and belonging to this church, particularly Trinity Chapel—Our Lady's Chapel—The Old Chapel—St. Catharine's Chapel—St. Lawrence's Chapel—New Chapel, &c. The before-mentioned chapel, appears by the architecture to have been built in the reign of Queen Elizabeth; over the door are the arms of that Queen, with the following inscriptions.

" At that time Deborah a Prophetess judged Israel.
" Judges IV. 4.

" Favour is deceitful and beauty is vain, but a woman that feareth the Lord,
" she shall be praised.
" Pro. XXXI. 29.

" Many daughters have done virtuously, but thou excelleth them all.
" Pro. XXXI. 30."

In this chapel the scholars from the free schools attended on Sabbath-days and holidays, as appears by the following account.*

" A. D. 1582, By the good advice, and mutual consent of the then Bailiffs,
" and of the Master and Seniors of St. John's College, in Cambridge, and of
" Mr. Thomas Lawrence, then Chief School Master ; the Chapel part of St.
" Mary's Church was repaired and beautified, at the School charges, to the
" intent, that upon all Sabbath-days, Hollidays, and half Hollidays, the Masters
" and Scholars should resort there to hear divine service, and to be instructed
" in the principles of religion ; where they attended for several years, until the
" Chapel adjoining the Schools was fitted up for divine service, and consecrated,
" and by a decree of the Lord Keeper, the Masters were discharged from their
" obligation to repair the Chapel, and the Masters, and Scholars allowed to
" attend there."

In this chapel are several monuments, particularly one of an armed Knight, in a niche on the north side, reclined at full length, with a lion under his feet; who†this is designed to represent, is uncertain, it seems to be the general opinion that it was designed for Hotspur, who was slain at the battle of Battlefield ; but it certainly was intended for some other person, as the figure is pourtrayed with the legs across, as usual for Knights Templars, which order was at that time destroyed.‡

* Mr. Hotchkiss's M. S. p. 97.

‡ The order of Knights Templars was established Anno 1118, all of them were arrested in France, in one day, being charged with great crimes, and having great riches, when 59 of them were burnt alive at Paris, October 13th, 1307 ; destroyed by Philip, King of France, 1311.—Hotspur was slain 1403.

† See note, page 23 this volume.—ED.

N

The following monuments, for their neatness, are worth notice.

IN THE CHAPEL.

A neat marble monument on the east wall, with the following inscription,
viz.

Hic Iacet
Rev^dm Vir Johannes Lloyd de Rug in Com: Merion.
Uxorem duxit Mariam Charlottam Relictam Thomae Pryse
de Gogerthun in Com: Cardigan.
Quae optimi Conjugis pie memor, moerens Hoc possuit,
Parentes, Frater, Soror, Privignus,
Omnes Cognati, Amici omnes,
Omnes deniq: qui Virtutes ejus cognôrant,
tam cari Capitis triste sentiunt Desiderium.
Quod vero maximum.
Animam ejus Coelos petentem,
Pauperum, quos Benignitate fovit singulari,
non vanae prosecutae sunt Benedictiones.
Obijt 2do Sept^bris An° 1758.   Ætatis 40.

IN THE CHANCEL.

Three neat marble monuments, viz.

I.

Near this place lies interred
The Body of *Mrs. Mary Lyster*, Spinster,
Daughter to *Sir Thomas Lyster*, of *Rowton*, Knight,
By his second Lady
Mary, Daughter to Sir *John Hanmer*
Of *Hanmer* in the County of *Flint* Bart.
Who departed this Life
The 19th day of September·
MDCCXXX.

II.

Near this Stone lies interred the
Body of MARY Wife of Rich Morhall of Onslow, Esq;
Amiable in Temper and Person
Exemplary in all the Virtues of her Sex
Blest above all with the Christian Graces, Piety, Resignation and Patience
Which were tried and triumphed through many Years of Pain and sickness.
Dear to her Husband, to her Friends, to the Poor,
She died lamented by all
in the 54th Year of her age April 18th 1765.

III.

A small neat monument, inscribed, to the memory of Humphry Lloyd, Esq. of Averbechar, in the County of Montgomery, who died Feb. 13th, 1705.

At the west end of the church, is a neat organ, dedicated in July, 1729, when a sermon was preached on the occasion by the Rev. Mr. John Lloyd.

The organ was made by John Harris, and John Byfield, 1729.

In the belfry are a new peal of eight bells, cast by Messrs. Peck and Chapman, of Whitechapel, London; they were opened by a society of change ringers in this town, March 14, 1776, and in the afternoon of the same day, a peal of grandsire triples was rung on them by the same society.

The east end of this church fell down by a great wind, on St. Simon and Jude's day, 1571; in that part of the church stood a window of costly workmanship and very neatly glazed; another window of the like workmanship was also blown down, and the leads of the church torn off.

The spire* belonging to this church, standing upon an elevated part of the town is seen at a great distance, and is a great ornament to the town, but has at several times suffered greatly from high winds, viz.

A. D. 1572. Blown aside by wind.
   1663. The cock taken down and a new one put up, by scaffolds being fixed from the upper holes, the steeple repaired at the same time, cost £72.
   1665. The cock blown down.
   1686. The cock and bar blown down.
   1690. Twelve yards taken down, being damaged by an earthquake. Cost £30.
   1739. The cock blown aside.
   1754. The spire shattered by an high wind, several yards taken down and rebuilt.
   1756. The new built part again blown aside, 25 feet taken down and rebuilt.

The last time of the spire being rebuilt, the work was performed by Mr.

---

* In the year 1818 it was discovered that the upper part of the spire was loose; ten feet six inches were taken down and restored by the late Mr. Straphen, for which he received £170; the spire was also raised by him two feet ten inches. The height of the tower, according to his admeasurement, is 78 feet 4 inches, of the spire to the top of the capstone 137 feet, from the capstone to the cock, 4 feet 9 inches, whole height 220 feet.—EDITOR.

William Thompson, of Litchfield, who on the 18th Sept. 1756, finished the building, and took the dimensions of it, viz.

	Yds.	F.	I.
The height of the tower,	24	2	9
The spire to the ball,	44	0	10
The ball in diameter,	0	1	3
From the ball to the back of the cock,	1	1	6
Total	71	0	4

When the cock was blown aside in the year 1739, one Cadman undertook to take it down, and accordingly in the month of January took it down and put it up again; and after several exploits performed, on a rope fixed from the top of the spire to a tree in a field called the Gay, on the other side the river Severn, and to several other places, he, upon Candlemas day, after beating a drum, firing pistols. &c. attempted to fly or slide down the rope across the river, when the rope failing, he fell down* in St. Mary's Fryars, and was dashed to pieces.

---

* Few events in the History of Shrewsbury for the last century have excited and retained so great a portion of feeling and of interest as the fate of Robert Cadman. There is indeed something so terrific in the idea of a man falling to the earth from such an immense height, his body bounding from the ground by the force of the fall, and in the presence of so many spectators, that we shudder at the picture presented to our imagination, and anxiously enquire after every particular relative to the subject of so appalling a disaster.

Mr. Hutton in his History of Derby, (cited by Ireland in his Views on the Severn,) gives the following account of Cadman's exploits at that place :—

"A small figure of a man, seemingly composed of spirit and gristle, appeared at Derby, (October, 1732) to entertain the town by sliding down a rope! One end was to be fixed at the top of All Saints' steeple (the loftiest in the town) and the other at the bottom of St. Michael's, a horizontal distance of eighty yards, which formed an inclined plane extremely steep! A breast-plate of wood, with a groove to fit the rope, and his own equilibrium, were to be his security while sliding down upon his belly, with his arms and legs extended. He could not be more than six or seven seconds in this airy journey, in which he fired a pistol and blew a trumpet. The velocity with which he flew raised a fire by friction, and a bold stream of smoke followed him! He performed this wonderful exploit three successive days, in each of which he descended twice, and marched up once; the latter took him more than an hour, in which he exhibited many surprising atchievements, as sitting unconcerned with his arms folded, lying across the rope upon his back, then his belly, his hams, blowing the trumpet, swinging round, hanging by the chin, the hand, the heels, the toe, &c. The rope being too long for art to tighten, he might be said to have danced on the slack."

The late, Reverend Historians of Shrewsbury inform us, that "The Salopian publick were prepared to witness Cadman's feats, by the following hand-bill:

"This is to give Notice to all Lovers of Art and ingenuity,

Salop, Jan. 24; 1739, 40,

That the famous *Robert Cadman* intends to fly from off *St. Mary's* Steeple over the River *Severn on Saturday next*, flying up and down, firing off two Pistols, and acting several diverting Tricks and Trades upon the Rope, which will be very diverting to the spectators.

N. B. The aforesaid *Robert Cadman* having no one but his Wife to collect what Money Gentlemen and Ladies are pleas'd to give him, he desires the Favour of those which are at a distance, either to send their Servant with it, or else he intends to wait on them at their own houses.

"This was not the first time that a similar exhibition had been performed here. Sept. 8, 1732, "A

He was buried at the foot of the steeple, and a small monument placed in the wall, over his grave, with the following inscription :—

> Let this small Monument record the name
> Of Cadman, and to future times proclaim,
> How by'n attempt to fly from this high spire.
> Accross the Sabrine Stream, he did acquire
> His fatal end : 'Twas not for want of skill
> Or Courage to perform the task, he fell,
> No, no, a faulty Cord, being drawn too tight
> Hurried his Soul on high, to take her flight,
> Which bid the Body here beneath, good night.
>
> Feb. 2, 1739.   Aged 28.

	Yds.	F.	I.
The length of this Church from east to west is	44	0	0
The breadth	18	2	0
The cross aisles	30	1	4

The parish of St. Mary is extended a considerable way into the country, including the following townships, viz. Cotton—Berwick (where there is a chapel endowed by Sir Samuel Jones, Knt. and an alms-house)—Newton—Albrighton, (where there is a chapel, dedicated to St. John Baptist)—Woolascot—Astley and Clive, (to which chapel the Mayor and Head Master present)—Almond Park—Sansawe—and Leaton.

---

man slid or fled down a rope from the first holes or windows above the tower part of St. Mary's steeple. The rope at the other end was fastened to a post in a shop below the market cross. He also went up the rope, and beat a point of war near the middle, and drank a mug of ale. When he came down, he had a pistol in each hand, which he fired in his passage, arms and legs extended, with his head foremost." Cadman himself had just been employed to take the weather-cock down, which he had performed with success, and put it up again; displaying at that and other times various exploits. On the fatal day, the rope was affixed to the upper windows, within a few feet of the top of the spire, and brought down to the Gay meadow on the opposite side of the river. It is said, that just before he set out on his mad career, he found the rope a little too tight, and gave a signal to slacken it; but that the persons employed, misconceiving his meaning, drew it tighter. It snapped in two as he was passing over St. Mary's Friars, and he fell amid thousands of spectators. It was the time of the Great Frost, and the ground was so hard that the body, after reaching the earth, rebounded upwards several feet. In a former publication it was related, on authority which we then deemed conclusive, that his wife was in the mean time employed collecting in a hat the contributions of the crowd with the utmost apparent indifference. But we are happy to contradict this on testimony more authentic. When the poor woman beheld the sad fate of her husband, she threw away her money in an agony of grief, and ran to him in hopes of affording some relief."

It is generally believed that Cadman was a native of Shrewsbury. A venerable intelligent inhabitant says, " The precise spot on which he fell, was the Block House wall, about two yards from the wicket that now opens into St. Mary's Friars, and his epitaph was written by a Mr. Meredith, who at that time kept an academy in Draper's Hall." Some years ago a school boy, pertaining to the free schools wrote in chalk underneath Cadman's monument,—

> " Good night, good night, poor Bob Cadman,
> You lived and died just like a madman."
>
> EDITOR.

ECCLESIASTICAL JURISDICTION.

The Ministers of St. Mary's were always Officials as well as public Preachers, till the year 1651.*

In the School Bailiff's accounts the Minister is stiled Preacher of the Word —In the Parish Book, public Preacher—In ditto, page 110, her Majesty's (Q. Eliz.) stipendiary Curate—and in the reign of Queen Elizabeth, by a covenant from the Corporation to save the Queen and her successors harmless from the yearly stipend of £13. 6s. 8d. the minister is stiled, the Vicar of St. Mary's.

MINISTERS OF ST. MARY'S.

1578	Rev. Edward Bulkeley, D. D.	Resigned May 25, 1582.
1582	Rev. John Tomkies, A. M.	Buried at St. Mary's June 24, 1592.
1592	Rev. Thomas Laughton,	Resigned May 1597.
1597	Rev. William Bright,	Buried at St. Mary's Oct. 29, 1618.
1618	Rev. Samuel Brown,	Buried at St. Mary's May 6, 1632.
1632	Rev. James Betton, D. D.	*(Resigned on Promotion.)*
1644	*Rev. Nicholas Frowd, B. D.*	*(Only a few months.)*
1646	Rev. Samuel Fisher, M. A.	*(Compelled by the parish to resign.)*
1652	Rev. Francis Tallents, A. M.	Ejected August 24, 1662.
1662	Rev. Robert Fowler, A. M.	Buried at St. Mary's Jan. 29, 1678.
1678	Rev. Thomas Dawes, B. D.	Died January 10, 1714.
1715	Rev. John Lloyd, A. M.	Died May 19, 1743.
1743	Rev. Benj. Wingfield, A. M.	Died September 1763.
1763	Rev. Edw. Blakeway, A. M.	Presented October 21, 1763, *resigned* 1795.

*1795 Rev. John Brickdale Blakeway, M. A.   Died 10th March, 1826.
**1826 Rev. Hugh Owen, M. A.   Died 23rd December, 1827.
1828 Rev. William Gorsuch Rowland, M. A. is the present Official.—ED.

ST. ALKMUND'S CHURCH.   The exact time when this church was founded cannot be ascertained, nor is it altogether certain by whom.   In general it is agreed, a noble Lady of the name of Ethelfleda was the foundress, who (some copies say) was the daughter of Offa King of Mercia, and married to Kenwolfe, 13th King of the Mercians, but whether founded in his life, or after his death (she surviving him) is not determined.   Some other copies mention Ethelfleda a daughter of King Alfred as the foundress, and with most proba-

* Mr. Hotchkiss's M. S. vol. I.

** Memoirs, &c. of the Rev. J. B. Blakeway and the Rev. H. Owen, will be found in another place.—ED.

St. Alkmond's Church. *1778*.

Eng^d from the Original for Hulberts new edition of Phillips History of Shrewsbury by Cha Askey 1820

bility, as this Lady* was remarkable for public acts of munificence in the kingdom of Mercia, such as building churches, re-edifying towns, particularly Warwick, in the year 915. Notwithstanding different accounts vary, respecting the exact time of this church being built, all fix it at some time between the years 850 and 900.

King Edgar in 975, by the advice of St. Dunstan enlarged this church, and added to it several possessions, with ten Prebends, because he was of the race of St. Alkmond, descended from the noble family of the Kings of Northumberland.

Nehel Medicus, alias Nigellus de Medicis, clerk, and physician to Roger de Montgomery Earl of Shrewsbury, is mentioned in some old manuscripts belonging to the Abbey, as succeeding Godric Wiseune in a Prebend of this Church about the year 1068.

In the reign of King Stephen, Anno 1150, Richard de Belmeys, alias de Beaumeys, alias de Belmarsh, one of the Deans, at the request of Maud the

---

* There can be little doubt that Ethelfleda, Ethelfreda, and Elfleda, as she is variously denominated, the daughter of king Alfred, is the lady supposed to be the foundress of St. Alkmond's church. It is said " she was a woman of a very superior mind, and to masculine powers added Amazonian activity. The most splendid actions of her brother Edward's reign were the effects of her counsels; her time, her genius, and her talents, being devoted to the service of her country. On the birth of her first child, she separated from her husband, being deterred by the pangs and dangers of parturition from hazarding its recurrence; observing, that " it was beneath the daughter of a king to pursue any pleasure attended with so much inconvenience." From the time of this event she devoted herself to deeds of arms, and to acts of munificence and piety. She built and refounded cities and erected castles in different parts of England. Her valor made her so celebrated, that the titles of Lady, or Queen, were thought unworthy of her greatness, and she was dignified with those of Lord, or King."

King in his Vale Royal of England, (published 1656,) gives the following summary of her feats and performances. " Elfleda, the wife of Ethelred, ruled Mercia, with a strong hand, like an Amazonian Dame; for every year performing notable Feats. A.D. 913. May 6. she came with a great Army to a place called Sceargate, by Hoveden, and others; Strengate by Matth. West. and built there a strong Castle, and another on the West Bank of Severn, called Bridge, haply Bridgnorth in Shropshire. A.D. 914 in the Spring-time she goes to Tamworth, and builds there another Castle, and repairs the Town. From thence to Stanford, on the River Welland; but more truly Stafford, on Sow River, as Florence hath it, and repairs that Castle. A.D. 915. She builds Elesbury, and fortified Warwick, as Hoveden; or Wartham, as Matth. West. corruptly calls it. A.D. 916. She builds Cherenburgh, as Matth. West. Cyriebyrig, by Florence; Cereburih,† by Huntington, Wedsbury, and Runcorn. A.D. 917, July 30, She made Wars upon the Brittains, at the Castle of Brecknock, took it, and therein the Kings Wife, and 33 Prisoners. A.D. 918. She made War upon the Danes at Derby, assaulted the Castle, and took it, not without slaughter of four of her valiant Captains. A D. 919, She took the Town of Leicester from the Danes, and forced them to Terms of Composition; but that very year died at her Castle of Tamworth, July 13th, and was buried at Gloucester, in the Porch of St. Peter."

Sir John Leycester, in his Historical Antiquities of Cheshire, published in 1673, also makes particular mention of this most extraordinary princess.—EDITOR.

† Cereburih, undoubtedly the Chirbury of Shropshire. The Castle which once existed there is totally demolished.—ED.

Empress, gave his Prebend of Lilleshull, and Hetingeham in this Church towards founding, and for the use of an Abbey of regular Canons at Lilleshull, of the order of St. Augustine, which Abbey is said to be built in a wood, and dedicated to the Virgin Mary, as appears by the following extracts from Dugdale's Monasticon, vol. II. p. 144.

"Ecclesiam S^{ti.} Alcmundi Adelfleda Regina Merciæ fundavit—Rex Edgarus
"ampliavit, et decem Præbendas fecit.
"Phillippus de Belmeis dat. totam terram quæ continetur infra Watlingestreete
"and Merdiche. Canonicis de Ordine Arroasiæ et de Ecclesiâ S^{ti.} Petri Dorca-
"cestriæ egressis ad fundandam Ecclesiam in honorem Sanctæ Dei genitricis Mariæ.
"Walterus Coventrensis Episcopus, &c.—Itaque Ricardus Belmeys Decanus
"Ecclesiæ S^{ti.} Alcmundi de Salopia dedit—Præbendam suam propriam de Lilleshull
"and Effingham, ut Abbatiam ad honorem perpetuæ virginis Mariæ in bosco de
"Lilleshull ædificarent.
"Stephanus Rex dat. Præbendam Ricardi quam habuit in Ecclesiâ Sancti Alc-
"mundi Salopesberia—et omnes alias Præbendas prædictæ Ecclesiæ S^{ti.} Alcmundi.

"Henricus Rex confirmat, &c."

King John afterwards confirmed the above, with an additional grant of, "the church of St. Alkmond, with all its appurtenances in Lilleshull, Hetinge-"ham, Uckington, Longedon, Preston, Gobalt, Lee, Edbrightley, Henne-"cote, Dunthull, Cherleton, Preston juxta Moneford, and Wystanstowe." This collegiate church becoming appropriated to the Abbey of Lilleshull, has since been a vicarage, and is rated in the King's books at £6.

This church held in Shrewsbury, 21 houses of the burgesses, 12 of the Canons, and 2 hides of land of the city, which were the portion of the Canons.

In the town rental,* 9 Ed. IV. the Vicar of St. Alkmond's is charged 12d. *pro introitu Tenementi sui.*

The fraternity of the Holy Cross is there charged 6d.

In the reigns of Queen Elizabeth and King James, it stands charged on the Queen's and King's Bailiffs for the Cross of St. Alkmond.

In 1633 and 1657 it is charged on the fraternity of the Holy Cross of St. Alkmond.

St. Alkmond or Alcmund, to whom this church is dedicated, was the son of Alured King of Northumberland, who slew Mollo, alias Edelwold, and succeeded him in that kingdom, reigning afterwards with such dislike that he was expelled by his own subjects, and fled to the King of the Picts. Alkmond

* Exchequer, M. S.

his son was slain in the year 800, and buried at Lilleshull ;* some say he was killed by the Danes, and others that Ardulph, then in possession of the throne, sacrificed him for his own safety, he being at the head of a party in opposition, and growing very formidable ; his death being looked upon by his friends as a martyrdom, he was ranked among the Saints.

St. Alkmond's Church is an irregular square pile ;† the structure Norman Gothic, the pillars in the same style, in form of a single cylinder, which with semicircular arches, support the roof. At the east end is a neat altar piece of the Corinthian order, which was adorned and beautified at the expence of Alice the wife of Martyn Baldwyn, Esq. and daughter of Sir Thomas Jones, Lord Chief Justice of the Court of Common Pleas, Westminster ; who, with her husband's consent, gave £100 towards the same. She died Sept. 5, 1712, and was buried near the chancel.

---

* St. Alkmond, is stated by Higden, to have been slain in a battle which took place at Chelmesford, now Kemsford, in the county of Gloucester, between Ethelmunda, a petty Mercian prince, and Weofstan, Duke of Wiltshire, and that he was buried first at the White Monastery, afterwards at Derby. Whitchurch is by some supposed to be the White Monastery intended by Higden, while very enlightened authorities deem it quite probable that if there was a church of *stone* at Lilleshull in the ninth century, it would be called a *White Monastery.*—EDITOR.

† The whole, except the tower and spire, of the venerable church described by Phillips, was, it appears, *very injudiciously* taken down. Of this circumstance Messrs. Owen and Blakeway thus express themselves :—ED.

"The sudden fall of St. Chad's roused the parishioners of St. Alkmund to an examination of their church. Upon an accurate survey, little appeared defective ; but some decay in the roof of the chancel of no serious extent, and for the repair of which orders were issued. Soon afterwards, however, a few active parishioners, influenced by the suggestions of interested individuals, proposed the destruction of the old church, and the rebuilding of it on a more contracted scale, which, it was pretended, would be a great eventual saving. This advice was favourably received by the vestry, and a resolution unfortunately passed, with scarce a single dissentient voice, totally to demolish their curious, roomy, and substantial church, and to erect a new one, after a plan furnished by Messrs. Carline and Tilly, stone-masons of Shrewsbury, on a part of its site. An act of parliament was obtained for this purpose, the mere expence of which would have covered all the expence of repairing the old fabrick ; and a committee appointed, under whose direction the venerable structure was quickly levelled with the ground. The present church rose rapidly on its ruins, and was opened for divine service on Nov. 8. 1795. The whole expence of this hasty and ill-advised procedure amounted to about £4000. (including the value of the old materials), of which the contract with the builders was £3000. Less than one-third of this sum might have repaired, and newly pewed the old church, which would have thus been rendered not only incalculably more handsome and interesting, but likewise far more strong and commodious than that which has supplied its place. So far from exhibiting symptoms of decay, the ancient walls proved unusually sound and firm, and it was not without great difficulty that they were rent asunder and thrown down. When the unsightly incumbrances of galleries and pews were removed, previous to its destruction, the beautiful architecture of this venerable fabrick, mixed and discordant as were the styles, was most striking, and convinced many, when too late, of the real merit of the church which had so heedlessly been condemned to ruin. No care was taken to preserve the numerous grave-stones, brasses, tombs, and other ancient memorials with which the aisles and chapels abounded. They were involved, with very few exceptions, in the common havock ; *the brasses were sold by weight,* and the grave-stones dispersed and converted to common uses!"

O

At the west end is a neat singers gallery, built at the expence of the parish, in the year 1775, and in the front of it stands a neat time-piece.

THE FOLLOWING MONUMENTS FOR THEIR NEATNESS AND SIMPLICITY DESERVE NOTICE, viz.

On the north wall two elegant marble monuments.—One erected to the memory of Sir Thomas Jones, Knt. with the following inscription :—

In a Vault near this Place lies deposited the Body of Sir Thomas Jones, Knt. late Lord Chief Justice of the Court of Common Pleas, Westminster, to whose Memory Alice his 4th Daughter, and Executrix caused this Monument to be erected, having lived with him to his death, which happened in the 78th Year of his Age, A. D. 1672.

ON THE OTHER ADJOINING MONUMENT.

Beneath this Monument is deposited, the body of Thomas Jones, Esq. Son and Heir of William Jones, Esq. and Grandson and Heir to Sir Thomas Jones, Knt. sometime Lord Chief Justice of the Court of Common Pleas, Westminster.

A worthy Patriot of his Country.

He lived deservedly beloved and died a Representative in Parliament of this ancient Borough of Shrewsbury, whose strictest Piety, Exemplary Virtue, and extensive Charity, will consign him to a joyful resurrection, Obijt 31° Die Julij. A. D. 1715.
Ætatis suæ 48.

ON THE SAME TABLE IS THE FOLLOWING INSCRIPTION.

In Memory of Mary, the Wife of Thomas Jones, Esq.; second Daughter, and Co-Heir of Sir Francis Russell of Strensham in the County of Worcester, Bart. by Dame Ann his Wife, second Daughter of Sir Rowland Lytton of Knibworth in the County of Hertford, Bart. whose virtues she inherited and adorned,
By a true conjugal affection,
Sweetness of Manners,
And undissembled Piety.
She died Nov. 1, Anno 1712, Ætat, 43.

Beneath these Monuments, within iron railing, stands an old Gothic tomb,* the architecture of which appears to be that of the time of James I. Two full length figures reclined, are on the tomb, in the dress of the time, representing William Jones, Esq. and Eleanor his wife. On the Freeze of the tomb appears the following inscription.

> Gulielmus Jones Aldermanus Villæ Salopiæ et Ælianora uxor ejus jacent sub hoc monumento.

ALSO ON THE OTHER SIDE THE TOMB.

Gulielmus Jones Obijt Julij 13, A. D. 1612.

In the north east corner lies interred the body of Thomas Jones, Esq. On the wall over his vault, a brass plate† was fixed, with the following inscription, viz.

> In a Vault near this Place is deposited the Body of Thomas Jones, Esq. who was six times Bailiff of this Town, the first Mayor of Shrewsbury, and once High Sheriff of the County. He was buried the 3rd day of May, Anno Dom. 1642. Who out of a godly Zeal, and charitable devotion, did give and bequeath Fifty Pounds, the profit whereof to remain for ever unto the poor of this Parish.

Upon a large stone‡ near the vestry, are the effigies of a Knight in armour, and a Lady, in full length proportion. The following inscription (found among the writings belonging to the family of the Corbetts of Abright Hussey), was formerly upon the brass plate round the stone, viz.

> Hic jacent Thomas Corbett et Anchoreta uxor ejus filia Thomæ Barre Militis, et Dom' Aliciæ uxoris ejus, Sororis Dom' Johannis Talbott.

The following curious account is transcribed from a manuscript collection belonging to the late Rev. Dr. Taylor; the reader is at liberty to give what degree of credit to it he pleases.

" This yeare 1533 uppon twelffe daye in Shrowsbury, the dyvyll apearyd " in saint alkmonds churche there, when the preest was at highe masse, with " greate tempeste and darkeness, so that as he passyd through the churche, he

---

† This plate has been taken down and lost.

---

* This tomb, after the erection of the New Church, was placed *outside* the wall, near the vault where the remains of the worthy pair had been deposited, but from being exposed to the action of the atmosphere, and changes of the weather, it was considerably injured, and in consequence transferred to the Abbey Church, and repaired at the expence of Sir T. T. Jones, family representative of Mr. and Mrs. Jones.—EDITOR.

‡ Now in the Abbey Church.—ED.

" mountyd up the Steaple in the sayde churche, teringe the wyers of the sayde
" clocke, and put the prynt of hys clawes upon the 4th bell, and toocke one
" of the pynnacles awaye with hym, and for the tyme stayed all the bells in
" the churches within the sayde towne that they could neyther toll nor rynge."

Some accounts say, the enraged Devil made his appearance in the habit
of a Grey Friar; also that at his departure, he stamped his hoof upon the
trembling spire, and left it in the shattered state it at present appears in.

The spire belonging to this church, is reckoned a neat piece of architecture;
four yards of it were taken down and rebuilt in the year 1621.

	Yds.	F.	I.
The height of the tower from the ground is -	23	1	0
The spire to the back of the cock - - -	33	0	1
Total height	56	1	1

The repairing this steeple, and the fool-hardy frolics* of the performer of
the work, are related in the following account.†

" This yeare and in the monthe of Februarie, the Steeple of the churche of St.
" Alkmond's in Shrosberie was newe pointed by one George Archer of St Alban's by
" London, who beinge a very simple man and lame, the 22d day of Februarie being
" Saturday, and in the Afternoone of the same daye clymed up to the top of the same
" steeple, beinge 56 Yards of height from the bottom, with clowted Showes uppon hys
" feete, and brought down the sayd Coke beinge of Brasse and weighing 12 pounds,
" beinge also of sisse from the Bill to the ennde of the tayle, three quarters of a Yard,
" and in bredth from hys comb, to the bottom of hys Belly halfe a Yard lacking 2 Ynches.
" And the thirde daye of Marche beinge teusday, in licke manner clymm'd uppon and
" did put the sayde Coke uppon the topp of the sayd Steeple againe, turning it about
" soondrie tymes, standing upright uppon the Iron Crosse being a rayny daye, shakyng
" hys hands and leggs abroade, to the admiration of the beholders; who also the 10th
" daye of Marche followinge beinge Wednesday clymmd up to the sayd Steeple topp
" againe in lycke manner, tacking with hym a drume, and a longe Bowe and Arrowes,
" and standing upright uppon the crosse of the same, shott an arrowe out of the sayde
" Bowe—Also againe and last of all, the thirteenthe daye of Marche being Saturdaye,
" he clym'd up in lycke manner to the topp of the sayde Steeple, and turned the sayde
" cocke about lycke a Wheele, shakyng hys armes and leggs about, whooting and cryinge
" about the crosse almost 2 Houres, and so cam down sober as he always dyd, but goinge
" upp at every tyme drunke as hys manner was."

† From Dr. Taylor's M. S.

---

* In 1788 two-thirds of the spire were found decayed, and restored by one Cheshire of Coleshill,
a spire builder, when several feet were added to the height. After the finishing of the spire, one Alice
Sindford, a pauper in the House of Industry, was permitted by the builder to ascend the ladders,
which she accomplished with the utmost agility, very composedly turned round the weather-cock,
and descended without the slightest difficulty. The next day she desired permission to repeat her
dangerous exploit, but was very properly refused.—EDITOR, *from information by Mr. Davies, Artist,
Frankwell.*

J. St. Julians Church. 1778.

Eng.d from the Original for Hulbert's new Edition of Phillip's History of Shrewsbury by J. Forday.

	Yds.	F.	I.
St. Alkmond's Church is in Length inside -	34	0	0
Breadth - -	28	0	6

Patron - - The King.

VICARS.*

1551 Rev. George Crane	Buried April 15, 1591.
1591 Rev. Humphry Leech,	After a short continuance, resigned, and embraced the Roman Catholic religion
1591 Rev. Andrew Duker.	
1605 Rev. Thomas Lloyde,	Buried May 13th, 1642.
1618 Rev. Julines Herring,	Inducted 1618. Resigned 1635.
1635 Rev. Thomas Good, B. D.	Ejected by the Parliament 1644.
1645 Rev. Thomas Blake	Promoted.
1650 Rev. Richard Heath,	Ejected for non-conformity, Aug. 24, 1662.
1663 Rev. Richard Beeston,	Buried March 10, 1683.
1684 Rev. John Lowe,	Buried May 1, 1734.
1734 Rev. John Cotton	Died Dec. 26, 1757.
1758 Rev. Samuel Jones	Died 1763.
1763 Rev. Samuel Sneade,	Died Jan. 11, 1774.
1774 Rev, Richard De Courcy,	Inducted Feb. 9, 1774. (Died 1803.)

1806 Rev. Edward Lynzee, M. A.	Resigned Sept. 1818.
1818 Rev. John Wightman, M. A.	Inducted Oct. 10, 1818.—Ed.

ST. JULIAN'S CHURCH. It is uncertain when or by whom the Old Church was built; it is distinguished in several reigns as a Royal Peculiar, and Free Chapel, stiled, The Church of St. Juliana the Virgin, and also "*Chapella Regiæ, Sanctæ Julianæ.*" Half a hide of land in Downton belonged to this church. In the 7th Henry III. Anno 1223, the chapel of Ford was an appendant of it.

---

* Phillips's list of Vicars, is corrected by Messrs. Owen and Blakeway in the following particulars: " Andrew Daker occurs as Vicar in 1593;" " June 17, 1591, Humphrey Leech, M. A. of Brasen Nose College, was presented by Lord Keeper Egerton." Messrs. O. and B. do not believe Mr. Julines Herring was ever Vicar of St. Alkmund's, but only " Lecturer, put in by the Feoffees of St. Antholines." Their statement is, that the " Rev. Thomas Lloyd was presented by Lord Chancellor Egerton in 1607, and continued vicar till 1642;" that " Thomas Good, B. D succeeded, but the unsettled times in which he became vicar sufficently account for the omision of his institution in the Episcopal Registers "

The parish of St. Alkmond comprises only a small part of the town; chief portions in the vicinity of the church are, part of High Street, part of Pride Hill, St. Alkmond's Square, Fish Street, and Double-Butcher-Row. It has several insulated portions, as the Western half, the Castle-foregate, Hencot, Abrightlee, part of Harlescot, Denthill, and Preston Montford.—EDITOR.

In the 13th Richard II. 1390, St. Julian's was a Royal Peculiar, as appears by a letter of attorney, then given to Reginald Scryven, to prosecute the executors of the will of William Pryseley, wherein are these words, viz.

"In cujus rei testimonium cum sigillum nostrum est pluribus incognitum, sigillum
"Officialitatis Dom. Rectoris liberæ Capellæ Regiæ Sanctæ Julianæ Salop literis apponi
"procuravimus et nos Official: antedictus ad personalem rogatum dictorum Will. &
"John' Sigillum officii nostri presentibus apposuinus."

"Omnibus xi fidelibus ad quorum notitiam presentes literæ pervenerint: Officialis
"liberæ capellæ regiæ Ste. Julianæ salutem in domino.—Cum Tho. Cowper de eadem
"ab intestato obierit prætextu cujus eventus ipsius bonorum dispositio ad nostrum offi-
"cium dignoscitur pertinere, nos igitur ipsius animæ saluti pro animo affectantes, prout
"sua bona exfendere valeant, salubriter providere; dilectos nobis in Christo J. C. &
"R. L. administratores et executores dativos &c. constituimus per præsentes sigillo
"officii nostri sigillatas. Dat, Salop 19th Apr. 1446."

The revenues of St. Julian's, together with those of St. Michael's in the Castle, were annexed to Battlefield at the time that church was built, reserving only a small allowance for the minister.

The present structure is modern, the old building all except the tower being taken down in the year 1748. The foundation was laid in the month of August that year, and divine service was performed in the new erected church in August 1750. The galleries are supported by pillars of the Tuscan order, and upon those stand another row of pillars, of the Doric order, with a full entablature supporting the roof, and the whole of the inside of the church is neatly finished. The expence amounting to about £1000 was defrayed by the patron, Sir John Astley, and the parishioners, assisted by some other public spirited benefactors.

At the west end of the church stands an elegant time-piece, put up in the year 1777.

	Yds.	F.	I.
Length of the Church	27	1	6
Breadth	16	0	3

St. Julian,* to whom this church is dedicated, was of a noble family in Florence.

Present Patron,—Earl of Tankerville.

---

* If this church, as it appears to be the case, was originally dedicated to "St. Juliana the Virgin," no satisfactory reason has yet been given why it should not still retain the name of its patroness Saint "Juliana" rather than the abbreviated, if not corrupted name of "Julian." St. Juliana was a young lady of Nicomedia, in Bythynia, who at the age of eighteen, suffered martyrdom during the Dioclesian persecution in the year 303· We find a "Saint Julian" in the Roman Calendar who was an illustrious Spanish prelate and lived in the seventh century, and who is highly commended for his learning and amiable life. The *Saint Julian of Florence* mentioned by Mr. Phillips, was a another, and lived subsequently to the times of persecution, consequently could not be *Juliana the Virgin* to whom the church is dedicated.—EDITOR.

MINISTERS* SINCE 1689.

Rev. Maurice Harrison,	Died Dec. 26, 1689.
Rev. James Talbot	Presented 1689.
Rev. James Pearson	Presented 1720.
Rev. John Wingfield,	Presented 1756.

1791 Rev. Hugh Owen, M. A.	Resigned July 1826.
1826 Rev. Frederick Iliff, M. A.	The present vicar.—ED.

AUSTIN'S FRIARY, built for the Eremites of St. Austin. Their house stood adjoining to the Quarry on one side, to Severn on another, to waste land by Severn side on another, and to the town wall by Romboldesham (now Barker Street) on the south side. The ground on which this building was erected appears to have been the place where excommunicated persons, and such as died of the plague, and other contagious distempers were buried. King Henry III. gave a grant of this ground A. D. 1255, to the Friars of Coulon, which appears to be the first time of their settling here. The founder it is probable was one of the Stafford family, Speed says, Lord Stafford. Several persons of note slain at the battle of Battlefield, were interred in the burying ground belonging to this house. A small part near the river side is yet standing, and it appears by several adjoining vestiges to have extended a considerable way towards the Quarry, in the garden, now Mr. Hill's, and also towards Barker Street; at the bottom of which is a postern or gateway, through the town wall, which the Friars made by permission of the Bailiffs and Burgesses, as a way to their house.†

The endowment of this Friary was only £13. 1s. 8d. per ann. They had a chapel in Barker Street, which till lately was used as a malt-house, and in the year 1764, was bought of Mr. Brickdale by James Mason, Esq. since

† Exchequer M. S.

then it has been rough cast and converted into a coach-house and dwellings, by which means the old stone work, and antique church doors (before visible) are altered.

Two sorts of enormities rendered these Friars odious to mankind, and hastened their suppression; their first was, their practice of taking away children from their parents, which they often did with violence and threats, for the children, according their phrase, were devoted to the service of God; and paternal authority with the endearments of nature were thereby extinguished; this custom prevailed, till by the statute 4th Henry IV. Cap. 17. it was enacted, that no Friar of any of the four Orders, should take or keep children from their parents by force, which act was ordered to be perpetual.

The other abuse of these Friars was, their scandalous lewdness and venery, insomuch, that a lane in this town from their nocturnal pranks, is to this day called Grope Lane.

This order came first into England, in the year 1252, some of them being sent here by Lanfrank of Milan, their first General; they had their first house given them in Wales at a place called Woodhouse, which before belonged to the noble family of Turbervilles.* Their rule was prescribed by Pope Alexander the IVth.

In the 36th Henry VIII. Roger Lewis, alias Pope did homage, for the reversion of the Priory of St. Austin in Shrewsbury.

The remains of this building, and the land ajoining, are now in the possession of Thomas Jelfe Powis, of Berwick, Esq.†

FRANCISCAN OR GREY FRIARY. The house of the Franciscan Grey Friars, or Friar's Minors, stood near the Stone Bridge, great part of the building yet remains, is now a dwelling-house, and has for several years past been called from the late occupier, Mr. Yonge's Friars. We have no particular account of the time this house was founded, neither how endowed, or valued at the suppression; probably it was founded before Austin's Friars, as in the 30th Hen. III. A. D. 1246, John son of Ralph de Mortimer, is mentioned as a Grey Triar there. Geoffrey Lord Powis is said by some to be the founder, but Leland, in his Itinerary, V. 6, P. 10, says, " My Lord Powis saith that Hawise " Wife to the Lord of Powis, was the causer that the Gray Friers College in " Shr. (wher she lyith buried under a flat marble by Chorlton's Tombe) was builded."

* Dugdale's Monasticon, vol. II. p. 221.

---

† Mr. Powis conveyed the property in 1802 to Edward Hughes, Esq. of the firm of Price, Hughes, Edwards, and Jones. Bankers, who occupies a considerable portion of the scite on which the Friary stood as a Tan-yard. On the land adjoining the Friary or *Priory*, as it is now generally called, several genteel houses have been erected. Very interesting remains are still visible, though modern buildings are united to them and mixed with almost every portion.—EDITOR.

This order was first founded in the year 1209, by Francis de Assizi, and established by Pope Honorius III. in 1223, and the next year they settled in England. The religious who embraced this rule, took, out of modesty, the name of Minors, or Minorites; by their rule, they were not to preach, or take confessions in any Diocese, without express leave from the Bishop; but this article was not long observed by them, for they represented to the Pope, that Christians were ashamed to confess themselves to their own Pastors, that many scrupled to do it, because the Parish Priests themselves were guilty of the same sins confessed to them, in fine, that they had not the discretion to be secret; upon these accounts they petitioned for a dispensation, which was readily granted them.

The remaining part of the building belonging to the Grey Friars, was lately purchased by Mr. Hewitt,* whose heirs are now in possession of it.

DOMINICAN FRIARY, or House of Black Preaching Friars. This Order came into England, A. D. 1221, shortly after their first institution; their house in Shrewsbury stood in the field at the bottom of St. Mary's Water Lane, known by the name of St. Mary's Friars; some vestiges of the foundation yet remain there.† It is uncertain who was the founder, some say, one Richard, a native of Shrewsbury, about the year 1265; others say, it was founded by Lady Genneville. (Speed mentions a Friary belonging to the Dominicans, founded by one of the Charltons, in which, he says Lady Charlton lies buried; and also a Friary of Carmelites, dedicated to St. Mary, founded by a Genneville.) Two sons of Edward IV. were born in the Dominican or Black Friars here, viz. Richard, stiled Duke of York, whom Perkin Warbeck personated after he was murdered in the Tower, and George Plantagenet, who died before his brother, or doubtless had been murdered with him.

---

* Mr. Hewitt's daughters, co-heiresses, sold it to James Hewitt, whose son John sold it in 1792 to Mr. John Bishop of the Stamp Office, and Mr. Bromfield, architect and builder; Mr. Bishop's share was sold to the late Mr. Simpson, builder, and now belongs to his heirs; Mr. Bromfield dying a few years ago, his portion descended to his heirs. In modern times we call the *scite* and a portion surrounding. " St. Julian's Friars." The remains of the Friary have been converted into comfortable dwelling-houses; the walls of the garden can be traced a considerable distance up the adjoining meadow, now occupied by Mr. Stant.—EDITOR.

† The scite on which the Dominican Friary stood is now partly occupied as a timber yard, by Messrs. Smith and Son, and partly as a wharf, where the Union Wharf Company have built a neat dwelling-house, and commodious warehousing, occupied by Mr. Rees. In cutting the banks, and making a road to complete the wharf in the year 1823, many skeletons were discovered. also several stone coffins, ancient tiles, &c. The scite and meadow adjoining, is the property of Mrs. Corbet of Sundorne Castle, under lease to the Union Wharf Company, for a term, it is said, of 60 years.

EDITOR.

P

Those of this Order were called Dominicans from their founder Dominic de Guzman, a Spaniard, who long preached against the Albigenses; they were also called Predicants, because the design of their institution was, that they should preach against heretics. The Court of Inquisition was committed to the Dominicans, by which they became famous for their cruelties upon pretended heretics, of whom that court was judge.

ST. MICHAEL'S CHAPEL, in the Castle, was built by Roger de Montgomery. The revenues of it were given to Battlefield, when the collegiate church was erected there. Where it stood in the Castle is uncertain, probably it was demolished about the time the cannon, &c. were removed by order of King James II. for it appears* about that time, an order was made by the Corporation, that enquiry should be made after the stones taken away from the ruins of St. Michael's Chapel in the Castle. St. Michael being a warlike Saint, was generally made the patron of chapels in castles; Leland mentions a chapel dedicated to this Saint, over a gate at Ilchester.

ST. NICHOLAS'S CHAPEL. Great part of it is yet standing in Castle Street, on the left hand of the entrance to the Council House, now used as a stable belonging to Mrs. Lyster.

ST. CATHARINE'S CHAPEL, at Cotton Hill. It stood in a piece of ground adjoining the Turnpike, and is now the property of John Mytton, Esq. which piece of ground is to this day, called the Chapel Yard, and stands part in St. Mary's and part in St Julian's parish: Chapels dedicated to this Saint generally stood on hills, without great towns.

ST. BLASE'S CHAPEL, in Murivance. See further, in account of Chorlton Hall.

ST. MARY MAGDALEN'S CHAPEL. Uncertain were it stood.†

* M. S. In Scaccario, Salop.

---

† In the rear of the house, now Mr. Surgeon Arrowsmith's, bottom of Pride Hill, there are remains of a very ancient stone building, as there are also of another in the passage opening into Shop-Latch, from the rear of Messrs. Eddowes's, Mr. Parsons's, and other premises. Query, may not one of the two be the remains of St. Mary Magdalen's chapel? I merely submit the suggestion without offering an opinion.—EDITOR.

Besides Churches, under this class may be mentioned the following

MEETING HOUSES FOR DISSENTERS, &c.

The OLD CHAPEL, in the High Street, for those of the Presbyterian denomination. The present building was erected in the year 1715, at the expence of Government, the former having been pulled down by a mob. Mr. Bryan, and Mr. Tallents, ministers ejected from St. Chad's, and St. Mary's for nonconformity, in the 1662, were first concerned in forming a congregation here. The first Meeting House was entered October 25th, 1691, and upon the walls of it, the following inscription was placed, viz.

" This place was not built for faction, or a party, but to promote repentance and faith, in communion with all those who love our Lord Jesus Christ in sincerity."

Our help is in the name of the Lord who made heaven and Earth."

LIST OF MINISTERS.

1691 Rev. John Bryan, A. M.	Died A. D. 1699.
Rev. Francis Talents, A. M.	Died 1708.
1699 Rev. James Owen,	Succeeded Mr. Bryan. Died 1706.
1706 Rev. Samuel Benion, M. D.	Died 1708.
1708 Rev. John Gyles, M. D. ⎬	Succeeded Messrs. Talents and Benion.
Rev. John Reynolds, ⎬	Mr. Reynolds, Removed 1718.
	Dr. Gyles, Died 1730.
1721 Rev. Charles Berry,	Chosen instead of Mr. Reynolds; continued with Dr. Gyles, till 1730, and remained sole Minister till his death, 1741.
1741 Rev Job. Orton,	Resigned, and removed to Kidderminster, 1766.
1743 Rev. Francis Boult,	Removed to Wrexham, 1746.
1746 Rev. Moses Carter,	Succeeded Mr. Boult, and Died 1747.
1748 Rev. Joseph Fownes,	Succeeded Mr. Carter.

1766 Mr. Orton desiring an assistant in his part of the public service, the Rev. Mr. Benjamin Stapp, of Warrington, was invited to this station, and fixed at Shrewsbury, October 5, 1766. But a seperation ensued, which gave rise to the congregation assembling at the New Chapel. Mr. Stapp died in 1767, and was succeeded by the Rev. Mr. Ralph Harrison, now of Manchester, whither he removed in 1771. He was succeeded in 1774, by the

1774 Rev. Mr. SMITH,*   Who, with Rev. Mr. Fownes, are the present Ministers of this Congregation.

THE NEW CHAPEL, on Swan Hill, or Murivance. The Congregation meeting here, formed themselves into a distinct society, from those meeting at the Old Chapel, in 1766, and built this place of worship, in 1767.

MINISTERS.

1766 Rev. Robert Gentleman.	Removed to Caermarthen.
1779 Rev. Samuel Lucas,†	Chosen, upon Mr. Gentleman's resignation.

THE BAPTIST MEETING HOUSE, in High Street. A society of this denomination, appears to have been in this town, in the time of the commonwealth; and before that time, there were a number of them here, but whether they met together as a distinct society, is not certain.

MINISTERS SINCE 1680.

1680 Rev. Samuel Travers.	
Rev. Mr. Watkins.	
1718 Rev. Josiah Thompson,	Removed to Pershore, 1725.
1725 Rev. Robert Morris.	
1742 Rev. John Sedgfield,	Removed to Froome, 1745.
1745 Rev. John Oulton, Junior,	Removed to Rawdon, Yorkshire, 1748.
1748 Rev. William Morgan,	Died 1753.
1753 Rev. Rees Evans,	Removed to Tewksbury, 1757.
1759 Rev. Charles Rogers,	Removed to Exeter.
1762 Rev. John Pyne,	Removed, and formed a seperate congregation, 1773.

---

* In 1781, the Rev. Mr. Smith removed to Liverpool; he was succeeded as assistant to Mr. Fownes, by the Rev. Pendlebury Houghton, who removed to Norwich in August 1787. The Rev. John Rowe being invited here, preached his first sermon October 14th; same year Mr. Fownes died, Nov. 7th, 1789, aged 75, after a ministry of 40 years. On his death, Mr. Rowe continued sole minister till 1793, when Mr. Arthur Aikin became his assistant till June 1795, when he resigned, and was succeeded by the Rev. George Case. In 1798 Mr. Rowe removed to Bristol, leaving Mr. Case sole minister, which situation he still retains.

The opinions, &c. of this branch of the Protestant Christian Church, and of all the other religious communities in the town, will be found in another place.—EDITOR.

† The Rev. Samuel Lucas resigned in 1797, and was succeeded by the Rev. Thomas Weaver the present minister.—EDITOR.

1773 Rev. John Sandys.*

THE BAPTIST MEETING HOUSE in Barker Street.

MINISTER.

1773 Rev. John Pyne†.

Besides the above-mentioned, here are the following Meeting Houses, viz. one for Methodists‡ of Mr. Wesley's denomination, supplied by itinerant preachers.—One for the Quakers,§ built A. D. 1746. And a Chapel lately erected for Roman Catholics.‖

And here let it be mentioned to the honour of the Dissenters in Shrewsbury, that on the 17th day of February 1757, a petition was presented to the House of Commons and read, entituled, "A Petition from the Protestant Dis-

---

* Rev. John Sandys, who succeeded Mr. Pyne as pastor of the congregation remaining in Still-House-Shut, (now Golden Cross Shut) had the pleasure to have a new chapel erected for him in Dog-Lane, and opened 22nd September 1780, he however removed to London the year following, and was succeeded by Mr. Wykes, who was removed in 1783. He was succeeded by the Rev. William Smith, who not liking the temper of his congregation, or they not liking his, removed to London in October 1788. The church was afterwards, it appears, without a regular pastor till 1793, when Mr. John Palmer then in the Medical profession, was invited to undertake the charge. He was ordained April 13th 1796, and continued in the zealous discharge of his pastoral duties till July 1822, when from continued ill health he resigned, and was succeeded by the Rev. Manoah Kent, the present minister.—EDITOR.

† Mr. Pyne, for whom the chapel was erected in Barker Street, did not long uphold a congregation there, and what became of him I cannot learn, his congregation, it is said, afterwards met in Cole Hall. They, however, finally dissolved, a few joined the church in Dog-Lane, and the rest were scattered by the breath of dissension. The chapel is now the dwelling-house of Mr. Williams, builder.
EDITOR.

‡ Mr. Phillips mentions in another place, that "the Shearman's Hall, top of High-Street, was used for a meeting-house for Mr. Wesley and his followers." Their first building in Shrewsbury, purposely erected as a place of public worship, was in Hill's Lane, and which building or chapel was conveyed or bequeathed to that community by one Mr. Appleby, a truly pious and excellent man. Soon after the erection of their handsome and commodious structure nearly opposite the Theatre, St. John's Hill, the Wesleyan or Arminian Methodists disposed of their Meeting House in Hill's Lane to the Welsh Calvinistic Methodists, who have greatly improved the property and fitted up a very neat and complete chapel.—EDITOR.

§ The Quakers' meeting was also then where it now is, top of St. John's Hill; it was erected as early as the year 1746, and considerably enlarged in the year 1807.—EDITOR.

‖ The Roman Catholic Chapel, was in the days of Phillips where it now is, at the head of the Back Lane. The Rev. James Corne was then priest, who died Dec. 4th, 1817, aged 72. He was succeeded by a French Refugee, the Rev. Mr. Le Maitre who died June 16th, 1822. The Rev. Samuel Jones is the present priest.
There is doubt but that each of these denominations were at that period very few in numbers, and consequently considered by Mr. Phillips of minor importance.—Additional particulars hereafter.
EDITOR.

senters in Shrewsbury," &c. expressing their apprehensions, that in the bill then depending, for the better ordering the militia, it might be proposed that they should be exercised on the Lord's day, commonly called Sunday, and praying that no clause for that purpose might pass into a law.

The petition was referred to the committee upon the bill ; and the first and third Mondays of every month from March to October, both inclusive, and Tuesday, Wednesday, Thursday, and Friday, in Whitsun week, yearly, were the days appointed to exercise the militia.

In the second class, among charitable institutions, particular notice may be taken of the following, viz.

The HOSPITAL of ST. JOHN BAPTIST, with the Free Chapel of ST. GEORGE annexed, situate in Frankwell, "*juxta Portam que dicitur Walsh Gate in Villa Salop." Some records have it "Extra Portam Wallie," being certainly one and the same house, as appears from the following narrations.

In an old rental † of the town, taken the 30th Henry III. 1246, this hospital stood charged with the following yearly rents, viz.

	s.	d.
D'Hospital Sancti Johannis de Sopis sub Messuagio illo - -	0	1
D'Hospital Sancti Johannis de Terra que fuit Nicholai filij Emme -	0	3½
D'Hospital Sancti Johannis - - - - - - - -	0	2

Anno 1262. 48th Henry III. Sunday next before the feast of St. Barnaby the Apostle, the Bailiffs of Shrewsbury accounted for the toll or custom arising from St. George's Gate, by the hands of Randle Putor, viz.

	£.	s.	d.
	0	15	0
Another time in the same year - - - - -	0	3	0
49th Henry III. From St. George's Gate - - -	0	13	0
Again - - - - - - - -	0	7	0
Again - - - - - - - -	0	3	2

Hence we see all along the Welsh Gate was also called St. George's Gate, from the vicinity of the said hospital.

‡ Anno 1275, 3rd Edward I. In the week next before the feast of the translation of St. Thomas, the Bailiffs of Shrewsbury, expended in repairing the bridge of St. George, by Allan Bill, Surveyor of the work, as under :

To one Mason, for four days - - - -	16d.
Item, to two labourers serving him - - - -	18d.
Item, to Allan Bill, Surveyor, for two weeks - - -	12d.

* Pat. 15°. Richard II.   † In Scaccario Salop.

‡ In Scaccario Salop.

7th Edward II. William Vaughan* had licence to settle on the hospital of St. John, 14 messuages with 18d. rent: These were probably on the street called to this day St. John's Hill.

† 1369, 42d. Edward III. Richard Pygot Chaplain by his will, dated Thursday next before the feast of St James the Apostle, ordains his body to be buried in the Chapel of the Saints, St. John and St. George, before the Cross, and wills that all the choirs of the churches of the town of Shrewsbury, be invited to his exequies, and to have as the custom was: He likewise bequeaths three pounds of wax, to make two candles, of which, he gives one to St. Chad's Church, and the other to the said chapel. And to the parish Priest of St. Chad's, forty pence: And to every one of the houses of Mendicant Friars, forty pence: And wills that the hospital by him begun, should be finished out of his effects, if the same should extend so far. And that a tenement in Colneham which he had bought of Allice de Leye, should be assigned to the service of the blessed Virgin, in the church of St. Julian, *(dum lex permittitur)* if not, to be sold, and the money therefrom to be laid out in pious uses, and works of charity, for the salvation of his soul. The residue of all his goods, of what sort soever, to be at the disposal of his executors, Sir Thomas de Tyford, and others therein named.

VIto. Id. August, Anno Dni. Mittmo CCC LXIX. probatum fuit Test. &c. (Dorso.)

Which Richard Pygot, must be allowed to be a great benefactor, though not the founder.

‡ 1371. The custody of this hospital of St. John, was committed to Robert Harlescott, Chaplain.

16th Henry IV. Thomas Barker, Chaplain, Keeper of this Hospital of St. John Baptist, Salop, with the consent of his brethren, grants in fee-farm to John Kinton, and others, a certain piece of land, in Frankwell, to hold for 99 years, at the yearly rent of three shillings and four-pence. This fee-farm, is under the common seal of the said Hospital.

16th Henry VI. Thomas Thornes, and John Begott, Bailiffs of Shrewsbury, present Lewis Montgomery, to the Chantry, in the Hospital of St. John the Baptist, " *Juxta Portam, Walliæ, Salop.*" Which Chantry was lately founded by William Vaughan, on a licence obtained from King Edward.

27th Henry VI. The King granted to John Hampton, Esq. the Collation of the next Vacancy of the Hospital of St. George, without the Gate of Shrewsbury, whenever it should happen.

§ 1468. 8th Edward IV. The Bailiffs of Shrewsbury, received for Toll, or Custom of St. George's Gate, eleven shillings and three-pence.

---

* Pat. 7th Edward II. p. 2. m. 20.   † Orig. Penes Thomam Berrington Armiger.

‡ Pat. 44th Edward III. p. m. 14.   § In Scaccario.

1469. 9th Edward IV. The Prior of the Hospital of St. John the Baptist, in Frankvile, is charged by the Bailiffs of Salop, 5½d. rent, for certain lands, and tenements of theirs, in Frankvile.

† At the general Dissolution, it was valued at £4. 10s. 4d. per annum clear.

3rd Edward VI. The King granted to Robert Wood, the free Chapel of St. John, in Frankvile, with the endowments thereof.

By a rental of the town of Shrewsbury, taken 1686, Mr. John Scott, stands charged for the said Hospital yearly, 5½d. In the mayoralty of Sir Francis Edwards, Bart.‡

N. B. In the last-mentioned rental, the Heirs of Mr. William Sherrar, are charged for Cadogan's Chapel, in Frankwell, yearly, one penny. Now Cadogan's Chapel is supposed to have stood near the Bull in the Barn, and that there was a Cross there, called Cadogan's Cross; but as some have thought it dubious from this circumstance, where the Hospital of St. John stood, the following remarks upon both, will make it appear, that the Hospital of St. John, with the free Chapel of St. George annexed, stood at the end of the Welsh Bridge on the right hand, at a place now called the Stew, and that Cadogan's Chapel and Cross, were somewhere near the Bull in the Barn.

1. The Gate upon the Welsh Bridge, is called in the before recited account, St. George's Gate, and the Bridge, St. George's Bridge, from whence it is probable, the Chapel of St. George stood near it.

2. The Hospital of St. John Baptist, is said to be "*Extra Portam Walliæ*," which would be improperly said of it, if at a considerable distance; besides, it is probable, St. George's Chapel, was the Chapel belonging to the Hospital.

3. In 44th Elizabeth, it appears,* a grant was made of a piece of ground,† 11 yards square, which piece of ground is said to lie between St. George's Chapel, and a place called the Stew.

4. In Speed's Map, St. George's Chapel, is placed at, or near the place called the Stew, as are also the Almshouses, anciently called Collde's Almshouses; but in this Map, St. George's Almshouses, which we know are generally built near the church or chapel, from which they are denominated.

5. Cadogan's Chapel, and Cross, it is probable were without the town, for so most Crosses were, as Waring's Cross, on the Gorsty Bank, about a mile out of town, in the road to Oswestry—Spell Cross, beyond Coleham—

---

† M. S, In Office. Primit.   * In Scaccario.   ‡ Mr. Bowen's M. S.

† This piece of ground, formerly granted by the Corporation to some of the ancestors of the late Captain Griffiths, of Bicton, has lately been found (through the vigilant attention of the present Coroners, Mr. Bold Oliver, and Mr. Robert Hill, to the business of their offices) to have reverted to the Corporation, and has been by them sold to Mr. Edward Cullis.

Weeping Cross, beyond St. Giles's, &c. Supposing Cadogan's Cross and Chapel, to be near the Bull in the Barn, which appears probable, then the place where Millington's Hospital is built, was the yard belonging to it, as the name Chapel Yard, by which it is called, and by which name it was sold to the Trustees of that charity seems to indicate.

ST. GILES'S HOSPITAL, or Hospital of Lepers,* in the Abbey Foregate, was founded by King Henry II. who granted them, for their support and maintenance, the toll of all corn and meal sold in Shrewsbury market, also thirty shillings yearly, out of his farm, at Shrewsbury ; as appears by the following extract from the charter.

"Henry, by the Grace of God, King of England, Duke of Normandy "and Aquitane, &c. To William, Bishop of Chester, with the Justices, Sheriffs, "Bailiffs, and good men of Shrewsbury. KNOW YE, That I have given and "granted for perpetual Alms to the infirm of Shrewsbury, a Rent of Thirty "Shillings, out of my Farm in Shropshire, to be paid regularly by the hands "of my Sheriff for the time being."†

ABSTRACT OF KING JOHN'S CHARTER.

"John, by the Grace of God, King of England, &c. KNOW YE, "That we, for the Love of God, grant this Charter, to confirm to the Lepers "of St. Giles's without Shrewsbury, that they have out of every sack of corn "coming to Shrewsbury Market, a handful of both hands, and out of every "strike of wheat, a handful of one hand, as they enjoyed in the time of King "Henry our Father : Wherefore, &c. &c. Given under our hand and Seal, at "Woodstock, the 19th day of March, in the 5th year of our Reign."†

ABSTRACT OF KING HENRY 3d's CHARTER.

"Henry, by the Grace of God, &c. &c. KNOW YE, That for the love "of God, and for the Salvation of my own Soul, and for the Souls of my

---

* Lepers, or Lazers, were sick persons, removed out of Monasteries, to Cells, or Hospitals, always built out of cities and towns. Their usual maintenance was, from liberty allowed them to go upon every market day to the markets, and with a dish, called a clap dish, they would beg corn. Their sickness and loathsome appearance, giving great disgust, many witheld their charity, upon which account, they were afterwards restrained from begging at large, but permitted to send the Proctor of the Hospital, who came with his box, one day in every month, to the Churches, and other religious houses, at time of service, and there received the voluntary charity of the congregations.— This custom, is said to be the origin of the present practice of collecting by briefs.

† Mr. Elisha's M. S. S.

Q

" Ancestors and Heirs, we do grant and confirm this our Charter, to the Lepers*
" of the Hospital of St. Giles's without Shrewsbury, that they have a Horse
" Load of Dead Wood, out of my Wood called Linewood, (Lythewood) for
" their firing ; wherefore we will, &c. &c.   Given under the hand of the Rev^d.
" Father, Bishop of Chichester, our Chancellor, at Wenlock, the 11th of
" August, in the 16th Year of our Reign ——"†

MILLINGTON'S HOSPITAL, in Chapel Yard, Frankwell, was founded
and endowed, pursuant to the will of Mr. James Millington, of Shrewsbury,
Draper, who, by his last will, bearing date the 8th of February, 1734, appoints

Corbet Kynaston, of Hordley, William Lacon Child, of Kinlet, Richard
Lyster, of Rowton, John Mytton, of Halstone, John Powys, of Berwick,
Borlace Wingfield, of Preston-Brockhurst, Andrew Corbet, of Albright-Hus-
sey, Adam Ottley, of Pitchford, Richard Jenkins, of Abby Foregate, and
Thomas Hill, of Tern. Esqs. together with John Lloyd, Esq. Mr. Robert
Wood, Apothecary, and Mr. Thomas Barnes, Attorney, to be Trustees to his
Will, and appoints the said John Lloyd, Robert Wood, and Thomas Barnes,
to be his Executors.

After bequeathing certain lands and tenements, the testator directs,

That his trustees shall purchase, in the most public or convenient place,
in Frankwell, sufficient ground, to build thereon an hospital, with twelve
dwelling houses, and a common kitchen, for twelve poor decayed housekeepers of Frankwell, who are single persons, and have lived in good repute ; to
be approved of by the trustees ; and likewise a charity school for educating
twenty poor boys, and twenty poor girls, with a convenient school-house, and
habitations for a school-master and mistress, and to settle and establish a public
and perpetual hospital and charity school.

† Mr. Elisha's M. S. S.

---

* The lepers are succeeded by four poor persons, who inhabit the same number of alms-houses,
nearly adjoining the church of St. Giles, which was doubtless the chapel of the old hospital.   They
were rebuilt about half a century ago.   By what means the lands charged with their maintenance came
into the family of Prince does not appear : but their connection with it was as early as the beginning
of the 17th century, when Walter Wrottesley, Esq. of Wrottesley, whose daughter married Sir Richard
Prince, bequeaths £100 thereunto, and the said Sir Richard Prince occurs as " Master of the hospital
of St. " Giles," in 1632, and the same office is now held by the Earl of Tankerville, probably as
possessor of certain estates.   His Lordship nominates the alms-people, to each of whom he pays 1s. 6d.
per week, with a certain allowance of coals and an upper garment annually, the whole payment amounting to £19 per annum.   The original donation by Henry II. of thirty shillings per annum, is still paid
by the sheriff of the county, and is allowed to him in his " cravings" at the exchequer.—*Owen's Account of Shrewsbury.*

Further, that twenty poor boys, and twenty poor girls, inhabitants in Frankwell, if there to be found, otherwise out of the parish of St. Chad, in that part nearest to Frankwell, should be first chose; the children to be of the age of six years, or near it, and to be there educated, until they can read well, and repeat the church catechism by memory.

Also, That the trustees do appoint a discreet school-master and mistress, the former, to qualify the boys to be put out apprentices, and the latter, to instruct the girls in knitting and sewing, to make them fit for reputable services. The master's salary to be £10 yearly, (unless the chaplain be master;) the mistress's salary also to be £10 yearly, and both to be paid half yearly. If the master is a married man, and has a sober careful wife, she is to have the preference.

Also, The children to be cloathed twice in every year, for ever, at Midsummer and Christmas, with a decent suit of cloaths of 20s. value, to be provided by the trustees; and if any boys, after education here, should go to the free grammar school, all books wanting, and necessary for them should be provided. A discreet and episcopally ordained clergyman, chose by the trustees, is directed to read prayers every school day, at seven o'clock in the morning, and five in the evening, in summer, and at eight and four in the winter; and to have a salary of £20 yearly, to be paid quarterly. If the chaplain is master, then the £10 appointed for the master, to be paid to the chaplain, added to the £20 allowed for his salary.

Also, By the said will is further given, the yearly sum of £40 to two scholars, chosen by the trustees, who shall be admitted, and reside in Magdalen College, Cambridge, and who before such admission, had been educated at the said charity school, and free grammar school in Shrewsbury, if such are to be found in the said college, otherwise to two scholars, that shall be born in Frankwell, and educated at the free grammar school, having been one complete year upon the upper form in the head school, to be paid by half yearly payments, and within half a year after admission, and to continue eight years. The scholars to reside, keep their terms, and take their degrees, according to the statutes and customs of the college and university, not to be absent above three months in the year, and that not in term time, unless in case of sickness, or some other sufficient cause, to be allowed by the trustees. If any scholar, educated at the said charity and free grammar school, and admitted an exhibitioner in Magdalen College, shall take his degrees, and be ordained; in such case, the clergyman not so qualified must resign, and the trustees are directed to elect such exhibitioner in his stead, and to continue such method for ever.

A charity sermon is also appointed to be preached, at St. Chad's church, yearly, upon the 1st of August, (now the 12th) being the testator's birth day, unless it happen upon a Sunday, and then to be on the Monday following; for which, the preaching clergyman is to have twenty shillings.

When the boys attain the age of fourteen years, three of them, if so many there be, are directed to be put apprentices to husbandry business, or such trades as the trustees shall judge proper ; to have £7. 10s. given to each master, with each boy, and £2. 10s. to be laid out in cloathing ; also, £5. to be paid to such apprentices, who have behaved themselves well during their apprenticeship, and set up in business ; to be paid them at the end of twelve months, from the time of their first setting up.

Further, That the 12 poor decayed single housekeepers, inhabitants of Frankwell, or in that part of St. Chad's parish nearest to Frankwell, who are admitted into the hospital, after their admittance, shall be annually paid £3 10s. each, by quarterly payments ; also a load of coal for each, value 10s. on All Saints Day, and a new coat, gown, or upper garment, value 10s. upon St. Thomas's Day.

Also directs, That the trustees do on St. Thomas's Day, yearly, distribute to ten more poor decayed housekeepers in Frankwell, if there are so many, otherwise in the street or streets nearest to Frankwell, in the parish of St. Chad, ten new coats, gowns, or upper garments, of the value of 10s. each ; and when any vacancy shall happen in the hospital, that poor person is to be elected out of the ten, who has longest received the coats, or gowns, out of the hospital. And further, that twenty-two penny loaves shall be given to so many poor people in Frankwell, or places adjoining, who have been cloathed as aforesaid, every Sunday, provided they come to church, and attend during the time of divine service there.

No dissenter, or dissenters, of any sect or denomination whatsoever, to have any benefit from this charity, not even though born in Frankwell, unless of the true orthodox principles of the Church of England.

The trustees to meet yearly, upon Candlemas Day, (unless Sunday) to audit the accounts ; the expence of the day to be allowed, not exceeding forty shillings.

The real estate of Mr. Millington, the founder, was disputed in chancery, and went to the heirs at law ; his personal estate, about £8000, to the use of this charity.

Through the increased value of lands, the trustees* have been enabled to augment the master's salary to £16, the mistress's to £15, each of the poor houskeepers to £4, and also some of the other bequests in proportion.†

† A progressive increase in the value of lands since the time of Mr. Phillips has afforded succeed-

THE CHARITY SCHOOL,† in Back Lane, founded in the year 1724, pursuant to the will of Mr. Thomas Bowdler,‡ Alderman of Shrewsbury, who left £1000, to erect and endow a charity school, in the parish of St. Julian, for the education of poor children in the said parish, if such are to be found, if not, out of the parish of Holy Cross.

THE SUBSCRIPTION CHARITY SCHOOL,§ for instructing and

---

ing Trustees additional opportunities of extending the benefits of the institution, and of augmenting the salaries of its operative managers.

There are at present 25 boys educated, who are allowed one suit of clothes each, annually, and are supplied gratuitously with hats, shoes, stockings, and shirts twice a year. After the period of a scholars' education is completed, he is allowed £10 5s. as a premium to place him out apprentice to some good and reputable trade; he is also presented with a bible and a prayer book on leaving the school; and with a further sum of £5 after the term of his apprenticeship is expired, provided he has conducted himself in a becoming manner and completed the whole term.

Twenty-five girls are also educated, and supplied gratuitously with frocks, skirts, shifts, caps, tippets, aprons, stockings, and shoes, twice a year; and each girl is presented with a bible and prayer book on leaving the school, and also allowed the sum of £3 to buy suitable clothing to equip her for a decent service. On producing satisfactory testimonials of having conducted herself properly in her first service for one year, she is presented with an additional sum of three pounds.

	£	s.	d.
Present Master, Mr. Thomas Groves, salary	50	0	0
——— Secretary, Ditto Ditto Ditto	10	10	0
——— School Mistress, Mrs. Bishop, salary	42	0	0

To 12 Hospitalers TEN guineas, three tons of coal, and two gowns each, are allowed annually, besides house and garden rent free, and one shilling's worth of bread per week.

To 10 Hospitalers FOUR pounds each per year are paid, with gowns, bread, &c. as the others.

Chaplain to the institution, the Rev. J. Matthews, M. A. salary £50 per annum.

EDITOR.

---

† It is also called the Blue School from the dress of the Scholars. That honour to our town, to the kingdom, and to Literature, THE REVEREND SAMUEL LEE, professor of Arabic, &c. in the University of Cambridge, and Rector of Bilton with Harrogate, was sometime master of this school.

The present Master is Mr. Sharrat. Mrs. Humphreys is school Mistress.

Number of boys in the school 18. Ditto of girls 12.

EDITOR.

---

‡ Mr. Thomas Bowdler was very highly esteemed by his fellow townsmen. In the year 1705 he served the office of mayor. From some feeling or other he resigned the office of alderman in the year 1719. The corporation expressed their regret on the occasion, and spoke of him "as a worthy man," &c. He died a bachelor July 10th, 1724, and was buried in St. Julian's Church.

EDITOR.

---

§ SUBSCRIPTION CHARITY SCHOOL, or Brown School as it is often called from the dress of the cloathing poor children, begun in the year 1708. The children enjoying the benefit of this charity, were for many years, taught in a large room in the Sextry, or King's-Head Shut. Upon a change in the owners of the buildings, of which this room was a part, there was a necessity for the school to be removed, since which the scholars have been divided, and several inconveniencies have turned up; but a School House is now erected near the Abbey Church for this purpose, which is expected to answer the ends for which it is immediately intended.

THE RULES.

1. All subscribers of sixteen shillings a year, or upwards, are trustees, out of whom a treasurer is yearly chosen, who is impowered to call the trustees together, as often as he sees occasion: and every person subscribing the said sum of sixteen shillings a year, or upwards, has a right of recommending a child for every sixteen shillings subscribed.

2. A master is provided to teach the boys reading, who has also a share of the senior girls put under his care, and is allowed a salary proportioned to the number of scholars taught by him. A mistress is also provided, by whom the junior girls are taught reading, and all the girls instructed in plain sewing, and knitting.

---

scholars, is now the National School. From the adoption of Dr. Bell's System of instruction the original foundation of this school has undergone no essential change whatever.

THE RULES AT PRESENT ARE

1. That all Subscribers of one guinea and upwards be Trustees; and for every guinea subscribed, a child may be recommended to be instructed and clothed annually.

2. That each Subscriber be entitled to nominate, for every guinea subscribed, an additional child for education only, on payment of five shillings per annum for such additional child.

3. That no child be admitted under six years of age, without permission of the Committee.

4. That the children be taught reading, writing, and accounts, on the national system; and the girls also plain sewing and knitting.

5. That the children likewise be instructed in the catechism, and regularly taken to church on Sundays.

6. That books be provided at the expense of the charity.

7. That a General meeting of the Trustees be held yearly on the *First Tuesday in April*, to examine into the state of the school, and pass such orders as may be necessary for its government and support.

8. That seven Trustees be elected annually, at the general meeting, who, with the Treasurer and Secretary, do form a Committee, for the purpose of conducting the concerns of the school, any three of whom may act —*Occasional visits, it is hoped, also will be made by the subscribers in general, since nothing contributes so much to the success of such establishments as regular and frequent inspection.*

9. That a President be annually appointed, and a Sermon preached for the benefit of the Charity.

Present Master Mr. Blount, number of boys 127. Present Mistress, Mrs. Bennett, number of girls 104.

Salary of the Master £50 per annum. Ditto of the Mistress £26 per annum.

EDITOR.

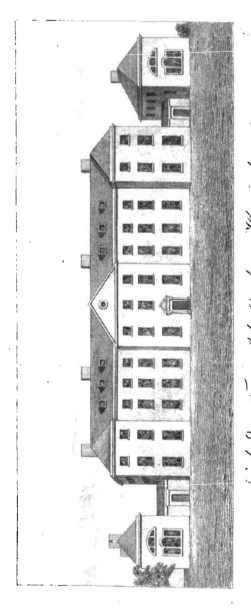

North East Front of the Orphan Hospital. 1776.

Eng.d from the Original for Hulbert's new edition of Phillips' History of Shrewsbury by C. Askin. [...]

3. The children are taught their catechism, with an explanation of it, and brought to church regularly every Sunday.

4. The scholars are to be upwards of eight, and under thirteen years of age.

5. The parents of the children are to provide them books, a number of which are provided for the purpose, off the society for promoting christian knowledge, which the trustees direct to be disposed of, at an easy rate.

THE ORPHAN HOSPITAL—A House for the reception of several Orphans from the Foundling Hospital at London, was first opened in Dog Lane, in the year 1759, and continued so, till the present large and elegant building was erected on the bank of Severn, opposite the Quarry. This house was begun in 1760, and finished in five years, by direction of proper persons, appointed by and at the expence of the managers of the hospital at London. Children were sent down in their infancy, and put out to nurse in the country for many miles about, under the inspection of neighbouring gentlemen, and at a proper age were brought into the house, where, under the care of proper masters and mistresses, the boys and girls were instructed in sewing, knitting, carding, spinning, and the several other branches of a woollen manufactory, begun and carried on there; until at a proper age to put out apprentices.

For several years past, the managers of the London hospital, have not thought proper to send any more children, the house of consequence, broke up, and has been for some time uninhabited, excepting in one part, where a considerable manufactory in the woollen branch is carried on, by Messrs. James and Thomas Baker. Some of the lodging rooms have also in the summer time (by permission) been occupied by some valetudinarians, who have for a time left the town, to enjoy the benefit and pleasure of so desirable, beautiful, and healthful a situation.

The expence of erecting this building, was above £12,000.* It consists of a front with two wings, and all necessary out-houses, and other conveniencies.

Application is intended to be made to the Governours of the Foundling Hospital at London. by the several parishes in this town, who have in view the renting of this House, to make use of it as a general Poor House: but the

* The history of this expensive building and of a *few only* of its inmates since the year 1765 to the present period would indeed be curious, but who is equal to the task? The most learned, the best qualified historians of Shrewsbury have left it unattempted. It would therefore be folly and presumption in me to make the effort. Some additional particulars will, however, be found in another place, at present I shall content myself with remarking, that shortly after the conclusion of Mr. Phillips's History, the Orphan House was made a receptacle for Dutch and French prisoners of war. In 1784 "An Act of Parliament was obtained to incorporate the five parishes of the Town and Meole Brace as far as concerns the

particulars respecting rent, time, &c. are not yet determined on by any of the parties.

ST. CHAD'S ALMSHOUSES, for decayed, and old men and women, in St. Chad's Church Yard. These houses were founded in the year 1409, by Mr. Bennet Tupton, alias Tipton, a common beer brewer, who dwelt in the College, in St. Chad's Church Yard. The following extract,* relates some particulars relative to the founder, and his family.

" This yeare 1409, one Bennett Tupton, being a common Beere Bruar,
" and dwellinge in St. Chadd's Churche Yarde in Shrousberie, now callid the
" colledge, founded the Almeshowses in the sayde St. Chadd's Churche Yarde
" in Shrousberie beinge then a Man at that tyme of 60 yeares of age."

" And, 1424 This Yeare and in the seconde Yeare of King Henry the 6th.
" one Bennett Tupton Beere Bruar dyed, who dwellyd in a brue howse in St.
" Chadd's Churche Yard in Shrousberie, which afterwards was, and nowe of late
" days, ys callid the colledge†, and was buried in St. Chadd's Churche; who

* Dr. Taylor's M. S.

---

poor, and to establish a general House of Industry." The Orphan House was therefore purchased with twenty acres of Land for £5,500, and about £700 was expended in repairs. In December the same year, the house was opened for the reception of Paupers, under the management of a Board of Directors, consisting of John Oliver, Esq. William Smith, Esq. Thomas Lloyd, Esq. John Maddock, Esq. Robert Jeffreys, Esq. John Bather, Esq. Mr. Joseph Gittins, Mr. John Lloyd, Mr. Charles Bage, Mr. John Jones, Mr. Thomas Hotchkiss, and Mr. George Lloyd.

The proportion of money to defray the expences of the establishment, to be paid by the united parishes, was fixed and ascertained " according to the average expenditure of each for twelve years, prior to the passing of the act, and which amounted in the whole to £2,761 16s. 8¼ per annum, viz.

	£.	s.	d.		£.	s.	d.
St. Chad	1276	15	11¼	St. Alkmond	271	0	6¼
St. Mary	479	18	5¼	Holy Cross and St. Giles	303	12	0¼
St. Julian	314	3	8	Meole Brace	116	5	11¼

These proportions being at length considered by the inhabitants of some of the parishes as disproportionate, in the year 1826 a new act was obtained repealing the former act, and directing that each parish shall pay the expenses of its own poor while in the house.

The directors continue in office for one year, are nominated by the vestries of their respective parishes, and elected by the Directors in office. One half the number retire each six months, so that the difficulties of an entirely new board of direction can never be experienced.—EDITOR.

† "The College of St. Chad adjoined the south-western end of the church. No plan remains to ascertain with exactness its original state. It has, however, been described to us, as it existed about seventy years ago, by an intelligent lady, who had passed the greater portion of a long life within its walls. From her account, it appears to have been an ancient structure of red stone, inclosing a small quadrangular court, shut out from the street by a wall twelve or fourteen feet in height, with a gateway,

" laft behynd hym a daughter of hys namy'd Blase Tupton, who cam by chance
" to be a Leeper, and made the Oryell which goythe alonge the west syde of
" the sayde Churche Yarde, and so cam a Loft to heare Servys through a Doore
" made in the Churche Walle, and so passy'd usually uppon the Leades unto a
" glasse wyndowe through which she dayly sawe, and hard dayly Servys as
" longe as she lyvy'd."

Though Mr. Bennet Tupton founded these houses, it does not appear that
he endowed them,* the first deed or grant we find any account of, is mentioned

---

the upper part or tower of which had been taken down. On the south side was a long range of building, before the entrance of which was a porch opening to a lobby that led to what was called the *Great
Chamber*, a spacious room with two fireplaces, on the south side. It was lighted by a Gothick bow
window, in which were some roundels of stained glass, glazed tiles, and a raised boarded platform for
the high table. Other chambers adjoined this. On the east side was a mound next the church yard,
from which extended a gallery or cloister, leading to the church; and on the spot now occupied by
the stables northward, was a terrace guarded by a low wall planted with sycamore trees."

" No plan remains by which we can point out the precise extent of the collegiate precinct, but
various circumstances conspire to prove that it embraced the whole south side of College Hill, and the
street called Murivance or Swan Hill as far as Caym's Place, now the residence of the Rev. Archdeacon Owen, which is separated from the college precinct by a substantial wall of old red stone. From
Caym's Place it passed, and apparently nearly in a straight line, into the street now called Belmont,
anciently Chedde Lode, or Priest Lode, which it followed till it reached the almshouses, and passing
along then to Kiln Lane, certainly comprised the Sextry, formerly the Sacristy, an ancient stone
building, still in part remaining, and giving to the alley in which it stands the name of Sextry Shut.
This building, in which were reposited the church plate, vestments, &c. was connected with the
church by a half timbered building which passed over Kiln Lane, and left an open passage for the
publick beneath it. This covered way was, no doubt, provided for the convenience of the sacristan
when he had occasion to pass to the choir. Mr. Phillips had seen MSS. which mentioned that the
shut next to that of the Sextry, called Steelyard Shut, was the residence of the prebendaries, and that
they also made use of this covered way, descending from it into the *Dimmery*, and from thence ascending by a flight of stairs into the church."—*Owen and Blakeway's History of Shrewsbury.*

---

* Tupton seems to have been content with erecting these houses, and made no provision for the
poor who were to inhabit them, unless the payment by the mercer's company proceeds from him.
David Ireland, alderman, bequeathed £100 for this purpose, to which his wife Catherine, who afterwards
married Robert Dudley, of Dudley, Esq. M. P. for this borough added £80. In lieu hereof her sons
Robert and Thomas Ireland settled, under the direction of their kinsman Judge Owen, the founder of
the Cundover family, an annual rent charge of £8 issuing out of their estate at Lythwood, which is still
paid by the owners of that estate, who nominate the paupers.*

The present allowance to the poor is not more than 16s. per annum, including two shillings and
two-pence annually paid by the company of mercers.

These alms-houses are wretched hovels, and by their projection into the street, are a great inconvenience to the public. The comfort of the poor inhabitants, and the public accommodation, call for
their removal to some other situation. The habitations were originally thirteen in number, but as there
is no fund for keeping them in repair two have fallen to decay.—*Owen's Account of Shrewsbury.*

---

* Mrs. Powys of Berwick House, and T. Parr, Esq. of Lythwood Hall, are the present nominators.
From some cause or other, the allowance to the poor inmates is reduced to 14s. 7¼d. each, per annum.

EDITOR.

R

in a subsequent deed dated 23d Eliz. 1591, between Richard Owen of Salop, Draper, and Roger Luter of Preston-Gobal's, Gent. which grant refers to certain covenants, agreement, &c. in indentures dated 20th of April, 7th Edward VI. 1554. (This last mentioned deed is lost, which was the original grant of £4 per ann. issuing out of Lythwood to these Alms-houses,) made between Thomas and Robert Ireland, Gents. on the one part, and Thomas Bromley, Knt. Geo. Hosyer, Thomas Byrington, Hugh Edwards, Gents. and others therein specified, being burgesses and inhabitants of Shrewsbury, on the other part, in trust by the said Irelands reposed in them, that they the said parties above-mentioned did grant and confirm, to Thomas Owen, Serjeant at Law, and eleven other persons therein mentioned, Burgesses and Aldermen of Shrewsbury, one yearly rent of £4 issuing out of one half of a certain wood, and woodlands, ground, and pasture, called Lythwood, which then late was the lands of the said Irelands; to have and receive the same in trust to them and their heirs for ever, to the intent that the said £4 should be yearly paid, and equally distributed to the poor in St. Chad's Alms-houses for their relief.

The next deed is dated 15th of March, 14th James I. 1616, assigned by the last surviving trustees, to John Webb and John Hunt, Gents. Burgesses and Aldermen of Shrewsbury on the one part, the Bailiffs and Burgesses of Shrewsbury on the second part, and the Church Wardens and Parishioners of St. Chad's on the third part. It is probable these trustees afterwards assigned to a certain number of others, as on a duplicate of a deed, in the parish Chest, mark'd No. 19, the name of Richard Lea, Gent. is indorsed, supposed to be the last surviving trustee, which name does not appear in the deeds there, mark'd N⁰ˢ 19 and 20. These last trustees neglecting to assign their trust, the possessors of Lythwood estate have the management of the said Alms-houses, viz. Tho. Jelfe Powis of Berwick, and Joshua Blakeway of Lythwood, Esqrs.

In order to preserve this charity in trust as before-mentioned, (which trust is now lost) the minister or reader of St. Chad's for the time being, was directed to read the above-mentioned deed publickly, before divine service, on one day in Whitsun-week yearly, for ever.

The present allowance to the poor in these houses, in consequence of the above grant, does not exceed 14s. per ann. to each; but the parish of St. Chad augments the charity by a weekly allowance to such of them who are parishioners. Leland in his Itinerary says, " The Mercers Company maintain these poor ;" if they do, it is at a very moderate expence, they paying only 2s. 2d. per ann. to all the houses, which being 13 in number, amounts only to the sum of 2d. to each.

ST. MARY'S ALMSHOUSES, in Ox Lane, near St. Mary's Church, were founded in the reign of Edward IV. about the year 1460, by Digery Waters, a Draper of Shrewsbury, who died the 28th July 1477, and was buried in Trinity Chapel in St. Mary's Church. The founder himself lived in the hall house among the poor people, and it was his constant practice to go with them to St. Mary's Church, where he would kneel among them in a long pew made for them and himself.† An effigy of the founder appears over the porch of the hall house, in the middle of the Almshouses,* with the name of Digery Waters round it, and opposite to that figure, another of the founder at full length, with a female partner, (probably his wife) who have stood there, hand in hand, during many storms and changes, both of men and manners. On the front of the said porch is the figure of Edward the IVth, with a long poetic inscription underneath, the same as under the same King's picture in Drapers Hall, which we shall copy when treating of that place.

The following Rules were agreed upon respecting these Houses, 29th Elizabeth, 1587.

"The Wardens of St. Mary's parish to name four poor people upon every

† Dr. Taylor's M. S.

---

* The Almshouses described by Phillips were sixteen in number, of the most wretched description, consisting of one single apartment 11 feet by 8, without any outlet, and were long a nuisance to the neighbourhood and the respectable street in which they were situated.

To the high honour of the Drapers Company these wretched hovels no longer exist, in the year 1824 they were entirely taken down, and fifteen new ones erected on the opposite side the street, after a design by Mr. John Carline, which are a credit to the Architect, to the Drapers Company, and the Town. Sixteen houses were comprehended in the design, but from some misunderstanding between the company and a proprietor of the property adjoining, the ground intended for one house has not been built upon; a small dwelling in the yard is however provided to complete the number, sixteen, and the whole are very comfortable indeed. The sum of £1. 2s. 3d. is paid quarterly to the poor occupants.

The following are the present rules to be observed by the inmates, as exhibited on a board in the gateway or entrance from Ox Lane, now St. Mary's Street.

1. " Any person who shall now, or at any time hereafter be permitted to enter upon either of these houses as occupier shall be tenant at will to the Drapers Company, and shall be liable to be removed, on receiving seven days notice from the masters or wardens of the said company.

2. No inmate shall, upon any pretence whatever, take in any lodger, nor shall any relatives or friends of the inmates reside with them, except by special permission in writing from the master or wardens of the said company.

3. The inmates must keep their respective dwellings clean and neat, must sweep before their doors at least twice every week, and upon no account throw any water, filth, or ashes into the church yard, or through their windows into the street.

4. Each inmate must attend divine service at St. Mary's church morning and evening every sabbath, except in cases of illness.

5. Any inmate violating either of these rules, and every one whose irregularity of conduct shall be complained of, and proved satisfactory to the company by any respectable neighbours, and especially by the Minister or Church wardens of the parish of St. Mary's, will be immediately expelled.

These Rules to be altered by the Drapers Company in such manner or as often as they shall think fit; such alterations shall be considered binding upon the occupiers."—EDITOR.

R2

" vacancy, and the Master of the Drapers Company, and the said Wardens
" to chuse one of the four.

" Their age to be above 50.—To be single persons, except in the hall
" house, where there must always be a man and his wife, and at the death of
" one of them, the survivor to go into a common house, and another man and
" his wife to be chose for the hall.

" Each person admitted, to bring with them a winding sheet, with 4d.
" wrapt up in it to pay for their burial.

" Each of the 14 houses to have 9 load of wood yearly, the hall house
" 12 load, and a bushel of corn every month."†

Several of the above-mentioned rules are not now observed, however
none are at present admitted but parishoners of St. Mary's, who have allowed
them, and paid by the Drapers Company, £2. 6s. 10½. per ann. at quarterly
payments, and an upper garment once in two years.

THE FREE SCHOOLS. King Edward VI. by his Letters Patent, dated
10th Feb. 1552, in the 6th year of his reign, directed that there should be
one Grammar School in Shrewsbury, to endure for ever, and appoints one
head Schoolmaster, and one under Master, also grants the Bailiffs and Burgesses all his tythes of sheaf-blade, grain, and hay, yearly, in the towns, fields,
parishes and hamlets of Astley, Sansaw, Cliffe, Letton, and Almond Park ;
and likewise all tythes of sheaf-blade, &c. in the towns, fields, &c. of Frankwell, Betton, Woodcot, Horton, Bicton, Calcot, Shelton, Whitley, and Welbach ; and also all rents and profits that may arise therefrom ; which tythe, &c.
did then extend to the clear yearly value of £20. 8s. He also appoints
the Bailiffs, with the Burgesses and their successors, to nominate and appoint
one Schoolmaster, and one under Master, and the said Bailiffs and Burgesses,
with the consent of the Bishop of Litchfield and Coventry, to make statutes
and ordinances.

By the aforesaid authority the Bailiffs appointed the Rev. Mr. Thomas
Ashton head Master, and Mr. Thomas Lawrence, Under Master of the said
school.

The above mentioned grant was procured from King Edward VI. by
Hugh Edwards,* of the college in Shrewsbury, Gent.

† M. S.

---

* " The college estates were, as we have seen, leased out by the crown in 1548 to a Mr. Beaton.
But the scite itself of the college was in the following year granted by Edward VI. to John Southcote and John Chaderton, and from them passed to the family of Edwards ; and in all probability to

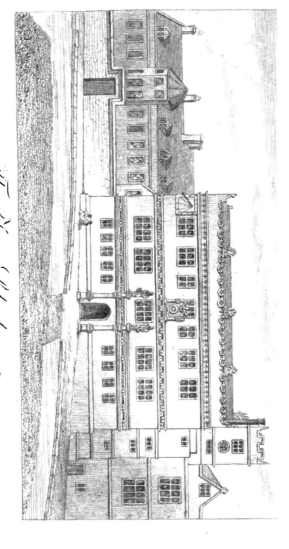

The Free Schools 1778

Engd from the Original, for Hulberts new edition of Phillips's History of Shrewsbury by Cha. Baker 1834

Queen Elizabeth, under the Great Seal of England, bearing date 23d of May, 1571, in the 13th year of her reign, granted to the Bailiffs and Burgesses of the town of Shrewsbury, the rectory of Chirbury, belonging to the priory of Chirbury, with all tenths of corn and hay, in Wylmington, Wooderton, Stockton, Chirbury, Winsbury, Dudston, Walcot, Hookleton, Prescot, Weston, Marynton, Tymbrick, Rorington, and Middleton, in the county of Salop, also all other tenths, oblations, profits, and emoluments whatsoever, belonging to the said priory.

She also gave the advowson, and right of patronage to the church, with all glebes, tithes, profits, and commodities thereunto belonging, which King Edward 6th. had leased in the first year of his reign to Wm. Bilmore, for £31 6s. 10d. per ann.

The lands called Provender's lands, in Shelton, of the yearly rent of three shillings and four-pence, were added by Queen Elizabeth to the above grants, for all which tithes and rents so granted, the trustees for the school were bound to pay the Queen and her successors, the yearly sum of £10. 12s. 3d. and likewise sundry other incumbrances, to pay to the Vicar of Chirbury, the Minister of St. Mary's in Shrewsbury, and to the Clive and Astley chapels within the parish of St. Mary.

She likewise granted all the tithes of corn, grain, and hay, in Albrighton, and all small tithes in the Castle-foregate, belonging to the late college of St. Mary, and also all her Highness's lands in Astley, and Sansaw, for which certain chief rent still continue to be paid, together with all the profits coming of the spiritual jurisdiction of the College of St. Mary, rented for £1. 6s. 8d. and the profits growing, or renewing of the Easter book, the whole let to Thomas Kelton, at £11. 5s. 9½. per ann.

After the decease of the abovesaid Thomas Kelton, his widow applied for a renewal of her lease of the tithes, upon which the Queen wrote to the Bailiffs, &c. on her behalf. The original letter is in the school-chest in the Exchequer, of which the following is a copy, obtained by favour of the Head Master.

Hugh Edwards, the descendant of an ancient family long seated at Kilhendre in the chapelry of Dudleston, and tenth in descent from Idon, upon whom his father Rhys Sais (a descendant of the great Tudor Trevor) settled his estates at Dudleston. Mr. Edwards, being a younger son, repaired to the capital for the purpose of engaging in commerce, and was of that city in 1549, when Edward VI. on December 14th, granted to him and William Knight, both of London, mercers, ten messuages, twenty-six gardens, and half a pigeon-house, parcel of the late dissolved college of St. Chad. But he was of Shrewsbury in 1551, when he was so instrumental in obtaining the foundation of our Free Grammar School, and seems to be the same who occurs by the name of Hugh ap Edwarde, as warden of the drapers' company here in 1562. He was buried at St. Chad's."
Owen and Blakeway's History of Shrewsbury.

The Queen's name is an exact copy of her own hand writing, except being reduced to onehalf its size in the original.

" By the Queen,

" Trusty and well beloved, we greete you well : Whereas among other " parcells of landes passed unto you by our late grante, there is contayned one " small parcell of tithes belonging to the parish of St Mary in that our towne " of Shrewesbury of the yearelye rent of 20 Markes or theareabouts, then, and " nowe in the tenure of Mary Kelton gentlewoman, widowe, whereof the yeares " are almost expired, Whereupon she hath made humble suite unto us, that " forasmuch as it is not nowe in our power to renewe hir estate in the sayd " tithes according as we use to extend like favours to our tenantes upon surren- " ders, the same being passed from us to you, and that it hath bene left to hir " by her late husband for a staie and relief, both to hir during hir lief and after- " wardes to hir children, to whom theire father deceased hath lefte but small " living besides, so as if this were taken from them theie were like to fall into " distresse : We have in consideration thereof been moved to recommend hir " suit unto you, that is, that upon surrender of hir presente estate you will make " unto hir a new Lease of the sayd tithes for the terme of 30 yeares, at the " rent accustomed, and without fyne, as at our request, wch we thinke we maye " the rather require at your handes, for that both the sayd parcell of tythes, " and manie other thinges, were in our late graunte, freely and without charge " by us given to you. And therefore we doe looke that this so reasonable a " request, being for the reliefe of a widowe and fatherless children, shall not " be denied, but rather graunted with suche favour and expedition as we may " have cause to thinke our late benefite to you bestowed on thankfull parsons. " Given under our Signet at the Mannor of Grenwiche the Sixtenth day of " November 1588, in the Thirtith yeare of our Reigne.

" To our trusty and well-beloved the Bayliffs, Burgesses,
  " and Head Schoolmaster of the Towne of Shrewes-   " ex **Flake.**"
  " bury that now be, and that hereafter for the tyme
  " shall be."

All these grants were made subject to such ordinances, as should be drawn up by Mr. Thomas Ashton the first master, and according to these ordinances the affairs of the schools have been conducted ever since.

There are now four masters, viz. one Chief or Head Master, two Under Masters, and an Accidence Master.

The School was originally a timber building, but in the year 1595 a fine range of stone building was finished, the ground floor of which is the Chapel. Prayers are read here every morning by the Head Master, (who is likewise Reader and Catechist) before the scholars go into school, and every evening when they go out. The Chapel was consecrated on the 10th day of May, 1617, by the Bishop of Lichfield and Coventry, the consecration sermon being preached by Dr. Sampson Price, a native of this town, and Vicar of Christ Church, London, who for his hatred of Popery, was called, "The maul and scourge of heretics."

Over the Chapel is the Library, which contains a large and valuable collection of books. One entire side consists of a great and elegant assortment, collected, and bequeathed by the late John Taylor, L. L. D. a native of the town, and educated here. At the one end of the Library is a repository of natural and artificial curiosities.

In the year 1630 another building was finished, joining to the former at right angles, in the same stile, and consisting of the same materials. The whole of the Attic story contains the three upper schools, being 82 feet in length. The ground floor, is the accidence school on one side the gateway, and the third master's house on the other. The middle story contains the upper rooms in the third master's house, and the accidence master's apartment, which has for many years been used as a writing school. The whole of the buildings with the masters houses make a very fine appearance, resembling a college, and handsomer than many in both Universities.*

The school revenue is now very large. The masters have handsome salaries. The foundation† (by the legacies of pious benefactors of latter times) is possessed of many valuable scholarships and exhibitions in both Oxford and Cambridge.

An account of the reception and entertainment of Sir Henry Sidney by the scholars here, is related in the chapter of Ancient History, to which may be added the following account transcribed from the same ancient manuscript.‡

‡ Dr. Taylor's M. S. S.

---

* Within these late years the Schools, Houses, &c. belonging to the Foundation have been greatly improved and beautified, to which have been appended by, and are the property of the present Head Master, handsome and commodious Halls, for the reception of Boarders on a very extensive scale. Some of the most Learned and Popular Men now in the United Kingdom have been educated at Shrewsbury School.—EDITOR.

† For some time previous to the year 1798, this noble foundation had been in a declining state; defects in its laws and government were urged as the cause, consequently a new act was obtained in the year above named, for the better government and regulation thereof. By this act the manage-

"This Yeare 1568 at Whytsuntyde was a noble stage playe, played at "Shrosbery, which lastyd all the holly dayes, unto the which cam greate num- "bers of people, of Noblemen and others, the which was praysed greately,

---

ment of the revenues, and the removal or discharge of the masters, who are reduced from *four* to *two*, is vested in the Bishop of Lichfield and Coventry as visitor, and thirteen trustees or governors, of whom the Mayor of the Town, for the time being is one. The appointment of masters rests solely in St. John's College, Cambridge: the salary of the head master, for the time being, not to be less than £120 per annum, clear of all deductions, over and besides the use and occupation of a school house to reside in, free of all taxes whatsoever. The salary of the second master not to be less than £80, clear of all deductions, with a house to live in, free of all taxes, &c. provided that the said masters do teach and instruct in the said school, such boys as are LEGITIMATE SONS OF BURGESSES of the Town of SHREWSBURY, GRATIS, and without ANY FEE, or reward whatever.

The nomination of Ushers and mode of instruction is within the sole power of the head master. The presentation to the benefices of St. Mary, Shrewsbury, to Astley, Clive, and Chirbury, is vested in the Corporation at large.

The following list of exhibitions from Shrewsbury School will shew the great advantages presented to meritorious scholars :—

" Four Foundation Exhibitions to St. John's College, Cambridge, £70 per Annum each, for Seven Years. Qualifications :—SONS OF BURGESSES ; in Default of these, Boys born in the Parish of Chirbury ; in Default of these, Boys born in the County of Salop. IN ALL CASES, Candidates to bring Certificates from the Head Master, of having duly attended the School for the space of Two Years immediately preceding, and also of their Learning, good Morals, and Behaviour. Electors, the Trustees of Shrewsbury School.

Four Exhibitions to St. John's College, Cambridge, Value about £15 each. To these the Col- lege elect any Boys from Shrewsbury School.

Four Scholarships, founded by the Rev. J. MILLINGTON, D. D. at Magdalen College, Cambridge, for any Boys who have been Two Years or more at Shrewsbury School, of which a Certificate is necessary from the Head and Second Master. For these Exhibitions, Residence is required during the greater Part of each Term. Present Value, Sixty Guineas a Year each. Electors, the Master and Fellows of Magdalen College, Cambridge.

A Bye-Fellowship, founded by the Rev. J. MILLINGTON, D. D. in Magdalen College, Cambridge, appropriate to a Boy educated at Shrewsbury School. Present Value, 120 Guineas per Annum. Elec- tors, the Masters and Fellows of Magdalen College.

Two Scholarships, by Mr. JAMES MILLINGTON :—1st. For Two Boys who are born in Frank- well, and go from the School in Millington's Hospital to the Royal Free Grammar School in Shrews- bury, and from thence to Magdalen College, Cambridge. 2d. In Default of these, to Boys educated at Shrewsbury School. Electors, the Trustees of Millington's Hospital. Present Value, £40 per Annum each.

Four Exhibitions to Christ Church, Oxford, founded by Mr. CARESWELL, for Boys educated at Shrewsbury School, being Natives of the County of Salop. Examiners, the Dean of Christ Church or his Deputy. Electors, Two or more Justices of the Peace for the County of Salop. In case any of the Schools cannot fill up their Vacancies, they must be filled up from Shrewsbury School ; or if from any of the other Schools, the Examination must take place at Shrewsbury. Present Value, £60 a Year each.

Two, by Mr. OSWALD SMITH, formerly Second-Master. Open to both Universities. Qualifica- tions, the same as for the Foundation Exhibitions. Electors, the Head Master, Second Master, and Minister of St. Mary's, Shrewsbury. Residence during the greater Part of each Term is required. Present Value, £25 each per Annum.

One, founded by Dr. TAYLOR, the learned Editor of Demosthenes. Open to both Universities, and to any Boys educated at Shrewsbury School. Electors, the Mayor of Shrewsbury, and the Head Master and Second Master. Residence as above ; present Value, about £23 per Annum."—EDITOR.

" and the chyffe actor thereof was one Master Aston, beinge the head Scoole
" master of the free Scoole there, a godly and lerenyd man, who tooke marve-
" lous great paynes therein."

In 1642, when King Charles kept his court at Shrewsbury, the following noblemen were lodged and entertained at the Free Schools, viz. At the house of the head master, Mr. Chaloner; Lord Keeper Littleton, Lord Viscount Grandison, Lord Archbishop Williams, Lord Cholmondeley, and Sir Richard Dyos. At Mr. Evans's the second master; Lord Grey of Ruthin, and Lord North and his brother.

Many men of note for their learning and eminent abilities, have been educated here, among whom were the following.—Sir Phillip Sidney, Knt.—Sir George Jeffries, Knt. Lord Chief Justice of the King's Bench, 1683, and afterwards appointed Lord Chancellor.—Sir Thomas Jones, Knt. Lord Chief Justice of the Common Pleas, 1683.—Dr. Sampson Price, Vicar of Christ's Church, London.—John Taylor, L. L. D. &c. &c. &c.

A LIST OF THE MASTERS.

HEAD MASTERS.

1562. Rev. Thomas Ashton,* Clerk.—At this time there were 290 scholars in the schools.—Resigned, 1568.
1568. Mr. Thomas Lawrence, a Layman, who was church warden of St. Mary's 1579. Resigned July 19, 1583.
1583. Rev. John Meighen, A. M.—Nominated by St. John's College, and admitted October 1.—At his admission there were in the highest schools 271 scholars. Received £100 to resign, 1635.
1636. Rev. Thomas Chaloner, Student of Jesus College, and elected by the College. Resigned 1646.
1646. Rev. Richard Pigott.—Nominated by the College, December 4.
1662. Rev. Thomas Chaloner.—Again nominated by the College.—Died 1664
1664. Rev. Andrew Taylor, A. M. Fellow of King's College.—Nominated by the College, November 12.—Formerly a scholar here.
1687. Rev. Richard Lloyd, A. M. Fellow of St. John's.—Resigned July 1, 1723.
1723. Rev. Hugh Owen, A. B.—Displaced by a decree of the Exchequer, in 1726.
1727. Rev. Robert Phillips, D. D. Admitted June 19, 1727.—Died October 11, 1735.

---

* Mr. Ashton resigned his office some years before his death, but he continued to cherish the seminary over which he had presided, with paternal care. He drew up the code of laws by which it was governed for above two centuries. He bestowed on it £120. of his own money, equal in effect perhaps to £1000. in the present day; and one of his latest acts was to visit it, when he preached a farewell sermon to the inhabitants of the town, after which, that "godlie father," (so he is styled in a cotemporary M S.) accompanied with the tears and blessings of Shrewsbury, returned to Cambridge, near which he died at the end of a fortnight, 1578.—*Owen's Account of Shrewsbury.*

S

1735. Rev. Leonard Hotchkiss, A. M.—Removed from the second School, October 17th.—Resigned 1754.

1754. Rev. Charles Newling, A. M. Fellow of St. John's College, Cambridge.—Admitted October 3rd, Richard Jones, Esq. then Mayor.—Resigned December 25, 1770.

1770. Rev. James Atcherley,* A. M. of Magdalen College, Cambridge.—Removed from the second school, and admitted Head Master upon Mr. Newling's resignation. William Smith, Esq. then Mayor.

SECOND MASTERS.

1562. Rev. Thomas Wylton.

—— Mr Thomas Lawrence,—Removed to the first school, 1568.

1577. Mr. John Barker.—Probably succeeded Mr. Lawrence in 1568.—Died 1607.

1607. Rev. Ralph Gittins, A. M.

1613. Rev. Andrew Studley.

1627. Rev. James Brook, A. M.

1631. Rev. Ralph Gittins.

1638. Rev. David Evans,

1659. Rev. Edward Cotton.—Died October 10, 1668.

1668. Rev. John Heynes, A. M.

1672. Rev. Oswald Smith, A. M.—Died July 26, 1715.

1715. Rev. Rowland Tench, A. M.

1718. Rev. Leonard Hotchkiss, A. M.

1735. Rev. John Mall, A. M.

1737. Rev. Humphrey Parry, A. M.

1754. Rev. John Brooke, A. M. third master, admitted into the second school, July 2nd, Richard Jones, Esq. Mayor,—Died Nov, 29, 1763.

1763. Rev. James Atcherley. A. M. and third master, was admitted into the second school upon the death of Mr. Brooke. Pryce Owen, M. D. Mayor. Rev. Charles Newling. A. M. head master.

---

* In the year 1798, after the new act came into operation, which, as previously stated, dispensed with third and fourth masters; handsome pensions for life were allowed on their retiring, as were also to the first and second masters on their resignation; each proportioned to the salaries they had previously been paid. The Rev. James Atcherley was succeeded by the present head master, the Rev. Archdeacon Butler, D. D. F. R. S. F. S. A. &c. to whose learning, talents, and perseverance the schools have been elevated to the highest degree of eminence.

The Rev. John Judwine, M. A. is the present second master.

In the choice of his assistants the head master manifests the greatest care and circumspection. The following gentlemen are considered admirably qualified for the important stations they occupy in the Schools :—

Rev. Frederick Iliff, M. A.	Mr. Thomas Butler, Son of the Head Master.
Rev. J. M. Wakefield.	Mr. Willis.
Rev. John Young.	Mr. Smith.

Upwards of Three Hundred Scholars are now under their care.—Editor.

1771. Rev. Thomas Humphries,* A. M. and third master, admitted into the second school in January. William Smith, Esq. then Mayor. Rev. J. Atcherley, A. M. chief schoolmaster.

THIRD MASTERS.

1562. Rev. Richard Atkys
1587. Rev. William Bailey.
1594. Rev. Ralph Gittins.
1607. Rev. Ralph Jones.
1627. Rev. David Evans, A. B.
1638. Rev. Robert Ogden.
1649. Rev. ——— Harrison.
1651. Rev. Isaac Solden.
1659. Rev. John Taylor, A. B.
1688. Rev. Henry Johnson.—Nom. by Col.
      Rev. Robert Matthews.—Nom. by Corp.
      N. B. Mr. Johnson was put into the place, but his right to it was to be tried, only his death, September 14, 1690, prevented it, and his competitor succeeded him.
1690. Rev. Robert Matthews.—Died February 12, 1701.
1701. Rev. Rowland Tench, A. B.
1715. Rev. Leonard Hotchkiss, A. M.
1728. Rev. Humphrey Johnson, A. B.
1735. Rev. John Brickdale, A. B.
1737. Rev. Arthur Vaughan, A. B.
1740. Rev. John Brook, A. B.—Admitted October 15.
1754. Rev. Alexander Hatton, A. M.—Admitted August 15, Richard Jones, Esq. then Mayor. Rev. Leonard Hotchkiss, A. M. chief schoolmaster.
1755. Rev James Atcherley, A. B. of Magdalen College, Cambridge —Admitted November 25. Edward Blakeway, Esq. Mayor. Rev. Charles Newling, A. M. chief schoolmaster, (See List of Head Masters.)
1764. Rev. Thomas Humphries, A. B. of St. John's College, Cambridge, who taught a flourishing school at Downton, near this town.—Admitted into the third school upon the promotion of Mr. Atcherley, January, 1764. Pryce Owen, M. D. Mayor. Rev. Charles Newling, A. M. chief schoolmaster.
1771. Rev, Samuel Johnson,† A. B. of St. John's College, Cambridge.—Admitted February, 1771. William Smith, Esq. Mayor. Rev. J. Atcherley, chief schoolmaster.

---

* 1783. On the death of Mr. Humphries the Rev. Samuel Johnson was admitted into the second school, and continued in his office till 1798, when he retired on a pension.—EDITOR.

† 1783. The REV. JAMES MATTHEWS, M. A. on the promotion of Mr. Johnson, was admitted into the third school, in which he continued till the constitution of the establishment was revised, when he retired on a pension. Mr. Matthews still lives, as active and erect as a man of thirty, cheering a most respectable circle of friends, by the intelligence and vivacity of his conversation, enjoying what the poet Thompson has designated—
——— "Heavens next best gift,
To that of Life, and an Immortal Soul—INDEPENDENCE." EDITOR.

FOURTH MASTERS.

1577. Mr. Roger Kent.
1588. Mr. Ralph Jones.
1607. Mr. Hugh Spurstow.
1649. Mr. —— Franklin.
1650. Mr. Robert Goddart.
—— Mr. —— Johnson.
1713. Rev. Leonard Hotchkiss.
1715. Rev. Alexander Hatton.
1754. Mr. Samuel Johnson.—Who before taught a flourishing private school in the town.
1764. Mr. Samuel Johnson, Junior.—Chose upon the resignation of his father.
1771. Rev. John Rowlands,*—Chose upon Mr. Johnson's promotion to the third school.

THE INFIRMARY, is the next charitable institution, which comes under our notice.

This useful charity (supported by voluntary subscriptions and benefactions) is extended not only to the town and county, but to all proper objects without distinction, from whatever quarter they may come ; provided their cases be such as come within the restrictive resolutions of the managers, and that they are recommended by a trustee.

This institution was first formed in the year 1745 ; a house commodious in every respect†, intended as a mansion house for a gentleman's family (being a grant from the Corporation to John Kynaston, Esq. of leave to build on the Town Wall), was fixed upon, and fitted up for the reception of patients, and opened on the 25th of April, 1747.

Out of 12,008 in-patients admitted from the first opening, 7127 have been discharged, cured, and 1189 relieved.—Out of 15,653 out-patients, 11,634 have been discharged, cured, and 680 relieved.

THE RULES OF ADMISSION ARE AS FOLLOWS :

No persons can be admitted, who are able to assist themselves, and pay for medicines.

Patients are admitted and discharged every Saturday, by the weekly board, between the hours of eleven and twelve.

No person can be admitted without a recommendation from a trustee, except in cases of accidents, or the most urgent necessity.

---

* 1798. The Rev. John Rowlands also resigned on a pension. This worthy and greatly respected gentleman died Nov. 15, 1815.—EDITOR.

† This building being found too small, and in many respects not very commodious, was taken down in the year 1827, and the present elegant building erected on its site.—EDITOR.

The Infirmary, 1775

Engraved from the original in Hulbert's now Aiken it Phillips History of Shrewsbury, 1858

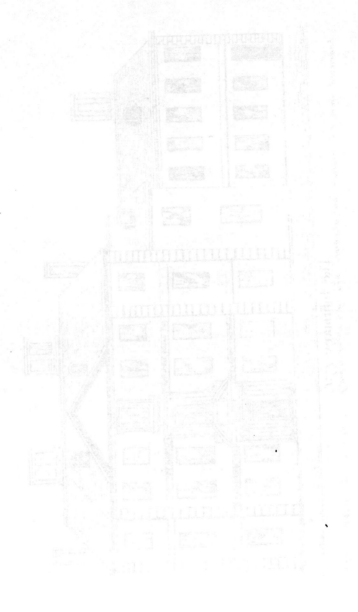

S...

	£.	s.	d.	DISBURSEMENTS.	£.	s.	d.
nd Dis-	6	5	9½	Coals, 136 tons 15 cwt.	118	9	9
PATIENTS in the ..	13	0	5	Mops, Brooms, Sand, Earthen and Tin Ware	18	6	6
Admitted since ..	6	9	3	Watch Nurses	13	4	0
..	3	1	8	Matron's Incidents, which include Washing			
				and Brewing	13	1	10½
				Stationery, Printing, Advertising, &c. ..	64	16	0
C				Carriage of Goods and Postage	7	10	10
R				Stipends, Wages, and Gratuities ..	227	1	1
DISCHARGED { B				Water	4	6	9
A				Insurance	3	10	6
F				Burials	16	9	7
B				Shaving the Patients	6	2	6
Dead ..					2037	16	7½
Remaining in the				Balance in the Hands of the Deputy Treasur-			
				er, exclusive of £25 in the Hands of the			
In-Patients admi...				Matron	757	6	9
April 25th, I							
——— Cured	£2795	3	4½		2795	3	4½
——— Reliev							

AB...ACT OF THE WHOLE ACCOUNT,

...firmary, on the 25th April, 1747, to the 24th June, 1826, inclusive.

	£.	s.	d.	DISBURSEMENTS.	£.	s.	d.
Balance of last ...ner				Expenses, as by former Accounts, to the			
Subscriptions	134296	11	4	24th June, 1825	134014	7	6
Subscriptions that ..				Expenses this Year, as by the above Ac-			
Benefactions and ..	2512	19	6½	count	2037	16	7½
Collected at St.							
being the Day					136052	4	1½
Cash from the s							
One Year's Rent				Balance in the Hands of the Deputy Trea-			
Stables				surer	757	6	9
One Year's Divi							
Consols	136809	10	10½		136809	10	10½
Half a Year's Di							

LACON CHILDE, ESQ. TREASURER.

Physicians. ...Extraordinary.

Joseph Sutton, Esq. Surgeon Extraordinary.

Mr. Edward Humphreys, }
Mr. Thomas Sutton, } Surgeons.
Mr. Henry Edward Burd, }

...SURER, MR. JOSHUA PEELE, SHREWSBURY.

...HENRY HIGGINS.—SECRETARY, MR. JOHN JONES.

In the y...
from the above 11s. 8½d. In the year 1826, fifty years afterwards, the Revenue, as it appears
Religion: W...ore astonishing may be the report of its advancing utility. Christians value your
the followers of *Paine* and *Carlisle?*—EDITOR.

th of April, 1747, to Midsummer, 1779.

After the opening in the several Years respectively ending at Midsummer.

		SECRETARIES.	MATRONS.	In-Patients admitted.	Out-Patients admitted.	RECEIPTS OF ALL KINDS. £.	s.	d.	PAYMENTS OF ALL KINDS. £.	s.	d.
Before the opening.		Rev. Mr. Orton.									
174	nd.	Mr. William Harland.	Mrs. Sandford.	78	45	1294	15	0	1294	15	0
174		Ditto.	Ditto.	166	117	1161	6	5	1168	5	2
174	..	.. .. ..	.. .. ..	177	124	1028	18	11	959	1	11
175	..	.. .. ..	.. .. ..	246	280	1036	16	3	950	2	11
175	all.	Mr. Samuel Winnall.	.. .. ..	290	337	1199	1	0	1362	3	8
175		Ditto.	.. .. ..	311	410	1558	12	2	1543	12	3
175	..	.. .. ..	.. .. ..	289	448	1348	4	4	1219	7	11
175	..	.. .. ..	.. .. ..	308	462	1428	6	0½	1517	6	10
175	..	.. .. ..	.. .. ..	311	430	1488	9	10½	1508	8	0
175	..	.. .. ..	.. .. ..	350	522	1242	3	2¼	1253	7	2½
175	..	.. .. ..	.. .. ..	365	562	1134	6	2	1230	5	9½
175	..	.. .. ..	.. .. ..	339	698	1458	11	6	1213	4	10½
175	..	.. .. ..	Mrs. Cross.	340	598	1503	9	10¼	1368	4	9
176	..	.. .. ..	Ditto.	332	562	1650	6	4½	969	16	10½
176	..	.. .. ..	.. .. ..	295	513	3105	7	6	3500	6	10½
176	..	.. .. ..	.. .. ..	340	541	1355	7	10¾	1550	13	9
176	..	.. .. ..	.. .. ..	377	526	1262	15	1	1533	3	10½
176	n r	Mr. Joseph Sparkes.	.. .. ..	385	485	1336	10	3½	1208	14	5
176		Ditto.	.. .. ..	407	507	1146	18	0½	1258	8	9½
176		.. .. ..	.. .. ..	396	501	1390	14	5¼	1064	3	10½
176	..	.. .. ..	.. .. ..	458	640	1169	12	8¼	1440	8	4
176	..	Mr. John Walker.	.. .. ..	453	591	2073	18	8½	2116	8	3
176	..	Ditto.	.. .. ..	460	615	982	3	5	1216	6	10½
177	..	.. .. ..	.. .. ..	441	606	1419	6	6½	1199	11	9½
177		Mr. William Jones.	.. .. ..	463	519	1461	18	3½	1126	15	4½
177		Ditto.	.. .. ..	477	505	1012	5	9	1334	9	2½
177	..	.. .. ..	.. .. ..	569	568	1513	5	8	1371	11	4
177	..	.. .. ..	.. .. ..	550	540	1584	18	4½	1852	1	5
177		.. .. ..	.. .. ..	586	573	1532	5	5½	1467	1	1
177		.. .. ..	.. .. ..	505	668	1459	19	3	1378	11	8½
177	..	.. .. ..	.. .. ..	520	616	1497	15	4½	1398	7	5
177	ord.	.. .. ..	Mrs. Harley.	502	591	1251	10	8	1400	15	4
17		.. .. ..	Ditto,	475	565				1346	13	4

William r ending at Midsummer, 1779, not being closed at the time when this
Deputy Trea f the Receipts for that Year could not be inserted herein.

[To face page 133.]

No subscriber's recommendation can be accepted, while his subscription is in arrear.

No persons having the itch, or any other infectious distemper, can be admitted as in-patients, nor any person troubled with, or subject to epileptic or convulsive fits.

When this charitable institution was first formed, a committee was appointed to fit up and furnish the house ; and the well-regulated statutes and orders then laid down by the said committee, still reflect honour upon them ; among the rest, the Rev. Mr. Orton, whose name appears in the annexed list of secretaries without fee or reward, undertook that office, and did the business for two years. Under the excellent management of those active trustees who attend the weekly and quarterly boards, this charity hath subsisted with increasing utility, and recommends itself to the notice of all such, who from sentiments and feelings of humanity, wish to encourage such institutions ; to all such, an ample field of charity presents itself, and invites them to add their names to the present respectable list of subscribers and benefactors to the Salop Infirmary.

N. B. The Physicians and Surgeons of the Town, regularly attend, and give their advice and assistance (gratis) to the unhappy objects who resort here, seeking for the blessing of health, and a release from pain and misery.

The progress, and present state of this institution, may be further seen in the annexed account, for which I am indebted to the present Secretary, Mr. Jones.

Under the third class of public structures, are to be ranked those, which were erected for public business, and first,

THE TOWN HALL, anciently called the Boothale, Bothale, and Guildhall. Boothale, comes from the Saxon word *Bote*, compensation, or making amends ; and Hall, as it is now used, for the place where matters relating to the government of a city or town, are transacted and settled ; and among other things, determining disputes, and making amends or satisfaction to the parties aggrieved.

To Boot, according as we use the word, implies what is given over and above in the exchange of things. Burgbote, was a tribute, or contribution paid towards the defence of castles, towns, &c. Gild, also signifies a tribute, so it is likely Guildhall, and Botehall, or Boothall, are synonimous terms, and mean the places where assemblies are held for the necessary service of the public, towards the erection and support of which, every one was *Gildare*, or to pay some small contribution. The grant of *Gilda Mercatoria*, was the ancient word of incorporation.

It is uncertain when the first building for this purpose was erected here, very probable one was built on the spot where the present hall stands, when the town was first incorporated, and was raised by the voluntary contribution of the inhabitants.

In the reign of Edward II. we find the Town-Hall here, was seized into the King's hands, as unwarrantably erected (from which we may suppose it was then newly built) but on the Burgesses making it appear they had power by charter, to make improvements where they thought fit, it was restored to them again.

The Hall at this time erected, was afterwards taken down, as appears by a deed bearing date 30th of Henry VI. A. D. 1452, and a new one (perhaps the present Hall) then erected, there was allowed by this grant forty marks out of the town stock, towards building this new hall, and a tower over the Exchequer.

The present is an old, low, timber building*, consisting of a large room 63 feet in length, and $25\frac{1}{2}$ in breadth, in which the assizes, sessions, and other courts are held; it is commodious, but in no respect elegant; adjoining to it is a large room, commonly called the Green Room, but more properly the agreeing Room, or chamber of concord, which room was altered and beautified in the year 1741. In this room the assemblies were generally held, until a larger and more elegant room, for that purpose, was lately built at the Lion Inn. At one end of the Green Room is the Exchequer, where the magistrates attend for transacting public business, on court days, and at other times. This separate building was erected in the year 1490, in it the town records, and archives are kept, it is a strong stone building, notwithstanding which it was broke into and robbed of £229. 7s. 6d. taken out of the school chest there, by two men on the 28th of November, 1613. They were both of them tried and convicted, at the town sessions before the Bailiffs and Recorder; one of them was hanged on the pillory, and the other, John Davis, a miller, pardoned by the King.

THE MARKET HOUSE, situate near the Town-Hall, and in the centre of the town, was built in the year 1595, as appears by the following inscription at the east end thereof, viz.

"The 15th day of June was this building begun, William Jones, and "Thomas Charlton, Gent. then Bailiffs, and was erected, and covered in "their time, 1595."

---

* In consequence of a fine of £2000 being laid upon the county by Judge Hotham in 1782, till a new Shire Hall could be erected, the old timber building was taken down, and in order to make the area before the new structure more handsome and convenient, several houses were purchased and also taken down. The present Hall was completed in 1785.—EDITOR.

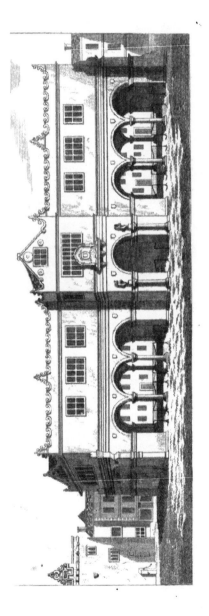

The Market House 1778.

Eng.d from the Original for Halbert's new Edition of Phillip's History of Shrewsbury by J. Ferday.

In 1685 posts were ordered to be placed under the arches to keep out carriages, and in the year 1719, Henry Jenks, Esq. then Mayor, laid the bottom with flag stones, and put up the iron railing.* Over the market place is a large room, let out by the Corporation to the Company of Drapers, who hold therein, every Thursday, a large market of Welsh cloths, and flannels†, of which great quantities are bought in this town, and sent abroad.

Before this building was erected two timber houses were upon the spot, designed to answer the same purpose, as appears by the following account.‡

"This Yeare 1567, Maister John Dawes of Shrosbery, and Alderman of "the sayde Towne, began and buylded two fayre hoyeses in the corne market "there, for the saffe placinge of corne from wether, so that the owners thereof "may stannd saffe and drye, the which buyldings was at his own coste and "charge; which place servyth for the inhabytants, as also strangers to walke "in, and the Lofte above for soondry profitable purposes."—To the above mentioned two houses, Mr. Humphry Onslowe added three others, in the year 1571, for the same purposes.

THE CROSS or MARKET CROSS, a building erected where the market for butter and poultry is held on Wednesdays and Saturdays, situate on the High Pavement. The first building erected here was of timber, and probably bore some resemblance to those called Crosses, yet remaining in some other towns and villages, in the form of an octagon, and ascended to by a flight of steps. This building however was taken down in the year 1705, and a new one erected, over the arches of which a leaden cistern was placed, as a reservoir for water from which the town was supplied. Before this time the reservoir for water was upon the town wall, near Mr. More's garden on Clarimond Hill, which, by means of horses, who worked the wheel, was forced up into several parts of the town. This building and work was held by Mr. Geo. Hosier,

‡ Dr. Taylor's M. S.

---

* The iron railing was not put up in Mr. Jenks's mayoralty, but in that of Edward Corbett, Esq. in 1738.—*Llewellin's Manuscript.*

† 1583, the Drapers bought flannels at Oswestry. 1585, at the Knockin. in 1621 they ceased to purchase at Oswestry. 1654 the Corporation ordered that the flannel market, over the Market House should be held on Thursday only; so the market continued till 1802, when it was removed to Welshpool, where the Drapers attend every other Monday. A few years after, the room in which the flannel market was held, was opened by Mr. Jonathan Perry, as an Auction Room; it has subsequently been occupied as a Depot for the clothing, &c. of the county militia.—*Llewellin's Manuscript.*

under lease from the Corporation, but in the year before-mentioned, he resigning the lease, a new one was granted by the Mayor and Corporation, to Robert Aldersley of London, to erect new works under the stone bridge, for which he was to pay 5s. per ann. and receive the profits. From this work, by means of a wheel, the water has been, and yet continues to be forced up into the reservoir over the Cross, from which the town is well supplied, at an easy rate. How long the works continued in the possession of Robert Aldersley, or whether the advantage arising therefrom answered his expectation, does not appear; however, they were afterwards, (together with all the Boylets below the stone Bridge,)in the posession of Mr. Gabriel Bingley, Upholder, who sold them to Richard Lyster, John Corbet, and John Powis, Esqrs.

In the year 1736 the pillars of the Cross, supporting the reservoir decaying and giving way through the great weight of water upon them; the proprietors took the building down, and another was erected, the cistern on the top of which held 600 barrels of water. This last mentioned building was so much damaged by the weight it supported, that in the year 1755 it was judged proper to take that down, the workmen who were appointed to survey it reporting that the floor of wood plank, supporting the cistern, was considerably damaged. The present building* was then erected, considerably larger and stronger than the former, with arched groin-work to support the bed of the cistern, which holds 1000 barrels of water.

The present proprietors† of the water-works are Lady Hill, Mrs. Lyster, of Rowton, and John Corbet, of Sundorn, Esq.

THE DRAPERS HALL; a large apartment or room, in a dwelling-house in St. Mary's church yard. Here the Company of Drapers meet to elect officers, and do business, but hold their feasts at some of the public Inns by direction of the master. The charter of this company bears date 1 Edward IV. A. D. 1461, that King uniting this company and the society of the blessed Trinity into one body. In the middle of their hall stands the abovesaid King's picture, placed there in the year 1659, having around and under it the following inscriptions, viz.

ROUND THE PICTURE.
" Edwardus IIII. Angliæ et Franciæ ex. Domino· Hiber.

UNDERNEATH.
" The Right noble Prince Edward the 4th, King of England and

---

* This building becoming very insecure, and altogether incommodious, was taken down in the year 1817, and the present was erected and completed the year following.—EDITOR.

† Whose Representatives have disposed of their interest to the New Water Works Company.—ED.

" Fraunce, Lord of Ireland. He raigned 22 years, and 5 Weeks. Died
" at the age of 52 years, buried at Windsor, 1483."

" This Yeare fourth Edward York's farre fam'd renowne,
" Circled his Temples, with great Albion's Crowne ;
" When over reading the memoriale
" Of Salop's Drapers ancient Hospitale,
" Founded in honour of the sacred Deity,
" He own'd and stiled them then, the blest Society ;
" And with his Parliament's sage approbation
" Deigned them his Charter for a Corporation,
" Which to confirme Himself was pleased to be
" The Royal Founder of their Companie,
" Granting immunities of large extent,
" Which stand his bounties, gratefull monument.

" Edwardo 4°· regi Anglorum gloriosissimo momumentum hoc posuit
" Pannoriorum Salopiensium grata Societas."

THE FOLLOWING PARTICULARS ARE SELECTED FROM SOME RECORDS BELONGING TO
THE DRAPERS COMPANY.

	£	s.	d.
" 7th Henry VII. 1492. They paid rent for the chamber of Sir John " Cleve their Priest, and also for the repairs of the chamber	8	0	0
" Same year paid rent for Sir John Pleyley their Schoolmaster 20d. " and for his school, 6d.	0	2	2
" 9th Henry VII. 1494. Paid the Priest's stipend	3	16	6
" ———— Paid for canvas, to make sheets for the Poor " Folk, in the Alms Houses	0	5	10
"Memorandum.—18th Henry VIII. 1527. John Corbet, Esq. is be-" come a brother of this fraternity, and hath agreed to pay to the com-"pany yearly, a Buck of season, and also a gallon of wine at his entry.			
" 1527. Paid to Sir Richard Forton, Chaplain, and to the Parish " Priest at a funeral, for a mass of Requiem by night	0	0	11
" Memorandum.—11th Eliz. 1559. The Company agree that their " Bailiffs shall give to Mr. Aston towards setting forth his play at " Whitsuntide	5	0	0
" Collected by assessment to build a new Hall.	100	0	0

" 25th Elizabeth, 1583. Ordered that no Draper set out for Oswestry on Mon-
" days before Six o'clock, on forfeiture of 6s. 8d. and that they should wear
" their weapons all the way, and go in company.—Not to go over the Welsh Bridge
" before the bell toll 6.
" 27th Elizabeth 1585. A market was held at Knocking, and a half-penny paid
" by the Drapers for every piece of cloth bought.

The Painting of " Digery Waters" and his wife formerly on the porch of the centre Alms House,
see page 123, is preserved in the Drapers Hall.—EDITOR.

T

"44th Elizabeth, 1602.—Agreed of good will to give the Minister at St. Alk-
"mond's 20s. for his pains in saying morning prayers in St. Alkmond's Church,
" and 6s. 8d. to the Clerk for lights.
"July 31, 1613. Gave the Bailiffs of the town 20s. towards entertaining the
" Judges of Assize.
"1614. Ordered 6s. 8d. per annum to the Clerk of St. Alkmond's for ringing
" the morning bell to prayers on Monday mornings at Six o'clock.*
"1621. Agreed to buy no more cloth in Oswestry.
"1649. The Welsh market in Shrewsbury altered from Friday to Thursday.—
" Ordered 20s. per annum to be given to the man who tolls the bell for market."

A considerable trade is carried on by the company of Drapers, and great quantities of cloth, &c. bought weekly in the market (on Thursdays) at Shrewsbury. Several acts of parliament have been obtained to secure and confine the trade, and several attempts made to lay it open, but the narrow limits of this publication, and the unexpected additional matter that has occurred under every chapter, prevent the intended publication of extracts from them.

THE MERCERS HALL, was formerly in the Sextry, or King's-Head Shutt, probably the same room in which the Charity School was kept, before the alteration of, and new building up that passage. Latterly their Hall was the house, now belonging to Mr. Symonds, apothecary†, in the High Street. This company, at present, have no Hall, but transact their public business at some one of the Inns, at the choice of the wardens.

A composition‡ or charter was granted to this company, united with the ironmongers and goldsmiths, on the 11th day of May 1480, by King Edward IV. at the particular request of Nicholas Pontesbury and Roger Adis, Wardens, the King being then present in Shrewsbury.

CONDITIONS OF THE CHARTER.

"That the said Company should, to the honour and laud of Almighty

* William Jones, Esq. left to the Drapers Company £1. 6s. 8d. to be yearly paid to the Vicar of St. Alkmond's for reading prayers on Monday mornings at Six o'clock, before the Drapers set out for Oswestry market; the money to be paid out of the profits arising from his lordship of Wigmore. This practice is now discontinued.

† Now Mr. Ward's Grocery and Tea-Warehouse.—ED.

‡ The composition it appears was *confirmed* by Prince Edward, son of Edward IV. on the 11th day of May 1480, and begins " Edward of my most drede lorde and fader Edward the fourth," &c. The validity of the charter was completely established by the verdict of a jury at the general Assizes for the county in August 1823.—EDITOR.

THE CASTLE, SHREWSBURY.

Published by C. Hulbert Shrewsbury

"God, our Lady St. Mary and St. Michael the Archangel, their Patron, together
"with the holy company of heaven; sustain and find a Priest, to do and say
"divine service daily, at the alter of St. Michael, in the College Church of St.
"Chad, and also give 13 poor men each of them one penny per week, to pray for
"the prosperity of our most dread Lord and Father Edward IV. our dearest
"Mother the Queen, the Kings Council, and for the fraternity of the said Guild,
"both quick and dead, and also to find the light made of wax, to be borne in the
"procession on Corpus Christi Day before the blessed Sacrament."

THE TAYLORS HALL, stood on the College Hill or Murivance, near
the corner turning to the walls, where Mr. Loxdale's house* now stands. At
present no Hall

THE WEAVERS HALL, was on the Wyle Cop, up a passage near the
middle, on the right hand going down. It lately belonged to Mr. Twiss, and
is now converted into two dwelling houses†.

THE CLOTH-WORKERS HALL, is an ancient building of red stone,
near the upper end of the High Street, when, or by whom built, is not known;
the company making but little use of it, have for several years past hired it.
For many years it was engaged as a Theatre; but is now used as a Meeting-
House for Mr. Wesley and his followers‡

Under the fourth, and last class of Public Structures and Institutions, we
shall (to close this chapter) take notice of buildings erected for defence—for
confinement of criminals, &c.—for mansion houses—and for public use and
ornament. And of buildings erected for defence, the first that presents itself
is

THE CASTLE, which is built of red stone, and stands on the neck of
land, where the winding of the River Severn forms a peninsula.—The entrance
from the town is of easy ascent, but steep on the other side; a natural mound
for the defence of the spot of ground beyond it.

---

* Now in possession of Thomas Loxdale, Esq. and is the residence of the Rev; E. Compson.—ED.

† Now the property of Mr. Rogers, and in the occupation of Mrs. Whitford.—ED.

‡ After the Cloth-Worker's Hall was discontinued as a Methodist Meeting House, it changed
tenants in quick succession, being at one period the auction room of Messrs. Hewitt and Hill, then
a court house during the re-building of the County Hall, sometime the watch house, but for these
last forty years it has been occupied as a dwelling house and tea-warehouse by the late Mr. Keate
and his successors, Messrs. Keate and Clarke.—EDITOR.

"When nature's hand this ground did thus advance,
" 'Twas guided by a wiser power than chance ;
" Mark'd out for such an use, as if 'twere meant,
" T' invite the builder, and his choice prevent."

DENHAM.

It has already been said, p. 59, that Roger de Montgomery, Earl of Shrews-bury, demolished several houses in order to build this Castle, the scite of which was then a part of the town, and well inhabited. The burgesses having their houses pulled down, and no abatement of their taxes, complained of the grie-vance ; but the Earl's two sons who succeeded him, were haughty, and regard-less of their complaints, though these no doubt, were in some measure redressed, when the Castle came into the possession of the Crown, upon the forfeiture of Earl Robert.

When this Castle became a royal fortress, the lands and demesnes that followed it, were parcelled out in serjeantries for the defence thereof upon occasion. The first tenure of that kind was the Serjeantry of Robert the son of Adam de Leyton, who was obliged to abide in this Castle fifteen days *cum una Balista* ; William the son of Warine did the same, 20th Edward I.—William de Wychard, held the manor of Cold Hatton, to keep ward in this Castle for twenty days, in time of war, at his own charges; besides many others. But such tenures, by degrees, grew obsolete, long before the statute was made that totally abolished them.—Commonly, the sheriff of the County had the custody of this fort, the better to enable him to defend his Bailiwick.

Henry de Alditheley, in the 11th Hen. III. was sheriff and constable of this Castle, and 17th Hen. III. constituted governour, in the room of John de Lacey, Earl of Lincoln. 41st Hen. III. John de Grey, of Wilton, was gover-nour. 44th Hen. III. James de Alditheley, son of the above-named Henry, was sheriff and governour. 3rd. Edward III. William de Mountacute, was governour. In the 16th Henry VI. Bowes Hampton, Esq; was appointed constable, with a fee of £10 per annum. 1 Edw. IV. the office of constable and keeper of the Gaol in the Castle, was committed to Roger Eyton. 7th Eliz. Richard Onslow had a grant of the scite of the Castle for 31 years, pay-ing a mark yearly.

Another officer belonging to this Castle was the chamberlain ; it being esteemed a place of great importance, great care was taken to have it kept in good repair, for the security of the marches. 7th Hen. III. Robert Lenfant and others, had the keeping of this Castle, and were allowed £27 for repairs, by virtue of the King's writ, directed to them for that purpose, which money the sheriff paid out of the tallage of the county, and it was allowed him in his accounts. 1 Hen. IV. Hugh Burnell, William Slepe, and Thomas Inkhole, were commissioners to enquire *de vasto et dilapidatione in castro Regis Salop tam in plumbo ferro fenestris.*

After the surrender of this Castle to the Parliament's forces in the year 1644, Colonel Mytton was made governour, but disliking the proceedings against the King, he laid down his commission, and Humphry Mackworth, son to Judge Mackworth, of Betton, was made governour. This governour appointed as lieutenant of the Castle, one Captain Hill, a prodigal drunken fellow, who, before the war, was a barber in Shrewsbury, but the townsmen and garrison hating him, when there was a prospect of the return of Charles II. they conspired against him, and in order to bring about their design, one of the townsmen was instructed to send for him out of the castle, to drink with him, at the Logerheads (now the Grapes,) an alehouse, near the Castle; when Hill was got without the gates, the soldiers shut them to, and cast his cloathes, boots, &c. over the wall; immediately the town was in an uproar, and Hill fled for fear of his life.

Soon after Colonel Hunt was made governour, and Mr. John Bromley, an honest and substantial burgess, was made lieutenant; but when King Charles II. was restored, he made Richard Hosier, eldest son of Colonel Hosier, governour. In the 15th of Cha. II. a *Quo Warranto* was brought against the charter of the town, and they were constrained to deliver up the Castle to the King. They afterwards purchased a confirmation of their charter, whereby all their liberties, &c. were confirmed, except the possession of the Castle, which remained in the King's hands.—(For further particulars, see Chap. 3.) In the time of King James II. all the cannon and match, of which there was several hundred weight, together with the greatest part of the muskets, were by the King's order removed to some other place.

This Castle was granted by Charles II. to Francis, Lord Viscount Newport, afterwards Earl of Bradford; after him, it came into the possession of his son Richard, Earl of Bradford; and is now in possession of John Newport, Esq.*

In the reign of Charles II. the Garrison here consisted of two companies, with their officers, under the following establishment:

	Per Day.			Per Month.			Per Year.		
	£	s.	d.	£	s.	d.	£	s.	d.
Entertainment for one company being 100 men, at 8d. per day,	3	6	8	101	7	9$\frac{4}{12}$	1216	13	4
A captain	0	8	0	12	3	4	146	0	0
A lieutenant, ...	0	4	0	6	1	8	73	0	0
An ensign, ...	0	3	0	4	11	3	54	15	0
Two sergeants,...	0	3	0	4	11	3	54	15	0
A drummer, ...	0	0	10	1	5	4$\frac{2}{12}$	15	4	2
One gunner's mate, ...	0	1	0	1	10	5	18	5	0
Fire and candles, ...	0	2	0	3	0	10	36	10	0
	4	8	6	134	11	10$\frac{1}{4}$	1615	2	6
	Per Day.			Per Month.			Per Year.		
The two companies with officers,...	8	17	0	269	3	8	3230	5	0

---

* Shrewsbury Castle now belongs to the Marquis of Cleveland, and is the occasional residence of Mr. Pelham, one of the knights of the shire.—ED.

Also an allowance of 7s. per week to a person, for locking and opening the gates of the town.

Signed,

T. Southampton,	-	-	-	Treasurer of England.
Edw⁴ Nicholas,	-	-	-	Principal Secretary of State.
Albermarle,	-	-	-	General.

THE TOWN WALLS were built so far as across the isthmus from the castle down to the river on each side, by Robert de Belesme, son of Roger de Montgomery, and were never assaulted, (Cambden says) except in the Baron's wars. The other part of the walls surrounding the town, were built in the reign of Henry III. who earnestly pressed the inhabitants to fortify and strengthen their Borough, lest the enemy should surprise them unawares, and this he recommended, as much for their own indemnity as his. This part of the wall was 32 years in building, and finished in 1252, to defray the charge of which the King at sundry times granted the Burgesses leases of the tolls of the town, and for the same purpose remitted them their tollage, particularly he gave leave to levy and gather once a week, for the space of four years, by way of toll, a farthing for every cart or carriage of goods sold in the town by the inhabitants of the county, but foreign carts were to pay one penny. Also for every horse load of goods one farthing, except wood and firing. Every horse, mare, cow, or ox, brought to the market, was to pay one farthing. Every ten sheep, goats, or swine, one penny. Every barge upon the river laden with goods, to pay four-pence. All which rates were ordered to be proclaimed by the sheriff through the whole county.

These receivings only amounting to an inconsiderable sum, the King afterwards remitted 100 marks, owing from the town, for this purpose.

That part from the north end of the abovementioned flank wall to the Welsh Bridge, called Roushill Wall, was built by Oliver Cromwell, in the year 1645, the old wall which went along the north side of the Castle Street and Pride Hill, being built upon with houses. The stone with which Roushill Wall was built, was brought from the ruins of Shrawardine Castle.

In an Exchequer Manuscript, without date, marked A. 2. P. 16. is the following memorandum respecting the several Gates of the Town, viz.

" Memᵐ de diversis clavis cum seris de diversis portis & posternis
" per Coronatores villæ Salop diversis custodibus deliberatis Viz.
" Clavum cum sera apud portam juxta Sturry's close.
" Dᵒ. ——————————— portæ exoppositæ Kayme place.
" Dᵒ. ——————————— portæ vocat Shepelache.

" D⁰· ——————————— portæ Claremont.
" D⁰· ——————————— portæ juxta Fratres August :
" D⁰· ——————————— apud Crepullgate.
" D⁰· ——————————— apud le Bulgerlode.
" D⁰· ——————————— apud Seynt Mary Waterlode."

In the above memorandum several gates or posterns are mentioned, to the keepers, of which the coroners of the town delivered bolts and locks for their security. Those at Shepelache and at Kaymeplace, no traces of the names remain, to ascertain where they were. That called Bulgerlode, was under the place formerly called the Gulph, at the bottom of the Wyle Cop. Cleremont, on the top of Clarimond Hill. Crepullgate, at the bottom of Knuckin Street. The names of the others point them out, and the Gates are yet remaining in Milk Street, Barker Street, and St. Mary's Water Lane*. One of the gates abovementioned, on Clarimond Hill, was often called Gate-poll, from poll, an old word for the summit, that being the highest part of the Walls. On the middle part of the flank wall between the lower Castle Gates, and the steps near the Rope Walk, stood an old Tower called Gerewald's Tower, or Gerewaldis Castle ; it was built on the bank of the ditch without the wall, part of it remained about the year 1716, but has since been taken down.

The principal Places of Confinement are the County Gaol, and the County, and Town Bridewell.

THE COUNTY GAOL†, was built in the year 1705 ; before that time, the Gaol was where the buildings called Windsor Square are, between the two Castle Gates, and while the town was a garrison, prisoners were confined in the Castle.

The following account of the present Gaol, taken from Mr. Howard's survey, will represent its present state, in a distinct and explicit manner.

" GAOLER, - - - - Samuel Wilding.
  " Salary - - - none.　£. s. d.
  " Fees, debtors - - - 0 9 0
  " —— felons - - - 0 14 4

---

* St. Mary's is the only remaining gate.—ED.

† The County Gaol, &c. described by Phillips, after the erection of the present new gaol, was converted into dwelling houses, workshops, &c.; it afterwards became a porter brewery; it now comprises a very respectable dwelling house in the occupation of the Rev. F. Iliff, several other good houses, various cottages for mechanics, &c.—EDITOR.

	£.	s.	d.
" Transports - - -	6	6	0

" License for beer and wine.

" PRISONERS.
      " Allowance.—Debtors—2 six-penny loaves a week each.
      " ———— Felons.—1s. 4½d. in bread a week each.
      " Garnish.—— lately cancelled.

" CHAPLAIN, - - - - Rev. Mr. Rowlands.
      " Divine Service.——Sundays and Thursdays.
      " Sacrament. - - The first Sunday in every month.
      " Salary. - - - £35.

" SURGEON, - - - - - Mr. Cooper.
      " Salary, none.——he makes a bill.

" APOTHECARY, - - - - Mr. James Winnall.
      " Salary, none.——he makes a bill.

" In the Gaol are separate court yards for debtors and felons, but the
" latter have no water; for this reason and because their day room is in the
" debtors court, both are commonly together. Here are commodious apart-
" ments for the master's side debtors, and a large free ward ·for the common
" side.—For felons there are two night dungeons, down eleven steps, that for
" men was about four years ago made more airy by an additional window, and
" it is, or should be daily freshened by an hand ventilator, which is in the room
" above. The day room for felons is small, men and women together. A
" court yard is lately inclosed for the women to which an infirmary should be
" added. At present when the Apothecary finds that a sick prisoner should
" have better diet, he orders the Gaoler to provide it, and signs his bill for the
" amount, which is readily allowed by the Justices at quarter sessions. The
" county allows transports convicted at the quarter sessions as much as those
" convicted at assize have from the King's allowance, viz. 2s. 6d. a week."

Every criminal sick and wanting cloathing, the Surgeon or Apothecary
orders the Gaoler to provide the same, and the county allows the expence.

The Justices of this county at the general quarter sessions, 11th January
1774, were so considerate and humane, as to prohibit the demanding from
prisoners at their entrance into this Gaol, any money for beer or ale. by the
name of Garnish or any other name, and to require that two or more fair
copies of their said order should be hung up in the most public places of the
Gaol, for the inspection of debtors and felons, that the unfortunate might not
be imposed on. The following Justices signed this order, viz.

Charles Baldwyn,	Thomas Powis,
Charles Bolas,	Thomas Harries,
Thomas D'Avenant,	Edward Pemberton,
Richard Hill,	Plowden Slaney, Esqrs.
Thomas Ottley,	John Fleming, L. L. D.

A table of the rate of fees, to be taken by the gaoler, from debtors and criminals, was settled and established by the justices at the quarter sessions, 14th July 1778, which rates were afterwards allowed and confirmed by two of the Judges. A copy of them would exceed the limits of our present plan of publication.

THE COUNTY BRIDEWELL, or House of Correction, is a building adjoining to the Gaol, with which it has a communication. The prisoners herein are allowed to attend upon divine service in the County Gaol.

Master.—John Baugh.

Salary.—£50.

THE TOWN BRIDEWELL, or Castle Gates*, is the room over the gateway; and is the prison for felons taken up in the town and liberties for small crimes, to be tried at the town sessions. In this house also vagrants and disorderly persons are confined and put to work.

Keeper.—John Meighen.

The principal ancient Mansion Houses in Shrewsbury of which we have any account, are the following, viz.

CHORLTON HALL (now the Theatre) at the bottom of St. John's Hill. This house was formerly a palace belonging to the Lords of Powis†, and probably was the place of their residence, for several centuries, after the palace of Brockwell Yisithroe (which stood where St. Chad's Church now stands) was burnt down in the time of the Saxon wars. It is not certain when, or by

---

* The Old Tower, last remain of the Castle Gates, was taken down in the year 1825.

† Ancient Powys was originally very extensive; for when entire it reached, in a strait line, from Broxton hills, in Cheshire, southwards to Pengwern Powys, or Shrewsbury, including a large tract in both these counties; from thence through the eastern limits of Montgomeryshire, comprehending all that county, part of Radnorshire and Brecknockshire; then turning northward included the Cwmwds (Commots) of Mawddwy, Edeirnion and Glynn Dyfrdwy, in the present County of Merioneth, and circuiting part of Denbighshire came along the hills to the east of the Vale of Clwyd, as far as Moel Vamma, including all the County of Denbigh, except the present Lordships of Ruthin and Denbigh; from thence eastward to the Broxton hills taking Molesdale, Hopedale and Maelor, in Flintshire. It appears by the articles of pacification between Henry III. and Llywelyn, the last Prince, that the limits of the Principality experienced but a small diminution from what they were in *Offa's* time, when it was agreed that the Dee should be the boundary from Wirral to *Castrum Leonum*, or *Holt*, and from thence a direct line to Pengwern Powys, or Shrewsbury. Wales was perhaps of much greater extent under the reign of Brochwel Ysgythrog, Prince of Powys, about A. D. 600, who was defeated by the Saxons at the battle of Chester.—*Cathrall's History of North Wales.*

U

whom built, but in the year 1326 appears to be in possession of John de Charlton, Lord Powis, who obtained leave of King Edward II. to fortify this his house with a wall of stone embattled.

This house was afterwards granted to Warine at 13s. 4d. rent, whose heirs still enjoy it.

The following extracts of grants describing the situation of Chorlton Hall are copied from an old book in the Exchequer, marked A 34.

" Henricus Gray Comes de Tankerville &c. (*i. e.*)

" Henry Gray Earl of Tankerville and Lord of Powis, gave to Thomas " de Bromley of Salop, Merchant, one messuage or dwelling house, called " Chorlton Hall, with the buildings and nine tenements, two cellars, with a " Garden, and all other lands belonging to the said messuage, lying in the " town of Salop, in length between a parcel of waste ground called, Behind " the Walls, on the one part, and in breadth between the land of William " Mytton, Esq ; and the land of John Grace. Dated Anno Henry VI. 24.

" Unam magnam aulum vocat Chorlton Hall, &c. (*i. e.*)

" One great Hall called Chorlton Hall, one great Stone* adjoining to the " said Hall, one large Cellar under the said Hall, and one great Garden " enclosed on either side with a stone wall, which (to wit the said Hall, Cellar, " and Garden) lie together in Salop, in a street called Shoplatch, extending in " length by the King's Highway, to that part of the King's Highway, leading " from the aforesaid street towards the Church of St. Chad. Dated Anno " Henry VI. 49."

THE BELL STONE, an ancient building† near Chorlton Hall, now be-

---

* In the original *una' magna' lapid' camer'*: the last word having escaped Mr. Phillips, he translates it *one great stone*, and has founded upon this error, the ludicrous conjecture, that the large pebble stone in Barker Street, near the house of William Owen, Esq. of Woodhouse, known by the name of the Bell Stone, was included in the lease.— *Owen's Account of Shrewsbury.*

† From the style of the architecture, the arms over the door, (a lion rampant and canton) and the initials E. O. in one of the windows, this house appears to have been erected by Edward Owen, alderman and draper, of Shrewsbury, and bailiff of the corporation in 1582, on the 8th of December, in which year he obtained a certificate of his genealogy and arms from Robert Cook, Clarenceux King of arms. His grandfather Howell Owen, of Machynlleth, ancestor likewise of the Owens of Lluullo and Bettws, was brother, by the half-blood, of Richard Owen, (bailiff of Shrewsbury in 1564, and four other years down to 1576) father of Thomas Owen, a judge of the Common Pleas, and founder of the family of Condover. From this Edward descended the Owens of Woodhouse.—*Owen's Acct. of Shrewsbury.*

In the year 1827, the Owens of Woodhouse sold this venerable mansion to Mr. Hazledine, by whom it has been completely repaired, but at the sametime entirely disrobed of its former rich mantle of antiquity. The large stone is preserved, and may be still seen in the front of the premises. Bell Stone is now the residence of Mr. Watson, solicitor, son-in-law of the proprietor, and it is justly esteemed one of the most splendid and capacious mansions in the town of Shrewsbury.—EDITOR.

longing to Mr. Charles Fowler. Various conjectures are made relative to the etymology of this name. Some are of opinion the ancient name was, The Ben Stone, the word Ben, being an abbreviation of Benedictine, and suppose this house to have belonged to some religious of that order, but it does not appear that there was at any time any house belonging to them in Shrewsbury, but the aforementioned Monastery. This house has been also called The Bent Stone, as supposed from the bent appearance of a large stone lying near the house. A large stone now lies near this building, and probably has lain where it now does or somewhere near it for several centuries, and might be the large stone mentioned in one of the just before recited grants of Chorlton Hall. A conjecture, as probable as any of the foregoing might be made, *viz.* That this stone (which now appears broken and much altered) formerly, either in colour or shape resembled a bell, and from that the house near it might be called The Bell Stone, *i. e.* the house at, or near the Bell Stone, however an absolute determination of this matter must be left to some one better informed, if any such there be.

VAUGHAN'S PLACE*; the old building adjoining to Murivance or St. Chad's Hill, on one side, and to a large court near the Market House on the other. This building is now rented by Mr. Peter Blakeway, by whom the vaults are used as a wine cellar, and the upper parts by Joshua Blakeway, Esq. as a warehouse. This is supposed by some, (or at least a part of it) to have been St. Blase's Chapel, which undoubtedly stood on that spot or near it, and indeed some parts of the chapel are still visible in a part of this building, the walls of which are near four feet in breadth. In latter times it has been called Vaughan's Place, and under that name is leased to the present possessor. John Mytton, of Halston, Esq. is the present proprietor,† into whose family it probably came by marriage. Hugh or Hubert de Burgh, a Chief Justice of England made this house his town residence; he had five daughters, heiresses, one of the Leightons of Wattlesbury married one of them, with whom they had that estate. One of the Myttons, another daughter, by which marriage they

---

* From the name, the Vaughans appear to be of Welsh extraction, and from their great possessions may be judged to have sprung from illustrious lineage in that principality. The spread eagle in their paternal coat should seem to point out Owayn Gwynnedd as their ancestor, but this is quite conjectural and uncertain.
  Eleanor the daughter and heir of Sir Hamo Vaughan married Reginald de Mutton, bailiff of Shrewsbury no less than five times from 1373 to 1390, a native, as there seems good reason to conclude, of the village in that name in the parish of Fittes, and to whom, we may suppose that she brought her patrimonial mansion of *Vaughan's Place.—Owen's Account of Shrewsbury.*

  † A few years ago the present Mr. Mytton of Halston, sold Vaughan's Place to Mr. Higgins, of Shrewsbury; part of it is now in the occupation of Mrs. Mercerot as a dwelling house; another portion offices for the town committee, and constables of the night. The cellars are appropriated as cells for night offenders, &c.—EDITOR.

became possessed of this cellar and old building, together with the Dinas Mouthwy estate. The other three daughters married neighbouring Gentlemen.

COLE HALL. The remains of a building so called, (which were considerable in the memory of several persons yet living) are in a timber yard situate in Dog Lane. It is not probable this was at any time a religious house, (as some have supposed) for nothing remains to favour that conjecture, although the present proprietor Mr. George Lomax* says he has found beadrolls, &c. about the building. These might have been used in private devotion, and several of the name of Cole, formerly living in this town, as appears by the list of Bailiffs, no doubt remains of this having been their Mansion House.

THE COUNCIL HOUSE. An ancient building, delightfully situated near the Castle. In Speed's map it is called "The Lord's Place," and appears by various accounts to have been the place of residence for the Kings of England and others of the Royal Family, together with the Lords Marchers, &c. when they came to Shrewsbury. Rowland Barker, Esq. was in possession of this house 1582, by a grant from the Corporation.† Here King James II. kept his Court August 25, 1687. And several of the Lords Marchers, particularly Sir Henry Sidney, the Earl of Arundel, and the Earl of Bridgwater, were nobly entertained here at the expence of the town.

This house was purchased off ———— Owen, Esq. of Condover, by Richard Lyster, Esq. and is now in the possession of his surviving widow.‡

THE THEATRE. (See Chorlton Hall) This building was fitted up for a Theatre, and opened in the year 1765.

THE ORIEL. It is not easy to say whether this house properly comes under the denomination of a Mansion House or not. The building called by this name, or a part of it yet remains on the left hand the steps going from St. Alkmund's Church Yard to Grope Lane. Most religious houses had a

† Exch. Book, C. 6, P. 4.

---

* The present proprietor of Cole Hall is the Earl of Tankerville. The upper part has for many years been occupied as a place of worship.—Ed.

‡ Still in the possession of the Lyster Family. A principal portion of it is under lease to Dr. Du Gard, who has expended a considerable sum in improvements, and it now ranks as one of the most delightful residences in the town or county.—Editor.

The Welsh Bridge. 1778.

Engraved from the original for Hulbert's new edition of Phillips' History of Shrewsbury. 1828.

building* of this kind before them, and Oriel College at Oxford is thought to have its name from such a circumstance.

Oriel or *Oriolum*, Lat. is by Spelman said to "denote a portal or porch, at the entrance into any place." The word seems to be of Saxon origin, in which language *Or*, is the beginning, *Ora*, a port or haven, which is an entrance from sea into land. And *Orl* an outward edge or border.

We shall conclude this Chapter with an account of the two Bridges; both of which are useful, and one of them greatly ornamental to the town.

THE WELSH BRIDGE. So called on account of the road from Shrewsbury to a considerable part of North Wales, lying over it.

This Bridge is very ancient, but it is not to be determined when or by whom built. It has been frequently repaired, and is by reason of its age, and the frequent floods forcing against it often receiving damage. By the foregoing account of St. John's Hospital and St. George's Chapel, it is plain this bridge, by reason of its vicinity to the said chapel, was called St. George's Bridge. On it, at the north end formerly stood an outer gate, used in later times as a guard house for soldiers at any time quartered in the town. This gateway being an interruption to carriages passing over the bridge, was taken down a few years ago. There yet remains at the end of the bridge adjoining to the town, a gateway and tower of neat workmanship, built Anno Dom. 1539. Over the arch on the north side stands an old figure of a man in armour, but who representing is uncertain. It is generally and almost universally allowed to represent Llewellin the last Prince of Wales, but the appearance of the figure itself, and some of its appendages, rather point it out as designed for

---

* In one of the great towers of Conwy Castle is a fine window, in form of an arched recess, or bow, ornamented with pillars. This, in ancient times, was an elegant part of architecture, called the *Oriel*, usual in the houses of people of rank, and appears from a Poem, of the very age in which the castle was built, to have been the toilet of the ladies; and probably this might have been that of Queen Eleanor :—

> " In her Oryall there she was,
> Closyd well with royal glas,
> Fulfillyd it was with ymagery ;
> Every windowe by and by
> On each side had there a gynne,
> Sperde with manie a dyvers pynne.‖†

‖ Part of the Poem of the *Squire of low Degree.*—See Mr. Wharton's Hist. Poetry. " The gynnes were the fastenings of the casements, which were often secured with pynnes of yvere (ivory)."
Cathrall's History of North Wales.

Edward the Black Prince,* son of Edward III. who died June 8, 1376. This statue had (it is likely) stood in some other place, for in one of the Corporation Order Books, is the following memorandum, viz.

"1695. Ordered that the King's (Prince's) Statue be provided for, and "the place assigned it to be on the Welsh Bridge."

This bridge consists of six arches, is 342 feet in length, and 12 feet in breadth.

THE EAST BRIDGE, commonly called the Stone Bridge, and now the New Bridge. The old Bridge standing here (taken down in 1768,) very probably was built by the founder of the Abby, Roger de Montgomery, as frequent disputes happened between the Abbots and the Corporation, relative to the repairing of it, which disputes were at one time set aside by the Abbot consenting to repair that end of the Bridge next the Abby, and the Corporation the other end next the town. And afterwards King Henry VIII. remitted to the town ten marks, on condition they should repair the Abbots part of this Bridge. (See Abstract of Charters, 34th Henry VIII.)

This Bridge was old, and being for the most part only 11 or 12 feet in breadth, and also a cosiderable length, consisting of 17 arches, carriages were frequently incommoded, and much damage done. In the year 1765, a subscription was set on foot to obtain an act of parliament for widening the said Bridge, and an order was made by the trustees to take down the stone gateway, which stood upon the Bridge.† When taken down, it appeared to have been repaired with stone brought from the ruins of some religious house, in the walls of it were several wrought stones, particularly one on the east side, with the arms of England and France thereon, it was 3 feet square, and appeared to be the one half of a tomb-stone. Behind this last-mentioned stone, were three Gothic arches, or niches, in which stood three images, viz. One of a mitred Abbot, another of a man with the ensign of the Holy Lamb in his arms, and in the middle niche, a woman with a book in her hand.

---

† In the year 1545, during the time of a great flood, this gateway, or a great part of it, fell down, on the 22nd of January, about 4 o'clock in the morning; at that time, a prisoner for felony was therein, the doors and windows were locked, bolted, and barred, and the prisoner chained; he fell with the building, and, notwithstanding his situation, was preserved, and afterwards pardoned, and set at liberty.

---

* The Rev. H. Owen supposes the Statue to represent Richard Duke of York, father of Edward IV. When the Tower was demolished, the Statue was removed to the end of the Market Hall, where it still remains. The Bridge was taken down in the early part of the year 1792.—ED.

150.

The Lent Bridge 1778.

Engraved from the Original, for Hulbert's new edition of Phillips' History of Shrewsbury, by Cha. Askew 1829

Upon the west side, over the gateway, or arch, were three shields; on that to the left was a talbot, passant, &c. being the crest of the Earls of Shrewsbury; in the centre, a plume of feathers, the crest of the Princes of Wales; and on the right hand, Azure, three leopards heads, Or, being the arms of the Corporation of Shrewsbury.

On the east side was painted the arms of England and France, and on a square stone on the right side of the gate, an inscription, signifying when, and by whom, the arch underneath it was re-built.

There were formerly two large and strong gates, or folding doors, of wood, studded with iron, under this gateway, which upon particular occasions were shut, except a small door for foot passengers, on the side of which was a lodging room for the keeper.

This building was entirely covered with lead, which when taken off, weighed 5 tons, 4 cwt, 2 qrs. 18 lb. and was sold to Mr. Davies, plumber, for £13 per ton. The whole of this building was given by the Corporation to the Trustees, towards repairing the Bridge, and was valued at £200.

On the 9th of June 1767, the first stone of the new part, intended for widening the old Bridge, was laid by Edward Smythe, Esq. son of Sir Edward Smythe, Bart. of Acton Burnell; and in sinking for a foundation, below the causeway, another causeway and channel appeared, at the depth of 5 feet 6 inches, the lower part of the Wyle-Cop, having at some former time been so much raised.

The next year, 1768, the plan being altered from the first design by Mr. Mylne, and subscriptions being very freely offered, another design was presented to the Trustees by Mr. Gwynn*, a native of the town, which plan was approved of, and an entire new bridge ordered to be built according to it. The new and old work was accordingly taken down, and on Thursday, June 29, 1769, there was a numerous and respectable meeting of the contributors, when Edward Vaughan, Esquire, Mayor, went in procession from the Infirmary to the River side, and the first stone of the Bridge was laid it a solemn manner, by Sir John Astley, Bart. who gave £1000 towards the building of it. The company then returned in proper form and order, with music, &c. and dined at the Raven Inn.

The following inscription (engraved on a plate of copper by Mr. Miles Longmire, engraver,) was laid in a cavity cut for that purpose, in the first stone, and a stone fitted to fill up the space above the copper plate, even, or level with the first course of the abutment.

* Besides the English Bridge, Mr. Gwynn built Atcham Bridge, and the Bridges of Worcester, Oxford, Henley, &c. The Rev. W. G. Rowland possesses a tolerable Portrait of this eminent Salopian architect.—Editor.

REGNANTE
GEORGIO TERTIO
PIO FELICE PATRE PATRIÆ
LAPIDEM HVNC OPERIS PRIMORDIVM
PVBLICÆ VTILITATI
OPPIDIQVE HVIVS ORNAMENTO SACRI
SVMMA MVNIFICENTIA
IOANNIS ASTLEY BARONETTI
PRÆNOBILIS ROBERTI CLIVE BARONIS DE PLASSEY
THOMÆ HILL ARMIGERI
ET S. P. Q. S.
PRIMVM SVSCEPTI
PLVRIMORVM ETIAM SALVTIS STVDIOSORVM COMMVNIS
EGREGIA ET VOLVNTARIA LIBERALITATE
MAGNA EX PARTE
DEO FAVENTE PERFICIENDI
POSVIT IOANNES ASTLEY BARONETTVS
IVNII DIE XXIX
MDCCLXIX
EDVARDO VAVGHAN ARMIG. PRÆTORE VRBANO
IOANNE GWYNN SALOPIENSI
ARCHITECTO.

IN ENGLISH.

In the Reign of George the Third, the Father of his Country, Sir John Astley, Bart. on the 29th June, 1769, in the Mayoralty of Edward Vaughan, Esq. laid this first Stone of a Work designed for the Public Utility, and for the Ornament of the Town, and which was first begun by the great Munificence of the said Sir John Astley, the Right Honourable Lord Clive, Thomas Hill, Esq. and the Corporation of Shrewsbury; and which, under the Divine Favour, is to be compleated principally by the extraordinary and voluntary Liberality of many other public-spirited Persons. Mr. John Gwynn, a Native of the Town, being the Architect of this Bridge.

This Bridge consists of 7 arches, is 410 feet in length, and 35 feet in breadth, having on each side, a flagged path for foot passengers, $3\frac{1}{2}$ feet in breadth.

THE FOLLOWING ACCOUNT, OF ANCIENT BUILDINGS

omitted by Mr. Phillips, are chiefly extracted from the Rev. Hugh Owen's invaluable little work. The descriptions being too copious for a note, they are given IN CONTINUATION.—*Editor.*

" THE WHITE HALL is so called from the practice, which, no doubt, has long prevailed of white-washing this respectable mansion of venerable red stone. It is one of those houses which belong to the period of Queen Elizabeth,—lofty, square, and compact: the roof finished with numerous pointed gables, the chimnies highly ornamented, and the whole crowned with an octagonal turret in the centre. The inside has been modernized. The ancient hall is now converted into a spacious parlour ; indeed, comfort and convenience are the general characteristics of this handsome mansion. The drawing-room is ornamented with several fine pictures, by some of the most eminent masters.

The gate-house is still standing. The Rev. Mr. Philip Wingfield, some-time Minister of St. Julian's, (who married a Prince) is said to have resided in this part of the building.

The ancient garden walls remain, abundantly replenished with curious fruit trees : some old mulberries and a lofty walnut, mark the venerable character of the place.

Richard Prince, Esq. the builder of this house had the distinguished merit of carving out his own fortune. His father, John Prince, is said to have lived in a house nearly opposite the north porch of the Abbey church ; and, as tradition affirms, on the void space, now a garden in the tenure of the Rev. Mr. Rowland.

It was in March 1578 that he commenced the building of the present mansion.* Of the completion of his undertaking, the MS. chronicle thus speaks. " March, 1581-2. The famous house in the Abbey Forgate, near the Abbot's " barn, was builded by one Master Prince, a lawyer, called *Master Prince's* " *Place.* It was four years in building, to his great charge ; with fame to him, " and to his posterity for ever."† In 1584, he took out a grant of arms (an

---

* " November 27th, 1592, " The dwelling-house of one Richard Prynce, Gent. near unto Shrews-" bury, and within the liberties and franchises thereof, was in the night-time broken and robbed ; who " being alarmed, got off, leaving their keys and horses behind them."—*Taylor's* MS. These last the officers of the corporation seized as waifs, but, a claim thereunto being set up by the Earl of Essex, they executed a bond to the servants of that nobleman for the delivery to him of the said horses ; and in the curious MSS. of the Rev. Mr. Hotchkiss, was a letter from the Bailiffs of this town to the Earl, requesting that the bond in question might be given up to them."

† " Churchyard in his Worthines of Wales thus speaks :—'· Maister Prince his house stands so trim " and finely, that it graceth all the soyle it is in.''

X

indispensable appendage to gentility in those days) in which, by an ermine cross, the herald seems to have intended an allusion to his probable elevation to the *judicial ermine ;* just as the stripes of the same colour, and azure in those of his countryman and contemporary, Sir Thomas Harries of Tong Castle, refer, there can be little doubt, to the robes of a judge, as the golden rings do to the degree of serjeant at law actually attained by this last eminent lawyer. His posterity subsisted in the male line for three generations, and at length ended in a daughter, who married Sir John Astley, Baronet, and was grandmother* of the Earl of Tankerville, now owner of this house and estate."

"JONES'S MANSION† stands at the corner of Ox-lane, leading to St. Alkmund's. It is in various styles, and exhibits the square mullioned window of James I's days, as well as the wide gable and clumsy sash of Charles II's time. The hall and great parlour are but little altered from their original forms. In the windows of the latter when Dugdale visited this town in 1663, were escutcheons of the arms of France and England, the Prince of Wales, Edward the Confessor, Mortimer, Talbot, Strange, Burnel of Holgate Castle, the Cross of St. George, &c.

This large house was built by Thomas Jones, alderman of Salop, who after having been six times bayliff, was by Charles I. appointed the first Mayor of the Corporation, and in 1624,§ served the office of high sheriff of the county."

"THE OLDEST TIMBER HOUSE‡ in Shrewsbury, is probably the lofty and spacious structure at the higher end of the Double Butcher-Row, now like

§ "The list of sheriffs in Mr. Phillips's Appendix, places the shrievalty of Mr. Jones a year later; but its true date is ascertained by the inscription in the text, and by the following entry on the books of the Draper's company. "1624, *Whereas Thomas Jones, a brother of this company, is High-* "*Sheriff;*" &c.

* Great Grandmother of the present Earl. White Hall is the residence of Lady Hanmer, and of her son Sir Thomas Hanmer.—EDITOR.

† The original character of this ancient building is nearly lost by modern alterations and additions, the Proprietor consulting, as of course he has a right to do, his own convenience and advantage, rather than the gratification of the curious or the antiquary.—EDITOR.

‡ The House which I at present occupy, five doors from the County Hall, High Street, is perhaps as old as any, if not the oldest dwelling in the Town of Shrewsbury; it is said to have been built in the reign of Richard II. The rooms are extremely low, not more than six and a half feet between the beams; the frame of timber is very old, fast hastening to decay, and had not every pains been taken to preserve the premises, they must ere this period have been a heap of rubbish. They are notwithstanding rather extensive, well situated and adapted for trade.—EDITOR.

the greater part of our ancient mansions, divided into several dwellings. With the exception of its square windows, this building is entirely of gothic architecture, and much resembles the wooden houses represented in many of the prints of Mr. Johnes' translation of Froissard, which were copied from illuminated manuscripts of the reign of Edward IV. The projecting stories are sustained by elegant springers, which, as well as the principal timbers, are enriched with carved work, consisting of small pointed arches, with trefoil and other ornaments. Along the ground story of the front is a cloyster of wooden arches, obtusely pointed, now hid by the butcher's shops, much enriched with carved work and delicate mouldings. The higher story is finished with numerous small dormants, with sharp pointed gables. At present this house forms two sides of a square, measuring about 60 feet each way, and is very lofty. Doubtless it has been a place of more than ordinary consequence, but it is not easy to say what was its original destination. As no hall and great chamber can be traced within the present remains, they do not seem to have been the residence of an opulent family, for those apartments are never wanting in ancient houses of the date and size of this, and it is far too sumptuous for common street architecture. The strong foundations of red stone, still visible in the adjoining narrow passage, called Grope, or the *Dark* Lane, probably made part of these premises, and inclosed a court, in which might have been a hall and other principal apartments. The cloyster gives it somewhat the air of an ecclesiastical building, and perhaps it was the *Oriel*, mentioned by Phillips, so called from its being inhabited by religious persons, connected with the neighbouring church of St. Alkmund, who perhaps were the Chauntry Priests of the guild of the Holy Cross. Or it may have been the town house of the Abbots of Lilleshull, erected on the site of the Saxon college of St. Alkmund, which was given to that abbey in the reign of Stephen. It is certain that the Abbots possessed a mansion somewhere in this part of the parish. The heads of religious houses had often residences in the capital city or town of their respective counties. The Abbot of Tavistock had his town house at Exeter, as had the Abbot of Haughmond at Shrewsbury. These were principally for their reception during the assizes, when they often sat on the bench with the King's Justices. The Abbot of Reading made one of the judges at the assizes for Berks; and the venerable Richard Whiting, last Abbot of Glastonbury, was dragged from the bench at Wells, where he was attending the assizes, and soon afterwards hanged without a trial near his own abbey, for not complying with the mandates of Henry VIII. for the destruction of his magnificent church and convent. This curious old house is now the property of Sir Richard Hill, Bart.* who, in 1796, purchased it from Mr. Studley, in whose family it had long remained. The Studleys were a family of considerable antiquity in Shrewsbury. Their

---

* Now the property of the Earl of Tankerville.—EDITOR.

pedigree in the visitation of 1623, ascends about four generations antecedent to that period. One of them will be found among the ministers of St. Chad's. John Studley was mayor in 1642."

" The noble timber house on the left hand of the High Street, near the turning towards Mardol, was the town house of the Irelands, of Albrighton, and was sold to the Corbets about the year 1720. This house when entire must have been grand and spacious. The front consists principally of four deep ranges of bow windows four stories high, very lofty, and on the pointed gables above each, are escutcheons of the arms of Ireland. The principal entrance as a very flat gothic arch. The premises are now divided into several good houses."

" At the bottom of the Wyle-Cop, and adjoining the stone bridge, is a large ancient mansion, erected probably by William Jones, alderman and draper, bailiff in 1580, and four other years, father of Thomas Jones, previously spoken of. It is a spacious pile, rude and irregular. A gateway with a round arch, too low for any modern carriage to pass, leads from the street to a small court surrounded by the house and its offices. The principal apartments are to the street, and the great chamber still remains in its original state, having a huge chimney-piece profusely adorned with grotesque carving, and a ceiling loaded with armorial bearings and other ornaments in plaister. A groupe of smaller buildings, close by the river's side, seem to have been the warehouses of the opulent merchant who erected the house, and there has been a back-way, to the adjoining quay, for the conveyance of his goods by water.

These premises were sold by Sir Thomas Jones, about thirty (now fifty) years ago, to Mr. Lloyd, builder, of the Abbey-Foregate, and devolved to his son-in-law, Robert Pemberton, Esq. who sold them to Mr. Hazledine.*

HILL'S LANE. The buildings which we have hitherto been describing are either of stone, or what is called half-timbered. Through the use of brick, which had been universally practiced by the Romans, was *revived* in England at least as early as the reign of Henry VI. when Middleton tower in Norfolk was built thereof, by the Lord Scales; yet that material could not have found its way to this town, for nearly the space of two centuries, if it be true, as tradition warrants, that the old house in Hill's-lane, with which we shall conclude the present catalogue, was the first brick building in Shrewsbury. From the dates still remaining on the leaden pipes, it appears that this mansion was erected in the year 1618, and it is said to have been built by William Rowley, an eminent brewer of this town."

---

* Mr. Hazledine has recently taken down this ancient mansion, and has erected several new brick dwelling houses on the scite. Some few coins of the reign of Elizabeth, were found amongst the rubbish. On a beam was inscribed the date of the erection of the building, 1575.—EDITOR.

"His eldest daughter and coheiress, Priscilla, married John Hill, Esq. of Shrewsbury, who resided with great hospitality in this mansion, and whose name is still preserved in that of the lane in which it stands, more anciently called Knuckin Street. Mr. Hill, who is said to have been one of the justices introduced by Farquhar into his comedy of the Recruiting Officer, died in 1731; whereupon this property descended to his two daughters, Priscilla, wife of Phillip Thomas, and Mary wife of Thomas Youde, as coheiresses to their mother: and it is now divided between the descendants of those ladies. The house, which is in the best and most highly ornamented stile of its day, with a profusion of decorations in stucco, and still in good preservation, was the residence of the learned and amiable Dr. Adams, when Vicar of St. Chad's, and is now used as a manufactory of woollens."*

* Belonging to Mr. Ramsbottom.—EDITOR.

CHAPTER VII.

EXTENT OF THE TOWN LIBERTIES.

" IN Edward the Confessor's reign, the City of Salop is said to contain
" 252 houses, inhabited by so many Burgesses, it is there stiled Civitat Sci-
" ropesberie."*

The following Places are mentioned* as in the Liberties, viz.

" Mela, Manerium, Rad. de Mortemer, q. Brace Mele.
" Salton et Ecclesiam, belong to the Bishop of Chester, but held of him
" by St. Chadd's.
" Sudstone, belonging to the Abbey of Wenlock.
" Mela, Manerium, Ep. Cest. q. Monkmele.
" Abbatia, cui Comes dedit Monasterium, S. Petri, ubi erat Parochia
" Civitatis ; quam Hugo Comes filius Rogeri liberam fecit ab omni Servitio et
" immunem ab omnibus."

The whole of the town and liberties was rated at 100 hides† of land, i. e.
10 or 12000 acres.

In the 6th year of King John they were thus described : "Villa de Salopes-
" biria cum Hundredo, ad illam pertinente, in Bosco et Plano, in Viis, et
" Semitis, in Pratis et Pascuis, in Aquis et Molendinis, in Stagnis et Vivariis, in
" Mariscis et Piscariis."

IN ENGLISH.

The town of Shrewsbury, with the hundred appertaining thereto,

* Doomsday Survey.

---

† It is scarcely necessary to offer any information as to what might be the exact quantity of land
designated a " Hide," were it not that authorities differ, some say it was such a quantity of land as
might be ploughed in a year with one plough, or so much as would maintain a family. Some say
sixty, some eighty, and some a hundred acres. Sir Edward Coke, holds that a Knight's fee, a hide,
a ploughland, a yardland, or an oxgang of land do not contain any certain number of acres. The
distribution of this Kingdom by hides of land is very ancient, mention being made of it in the laws
of King Ina. Henry 1st, had three shillings an acre for every hide of land in order to raise a
dowry for his daughter. This tax was called hidage.—EDITOR.

in woods and plains, in highways and foot paths, in meadows and
pastures, in water courses and mills, in lakes or pools, and fish ponds,
in marshes and fish markets.

HENRY III. A°· 40.

" Villan de Salopesbiria, et omnes Libertates et Liberas Consuetudines
" suas, et quod Burgenses possint appropriare in Terra et in Aqua juxta Liber-
" tates suas, salvis pourpresturis si quæ ad nos de Jure debeant pertinere."

IN ENGLISH.

The town of Shrewsbury, and all its liberties, and free customs,
and whatever the burgesses may be able to appropriate in land and
in water, near to its liberties, saving such encroachments (if any) which
ought of right to belong to us.

HENRY VII. A°· II.

" Villa Salopiæ ac Libertates ejusdem in omnibus & singulis, Villis, Villatis,
" Hamlettis, Terris et Tenementis intra Comitatum Salopiæ quæ sint extra
" dictam Villam Salopiæ ac Libertatem, Suburbia et Procinctum ejusdem intra
" Parochias et de Parochiis Ecclesiæ Collegiatæ S^{ti.} Ceddæ Ep^{i.} Ecclesiæ Colle-
" giatæ beatæ Mariæ, Ecclesiæ Parochialis S^{ti.} Alkmundi, et Ecclesiæ S^{tæ.} Juli-
" anæ Virginis in eadem Villa, et intra Limites et Procinctus cujus libet prædic-
" tarum Parochiarum extra Villam prædictam ac Procinctum, Suburbia et
" Libertatem ejusdem, ac in singulis Villis, Villatis sive Hamlettis de Hadnoll,
" Allerton, Acton Reynald, Myryton, Grilsbill, Hanwood, Onneslowe, Preston-
" Goball et Pemley, in prædicto Comitatu Salop, et quæ extra Libertatem et
" Procinctum dictæ Villæ Salopiæ similiter existunt."

IN ENGLISH.

The town of Salop, with the liberties of the said town, in all,
and every one of its towns, villages, hamletts, lands, and tenements,
within the county of Salop, which may be without the said town of
Salop, and the liberty suburbs, and precinct of the same, within the
parishes, and of the parishes of the collegiate church of St. Chad the
Bishop, the collegiate church of the blessed Virgin Mary, the parish
church of St. Alkmond, and the parish church of St. Julian the Virgin,
in the same town :   And within the limits and juridictions of any of
the before-mentioned parishes, without the town aforesaid, and the
precinct, suburbs, and liberty of the same, and in every of the towns,
villages, or hamletts of Hadnoll, Allerton, Acton-Reynald, Myryton,
Grilshill, Hanwood, Onneslowe, Preston-Goball, and Pemley, in the
county of Salop, and whatever may in like manner exist without the
precinct of the said town of Salop.

The extent of the Town Liberties, copied from an old Ledger Book in the Exchequer, marked A. P s (Post 11º· Hen. 7.)

" Nomina Villarum,* et Villatarum, et Hamblettorum intra Libertatem Villæ Salop.

" Eton juxta Pytcheford.
" Betton Straunge.
" Altemere.
" Sutton.
" Meole Bracy.
" Pullyley.
" Newbold.
" Welbache.
" Whytley.
" Hanwood magna.
" Hanwood parva.
" Horton.
" Woodcote.
" Aldemere Newton.
" Preston Gubbald.
" Lee.
" Herdwyk.
" Burghton.
" Yorton Allerton.
" Clyve.
" Sandsawe.
" Acton Reynald.
" Grylleshill.

" Hadnall.
" Edgbald.
" Meole Monachorum.
" Schelton.
" Onnyslowe.
" Bykton.
" Rossal parva.
" Calcote.
" Preston.
" Dynthyll.
" Leton.
" Wolascote.
" Berwych Leybron.
" Berwych Parva.
" Smethcote Haston.
" Adbright Huseye.
" Adbright Monachorum.
" Halescote.
" Astley Abrigtlye.
" Battlefield.   Pymley.
" Longnore.
" Derbald.
" Hencote."

HENRY VIII. Aº· 34.

The Town Liberties extended.—" Intra Limites et Bundas Parochiarum " Sⁱⁱ· Ægidii et Sᵗᵃ· Crucis juxta Villam Salop, *viz :* a Ponte lapideo et a Postis " in eodem, Ponte ab Antiquo fixis, olim vocato le Abbey-Bridge, et le Abbey- " forgate, per totum Circuitum dictarum Parochiarum, ac etiam in una Parcella " Terræ cum quatuor Tenementis ibidem vocat. Meryvalle intra Parochiam ·· Sⁱⁱ· Ceddæ Epⁱ. prope dictam Villam Salop."

IN ENGLISH.

Within the limits, and bounds of the parishes of St. Giles, and

* King Edward II. sent his letters to all sheriffs enjoining them to return into the Exchequer an exact account of the names of all the villages and their owners, in every county; these returns of the sheriffs being all put together, is called Nomina Villarum, remaining still in the Exchequer.

Holy Cross, near the town of Salop, *viz :* From the Stone Bridge, and from the posts, of old fixed in the same bridge, called the Abbey Bridge, and the Abbey-foregate, through all the circuit of the the said parishes : And also in one parcel of ground with four tenements there, called Merryvale, within the parish of St. Chad the Bishop, near the said town of Salop.

———————————

N. B. For a modern account of the TOWN LIBERTIES see the Editor's additional particulars.

Y

CHAPTER VIII.

INTERNAL POLICE.

IN order to enable the reader to form proper ideas relative to the ancient and present Government of Shrewsbury, it will be necessary to have recourse to the several Charters that have been granted by successive Princes, to confirm and enlarge its privileges. The following are Abstracts from these Charters, in the order they were granted ; to which are added, some particulars relative to the present Government of the Town.—Also, a selection of Orders issued by the Corporation at different Times, relative to their Government, and management of their Affairs.—With correct Lists of the Bailiffs, Mayors, and Recorders, from the earliest Times.—Also, the present Justices of the Town, and Members of the Body Corporate.

ABSTRACTS OF GRANTS AND CHARTERS.

The Burgesses of Salop had priviledges under King Edward, before the Conquest, and paid *de Galbo* £7. 16s. 8d. per ann.—*Note.*—All the first Charters are granted to the Burgesses, and all the profits granted, with the forfeitures and amerciaments, are said to be for their benefit.

William I. granted the Town and County to the Norman Earl, Roger de Montgomery, then made the first Earl of Shrewsbury, to whom the Burgesses paid for the Town £40 per annum.

Henry I. upon the forfeiture of Robert de Belesme, son of Roger de Montgomery, seized the Town into his own hands, and granted the first Charter to the Burgesses, which is refer'd to in the subsequent Charters, but is not extant.

1st Richard I. 1189, the King by the first Charter extant, granted the Town, with all its appurtenances, to the Burgesses, for 40 marks of silver per ann. with all its priviledges and free customs, which they enjoyed in the reign of Henry I. Ten marks of which were for a brace of hunters, which they were used to provide.*

* Exch. 2 Book, P. 49.

1st John, 12th April, 1199, the King grants the Burgesses all the priviledges they had enjoyed under Henry I. and enjoins, that no one should disturb them under the penalty of ten pounds.*

1st John, 20th April, 1199, he grants the Burgesses to hold the Town of him, at 40 marks of silver, (as before) and to chuse two substantial discreet Burgesses, and present them to the Sheriff, who, when he gave up his accounts, was to present one of them to the Chief Justiciary, at Westminster ; and they were not to be moved from their office in the Bailiwick, while they behaved well, unless by the Common Council of the Town.†

And also to chuse four substantial discreet Burgesses, to hold the Pleas of the Crown, and to have inspection over the Præpositi themselves.

Also confirms the priviledges and free customs they had under his father.‡

6th John, 24th February, 1204, he grants to the Burgesses the Town, and also the Hundred belonging to it, for 45 marks, to be paid into the Exchequer, at Easter and Michaelmas, 5 marks of which were for the increase of the farm, and ten for a brace of hunters.—Also,

To hold all Pleas, except those belonging to the Crown.

To chuse by their Common Council, as before, two Præpositi, who should keep faithfully the Government of the Town.

Also, to chuse by their Common Council, two substantial discreet Burgesses, to keep the Pleas of the Crown, and to see that the Præpositi§ behaved justly to poor and rich.

That all in scot and lot with the Burgesses, should be partakers with them in all their aids, assizes, tolls, and benefits, as they were wont.

That the Burgesses there, should be impleaded for their tenements, only in the borough.

Grants a power to distrain within the borough, for debts contracted there, Also,

To receive due toll and custom of all the Welsh, that came into the town with merchandize, as they were used to have. ‖

Grants assize of victuals, by the *Probi homines*, under a forfeiture.

Forbids any burgess to alienate any tenement in mortmain.

Grants to be governed by the laws, *Bretol et Baronie et Angleterie.*

Also, a Fair, on the 1st of June, and two days following.¶

---

* Excheq. 2 Book, p. 49.   † Exch. 2 Book. p. 49.   ‡ Exch; 2 Book, p. 49.

§ The business of these Præpositi, or Governours, afterwards called Bailiffs, seems to have been to receive the rent of the town, and account to the Crown for it.

‖ It hence appears they received toll (perhaps) before the Conquest, or under Earl Roger. By an agreement 33d Henry III. between Thomas Corbett, Lord of Cause and the Burgesses, they quit claim from all the Welsh that were tenants to the said Corbett. 4 Book, p. 43.

¶ Exch. Book 2, p. 50.

Y2

11th Henry III. March 2, 1226. The King grants the same as the last Charter, and confirms it,

Also, The burgesses to be a *Guilda Mercatoria cum Hansa.*

—— If any ones slave staid a year and a day in the said Guild, and paid scot and lot, he could not be demanded back by his master, but should be free.

—— An exemption from pontage, toll, and all exactions, granted to the Burgesses throughout the whole kingdom, except in London.*

—— That none should buy raw hides, nor undressed cloth, but such who were in scot and lot, assize and tallage, with the Burgesses, which priviledge had been before granted by King John, for which the Burgesses, &c. paid into the Exchequer a palfrey, and 20 marks yearly.†

40th Henry III. August 10, 1256. The King grants to the Burgesses, the return of writs concerning the town.

Also, To answer by themselves to the Exchequer for their debts.

—— That their goods should not be seized for any forfeiture made by their servants.

—— That if a Burgess die elsewhere, his goods should be restored to his heirs.

—— That they should not be summoned before foreigners, but before Burgesses, their peers.

—— Licence to appropriate to themselves lands in the borough.

—— That no sheriff, or officer, should take distresses within the liberties.

—— Confirms all their ancient priviledges.‡

—— That the Burgesses should not be arrested, nor their goods seized.§

49th Henry III. September 24, 1265. The King grants the Burgesses, for their fidelity to him and his son, exemption from murage throughout his kingdom. ‖

Edward II. 13th year, February 2, 1319. Granted a Charter of confirmation of the 4 Charters of Henry III. by an Inspeximus.¶

March 3, 1326, Edward III. recites that Henry III. had granted a Fair on St. Clement's Day, (November 28), and that King Edward II. had granted a Fair on St. James's Day, instead of which, he grants a Fair on the Eve of St. Matthew, the Day, and the two following days, with all their liberties and customs.**

---

* Exch 2 Book, p. 52.   † Exch. 2 Book, p. 54.   ‡ Exch. 2 Book, p. 55.
§ Exch. 2 Book, p 56.   ‖ Exch. 2 Book, p. 57.   ¶ Exch. 2 Book, p. 57.

** The Grants here mentioned of Henry III. and Edward II. are not to be found.—The town had but two Fairs, till the Charter of Henry VIII. which two must be the above-mentioned of St. Matthew, and that on the Wednesday before Whitsunday. The Abbey Foregate Fairs must be in grants to the Abbots; and the two others were granted by Charles I.—See p. 15.—Henry I. granted the Abbot a Fair, *ad vincula S⁺ʰ. Petri,* for three days.—See Exch. 4 B. p. 88 and p. 101. A Fair is said to be granted by Earl Roger, on the first of August, with the toll, and all the profit. For the Grant of Edward III. see Exch. Book 2, p. 58.

The same King, May 12, 1328, Granted a Licence to erect a Town Mill. October 25, 1328. A Charter of confirmation of former Charters.*
March 10, 1336. Another Charter of confirmation.

May 15, 1341. He confirms and enlarges former Charters, and grants the Bailiffs power to attach, imprison, to hold a Sessions, and to try causes, which powers were granted at the request of Lord Arundel, and other Noblemen in Parliament.†

March 5, 1376. He granted another Charter of confirmation of a Charter of Henry III.‡

Richard II. in his first year, January 27, 1377. Granted a Charter of confirmation of all former Charters.§ And November 22, 1388. Another Charter of confirmation of former Charters, ‖ and two years after, viz. 1390, the Earl of Arundel being commissioned by the King to end certain disputes among the Burgesses, ordered, that for the future good government of the town, the commonalty should elect out of themselves, twelve of the most sufficient persons, who should continue in their offices two years, from the Feast of St. Giles the Abbot; upon which the following twelve persons were elected for that purpose, who may be accounted the first Aldermen of Shrewsbury. Viz.

Thomas le Skynner	Thomas Pryde
Rich. de Pontesbury	John Perle
Rich. de Beorton	Reynald de Mutton
Will de Byrinton	John Geffrey
Rich Stury	Ja͞ Dyer
Robͭ de Thornes	John le Tyler.

Accordingly the twelve persons so chosen, together with the Bailiffs, made a Corporation, for the better government of the town, which was confirmed by the King, in the 22d year of his reign.

19th of Richard II. February 7, 1395. The King granted, that if the Lords of the Marches attached any Burgesses for actions, that did not arise within their own Manors. it should be lawful for the Bailiffs to attach them or their Bailiffs, when they should be found in Salop, till they had made satisfaction; in the same manner as at the cities of London and Bristol¶.

The same King in his 22nd year, June 31, 1398. In another grant recites a composition that was made in the Abbey of Shrewsbury 13th the same reign, about the method of chusing 2 Bailiffs, 6 Cessors, 2 Coroners, Auditors, Serjeants, &c.**

---

* Exch. 2 Book, p. 59.
† Exch. 2 Book, p. 60. This is the first time Bailiffs appear to be named in the Exchequer Records.
‡ Exch. 2 Book, p. 63. § Exch. 2 Book. p. 64. ‖ Exch. 2 Book, p. 65.
¶ Exch. 2 Book, p. 66. ** Exch. 4 Book, p. 46.

1399. About Whitsunday, Robert de Thornes and William de Byrinton, were by virtue of a new composition of the town, removed from their offices of Bailiffs, and Thomas de Paunceley, and Richard Alderscote, were elected in their stead for that year, and continued in office the year following.

Henry IV. in his first year, September 28, 1400. Granted to the Bailiffs and Burgesses, *probis hominibus et Communitati*, A Charter of confirmation of former Charters, and Privileges, and recites the letters patent of June 31, 22d of Richard II. confirming the composition of the 13th of Richard II. made in the Abbey of Salop, before Lord Arundel and Surry, the Abbot, and many others, by the two Bailiffs Robert de Thornes and Hugh Wigan, and 12 persons chose by the Commonalty.—The 2 Bailiffs were to be sworn to chuse indifferently 25 Burgesses, which 25 were to elect the new Bailiffs, each Bailiff to have £10 per ann. in rent, or £100 in merchandize, and to be housholder resident —The said 25 were also upon oath to chuse 6 Cessors, and 2 Coroners, which 2 Coroners were to survey every week, all manner of works touching the said town, and to have for their fee 12d. between them.—Each Bailiff's fee 40s. and a robe of 5 ells of cloth, at 4s. per ell.—The Town Clerk's fee was 40s. his livery 20s. and 26s. 8d. allowed him for parchment, and his pains in writing the court rolls and acccounts.—The Steward's fee and livery the same. —The election to be on the Sunday after the feast of St. Giles, before six persons to be elected by the Commons.—That no resident Burgess should be absent on the day of election.—That the Bailiffs should make Serjeants, for whom they could answer, the Serjeants to account for issues and estreats of courts and Bibsters* fines, every quarter—Tensors† fines, to be levied before the feast of St. Catharine.—No Serjeant to take any fee for any thing that comes into the town, unless of such as shall be found of record. The Bailiffs and 6 Cessors to deliver each Serjeant a bill sealed with the office seal, of all fees due and found on record, and that they be sworn to take no other.—The collectors of toll and murage, to be chosen annually.‡

Henry VI. in his 23rd year, June 7, 1445, granted to the Bailiffs and Burgesses, felons goods, forfeitures, deodands, &c. for the use of the Burgesses.—That the Bailiffs should be Escheators, and receive the goods and chattels called mayonor, for the use of the Burgesses.—Also grants pleas.— That the Bailiffs should be Justices, and forbids county Justices to act in the borough.—The Bailiffs to determine between merchants, and to attach for debts.

24th of Henry VI. January 12, 1445.—The King confirmed and enlarged the Bailiffs authority to try causes.—Grants that the Recorder, who must be

---

* Now called Alesellers, who were fined at every Court Leet.
† Not being Burgesses, paid such fine as the Court Leet set upon them.
‡ It hence appears there was toll or custom due before the charter of Henry VI. See page 18, of Bailiffs accounts, June 1, 1st of Henry V.

legis peritus, be a Justice, and be joined with the Bailiffs, or one of them to hold gaol delivery.—Also that the Coroners impannel Juries.—Recites that March 15,* 20th of Henry VI. the King had granted toll for ten years, for the repairs of the walls and bridges, because the inhabitants had resisted the incursions of the Welsh, and Owen Glendour,† and he now makes that grant perpetual, by authority of Parliament.

* The charter of March 15, 20th of Henry VI. is wanting, but is recited as above and in that of December 14, 11th of Henry VII.

---

† Owen Glendour, Glendower, or Owain Glyndwr, has been sometimes called the Wallace of Wales. The precise date of his birth is uncertain, some fixing it at May 28th, 1349, others on the same day in 1354. The place of his nativity is better ascertained to have been Trefgarn, in Pembrokeshire, where he was born of Ellen, a lineal descendant from Catherine, daughter and heiress to Llewellyn, last Prince of Wales. His father's name was Gryffyd Vychan, *(Vaughan.)* At an early age he was sent to London for education, and afterwards entering himself of one of the inns of court, studied for the English bar, but relinquished the profession on being appointed scutiger to Richard II. Jolo Goch, a contemporary bard, gives a splendid description of his family mansion, or rather palace, and indeed he appears at this time to have exercised considerable feudal influence, carrying on with great spirit a contest of some duration with Reginald lord Grey de Ruthyn respecting an estate called Croesau, in which he was for a time successful; but on the deposition of his royal patron by Henry of Bolingbroke, his old antagonist took advantage of the unsettled state of the country to renew his usurpation. Nor did his evil practices end here, for Grey, being charged with the delivery of a summons to Owen from the new king to attend him on his Scotch expedition, purposely neglected to deliver it, and Glendour being in consequence outlawed for disaffection, his enemy seized upon all his lands, and the parliament treated his remonstrances with contempt. Glendour, in revenge, rushed into rebellion, forcibly dispossessed Grey of his lands, and having succeeded in raising a considerable force, caused himself to be proclaimed prince of Wales, September 20. 1400. To this strong measure he is said to have been mainly incited by some traditional prophecies of Merlin; and certain it is, that many of his countrymen of consideration were induced, by the same motives, to join his standard. In one of the battles fought on this occasion in, 1402, he made prisoner his old enemy, the lord Grey, the price of whose ransom was fixed at 10,000 marks, and a stipulation of neutrality, which latter was cemented, or rather converted into amity afterwards, by Jane, Owen's third daughter, becoming lady Grey. Having defeated the king's troops under sir Edward Mortimer, Henry put in motion against him three grand divisions of his army, but retiring to the mountains he foiled all attempts to bring him to action, and the rebellion of the Percys breaking out, joined the coalition, causing himself at the same time to be formally crowned at Machynlleth in Montgomeryshire, "Sovereign of Wales." The rashness of Henry Percy brought on the fatal battle of Shrewsbury before all his Welch auxiliaries had come up. Their Prince, however, is said to have been so near as to have reconnoitered the action from the top of a lofty tree; (See page 28. this volume.) but seeing all was lost, directly retreated and continued his marauding warfare. This he kept up with various success, occassionally assisted by Charles, VI. of France, with whom a treaty of his is yet extant, dated 1404, in which he is styled "Owenus Dei gratiâ Princeps Walliæ." Finding it impossible to subdue, Henry in 1415 condescended to treat with him; but Owen died on the 20th of September in that year, during the negociation, which was however continued and ratified by his son Meredyd ap Owen, February 24, 1416. Direct descendants of his are yet living in the family of Moninzton, settled at the place of that name in Herefordshire; which is also assigned, by tradition, as the burial-place of Glendower.

The Vaughans of Nannau, Hengwrt, and Rûg, in Merionethshire, all branches of one family, are lineally descendants of Owain Glyndwr; and Grufydd Hywel Vaughan, Esq. of Rûg, possesses now a large portion of those domains which once belonged to his ancestor. This gentleman has also in his possession an elegant and highly-prized memorial of the Chieftain: it is a case, containing a

24th Henry VI. July 20, 1446. An act of Parliament was passed, which recites divers compositions made by the Bailiffs and Commonalty of the town of Shrewsbury, for the good government thereof, which had been confirmed by Parliament to endure for a time, which were in a schedule annexed, and are by this act made perpetual, and authorizes the Bailiffs to sue for the penalties therein mentioned, either in their Guild Hall, or in Westminster.

28th of Henry VI. An act of Parliament was passed, being a reassumption of grants.

2d of Edward IV. A charter of confirmation of former grants was given.*

10th of Edward IV. 1469, April 10. Two acts of Parliament were passed againt the Welsh, who might be tried in England, at the request of the Bailiffs and Burgesses of Salop.

18th Edward IV. April 10, 1478. By an order of the Council of the Marches, Lord Bishop of Worcester President, Lord Rivers, the Prince's Uncle and Governor, and others present; any stranger who staid in town above two days, might be taken up by the Wardens, and four Assistants of a company, and be imprisoned by them, and those who did not obey their Wadens, were to be put out of their craft.†

7th of Henry VII. An act of reassumption of the 10th and 15th of Henry VI. was obtained, with a proviso, that nothing therein should be prejudicial to the letters patent of December 12, 1st. of Henry VII. to the Bailiffs and Burgesses of Salop.‡

11th of Henry VII. December 14th, 1495. The King confirms his own Charter of Dec. 12, 1st of Henry VII. wherein he remits to the Bailiffs, Burgesses, and Inhabitants, in regard for their decay, 10 marks of the town rent§

---

* Exch. 2 Book, p. 80.   † Exch. 2 Book, p. 224.

‡ The Grants here mentioned of 1st of Henry VII, and the act of 7th of Henry VII, are not to be found. That of the 1st of Henry VII. is recited in the Charter of December 14, 11th of Henry VII.

§ The town rent was 30 marks, and 5 marks for the increase of the fee-farm, viz. £23. 6s. 8d. In the year 1650 the town purchased the fee-farm off the Parliament's Trustees, for £182. 6s. 8d. as appears by the Bailiffs accounts, fol. 1652, which afterwards proved a void purchase.

---

dagger, and a knife and fork; the three are in the same sheath, but each in a separate compartment, richly ornamented with silver; the knife and fork are rather slender, and the dagger is about seventeen inches long, twelve of which constitute the blade, which tapers to a point; at the end of the handle is the family coat of arms—a Lion rampant, and three Fleur-de-lis, very curiously and neatly engraved. The principal part the handle is inlaid with black and yellow wood, and hooped with silver; the haft is a piece of the same metal : the knife and fork are obliged to be sheathed first, when the hilt of the dagger covers them, consequently the latter must be drawn first. The building where Glyndwr assembled the states of the principality, still exists in Machynlleth. part of it is now, or was lately, a Butcher's Shop.—*Thomas's Life of Glendower, and Cathrall's History of North Wales.*

for 50 years.—Also grants a view of Frank Pledge, *viz.* Court Leet.—Assize of bread and beer, fines, and waifs, through all the liberties and hamlets.—Return of writs.—The Bailiffs to be Escheators, and the Escheators of the county not to intrude.—To take cognizance of Pleas touching lands, &c.—The Bailiffs to be Justices.—The Recorder, with the Bailiffs, or one of them, *to* hold Gaol Delivery.—To attach.—No Sheriff to intrude.—Grants felons goods.—Forfeitures.—Hidden Treasures, &c. to the use of the Burgesses.—Also Toll, the same as Henry VI.—Exemptions from tenths and fifteenths, to all the inhabitants.—The Inhabitants to have divers priviledges, but not to be of the Guild, except admitted.—And confirms all former Grants, Priviledges, &c.*

34th Henry VIII. April 16, 1542. The King in a Grant recites the Charter of November 24; 6th Edward IV. and the several priviledges the Abbot of Shrewsbury thereby had, within his manor of the parish of the Holy-Cross and St. Giles, and in Meryvale, and that he (the Abbot) had surrendered all to the King, January 24, 31 Henry VIII. And the King grants to the Bailiffs and Burgesses all the same priviledges in that Manor, which the Abbot before enjoyed there.† He also remits to the town for ever the ten marks, which Henry VII. had before remitted for fifty years, on condition that they should repair the Abbot's part of the Stone Bridge.

I Edward VI. December 12, 1547. The King granted a Charter of confirmation of all former Charters.‡

28th Elizabeth, April 2, 1586. The Queen enlarged the borough, by uniting the Abbey-Foregate to it.—Granted the Bailiffs and Burgesses to be a Body Corporate, and to have all the priviledges the Bailiffs and Burgesses had before, and also those which the Abbot had in the parish of Holy-Cross, St. Giles, and Meryvale.—Also to have a Common Seal.—To chuse two Bailiffs, a Town-Clerk, and other Officers, out of the Burgesses inhabiting the town and liberties, or the Abbey-Foregate.—The Abbey-Foregate to be in scot and lot with the Burgesses.§—To be a suburbs united to the town, and to be called the Stone Ward.—Also a Court of Conscience, the Bailiffs to be Judges, not exceeding 40s.—The Bailiffs to hold a Court of Record, every Tuesday, for all pleas and actions of trespasses, with a power to levy fines, and to make six Attornies of their Court. ‖—The inhabitants not to be compelled out of their town to appear before foreign Justices.—To make records, inrolments of deeds, estates, &c.—To receive recognizances between merchant and merchant.—To chuse six Aldermen past the chair to be Justices.—The Recorder, with the Bailiffs, or one of them to hold Gaol Delivery.—The Town Coroners to be Coroners in the Abbey-Foregate.—Liberty to acknowledge writs of right, pleas, &c.—The

* Exch. Book, p. 96.   † Exch. 2 Book. p 99   ‡ Exch. 2 Book, p. 99.   § Exch. 2 Book, p. 113.   ‖ Exch. 2 Book, p. 116.

z

Bailiffs to have return of writs.—A view of frankpledge.—Assize of bread.—
The Bailiffs to be Clerks of the markets and Escheators.—Grants a Water-Bai-
liff.- That the Bailiff's and Recorder, with such as they should take to them,
might correct and alter customs according to law.—Also, grants forfeitures,
felons goods, deodands, waifs, &c. to the use of the Burgesses.—Leave to levy
fines.—Exemption from tenths and fifteenths.—Also, recites a grant of the
castle, January 25, 7th Eliz. to Richard Onslowe, for 31 years, and grants it
to the town for ever, paying for rent £13 4s. per annum.   Also a Licence to
purchase in Mortmain, to found Preachers in Salop, to last for ever.—None but
Burgesses to merchandize.—None to be admitted Burgesses, but by the consent of the Bailiffs and Burgesses.—And confirms to all Burgesses and Inhabitants, their usual Liberties, Customs, Priviledges, &c. not to be interrupted.*

   14th Charles I. June 16, 1638.   The King by a grant recites, that the Freemen and Burgesses of Salop, have used divers prescriptions and customs, from
time immemorial, and have also several priviledges granted by former Charters.†
Also recites Queen Elizabeth's Charter.—And appoints one supreme Magistrate,
forming a Body Politick, by the name of the Mayor, Aldermen, and Burgesses,
capable to purchase and alienate, to sue, and to be sued, and to have a Common
Seal.‡—To be within the town and liberties, one Mayor, twenty-four Aldermen,
and forty-eight Assistants, these to be called the Common Council of the town,
the Aldermen and Assistants to council and aid the Mayor, and in some cases,
the senior Alderman.—Thomas Jones, Esq. appointed the first Mayor, to take
an oath, and continue in office, till the Friday after St. Bartholomew, in 1639.§
The senior Alderman to be elected Mayor, on the Friday after St. Bartholomew,
and to be sworn into office on the Friday after Michaelmas.   If he refuse, or
die, the next senior Alderman to be chose.‖—During any vacancy or occupation
of a Mayor, the senior Alderman to take the oath, and officiate as Mayor, and on
his refusal, the next senior.¶—The Aldermen to take their oaths, and continue
for life.**—An Alderman to be elected by the majority of Aldermen remaining,
out of the Assistants.—An Assistant to be elected by the Mayor, and greater
number of the Assistants, out of the Burgesses.††—The Mayor, Aldermen, and
Assistants, constantly to reside in the town or liberties.‡‡—Two Chamberlains
to be chose by the Mayor, Aldermen, and Assistants, on the Friday after
Michaelmas, for one year.§§—Timothy Turner appointed Recorder, and after
his death the Mayor, Aldermen, and Assistants, to elect an honest man to be Recorder during life.‖‖—Thomas Owen, Esq. appointed Town Clerk, with power
to appoint a Deputy, and after his death or departure, the Mayor, Aldermen,
and Assistants to elect an honest man to be Town Clerk, during life.¶¶—The
Recorder, Steward, and Town Clerk, are allowed to appoint Deputies.**—The

---

* Exch. 2 Book, p. 124.   † Exch. 2 Book, p 137.   ‡ Ditto, p 139.   § Exch. 2 Book, p. 141.
‖ Exch. Book 2, p. 142.   ¶ Ditto p. 144. ** Ditto, p. 145. †† Ditto, p. 146. ‡‡ Ditto, p. 147.
§§ Ditto, p 147.   ‖‖ Ditto, p. 49.   ¶¶ Ditto, p. 150. ** Ditto, p. 152.

Mayor, Aldermen, and Assistants to chuse two Coroners, and no Coroner of the county to act within the borough.*—They to chuse four Auditors.†—They to chuse a Sword Bearer, the Sword to be carried where the Maces formerly were, but not erect in any church.—They to chuse on the Friday after Michaelmas, three Serjeants at Mace, to carry their Maces before the Mayor, and to attend Courts.‡—The Serjeants may appoint their Yeomen, to serve processes, warrants, &c.§—The Mayor, &c. to chuse all other Officers that have been usually chosen, and on an equality of voices, the Mayor to have two votes.—If any person elected to any office refuses to act, the Mayor, Aldermen, and Assistants may disfranchise him, or fine or imprison him, the fine to be to the use and support of the whole body.—The Mayor, Recorder, and Steward to frame oaths.∥— The Mayor, Aldermen, and Assistants may remove from office, any Mayor, Alderman, or Assistant for non-residence or mal-practices in their office.—To have a Council House, for Meetings, Courts, &c.¶—A power is granted them to make bye-laws for the government of the town.—The Mayor, Aldermen, and Burgesses may have a Court of Record in the Guild Hall on every Tuesday, before the mayor and Recorder.** A power is granted to attach.—Six Attorneys of the Court to be named by the Mayor.††—The Mayor, the Bishop of Litchfield and Coventry, the Recorder, Steward, the three senior Aldermen, and the Alderman who was last Mayor, to do all the offices of justices, to take oaths, &c.— The Mayor, Recorder, and Steward, or two of them, whereof the Mayor to be one, to hold gaol delivery. The Coroners to return Juries, &c.‡‡—To be six Constables within the walls, two in each ward, to be sworn at the Court Leet.§§ Also, a Fair granted on the first day of December, and another on the Wednesday after Easter.—Piccage and stallage is granted, and the same toll as the Bailiffs and Burgesses had at other fairs.—Also, confirms Queen Elizabeth's licence to purchase in Mortmain.∥∥—Confirms all customs by prescription, or grant, tolls, piccage, stallage, murage, pontage, &c. as full as the Bailiffs and Burgesses ever enjoyed them;¶¶ and confirms all former grants, notwithstanding an act 23d Henry VI. for the preservation of the town, and another Ist Edward IV.

15th Charles II. By the statute of 13 Charles II. Ch. 1. for the regulating Corporations, it is enacted, that no Charter of any Corporation in England, &c. should at any time then after be avoided, for or by reason of any act, or thing done, or omitted to be done, before the first day of the parliament.— Yet, in the 15th Charles II a *Quo Warranto* was brought against this Charter, and the town constrained to surrender the Castle to the King, and to purchase* a confirmation, which is granted by Letters Patent under the Great

* Ditto, p. 153.   † Ditto, p. 154.   ‡ Ditto, p. 156.   § Ditto, p. 158.   ∥ Ditto, p. 160.
    ¶ Ditto, p. 161.   ** Ditto, p. 163.   †† Ditto, p. 165.   ‡‡ Exch 2 Book, p. 166 and 170.
        §§ Exch. Book, p 171.   ∥∥ Ditto, p. 173.   ¶¶ Ditto, p. 174.

* The new charter cost about £100.—*Llewellin's Manuscript.*

z2

Seal of England, dated July 6, 16th, Charles II. whereby Queen Elizabeth's Charter, and this, and all other liberties, &c. except the Castle, are confirmed; but there is a proviso, that none hereafter shall be chosen to the office of Recorder, Steward, or Town-Clerk, without the King's approbation.

By the above-mentioned statute of 13th Charles II. for regulating corporations, Lord Newport, and several other country gentlemen were appointed to place and displace the Aldermen and Council in Shrewsbury.—Richard Bagot, then Mayor, was displaced, and Robert Forster, put in his room, ten Aldermen were put out, and twenty new ones appointed to make the number full, viz. twenty-four; thirty-two of the Common Council were displaced, or taken to be Aldermen, and sixteen new ones made to make that number full, viz. forty-eight.

King James II. afterwards granted a new* Charter to the town, but the old one was restored again in 1688, and is that by which the Corporation now acts.

In the before-mentioned Grant of Edward III. dated March 3d. 1326, together with the annexed Note, the several Grants of Fairs to the town of Shrewsbury are mentioned.

THE FOLLOWING IS A LIST OF THEM, AS NOW KEPT.

NAMES.	TIME HELD.	GRANTED.	COMMODITIES, &c. SOLD.
First Horn-Market.	Last Saturday in February.	By Corporation, 1762.	Horned cattle, horses, &c.
Second Horn-Market	Saturday after the 15th of March.	By Ditto, 1702.†	Horned cattle, horses, sheep, swine, cheese, &c.
Easter Fair.	Wednesday after Easter.	By Charles I. 1638.	Horned cattle, horses, sheep, swine, cheese, and linen cloth.
Whitsun Fair.	Wednesday before Whitsunday.	By King John, 1204.	Horned cattle, horses, sheep, swine, cheese, and linen cloth.
Midsummer Fair.‡	July 3d.	To the Abbots, by Henry I.	Horned cattle, horses, swine, sheep, cheese, linen cloth, and wool.
Lammas Fair.‡	August 12th.	To the Abbots, by Earl Roger.	Ditto, Ditto.
St. Matthew's Fair.	October 2d.	By Edward III, 1326.	Horned cattle, horses, sheep, swine, cheese, butter, cloth.
St. Andrew's Fair.	December 12th.	By Charles I. 1638.	Ditto, Ditto.

† At the request of Mr. Methusalem Jones, of Underhill.
‡ Principally held in Abbey-Foregate, and called Abbey-Foregate Fairs.

* 1684, June 13th, the old charter was surrendered to King James with the town seal, and taken up to London by Lord Chief Justice Jones and others.—*Llewellin's Manuscript.*

Besides fairs,* the town is exceedingly well supplied with all sorts of provisions on the weekly markets, Wednesdays and Saturdays.

On the first Friday after St. Bartholomew's day, in every year, the Mayor is chose, by the Aldermen and Assistants, and sworn into office the first Friday after Michaelmas day.

Four General Quarter Sessions are held every year, *viz.*

The Friday in the first week after Epiphany.
———————————————————— the close of Easter.
———————————————————— the translation of Thomas a Becket.
†——————————————————— the feast of St. Michael.

The Mayor, and some of the Justices attend in the Exchequer, every Tuesday, between the hours of twelve and two, to transact public business; and through the vigilant attention of some who have filled up the offices of magistracy, many useful regulations have from time to time been made, for the preservation of order, and to promote the convenience and happiness of the inhabitants.

The following Orders issued by the Corporation, and selected from Exchequer books, will afford some information and amusement, as in several respects, they shew the difference between past and present times, and are an addition to the historical account of the town.

---

* The FAIRS are at present twelve in the year, and are held the second Tuesday and Wednesday in every month. This modern regulation has been greatly censured by some, while on the other hand the absolute certainty that no change takes place in the date or time of the Fairs, enables Farmers and Dealers to attend, without meeting with a disappointment. There remains, notwithstanding, one troublesome difficulty, viz. the Horse Fairs are sometimes held in the Abbeyforegate, sometimes on the Welsh Bridge, at other times in the Castleforegate.

The Cheese Fairs were formerly held *entirely* on Pride Hill, to the great inconvenience of carriages passing through the town in that direction, but to the great advantage of the inhabitants of that neighbourhood, who usually devoted their houses, shops, cellars, &c. to the warehousing and weighing, of butter and cheese, for which the farmers paid for butter, 6d. per tub, and for cheese, 6d. per cwt. When I was the proprietor of the premises, now Mr. Wildig's China Warehouse, &c. I received as much as fifteen pounds in one day for warehousing and weighing. Since the erection by Mr Newton of the commodious New Market at the Welsh Bridge, the advantages enjoyed by the residents of Pride Hill have been gradually declining.

Shrewsbury Fairs are in general numerously and respectably attended. The Shropshire Farmers are comparatively speaking wealthy men, some of them are very extensive land proprietors. Mr. W. B. Price of Felton Butler, who constantly attends the fairs and markets in person, has not only large estates, but is a Banker; his property is estimated at not less than £200,000.

The Dealers, Factors, or MERCHANTS, as they may be termed, who purchase at our Fairs, are many of them men of considerable property also, having establishments in London, Liverpool, Bristol, &c.

The first Monthly Fair, according to the new regulation was held the second Wednesday in January, 1819.—EDITOR.

† The Sessions for the Michaelmas Quarter are now held the Friday in the week, *next after* the 11th of October.—EDITOR.

ORDERS, &c.

HENRY VIII.

1516 Ordered that a Thanksgiving be made for the birth of a Princess, at St. Mary's Church, by all the Choirs of the town.

1519 Ordered that Tensors selling ale, should pay 6d. quarterl.y— (*Note.* Tensors, were such as not being Burgesses, yet traded in the town, for which liberty they paid such fines as by the Court Leet were set upon them.)

—— Orders were taken by the Bailiffs and Aldermen, for regulating the bakers in making loaves.

—— Brewers were ordered not to use hops in their brewings, under the penalty of 6s. 8d.*

—— Alesellers ordered to pay 6d. quarterly.

—— Burgesses to have the first licences, and to sell ale at 2d. per gallon, also to use sealed measures.

1528 Ordered that country bakers be allowed to sell bread in town.

1531 Ordered that vintners do not sell their Malmsey wine, above 16d. per gallon.

1535 Agreed to find a hogshead of wine, four lambs, and twelve capons, for the King's Commissioners, at the Abbey of St. Peter's, Salop.

—— Ordered that no one shall sell ale for more than one penny per gallon, and the meaner sort for no more than a farthing.

1536 Agreed to call the Burgesses of the town before the Bailiffs, to know whether they will serve the town with flesh, at the following rates, *viz.* beef, pork, mutton, and veal, at a farthing a pound ; or else they would find other persons to do it.

—— Order that the brewers sell the best ale at one penny farthing a gallon.

—— Ordered that the Clerk of St. Alkmund's have 40d. half-yearly, for ringing the watch bell, at four o'clock every morning.

ELIZABETH.

1558 Ordered that all such who are or have been Bailiffs, and their wives, should wear scarlet gowns, on all scarlet days.

—— Ordered that unless the Bakers Company pay £4 6s. 8d. yearly, which has been paid time out of mind to the Corporation, and called the Serjeant's Fee, that foreign bakers shall be allowed to bake and sell bread in town.

—— Ordered that Cadogan's Tower, (See page 36,) be let for 48 years, at 2s. per annum. The Bailiffs reserving a power to re-enter in case of war.

---

* Hops were in use some time before this, for in 1428, the Parliament were petitioned to prevent the use of them, as being a wicked weed.

—— Ordered that a Bailiff arresting a person by a Sheriff's Writ in town, forfeits £20.

—— Ordered that country bakers sell bread in town, on Wednesdays and Saturdays, between the hours of ten and three.——Also, that foreign butchers may come in to sell flesh, upon Saturdays, and have a place appointed them near St. Alkmond's Church.

1598 Agreed to disburse £820. for the relief of the inhabitants of this Corporation, in the present extremity and dearth.

—— Ordered that John Salter, for abusing the Judges servants, be degraded, and discharged of his Burgesship. C 6. p. 34.

1600 9th July, Agreed that Adam Mytton do find the Judges a house, and all other necessaries at the next assize for £3. 6s. 8d. in respect of courtesy, and £3. 6s. 8d. to the High Sheriff for house rent for the Judges.

1601 Ordered that Randle Hughes be discharged as a Burgess, for speaking opprobrious words against the Bailiffs.

1602 Agreed that Mr. Thomas Lawrence, Head Schoolmaster, being grown poor, be allowed £5. and 50s. in hand out of the Corporation revenues, for his great pains in procuring good order in the Free Grammar School.

JAMES I.

1603 Ordered that no man should be Town Clerk, but a Burgess of the town, and Utter Barrister.

1609 Agreed that the fee-farm chief rent* of this town be purchased from the Crown, and the charter of the town renewed. C. 6. p. 127.

—— Agreed that the Coroners view and present all doors made through the Town Walls, and if not made up to be fined. C. 6. p. 131.

1610 Ordered that £3. 6s. 8d. each, be allowed to the Bailiffs for charges of sessions dinner.

1613 Agreed that the Bailiff's treat with the Commissioners, for levying a tax on the inhabitants for aiding the marriage of Lady Elizabeth, the King's eldest daughter. C. 6. p. 165.

—— Ordered that the town provide 100 trained soldiers, to continue therein for the defence of the Corporation.—And two persons in each street to search for vagrants. C. 6. p. 167.

1618 Ordered that the school boys play only on Thursdays in the afternoon, unless at the request of some men of honour, and then to grant Tuesdays in the afternoon, by consent of Mr. Bailiffs. C. 6. p. 22.

1619 Ordered that the country butchers shall come in, and a new shamble be set up for them near St. Alkmond's Church.

---

* The chief rent was £23. 6s. 8d.—*Llewellin's Manuscript.*

—— Ordered that 5 marks yearly be paid out of the town's treasury to Mr. Lloyd, so long as he reads prayers in the morning at St. Alkmond's.—Also that the Corporation endeavour to compel the Wardens of the the Bakers Company, to pay their old annuity of £4. 6s. 8d. to the Corporation.

1623 Agreed to give £1. 6s. 8d. per ann. for ringing at St. Julian's, at four in the morning, and tolling at six and twelve. (*Note*, this was first ordered in the year 1557, by Mr. John Holliwell, one of the Bailiffs, and from him called Holliwell's Knell. This has been discontinued several years.)

CHARLES I.

1632 Agreed that country butchers be allowed to sell their flesh-meat on Wednesdays and Saturdays, near St. Julian's and St. Alkmond's Church yard walls, from eight o'clock in the morning to three in the afternoon, and that a proclamation be published, and £10 be allowed for erecting shambles.

1642 Agreed that considering the great distractions that are now in this Kingdom, and the great fears the inhabitants of this Corporations are in, that they do, by one consent join together for the preservation of the peace of this town and liberties, against all unlawful force, and that no person or persons do wear or bear any colours of any side or party. And also that all men of abilities, do provide arms for the defence of themselves and the town, and that all strangers do forthwith avoid the town.—Also agreed, that if the King's Majesty (Charles I.) comes to this town, that then he shall have free access into the town, and that the town do make the best entertainment for him these troublesome times can afford.

1643 January 31, Agreed that as Prince Rupert, his Highness, is shortly expected to come to this town, that an assesment of £1000 be raised for him at one payment.

1644 Ordered that the streets of the town should be kept clean, during the present sickly time.—Also that the Bailiffs raise what they can from the innkeepers and traders, towards the entertainment of the Judges.

1650 Ordered that the Pest House at Kingsland shall be repaired.

1651 Agreed that as the day of thanksgiving for the taking of this town by the Parliament's forces, falls out on a Sunday, the same shall be observed on Tuesday next, February 24. The whole House to appear in their scarlet robes and gowns, and the Wardens of the several Companies, to attend divine service, or forfeit, Aldermen 2s. Wardens and Assistants 1s each.

1654 Ordered that all due care should be taken for the preservation of the town during the plague.

1658 September 8, Ordered that Richard Cromwell, Lord Protector, shall be proclaimed.

1660 Friday May 11, Ordered that King Charles II. be proclaimed, and that the Aldermen and Assistants who were rejected by the Parliament's forces, be restored.

1663   Ordered that the Castle be surrendered to the King, and his successors.

1664   Ordered, for want of ladders in case of fire, to take down Maypoles and make some.

1669   Ordered that the butchers and bakers, brewers and alesellers, be summoned to contribute to the charge of holding the assizes.

1669   Ordered that a Ducking Stool be erected, for the punishment* of all scolds.

1677   Ordered that as soon as the chimes at eight o'clock have done going, they immediately begin the eight o'clock bell, at St. Chad's, and ring a quarter of an hour; and when ended there, St. Alkmond's great bell to ring a quarter of an hour; and when ended, the nine o'clock bell to begin at St. Mary's, and to ring a quarter of an hour; or the Sextons of the several parishes not to be allowed any thing by the Corporation.

1678   Ordered that all inn-keepers, and victuallers, with other public housekeepers, hang out lights, each dark night, from six in the evening till nine at night, under a penalty of 3s. 4d.

1684   June 13, Agreed at a full Assembly, that the Charter of the town of Shrewsbury should be surrendered and yielded up to his Majesty, when his pleasure is to require it.   And that Mr. Recorder, and Mr. Edward Kynaston, draw up a Petition to his Majesty, signifying the contents of the Order for that purpose; and that Collins Woolrich, Esq. Mayor, do please to attend Lord Chief Justice Jones, with the Order, and to take with him such other persons of quality, as he shall think fit.

A LIST OF THE BAILIFFS AND MAYORS OF
SHREWSBURY.

Reimerus, was one of the first Bailiffs, after the Conquest, he is among the Benefactors to the Abbey, stiled Reimerus Præfectus, alias Præpositus.†

Edricus, somewhat later, who in a Grant to an Hermitage at Sutton, is stiled Edricus Præpositus. †

† Dug. Mon. V. 1. p. 376.

---

* There is the *iron* headstall of a bridle, now in the Town Hall, formerly used for the same purpose.—EDITOR.

A a

The following Persons served the office of Bailiffs, but uncertain in what years, till the 46th EDWARD III.

John Villanus
Simon Granegos
John de Paumer
Laur. fil. Edwin
John le Vileyn
John Burgh
Andw. fil. Hubert
Henry fil. Ivon
Richard Siche
Luke fil. Walter
Tho. Champeneys
William Vahan
John Villanus
Hugh Colley
Simon de Stafford
Wil. de Parmenter
Galf. fil. William Randolf
Thomas Colle
John Roberd
John de la Pole
Hugh le Donsowe
Tho. de Bykedon
Nicholas Ive
Nich. Pycheford
John fil. Hugh Villani
John Russel
John Stury
Wil. de Parmenter
John de Upton
John de Foryate
Rich. de Beorton
Reg. Skryven
Will. Longnore
Tho. le Skinner
John Geffrey
Will. de Biriton
John Stury
John Schetton
John Stury
Tho. de Biriton
John Stury
Richard Russell
Robt. de Thornes
Will. Longnore
John Stury
Will. le Skinner
Will. de Biryton

Tho. de Mutton
Roger de la Yate
John Stury
Will. de Biriton
Thomas Gamel
Rich. de Weston
John Stury
Will. le Skinner
Reginald Perle
Roger de la Yate
Thomas Gamel
Will. de Smethcote
Wal. de Smethcote
Robert de Upton
Reginald Perle
John de la Toure
John Stury
Will. le Skinner
Thomas Colle
John Stury
John Sherry
John de la Toure
John de Weston
Thomas Ive
John Rayner
Thomas Colle
John de Walesche
Thomas Vaghan
Nicholas Ive
Tho. de Bykedon
John Rayner
Galf Randulph
John Baldewyne
Gr. Montisgomeri
John Hagwas
Tho. de Bykedon
John Rayner
Hugh fil. Robert le Dousowe
Tho. de Bykedon
Reginald Perle
Hugh le Donsowe
Nicholas le Child
Roger Pride
Nich. le Spicer
Tho. de Bykedon
John Baldwyn

Reginald Perle
Wil. le Parmenter
Tho de Bykedon

KING JOHN.

Allan Villanus

HENRY III.

Galf. Randolf
Richard Berry
1246 Hugh le Villeyn
Peter fil. Martyn
1277 Richard Borry
1298 Tho. de Bykedon
1304 William Vaughan
1305 Hugh le Donsowe
Tho. de Bykdon
John Gamel
Alan Clement
John de Perle
Henry Wildegos
Hugh Barnard
William Vaghan
Richard Sturry
Robert Pally

EDWARD III. 46th YEAR.

1372 Tho. de Byryton
Roger de Yate

1373 John Sturrye
Regin. de Mutton

1374 R. de Pontesburye
John Jeffrey

1375 W. de Withyford
Rog. de Yate, alias de Loriat

1376 Regin de Mutton
Thomas de Preede

RICHARD II. BEGAN HIS
REIGN, JULY 16, 1377.

1377 Will. de Longnore
John Jeffrey

1378 Will. de Birington
James le Dyer

1379 Ric. de Beorton
Will de Weston

1380 Will. de Byriton
Tho. Preede

1381 Tho. le Skynner
Ric. Russel

1382 Will. de Birington
Hugh le Donfowe

1383 Tho. le Skynner
Thomas Preede

1384 Will. de Birington
Regin. de Mutton

1385 Will. de Birington
Hugh Wygone

1386 John Jeffrey
Regin. Mutton

1387 Richard de Stury
Will. de Byrington

1388 Robert Thornes
Hugh Wygone

1389 Hugh le Donfowe
James le Dyer

1390 Regin. de Mutton
Robert Grafton

1391 Sim. de la Towre
Randle de Forde

1392 John Geffrey
Will. Byrington

1393 Thomas Preede
Will. de Willely

1394 John Tyler
Ric. Awlderscott

1395 Will. de Byrington
Regin. Scryven

1396 John Geffrey
Jas. le Dyer, alias
Dygber

1397 Will. de Willeley
Michael Gerrard

1398 Robert Thornes
Will. de Birington*

---

* " Robert Thornes and William de Birington were removed on Tuesday before Whitsuntide, 22nd Richard II, 1399. " The circumstances attending their removal," say Messrs, Owen and Blakeway, are singular and deserving of notice."

"In the oldest book of the corporation marked A, are articles of accusation against one John Raves, one of the underbailiffs (i. e. what are now called serjeants-at-mace) of Shrewsbury. One of them runs thus : " And that the said J. R. on the 16th day of April, 22nd Richard II, at Shrewsbury, excited and procured many men of the community of the aforesaid town to rise and kill R. Thornes and W. Biriton, bailiffs, and other good and lawful men having the government and rule of the town. By pretext (i. e. reason) of which excitation and procuration the said bailiffs and the rest despaired of their lives." The election of Paunteley and Aldescote is thus entered in the same book :

" Electio Ballivorum de novo A°. xxij^do.

" Memorand. quod. die mart' prox' ante fest' Pentecost' anno r. r. Ric'i secundi xxij^do Robert' Thornes & Will' de Byriton remoti fuer' de officio Ballivor' virtute composicois ville Salop in presencia Hugonis Burnell militis unius Justic' d'ni Reg', Joh'is Beostan, Mathi del Mer & alior' generosor' tunc ibid' existencium ac omnium burgencium & communitatum ejusdem ville. Et eodem die & loco Thomas de Paunteley & Ric'us Aldescote ellecti sunt ad officium Ballivorum ville predicte & coram prefatis personis jurati, prout dicta composicio exigit & requirit."

" How sir Hugh Burnell, baron of Holgate, and a justice of peace for Shropshire, at a time when that commission was confined to a very few of the very highest personages in every county, and how the gentlemen mentioned above, with all the governing part of the town, yielded to a compliance, which appears to us so weak, with the demands of a furious rabble, we are left to conjecture. A slight glance at the great events which were now passing in the kingdom may afford a probable one. Tuesday before Whitsuntide, 22 Rich. II. the day when these bailiffs were turned out in consequence of the riotous proceedings, was the 20th of May, 1399, not a week before the King embarked for Ireland, leaving the kingdom very generally disgusted by his gross injustice to the banished duke of Lancaster, who, availing himself of that popular feeling, soon after thrust his oppressor from the throne. Burnell was a secret but warm adherent of the duke; but whether the Shrewsbury tumult was connected with that great revolution must be left to the judgment of the reader. The bailiffs would of course support the legitimate government of Richard : Raves and his associates broke forth perhaps in favour of the usurper Henry IV."

HENRY IV. SEPT. 30. 1399.

1399 Tho. de Pawnceley
Ric. Awlderscott

1400 James le Dyer
Thomas Porter

It is recorded in an old Book in the Excheq. marked A. P. 48, that Thomas Skynner, and Reg. de Mutton, were Bailiffs, between those of 1400 and 1401.

1401 Robert de Grafton
Will. de Birinton

1402 Robert Thornes
John Scryven

1403 Sim. de la Towre
William Forster

1404 Thomas Skynner
Richard Sturry

1405 William Towre
Will. Berington,Died
John Perle, Elect.

1406 John Perle, Junr.
John Scryven

1407 John Glover
David Rathbon

1408 Richard Sturry
Nicholas Shotton

1409 Robert Thornes
Sim. de la Towre

1410 John Perle, Junr.
William Towre

1411 Nicholas Gerrard
William Hoorde

1412 David Holbache
Richard Stury

HENRY V. MARCH 20, 1413.

1413 John Gamel
John Glover

1414 Nicholas Shotton
Robert Horsley

1415 David Rathbon
John Shelton

1416 Roger Corbet
John Perle

1417 Roger Corbet
John Perle

1418 William Hoord
John Forster

1419 David Rathbon
J. Northampton

1420 John Glover
Rob. Whitcombe

1421 John Shelton
Robert Horsley

HENRY VI. AUGUST 31, 1422.

1422 John Perle
Nic. Shotton

1423 John Towre
Vryan Semper, alias St. Piere

1424 John Gamel
John Glover

1425 John Shelton
William Forster

1426 Rob. Whitcome
Will. Burleigh

1427 William Towre
William Hoorde

1428 Nicholas Shelton
John Pawnton

1429 Roger Corbet
Richard Hoord

1430 Thomas Forster
Vrian Semper

1431 William Hoord
John Shelton

1432 Rob. Whitcome
Thomas Thornes

1433 Nich. Shelton
John Knight

1434 Thomas Forster
Will. Burleigh

1435 Richard Hoorde
John Fowlke

1436 Thomas Thornes
John Beggett

1437 Rob. Whitcome
John Scryven

1438 John Gamel
Rich. Burleigh

1439 Will. Burleigh
Thomas Ottley

1440 Thomas Thornes
Thomas Mytton

1441 Rob. Whitcome
John Mytton

1442 Richard Burleigh
John Gamell

1443 John Fowlke
Thomas Ottley

1444 Will. Burleigh
Richard Stury

1445 Robert Eyton
William Bastard

1446 Thomas Forster
Adam Goldsmith

1447 John Knight
J. Fowlke, Died
J. Gamell, Elect

1448 Will. Burleigh
Richard Stury

1449 Roger Eyton
John Hoord

1450 Robert Scryven
Thomas Lloyd

1451 John Gamell
William Bastard

1452 Richard Stury
Richard Burleigh

1453 John Cole
Phillip Grace

1454 William Burleigh
Robert Scryven

1455 Roger Eyton
John Trentam

1456 Richard Stury
John Hoord

1457 Nic. Fitz. Herbert
Roger Adis

1458 Robert Scryven
Nicholas Stafford

1459 John Trentam
Tho. Byrington

1460 John Knight
John Grafton

EDWARD IV. MARCH 5,
1461.

1461 Thomas Wynnes
Thomas Stone

1462 Thomas Lloyd
William Ottley

1463 John Baxter
Hugh Hosier*

1464 Richard Stury
Thomas Mytton

1465 Roger Knight
John Coulton

1466 John Cole
Edward Easthope

1467 John Trentam
Thomas Ottley

1468 Thomas Mytton
Tho. Goldsmith

1469 William Ottley
Tho. Pontesbury

1470 Roger Knight
John Baxter

1471 Hugh Hosier
Richard Wantner

1472 Thomas Mytton
John Trentam

1473 Thomas Ottley
Tho. Pontesbury

1474 William Ottley
Roger Horton

1475 John Cole
Rob. ap Egnion

1476 Thomas Mytton
Thomas Thornes

1477 John Hoord
Roger Knight

1478 Thomas Ottley
Tho. Byrinton

1479 Tho. Goldsmith
William Sugdon

1480 Thomas Mytton
Tho. Pontesbury

1481 Thomas Thornes
John Baxter

1482 John Hoord
J. Gyttyns, sen.

EDWARD V. APRIL 9, 1483.

RICHARD III. JUNE 22,
1483.

1483 Rich. Wantnor
John Ottley

1484 Thomas Mytton
Roger Knight

HENRY VII. AUGUST 22,
1485.

1485 Thomas Thornes
Nic. Pontesbury

1486 John Hoord
John Baxter

1487 Rich Wantnor
John Ottley

1488 Thomas Mytton
Roger Knight

1489 Thomas Thornes
Tho. Pontesbury

1490 John Gyttyns
Robert Thornes

1491 Thomas Trentam
Florice Semper

1492 Thomas Mytton
Nic. Pontesbury

1493 Will. Cole
Will. Pontesbury

1494 John Gyttyns
Lawrence Hosier

1495 Nic. Waringe
Hugh Walker

1496 Thomas Mytton
Edward Hosier

1497 Roger Thornes
Richard Forster

1498 William Cole
Lawrence Hosier

1499 John Lloyd
Nic. Pontesbury,
Died.
Nic. Waringe, Elect-
ed.

1500 Thomas Mytton
Thomas Trentam

* Hugo Pimley, M. S.

B b

1501 Thomas Knight
Edward Hosier

1502 William Cole
Richard Dycher

1503 Richard Mytton
Tho. Wythiford

1504 Roger Forster
Thomas Mytton Died
William Mytton,
Elected

1505 Roger Thornes
Thomas Knight

1506 Richard Lyster
Edward Hosier

1507 Tho. Trentam
Edward Knight

1508 William Mytton
Tho. Wythyford

HENRY VIII. APRIL 22,
1509.

1509 Roger Thornes
Thomas Knight

1510 David Ireland
Nic. Waringe, Died.
Edward Hosier,
Elected.

1511 Tho. Trentam
Sir Thomas Kynas-
ton

1512 Tho. Trentam, junior
William Mytton,
Died
Richard Mytton
Elected

1513 Thomas Knight
William Jenyns

1514 Richard Purcell.
Roger Luter

1515 Robert Dudley
Roger Thornes

1516 Tho. Trentam
Tho. Hosier. junior

1517 Thomas Knight
Willam Jenyns

1518 Richard Mytton
Richard Purcell

1519 David Ireland
Tho Wytheford, Died
Rog. Luter. Elect.

1520 Randle Biston
Edward Bent

1521 Roger Thornes
Thomas Hosier

1522 Robert Dudley
Edward Cole

1523 Adam Mytton
William Jenyns

1524 David Ireland
Randle Biston

1525 Roger Thornes
Thomas Hosier

1526 Robert Dudley
Edward Bent

1527 Adam Mytton
William Bailie

1528 Edward Cole
David Ireland

1529 Thomas Hosyer
Randle Biston

1530 Roger Thornes
Richard Brickdale

1531 Robert Dudley
Adam Mytton

1532 Tho. Byrington
Nicholas Purcell

1533 Edward Cole
Thomas Hosier

1534 Richard Hussey
Will. Bailie, died
John Waters, Elected

1535 John Thornes
David ap Owen

1536 Roger Lewis, alias
Pope.
Nicholas Purcell.

1537 Edmund Cole.
Adam Mytton.

1538 Tho. Byrington
Thomas Ireland

1539 Richard Atkis
David ap Owen, died
Rich. Brickdale,
Elected

1540 Nich. Purcell
John Mackworth

1541 Adam Mytton
Edward Hosier

1542 Richard Mytton
Tho. Byrington

1543 Thomas Ireland
Roger Luter

1544 Humph. Onslowe
Nicholas Purcell

1545 Tho. Montgomery
Richard Dawes

1546 Adam Mytton
Roger Lewis, alias
Pope.

EDWARD VI. JANUARY 28,
1547.

1547 Edward Hosier
Will. Whittakers

1548 Tho. Byrington
John Mackworth

1549 Richard Mytton
Hump. Onslowe

1550 Nicholas Purcell
Thomas Ireland

1551 Roger Luter
Rich. Whittakers

1552 Sir Adam Mytton
Roger Lewis, alias
Pope.

MARY, JULY 6, 1553.

1553 Richard Mytton
Richard Dawes

1554 Nicholas Purcell
Robert Ireland

1555 Hump. Onslowe
Tho. Byrington

1556 Tho. Montgomery
John Dawes

1557 Richard Mytton
John Mackworth

ELIZABETH, Nov. 17, 1558.

1558 John Evans
John Holliwell

1559 Robert Allen
Rich. Owen, jun.

1560 Tho. Montgomery
William Teuche

1561 Richard Mytton
Richard Dawes

1562 Roger Luter
Rich. Owen, jun.

1563 Hump. Onslowe
George Higgons

1564 Rich. Owen, Sen.
George Leighe

1565 Richard Purcell
William Peers

1566 Robert Allen
Rob. Ireland, jun.

1567 Richard Mytton
Thomas Stury

1568 George Leighe
Ric. Owen, Senior

1569 George Higgons
George Proude

1570 Hump. Onslowe
Hugh Beanes

1571 William Peers
Thomas Burnell

1572 Thomas Sherrer
William Lowe

1573 Richard Owen, senior
Richard Powell

1574 George Leighe
George Higgons

1575 David Lloyd
John Okell

1576 John Dawes
Richard Owen

1577 Thomas Sherrer
Thomas Charlton

1578 William Weale
Roger Harris

1579 Rob. Ireland, jun.
John Perche

1580 William Jones
William Heringe

1581 Thomas Sherrer
Thomas Lewis

1582 William Tench
Edward Owen

1583 George Higgons
Michael Chambre

1584 John Dawes
John Webbe

1585 Richard Owen
Richard Dawes

1586 Thomas Sherrer
David Lloyd

1587 George Higgons
William Jones

1588 John Perche
Nicholas Gibbons

1589 Thomas Lewis
John Davies

1590 Thomas Sherrer
Thomas Burnell

1591 Richard Powell
Edward Ireland

1592 Robert Ireland
Michael Chambre

1593 Edward Owen
Humphry Hughes

1594 David Lloyd
Thomas Lewis

1595 William Jones
Thomas Charlton

1596 John Webbe
Nicholas Gibbons

1597 Thomas Burnell
Rich. Cherwell

1598 John Perche
Richard Dawes

1599 Thomas Edwards
Edward Owen

1600 William Jones
Thomas Lewis

1601 Richard Higgons
Thomas Jones

1602 John Perche
Roger Marshall

JAMES I. MARCH 24, 1603.

1603 Edward Owen
John Hunt

1604 R. Cherwell, Died
Tho. Lewis, Died
Ed. Donne, Elect.
Rob. Betton, Elect.

1605 Robert Langley
Robert Stevens

1606 William Wilkes
Arthur Kynaston

1607 William Jones
Andrew Lewis

1608 Richard Higgons
John Nichols

1609 Robert Betton
John Garbett

1610 Thomas Jones
Hugh Harris

1611 Thomas Wolley
John Hawkeshead

1612 Robert Langley
Rowland Jenks

1613 Richard Hunt
Richard Betton, died
Thomas Gardener,
Elected

1614 John Gardener
Thomas Fawkener

1615 Thomas Jones
Roger Blakeway

1616 John Nichols
Richard Wynne

1617 Edward Donne
Tho. Wingfield

1618 Arthur Kynaston
John Garbett

1619 George Wright
Richard Gibbons

1620 Roger Pope
Howell Vaughan

1621 Sir William Owen
Thomas Jones

1622 Robert Stevens
Richard Hunt

1623 Tho. Wingfield
Leonard Hinckes

1624 John Studley
Tho. Matthews

CHARLES I. MARCH 27, 1625.

1625 Thomas Knight
Charles Benyon

1626 Richard Pershouse
Richard Lewellin

1627 Thomas Jones
Robert Stevens

1628 William Rowley
Ed. Donne, Died
R. Gibbons, Elect

1629 Robert Betton
Daniel Lewis

1630 George Hunt
Simon Weston

1631 Richard Hunt
Thomas Knight

1632 George Wright
Owen George

1633 John Poyner
Andrew Griffiths

1634 Charles Benyon
Thomas Haynes

1635 Thomas Jones
John Proude

1636 Thomas Nichols
Simon Weston

1637 Richard Llewellin
John Whitwick.

———

In 1638, KING CHARLES I.
granted to the Town
a new Charter, incor-
porating them by the
Names of the Mayor,
Aldermen, and Bur-
gesses of Shrewsbury

1638 Thomas Jones, first
Mayor
1639 Robert Betton
1640 Hugh Harris, Died
Tho. Wingfield
Elected
1641 Richard Gibbons
1642 John Studley
1643 Robert Betton
1644 Charles Benyon
1645 Thomas Nichols
1646 Thomas Knight
1647 Richard Llewellin*
1648 Owen George

The Common-Wealth of
England, Jan. 30, 1649.

1649 Thomas Hayes
1650 John Prowde
1651 Charles Benyon
1652 Richard Cheshire
1653 John Rowley
1654 John Cooke
1655 Adam Webbe
1656 John Lowe
1657 Thomas Hunt
1658 John Betton
1659 John Walthall

CHARLES II. MAY 29, 1660

1660 Andrew Vivers
1661 Richard Bagot, Dis-
placed.
Robert Forster,
Elected
1662 Sir R. Prince, Knt.
1663 John Langley
1664 Edw. Kinnaston
1665 Francis Burton
1666 Richard Waringe
1667 John Harding
1668 Samuel Lloyd
1669 Richard Taylor
1670 Thomas Cotton

* 1647 Richard Llewellin, Bailiff of Shrewsbury, left a piece of land, near the Prill Gutter, called Bells Croft, to put out boys apprentice in St. Chad's Parish only. The present Mr. Eddowes, Bookseller receives the rents, and places the apprentices to proper masters. This Richard Llewellin had a Tanyard in Barker Street: see his will in Doctors Commons, 1654.—*Llewellin's Manuscript.*

1671 Roger Griffiths
1672 Samuel Jevon
1673 Rowl. Middleton
1674 William Thynne
1675 John Severne
1676 George Hosier
1677 Robert Forster
1678 Edward Philips
1679 Arthur Hinckes
1680 John Harwood
1681 George Llewellin
1682 Edward Gosnell
1683 Collins Woolrich
1684 John Wood, Died
    Robert Wood, Elect.

JAMES II. FEBRUARY 6, 1684

1685 Sir Fra. Edwards
    Bart.
1686 Thomas Badewin
1687 Richard Salter
1688 Rich. Muckleston

WILLIAM III. & MARY II. FEB. 13, 1689.

    Rich. Muckleston,
      Displaced.

    Roger Griffiths,
      Elect. and Disp.

    Collins Woolrich,
      Elect. and Disp.

    John Hill, Elected.

1689 Jonathan Scott
1690 Samuel Thomas
1691 Charles Kinaston
1692 John Hollier
1693 Arthur Tong
1694 Samuel Adderton
1695 Simon Hanmer
1696 John Kinaston
1697 Robert Shepherd
1698 Andrew Johnson
    C C

1699 Moses Reynolds, died

    Richard Presland,
      Elected

1700 John Kinaston
1701 Robert Phillips

ANNE, MARCH 8. 1702.

1702 Rowland Bright,
      Died

    Thomas Harwood,
      Elected.

1703 William Bowdler
1704 William Leighton
1705 Thomas Bowdler
1706 John Twiss
1707 John Felton, Died.

    William Smith,
      Elected.

1708 Samuel Cooke
1709 William Clemson
1710 Walter Pateshull
1711 William Turner
1712 Jonathan Scott
1713 Edward Jones

GEORGE I. AUGUST I, 1714.

1714 James Blakeway
1715 Thomas Phillips
1716 Joseph Muckleston
1717 William Kinaston
1718 Sir C. Lloyd, Bart.
1719 Henry Jenks
1720 Thomas Morhall
1721 Michael Brickdale
1722 Edward Gregory
1723 Matthew Travers
1724 Thomas Lindop
1725 Samuel Elisha
1726 John Adams

GEORGE II. JUNE 11, 1727

1727 Joseph Jones

1728 John Fownes
1729 Godolphin Edwards
1730 Rich. Woolaston
1731 Abraham Davies
1732 Richard Lloyd
1733 John Lacon
1734 John Rogers
1735 Sir Rich. Corbett,
    Bart.

1736 Charles Bolas
1737 Robert More
1738 Edward Corbett
1739 Broth. Griffiths
1740 Edward Twiss
1741 Trafford Barnston
1742 William Turner, Jun
1743 Edward Elisha
1744 Francis Turner
    Blithe

1745 John Langley
1746 Isaac Pritchard
1747 James Downes
1748 William Atkiss
1749 Thomas Fownes
1750 John Adams, Jun.
1751 William Oswell
1752 Thomas Wynne
1753 Richard Jones
1754 John Cotton
1755 Edward Blakeway
1756 Baldwyn Leighton
1757 John Oliver
1758 John Bennett
1759 John Ashby

GEORGE III. OCTOBER 25, 1760.

1760 John Rocke
1761 Henry Adams
1762 Robert Lord Clive
1763 Pryce Owen, M. D.
1764 Richard Vaughan
1765 Charles Bolas
1766 John Kinchant
1767 Thomas Wingfield
1768 Edward Vaughan
1769 William Oswell
1770 William Smith

1771 Edward Atkis	1774 Thomas Loxdale	1777 Charlton Leighton
1772 John Vaughan	1775 William Owen	1778 Noel Hill. Esqrs.
1773 James Winnall	1776 Robert Corbett	

CONTINUATION

From the year 1778, to the year 1828.

1779 Edw. Cludde of Orleton	1795 William Cludde of Orleton	1814 Rich. Phillips. Died Wm. Harley. Elect.
1780 Joshua Blakeway	1796 Henry Bevan	1815 Samuel Tudor
1781 Robert Pemberton	1797 Joseph Loxdale	1816 Sir John Betton, knt.
1782 John Flint	1798 Nathaniel Betton	1817 Joshua Peele
1783 John Oliver	1799 Joseph Carless	1818 William Egerton Jeffreys
1784 Samuel Harley	1800 Richard Bratton	
1785 James Holt	1801 Edward Stanier	1819 Rev. Hugh Owen
1786 Richard Rocke of Trefnanney	1802 Edward Burton	
1787 Thomas Kinnersley of Leighton	1803 General Baldwin Leighton	GEORGE IV. JANUARY 29, 1820.
1788 Wm. Oakeley of Tanybwlch co. Merioneth	1804 Philip Michael Williams	1820 Edward Cullis
	1805 William Wilson	1821 Samuel Harley
1789 Bold Oliver	1806 William Prissick	1822 Rice Wynne
1790 John Bishop	1807 Charles Bage	1823 Jonathan Perry
1791 Thos. Eyton of Eyton	1808 Robert Pemberton	1824 Hon. & Rev. Richard Noel Hill
1792 Rev. John Rocke	1809 Joseph Bromfield	
1793 Rev. Edw. Blakeway	1810 Thomas Lloyd	1825 W. Brayne
1794 Captain Thos. Pemberton	1811 Sir John Hill, bart. of Hawkstone	1826 Rev. Richard Corfield of Pitchford
	1812 John Lee	1827 Thomas Du Gard
	1813 William Coupland	1828 William Cooper
		EDITOR.

RECORDERS, SINCE 1582.*

1582 Sir George Bromley, Knt.	1638 Timothy Turner, Esq. Appointed by the new Charter.
1627 Sir John Bridgman. Bart.	
1638 Humphrey Mackworth, Esq.	1654 William Jones, Esq.

* " As early as the year 1473, John Phelypps was Recorder, and the first who held that office.
1491. Roger Montgomery was elected.
1508. George Bromley. In 1511 it is ordered that he have a fee of £1: 6s. 8d. as recorder, and that his former grant be resumed. He was still recorder in 1527.

1687 Earl of Powis
1695 Francis Berkley, Esq.
1710 Robert Middleton, Esq.
1733 William Kinaston, Esq.

1747 Earl of Powis
1771 Robert Lord Clive
1775 Edward Lord Clive*

1532. Thomas Bromley, elected on Wednesday after Easter, with " £4. fee as long as he is abiding in the town. and that he shalnot be of counsell with thabbot of Salop, ner no burgess or inhabitant, and so doying to have £5. of fee."

Reginald Corbet. We have not found the date of his appointment, but it is entered on our books 27 Dec. 2 Eliz. (1559) that " Mr. Reynold Corbett, recorder, is made a justice of the Court of Common Pleas."

Sir John Throgmorton, 1569, 1574.

Sir George Bromley, 1582. ob. 1588.

Thomas Owen, esq. serjeant-at-law, 1592.

Richard Barker, esq. barrister-at law, 1603, 1613."—*Owen and Blakeway.*

---

* Edward Clive, Earl of Powis, Viscount Clive, of Ludlow, Baron Herbert, of Chirbury, both in the county of Salop; Baron Powis, of Powis Castle, in the County of Montgomery, Baron Clive, of Plassey, in Ireland, and Baron Clive, of Walcot, in the county of Salop ; D.C.L., Lord Lieutenant of the county of Salop, and of the county of Montgomery, Recorder of Shrewsbury, late Governor of Fort St. George, Madras, &c. was born March 7th, 1754.

While only an Irish peer, his Lordship sat in Parliament for the borough of Ludlow. On the 13th of August, 1794, he was advanced to the English peerage, by the title of Baron Clive, of Walcot, in the county of Salop. In the year 1802, he was appointed Governor of Madras, whither he immediately repaired, but returned in the spring of 1804. On the 3rd of May in that year, the unanimous thanks of both Houses of Parliament were voted to his Lordship for the important services which he had performed in India, during the late Mahratta war. Eleven days afterwards—May 14—he was created Baron Powis, of Powis Castle, Baron Herbert, of Chirbury, Viscount Clive, of Ludlow, and Earl of Powis—a dignity to which he may be considered to have been entitled by his marrying the heiress of the Powis estates. In 1805, the Earl was nominated to the Lord Lieutenancy of Ireland ; but, in consequence of the death of his friend, Mr. Pitt, of whose measures he had been a warm supporter, the appointment was not carried into effect.

It was on the 7th of May, 1784, that, as Lord Clive, he married the Lady Henrietta Antonia Herbert, daughter of Henry Arthur, Earl of Powis, and sister of George Edward, the last Earl, on whose decease, in 1801, the title became extinct. By this marriage, his Lordship has had issue :—

1. Edward Viscount Clive, M. P. for Ludlow, born March 22, 1785, married, in 1818, the Lady Lucy Graham, third daughter of James, Duke of Montrose, K. G. &c.—2. Robert Henry, M. P. for Ludlow, born in 1789, married, in 1819, Harriet Windsor, daughter of the late, and sister of the present Earl of Plymouth ;—3. Henrietta Antonia, born in 1786, married, in 1817, Sir Watkin Williams Wynn, of Wynnstay, in the county of Denbigh, Bart ;—4. Charlotte Florentia, born September 12, 1787, married April 29, 1817, to His Grace, Hugh, Duke of Northumberland —*La Belle Assemblee.*

The family of Clive, says Lysons, in his Magna Britannia " were originally of CLIVE, in the parish of Middlewich, in the county of Chester, and settled at Huxley at an early period, by marriage of an Heiress of that place and name ; Sir George Clive, who in consequence of his ancestors marriage with the Heiress of Styche, was of Styche in Shropshire and of Huxley, had two sons, one of whom was ancestor of Lord Clive, the Heiress of the other, in whom the male line of the Huxley branch ended, married into the Wilbraham Family ; the Heiress of a younger branch, of the which remained at Clive Hall, married into the Family of Hulse. Clive Hall, now a Farm House, belongs, under the will of the Rev. John Hulse, to the University of Cambridge."

In the register of the Parish Church of St. Mary, Shrewsbury, there is the following entry :— " 1645, March 5, Burred, old Mr. Clive of the Stich in our Chensull," which Messrs. Owen and

cc2

According to the Charter, 14th Charles I. the Mayor—the Bishop of Lichfield and Coventry—the Recorder—Steward—three senior Aldermen— and the Alderman who was last Mayor, are to act as Justices of the Peace, within the town and liberties. The stile or address of the Corporation has varied in successive reigns, according to the Charters, or Grants of incorporation, viz.

WILLIAM I.   Civitas Sciropesberie, Scropesbery, Urbs Scroburiæ. Burgenses, de Sciropesberie.

Without Date. Communitas Municipii Salop. Ballivi Libertatis Villæ Salop.

HENRY II.   Burgenses de Salopesberi.

RICHARD I.   Villa de Salopesbirie Burgenses de Salopesbiri

JOHN.   Præpositi* et Burgenses de Salopesbyriæ

Blakeway say "was Ambrose Clive, Esq. second son of Sir George Clive of Styche. He had been Fellow of St. John's College, Cambridge, but succeeded to the patrimony of his ancient family on the death of his Nephew, George, and was lineal ancestor in the fifth degree to the present Earl of Powis."   EDITOR.

* The chief magistrate of Shrewsbury in the Norman times was a provost (præpositus); whose office it was to collect the burgesses' rents.

REINER the provost, or, as he is sometimes called, prefect, who gave land in the town fields of Shrewsbury (campis urbis) to the Abbey of Shrewsbury, pro filio quem fecit monachum, in the time of Henry I. when Richard de Belmeis was steward, is the first upon record.

AILRIC RUFFUS, who gave the same monks other land in the same fields, was perhaps another, and may have been the same with EDRIC the provost.

ROBERT the prefect, the son of Andrew the clerk, bequeathed the same monks all his land in the fields after his mother's death.

EDRIC.

PETER the provost appears to have been brother of John son of Clement son of Peter burgess of Shrewsbury: which John was a benefactor to the abbey.

RICHARD RUSTICUS. Chartulary of Haughmond abbey. He occurs both singly and as colleague with another: and may have been the connecting link between the single and double provosts.

We find no other names of provosts while the office was held by a single person: i. e. while the appointment was in the earl or king. In whom it was vested when Henry II. gave or restored to the burgesses of Shrewsbury free customs, does not appear. But from the time (1199) that king John empowered them to elect *two* of their body annually to hold the *prepositure* or provostship of the town, we are sure that it was governed by two provosts till the middle of Edward I.'s reign, when that title was changed to *bailiff:* and though the regular series of our FASTI CONSULARES does not commence till 1372, yet the attestations of private deeds preserve the names of a considerable number of these annual officers under both their titles. Unfortunately, the practice of dating deeds was not fully established in England before the close of Edward I.'s reign: so that of many of these magistrates we are unable to fix the year with certainty.—*Owen and Blakeway.*

HENRY III.	Ballivi et probi Homines Salopiæ
EDWARD I.	Homines Salopiæ,
	Civitas Salopiæ (so found by a trial at law)
	Communitas Villæ Regis Salopiæ
EDWARD II.	Homines Salop
RICHARD II.	Ballivi probi Homines et Communitas Villæ Salop.
HENRY VI.	Ballivi et Burgenses Villæ Salop.
	Ballivi Libertatis Villæ Salop, ac communitas ejusdem Villæ.
	The Bailiffs, twelve Aldermen, twenty-four Councellors, and the Commonalty of Salop.
CHARLES I.	The Mayor, Aldermen, and Burgesses of Salop

N. B. According to this Charter, the Body Corporate is to consist of the Mayor twenty-four Aldermen, and forty-eight Assistants, or Councellors.

The following is a List of the present House,* (1778) in which there is now a considerable vacancy.

CORPORATION.

Noel Hill, Esq. MAYOR.   Edward Lord Clive, RECORDER.

ALDERMEN.

Robert More, Esq. Senior	John Rocke, Esq.	Edward Atkis, Esq.
J. Langley, Esq. Steward, and 2d. Ditto	Pryce Owen, M. D.	John Vaughan, Esq.
T. Fownes, Esq. 3d. Ditto	Charles Bolas, Esq.	James Winnall, Esq.
Edward Blakeway, Esq.	John Kinchant, Esq.	Thomas Loxdale, Esq.
Baldwyn Leighton, Esq.	Thomas Wingfield, Esq.	Town Clerk
John Oliver, Esq. Deputy Recorder	Edward Vaughan, Esq.	Robert Corbett, Esq.
	William Oswell, Esq.	Charlton Leighton, Esq.
	William Smith, Esq.	

---

* How few of the above members of the corporation of our venerable town have survived the lapse of fifty years, those who still live have witnessed many changes in men and their circumstances within that period. In the next half century still greater changes may take place. May the Divine Providence preserve our Nation and our Town in Prosperity and Peace,—EDITOR.

ASSISTANTS.

Rev. W. Gorsuch, Clerk
Andrew Corbett, Esq.
Mr. Joseph Plymley
Mr. John Allat, Chamberlain
Robert Clavering, Esq.
Mr. James Cross
Sir Tho. Edwards, Bart.
Mr. Richard Plumer
Mr. James Holt
Mr. Bold Oliver, Coroner
Mr. John Bishop

Mr. Robert Pemberton
Robert Devereaux, Esq.
Mr. Thomas Hill
John Davies, Esq.
Mr. Lacon Bennett
Mr. William France
Mr. John Flint
Mr. John Oliver
Richard Rocke, Esq.
John Hollings, Esq.
Mr. George Lomax
Mr. Samuel Winnall

Mr. Robt. Hill, Coroner
Mr. Samuel Harley
Mr. Richard Flint
Mr. Rowland Littlehales
Mr. William Harris
Joshua Blakeway, Esq.
Mr. Samuel Yardley
Mr. John Houldston
Edward Cludde, Esq.
Thomas Eyton, Esq.
Mr. John Yeomans
Mr. Thomas Loxdale

SWORD BEARER.   Mr. John Thomas.

SERJEANTS AT MACE.

Richard Evans   James Burley   John Cooper

SERJEANT'S YEOMEN.

John Meighen   Joseph Humphreyson   Thomas Wright

Several assistants are elected, and others nominated to fill up the vacancy but have not yet been sworn into office.

In the year 1828, being fifty years after Mr. Phillips's list was published, we find the body corporate composed of the following highly respectable members :—

RECORDER.

Edward Earl of Powis, since 1755.

DEPUTY RECORDER.

Joseph Loxdale, Esq. since 1786.

STEWARD.

Joseph Loxdale, Esq.* (the above) since 1787.

---

* Mr. Loxdale is also Clerk of the Peace for the County, and a Magistrate for the Town and Liberties.—EDITOR.

TOWN CLERK.

Thomas Loxdale, Esq, since 1793.

MAYOR.

William Cooper, Esq,

ALDERMEN.

Thomas Kynnersley
William Cludde
Joseph Loxdale
Richard Bratton, Esquires
Sir Baldwin Leighton, Baronet
Philip Michael Williams
Thomas Lloyd
William Harley
Samuel Tudor, Esquires
Sir John Betton, Knight
Joshua Peele
William Egerton Jeffreys

Samuel Harley
Rice Wynne
Jonathan Perry, Esquires
The Hon. Richard Noel Hill, Clerk
William Brayne, Esquire
Richard Corfield, Clerk
Thomas Du Gard. M.D.
Robert Gray
Joseph Loxdale, the younger
Thomas Farmer Dukes
Thomas Tomlins, Esquires

ASSISTANTS.

Robert Hill, Gentleman, Coroner
Thomas Loxdale, Esq. Town Clerk
Edward Earl of Powis, Recorder
William Lloyd, Esquire
Richard Loxdale, Gentleman
Thomas Noel Lord Berwick
Sir Edward Kynaston, Bart. Clerk
George Wingfield, Gentleman, Coroner
Jonathan Scott, Esquire
The Right Hon. William Noel Hill
Joseph Corbett, Clerk, Archdeacon of Salop
William Lee, Carver
William Wood, Gentleman
Samuel Hartshorn, Mercer
John Wingfield, Clerk
Edward Bather, Clerk, Archdeacon of Salop
Panton Corbett, Esq. M.P.
John Bather, Esquire
Samuel Butler, D.D. Archdeacon of Derby
Joseph Sutton, Esq.
Thomas Higgins, Druggist, Chamberlain
John William Smith, Esquire
Thomas Wood Loxdale, Gentleman
John Bowdler, Grocer

Thomas Higgins, jun. Surgeon, Chamberlain
John Cresset Pelham, Esq. M.P.
Edward Cludde, Esquire
John Harley, Gentleman
John Wingfield, Esquire
Edward Herbert Lord Viscount Clive
The Hon. Robert Henry Clive
John Loxdale, Gentleman
George Ashby Maddock, Clerk
James Loxdale, Esquire
John Williams, Gentleman
Richard Drinkwater, Woolstapler
James Watkins, Ironmonger
John Topp, Clerk
Francis Knyvett Leighton
Andrew Vincent Corbet
Uvedale Corbett, Esquires
John Eaton, the younger, Gentleman
William Vaughan, Clerk
James Edward Compson, Clerk
Joshua John Peele
Robert Burton
Joseph Shepherd, Esquires
Thomas Harley Kough, Gentleman

OFFICERS PERTAINING TO THE CORPORATION.

SWORD BEARER.

Edgar Abbott.

SERGEANTS AT MACE.

Edgar Abbott,—David Cowley.

SERGEANT'S YEOMEN.

Abraham Pearson,—Richard Ganderton,—Samuel Farlow, and John Hayward.

BELLMAN.

William Schofield.

CHAPTER IX.

ELECTIONS.

Much animosity having taken place in Shrewsbury, relative to Elections, and the minds of the inhabitants yet remaining in an unsettled state; these things, together with the situation of the Editor, induce him to ask the favour of his Fellow Burgesses and Townsmen, to excuse him, if under this head, he only mentions matters of fact, in a chronological way, without making any observations, or remarks of his own.

SHREWSBURY is a Borough by prescription, and sends two Members to Parliament, who have sometimes been chosen by the Burgesses at large, wheresoever inhabiting, and sometimes by the inhabiting Burgesses only.

1709.—The first controverted Election for the Borough, was in this year; Sir Edward Leighton, petitioned against John Kynaston and Richard Mytton, Esqrs. when Sir Edward, and Thomas Jones, Esq. were declared the sitting Members.

The question was, Whether the right of Election was in the Burgesses at large, or in the inhabiting Burgesses? And the same was determined as follows.

"20ᵗʰ day of Decemʳ· 1709. Resolved, that the right of Electing Bur-
" gesses for the Borough of Shrewsbury, in the County of Salop, is only in
" the Burgesses inhabiting in the said Borough, or in the Suburbs thereof,
" paying Scot and Lot, and not receiving Alms, or Charity."—See the Report on the Journal.

To support this resolution an indenture was produced returned Anno 1478, and also an indenture, 1st Mariæ, and another, 2d Phillippi et Mariæ. The Burgesses therein are particularly named, and are called *Homines Burgenses ac Comorantes infra Vill, et Burgum predict Inhabitan.*

1714.—Came on to be heard before the House of Commons, 2 *Jovis,* 27 *die Maii,* the Petition of Corbet Kynaston, Esq. and several Burgesses, complaining of an undue Election and Return for the Borough of Shrewsbury.— This Election was the year preceding: The Poll began on Monday, the 31st day of August, 1713.

DD

Edward Jones, Esq. MAYOR.

CANDIDATES.

Thomas Jones, Esq.
Edward Cressett, Esq.
Corbet Kynaston, Esq.   The Petitioner.

Upon considering the Petition, the House resolved, 2 *Jovis, 27 die Maü,* 1714.

Resolved,—That the right of Electing Burgesses to serve in Parliament for the Borough of Shrewsbury, in the County of Salop, is in the Mayor, Aldermen, and Burgesses of the said Borough.

2 The Petition of John Powell, Robert Pearson, and several others, whose names are subscribed thereto, being Burgesses of, and inhabiting in the town of Shrewsbury, being read,

Resolved,—That the said Petition, complaining of an undue election and return of Edward Cressett, for the said Borough of Shrewsbury, is frivolous, vexatious, and scandalous.

That the said Petitioners do make satisfaction to the said Mr. Cressett, for his costs and expences.

1714—Upon the accession of King George II. Corbet Kynaston, and Thomas Jones, Esqrs. were elected.

1721. March 24.—An Election for the Borough.

Michael Brickdale, Esq. MAYOR.

CANDIDATES.					VOTES.
Corbet Kynaston, Esq.	-	-	-	-	- 722
Richard Lyster, Esq.	-	-	-	-	- 695
Sir Richard Corbett, Bart	-	-	-	-	- 644
Orlando Bridgman, Esq.	-	-	-	-	- 643

The two former were returned, and a Petition lodged in the House of Commons, complaining of an undue Election. Upon hearing the Petition, the Abbey-Foregate, was deemed no part of the town, and Mr. Kynaston, and Mr. Lyster, were thrown out, after sitting two sessions. The House resolving, 9th April, 1723. *Verbatim,* as 20 *die Decembris,* 1709.*

---

* The Resolution referred to is the following :—1723, 9th April. The Right of Election is only in the burgesses·inhabiting in the said borough, or in the suburbs thereof, paying scot and lot, and not receiving alms or charity.

" That the *whole* parishes of St. Chad, St. Mary, St: Alkmond, St. Julian, the Holy Cross, and

In 1727—Sir John Astley, Bart. and Richard Lyster, Esq. were returned, without opposition.

1734, April.—An Election for the Borough.

John Lacon, Esq. MAYOR.

CANDIDATES.				VOTES.
William Kynaston, Esq.	-	-	-	269
Sir Richard Corbet, Bart.	-	-	-	265
John Mytton, Esq.	-	-	-	201
Richard Lyster, Esq.	-	-	-	199

At this Election the number of Voters being reduced, was owing to the admission of none but such who were inhabiting Burgesses, and who were such by birth or favor.

1735.—The Mandamus Cause, which had been brought to trial in 1733 and passed by the Judges, was this year tried by Corbet Kynaston Esq. in the Court of King's Bench. He gained his point, which occasioned great rejoicings in the town and country about Shrewsbury: but the Corporation threw in a writ of error, determining to appeal to the House of Lords, yet this determination appears to be superseded, by a flaw or error in the first judgment, upon which the Corporation refused to admit Mr. Kynaston. He brought on a trial at common law to recover costs, but was nonsuited on account of the Jury being chose by the sheriff, whereas they should have been chose by the Coroners. It is observable, that the Jury in 1732, were chose by the Coroners, and the trial put off because they were not chose by the Sheriff. Mr. Kynaston the following year brought on a trial at common law, but did not gain his point; he moved again at the King's Bench, but that Court stopt the proceeding.

The next return in 1741, was without opposition; Sir Richard Corbet, Bart. and William Kynaston, Esq. were elected Members.

St. Giles, and the several vills of Hadnal, Acton Reynold, Meriden, Hanwood, Grinsell, Ollerton Onslow, Preston Gubbald, Pimley, and Merival, are not within the borough of Shrewsbury, or the suburbs thereof.

That the several vills of Bicton, Betton, Alkmere, Longnor, Calcot, Whitley, Welbatch, Upper and Lower Rossal, Shelton, Oxon, Woodcot, Horton, Munkmeal, and Goosehill, in the parish of St. Chad; Great and Little Berwick, Almond Park, Newton, Albright Hussey, Cotton Hill, Leaton, Astley, Merrington, Wollascot, Sansaw, and Clive, in the parish of St. Mary; Hencot, Albright Lee, Preston, Montford, Dinthill, and Arlescot, in the parish of St. Alkmond; and Pulley, and Shelton, in the parish of St. Julian; are not part of the ancient borough of Shrewsbury, or the suburbs thereof.

That the parish of Holy Cross and St. Giles is no part of the ancient borough of Shrewsbury, or the suburbs thereof.—EDITOR.

DD2

In 1747, an opposition again took place: The days of election were June 29, and 30.

Isaac Pritchard, Esq. MAYOR.

CANDIDATES.	VOTES.
William Kynaston, Esq. - - - -	155
Sir Richard Corbet, Bart. - - -	150
Robert Pigott, Esq. - - ' - -	140
Richard Prince Astley, Esq. - - -	135

Burgesses refused, who voted for Pigott and Astley, - 22
Tradesmen offered to be Burgesses, but were refused, - 42

In 1754, Thomas Hill and Robert More. Esqrs. were returned, without opposition.

In 1761, Thomas Hill, Esq. and Robert Lord Clive, were elected, without opposition.

In 1768.—The day of election, March 18.

Thomas Wingfield, Esq. MAYOR.

CANDIDATES.	VOTES.
Noel Hill, Esq. - - - - -	233
Robert Lord Clive, - - - -	149
William Pulteney, Esq. - - - -	97

In 1774,—Days of Election, October 11, 12, 13 and 14.

Thomas Loxdale, Esq. MAYOR,

CANDIDATES.

Robert Lord Clive, Charlton Leighton, Esq. William Pulteney, Esq.

STATE OF THE POLL.

LORD CLIVE.	MR. LEIGHTON.	MR. PULTENEY.
Burgesses Polled - 211	179	171
Afterwards rejected - 1	1	
210	178	171
Freemen offered - 99	60	170
309	238	341
Burgesses objected to 18	9	28
Total - 327	247	369

The 19th of the following month. (November,) came on in the Court of King's Bench, Westminster, before a special Jury, a Trial at Bar, upon a Writ of Mandamus, for settling the long contested Question concerning the Rights of the Freemen in this Town, against the Corporation. After eleven hours hearing evidence on both sides, a Verdict was given in favor of the Freemen.—And in March following the Committee of the House of Commons, appointed to try the Shrewsbury Election, after a short hearing, on the 8th, determined, That the Right of Voting of the Freemen of Shrewsbury, was established by the former Verdicts, and Judgments upon each, obtained in the Court of King's Bench. In consequence of this they declared, that Mr. Leighton, the sitting Member, ought not to have been returned, and that Mr. Pulteney,* was duly elected.

A LIST OF THE COMMITTEE.

Names.			Members for
John Ord, Esq. Chairman.	-	-	Midhurst.
William Ewer, Esq.	-	-	Dorchester.

---

* In the year 1771, Sir William (then Mr.) Pulteney, having lost the election in the contest of 1768, brought forward this cause in the name of one Baxter. On the trial of that cause, the Corporation contended, that the two customs, which the plaintiff alledged to be immemorial, were only introduced by a Bye-Law of 1642, which Bye-Law was repealed in 1733. The Plantiff maintained that the Bye-Law was only declaratory of the ancient custom, which could not, therefore, be affected by the repeal of such Bye-Law. The jury found for Plaintiff. Baxter, in consequence of the judgment in his favour, sued out a peremptory Mandamus, and was admitted to his freedom. But the Corporation still refused to admit other persons who claimed under the same customs. In the case of Baxter they had moved for a new trial, which was refused ; but a second Mandamus being obtained against the Corporation, they moved that this cause might be tried at the Bar. This was granted by the Court. This Mandamus was tried in Michaelmas Term, November 19, 1774. and determined as before, and there has been no application since for a new trial.

But at the General Election in 1774, Sir William Pulteney having petitioned against the Return of the late Lord Clive, and the late Sir Charlton Leighton, the committee determined in his favour, in consequence of the above decision of the Court of King's Bench, and Sir William Pulteney was seated in the room of Sir Charlton Leighton. Lord Clive died *pendente lite*, and was succeeded in the representation of the borough by Mr. Corbet of Sundorn: The Corporation after this submitted, and have sworn in all who have applied to be burgesses, if born in the town, or having served a legal apprenticeship, on the payment of a fee of admission, which I understand is about seven guineas.*

Sir William Pulteney succeeded in finishing the work, begun so many years before *by another person*, for which he is indebted to two powerful circumstances. His present Majesty had early in his reign given his assent to an Act of Parliament for making the Judges independent, and another Act also received his sanction (called Grenville's Bill) to regulate Controverted Elections. Hence the power of the Minister had ceased to operate, at least so far as to controul these matters. Justice had its due course ; the Corporation, as hath been stated, much to their honour, acquiesced in the decision, and in 1796 all dispute about the Mandamus Cause ended ; though it is still open to the Corporation to renew the question at pleasure, for every fresh claimant creates a separate case ; but they have wisely determined otherwise.—*Short Account of the Mandamus Cause, Published in* 1806.

* July 1830. The fee for the admission of a Burgess on the ground of having served a legal apprenticeship is Seven Pounds ; for a born Burgess, that is the son of a Burgess, and born in the town, £1. 3s. 7d.—Editor.

William Chaffin Grove, Esq. - -	Weymouth.
Edwin Lascelles, Esq. - - -	Yorkshire.
John Elwes, Esq. - - -	Berkshire.
Lucy Knightly, Esq. - - -	Northamptonshire.
Richard Aldworth Nevil, Esq. - -	Grampound.
Charles Brett, Esq. - - -	Lestwithiel.
John Darker, Esq. - - -	Leicester.
Grey Cooper, Esq. - - -	Saltash.
Sir Cecil Wray, - - - -	East Retford
George Bridges Brudenell, Esq. - -	Rutlandshire.
Daniel Lascelles, Esq. - - -	Northallerton.

NOMINEES.

Right Hon. Thomas Townshend, Esq. -	Whitchurch.
Henry Herbert, Esq. - - - -	Wilton.

Upon this determination, Mr. Pulteney took his seat, and John Corbet, of Sundorn, Esq. was on March 17th, elected in the room of Lord Clive, who died the 22d of November preceding.

A LIST OF MEMBERS CHOSEN AT GENERAL ELECTIONS FOR THE TOWN OF SHREWSBURY.

1478	Robert Benyon, Esq.*	John Guttons, Esq.
1492	William Mutton, Esq.	Lawrence Hosyer, Esq.
1520	Edmund Cole, Esq.	Adam Mutton, Esq.
1530	Robert Dudley, Esq.	Ditto.
1654	Richard Cheshire, Esq.	Humphrey Mackworth, Esq.
1656	Samuel Jones, Esq.†	Ditto.
1658	William Jones, Esq.	Ditto.
1660	Samuel Jones Esq.	Thomas Jones, Esq.
1661	Robert Leighton, Esq.	Ditto.
1678	Sir Richard Corbett, Bart.	Edward Kynaston. Esq.
1681	Ditto.	Ditto.
1685	Sir Francis Edwards, Bart.	Ditto.
1688	Ditto.	Andrew Newport, Esq.
1690	Richard Mytton, Esq.	Ditto.

* Elected by the inhabiting Burgesses.

† These Members at this election offered to serve at their own charge; before that time they were paid by the borough, as appears by an order in one of the Exchequer books 1588, to assemble the Burgesses, in order to levy a fine on the town, to pay £9 due to Thomas Harris, one of the Members for the borough, being wages for 90 days attendance, at 2s. per day. In 1524 assessors were appointed to regulate the expences of the town Members; before that time they were paid 20d. per day, agreeable to an order 17th Edward II.

1695 John Kynaston, Esq.	Ditto.
1698 Ditto.	Richard Mytton, Esq.
1701 Ditto.	Ditto.
1702 Ditto.	Ditto.
1705 Ditto.	Ditto.
1709 Sir Edward Leighton, Bart.	Thomas Jones, Esq.
1713 Corbet Kynaston, Esq.	Edward Cresset, Esq.
1714 Ditto.	Thomas Jones, Esq.
1721 Sir Richard Corbett, Bart.	Orlando Bridgman, Esq.
1727 Richard Lyster, Esq.	Sir John Astley, Bart.
1734 Sir Richard Corbett, Bart.	William Kynaston, Esq.
1741 Ditto.	Ditto.
1747 Ditto.	Ditto. Died.
	Thomas Hill, Esq. Elected.
1754 Thomas Hill, Esq.	Robert More, Esq.
1761 Ditto.	Robert Lord Clive.
1768 Robert Lord Clive.	Noel Hill, Esq.
1774 Ditto. Died:	William Pulteney, Esq.
John Corbet, Esq. Elected.	

N. B. In 1709 the House of Commons resolved, that none have a right to vote in electing Members for Shrewsbury, but Burgesses living in the town, and paying to church and poor. In 1714, upon the petition of Corbet Kynaston, Esq. they resolved, that foreign Burgesses had a right to vote.

Parliaments were triennial from November 1694 to 1716, when an act passed for septennial ones.

CONTINUATION.

1780 Sir Charlton Leighton, Bart.	William Pulteney, Esq.
1784 The same.	The same.

N. B. On the death of Sir Charlton Leighton, John Hill, Esq. was elected.

1780 John Hill, Esq.	William Pulteney, Esq.

1796. This is generally referred to by our fellow Townsmen, as the *great election*, owing to the very extensive and protracted contest between Mr. John Hill, the (former Member) of the House of Hawkstone, and the Hon. William Hill, of the House of Attingham. At the conclusion of which contest, the numbers were for

William Pulteney, Esq. - - - -	370
Hon. William Hill - - - - -	242
John Hill. Esq. - - - - -	153

This struggle between two great and greatly respected families, related to each other, was the cause of numerous and lasting animosities among the Gentry, Burgesses and Inhabitants of the town and vicinity. At the same time, many Innkeepers, &c. made their fortunes during the excess of riot and revelling, the six months *Saturnalia* occasioned.

1802 Hon. W. Hill.	Sir William Pulteney.
1806 The same.	Hon. H. G. Bennet.

In 1806 Thomas Jones, Esq. was the unsuccessful Candidate. This was a very severely contested election. The Candidates most directly opposed were Mr. Bennet and Mr. Jones, and singular enough to remark, the partisans of Mr. Bennet, who was a Whig, where principally Tories ; and the Partisans of Mr. Jones, who was a Tory, where chiefly Whigs. At the close of the poll the numbers were for the

Hon. W. Hill. - - - - -	589
Hon. H. G. Bennet. - - - - -	370
T. Jones, Esq. - - - - -	351

In 1807 there was a second contest between Mr. Bennet and Mr. Jones, when Mr. Bennet was the unsuccessful candidate. The numbers were for the

Hon. W. Hill, - - - - - -	538
Thomas Jones, Esq. - - - - - -	345
Hon. H. G. Bennet, - - - - -	321

On the death of Sir Thomas Jones, Nov. 26, 1811, the Hon. H. G. Bennet was elected.

1812 Lieutenant General Sir Rowland Hill, and the Hon. H. G. Bennet.

Benjamin Benyon, Esq. was, on this occasion, the unsuccessful candidate. The numbers were,

Hon. H. G. Bennet, - - - - - -	724
Lt. Gen. Sir R. Hill, - - - - - -	512
B. Benyon, Esq. - - - - : -	336

On Sir Rowland Hill's elevation to a Peerage, May 3, 1814, Richard Lyster, Esq. of Rowton Castle, and Benjamin Benyon, Esq. became candidates for the vacancy ; when after a smart struggle Mr. Lyster gained his election.

For Mr. Lyster, - - 551.—Mr. Benyon, - - 286.

1819 R. Lyster, Esq.   Hon. H. G. Bennett.

On the death of Mr. Lyster, May 3rd, 1819, John Mytton, Esq. of Halston Hall, and Panton Corbett, Esq. of Leighton Hall, offered themselves as candidates. This contest was spirited, and carried on with laudable temper and reciprocal good nature.

The numbers for Mr. Mytton were   -   -   384
Mr. Corbett,   -   -   -   287

1820 Panton Corbett, Esq.   Hon. H. G. Bennett.

1826 The same   Robert A. Slaney, Esq.

T. Boycott, Esq. was the unsuccessful candidate. The contest was sharp, but not of long continuance. Numbers who polled for

Mr. Corbett - - - - - - - - 627
Mr. Slaney - - - - - - - - 387
Mr. Boycott - - - - - - - - 276

1830. On the death of George the Fourth, and the accession of William the Fourth, parliament was dissolved, and the representation of the Borough again contested.

The Candidates were the former members and Richard Jenkins, Esq. Mr. Corbett was the unsuccessful Candidate. The numbers polled were for

Mr. Jenkins - - - - - 754
Mr. Slaney - - - - - 563
Mr. Corbett - - - - - 445

It has been remarked, "that in no recently contested Election for the Borough of Shrewsbury, has the omnipotency of gold been so clearly demonstrated."

The following particulars are copied from the Salopian Journal of August 4th, 1830, the day on which the members were chaired.

At the conclusion of the Poll, Monday, 2nd of August, Mr. Corbett is stated to have declared in his Speech to the Electors, &c. "It was not his " wish to alloy the gratification that would arise to many persons from the result " of the poll; but he felt that he had been justified in his extension by the " promises of support and the expressions of kindness made to him prior to its " commencement. The promises that had been made to him were about 600, " and if all the Burgesses who made them had kept them, they would have " placed him in the proud situation to which he had aspired; but he was sorry

EE

" to say that about 160 had broken their sacred word and polled against him,
" for what reasons, or under what influence they best knew, and he did not stop
" to enquire. For eleven years he had attended to the interests of the Bur-
" gesses of Shrewsbury, and on looking back he could not lay his finger upon
" a single vote which he could wish to recall; and although on some occasions,
" and more particularly on one great question, he had been unfortunate in dif-
" fering in opinion from some of his constituents, yet even on that question he
" ventured to prophesy that the time would come, and he thought shortly,
" when those who had differed with him on that question would think he had
" done right." Mr. Corbett then returned thanks to the 445 voters who had
polled for him, and said " they could bear testimony that he had not used any
" undue influence to obtain their votes, or asked for more than a single vote
" from them."

The Editor of the Journal observes,—" We have since learnt on good
authority that the numbers stood thus:—

Promises to Mr. Corbett - - - - - - 607
Votes polled for him by persons who had not promised him 61
___
668

Polled for Mr. Corbett - - - - - - - 445
Polled against him, having promised to support him - - 167
Tendered for him and rejected - - - - - - 3
Did not come up to poll, having promised Mr. Corbett - 53
___
668."

While there is too much reason to believe the above statement to be correct, in justice to the successful candidates, it must be recorded, they were
themselves indefatigable; and their agents, both professional and otherwise,
were not only very numerous and respectable, but zealous and active. Those
of Mr. Corbett were equally respectable, and equally anxious to serve their
leader, but being few in number, and under particular limitations as to influence, they had not an equal chance of success.

EDITOR.

CHAPTER X.

ANECDOTES OF EMINENT AND LEARNED MEN, WHO WERE BORN OR
INHABITED IN SHREWSBURY OR ITS NEIGHBOURHOOD,

WITH A LIST OF THE EARLS OF SHREWSBURY.

RICHARD PLANTAGANET, second son to King Edward IV. and Elizabeth his Queen, was born at Shrewsbury, Anno 1472. He was created Duke
of York, by his father, and affianced to Anne the daughter and heir of John
Mowbray, Duke of Norfolk. He was murdered, with his brother King Edward
V. in the Tower of London, by the instruments of his cruel uncle, Richard
Duke of Gloucester, in order to make his way to the Throne; though a report
that he was alive after King Richard's death, and that he had been conveyed
away to his aunt Margaret Duchess of Burgundy, was a ground for some male-
contents to set up Perkin Warbeck, under his name and person, to claim the
Throne, when Henry VII. had got possession of it, which caused that King
some danger, but more trouble to suppress it.

GEORGE PLANTAGANET, brother to Richard, the youngest son of the same
King and Queen, was also born at the Black Friars here. He died in his
infancy.

ROBERT OF SHREWSBURY, Bishop of Bangor.—In the reign of King John,
Anno 1197, that King being engaged in a war with Llewellin Prince of Wales,
imprisoned this Bishop in his own Cathedral, and for his ransom obliged him
to pay three hundred Hawks, a bird we may suppose then plentiful in this
nation. This Bishop wrote the Life of St. Wenefride, before mentioned; in
which he relates many miracles wrought by her, at the request of the men of
Ruthin, in Wales. It is remarkable of this Bishop, that by his will he ordered,
his body should not be buried in his own Cathedral, but in the middle of the
Market-Place, in Shrewsbury, where he was born. Dr. Fuller, when he mentions this circumstance, desires " it might not be imputed to his profaneness,
" but either to his humility, as not worthy to lie in Holy Ground, or to his fear
" lest in those times of civil commotion and disturbances, his body would be
" disturbed sooner, if laid in a Church, than in a Market-Place."—He died
Anno 1215.

EE2

RALPH OF SHREWSBURY, so called from being born here. He was Bishop of Bath and Wells, in the reign of King Edward III. but because he was consecrated without the Pope's knowledge, he was forced to pay a large sum for his presumption. He was a great benefactor to his Cathedral, giving not only a large sum of money, but also a strong chest with iron bars to keep it in ; which chest, in Queen Elizabeth's days was broke open and robbed. He erected and endowed a spacious structure for the Vicars Choral of his Cathedral to inhabit together, and with great expence enlarged the Bishop's Palace, beautifying and fortifying it as a castle. He sat Bishop thirty-four years, died August 14, 1363, and was buried in his own Cathedral.

SIR GILBERT TALBOT, the son of John, second Earl of Shrewsbury of that name. He was High-Sheriff of Shropshire, 3rd Richard III. and in the year of his shrievalty, he raised an army for the support of Henry Earl of Richmond, afterwards Henry VII. as related already in the third Chap. of Ancient History. For this and other services, when the Earl came to the Throne, he gave him a large estate in Worcestershire, made him Governour of Calais, and Knight of the Garter ; and from him the Earls of Shrewsbury, from the 14th Jac. I. are descended. While he was Governour of Calais, King Henry VIII. fearing lest that important place should be surprised by the French, sent orders to Sir Gilbert, to fortify it well ; in answer to which, he sent to inform his Majesty, " That he could neither fortify, nor fistify without " money, of which his Majesty had sent him none."

EDWARD BURTON,* Esq. of Longnor,† a small village,‡ near Shrewsbury. He was a zealous assertor of the Gospel, all Queen Mary's days, and is by

---

* The family of *Burton* was seated for many centuries prior to 1460, at Richmond, co. York. Sir Edward Burton, for his services to the House of York in 14 battles, had the singular honour of knight banneret conferred upon him by Edward IV. in 1460, after the battle of St. Albans. Sir Edward settled at Longner, co. Salop, and from him descended his son, Sir Robert Burton, knt. had the first grant of arms, May 23, 1478; his son, Edward, *m.* Jocosa Coyney; he *d.* 1524: their eldest son, John, *m.* Elizabeth Poyner, and *d.* 1543; Edward, his eldest son, *m.* Anne Madock; he *d.* 1558, and was buried in the garden at Longner, Thomas his eldest son, succeeded at Longner, where his descendants in the female line, who have assumed the name and arms of *Burton*, still remain. Edward, the 2nd son of Edward of Longner, was father of Thomas Burton, of Buncraggy, who settled in Ireland in 1610, and *m.* Anne, daughter of Thomas Shepherd, of Baycote, co. Hereford, Esq. from whom descended in the 4th degree, Francis Burton, Esq. *b.* Dec. 1, 1696, representative in parliament for co. Clare, and a privy counsellor, *m.* Mary, 3rd daughter of lieutenant-general Henry Conyngham, of Slane Castle, and sister of Henry, Earl Conyngham, and *d.* March 20, 1743, leaving issue by her, (who *d.* 1737,) 1. Francis Pierpoint; 2. William, of Slane Castle, *b.* 1733, teller of the exchequer, vice-admiral of Ulster, governor of Donegal, a privy counsellor, and formerly a lieutenant-colonel of the 12th regiment of dragoons, *d. unm.* May 31, 1796; 3. Mary, *d. unm.* 4. Alice, *m:* Sept. 22, 1743, Sir George Gore, Bart. and *d.* April 23, 1745.

† Now generally written Longner. ‡ Not a village, but an insulated part of St. Chad's parish.—ED.

Mr. Fox, in his Acts and Monuments, named among those who by various ways and means, escaped persecution. He, one day sitting in his parlour alone, meditating on the troubles of the times, and the deliverances he and others had found, though many had suffered; while he was thus reflecting, he heard a general ringing of all the bells in Shrewsbury, which he concluded must be for the Accession of the Lady Elizabeth to the throne, by the death of Queen Mary. Longing to know the truth, and not daring to send any of his servants to enquire, he sent his eldest son, a youth about sixteen years of age, ordering him, if the bells rang for the Lady Elizabeth's Accession, to throw his hat up into the air, at some place from whence he might see it, to gratify his expectation : the young man, finding it was as expected, threw up his hat, which his father seeing, was suddenly affected with such extremity of joy, for the liberty and comfort God's people had a prospect of, that he retired from the window, where he saw the sign, with difficulty gained a chair, and immediately expired.—By his last will he ordered, that his body should be buried in the parish Church of St. Chad, in Shrewsbury, and that no Mass-monger should be present at his interment. His friends, designing to execute his will in this respect, brought his corpse to the Church, and were there met by the Curate, Mr. John Marshall, who said that "Mr. Burton was an Heretic,

---

Francis Pierpoint, the eldest son, succeeded as the 2nd Lord Conyngham, April 3, 1781, and *m.* March 19, 1750, Elizabeth, eldest daughter of the Right Hon. Nathaniel Clements, and sister of Robert, Earl of Leitrim, and by her, (who *d.* Oct. 31, 1814,) had issue, 1. *Henry*, the 3rd lord; 2. Francis-Nathaniel, twin brother of the earl, *b.* Dec. 26, 1766, colonel of the Clare militia; *m.* June 4, 1801, Valentine-Alicia, 2nd daughter of Nicholas, Lord Cloncurry; 3. Catherine, *m.* March 26, 1786, the Rev. John Shirly Fermor, of Sevenoaks, co. Kent, *d.* March 1814; 4. Ellena, *m.* Dec. 11, 1777, Stewart Weldon, Esq. *d.* April 12, 1815; 5, Henrietta. His lordship *d.* May 22, 1787, and was succeeded by his eldest son, *Henry*, the 3rd baron, who was created a viscount, Dec. 6, 1789, and advanced to the dignity of Earl Conyngham, Nov. 5, 1797.—*Debrett's Peerage.*

No doubt the editor of the Peerage quoted, had good authority for stating, " that the family of Burton was seated for many centuries prior to 1460 in the *county of York*." But William Burton, author of a Commentary on the "Itinerary of Antoninus," and kinsman of Francis Burton, who resided at Longner Hall in the middle of the 16th century, says, "The Burton's WERE OF SHROP-SHIRE, a family sometime for no ordinary relations very gracious with the several princes of the Royal House of York," &c. &c. He also gives an account of the death, &c. of his ancestor, the Edward Burton, who died of joy, differing only in very minor particulars from that given by Mr. Phillips. This writer, who is highly commended by Ant. Wood, was the son of William Burton, of Atcham, born in Austin-friars, London, in the seventeenth century; and being admitted into Glou-cester-hall, Oxford, he took the degree of bachelor of civil law, and, leaving the university, was master of the free-school of Kingston-upon-Thames. He was a good linguist, an excellent critic and antiquary, very much esteemed by the learned of his time, and particularly by the famous archbishop Usher. He died in 1657. He was not only a learned but useful writer. Copies of the Commentary on Antoninus's Journies have been recently sold by auction at three pounds. His " Researches into the Phraseology, Manners, History, and Religion of the Ancient Eastern Nations, as illustrative of Sacred Scripture," is a compilation of considerable value to the Biblical Student. Among his other works are Græcæ Linguæ Historia, and Veteris Linguæ Persicæ.—EDITOR.

and should not be buried in " his Church." (This being the day of Queen Elizabeth's Coronation, the Popish Priests were yet in place.) One of Mr. Burton's friends replied, " As to his being an Heretic, God would judge that " at the last day." The Curate replied, "Judge God, or judge Devil, he " shall not be buried in this Church." His friends were obliged to carry his body back again,* and bury it in his own garden, near the fish-ponds. A monument was set over him, which being injured and defaced with the weather, Edward Burton, Esq. his grandson, in the year 1614, at the request of Sir Andrew Corbet, Lieutenant of Shropshire, re-edified the tomb, that the memory of this holy man might be preserved, on which was placed the following inscription.

" Here lieth the Body of Edward Burton, Esq.
" who deceased, Anno Domini 1558.

" Was't it for denying Christ, or some notorious Fact,
" That this Man's Body Christian Burial Lack't?
" Oh no, (not so.) His faithful true Profession
" Was the chief Cause which then was held transgression.—
" When Popery here did reign, the See of Rome,
" Would not admit to any such, a Tomb
" Within their Idol Temple Walls. But he,
" Truly professing Christianity,
" Was like Christ Jesus, in a Garden laid
" Where he shall rest in Peace, till it be said,
" Come, faithful Servant, come receive with me,
" A just reward for thy Integrity."

---

* Similar but even more distressing was the case of the body of William Glover, who though he escaped the hands of the Papists during his life, may be properly enough reputed a Martyr after his death. He died at *Wem* in this county, and being brought to the parish church, there to be buried, one *Bernard*, who was then the Curate, and so continued, when Mr. *Fox* wrote this Part of his Martyrology, would not suffer his Body to be interred, but rode to the then Bishop of *Coventry* and *Litchfield*, Dr: *Ralph Baines*, to certify him of the Matter, and take his Order, and advice what he should do. In the mean Time the Body lying unburied a whole Day; One *Richard Morrice* a Taylor in the Night-time, attempted to bury him, but was hindred by one *John Thorlin* and others, from so doing, so that the Corpse lay above ground without Sepulture two Days and a Night, till *Bernard* the Curate returned with the Bishop's Letter, directed to the Parish of *Wem*, to this Effect :— " That he understanding that one *Glover*, an Heretick, was dead in the Parish of *Wem*, which " *Glover*, for all the Time of his being in this Country, hath been known for a Rebel against our Holy " Faith and Religion, a Contemner of the Holy Sacraments and Ceremonies used in Holy Church, and " hath separated himself from the Communion of all good Christian Men, and never required to be " reconciled to our Holy Mother Church, and in his last Days did not call for his ghostly Father, " but died without all Rites belonging to a Christian Man. I thought it good not only to command " the Curate of *Wem*, that he should not be buried in Christian Man's Burial, but also will and com-" mand all the Parish of *Wem*, that no Man procure help, or speak to have him buried in Holy " Ground, but especially the Churchwardens, to assist the Curate in hindering and letting that he be

SAMPSON PRICE, D. D. the son of Thomas Price, Vicar of St. Chad's, in Shrewsbury, was born in that Parish. He received his university learning in Exeter College, Oxford, where he took all his degrees in divinity, being made a Doctor in 1617. He was afterwards appointed University Preacher, and from a Lecturer of St. Martin's church in Oxford, was made the same at St. Olave's in Southwark, Chaplain in Ordinary to King James I. (and so continued to King Charles I.) and Vicar of Christ-church, London. He was a ready and frequent Court Preacher, and being zealous against Popish doctrines was much resorted to and admired, being usually styled by his hearers, " The maul or scourge of heretics." He published seven sermons, and lies buried under the Communion Table in Christ-church. He died in 1630.

MR. THOMAS CHURCHYARD was born in this town. He wrote a book in verse on the Worthies or Worthiness of Wales, including Shropshire, wherein he calls Wales the Park, and the Marches the Pale. He also wrote in verse, " A description and discourse of paper, and the benefit it brings, with the " setting forth of a paper mill, built near Dartford, by a High German, " called M. Spilman, Jeweller to the Queen, 1588."

N. B. This appears to be the first paper mill erected in England.

Mr. Churchyard wrote the following epitaph for himself, at which time it seems probable that he was but in poor circumstances.

> " Come Alecto, lend me thy torch,
> " To find a church yard, in a church porch ;
> " Poverty and Poetry his tomb doth enclose,
> " Wherefore good neighbours, be merry in prose."

He died about the 11th of Queen Elizabeth's reign, 1570.

EDWARD WOLLEY, D. D. of Oxford, but educated in St. John's College, Cambridge. He was one of the Chaplains in Ordinary to King Charles I. and adhering to his Majesty's cause in the grand rebellion, retired with the King to Oxford, to attend on him and preach sometimes before him there. When his Majesty's cause declined, he suffered as other Royalists did, notwithstanding which he afterwards attended King Charles II. in his adverse

---

" not buried neither in the Church or Churchyard. And I also charge those that brought the Body " to the Place, to carry it away again at their own charge, as they will answer it at their peril. At " *Ecclesch 6 Sept.* 1558." By Virtue of this Letter, those Persons who had brought the Corpse to be buried, were forced at their own Charge to carry it back again, and because it was so corrupted, and smelt so strong, that no man could come near it, they were fain to draw it with Horses into a Broom-field, and there bury it.—*Magna Britannia.*

state, enduring many hardships in his service. After the restoration of his Master, he was made Rector of Finchingfield in Essex, in order to settle the inhabitants there in loyal principles, and to endeavour to invalidate the doctrines of the independent Minister, Mr. Stephen Marshall. In 1665 he was promoted to the episcopal see of Clonfort, and Kilmacogh in Ireland, to which he was consecrated at Tuam 16th April, and sat there several years, being held in great veneration, for his admirable way of preaching, and exemplary conversation.

MR. THOMAS CHALLONER, of this town, was an admirable Greek scholar and school-master, in the Free School here. This part of the kingdom was beholden to him for keeping up the principles of loyalty, which he instilled into a vast company of young gentlemen, who were educated by him; for which, falling under the frowns of the opposite party, he was fined sixty pounds.

COLONEL BENBOW,* a noted Royalist, and very active in King Charles the Second's cause, at the battle of Worcester, was shot to death in this town, October, 1651.—See Chap. III. Ancient History, p. 44.

ADMIRAL JOHN BENBOW, Vice-Admiral of the Blue Squadron, and one of the most gallant officers this kingdom has produced, was descended of an ancient family in Shropshire, and born on Cotton-Hill in this town, about the year 1650. He was early initiated into the sea service, and after acting for

---

* Twenty-seven years after the death of *Captain* Benbow, as he is called in the parish register of St. Chad, and on his grave stone, Lloyd in his celebrated "Memoirs of the Lives, Actions, Sufferings and Deaths of Noble and Excellent Personages," styles him *Colonel,* which work very probably, Mr. Phillips might have seen. The following are the particulars given by Lloyd:—

"Col. *Benbow* fell *Oct.* 1651, having been observed active in the engagement at *Worcester,* being shot to death at *Shrewsbury;* a person very observant in his carriage of that Rule in *Mr. Herbert.*

> "Slight not the smallest loss, whether it be
> In Love or Honour, take account of all;
> Shine like the Sun in every corner, see
> Whether thy stock of credit swell or fall,
> Who say, I care not, those I give for lost;
> And in his habit of this,
> Affect in things about thee cleanliness;
> That all may gladly hoard thee as a flow'r,
> Slovens take up their flock of noysomness
> Before hand, and anticipate their last hour.
> Let thy minds sweetness have his operation
> Upon thy Body, Cloaths, and Habitation."

With pleasure I correct the remark in a note, page 44, "That no traces of Benbow's grave "stone now exist;" the humble memorial certainly does exist, and the inscription which was nearly, if not totally, illegible, has subsequently been restored.—EDITOR.

some time as master of a Merchant ship, was introduced into the navy, by the following incident: Having in an engagement with a Sallee rover, taken thirteen of the enemy, he caused their heads to be cut off, and thrown into a tub of pork pickle, and upon his arrival at Cadiz, went on shore, followed by a Negro servant, with the Moors heads in a sack; the officers of the revenue demanded to see the contents, which the Captain told them were salt provisions for his own use; but upon their still insisting to look into the sack, Mr. Benbow replied, sternly, "I told you they were salt provisions for my own "use; Cæsar, throw them down upon the table, and gentlemen, if you like "them, they are at your service." The King of Spain was so charmed with this adventure, that he recommended Mr. Benbow to King James II. of England, who gave him the command of a ship of war. From this time he rose by pure merit, without any Court interest or intrigue, to the first offices in the navy, signalized himself, by several descents upon the French coast, pursued the famous Du Bart, whom, however, he could not overtake, and asserted and maintained the honour of the British flag in the West Indies, and wherever else he commanded. But the greatest and most important action he ever performed was in 1702, when, with his own ship, assisted by two others, (for all the rest of the Captains shamefully declined fighting) he maintained a desperate battle against a whole French squadron, for the space of four days, and in the morning of the fifth, had his right leg shattered to pieces by a chain shot. Such was his undaunted spirit, that when in this miserable condition, he was carried down to be dressed, and one of his Lieutenants expressed great sorrow for the loss of his leg, be briskly replied, "I am sorry for it too, "but had rather have lost them both, than to have seen this dishonour brought "upon the English nation: But, do you hear, if another shot should take me "off, behave like brave men, and fight it out." He recovered from the fever produced by this accident, but vexation at the bad behaviour of his Captains, (two of whom were afterwards shot for cowardice) co-operating with a consumption, with which he was now seized, put a period to his life, November 4, 1702.

The picture of this brave man, who was an honour to the town of Shrewsbury, is placed, by the Corporation's orders, on the left hand, over the Justice's Bench in the Town Hall.*

A LIST OF THE EARLS OF SHREWSBURY.

I. 1067. Roger de Montgomery, created Earl of Shrewsbury by William I. He was one of his chief favourites and a commander at the battle of Hastings, died 1094, and was succeeded by his second son.

---

* Now in the Grand Jury Room of the present Hall. For many anecdotes and interesting particulars of the gallant Admiral see the Salopian Magazine for 1815.—Editor.

FF

II. 1094, HUGH MONTGOMERY, who was slain in Anglesea, by an arrow, in an action with the King of Norway's forces.—See p. 13.

III. 1098, ROBERT MONTGOMERY, alias ROBERT DE BELESME, eldest son of Earl Roger, succeeded his younger brother Hugh. He had a vast estate in Normandy, but revolting from Henry I. he lost his estates in England, and being obliged to fly, was afterwards seized in Normandy, and sent prisoner to Wareham in Dorsetshire, where he died, and the title became extinct.—See p. 14.

IV. 1442, SIR JOHN TALBOT, Knight, was created Earl,* by King Henry VI. He was twenty years in the King's service abroad, and for his valour had many signal honours bestowed on him. At the siege of Chastillon, his horse was shot under him, and he being dangerously wounded, died July 20th, 1453, and was buried at Roan, in Normandy, but afterwards removed to Whitchurch† in Shropshire.

---

* It does not appear that he had any possessions in Shrewsbury, unless it might be a mansion called *Talbot Inne*, of which his grandson the third earl died seised, and which seems to have been situated in Dogpole. But from his *mother* he derived the great inheritance of the Le Stranges of Blakmere near Whitchurch, in the *county* of Salop, and it was from this, and not from the town its capital, that the title of this distinguished warrior was originally designed to be taken, though the subsequent usage of his descendants has denominated them Earls of SHREWSBURY.

Owen and Blakeway's History of Shrewsbury.

† " *Whit-church*, or *de Albo Monasterio*, called also *Blackmere*, because the Manor-house of this Town stands upon a large Mere, which, from the Blackness of the Water, was called *Blackmere*. This Manor was the Estate of the Family of *Blancminster*, or *de Whit-church*; the last of which Family leaving only 4 Daughters and Heirs, this Manor by one of them, passed in Marriage to *Robert Le Strange*, (whose Family was so named, because they were Strangers brought into *England* by King *Henry* II. and soon after far spread and propagated) whose Son *John Le Strange* was called *Le Strange* of *Blackmere*, from his Seat near the Mere, of which before. This Manor continued some Successions in the Family of *Le Strange*, and *John Le Strange*, the Grandson of the above-mentioned *John*, being in Favour with K. *Edw.* III. obtained a Charter for free Warren of the said Prince for his Manors of *Whitchurch*, and other Lordships in this County. He died seized of this Manor, and left it to his Son *Fulke*, whose Descendant and Nephew by his Brother *John*, coming into Possession of this Lordship, obtained of King *Edward* III. a Charter for a Fair to be held yearly at *Whitchurch*, upon the Eve, Day and Morrow of the Feast of the Apostles of S. S. *Simon* and *Jude*, 28 *Octob.* This *John* left a Daughter for his Heir, but she dying without Issue, her Aunt *Ancharet* became her Heir, being then 22 Years old, and married to Sir *Richard Talbot*, Knt. she brought it into his Family, in which it continued long, as will presently appear.

Sir *Richard Talbot* being possessed of this Manor, died seized of it, 20 *Rich.* II. leaving it to his Son *Gilbert Talbot*, who dying 7 *Hen.* V. left a Daughter named *Ancharet* his Heir, then but two Years old, *Beatrix* his Wife surviving him, who tho' she was a *Portuguese*, and illegitimate, the King accepted as a free Denizen, and confirmed to her this Manor, with the Advowson of the Church, and some other Estates, which had before been settled on her for Term of Life. *Ancharet*, the Heir of *Gilbert*, died about two Years after her Father, and *John* her Uncle became her Heir. He was so famous for military Exploits, that he was made Earl of *Shrewsbury*, and the World's Wonder. He was killed before *Chatillion* in *France*, by a Cannon-shot, and was brought to this Town to be buried,

V. 1453, JOHN TALBOT, his son, succeeded, and was slain at the battle of Northampton, July 10th, 1460.

VI. 1460, JOHN, son of the above, succeeded him in the Earldom, when he was only twelve years old. He was appointed Chief Justice of North Wales, and one of the King's Commissioners. Died June 28th, 1474.

---

leaving this Manor, and other great Estates to his Son and Heir *John*, whom he had by *Maud* his first Wife, one of the Heirs of Sir *Thomas Nevill* Lord *Furnival*. This *John* left this Manor to his Son of the same Name, as did also this *John*; but *Christopher Talbot* his fourth Son, Archdeacon of *Chester*, was Rector of this Church. We find no farther Account of this Manor, and so suppose it continued in the *Shrewsbury* Family, till it was extinct in the last Duke, as we have shewed above.

The Church here is a Rectory valued in the King's Books at £26 4s. 4d. *ob.* in the Patronage of the *Shrewsbury* Family till lately. In it are several Monuments for the *Talbots*; but the most remarkable is for our *English Achilles*, John Talbot, the first Earl of *Shrewsbury* of this Family. It stands in the South-Wall of the Chancel, and deserves our Notice for the Plainness of it, according to the Custom of the Age."

" *Orate pro anima Prænobilis Viri, DOMINI IOANIS TALBOT, Quondam Comitis Salopiæ Domini Strange de Blackmere, & Mareschalli Franciæ Qui obiit in Bello apud Burdenos.* VII IVLII MCCCCLIII.

Pray for the Soul of the Right Honorable Lord, JOHN TALBOT, some Time Earl of *Shrewsbury*, Lord *Talbot*, Lord *Furnival*, Lord *Verdon*, Lord *Strange* of *Blackmere*, and Marshal of *France*, who died in Battle at *Burdeos*. the VII of JVLY MCCCCLIII."

Magna Britannia.

The present church, which is a handsome stone structure of the Tuscan order, was erected on the scite of the former, a Gothic building, which fell down from age and decay; it was finished in the year 1722, and cost nearly £4000. The whole building is very regular, and consists of a large nave with side aisles. The galleries are very convenient, and the whole interior handsomely fitted up. The monuments of the Talbots were removed from the ruins of the old church, and preserved in the new. The church-yard which is spacious and pleasant, presents to the imagination of a visitor, the idea of a commodious and comfortable resting place. Nearly adjoining the church-yard is the tasteful residence of Mr. Harper, solicitor.

The Free Grammar School, founded by one of the Talbots who was rector of Whitchurch, is a Seminary of high character and respectability. The Rev. William Kent is first master, and the Rev. John Evans second master. Mr. Evans is author of a valuable Synopsis of the Evidences of the Christian Religion, a Poem on the Statue of Laocoon, &c.

Whitchurch is a place of some antiquity, and formerly had a castle, some parts of the walls of which, it is said, were standing in the year 1760. It contains 20 inns or taverns, and has several handsome and extensive shops, particularly that of Mr. Evanson, Druggist, Glass dealer, &c. The population of the parish may be estimated at the present period at more than 6000 inhabitants. The Rectory is one of the richest in the county, and in the gift of the Bridgewater family, to whom the estates, formerly possessed by the Talbots, now belong.—EDITOR.

FF2

VII. 1474, GEORGE TALBOT, succeded to the Earldom at five years old.* Died at his Manor of Wingfield, in Derbyshire, July 26th, 1541, and was buried at Sheffield.

VIII. 1541, FRANCIS TALBOT,† son of George, and his heir, was born at the Castle, in Sheffield, and called up to Parliament during the life of his father. In the Parliament 2nd Elizabeth, he was the only peer besides Viscount Montague, who opposed the bill for abolishing the Pope's supremacy, and reformation of religion. He died September 21st, 1559.

IX. 1559, GEORGE, only son of Francis, and his successor. He had the

---

* When little more than six years of age was made a Knight of the Bath, with Edward, Prince of Wales, and others; and previous to the battle of Bosworth, the forces of this Earl of Shrewsbury, consisting of 2000 men, were led by his uncle, Sir Gilbert Talbot, to the assistance of Henry Earl of Richmond against King Richard the Third; and having given him the meeting at Newport in Shropshire, accompanied him to the battle fought near Bosworth, on the 22nd of August, 1485, where Sir Gilbert Talbot commanded the right wing of the Earl of Richmond's army; and for this service was knighted in the field, and made a Knight Bannerett on the 28th of October following, (l. H. VII.)

In the 1st. year of Henry VII. the Earl of Shrewsbury had livery of his lands. In the 2nd of Henry VII. he met the King near Nottingham, in his way to the battle of Stoke, fought against Lambert Simnel, on the 16th of June, 1487, and having shared in the victory that day obtained by the King, he, for the reward of his services, was immediately afterwards made a Knight of the Garter.
Blore's Manor of Winfield.

† In the 2nd of Edward VI. he was sent into Scotland with 15,000 men, against the Scots and French, whom he compelled to raise the siege of Haddington; and, after having victualled and reinforced the town, and made an ineffectual attempt to bring the enemy to action; he destroyed Dunbar, and then returned into England. It is said by Holinshed, that when the noble Earl of Shrewsbury entered Haddington, he found the distresses of his gallant countrymen, by whom it was garrisoned, had been so great, that he could not refrain from tears.

The same year he was appointed Justice in Eyre of the forests north of Trent: and, in October 1549, (3. E. VI.) he was one of the Lords who signed the first proclamation declaring the Protector, Somerset, a traitor: in consequence of which, Somerset was, for a while, committed to the Tower. The Earl of Shrewsbury was of the Privy Council to King Edward; one of the chief mourners at the King's funeral; and after the death of the King, being one of the Lords of the Council who had engaged their allegiance to Lady Jane Grey, he subscribed the letter to Queen Mary, dated the 9th of July 1553, denying her right to the Crown. But this was so little resented by Mary, that on her accession to the Crown he was immediately pardoned; and soon after appointed President of the Council in the North, and Lieutenant of the Northern Counties.

He left behind him the reputation of the chiefest counsellor, "and most eminent scholar of his age;" and was buried with his father at Sheffield; but without a monument. His heirs, probably, considering his name as too great for eulogism, and as incapable of being rendered more durable by brass or marble.—*Blore's Manor of Winfield.*

custody* of Mary Queen of Scots, committed to him, and 15th Eliz. was for that service made Lord High Steward of England. He died Nov. 18th, 1590.

X. 1590, GILBERT TALBOT. Died at his house in Broad Street, London, May 8th, 1616. and was buried with his ancestors at Sheffield.

XI. 1616, EDWARD TALBOT, brother to Gilbert Talbot, and the next male heir. He died in London, without issue, February 8th, 1617, and was buried at Westminster.

XII. 1617, GEORGE TALBOT, descended from the second son of John the Fifth, Earl of Shrewsbury, and second of that name. He dying unmarried, April 2nd, 1630, was succeeded by his nephew.

XIII. 1630, JOHN TALBOT, who died February 8th, 1653.

XIV. 1653, FRANCIS,† son of John, was killed in a duel, by George Duke of Buckingham, March 16th, 1667. John, his second son, was also slain in a duel, by Henry Duke of Grafton.

XV. 1667, CHARLES, eldest son of Francis. He was created Duke of Shrewsbury by King William III. and died without issue at Isleworth, February 1st, 1717.

---

* The Queen of Scots was first committed to his custody in January 1568, (11 Eliz.) in the castle of Queen Elizabeth, (belonging to the Duchy of Lancaster) at Tutbury in Staffordshire; and continued under his care till the month of September 1584. In this service he preserved his fidelity to Elizabeth unshaken; but he was so perpetually teized by her suspicions, and those of her ministers, that his office, which might otherwise have been desirable to so great a nobleman, as a distinguished mark of honour and confidence, appear to have inflicted upon him a severity of punishment little inferior to that of his unfortunate captive. The fear of Elizabeth's displeasure induced him, at times, to a moroseness in his behaviour to Mary, which implanted in her bosom sentiments of distaste and resentment, that her high spirit could not be subdued by her sufferings to dissemble; whilst, at other times, by real or colourable marks of kindness, and attention to Mary, he drew upon himself the malevolence of a wife, ever alive to jealousy, and prepared to empoison his comforts; and the suspicions and rebukes of his Queen, who had no trifling satisfaction in mortifying and humiliating the greatest of her subjects.

His Lordship was buried in the church of Sheffield, where he had erected for himself a costly monument, which still remains, to preserve his memory.—*Blore's Manor of Winfield.*

† George Lord Talbot dying before his father, without issue, Francis, brother of George, and eleventh Earl of Shrewsbury, succeeded; who in 1651 (whilst his father was living) raised a company of sixty horsemen, and carried them to the assistance of King Charles the Second at the battle of Worcester; and escaping with the King, after the defeat of the royal army, he was one of the few persons of the King's party, who had the good fortune to ensure their safety by flight out of the kingdom; and having survived the restoration, died the 16th of March, 1667, of a wound received in a duel with George Villiers, Duke of Buckingham.—*Blore's Manor of Winfield.*

XVI. 1717, GILBERT TALBOT, descended from the 13th Earl of Shrewsbury, and tenth of that name. To him the title of Earl only, descended, and he being a Romish Priest, his brother George enjoyed the honours. Gilbert died December 12th, 1743, and was buried at Albrighton. George died December 12, 1733.

XVII. 1733, GEORGE, the present Earl* of Shrewsbury, was born December 11th, O.S. 1719. Married November 21st, 1753 to Elizabeth, daughter of the Hon. John Dormer of Peterly, in Buckinghamshire, Esq. afterwards Lord Dormer.

TITLES. George Talbot, Earl of Shrewsbury, in England, Wexford, and Waterford, in Ireland ; Baron Talbot, Strange (of Blackmere) Furnival, Verdon, Lovetot, Giffard (of Brimsfield) Comyn (of Badenagh, or Badenoch) Valence, and Montchensy.

CREATIONS. Baron Talbot, by writ of summons to Parliament, June 5. 1330, 4th Edward III. Strange of Blackmere, in com. Salop. Furnival, Vernon, Lovetot, Giffard of Brimsfield, in com. Glou. and Comyn (Cumming) of Badenagh, a family in Scotland, Valence, and Montchensy, the names of families : Earl of Shrewsbury, May 20, 1442. 20th Hen. VI. Earl of Wexford, and Earl of Waterford, July 17th, 1446, 24th Hen. VI.

ARMS. Gules, a Lion rampant, within a Border engrailed, Or.

CREST. On a Chapeau, Gules, turned up Ermine, a Lion, Or, his Tail extended.

SUPPORTERS. Two Talbots argent.

MOTTO. " PREST D' ACCOMPLIR."

CHIEF SEATS. At Isleworth, in the county of Middlesex. Grafton Park, near Bromsgrove, in the County of Worcester. Alton Castle, near Cheadle, in the County of Stafford ; and at Heythorpe, near Woodstock, in Oxfordshire.

---

* GEORGE, the 17th Earl of Shrewsbury, (following Phillips's arrangement,) died 22nd July, 1787. CHARLES, the 18th Earl of Shrewsbury, succeeded his uncle George, 22nd July, 1787. Married September 12th, 1792, Elizabeth, eldest daughter of James Hoey, Gent. of Dublin. He died without issue, April 5th, 1827, when his nephew John, the present Earl, succeeded.—EDITOR.

ADDITIONAL ANECDOTES,

AND SELECT

MEMOIRS OF EMINENT AND LEARNED MEN BORN, OR RESIDENT IN
THE TOWN OF SHREWSBURY AND NEIGHBOURHOOD,
OMITTED BY MR. PHILLIPS, OR WHO HAVE DIED SUBSEQUENTLY TO
HIS HISTORY BEING WRITTEN.

ODERICUS VITALIS, one of our best early historians was the son of Odelirus,
a priest of Attingham, (Atcham) where he was born in 1074. At five years of
age he was sent to the seminary of St. Peter, at Scrobbesbyrig, to which his
father was a large benefactor. Here he remained until he attained his tenth
year, when he was placed in the Benedictine abbey of Uticum, in Normandy,
where, in his eleventh year, he received the tonsure of the order, and was then
named Vitalis, because his first acceptance of the rule of St. Benedict happened
on that saint's day. His great ecclesiastical work is a history of his own times,
of which a fragment was published by Camden, in the collection of English
historians sent to the press by him from Frankfort in 1603. He called it the
Caen fragment, and supposed it to have been written by William de Poictou,
archdeacon of Lesieux. The whole work was printed by Du Chesne, in his
grand and accurate edition of Norman writers.—*Beauties of England & Wales.*

WILLIAM THORPE, who having for 20 years and more travelled up and
down the nation propagating the gospel doctrines, then lately received by John
Wickliffe, and among other places, where he chiefly abode, preached much at
Shrewsbury, was at length apprehended and imprisoned by Archbishop Arundel at Saltwood Castle in Kent, where having remained some time, the Archbishop having no particular charge against him, and but a suspicion of heresy,
offered him his liberty " If he would swear to him to forsake all the opinions
" which the sect of the *Lollards* held, and hereafter neither privily nor openly
" hold or teach any such opinion, nor favour any man or women, young or
" old, that holdeth them, but to the best of his knowledge and power shall
" withstand such disturbers of Holy Church in every diocese where he should
" come, and them that will not leave their false and damnable opinions, he
" will make known their names to the Bishop of the diocese, in which they
" are, or his Ministers, and more-over shall preach no more, till he should un-

" derstand by good witness that he had utterly abandonded his heretical opi-
" nions and doctrines, which he had before held and taught." William Thorpe
answered to this proposal, " That if he should consent to it, he should do a
" thing unlawful and deem himself accursed, by becoming an appealer and a spy
" for every bishop, and be the cause of the death both of men and women
" both ghostly and bodily : for many of both sexes that stand now in the way
" of salvation, if he should inform of them to the bishop and his merciless
" ministers, would forsake the ways of truth to avoid the troubles and persecu-
" tions which they would lay upon them to constrain their consent to their doc-
" trines." This answer provoked the Archbishop so much, that he told him,
that he was not willing to leave his old errors he saw, and therefore added, that
he should quickly either consent to his ordinance, and submit to his decrees,
or else by S. *Thomas* he should be degraded, and follow his fellow (William
Sautrey, a little before marty'd) into *Smithfield*. William Thorpe, after some
further discourse with the Archbishop, who was impatient for a direct answer,
said, " I tell you at one word, I dare not for the dread of God, submit to you
" after the tenure and sentence that you have rehearsed above to me."

The Archbishop having thus dealt with William Thorpe, according to St.
Paul's advice, (as he speaks) " If it may be, as much as in us is, we ought to
" have peace with all men ;" and not prevailing, came to a more close accusation of him, and produced a certificate sent to him from *Shrewsbury*, under the
Bailiff's seal, witnessing his errors and heresies to this effect :—

" The third Sunday after Easter, in the year of our Lord, one thousand
" four hundred and seven, William Thorpe came into the town of *Shrewsbury*,
" and through leave granted unto him to preach, he said openly in St. Chad's
" church in his sermon—That the Sacraments of the Altar after the Consecra-
" tion was material Bread ; and that Images should in no wise be worshipped ;
" and that men should not go on Pilgrimages ; and that Priests have no title
" to Tithes ; and that it is not lawful for to swear in any wise."

William Thorpe having heard the certificate read, awswered, " That he
" never preached or taught so either openly or privily ;" but the Archbishop
replied—that he would give credence to those worshipful men of Shrewsbury.

Upon this denial of William Thorpe, it was moved by the doctors then
present—that the Archbishop should appose and examine him in all the points
that were certified against him, that they might hear his answers from his own
mouth, and be witnesses of them.

Other discourses passed at this examination by the Archbishop, but all
concluded with this question—Wilt thou submit to the Ordinance of Holy
Church, or no ? But he promising it no further than was agreeable to God's
law, his submission was rejected, and he was remanded to prison. What became of him afterwards, is not known : It is not found that he was burned.
It is most probable, that being committed to prison, he was either secretly made
away, or died of sickness and hard usage.—*Magna Britannia.*

PETER STUDLEY, M. A. minister of St. Chad's church in 1628. He was a native of the town, being third surviving son of Thomas Studley, draper. He had not been many years at St. Chad's before the part which he took in a tragical event, exposed him to the ill-will of a powerful and not very merciful party, which the ensuing convulsion in the state enabled them to gratify by destroying the tranquillity of his remaining years. The event we allude to was the barbarous murder perpetrated by a young farmer of Clun, Enoch ap Evan, upon his aged mother and younger brother, in July 1633. The murderer was a zealous schismatick, and Mr. Studley, who visited him assiduously while he lay in prison, wrote a book, to prove that his crimes were the entire fruit of those principles. The puritans, on the other hand, contended vehemently that they were the mere effect of insanity. The truth probably lay, as is often the case, between the two extremes. Few, who read the book, will doubt, that the poor man had an intellect decidedly deranged : but it seems as little to be disputed, that religious animosity gave the last fatal turn to his disorder. Whatever were the fact, no one will wonder that Mr. Studley's work, which appeared with the *Imprimatur* of the bishop of London's chaplain, excited the utmost rage of the puritanical party, of whom, according to his account, there was no want in this town. It was probably this that induced him to resign St. Chad's in 1637. He occurs in 1639 as rector of the second portion of Pontesbury : but did not long continue there undisturbed, being among the first of the clergy whom the House of Commons summoned before them as delinquents in 1641. His book, which was deemed of so much consequence, that an answer to it was now, at the end of eight years, published by order of the house, was, doubtless, the cause of so iniquitous a proceeding ; for there was nothing else to alledge against him. As long, however, as Shropshire continued free from the incursions of the parliamentary forces, Mr. Studley, it is probable, did not much regard the thunders of the House. But when they became masters of it, he was " turned out of his rectory and well-furnished house: and so horribly dealt with, that he was denied the use of one of his own books, which he desired he might borrow for a short time." He was buried at Pontesbury 15 July, 1648, leaving behind him the character of a pious and good man.—*Owen and Blakeway's History of Shrewsbury.*

AMBROSE PHILLIPS, an eminent Loyalist Divine, Rector of the first portion of Westbury, was sequestered by the parliamentary committee of Salop in 1645, and he was ejected the next year by a party of soldiers. He had then a wife and ten children, who were turned out of doors. He was afterwards permitted to rent the tithes, but when his barns were full, the committee sent an order, and seized all the tithes and profits, so that from thenceforth his family was forced to subsist by charity chiefly, for though he had a tenement of £30 per annum, he could never get above £6 a year clear, and would have taught a school, but could not be allowed that liberty. He lived to be restored, but not without great opposition from the adverse party.—*Magna Britannia.*

GG

SILAS DOMVILLE, a native of Harley, and educated at Shrewsbury, a busy man against the king during the wars; but when they ceased, though by his father's interest he was made a sequestrator in Herefordshire, and had great power there; yet he used the Royalists so civilly and obligingly, that he was beloved by all the King's party. His father bought a good estate in church lands, and settled it upon him, with a moiety of the Bishop's palace of Hereford for a seat, but upon the King's restoration he lost all, and was in a manner ruined; but his civility to the Royalists had gotten him such friendship among them, that they procured him the place of Commissary of the Ammunition and warlike provisions at Dunkirk, and five years after, by the endeavours of Sir Paule Neile, he was made keeper of the King's stores for shipping, and other marine affairs at Harwich, a sea port town in Essex, where he died. He was bred a scholar, and studied some time at the university, viz. at New Inn, Oxford, but never took any degree; yet he had all the accomplishments of a scholar. He was a great lover of antiquities, and had some good MSS. out of the libraries of the cathedrals of Hereford and Worcester, among which was the original grant of King Edgar, about the sovereignty of the sea, and a treatise in hieroglyphicks finely painted, about the philosopher's stone, for which King Charles II. offered him a hundred pounds, but he refused it. He had good skill in music, and composed several anthems and lessons, as also in the mathematics and tongues. He wrote a History of Gavelkind, Lond. 1663; a Description of Harwich, and some observations upon some special occurrences in our English history, besides several pamphlets in the time of the rebellion, which he would not own. He died in 1678, and was buried in the chancel at Harwich, much in debt, so that his creditors got his MSS. and goods.—*Magna Britannia.*

THE REV. JOHN BRYAN was ejected from the living of St. Chad's. He was the eldest son of Dr. Bryan of Coventry. At an early period he was sent to the University of Cambridge, and entered of Emanuel College and Peter House, where he spent many years. Soon after he left college, he became domestic chaplain to the Earl of Stamford, lecturer of Loughborough, and minister of Didlebury, in this county. In 1652, he removed to the abbey-parish, Shrewsbury, where he was much respected. He soon received an invitation to the vacant living of St. Chad's, where he remained till August 24, 1662. He was twice imprisoned along with Mr Tallents and others, but in the last instance, he, with great difficulty, contrived to make his escape. Upon his refusal of the Five-mile act, 1666, he was constrained to remove, with his family, to Shiffnal, and used to go by night to officiate at Shrewsbury. The Indulgence act of Charles the Second, in 1672, gave him and his colleague, Mr. Tallents, a little respite from fear and interruption in their religious exercises. During this period he preached in the house of a Mrs. Hunt, noted for her piety, and her partiality to the ejected ministers. This season of repose, however, did not long continue. In 1683, new troubles arose. On the evidence of two maid servants, Mr Bryan was convicted of preaching, and fined £40. Afterwards he and Mr. Tallents were put into the crown-office; and he was forced once more to leave the town. The liberty granted in 1687, by the succeeding monarch, James, again restored him to his ministerial vocations with Mr. Tallents, and a regular dissenting congregation being formed, these two ministers continued together till the death of Mr. Bryan, August 31, 1699.

Beauties of England and Wales.

The Rev. Francis Tallents, was born at Pelsley, near Chesterfield, Derbyshire. About 1642, he travelled as tutor to the sons of the Earl of Suffolk. On his return, he was chosen Fellow of Magdalen College, and was afterwards Senior Fellow and President. As a tutor he was justly celebrated, and had among his pupils Sir Robert Sawer, and Dr. Burton. In 1652, he left the university, and became minister of St. Mary's. 1656, in the parish church of Ellesmere, was exhibited one of those public disputations about doctrine, for which that period was noted and disgraced, and Mr. Tallents was chosen moderator, an office for which his great learning and greater prudence eminently qualified him. The disputants were Mr. Porter, of Whitchurch, and and Mr. Haggar, a Baptist.—The subject was the necessity and validity of infant and adult Baptism. In this business Mr. Tallents is said to have acquitted himself with credit. The restoration of the exiled Charles gave him great pleasure; but the act of Uniformity blasted all his hopes of accommodating himself to the established state of ecclesiastical affairs. After his ejection, he annually observed Bartholomew-day as a day of fasting and prayer; and it was not till after the lapse of several years that he could bring himself to undertake any stated work in the ministry, or to lay aside the use of the liturgy, to which he had always been accustomed, and which he had ever justly admired for its antiquity and excellence.

In 1670, he travelled into France, as tutor to Mr. Boscawen, and Mr. Hampden, two young gentlemen of fortune. At the expiration of two years and a half, he returned to Shrewsbury, and joined Mr. Bryan in preaching to the dissenters there, and in conducting an academy for the education of dissenting ministers. In 1685, he was sent a prisoner to Chester for these labours; but on the defeat of the Duke of Monmouth in the West, he was liberated, and going to London, he led a private life. During his absence from Shropshire, in 1686, he was calumniated as a papist, by a fanatic who pretended to have found, in a desk which he had left at Shrewsbury, "such vestments as priests say mass in, full of crosses and images; and a book in which were the names of such as were admitted into the order of the jesuits." This "no-popery" slander had its foundation in a piece of an old white damask bed scolloped, and a book, containing the names of his pupils at Magdalen College. The matter produced some successful prosecutions, and then dropt. In 1687, he returned once more to the assistance of Mr. Bryan, and, though he was a man of very great moderation and favourable to occasional conformity, in 1691, he

GG2

finally entered into his new place of worship, on the walls of which he caused to be written "That it was not built for a faction or party, but for promoting repentance and faith, and in communion with all that love our Lord Jesus Christ, in sincerity." He died April 11, 1708, in the eighty-ninth year of his age, and was buried in the church, from which he had been ejected. Mr. Tallents was a man of considerable erudition and great industry. He published besides several works on controverted points of divinity, "A View of Universal History: or Chronological Tables." They were finely engraven, on sixteen copper-plates, in his own house. In his eighty-fifth year, he wrote a short History of Schism, for the promoting of Christian moderation, which was answered by a person signing himself S. G. whose book was replied to with effect by Mr. Tallents. He left behind him many MSS. of importance, particularly a journal of his travels, which was formerly in the hands of the Rev. Job Orton; but so blotted and soiled, as to lose much of its value.—*Beauties of England and Wales.*.

DR. JOHN THOMAS, Bishop of Salisbury, was a native of Shrewsbury. Of this Prelate some curious particulars are recorded by Bishop Newton. "There were," says that writer, in his own life, "at that time two Dr. Thomas's who were not easily distinguished; for somebody was speaking of Dr. Thomas; it was asked which Dr. Thomas do you mean? Dr. John Thomas,—They are both named John. Dr. Thomas who has a living in the city.—They have both livings in the city. Dr. Thomas who is Chaplain to the King.—They are both Chaplains to the King. Dr. Thomas who is a very good preacher.—They are both very good preachers. Dr. Thomas who squints.—They both squint.' They were afterwards both Bishops. Dr. Thomas was Chaplain to the English factory at Hamburgh, and was accustomed to go from thence to wait upon George II. at Hanover, on that King's frequent visits to his electoral dominions. After some time the King asked him whether, if he could obtain some preferment from the crown, he would not gladly leave Hamburgh to settle in England? He replied, that his Majesty's father had made him the like gracious offer, and he had declined it, because there were many eminent merchants with whom he lived much at his ease, and who were very kind and liberal to him; but now the case was altered, a new race was springing up, and he should think himself very happy under his Majesty's patronage and protection. He was desired to mention the preferment that would be most agreeable to him, and he pointed out one of the royal prebends. His Majesty intimated that it was not in his power to "get him any such thing, because his ministers laid their hands upon them all as necessary for his service," but he proposed to make him his Chaplain and to give him a living, and promised the next time he came to Hanover to take him over as his Chaplain; "and then," said the King, "if a Deanery or Prebend should fall, you will have a good chance of it."—Dr. Thomas, agreeably to this plan, returned to England, had the living of St. Vedast, Foster-lane, was appointed one of the

King's Chaplains, and in the spring ensuing, when the King was making preparations for Hanover, he sent word privately to the Doctor to prepare himself, and to have every thing in readiness to put on board by a particular day. The minister having been informed of the King's order, assured Dr. Thomas that he could not go, as another person had been fixed upon for that appointment long before. Dr. Thomas answered, that he had received his Majesty's express command, and should certainly obey it: he accordingly attended the King, and not the clergyman who had been nominated by the minister. It happened that during the summer the Deanery of Peterborough became vacant, and Dr. Thomas kissed the King's hand for it; at the same time the Duke of Newcastle wrote to him from England, that he had engaged that Deanery, and if the Doctor would waive his turn, he would certainly procure for him a better. Dr. Thomas wrote in answer, that as the King had been graciously pleased to give him the Deanery, he could not with any decency decline his Majesty's royal favour, but his Grace might vacate it by giving him a better thing, as soon as ever he pleased. In 1743, he was nominated to the see of St. Asaph, but before consecration removed to Lincoln in 1744, and was translated to Salisbury in 1761. He is buried in the cathedral of Salisbury, in which there is a monument to him. He was a very pleasant, facetious man, but had the misfortune of being deaf. Dr. Thomas was of Cambridge, and always attended the Duke of Newcastle in his visits to that University where he was remarkable for his good sayings. He was concerned in writing the celebrated periodical paper, called the Patriot, when at Hamburgh, being very well versed in the German language."—*Owen's Account of Shrewsbury.*

DR. JOHN TAYLOR, a learned critic and philologist, was born here in 1704. His father was a barber, but his son, whom he could not get to dress a wig or shave a beard, so perpetually was he poring over his books, was patronized by Edward Owen, Esq. of Condover, and at his expence placed at St. John's College, Cambridge, where he regularly took his degrees. A difference of opinion with his patron on political subjects having destroyed his hopes of ecclesiastical preferment induced Mr. Taylor to abandon the church for the practice of a civilian. But he had now established his character as a scholar and become a tutor and fellow of his college. In 1730 he was selected to speak the music speech, before the University. In 1732 he was appointed Librarian, and 1734 Registrar of the University. He now resided almost entirely at Cambridge, and employed himself in superintending the publication of some valuable editions of the classics. His erudite acquirements now gained him great respect and esteem. In 1744, he was appointed chancellor of the extensive diocese of Lincoln, previous to which it was intended to have employed his superior talent in a civil situation, as under secretary of state to Lord Granville. In 1751, he was presented with the rectory of Lawford in Essex, and in 1753, he became Archdeacon of Bucks. His " elements of civil law" was drawn up for the use of his pupils, the marquis of Bath and his brother. In 1755, he was attacked by the imperious and dogmatical Warburton, whose school he zealously opposed. In 1757 he was nominated a canon residentiary of St. Paul's; this was the highest preferment he obtained, and shortly after he left Cambridge to reside in London. Here he was employed in arranging the first volume of his celebrated edition of Demosthenes; but ere he had accomplished his design, he was called into another state of existence, on he 14th of April, 1766.

Dr Taylor's private character was amiable; his temper was social, and he was possessed of talents which were well calculated to adorn and amuse society. His income, which was ample, was chiefly employed in purchasing books, so that at his death his library was very extensive and valuable. This, with the residue of his fortune, for the support of an exhibition at St. John's, he bequeathed to the Free School of his native town, where he imbibed that habit of study, which laid the foundation of his future eminence.—*Stranger in Shrewsbury.*

Dr. Edward Waring, M. D. was born in 1734. The early part of his education he received at the Free Grammar School, Shrewsbury, whence he removed to Cambridge, in 1753. Here his talents for abstruse calculation soon developed themselves; and at the time of taking his degree. he was considered a prodigy, and the name of senior wrangler, or the first of the year, was thought scarcely a sufficient honour to distinguish one who had so far outshone his contemporaries.—Waring took his bachelors' degree in 1757; and the Lucasian professorship becoming vacant before he was of sufficient standing for the masters' degree, which is a necessary qualification for that office, the defect was supplied by a royal mandate, through which he became master of arts in 1760; and shortly after, Lucasian professor. In 1762, he published his Miscellaneous Analytica; one of the most abstruse books written on the abstrusest part of algebra. This work extended his fame over Europe; and he was elected, without solicitation member of the societies of Bononia and Gottingen, and received flattering marks of esteem from the most eminent mathematicians at home and abroad.

Mathematics did not, however, engross the whole of his attention. In 1767 he was admitted to the degree of doctor of physic; but whether from the incapacity of uniting together the employments of active life with abstruse speculations, or from the natural diffidence of his temper, for which he was peculiarly remarkable, the degree which gave him the right of exercising his talents in medicine was to him merely a barren title. His life passed on marked out chiefly by discoveries in abstract science, and by the publication of them in the Philosophical Transactions or in separate volumes under his own inspection. Having married, the Doctor quitted Cambridge, with a view of residing at Shrewsbury; but the air or smoke of the town being injurious to Mrs. Waring's health, he removed to his own estate at Plealey, near this place, where he died in 1797, universally esteemed for inflexible integrity, modesty, plainness, and simplicity of manners. They who knew the greatness of his mind, from his writings, looked up to him with reverence every where; but he enjoyed himself in domestic circles, with those chiefly among whom his pursuits could not be the object of admiration or envy.

In the mathematical world, the life of Dr. Waring may be considered as a distinguished era. The strictness of demonstration required by the ancients had gradually fallen into disuse, and a more commodious, though almost mechanical mode, by algebra and fluxions, took its place, and was carried to its limit by the professor. Hence many new demonstrations may be attributed to him, but 400 discoveries can scarcely fall to the lot of a human being. If we examine, thoroughly, those which our professor would distinguish by such names, we shall find many to be mere deductions; others as in the solution of biquadratics, anticipated by former writers. But if we cannot allow to him the merit of so inventive a genius, we must applaud his assiduity; and, distinguished as he was in the scientific world, the purity of his life, the simplicity of his manners, and the zeal which he always manifested for the truth of the gospel, will entitle him to the respect of all who do not esteem the good qualities of the heart, inferior to those of the head.

Stranger in Shrewsbury.

DR. CHARLES BURNEY, an eminent musician, was born at Shrewsbury in 1726, and was educated at the free grammar school. He afterwards became the pupil of Mr. Baker, the organist of Chester Cathedral. In 1741 he returned to Shrewsbury, and from thence, in 1724, went to London, and was chosen organist of St. Dionis, Backchurch. He afterwards resided nine years at Lynn. Returning to the metropolis, he obtained in 1769 the honorary degree of doctor in music, at Oxford. The year following he travelled through France and Italy, of which tour he published an interesting account in 1771. The next year he travelled through the Netherlands, Germany, and Holland. Of this journey he published an account in two volumes.

The first volume of his history of Music appeared in 1776, and the remaining four volumes came out at different intervals, the last being published in 1789. The next important work which proceeded from the pen of Dr. Burney was a history of the musical festival, in commemoration of Handel, in 1758, 4to. In 1796, he published the life of Metastasio, in three volumes, octavo. Besides these productions, he wrote "The cunning Man." "An Essay towards the history of Comets." The "Plan of a musical school," and "An account of Little Crotch, the infant Musician."

Dr. Burney resided for some time in the house that had been occupied by Sir Isaac Newton, near Leicester square, but, on being appointed organist of Chelsea college, he removed thither, and died in May, 1814.

He had a numerous family, among whom were, 1. James Burney, a Captain in the navy, and the companion of Cook. This gentleman published some valuable works. 2. Charles Burney, an eminent scholar and divine, who died in December, 1817, and whose library was purchased by parliament and presented to the British Museum. 3. Frances, who married a French officer named D'Arblay. She is known by Eveline, Cecilia, Camilla, and the Wanderer. 4. Sarah Harriet, the author of some novels of merit.

Various Authorities.

Dr. SNEYD DAVIES was born at Shrewsbury, and was educated at Eton, from whence he removed to King's college, Cambridge, where he became D. D. in 1759. Dr. Cornwallis, bishop of Lichfield and Coventry, gave him a canonry in his cathedral, and presented him to the mastership of St. John's hospital at Lichfield. He was also archdeacon of Derby, and rector of Kingsland, in Herefordshire. Dr. Davies wrote several ingenious poems in Dodsley's and Nichol's collections.—*Various Authorities.*

Dr. WILLIAM ADAMS, a most exemplary divine, was born at Shrewsbury, in 1707, and at the age of thirteen entered Pembroke college, Oxford, where he took his master's degree in 1727, and became fellow of the college.

In 1732 he became minister of St. Chad's, Shrewsbury, and in 1756, took his doctor's degree, and was at the same time presented to the rectory of Cound, in this county. In 1775, he was elected master of his college, on which occasion he resigned the vicarage of St. Chad, and was soon after made archdeacon of Landaff.

He died at Gloucester, of which cathedral he was prebendary, in 1789, aged 82.

Dr. Adams was one of the most intimate friends of Dr. Johnson, who held him in high esteem. Besides some occasional sermons, collected into one volume, octavo, he published an answer to Hume's Essay on Miracles, octavo, 1752. Dr. Adams was on terms of the most intimate friendship with the Rev. Job Orton.—*Various Authorities.*

REV. JOB. ORTON was born in the year 1717, in High Street, Shrewsbury, in a house which formerly stood on the scite (or nearly adjoining) on which stands Messrs. Beck and Co's Bank. His father was a respectable grocer, of honest and upright principles, and of the most industrious habits. Such was the attention of Mr. Orton to his business, that it became a provincial proverb, and nothing was more generally introduced, as a sort of an appeal in the confirmation of a circumstance or narrative, than " It is as sure as that Job Orton is in his shop."

Nurtured in the lap of piety and honest integrity, young Job, when of proper age, was sent for education in grammar learning to the free school of his native place, where he enjoyed as great advantages for classical knowledge as in most public schools, and spent somewhat more than eight years, with becoming diligence and proportionable improvement. In 1733, he was placed under the care of Dr. Charles Owen, a dissenting minister, at Warrington, in Lancashire, who possessed considerable learning, great piety, and most amiable manners, and had usually two or three young men under his tuition. After continuing with him one year, Mr. Orton spent a month in the family of Mr. Colthurst, a worthy minister at Whitchurch, in Shropshire, with whose church he first joined in the communion of the Lord's Supper. In 1734, he entered a pupil in the academy under the care of Dr. Doddridge at Northampton, where he continued about seven years, excepting during an interruption of about seven months, which the ill state of his health obliged him to spend at his father's house. Before he went first from home, he had been bound apprentice to his father, that, if he should not be inclined to any of the learned professions, he might be a freeman of the town of Shrewsbury, and engage there in business; but his inclinations were always to the christian ministry, from a pure desire of contributing to the religious improvement and everlasting happiness of mankind; and to qualify himself for this work were all his studies directed. Such were the ability and diligence with which he prosecuted his literary course at Northampton, that in March 1738-9, he was chosen assistant to Dr. Doddridge in the academy; and he began his lectures in this capacity, with instructing the junior students in the classics and geography. About the same time he was examined by a committee of neighbouring pastors, as to his qualifications for the ministerial office, and received an ample testimony of their approbation. From this time he continued to preach occasionally in all the neighbouring congregations, excepting on the first Sunday of every month, when he generally assisted Dr. Doddridge at Northampton. During the vacations, which lasted two months, the doctor staid at home the former month while Mr. Orton paid a visit to his friends and relations. In the second month he returned to Northampton, and took care of the congregation, while Dr. Doddridge made his excursions to London, or other places. In this early part of his life, Mr. Orton's acceptableness as a preacher occasioned invitations to be sent to him from several congregations) to settle with them as their minister; but he thought it best to decline them, as he was already engaged in a very useful employment, and had daily opportunities of improving himself, superior to what he should have had in any other station. In the year 1741, vacancies having taken place in both the presbyterian and independent congregations at Shrewsbury, the two societies concurred in an invitation to Mr. Orton to accept the pastoral charge among them, promising that in that case they would unite together in one church; he was accordingly ordained. The circumstance of such a pleasing coalescence of two different denominations of Christians, the unanimity of the application, the prospect of an agreeable settlement, and of a considerable sphere of usefulness, induced him to accept of the invitation, though not without a becoming diffidence in himself, and a deep sense of the peculiar delicacy of such a charge.

In October 1741, Mr. Orton removed to Shrewsbury, and preached his

HH

first sermon to the united congregations. The loss of his father which happened soon afterwards, not only proved a great personal affliction to him, but brought upon him such a weight of cares, in addition to his various duties as a minister, that his health was materially injured ; in consequence of which he was under the necessity of having an assistant. He was obliged, also, in the year 1742, to take a journey to Bath, where the waters afforded him some relief. In the same year he was solemnly ordained to the pastoral office, when thirty ministers* were present at the service. In the year 1746, he was invited by the large and respectable congregation at the new meeting in Birmingham, to be their co-pastor with Mr. Bourn ; but, though he had a high esteem for the people of that society, he was induced, from various motives, to continue where he was already comfortably and usefully settled. In 1748, Mr. Joseph Fownes was chosen assistant to Mr. Orton ; which connection was highly agreeable to both parties, they having always lived together in the utmost harmony and friendship. In the year 1751, the death of Dr. Dodddridge, though for some time expected, was a painful event to Mr. Orton, who thereby lost his much honoured tutor and friend. By the will of the doctor he was appointed to preach his funeral sermon, and was left all such of his papers as he might choose. In the spring after the doctor's death, the congregation at Northampton invited Mr. Orton to become their pastor. This circumstance alarmed the people at Shrewsbury, who under apprehensions lest he should listen to the application, sent him a most respectful, affectionate, and unanimous address, to intreat that he would not leave them. A separate address to the same purpose was made to him by the young persons of the society. But various circumstances combined, determined him not to remove to Northampton, and he declined the invitation, after taking some time to consider of it, which he thought was a piece of respect due to the congregation of his late friend. Soon afterwards he was applied to by a considerable congregation in Westminster, to succeed their late pastor the Rev. Obadiah Hughes; but he immediately rejected this proposal, both from a disinclination to settle in London, and from a firm persuasion that neither his health, nor his abilities, nor his sentiments, qualified him for a situation in the metropolis.

From this time nothing material occurred in the course of Mr. Orton's ministry at Shrewsbury, till the year 1765, when his bodily infirmities had arisen to such a height, that he was quite disabled from continuing his public work. On the fifteenth of September, therefore, which was his birth-day, he delivered his last sermon to his congregation. Several times after this he administered the Lord's Supper, but he durst not undertake to preach any more.

---

* The ordination sermon was preached by the Rev. Joseph Mottershead of Manchester, a near relative of my maternal grandfather, author of a volume of Practical Sermons, and various other pious works. A small Bible, once the companion of Mr. Orton. I have the great pleasure now of possessing; also an Original Letter of his, presented to me by the late Rev. T. Stedman, more than 20 years ago.

EDITOR.

On Mr. Orton's declining the office of minister, a contest took place with respect to the choice of an assistant to Mr. Fownes, which terminated in a division of the congregation. The larger number of the society having thought it their duty to provide themselves with another place of worship, Mr. Orton concurred with them in opinion, and esteemed himself bound to countenance them as a christian, a dissenter, a minister, and a friend to liberty. This circumstance, however, did not occasion any dimunition in the friendship between Mr. Fownes and Mr. Orton; but the separation had the effect of exciting a bad spirit in several persons of both parties. To such a height was this carried, that Mr. Orton's situation at Shrewsbury was rendered very uncomfortable, and it also produced an unfavourable effect upon his health. He therefore found it necessary to retire to some other place; and in the year 1766 he removed to Kidderminster, principally for the advice of Dr. Johnstone, a very able and skilful physician, who always proved himself a faithful and a tender friend. Here Mr. Orton spent the remainder of his days, zealously intent on promoting the interests of religion, though the state of his health prevented him from appearing again in the pulpit. What he could not perform as a preacher, he was solicitous to effect as a practical writer.

In the spring of 1783, his complaints multiplied so fast upon him, that there was no prospect of his continuing much longer in life. He died on the nineteenth of the following July, in the sixty-sixth year of his age. Our author's talents as a preacher are thus delineated by Mr. Fownes, in the sermon which he delivered after his death. " Mr. Orton was master of a great variety of styles, and I have frequently heard him in the course of his public services adopt them all with success. But the general character of his preaching was rather of a practical, serious, and affectionate turn, than distinguished by laboured and long continued trains of reasoning. To the excellence of his private character, the following extract of a letter from Dr. Johnstone to Mr. Stedman bears honourable testimony.

" Indeed, my friend, we shall not see his like again; we shall not see knowledge so extensive joined with such humility, such wisdom and discernment of the human character and of human life, so determinately employed in doing good to all around him, and to diffuse happiness in the large circle of human society. He truly had the wisdom of the serpent and the innocence of the dove. Of the seventeen years which he passed in Kidderminster, I spent most usefully and happily, daily, many hours in his company; his counsel, always skilful, was faithful and benevolent. I do not remember I ever spent ten minutes in his company, without being witness to some benevolent design or some benevolent action."

Dr. Kippis, at the close of his biographical memoir of this excellent man, observes, " that Mr. Orton, who so long resided at Kidderminster, the principal seat of Mr. Baxter's ministerial usefulness, had a considerable resemblance in certain respects, to that famous divine. In extent of abilities, Baxter was undoubtedly greatly superior to Mr. Orton, and he prodigiously exceeded

HH2

him in the multiplicity of his writings ; but with regard to the nature of their practical works, and the strictness, we had almost said the rigidness, of their personal piety, there was no small degree of similarity. Both of them display, in their productions, the same ardent zeal to excite the attention of men to their eternal concerns, and urge these concerns with peculiar energy and pathos."—*Editor, from Published and Original Sources.*

The late Mr. Thomas Wood, first publisher of Phillips's History of Shrewsbury, Printer and Proprietor of the Shrewsbury Chronicle, &c. was a native of Painswick, Gloucestershire, in which town or village, his father, Mr. Stephen Wood, was a clothier of some eminence for a long series of years. Thomas, the subject of this article was, it is believed, his third son, and having been fully trained up to the active business of his father, and appointed by him to undertake the journeying department, (which he had pursued for several years) had an opportunity about the year 1769 of surveying the interesting *arcana* of printing, at, it is understood, the town of Birmingham, when finding a strong desire to arise in his mind to acquire the full knowledge of so astonishing an art as that which in early ages constrained the inhabitants of Germany to identify its production with the absurdities of magic or conjuration, or with the secrets of a cabalistic junto, the idea of which, in these enlightened ages, we treat with ridicule, though such was the fact in the beginning of the fifteenth century. Mr. Wood being then twenty-three years of age, after consulting his friends in Gloucestershire, articled himself for two years with Mr. Miles Swinney, printer, of Birmingham, who observing Mr. Wood's astonishing advance, from day to day, in a general acquaintance with every branch of printing discoverable in a provincial office, and having, on the expiration of the period just named, remarked frequently to his friends, that he " never met with an apprentice who, in the customary period of seven years, became so completely master of the trade he was connected with in its various ramifications," and knowing that his constitutional meekness of temper, deliberate judgment of mind, integrity of morals, and unwearied industry, rendered him an admirable ally, if he should feel inclined to carry into effect what he had long been wishing for and designed, viz. the establishment of a second newspaper in the populous and increasing town of Birmingham ; determined immediately on the execution of his project, and in the year 1771 the *Birmingham Chronicle* was immediately commenced. But the habits of Mr. S.* and those of his coadjutator were but of a dissimilar nature and tendency ; and Mr. W. having learned, again and again, the need of a weekly publication in Shrewsbury, resolved, as soon as he could help Mr. Swinney

---

* No disrespect is wantonly offered to the memory of Mr. S. (who is not living at this time) but knowing many circumstances which would ratify the expression used, I merely allude to facts.—T. W.

in the completion of a chart or directory for his own management of the infant newspaper ; and in full concurrence with the approbation of Mr. S. to comply with the advice of his Shrewsbury and Shropshire friends, concerning the opening referred to, so that a dissolution of partnership having taken place, the Shrewsbury Chronicle was commenced by Mr. W. on Pride Hill, in that town, about the middle of November 1772, on the principles of English Loyalty and unfeigned attachment to the person and throne of the King, unchangeable advocacy of the Protestant ecclesiastical establishment of the country, and zeal for the honour of God, in a due regard for all which, (whatever may be the disposition to amalgamate in the political questions of this falsely called liberal age) the safety of the Constitution is immediately and specifically connected ; and notwithstanding the multiplied cynical opinions of " existing only three months," then " six months," " a twelvemonth, two years," &c. that prevailed at first among the murmurers of the age, the Chronicle had for nearly twenty-nine years pursued " the noiseless antijacobinical tenour* of its way," when the amiable and benevolent, unprovoked and unprovoking, loyal, virtuous, and universally respected Thomas Wood departed this life, April 7, 1801,† aged 54, of whom it has been well expressed—

> "Thy worth, thy friendship ever call to mind,
> " And say—where can we such another find?"

Nor will it be thought superfluous in delineation of the character named, if there be in the close of this article an allusion to three particulars in which the unvarnished truth of the foregoing statements will be immediately remembered by many. ATTACHED as Mr. Wood was to the PRINCIPLES AND BASIS OF THE GOVERNMENT UNDER WHICH HE LIVED, the conspicuous LOYALTY of his weekly newspaper was not merely approved by the general inhabitants of the town and county of Salop, who have uniformly regarded the boasted principles of "liberalism" with the jealousy and dislike that an undissembling friend to his country cannot but feel, but in taking his annual journey or occasional rides to the various parts of the Principality of Wales, in which his loyalty was revered as his person and family were beloved, the arrival of their friend, was hailed by the Cambrian Patriots, (when the event was expected more

---

* So spelt by the learned Dr. Johnson, therefore the modern spelling (tenor) is erroneous.—T. W.

† The Rev. R. De Conroy, in a most affecting discourse from the pulpit, paid a last tribute of respect to the memory of Mr. Wood, in which discourse he intimated his own expectation of being speedily called to follow. His text on the occasion was, " Blessed are the dead who die in the Lord from henceforth ; yea saith the Spirit for they rest from their labours, and their works do follow them." The church was not only *crowded* but *surrounded* by affected hearers, and the impression then made upon many hearts, we have reason to believe, was deep and lasting.

> " So die the just, the gen'rous and the kind ;
> " And dying, breathe their blessings on mankind."

EDITOR.

especially) with feelings and attestation of the most gratifying kind ; and no small exultation of mind do his son-in-law, the publisher of this work, and other relatives experience, in finding from time to time, in the warm-hearted sons and daughters of the intrepid CARACTACUS, an emanation of the same feelings towards themselves, proceeding as it does from the fountain of that esteem for the "*first founder of the Chronicle*," which terminates only in human dissolution.

Amidst all the mildness of disposition, and evenness of temper, for which Mr. W. was so UNIVERSALLY ESTEEMED, (so that by some of his most intimate friends he was commonly spoken of as their good friend Moses) his ADHERENCE TO PRINCIPLE was serious, constant, and inflexible. Tried as his temper was, from time to time, by the contravening endeavours of a refractory hydra-headed opposition, about the periods of the American War and French Revolution, with regard to the political ground on which he stood, HIS FIRMNESS FAILED HIM NOT ; and though desirous as he was, being a Member of the Church of England, to keep "the Unity of the Spirit in the bond of peace," to avoid the occurrence of wanton or party offence, no inducement of pecuniary benefit, nor hope of being in favour with the great, could on any occasion whatever tempt him to profane or disregard the Sabbath. Instances of a remarkable self-denial IN THIS WAY, and when the risque of displeasing some of the nobility of the county was inevitably run, might be circumstantially detailed, were human applause the object contemplated in writing this article ; but a far greater plaudit and consolation of mind was enjoyed by Mr. Wood, in the undissembling testimonies of esteem that his dearest friends thought proper to make known, the approbation of his conscience, and the pleasure of the Supreme Being, who caused the event of his integrity, in some of the cases referred to be of the most gratifying nature, WITH RESPECT TO SECULAR advantage, which a yielding to the dictates of an imbecile mind (in the nature of things) would effectually have precluded ; and it is worthy of remark, that at the end of every year, in his private cash book, there was regularly made, in his own hand writing, an acknowledgement of gratitude to the Merciful Disposer of events, that he was not unconscious of the benificence of the Deity, whose compassion is, at all times, specially shewn forth in behalf of " them that fear him."

The CHARACTERISTIC BENEVOLENCE, connected with the absence of whatever is identified with avarice, or an habitual grasping after lucre, or a pursuit of popular acclamation, by an uncourteous meddling with questions of local dispute, where a retiring modesty of temper would be more amiable and praiseworthy, form the only other feature of excellence in the character of Mr. Wood that needs to be here adverted to. Faulty as is the disposition of that man, who having a considerable family to provide for, is not careful and strict in the *collection of his debts*, the failing named is worthy of being classed amongst those errors IN HIS character, which

" Lean'd to Virtues's side."

The complaint of " difficulties" or " inconvenience," the semblance of poverty, and even the intreaty of delay, would always keep back the hand of the benevolent Thomas Wood from the attempt of obtaining payment by measures of coercion; and it was not till after his decease that a gentleman of the legal profession, conversing with one of Mr. W's debtors on the circumstance of his arrest, which could not be avoided, unless the debt which had been of twenty years running was intended to be given up, received this answer from the defaulter;—"I dont believe that Mr. Wood would have thought of sending me to gaol, had we dealt together AS WE HAVE DONE for fifty or a hundred years." The losses he sustained in this way, from first to last, were numerous and great, and during the career of his trading concerns in Shrewsbury, may be fairly computed at ten or twelve thousand pounds; but even these losses, when coupled with the acts of his unsparing benevolence towards the needy and the embarrassd, prove the truth of his character to have been such, that if he was known through the kingdom by the name of the " religious printer," it was equally evident that he " SHEWED HIS FAITH BY HIS WORKS." In fine, there are still living in Shropshire and North Wales multitudes to attest that the following character of Mr. Wood, freely inserted in, perhaps, twenty provincial papers, within a few days after his death, gives (NOT *an overstrained or fulsome, but*) a true description of the man :—

" How much and how deservedly the loss of this most worthy man is to be
" lamented by his family, and by society at large, may be fairly estimated by
" a consideration of the many virtues which adorned his character in public
" and private. In all his connections, and in every department of life,
" whether civil, social, or domestic, in all the tender relations of husband,
" father, master, and in all the offices of friendship, his temper and whole
" deportment exemplified the purest principles of christianity. No wonder
" that his last moments, resembling so uniformly the tenour of his life, and
" cheered so much by the hope of the gospel, should be distinguished by
" patience and placidity, and that under the bright prospect of a happy
" immortality, the end of such a man should be peace."—T. W.

My Reverend and esteemed relative,* the writer of the above article, particularly requested that no alteration whatever should be made, either in word or sentiment, in what he had written, with which desire I have most scrupulously complied.—EDITOR.

---

* The Rev. Thedosius Wood, Vicar of Leysdown, Kent.

The Rev. R. De Courcy, M. A. Vicar of St. Alkmond's Shrewsbury, was born in the year 1744. He was a native of Ireland, a descendant of the ancient family of De Courcy, of whom was John De Courcy, celebrated in Irish history for his extraordinary prowess and heroism.* He was also distantly related to the family of the Earl of Kinsale.

Early in life he had very serious impressions and an unconquerable desire for the work of the ministry; to complete his design he entered himself a member of Trinity College, Dublin, where he acquired considerable eminence, and was designated "a young man of great promise." At the age of twenty-three he received deacons orders in the Cathedral Church of Clonfert, but in consequence of some offence given to the Bishops of Ireland, (probably by his zeal, which was then considered Methodism) he could not in his native country obtain priests orders.

In the year 1768 he came over to England, where attracted by the fame of the Rev. George Whitfield, who was then in London, he visited him,

* John De Courcy was never satisfied nor reconciled to the manner by which King John obtained the throne; he treated his conduct as equally lawless and cruel, and openly charged him with the murder of Prince Arthur. John, stung with this reproach, summoned him to repair to his presence, which De Courcy at first peremptorily refused. However, on considering that he was not in a condition to withstand the power of the king, he at last consented to do homage to John, on receiving a safe conduct, but which was not respected by that unprincipled tyrant. For De Courcy, immediately on his arrival in England, was condemned to perpetual imprisonment, and remained neglected until a champion from Philip, King of France, appeared at the court of John, and offered to maintain by wager of battle his master's claims to certain castles and domains in the duchy of Normandy.

None of the English courtiers seemed disposed to encounter this gigantic challenger, at which John was exceedingly mortified, till reminded that the bodily strength of De Courcy was not inferior to that of the French champion. De Courcy, in consequence, is invited to support the honour of his country; and after repeated denials, is at length prevailed upon, not for the sake of John, to whom he bore an implacable enmity, and who had treated him so injuriously, but for the honour of the crown and kingdom to accept the challenge. He desired his own sword to be brought from Ireland: the rigour of his confinement was softened, and his strength repaired by due care and nourishment. The day of this important decision at last arrives. The Princes and nobles of France and England are assembled in the utmost expectation. The Frenchman first appears; De Courcy prepares himself with great composure, and when he enters the lists, the Frenchman having surveyed him minutely, and being terrified by the stern aspect, and the colossal stature of his antagonist, declines the combat, and flies from the field.

Philip and John, who are said to have been witnesses of this triumph of De Courcy, entreated him to give some proof of his bodily strength, as they had been disappointed in their expectations of his hardy combat with the Frenchman. In compliance with their desire, he ordered his attendant to drive a stake into the ground, on which he placed a coat of mail and a helmet. Then drawing his sword, and looking with a threatening aspect on the princes, he struck it through the armour so deeply into the stake that no one but himself could draw it out. The princes expressed their astonishment, not only at his vigour, but at the menacing looks which he had darted at them both; He answered them with a rude and sullen violence, that, had he missed his blow, he should have struck their heads. The importance of the service achieved by intimidating the challenger, atoned for these passionate expressions. John gave him his liberty, and restored him to his possessions; and, it is added, that on this occasion he also granted to De Courcy and his heirs the privilege of standing covered in their first audience with the King of England.—*Museum of the World, from Galt's Sketches.*

and for some time officiated at the tabernacle; he afterwards, for a short period, preached in the chapels of Lady Huntingdon, but not being satisfied with that connexion, he became chaplain to Lady Glenorchy, and preached at her chapel in Edinburgh, where he was extremely popular. His ardent attachment to the discipline of the Established Church of England and Ireland induced him to engage as curate of Shawbury, in the County of Salop, where he continued four years, and obtained priest's orders. In 1774 he was presented by the Lord Chancellor to the Vicarage of St. Alkmond's, Shrewsbury.

Having preached in unconsecrated places of worship, Mr. De Courcy was considered by many of his parishioners as little superior to an Itinerant Methodist Preacher, he consequently met with considerable opposition; at the same time the more zealously pious of the Established Religion, and many respectable dissenters in the town became his active friends and advocates. A rather clever and satirical Poem, entitled "St. Alkmond's Ghost," written under the signature of Clio, by a Mr. Williams,* an eminent Auctioneer of Shrewsbury, caused no inconsiderable agitation, and was designed to support Mr. De Courcy's cause. From this Poem the following lines are selected. The author lays the scene of his vision in St. Alkmond's Parish, and assumes the character of a Salopian Butcher.

'Twas that sad Night, when *Reverend Sneade* in Death
Resign'd at once his *Vicarage* and *Breath;*
About the Hour *(as runs the Village talk)*
When *shrouded Spectres* haunt the *Yew-tree Walk,*
Fancy was left, *prophetic of some Change,*
In the wide World of *Intellect* to range:
Methought I stood, unshelter'd and alone,
Where *Alkmond's Dead in mould'ring Heaps are strewn.*
From the dark Mansions of the dreary Tomb,
Old Alkmond's Ghost stalk'd horrid thro' the Gloom:
A dismal Paleness all his Looks express'd,
And steaming Sulphur wav'd his sable Vest,
When thus the Ghost,—(but first he wav'd his hand)
Bespoke aloud the visionary Band:
" Sons of my Labours, while confin'd to Earth,
" And still my subjects in the realms of Death:
" With sad Regret, I see my Pow'r decline:
" At least, in this thrice hallow'd Dome of mine,
" And lo! as jealous of my rising Fame,
" A *Rival starts !—D-C—y* is his name;
" *Hibernian* born, the Insect of an Hour!
" The Child of Fortune, but the *Lie* of Pow'r!
" He comes! (base Idol of deluded Brains,
" *Enthusiastic*, as his poison'd strains;)
" He comes—to brand me with opprobrious Names,
" And judge my *System* to eternal Flames:

---

* He died at Shrewsbury, September 21, 1785. A portrait of him, in oil, has for many years adorned the front parlour of the White Hart Inn, in this town.—EDITOR.

II

" In *native Bronze*, methinks I see him stand,
" Adjust his Robes, and proudly wave his Hand,
" While from his Lips, a Flood of Fury pours,
" That *Tart'rus* shakes and all my *neighb'ring shores.*"

In 1775 Mr. De Courcy married the lovely and accomplished Miss Dicken, only daughter of Thos. Dicken, Esq. of Wollerton, near Hodnet, by whom he had six children. He was a man of rare abilities, of a warm and generous heart; his sermons were chiefly extemporaneous, but elegant and finished; his action was graceful, and his appearance in the pulpit altogether preposessing; his doctrines, though Calvinistic, were, as he believed, the pure orthodox doctrines of the Church of England, these he most zealously defended; he also warmly engaged in a controversy with the Baptists, in which he unfortunately lost his temper, and was keenly satirized by his opponents as " The good vicar in a bad mood."

In all Mr. De Courcy's controversies, his warm and generous friend, Thomas Wood, Proprietor of the Shrewsbury Chronicle, was his Printer and Publisher, who, when the success of his publications did not remunerate their author, the printer would cancel all obligation and take upon himself the sole responsibility. A Three Shilling publication entitled " The Rejoinder" was printed, but never offered to the public.

As the Vicar of St. Alkmond's Mr. De Courcy was highly esteemed by his congregation; the fruits of his ministry and the witnesses of his zeal and fidelity are still numerous in the town of Shrewsbury and its vicinity.

To the Printer of the Shrewsbury Chronicle and his family, Mr. De Courcy was most ardently attached. To a relative* of that family he addressed a letter of " solemn counsel," which was published, and as a composition does credit to the author's talents and his heart. The following letter to Mr. Joseph Wood† contains many fine sentiments and most suitable advice.

MR. JOSEPH WOOD,

Having received express permission from your Father and Mother to address Captain Bass on the subject which appears to occupy so much of your attention at present, and taking it for granted that the Captain would not return again to Shrewsbury, I sent him a letter to London, under cover to my son: his Naval appointment however being postponed, I find by the note which I received from him this morning, that he has been obliged to return; I inclose the note for your perusal, because the contents of it are as favourable as your most sanguine wishes could desire or anticipate, as far as respects the *inclination* of the Captain; and

---

* Mr. Samuel Horlick, of Painswick, Gloucestershire.

† Mr. Joseph Wood was a young man of considerable mental acquirements, of genuine loyalty, undaunted courage, and unconquerable zeal. He served in the British Navy as a Midshipman nearly six years, in which capacity he had on various occasions distinguished himself as a most skilful enterprising young officer, and was on the point of being promoted, when he bravely fell on board the Wolverine Gun Brig, while engaged with two French Privateers, contending for the honour of his country, by the side of his Captain, March 24th, 1804, in the 23rd year of his age.—EDITOR.

I have no doubt when his own appointment takes place yours will immediately follow. This is a very important step Sir that you are going to take. To embark in life, which, whether we enter upon it by Sea or Land is a sort of stormy sea at best, requires thought, and very serious deliberation: and to take this first step on an *element* of which you know comparatively nothing, requires not a little of that kind of courage which teaches a young man to be cautious without being timid, and resolute without being rash. I do not say this to discourage you. The great Governor of the Universe is the God of the Ocean as well as the Land, and his Almighty protection extends to the remotest part of the world, as well as to all circumstances of danger or difficulty in which his Providence may place us.

A *Christian*, (be sure that *you* are one,) is warranted to take the comfort of this blessed truth, through all the changing scenes of life, in trouble and in joy, for it is *his* great privilege to " trust in the Lord at all times," and then whatever happens all will be well. My principal view in what I have said is to give encouragement, and to excite to prayer; it may be very different in Naval tactics, but it is an invariable rule in christian discipline, that the best way for a christian soldier to fight, or at least to prepare for fighting, is *upon his knees*. Here is great room for advice, but as Solomon will give it you much better than I can, I refer you to *him*. Prov. iii, 6, and again, Prov. xxiii, 26, yet he again would refer you to his father. " And thou Solomon, my son," 1st Chron. xxviii, 9. Read these passages and treasure them up in your mind. Be assured I shall pray that as your name is *Joseph*, the same blessings in substance may attend you, that rested " on the head of him (your NAMESAKE) that was separate from his brethren." Gen. xlix, 26.

I thank you for your elegant *letter*, for the *paper* it contained, for your own *remarks* on the character and achievements of Lord Nelson, and for the poetic *distich* in which you celebrate the praise of that great naval commander.

Nothing, you will perceive, that you have done me the favour to communicate has escaped my notice, and merely to say I am much pleased with it is saying too little; be assured then, that I think myself much obliged; my obligation, however, will be much increased, if you will request Mrs. Wood* to distribute the inclosed *half guinea* in what proportion, and to what pensioners on her bounty she thinks proper.

With affection to her, to your Father, and all the Family, I remain,

Your very Sincere Friend,

The Mount,
December 27, 1798.

R. DE COURCY.

---

* The following character of Mrs. Wood appeared in the Obituary of the Gospel Magazine, for November 1808.

"On Sunday, the 28th of August, departed this life, in the 64th year of her age, Mrs. Mary Wood, relict of the late Mr. T. Wood, printer of the Shrewsbury Chronicle. To enlarge on the numerous excellencies of this much respected woman, or to describe the effects which during the greater part of an useful life, were so evidently produced (both in a mental as well as a corporeal point of view) on that rank of society among which she resided, would not only be offering a panegyric to her memory, expressly contrary to her own desires, but virtually ascribing praise to the personal dispositions of the creature, rather than to that Divine Being " from whom all holy desires, all good counsels, and all just works do proceed." Suffice it, therefore, to say, that that unshaken faith which was built on the irrevocable promises of God, and which was the operating cause of anything that in the sight of the world appeared " lovely or of good report," remained her strong consolation in the approach of death. Relying on the faithfulness of Him that hath promised, she could with a calmness and confidence, a rapture and transport (only to be inspired and produced by THE GOSPEL) meet " the last enemy" as one disarmed of his sting; and in bidding adieu to a world of sin, sorrow and pain, could exclaim in the language of faithful Simeon, " Now Lord, lettest thou thy servant depart in peace; for mine eyes have seen thy salvation."

As we before intimated, the doctrines believed and taught by Mr. De Courcy were those of Particular Redemption; hence in the controversy between the Rev. A. Toplady, Mr. Richard, afterwards Sir Richard Hill, and the Revds. John Wesley, and John Fletcher, he supported the opinions of the two former gentlemen.

In the year 1782 Mr. De Courcy published, "Seduction; or the Cause of Injured Innocence Pleaded," a Poem, addressed to the author of the "Villainy," with a preface, stating the melancholy but authentic facts on which the subject of the Poem is founded."

The circumstances will be fresh in the recollection of many of my readers. A Colonel Winwood who resided in Shrewsbury, was accused of being the seducer of an amiable young lady, a Miss F——r, his ward; this he denied, and charged the guilt of the deed on his own footman. The lady on being informed of the Colonel's attempt, "fired with indignation and shocked with horror, disclosed the whole," which brought on the Colonel the hatred and disgust of every individual who believed *her* story.

The Poem has certainly less of poetry in it than we should have expected, considering Mr. De Courcy as a scholar and orator of such distinguished eminence. On the same occasion, the year following, he published "the Seducer convicted on his own evidence." Each publication was anonymous. A reward of 50 guineas was offered by the Colonel for a discovery of their author. Mr. De Courcy also published "Jehu's Looking Glass," "Nathan's Message to David," a Sermon, Two Fast Sermons in 1776, Two ditto in 1778, "Hints for suppressing the profanation of the Lord's Day," "Letter to a Baptist Minister," "A Reply to Parmenas," "Self-Defence not inconsistent with the precepts of Religion," addressed to the members of the North Shropshire Yeomanry Cavalry; but the chief publication during his life time was "Christ Crucified," a popular and admirable work. His posthumous pieces have been very justly esteemed, they were published by subscription in one vol. 8vo. price £1. 1s. and were the means of raising a fund for the benefit of his widow, who survived him till within a short period of the present time. This upright and faithful minister died Nov. 4th, 1803, aged 59 years, in the full assurance of eternal happiness, exclaiming in the moment of departing nature, "Thanks be to God for my salvation."

To the labours of Mr. De Courcy, Shrewsbury is deeply indebted for much of the pious feeling and love of evangelical preaching which now prevails in the town. To his friend, Thomas Wood, the town and county of Salop owe much of that love of their country, and those loyal sentiments which are found to blossom and flourish in the towns and villages of the *fourth division of the ancient Cornavi*; each will be long remembered by the virtuous and the good, who lived within the circle of their respective labours and usefulness.

EDITOR.

SIR WILLIAM PULTENEY, BART. representative for Shrewsbury in seven successive parliaments. His name was originally Johnstone, and he practiced at the Scotch Bar. By his marriage with the heiress of the house of Pulteney, he became possessed of a very large fortune, which was not likely to be diminished in his hands, and he was then induced to take the name of Pulteney. He was a useful and intelligent speaker in parliament, though by no means a graceful and eloquent orator. What he said, however, always contained substantial matter, and was marked by plain sense. His vast fortune placed him above the usual temptation by which public men are too often led to convince the world that their pretensions to patriotism are founded merely on self-interest. He was therefore occasionally a supporter and an opposer of the measures of administration, and might be said to hold an independent character. He was, however, on the whole, to be considered as a friend to government. He married for the second time, in 1804, the widow of the celebrated Andrew Stuart, who took so memorable a part in the famous Douglas cause, in favour of the Hamilton side, and whose letters to Lord Mansfield on that subject are models of accurate investigation, as well as of acute and solid reasoning. Sir William Pulteney had a daughter by his first marriage, the Countess of Bath, who was his only issue. She married Sir James Murray, who took the name of Pulteney. Sir William's disorder was the gravel. He was so sensible of his approaching dissolution, that he predicted almost the hour of his decease. In the latter part of his life, he was remarkably abstemious, his food was composed of the most simple nourishment, principally bread and milk. In the apartment where he chiefly resided but little fire was used, because he found his health better by it. He died in London, June 5th, 1805, aged 84 years, and was interred in Westminster Abbey, where the remains of many of his ancestors are deposited. Sir William was supposed to be the richest commoner in the kingdom; it is said his funded property amounted to near two millions sterling; and he was the greatest American stockholder ever known.—*Monthly Magazine.*

MR. GEORGE BAGLEY, a man whose literary attainments, as a self-instructed scholar, have very rarely been equalled. He was the son of reputable parents, who, in the decline of life, suffered from adversity—the filial affection of their son, however, rendered the evening of their days peaceful and happy—his genius and industry supplying their various wants. Mr. Bagley was an *original*—his religious Creed was peculiarly his own—his opinion that the spirits of serpents, and all other animals of the same nature, are what are called evil spirits, was no less singular than the ability with which he could defend the notion. He also considered the final destruction of these evil spirits, and the spirits of wicked men, as a sure consequence of the just indignation of the Divine Being.

In 1804, Mr. B. published Grammars of Eleven Languages; in the year following, a Compendium of the Mathematics; in 1806 Dialogues in Six Languages; in 1808, a calculation on the nativity of Bonaparte, and a prediction on the period of his death, which he supposed would happen in 1810; but in this he was disappointed.

To show that he had some reason for believing in the truth of Judicial Astrology, Mr. B. would relate a great variety of facts, amongst which he referred to a prediction of his own, previous to his marriage with Mrs. Bagley, who still survives him. Notwithstanding the exact day of his marriage was finally fixed, and no one could foresee the possibility of disappointment, Mr. B. persisted in it, even when on the way to church, that he knew from Astrology, he could not be married on that day. The event verified the prediction—On the arrival of himself, his intended bride and their friends at the altar of Hymen, there was no priest to perform the marriage rite. Some unavoidable circumstance had occurred to prevent his attendance, and the company returned to their homes, not a little astonished as well as disappointed; the next day the happy knot was tied. This excellent man had the universal esteem of his fellow townsmen. He fell a sacrifice to his love of music and literature—intense study having laid the foundation of the disorder which terminated his existence, October 1st, 1812, in the 54th year of his age.—EDITOR.

THE REV. FRANCIS LEIGHTON, was the only son of Herbert Leighton, Esq. a captain in the army, and equerry to Frederick Prince of Wales, (eldest son of Daniel Leighton, Esq. lieutenant-colonel of the 4th regiment of Dragoons, who was the eldest son, by the second marriage, of Sir Edward Leighton, Bart. of Wattlesborough Castle and Loton, in the county of Salop;) and was born at London in the year 1747. He entered at an early period of life, into the 3rd regiment of Dragoons. But he quitted the army on his marriage, and took orders. To the manly, honourable, and generous spirit, which most loftily distinguish, where they do distinguish, ancient family, and to the frankness, valour, and loyalty, of his early profession, Mr. Leighton added the firm faith, the warm piety, the extensive benevolence, the active charity, of a Christian and a Clergyman. His talents were of the brightest lustre; his acquirements vast, diffusive, elegant, and profound. In his early youth he was prevailed upon to print a collection of poems, inscribed to his great-uncle Gen. Francis Leighton, under the title of "The Muse's Blossoms." As a scholar and linguist, the extent of his information was astonishing: and in this respect he was scarcely surpassed by any of his contemporaries, unless, perhaps, by the late estimable and lamented Sir William Jones.

While yet but a subaltern in the army, and engaged in all the gaieties of that time and mode of life, Mr. Leighton did not intermit his acquaintance with the Greek and Roman Classics. He did not commence his researches into the Welsh language, and its cognate dialects, Gælic, Irish, Manks, Breton, and Cornish, in which his knowledge exceeded that of most of the natives, till he came to settle at Shrewsbury, and conceived the plan of an "History of

Shropshire." He never willingly gave any thing to the public, except the juvenile Collection already mentioned, which, perhaps, was wrested from him by the authority of his elders. His account of the Wroxeter Baths, in the ninth volume of the Archæologia, was only a communication to Mr. Gough (with whom he occassionally corresponded, and who has acknowledged his obligations in his edition of Camden,) for the purpose of explaining the Drawings of Mr. Telford. His few communications to the gentleman's Magazine were anonymous: and the two excellent Sermons (one of them on the recovery of his Majesty, for whose character, both regal and domestic, he cherished an ethusiastic veneration,) which he committed to the press, were restricted to a private circulation. At an earlier period, he had meditated an "History of Shropshire;" but circumstances on which it would be invidious to dwell, but which we cannot cease to lament, prevented this design from being carried into effect. If it had been executed, it is probable the world would have seen a topographical work superior to any that has ever appeared in this country. His charities were extensively munificent, and judiciously discriminated; and his best eulogium will be read in the lamentations of his poorer tenants and indigent neighbours. He died November 7th, 1813, in the 66th year of his age.—*Gentleman's Magazine.*

MR. JOSEPH PARRY was born in the township of Whixall, near Wem, in the year 1736. His father was a weaver, of an unsullied character, and very much beloved in the neighbourhood of his residence. At a very early age, he was placed out to service, in the family of that excellent man, the Rev. Job Orton, of Shrewsbury, of whose principles he always spoke with the greatest veneration. Mr. Parry was afterwards apprenticed to a hatter, in Wem, where he endured many hardships; and, where as he would frequently express it, *"Nothing was left in the cupboard after meals."* Notwithstanding all his sufferings, to this situation he was perhaps indebted, in a great measure, for those industrious habits which accompanied him through life.

Mr. Parry served his complete time as an apprentice, with great patience and fortitude. He afterwards left Wem, and was employed as a journeyman by a respectable hatter in Shrewsbury; from whence he removed to the metropolis, where, under the preaching of the Rev. W. Romaine, he received those religious impressions, and was established in those principles, commonly termed Calvinistic, of which, whether orthodox or erroneous, he was a most distinguished ornament.*

Still fond of his native county, Mr. Parry returned to Shrewsbury, where he married Miss Alice Pearce, haberdasher, who being a young woman of excellent character, and of a religious turn of mind (though differing in senti-

---

* Mr. Parry was of the denomination of the Independents—a Deacon, and at the time of his death the oldest member in the congregation assembling in the Swan Hill Meeting House.—EDITOR.

ments from Mr. Parry, being a follower of the Rev. J. Wesley,) yet she was in every respect a most suitable companion. Both were liberal in their sentiments, nor ever did a difference of opinion cause a moment's dispute.—Mr. Parry's House, like his purse, was open from the period of his marriage to the day of his death, for the truly sincere of every denomination.

About the year 1783, Mr. Parry lost his excellent helpmate, and a severe shock it proved; but she died in the full assurance of everlasting happiness.

Mr. Parry is perhaps the most extraordinary instance we have on record, since the days of Mr. Thomas Firman,* of extreme liberality, supported *only* by *industry*, being accompanied with success, and crowned with considerable affluence: for notwithstanding Mr. Parry's seemingly limited business, his great benevolence, and constant losses. *for many he had*, he died in possession of £12,000, the chief part of which, dying without issue, he judiciously distributed among his relations, and the remainder to the following benevolent purposes:—

London Missionary Society	£1000
Shropshire Itinerancy	1000
For the Education of young Dissenting Ministers	400
Bible Society	100
Salop Infirmary	50

This highly respected good man lived to the venerable age of 79 years, and died April 26th, 1816.—Editor.

Rev. John Palmer, Pastor of the Baptist congregation, meeting in Dog-lane, was born at Tenbury in Worcestershire, and educated for the medical Profession, to which he served a regular apprenticeship; he afterwards became an assistant to Mr. Tudor, an eminent and highly respectable Surgeon of Shrewsbury; while in this situation he commenced his ministerial exertions, and was finally ordained Pastor of the Baptist Church. Among these people he laboured

---

* Mr: Thomas Firman, a person memorable for public benefactions and charities, was born at Ipswich in 1632. As soon as he had been made free, he began to trade for himself, with a stock not exceeding £100, which, however, he improved so far, as to marry, in 1660, a citizen's daughter with £500 to her portion. This wife did not live many years, but, after bringing him two children, died, while he was managing some affairs of trade at Cambridge; and what is very remarkable, he dreamed at the same time at Cambridge, that his wife was breathing her last. Afterwards he settled in Lombard-Street, and grew so famous for his public-spiritedness and benevolence, that he was taken notice of by all persons of note, and especially by the clergy.

In 1664, he married a second wife, who brought him several children: nevertheless, his benevolent spirit did not slacken, but he went about doing good as usual. The Plague in 1665, and the Fire in 1666, furnished him with a variety of objects. He went on with his trade in Lombard-Street, till 1676: at which time his biographer supposes him to have been worth £9000, though he had disposed of incredible sums in charities.—*Simpson's Discourse on Benevolence.*

with great diligence and success. The benefits arising from his ministry were not confined to the Town or County of Salop; Wales and various other parts of the kingdom were the scenes of his successful labours.

He was a man of no common talents, he possessed great versatility of genius. He spoke with fluency, and would versify with the utmost quickness; many of his verses which I have seen, and some I now possess, would not be discreditable to the heart or the pen of James Montgomery. Mr. Palmer's sermons were generally of a colloquial character, he would, however, sometimes attain to the sublime. His sermon on the death of the Princess Charlotte was popular at the period, and passed through two editions. He died May 15th, 1823, having just entered on his 56th year.

Mr. Palmer was not only a laborious and faithful Pastor, but he had the character of being a sincere friend. His charities were numerous considering his property, and in all his endeavours to relieve the wretched, or to assist those whom he believed had claims on his protection and care, as relatives, or otherwise, he experienced the unwearied assistance of the lady to whom in the year 1808 he had the happiness to be united.—EDITOR.

REV. THOMAS STEDMAN, M. A. was born at Bridgnorth, Shropshire, Dec. 14th, 1745, of good and respectable parents. He could number among his ancestry, with a triumph of a professional as well as a congenial kind, *one* in particular, who made a noble sacrifice to conscience and integrity, Rowland Stedman, a native of Diddlebury, in the same county; and distinguished, according to Calamy, by learning, piety, and zeal. He was ejected from his living of Oakingham, Berks. The subject of this memoir having encountered the disadvantage of removal to different schools, the last of which was that of Shrewsbury, he took rather an unusually long time to deliberate on his future profession, but, fixing on the Church, he entered at Pembroke College, Oxford; and proceeded regularly to the degrees of B. A. and M. A. On quitting the University, and entering into holy orders, he had the good fortune to become curate to Dr. Stonehouse, rector of Great and Little Cheverel, Wilts through the friendship and recommendation of that excellent man, Job Orton. Thus was formed and matured a friendship, which had the happiest effects on his future conduct as a man and a clergyman, and constituted the joy and pride of his whole life. In this retreat, so congenial to his taste, and beneficial to the studies of the raw, unfledged divine, he spent the happiest days of his life. With an orderly and docile people to instruct, his labours were blest, and and many "owned the seal." And, among what the great Lightfoot called his "russet coats," he could number "the shepherd of Salisbury Plain," whose simple annals have been recorded by Mrs. Hannah More. There he could apply the words of his divine Master, "his sheep heard his voice, and followed him." In 1775, he was unexpectedly presented to the living of Wormington, Gloucestershire, to which he was instituted by the celebrated Bishop War-

KK

burton whose great mind, then rapidly falling to decay, produced on our young clergyman an impression he never afterwards lost. In allusion to this humiliating and affecting lesson, he would often emphatically repeat those lines of the poet,

> " From Marlbro's eyes what streams of dotage flow,
> And Swift expires, a driv'ller and a show !"

In 1788, he was called to a more active sphere of duty, at Shrewsbury, the scene of his education ; having been presented to the vicarage of St. Chad. Owing this piece of preferment to the kind exertion of a valued and, through a long life, much respected friend ; he entered on his arduous duties with conscious diffidence. But though brought into contact, never into *collision*, with jarring sects and parties, more especially on one great, rather than memorable, occasion ; he had the singular felicity of being respected by all. Good sense, conciliating manners, and an invincible love of peace, enabled him to steer clear of those rocks, which sometimes prove hurtful, if not fatal, to the labours of the pastor. Respectful, but not obsequious ; humble, but not servile ; independent, but never dogmatical or dictatorial ; his conduct, public and private, was ever marked with propriety—at the same time that his integrity was so un_ questionable, that he never gave offence, save to those who mistook the purity of his motives.

In 1785, he married Catherine, niece of the Rev. Dr. Adams, his predecessor at St. Chad's and master of Pembroke College, Oxford : the learned and gentlemanly antagonist of the acute but sophistical Hume, in his justly celebrated answer to the "Essay on Miracles," of that philosopher and sceptic. By this amiable woman, and best of wives and mothers, he left five children.

But it is time to view him more particularly in his pastoral character : and herein it was apparent that *love to God and man* inspired and invigorated all his labours. His discourses were plain and simple ; exhibiting the most cheerful and encouraging views of religion, the most comprehensive and enlarged notions of the Christian covenant. He rarely discussed points of a merely doctrinal nature, or perplexed his hearers with subtleties and distinctions, in stating different modes of faith. *God is love,* was the groundwork and master-principle of his discourses, as well as his constant theme : and with this ample shield he could repel every narrow, selfish, and demoralizing doctrine and opinion so derogatory to the divine goodness, so contrary to every notion of justice, and subversive of practical holiness.*

---

* The following may possibly furnish an useful hint. In his sermon-case were deposited a few choice heads of some of his favourite divines and preachers. With these he would refresh his memory immediately before he stood up to preach. Hence, if his energies were inclined to slumber at the moment they were most wanted to give effect to his discourse ; a glance at a Hooker or a Tillotson, a Baxter or a Doddridge, seldom failed to kindle a congenial flame.

At the bed of the sick he gave full vent to his feeling. Whilst he laid the axe to the root of the tree, and impressed on the sinner the necessity of repentance, and amendment of life; he was ever forward to catch with delight the faintest spark of contrition, the slightest symptom of returning convalescence: these he was extremely cautious of quenching by too rigid and harsh treatment, especially at so critical a juncture; or of afterwards overlaying by too severe exactions.

From the laborious concerns of a large and populous parish, and incessant devotion " angulis et libellis," to his "books and his retirement;" he nevertheless found time to give to the world some highly useful publications. Besides several sermons on particular occasions, and useful and popular tracts; the "Letters to a Young Clergyman" (himself) from his inestimable friend, the Rev. Job Orton, form one of the most valuable manuals for the use and direction of the younger clergy, which have ever been published. To these he added a second volume of " Letters (to himself), from the Rev. Sir James Stonehouse, Bart.;" a name he never mentioned but with respect, and the most tender affection. In 1790, followed " Letters to and from Dr. Doddridge," published from the originals in his own possession: and subsequently, " Letters from Bishop Warburton to Dr. Doddridge."

In the summer of 1825, he made a long journey for the purpose of once more seeing his beloved children, and their respective families, in Shropshire, Middlesex, and Essex, He frequently intimated that this would be his last, though no symptoms were visible to confirm the presentiment: " his bow abode in strength;" his step was still firm, his body erect, his faculties alert; with occasional failures of memory. In November, however, it appeared, that he had not been wrong in his conjecture. A sharp fit of the gout brought on a general reduction of system, from which he had not sufficient power to rally. The wheels of nature could proceed no farther; and the machine stood still. This event took place Dec. 5th, 1825. Thus died this truly amiable and venerable man, in the 80th year of his age, and the forty-second of his ministry.—*Post funera virtus*. Death stamps the estimation of the man, and fixes his worth. As he had lived in the affections of his flock; so, at his somewhat sudden, though gentle removal, he received at their hands the most unequivocal marks of respect; shops and private dwellings stood closed on the morning of his funeral. His pall was supported by eight of the clergy of the town; upwards of fifty respectable parishioners* *voluntarily* accompanied his remains to the grave; and even

---

* Amongst these were associated professors of most, if not all the religious denominations in Shrewsbury. As he had not a particle of bigotry in his own composition, so was there not a heart in the whole town, sincerely impressed with the importance of true religion, that could for a moment indulge an intolerant feeling towards Mr. Stedman The last time the Rev. John Wesley visited Shrewsbury, Mr. Stedman was one of the Clergymen who on the occasion attended the Wesleyan Meeting House. At a subsequent period, after the interment of Mr. Jebu, Mr, Stedman attended the preaching of that gentleman's Funeral Sermon in the Methodist Chapel, Hill's Lane; after the Service was ended he inquired of the minister *what he should receive* for preaching the Sermon, when being informed it was purely gratuitous, on parting he conveyed a guinea into the hand of the preacher.—EDITOR.

KK2

the commercial pursuits of a large town seemed partially suspended in the payment of this last tribute of affectionate respect to the virtues of the deceased venerable pastor.—*Imperial Magazine*.

Rev. J. B. Blakeway, F. S. A. was born in the town of Shrewsbury, on the 24th June, 1765—and his father Mr. Joshua Blakeway, had the fortune to obtain a Prize of £20,000 in the State Lottery; a portion of this sum he expended in the erection of an elegant mansion, about 3 miles from Shrewsbury, called Lythwood Hall, now the property and residence of Thomas Parr, Esq. It appears from a brief memoir of this most estimable man in the Gentleman's Magazine for April 1826, that "the first instruction in learning he received, was in the house of the Rev. Mr. Howard, of Oldbury, near Bridgnorth, excepting what had previously been given to him by his parents. From seven to ten years of age he was a scholar of Shrewsbury School, whence he removed to Westminster; from thence he removed to Oxford, where his progress in Literature was evinced by the most rapid advances. His faculty of acquiring both ancient and modern languages was remarkable. He was at that period intended for the bar. From a change in his prospects in life his purpose was altered, and he abandoned the design; and in 1794 he was ordained by the Bishop of Lichfield and Coventry; in 1794 he was presented to the living of St. Mary, in Shrewsbury, and upon the death of his uncle, the year following, he succeeded to the Rectory at Neen Savage; in 1795 he was instituted to a third living, Felton, in the County of Somerset. In 1797 he married the daughter of Thomas Wilkinson, Esq. of Amsterdam. In 1800 he was inducted to a fourth living, that of Kinlet, in his native County, In 1816 he resigned the livings of Felton and Kinlet, in order that he might have the pleasure of residing in Shrewsbury without the fatigue of changing his residence. Mr. Blakeway was considered a very plain, but elegant and solemn preacher; with the Holy Scriptures he had a most profound acquaintance; but the study which he followed with most unwearied fondness throughout the whole of his life, was that of Antiquities. On April 30th, 1807, he was admitted a member of the Society of Antiquaries."

"He had explored," says the Author of the Memoir to which I am inindebted, "the antiquities of his native county with a perseverance, which we may confidently say was never exceeded by any other antiquary; and we cannot help deploring it as a serious loss to the country at large, that death should have snatched him away, before he had arranged the voluminous collections which he had made for a History of Shropshire. His power of giving a real interest and value to these subjects was most successfully displayed in the History of Shrewsbury, which was begun by him in the year 1822, with the assistance of Archdeacon Owen, a most intimate friend and brother antiquary: and it is remarkable, that his life was terminated, just as this valuable work had received its completion. The last number was printed, but not actually delivered to the subscribers, when that melancholy event happened, which so awfully and abruptly termimated all his labours."

"Though Mr. Blakeway wrote so much,—indeed he was always writing—and has left many compositions behind him on various subjects, which had evidently cost him considerable pains, the works which he published were not many. The greatest literary undertaking in which he was engaged was "The History of Shrewsbury," which has been alluded to above. At different times he printed three Sermons, one in 1799, entitled, "A Warning against Schism," preached before two friendly societies in St. Mary's, Shrewsbury: another in 1805, also preached at St Mary's upon the occasion of the victory at Trafalgar, and entitled, "National Benefits a Call for national repentance:" and a third in 1816, preached in the church of St. Julian, Shrewsbury, at the anniversary meeting of the Salop District Committee of the Society for promoting Christian Knowledge, entitled, "Attachment to the Church the Duty of its Members."

In the year 1813 he published a pamphlet, entitled, "An Attempt to ascertain the Author of the Letters of Junius." Mr. Blakeway wished to assign the writing of these celebrated letters to Horne Tooke. In 1815 he published a short Supplement to this "Attempt," and in 1816 he put forth a small tract upon the subject of regeneration. It may be added that he was an occasional contributor to the pages of the Gentleman's Magazine, and was the Author of the biographical sketch of the Rev. Francis Leighton."

The illness which brought him to his grave was caused by a tumour in his side, which had been forming for some years. He expired without apparent pain and in full possession of his faculties, on Friday, March 10, 1826, in the 61st year of his age."

Every lover of our "good old town" was deeply affected by the unexpected event.

Tributary lines to his memory appeared in the next Salopian Journal following his demise, by a youth nearly related to the Editor of this work, from which the following are extracted.

> "Oh, weep, Salopia! let thy manly grief
> Shine on that fittest shrine, thy History's leaf;
> One hand shall now record thy deeds no more,—
> Oh, let thy tears that deepest loss deplore!
> One spacious heart, that beat with fervour true
> For thee, Old Town! the dearest to his view,
> Cold as thy rock, shall throb no more, as erst,
> To hear thine ancient loyal pride rehearst;
> But its last throe hath broke the ties that bound
> Thee to its core. and thou hast felt the wound.
>
> Near his loved church his earthly frame will rest,
> By Learning honour'd, and by Friendship blest;
> While his freed Spirit, buoyant in its faith,
> Soars from the stormy realms of sin and death;
> And meets triumphant, with approving brow'
> The God he served and worshipp'd whilst below.

Prophetic Sage! how late thy voice foretold
The parting hour thy friends so soon behold :*
How to all hearts—to manhood, age, and youth—
It breath'd th' unutterable force of Truth:
" Soon shall these walls repeat my voice no more,
" Soon shall new footsteps tread this sacred floor ;
" New forms shall bend in prayer, new voices raise
" Through these still venerable aisles their praise :
" While we, commingled with our native earth,
" Leave but the noiseless record of our birth ;
" Then let us live,—Oh! let me, Lord, so run
" My course in peace, that, when that course is done,
" Calm as the just, Oh, may my death-bed shine !
" And like his latter end, Oh, Lord, be mine !

C. A. H.

On 13th of Nov. 1825, he preached from those impressive words, *" *Let me die the death of the righteous, and let my last end be like his :* on which occasion he made use of the affecting remarks to which the youthful author alludes.

EDITOR.

Rev. HUGH OWEN, M. A. F. S. A. Archdeacon of Salop, &c. was the only son of Dr. Owen, an eminent physician of the town of Shrewsbury. The Archdeacon's mother was Bridget, only daughter of John Whitfield, Esq. a respectable surgeon.

Of the early years of Archdeacon Owen, I have not any particular information He was a student of St. John's College, Cambridge, and in 1788 took the degree of B. A., and in 1807 that of M. A. His church preferments prove the high estimation in which he was held by the patrons of livings and prelates of his time. In 1791 he was presented to the living of St. Julian, Shrewsbury, by the late Earl of Tankerville; in 1803 to the Prebendary of Gillingham Minor, in the Cathedral of Salisbury, by Bishop Douglas. In the year 1819 he was presented to a portion of Bampton, by the Dean and Chapter of Exeter ; in 1822 he was preferred to the Prebendary of Bishopshull, in the church of Lichfield, and to the Archdeaconry of Salop, by Bishop Cornwallis. On the death of his friend, the Rev. J. B. Blakeway, he succeeded to the Royal Peculiar of St. Mary, Shrewsbury ; he also held for some years the living of Stapleton, about six miles from Shrewsbury.

On accepting the Royal Peculiar of St. Mary, the Archdeacon resigned the living of St. Julian. This circumstance was no less grievous than unexpected on the part of the congregation,† considering that for thirty-one years he had been their parish priest, their regret, however, was considerably diminished by the excellencies of his successor.

---

† I was myself many years one of his parishioners, and can speak of the universality and sincerity of attachment felt and manifested towards him. And his memory is endeared to *me and mine* from the recollection that HIS was the voice which pronounced this blessing—" The Lord mercifully with his favour look upon you, and so fill you with all spiritual benediction and grace, that ye may so live together in this life, that in the world to come ye may have life everlasting."—EDITOR.

As a Minister of the Establishment, his doctrines were truly liberal, maintaining the Arminian interpretation of the Articles of the National Church. His sermons were seldom long, but always full; nothing wanting, nothing redundant. His delivery was solemn and impressive. In his parochial duties he was indefatigable; ever attentive to the sick poor of his flock, he would enter the most humble dwelling, pray and converse in the spirit of an apostle, and with the utmost cheerfulness relieve the wants of the wretched.

As an Author, a little work, published in 1808, without his name, entitled "Some Account of the Town of Shrewsbury," would have been sufficient to have handed his learning and talents down to posterity in the annals of his native town. But this may be considered as the preface only to that work, which in conjunction with the Rev. Mr. Blakeway, was ushered into the world, as, the "History of Shrewsbury," in the year 1826. This work has immortalized its Authors, and will live as a standard History of our venerable town, long as records shall endure. It is to be lamented that they were prevented, through complaints of the expensiveness of the work, by some subscribers, from completing their invaluable labours; hence we have not in the whole work any description of the Public Buildings, or Institutions in the town excepting those of an Ecclesiastical nature. That they were so prevented, I had the declaration from the Archdeacon himself. As an antiquary his knowledge was extensive and profound. As a magistrate, while filling the office of Mayor of Shrewsbury, he was prudent and upright. As a Dignitary, or superior officer in the government of the Church of England, he diligently visited the churches within his Archdeaconry, directing every necessary repair or improvement with taste, judgment, and economy.

This excellent divine, historian, and antiquary died Dec. 23d, 1828, aged 66 years.   EDITOR.

JONATHAN SCOTT, Esq. L. L. D. This eminent oriental scholar was brother to the present Henry Scott, Esq. of Beslow Hall, in this County. He had three other brothers who entered early in the service of the Honourable the East India Company, and were distinguished by their talents and their valour. At the Free Schools of Shrewsbury this eminent Orientalist received the chief portion of his Classical Education.

So early as at twelve years of age he left his native country for India; a circumstance fortunate to himself, and no less so to the cause of Oriental Literature. While in India he had the honour of serving as Captain in the Company's service, and also received the appointment of Persian Secretary. His knowledge of the Hindostanee Language qualified him for undertaking the translation of various interesting and valuable works, particularly a Translation of the Memoir of Eradut Khan, an Hindostanee Nobleman; and also of Ferishta's History of Deccan, Bahaar Danush or Garden of Knowledge. He translated likewise Tales, Anecdotes, and Letters from the Arabic and Persic. We are indebted to Dr. Scott for what is esteemed the best Edition of the Arabian Nights Entertainment. He published also an Historical and Political View of the Deccan.

On his return to his native country he had the honour of being appointed Oriental Professor at the Royal, Military, and East India Colleges; and had the Honorary degree of L. L. D. conferred upon him by the University of Oxford in 1805. Dr Scott was a peculiarly modest man, the first to discover merit in others, and the last to acknowledge any in himself. In the circle of friends who had the advantage of his acquaintance, in the town of Shrewsbury, he was greatly esteemed. He died February 11th, 1829, at the advanced age of 75.—EDITOR, chiefly.

Having already considerably exceeded the limits assigned to this portion of our History, I can therefore only add, a brief catalogue of Authors, whose literary labours have chiefly been confined to subjects, connected with the town or vicinity :—

Mr. HENRY JONES, Author of the Shrewsbury Quarry, Earl of Essex, Kew Gardens, Isle of Wight, &c.

Mr. THOMAS MINSHULL, Author of a Guide to Shrewsbury, Poems, &c.

Mr. EVAN THOMAS, commonly called Prince Thomas the Astronomer, Author of numerous little Poems of a local nature, Prefaces to Almanacks, &c.

Mr. JAMES MASON, an elegant Scholar and Writer.

Mr. CHARLES BAGE, a man of considerable talents, Author of some excellent Electioneering Pamphlets, Addresses, &c.

Mr. THOMAS BROCAS, Author of an Electioneering Pamphlet and several publications in defence of Universal Redemption.

Mr. THOMAS HOWELL, Author and Publisher of the Stranger in Shrewsbury.

EDITOR.

CHAPTER XI.

THE ENVIRONS.

THE principal places worth notice in the vicinity of Shrewsbury are Wroxeter—the Quarry—and Kingsland.

The most noted place for antiquity is Wroxeter, about five miles from Shrewsbury, near the London road,* and generally supposed to be Uriconium,†

---

* Or Watling Street, which was one of the Prætorian or Consular highways, made by the Romans for the better marching their armies. This road was thrown up considerably above the level, and the sides kept up with large stakes drove into the ground, and lesser wood wove between them; these were called by the Saxons, Watles, from which the road had its name. Hov. p: 248. Camb. Brit. p. 343. English Atlas, p. 638.

---

† "*Wroxeter*, an ancient Town, situate upon the *Severn* near the joining of the River *Tern* with it. It is supposed by our Antiquaries to be the *Uniconium*, a *Roman* Station, as *Antoninus* calls it; but *Ptolemy* will have its name *Viroconium*; *Ninninus* calls it *Caer Uruach*; the *Saxons Wrekon- cester*; but we *Wreckceter* and *Wroxeter*. Ancient Records write it *Wroxcestry*, *Wroxcestre*, and *Wrockcestre*: N. B. We own ourselves much indebted to one *Mr. Jones* of *Shrewsbury*, for his Informations in his Letter to *Mr. Wellins*, of divers things relating to this place, *Longnor* and *Acton Burnel*. It was the Metropolis, (says *Mr. Cambden*; but *Mr. Burton** from *Ptolemy*, makes it the second of the two chief Cities) of the *Cornavii*, built probably (says *Mr. Cambden*,) by the *Romans*, when they fortified the bank of the *Severn*, which is more easily fordable here than in any other Place between it and the Mouth of it. It was very much shattered by the *Saxon* Wars, and quite destroyed in the *Danish*; and is now a very small Village, inhabited only by Country People, who frequently plough up ancient Coins that bear Witness of its Antiquity.

Mr. Cambden refers the Decay of it to the *Danish* Wars; (and indeed it was burnt without Dispute, because the Way where the Fire went is easily traced by the Blackness and Rankness of the Soil) but if we hold it to be done by the *Danes*, we shall much diminish the Antiquity of *Shrewsbury*, which rose out of the Ruins of it, as is generally believed, and can never be able to answer the Argument brought to prove it of greater Antiquity much, taken from the Coins found there, which are some of them of Gold, (but those are rare) some of Stone, red, green and blue, and others of Silver, very commonly met with, and the rest of Brass, Copper, and mixed Metals, all of them *Roman*. From whence we may very well infer, that the Destruction of this City was before the Coming of the *Saxons* into *Britain*, or at the latest, in their Wars with the *Britains*; for if it had continued to the *Danish* Times, there would certainly be some of the *Saxons* Coins mixed with them. To confirm this Opinion, the Name given it by the *Saxons*, which is *Wreken-cester*, (from which the modern Name of *Wroxeter*, is taken) may be used, because it signifieth a Castle or Town, wracked or destroyed, implying, that when they came into *Britain* they found it demolished. The Coins that are found here are called *Dinders*, and are so worn and decayed, that there is not one in ten found, which hath the Inscription perfectly legible, or the Image distinguishable.

But whenever or by whomsoever it was demolished, it hath certainly been a Place of very great Antiquity, as appears from several Remains of the *Romans* Burials, Urns and other Works. And first as to their Burials in searching into their Places of Interment, there have been taken out of the Jaw-bones of Men, Teeth near three Inches long, and three Inches about, and Thigh bones have

* Vide page 204.

one of the cities of the Cornavii, the ancient inhabitants of these parts. This city was also called Wreckencester, which is manifestly retained in the name of the adjacent hill to this day.

What manner of a town this was under the Romans is lost to us at this distance of time, and whether built by them or the Britons is uncertain, but that it was fortified by the Romans is very likely, because the river Severn has more fords hereabout than in any other place. The foundation of a bridge is sometimes discernable at low water, which was at first discovered by some workmen erecting a wear upon the river. The town is situated upon the confluence of Severn and Tern. The circumference of the walls took up about three miles, was built upon a gravel full of pebble stones; they were three yards broad, with a deep trench on the outside, which may be traced in several places to this day. The remains of the wall or old buildings are called by the present inhabitants, the old works of Wroxeter, being about twenty feet high, and an hundred feet in length, made of hewn stone, distinguished with seven rows of British bricks at equal distances, and arched within, after the manner of the Britons. Where these remains appear, it is thought the Citadel

been lately found by the Inhabitants, full a Yard long. Now their Way of burying their dead Bodies (when they did not burn them, and put the Ashes into Urns) was this, as hath been observed. First they made a deep wide Grave, at the Bottom of which they laid a Bed of very red Clay, and upon it laid the Body, and then covered it with the same Clay, over which they placed a thin Sort of Slates to fence the Clay against the Earth or Mould, which being thrown in upon it, would otherwise have been apt to break through to the dead Body. Lastly, they filled the Grave, and covered it with great Stones, sometimes five or six upon a Grave; but their Weight hath long ago sunk them into the Ground. As to the Urns, there have several of them been found whole in the Memory of Man, when they have had Occasion to dig three or four Foot deep in their sandy Land; for as the dead Corpses were buried in a red Clay, so their Urns were lodged in a red Sand. Some other *Roman* Works have been found here; for a few Years since, in a Place that was observed to be more barren than the rest, there was found in digging, a square Room, walled about with four Ranks of small Brick Pillars to support a double Floor made of Mortar, which is supposed to have been a Sudatory or sweating House for the *Roman* Soldiers.

The Manor of this Town was anciently the Estate of *John Fitz-alan*, in the Reign of King *Henry* III. and after his Death, which happened 24 *Hen.* III. *Hawise* his Wife, was by the King's Precept, sent to *John L'Estrange*, the High Sheriff, to assign her a Dower, allotted this and some other Manors in this and other Counties. He was succeeded in his Estate by his Son and Heir *John*, who 38 *Hen.* III. obtained a Charter of free Warren in all his demesne Lands in this Town, and other Places in this County. His Posterity enjoyed this Manor divers Successions; for *Thomas Fitz-allan*, Earl of *Arundel* and *Shrewsbury*, died possessed of it, 13 *Octob.* 1415, 3 *Hen.* V. and *John Fitz-allan*, 13 *Hen.* VI."—*Magna Britannia et Hibernia.*

To the valuable work from which the preceeding particulars are extracted, Mr. Phillips was no doubt very much indebted in the compilation of his History. The Village of Wroxeter is delightfully rural, and the Inhabitants sustain the character of great respectability. The Church contains sepulchral monuments of Sir Thomas Bromley, Lord chief Justice of England, one of the executors of Henry the Eighth's will, who died in 1555; Sir Richard Newport, his grandson, ancestor of the Earls of Bradford, 1570; Francis, the first Lord Bradford, 1708; Andrew, his brother, 1699; his son Thomas, Earl of Torrington, 1719, &c. A massive Fragment of a Wall defying time and destruction, still rears its venerable head in a field adjoining the road from Ironbridge to Shrewsbury. The dimensions of the remains have recently been given as 60 feet in length, and 24 in height.—EDITOR.

stood, and what favours the opinion is, the unevenness of the ground and the rubbish of walls lying thereabouts. It is conjectured by some that the blackness of the soil in some places proceeds from the fire which burnt that town, but it can hardly be supposed, that the footsteps of such a casualty should remain so long. The Roman coins found here are a proof of the antiquity of the place; the inhabitants call them Dinders, a corruption of the Roman *Denarius*, but they are so rusty and decayed that the inscription is scarcely legible of one in ten, or the image to be distinguished. None of the Saxon coins were ever found here, which is a proof the place was destroyed before the Saxons came here and settled in different places south of the Severn. The graves that have been met with here are deep and wide, the corpse inclosed in red clay, the graves faced on the sides with slates, and then covered with stones, sometimes five or six upon one grave; bones have been found that were interred after this manner which contributed to their preservation several hundred years, and teeth have been taken out of the jaw-bones of men, near three inches long, and thigh-bones near a yard in length. Several urns have been found after digging three or four feet deep in the earth, and it has been observed, that as bodies here in general are found in a red clay, so urns are found deposited in a red sand. From hence the Roman way went to the Strettons.

THE QUARRY. A large piece of land adjoining the town on the southwest side. This was formerly waste land, and probably received its name from a small quarry of red stone worked there in the Dingle. This land in several old manuscripts is called "Behind the Walls."

The Corporation, in the year 1569 leased the Quarry to three persons for ten years, at a red rose yearly, on condition that they should bring the water from Brodwell near Crow Meole, as high as it would run in the town of Shrewsbury, to be brought in leaden pipes, the first 700 yards to weigh 28lb. each and to be two inches and three quarters in bore, the next 700 yards to weigh 22lb. each, and to be two inches in bore, and the rest to weigh 16lb. each yard, and to be one inch and a half in bore. They were to have all the lead and stone then belonging to the conduit, except the cistern on Mardol Head, and that on the Wyle Cop. By this means the water was first brought into the town, the work was compleated in the year 1574, and then the conduits were first opened at the upper end of Shoe-maker's Row*—Mardol Head—the Apple Market†—the Sextry Wall ‡—and the Wyle Cop.

On this place (the Quarry) in former days the Salopians exercised themselves in the sports and diversions of the age. In the reign of Queen Elizabeth one Aston exhibited several dramatic performances here, some formed

---

* Single Butcher Row.   † Green Market.   ‡ Near the Chapel in High Street.

LL2

upon moral romance, and some on scripture history. The place of exhibition was on the top of the rope walk, a bank there cut in the form of an amphitheatre, with seats thereon are still visible.* These performances were in general acted about Whitsunday, and from thence called Whitsun Plays,‡ by some Mysteries. They were probably the first fruits of the English theatre, which, as Mr. Warton† observes, were in general confined to religious subjects.

---

* In the reign of James I. the Bailiffs and Burgesses of Salop, defendants, in answer to a bill of complaint of Roger Pope, Esq. say, that the quarry had always been used for agisting of Cattle, for musters of Soldiers, and other laudable exercises, and recreations.—7th James, 1610, Richard Higgins. of Salop, deposed in Chancery, that the Dry Quarry ever was used for bull-baitings, stage plays, &c. by consent of the bailiffs. Exch. M. S.

. † History of English Poetry, I. 237.

---

‡ Hanshall in his History of Cheshire, citing Rogers's Manuscripts, gives the following particulars relative to the " Whitsun Playes," formerly acted in the City of Chester :—

" These playes (says Rogers) were the worke of one Randall Higden, a Monke in Chester Abbeye, whoe in a good devotion translated the Bible into several partes and playes, soe as the common people might learne the same by their playinge; and also by action in their sighte, and the first time they were acted, or played, was in the time of Sir John Arnewaye, about the first year of his Maioralty, about A. D. 1328 ; we must judge this Monke had no evil intention, but secret devotion therein. soe alsoe the citizens, that did acte and practise the same, to their great coste. Here I must showe the manner of the performinge of these anchent playes, (which was) all those companies and occupations, which were joyned together to acte, or performe their several partes, had pagents, which was a building of a great height, with a lower and higher rowme, beinge all open, and set upon fower wheels, and drawne from place to place. where they played. The first place where they begane, was at the Abbeye Gates, where the Monks and Churche might have the first sighte ; and then it was drawne to the high crosse before the Mayor and Aldermen, and soe from streete to streete, and when one pagent was ended another came in the place thereof till all that were appoynted for the daye were ended ; thus of the manner of the playes, all beinge at the Citizen's charge, yet profitable for them ; for all, both far and near, came to see them."

" Now follow what occupations bring forth at their charges the playes of Chester, and on what dayes they are played yearly. These playes were sett forth, when they were played upon Mondaye, Tuesdaye, and Wednesdaye in the Whitsun weke."

" 1. The Barkers and Tanners bringe forth The falling of Lucifer.—2. Drapers and Hosiers, The Creation of the World.—3. Drawers of Dee, and Water-leaders—Noe and his Shippe.—4. Barbers, Wax-chandlers, and Leeches —Abraham and Isacke.—5. Cappers, Wire-drawers, and Pinners—King Balak, and Balam, with Moses.—6. Wrights, Slaters, Tylers, Daubers, and Thatchers—The Nativity of our Lord.—7· Paynters, Brotherers, and Glaziers—The Sheppard's Offering—8. Vintners and Merchants—King Herod and the Mounte Victorial.—9. Mercers and Spisers—The three Kings of Coline. These nine Pagents above written, be played on the firste daye."

" 1. Gouldsmiths and Masons—The slayinge of the Children by Herod.—2.Smithes, Forbers, and Pewterers—Purification of our Ladye.—3. Bouchers.—The Pinackle with the Woman of Canaan. 4. Glovers, and Parchment-makers—The arisinge of Lazarus from Death to Life.—5. Corvesers and Shoemakers—The coming of Christe to Jerusalem.—6. Bakers and Millners—Christe's Maundye, with his Disciples.—7. Boyers, Fletchers, Stringers, Cowpers, and Torners—The Scourginge of Christe.—8. Ironmongers and Ropers—The Crucifieinge of Christe.—9. Cookes, Tapsters, Hosiers, and Innkeepers—The Harrowinge of Hell. These nine Pagents above written, be played upon the Seconde Daye, being Tuesdaye in Whitson Weke."

" 1. Skynners, Cardmakers, Hatters, Poynters, and Girdlers—The Resurection.—2. Sadlers and Fusters—The Castell of Emmaus, and the Apostles.—3. The Taylors—Ascension of Christe.—4. Fish-

In 1565 Julian the Apostate and another performance of Mr. Aston's, the name of which is not mentioned, were performed on the above-mentioned spot before a large audience, when, (notwithstanding much of the gross and ridiculous appeared) the Salopian audience (not so refined and gay as their descendants) listened with admiration and devotion. The Queen (Elizabeth) came so far as to Coventry, on a journey to Shrewsbury, intending to see one of these performances, in the year 1565, but her Majesty not having proper information

---

mongers—Whitsunday—the making of the Crede.— 5. Shermen—Profetts afore the Day of Dome. 6. Hewsters, and Bell-founders—Antechriste—7. Weavers and Walkers—Domesday. These seven Pagents above-written, were played upon the Thirde Daye, beinge Wensedaye in Whitson Weke."

"These Whitsun playes were played in A. D. 1574· Sir John Savage, Knight, beinge Mayor of Chester, which was the laste time they were played,"

At this period it was the general fashion to Dramatize Scripture History and Scripture Facts. From the earliest ages of the Christian Church, indeed, this abuse of the Holy Book had in a greater or lesser degree prevailed.

Appollinarius, who lived in the time of the emperor Julian, wrote religious odes, and turned particular histories, and portions of the Old and New Testaments into comedies and tragedies, after the manner of Menander, Euripides, and Pindar. These were called Mysteries, and were the first dramatic performances. The first dramatic representation in Italy, was a spiritual comedy, performed at Padua, in 1243; and there was a company instituted at Rome, in 1264, whose chief employment was to represent the sufferings of Christ in Passion Week. The Rev. Mr. Croft, and the Hon. Topham Beauclerc, collected a great number of these Italian Plays or Mysteries; and at the sale of their libraries, Dr. Burney purchased many of the most ancient, which he speaks of as being evidently much earlier than the discovery of Printing, from the gross manner in which the subjects are treated, the coarseness of the dialogue and the ridiculous situation into which most sacred persons and things are thrown.

1313, Philip the Fair, gave the most sumptuous entertainment, at Paris, ever remembered in that city. Edward II. and his queen Isabella, crossed over from England with a large retinue of nobility, and partook of the magnificent festivities. The pomp and profusion of the banquetings, the variety of the amusements, and the splendour of the costume were unsurpassed. On the occasion Religious Plays were represented, of the Glory of the Blessed, and at other times with the torments of the Damned, and various other Spectacles. The Religious Guild, or fraternity of Corpus Christi at York, was obliged annually to perform a Corpus Christi play. But the more eminent performers, of mysteries were the Society of Parish Clerks of London. On 18th, 19th, and 20th of July, 1390, they played Interludes at the Skinner's Well, as the usual place of their performance, before king Richard II. his queen, and their court; and at the same place, in 1490, they played the Creation of the World. The first trace of theatrical performance, however, in this country, is recorded by Matthew Paris, who wrote about 1240, and relates, that Geoffrey, a learned Norman, master of the school of the abbey of Dunstable, composed the play of St. Catherine, which was acted by his scholars. Geoffrey's performance took place in the year 1110, and he borrowed copes from the sacrists of St. Albans, to dress his characters.

In the reign of Henry VII. 1487, that king, in his castle at Winchester, was entertained on a Sunday, while at dinner, with the peformance of Christ's Descent into Hell; and, on the Feast of St. Margaret, in 1511, the miracle play of the Holy Martyr St. George, was acted, on a stage, in an open field at Bassingborne, in Cambridgeshire, at which were a minstrel and three waits, hired from Cambridge, with a property-man and a painter.

In the church-warden's book of accounts for Tewkesbury, A. D. 1578, is this entry,—" Pay'd " for the player's geers, six sheepskins for Christ's Garment's." And in an inventory recorded in the same book. 1585, are these words, " And order eight heads of hair for the apostles, and ten beards " and a face or vizer for the devil."—This shews that mysteries, as plays were then called, were probably acted in the churches.

EDITOR.

mistook the time, and when she came to Coventry, hearing it was over, returned to London. Two years after, *viz.* in 1567, the theatrical representation of the Passion of Christ was exhibited in the same place, by the aforesaid performer.

This large and extensive piece of ground, is pleasantly situated by the side of the River Severn, the pasture is yearly let to the inhabitants, and the profits arising thence, distributed among the Burgesses. The lower walk along by the River Side, is 540 yards in length, well shaded with lime trees, planted here by Henry Jenks, Esq.* in the year of his Mayoralty, 1719, and is extremely pleasant. In the middle of this walk is a double alcove, or summer-house, with seats fronting both the River and the Town, built in the year 1734.† Three walks lead from the town down to the lower walk, and two others cross the tops of them, one from St. John's Hill to the tower, made by direction and in the Mayoralty of Mr. John Cotton, Anno 1775; the other from the Reservoir to the top of the hill near the Dry Dingle, Anno 1759, in the Mayoralty of Mr. John Bennett.

> " The waving Walks, the woody Hills appear,
> " In all the Liveries of the lavish Year,
> " Complete in every part, complete the whole,
> " Whilst Severn gives the finished Scene, a Soul.
> JONES'S QUARRY, p. 6.

KINGSLAND, is an extensive piece of ground on the opposite side of Severn from the Quarry. It belongs to the Corporation, and is in the parish of Meole Brace. Upon what account it received the present name, it is not easy to say; probably it was waste land belonging to the Crown, and granted to the Corporation, as it is in some old writings mentioned as uninclosed. The first accounts I have been able to get relative to this piece of ground are, that in the year 1529, at a Common Hall, the Common Pasture of Kingland was set for three years at £3 per year,‡ and in 1586, ordered to be inclosed.

The Annual Horse Races were formerly on this spot, it was then considerably larger, many enclosures having of late years been made on the out parts. In 1724, the whole of this land was let to Mr. Richard Morgan, of Shrewsbury, who sowed it with corn. At the Annual Meeting of the several

‡ Excheq, M. S. Lib. I.

---

* 1720, agreed that Henry Jenks have a Lease of the Tower in the Quarry for three lives, and for 21 years after the three lives expire.—*Corporation Books, as cited in Llewellyn's Manuscript.*

† Now destroyed.

Companies, (the Show†) the tradesmen threatened to throw the corn down to get to their Arbours, but were prevented by a promise that they should never be hindered again ; notwithstanding which, the next year, some part of it was again sowed, and at the Show the Clothiers Company obliged Mr. Morgan to cut down so much, as would give a free passage to their Arbour.

---

† In the Shrewsbury Chronicle of June 6th, 1825, appeared the following humourous description of this exhibition :—

"SHREWSBURY SHOW was exhibited on Monday in rather better style than of late years. The weather was favourable; the tradesmen were in a great measure unanimous ; the country-folks attended in multitudes, decked out in all the gaiety and variety of summer. About half-past one the "trades" had mustered in Raven-street, and shortly after they proceeded to Kingsland in the following order :

AT THE HEAD OF THE PROCESSION CAME THE

Shoemakers—Preceded by Crispianus dressed in the uniform of an officer "sixty years since," with sword and gorget ; his cocked hat ornamented with a bouquet of blue and white ribbons ; by his side Crispin in a leather surtout, with his mace surmounted by the boot, their horses led by their 'squires, and preceded by a halberdier.—Next came the

Tailors—Preceded by three Antiques, bearing two bodkins, each half-a-yard in length, with shields ; the third carrying a battle-axe.

Butchers—The Masters' procession was headed by two men with swords and shields ; the Apprentices by the king, with a lofty cap of every-coloured feathers. his chaplet enriched with thousands of trinkets ; a cleaver in his hand surmounted by a griffin ; his horse covered with net-work and led by a squire ; the boys dressed in white frocks.

Bricklayers—His Majesty, "Henry the Eighth," preceded this Company, his face covered with a pot-full of red raddle, and a pair of monstrous black-lead mustachoes ; dressed in a gorgeous blue puffed robe, with scarlet mantle, his rotundity kept from bursting by a richly embroidered waistcoat, his hat bordered with ermine, and a plume of white feathers ; a sceptre in his hand, his horse led ; the Apprentices were preceded by a King dressed in white, a profusion of sashes and belts, with "God save the King" inscribed on a sash over his shoulder, his cap ornamented with blue, white, and green feathers, his horse caparisoned and led.

Apprentice Smiths, &c.—The King, with a beautiful crown bordered with ermine, a noble plume of feathers ; the robes white, with red and black sashes. Before him came the Chancellor, carrying the crown, attended by two beef-eaters, with swords and shields ; and a Vulcan, smoking hot from the forge, armed with a blunderbuss, which he fired off at intervals, to the great terror of all the old women.

Hairdressers—The Queen, seated on her grey horse, and led by a groom. Her long flowing robe of white, ornamented with blue drapery, and bordered with knots of crimson and green ; her gown of white silk gauze, ornamented with sixteen rows of pink, and a plume of crimson and white feathers.

Painters, Sadlers, Booksellers, &c.—The Apprentices preceded by "Cupid" on horseback ; his plume of white feathers, his dress white, with blue sash ; in his hand the pallet and brushes ; his horse led by two pages. The Masters, (a numerous company of whom were present) preceded as usual with the horse gaily caparisoned, with blue tapestry saddle cloth, and led by a groom.

In this order (each trade having its music, and its banners) the procession marched through the Town. The Hon. and Rev. Richard Hill, the Mayor, attended by a respectable party of the Corporation and Gentlemen of the Town and Neighbourhood, set out from the Town-Hall about 2 o'clock, and were greeted with great applause on their arrival at Kingsland."

The crowd on Kingsland throughout the whole of the day, was great ; and various were the means provided for their entertainment. "Ups-and-Downs,"—"Jerry go-rounds,"—"Rowley Powleys,"&c.

The several Companies in Shrewsbury who were incorporated, had formerly Arbours on this ground, to which they resorted on the Show Day, some of them have been taken down, but there are ten or twelve remaining, to which the Companies go on the Show Day, which is the Monday Fortnight after Whitsunday, where the Mayor and his Attendants are entertained by them, and then return into town, in the same order of procession as they went out. It may be expected, an account should be here given of the Origin of the Show ; that it is the remain of an ancient Religious Procession, will appear from the following account.—Among the numerous Feasts observed by the Romish Church, that of *Corpus Christi, viz.* The Feast of the Holy Sacrament or Body of Christ, is distinguished by particular marks of respect, insomuch, that on that day, the richest church treasures are brought out to grace the procession and honour the presence.

On the Thursday following the Week of Whitsunday, it was the custom of this town, as appears by the Preambles to several of the Companies Charters, for the respective incorporated Companies, preceded by the Masters and Wardens, to attend the Bailiffs, Aldermen, and Commonalty, to St. Chad's Church, with the colours and devices belonging, and suited to each company or craft.

In this Procession the Holy Sacrament was borne under a rich canopy, supported by Priests, and after hearing Mass, the whole of the company returned from church, keeping the respective places assigned them ; the parties being subject to a fine for non-attendance, or non-observance of order.

Upon several incorporated Companies, it was obligatory to provide certain necessaries for the Procession, such as wax-candles, &c. which were carried before the Host, and afterwards placed before the Holy Altar of St. Michael the Archangel, in St. Chad's Church.

This Procession was on the Thursday before that Monday, on which the Show or Procession is now held ; and the Days of Entertainment, or as they are called in the Charters, the Days of Disport and Recreation for the several Companies, were at some other time, fixed by the Masters or Wardens.

It seems probable that this procession was continued in the manner above related, until the time of the Reformation from Popery, when the Salopians, though prohibited from attending Mass, yet were determined to retain as much of the ceremony as they could, and accordingly fixed upon the Monday following *Corpus Christi,* for their Procession, and chose an entertainment at Kingsland for their bodies, in lieu of assembling before the Altar of St. Michael the Archangel, to pray for their souls.

The most probable reasons why the Day was changed from Thursday to the Monday following, seem to be these ; though prohibited going to church on that day to hear Mass, they might think it improper to observe it as a day of recreation ; and also Coventry Show and Fair, falling always on the following day, (Friday) many of the inhabitants attended there, and many in the country round about were prevented coming here.

Just below the Shoemakers' Arbour, on this ground, Mr. Thomas Anderson was shot* on the 11th of December 1752, for deserting from Sir John Ligonier's regiment of Dragoons. His trial began at Worcester, November 16th, and lasted three days; from thence he was removed to Shrewsbury, where

---

* " Thomas Anderson was a Roman Catholic, a native of Yorkshire, the descendant of a Gentleman; he had a very liberal education, was well versed in the modern languages, and travelled into most parts of Europe. He occasionally went by the several names of Milbank, Sympson, and Douglas; by the first of these he passed, when he inlisted himself into Sir John Ligonier's Regiment of Dragoons, in the year 1746; but it was soon discovered that his real name was Anderson. The Regiment being quartered in the city of Worcester, about three years ago, he obtained a furlough for a few days, but instead of returning, he went abroad, and it is said, was at Prague, Hanover, and other places in Germany; after which, coming to Perth, in Scotland, he passed by the name of Charles Douglas; where being suspected of treasonable practices, himself, and his servant (Thomas Jones), were taken up, and after some examination sent prisoners to Edinburgh, where he was confined in the Castle, and though he was several times examined before the Lord Provost, &c. yet nothing could then be proved upon him, and therefore he was to be set at liberty in a few days; but in the mean time, a letter being intercepted, it was discovered that his name was Thomas Anderson, and that he belonged to Sir John Ligonier's Regiment. Soon after this he was sent from Edinburgh, under a strong guard, who were met at Lichfield by an Officer's guard from Worcester, consisting of a Cornet and 25 privates, who conveyed him to Worcester, to take his trial for desertion. On Thursday November the 16th last, between nine and ten o'clock, he was brought under a strong guard from the County Goal in Worcester, to a General Court Martial, and put upon his trial, which did not end till Saturday about noon. Each day there was an incredible number of persons present, who not only observed, with much satisfaction, the great candour and impartiality of the Court in their proceedings, but likewise the suitable deportment, becoming fortitude, and genteel address of the prisoner, and it is thought there never was before known so long and remarkable a trial of a person for desertion only. The proceedings of the Court, with their opinion, were sent to London that evening, to be laid before his Majesty.

" On the Tuesday following he was brought out of the Castle, and handcuffed, and put on horseback; in which manner (one of the dragoons who rode next him holding the bridle,) he proceeded through the city, under guard of the troops, marching for Shrewsbury. The first day's march was to Kidderminster, where Mr. Anderson was lodged at the Talbot Inn, under a very strong guard.

On Thursday they arrived in Shrewsbury, where Mr. Anderson was immediately committed to the County Goal. During his confinement there, two centinels, with their muskets charged and bayonets fixed, were placed in the room with him night and day; and no persons admitted to see him, or any letter to pass to or from him, without proper inspection.

On the Monday following a letter came from London to the Commanding Officer there, with orders for his execution, which was fixed for Monday the 11th of December. In the mean time there were several petitions sent to London in his behalf, viz. one from Lancashire, another from Yorkshire, one from Worcester, and another from Shrewsbury; but all in vain; for on Thursday the 7th instant several letters came to Shrewsbury, confirming his former sentence. And accordingly, on Monday the 11th of December, about ten o'clock in the morning, he was conducted from the County Goal by the troops quartered there, with their Officers, together with the Mayor of Shrewsbury, and proper attendants, to Kingsland, which was the place of execution, dressed in a handsome suit of black velvet. When he came there, he addressed the Mayor and Officers in a very handsome speech, thanking them for all their favours, and acknowledged that he was a deserter, and the justice of his sentence. He then addressed himself to his brother soldiers very affectionately; begged of them to take warning by his unhappy conduct, and desired them to stand fast to their colours; he particularly spoke to the persons who were to shoot him, assuring them he freely forgave them, and hoped they would pray for him. He then kneeled down on a white cloth spread for the purpose, and prayed a considerable time: after which he again spoke to the Major, desiring him to take care to distribute a small favour he would leave to the persons who were to take away his life, and took a purse of gold out of his pocket and laid it on his coffin, which he desired them to accept, as a token of his respect and forgiveness; he

MM

orders were received for his execution.—In the mean time, several petitions were sent to London on his behalf, viz. one from Yorkshire, the place of his birth ; one from Lancaster ; one from Worcester, and another from Shrewsbury ; but all to no purpose; for on Monday, December 11th, about ten o'clock in the morning, he was conducted from the Goal to Kingsland, under a guard, attended by the regiment, with the Mayor of Shrewsbury and his attendants ; he was dressed in a suit of black velvet, and appeared with great composure.—Five soldiers were appointed to shoot him, but only three fired. The balls from the two first entered, one into each breast, and the third shot him through the head. He was buried in St. Mary's Church-yard the same day, and agreeable to his own desire the following inscription was placed upon his tomb-stone, viz.

"THOMAS ANDERSON,
Youngest Son of George Anderson, Esq.
Was born January 13, 1720, at Gales, near Richmond, Yorkshire.
Departed this life, Dec. 11, 1752. Aged 31.

STOP TRAVELLER !
I've pass'd, repass'd, the Seas and distant Lands ;
Can find no Rest, but in my Saviours's Hands.

---

then went to prayer for about ten minutes ; after which he took off his hat and wig, and laid them on his coffin, and put on a white cap, tied with a black ribband, which he soon drew over his face. He then took a handkerchief, one end of which he held in his mouth ; he prayed privately about five minutes, and then dropped the handkerchief out of his mouth, which was the signal for the soldiers to fire, which they immediately did by command of the officer; six men were appointed for this purpose, three only of which fired upon him, the rest being reserved in case he should not be quite dead ; but he was dispatched immediately, for one bullet went through his right breast, another through his left, and a third through his heart. However, for fear any symptoms of life should appear, another of the soldiers shot him through the head. A Corporal was then ordered to search his pockets, out of which he took a few papers, but of no importance.

The soldiers then marched round him, one by one ; after which the Undertaker delivered six pair of mourning gloves to the Major, which Mr. Anderson desired might be given to the soldiers he directed them for.

"He was carried in a hearse from Kingsland, and handsomely interred in St. Mary's Church-yard, Shrewsbury.—His behaviour during his confinement, and at the place of execution, was very becoming."

The above is a copy of a paper sold about the Streets after Mr. Anderson's execution, and was printed by a grandfather of Major Lathrop Murray, who was transported for bigamy. For this information, originally published in the Salopian Magazine, I am indebted to Mr. Tarbuck, a venerable and intelligent Inhabitant of Shrewsbury, and also for the following particulars :

"The execution of Anderson took place on Kingsland, about four yards from the door of the Butcher's Arbour. After he was shot the body was stripped, when the colours of the Chevalier Stuart were found next his skin, in a sash given him by the Chevalier when in Scotland, as a mark of his esteem for Anderson's activity in the rebellion of 1745, from which the kingdom was just emerging.

The axe and the gibbet having been glutted with victims, the Bullet was deemed the most Summary way of dispatching the unfortunate Anderson, and the reason for shooting him at Shrewsbury was—EXAMPLE ; for there had been a sanguinary contest between the soldiers and town's-people, on the 10th of June preceding, and much blood had been shed : it was the pretender's birth-day, and Mr. John Richards, a master builder, had been paying his men at the Crown, near the Butter Cross : these men wore white roses (which in those days were esteemed symbols of sedition,) and were overheard singing " Charley over the Water," and other popular airs in vogue during the Rebellion. the patrole resented this, and both sides fought with great violence, as wherever thrones and kingdoms are disputed, the passions, prejudices, and interests of mankind are always opposed."—EDITOR.

CHAPTER XII.

A CHRONOLOGICAL ACCOUNT OF REMARKABLE OCCURRENCES, NOT
REDUCIBLE TO, OR OMITTED UNDER THE FORMER HEADS.

ANNO 961, Land about Shrewsbury sold for one Shilling an acre. The
price of an ox was 2s. 6d. a cow, 2s. a sheep, 1s. a swine, 8d.

1010. A great earthquake felt here.

1110. A great earthquake, and a severe winter, with great mortality of
men and cattle.

1225, Weights and measures were regulated. Three gallons of ale sold
for one penny in the town, and four out of the town.

1296, It appears by an agreement then made, between the Abbot and the
town, that there were four islands in the River Severn, between the Stone Bridge
and St. Mary's Water-Lane, three of which were, one with another, 200 feet
in length, and one of them 64 feet in breadth. The three last mentioned were
near the Bridge, and the other at the Monks Garden, near Merrivale.

1315, The price of provisions settled by order of the Bailiffs, *viz.* A corn-
fed ox, 24s. A grass fed ditto, 16s. A cow, 12s. A fat mutton, 20d. A mutton shorn, 14d. A fat hog of two-years old, 3s. 4d. A fat goose, 2d. A hen,
1d. A capon, 2d. Two chickens, 1d. Four pigeons, 1d. Twenty-four
eggs, 1d.

1326, Hay at 5s. per load.

1347, Price of provisions, *viz.* A fine horse 6s. 8d. The best fed ox, 4s.
A cow, 1s. A steer or heifer, 6d. A weather, 4d. An ewe, 3d. A lamb, 2d.
An hog, 5d.

1400, Sir Thomas Pierce, beheaded at Shrewsbury.

1421, Rees ap Doe, a Welsh Esquire, was hanged and quartered here, for
treason.

1427, A bye-law was made against swine wandering about the town, under
pain of cutting off an ear for each of the two first offences, and forfeiture for
the third.

1433. A new composition was granted by the Bailiffs, to the company of
fishmongers.

1454, Corn was so plenty, that a quarter (8 strikes) of Wheat, was commonly sold for 12d. or 14d. Rye, for 10d. Malt for 16d. or 17d.

MM2

1478, John, Bishop of Worcester, President of the Prince's Council, and Anthony, Earl Rivers, Uncle and Governour to the said Prince, and others of his honourable Council, being in the Town-Hall in Shrewsbury, by the assent of the officers, ministers, and inhabitants, made certain ordinances for the good rule and tranquility of the town.*

1490, Wheat sold for 20d. per bushel.

1492, Wheat sold for 6d. per bushel.

1493, Wheat sold for 4s. per bushel.

1498, Wine sold for 40s. per tun, Wheat for 6d. per bushel.

1499, Register books ordered in every church.

1509, Provision was made by an Act of Parliament, for the repairing decayed houses, and building upon waste ground, in Shrewsbury. Anno I Hen. VIII.

1519, A general Chapter of the Grey Friars held here.—See Chap. VI. p. 104.

1520, Griffith Wickham, drawn through the town, and afterwards hanged.

1523, Shrewsbury made the See of a Suffragan Bishop,† stiled Suffragan of the Realm of England.—Twenty-five other towns, had a like appointment at the same time.

1524, Wheat sold for 6d. per bushel, Rye, for 4d.

* Charter of the Weaver's Company.

---

† Suffragans, so called, quia *suffragantur*, because they are *assistant*, to the bishops of the dioceses, were very ancient in the primitive church, under the name of chorepiscopi, or *rural* bishops. When they obtained a footing in England does not appear : but on the episcopal registers of Lichfield is the " commission of a suffragan," of the date of 1398. These assistant bishops had hitherto derived their titles from towns or villages in Ireland or in Italy, or in partibus infidelium (those parts of Greece or Asia Minor, which having once been Christian, were now within the Turkish dominions,) as the vicar of Baschurch, whose commission is abstracted above, was bishop, perhaps, of Tibur or Tivoli. But this was no longer to be the case ; Henry the VIII. did not choose that any prelates with foreign titles should exercise authority within his realm : and therefore the act before us names twenty-six borough towns dispersed over the kingdom, which should hereafter " be taken and accepted for sees of bishops suffragans," and every archbishop or bishop who should be disposed to have a suffragan shall choose two honest and discreet spiritual persons being learned and of good conversation, one of whom, after allowance by the king, shall be consecrated by the archbishop of the province within which the town from which he derives his title is situate. One of these towns thus selected is Shrewsbury. The choice was judicious, on account of the great extent of the county, and its distance from the cathedral cities between which its spiritual jurisdiction is divided : and it is impossible not greatly to regret that the statute was so seldom enforced even at the period of its enactment, and, though still existing as a law capable of being put in action at the will of any bishop who may desire it, has long since ceased to be in use. One only BISHOP OF SHREWSBURY has occured to our enquiries : Lewis Thomas, late abbot of Kynmer, (i. e. Cwmhir) who was consecrated suffragan bishop of the see of Salop by archbishop Cranmer, June 24, 1537 : he was also instituted to the rectory of Llantwroc in Wales, and died in 1560 or 61.
Owen and Blakeway's History of Shrewsbury.

1531, Lord Rees ap Thomas, beheaded here.

1532, John Goldsmith, drawn through the town, and afterwards hanged, for coining money.

1539, One Richard Brewer, the son of John Brewer, passing through the gate on the Wesh Bridge, a sudden gust of wind blew the gate to, which caught his head between that and the post, and squeezed his brains out.

1541, This year, Thomas Davies, Serjeant to Mr. Nicholas Purcell, one of the Bailiffs, murdered one Carr, a journeyman shoemaker as he was passing over the Welsh Bridge; he fled to Calais, but was afterwards pardoned.

1542, Rowland Lee, Bishop of Litchfield and Coventry, the first Lord President of the Marches, was buried on the 30th of January, before the High Altar in St. Chad's Church, under a tomb of black marble.

1547, This year, Adam Mytton, and Roger Pope, the Bailiffs, ordered the picture of Our Lady to be taken out of St. Mary's Church, the picture of Mary Magdalen, and the picture of St. Chad, out of St. Chad's Church, and burned in the Corn-Market, Anno I Edward VI.

1552, The Magistrates of this town were restrained by Act of Parliament 5th Edward VI. from licensing any more than three persons to sell wines within the town. By the same Act, a certain number only, were allowed in the following towns, viz.

London,	40	Exeter,	4	Southampton,	3
York,	8	Salisbury,	3	Canterbury,	4
Westminster.	3	Glocester,	4	Winchester,	3
Bristol,	6	Chester,	4	Oxford,	3
Lincoln,	3	Hereford,	3	Cambridge,	4
Hull,	4	Worcester,	3	Colchester,	3

1554, Lord Chief Justice Bromley, Alderman of Shrewsbury, and free of the Drapers Company, died at Eyton, and was buried at Wroxeter.

1563, An order was published by the Bailiffs, that no foreigner should be free of this town, without paying £10, and all the ordinary fees.

1565, This year the persons who were met together to chuse Bailiffs for the ensuing year, on the Friday after Michaelmas, not agreeing in their choice, they were obliged to stay in the Hall twenty-five hours without meat or drink, till they were agreed.

1570, Two men were killed by the falling of the clapper out of the third bell, while they were ringing the great bell, commonly called St. Wenefride's Bell, at the Abbey Church.

1571, Mr. Humphrey Onslow, one of the Bailiffs, built the Chapel of our Lady in St. Chad's Church, repaired the pavement in Frankwell, and paved all the great causeway, from the Lord's Place (the Council House) to the Cross, at his own cost.

1576, On the 20th day of December, a luminous appearance in form of a cross was seen in the air, over the town, which continued half an hour.

1577, Edward Clarke, a butcher, was deprived of his Burgesship and imprisoned, for abusing, and striking Mr. Dawes, one of the Bailiffs.

1579, The 10th day of August the assizes were held here, a great deal of business was done, one of the Judges sat under the new building at the Market House upon a scaffold.

1580, A general muster of all the inhabitants of Shrewsbury, in the Quarry, before the Bailiffs, by the Queen's order.

1581, March 24th, One John Capper, Clerk of the Abbey Church, was drawn through Shrewsbury and afterwards hanged at Kingsland, for treason.

1582. February 4th, One John Prestige, alias Hill. (so called because he lived with a Priest whose name was Hill,) was hanged upon a gibbet erected on the green, by the water side, near the Abbey Mill, and opposite his own house, for the murder of his wife, by throwing her over the Stone Bridge into Severn. He hung there three days.

Mr. Prince's house, (late Sir John Astley's, now Mr. Wingfield's) in the Abbey Foregate, was begun this year, and was four years in building.

1583. The assizes begun the 22nd July, and continued two days and a half, the Judges lay at Mr. Onslow's house, and the Sheriff at Mr. Purcell's. The Sheriff came in with the Judges, attended by forty-two horsemen, being all his own men, and all in the same livery. He kept open house all the time of the assize.

This year, on the 3rd of October at night, the stone cross in St Julian's Church-yard was pulled down.

Also, Friday, October 4th, being the day before the election of Bailiffs, the then present Bailiffs made proclamation through the town, that no scholars, boys, or apprentices, should that night go abroad to disturb the town with unseasonable noises, fightings, and discord, which was usually the case on that night. Also, that householders should not suffer their servants or others to go out of their houses after night, upon pain of £10. This order was observed, and all quiet.

In December this year a servant of one Richard Gardner of this town, fell into a furnace of boiling water, and was scalded to death.

1584. Robert Lord Dudley, the Earl of Essex, and Lord North, came to Shrewsbury, before whom several orations were made by the Free-School scholars.

On the 17th of July this year, a stage-play was acted in the High Street, near the Apple-Market, by the Earl of Essex's men.

1585. On the 15th day of May, Lord Robert Devereux, Earl of Essex, came through the town, before whom the Free-School scholars made several orations, as he passed through the Castle Gates ; they standing there in battle array, with bows and arrows.

This year, in December, while some men were digging a saw-pit, in the Horse-Fair, in Frankwell, they found the head and bones of a man, which had lain there a long time ; on examining the head, a round hole appeared, as though made with a pole-axe or bill ; it is probable, being privately murdered, he was buried there ; but nothing further was ever known relative to it.

1588.   One Richard Reynolds, of Bagley, near Cockshutt, in this county, was on the 19th day of July, being the second day of the assize, put into the Pillory, in Shrewsbury, by order of the Privy Council, and had both his ears cut off, by Richard Stubbs, then appointed by the Bailiffs to be executioner. His crime was setting fire to a sheep-cote of one Gammer, his brother-in-law, wherein was a great number of sheep, and all burned.

This year, on the 22nd day of January in the night, the prisoners confined in the Goal in the Castle, found means to unfasten their bolts and links, and so far got themselves at liberty in the Prison ; they pulled down several stones out of the wall, on that side towards the Free-Schools, designing to get out there, but the earth on the outside being above the breach they had made, they were prevented ; at length with their noise, some of the goaler's men were awakened, who called him up, but in attempting to put bolts on their hands, they opposed, and raised a mutiny, but assistance being called in, they were properly secured.

In May this year, great disturbances were in the town, occasioned by the setting up May-poles, and making bonfires, before the Shearmens-Hall, and in other places.   Mr. Tomkies, Minister of St. Mary's, and public Preacher, appeared among the people, and endeavoured to dissuade them against such proceedings ; but he was ill-used by the populace, and the disturbances increased, until the Bailiffs interfered and put a stop to them.

1590.   July 24th, a scaffold was set up in the Corn-Market, on which an Hungarian, and others of the Queen's players, performed several extraordinary feats of tumbling, rope-dancing, &c. such as had never before been seen in Shrewsbury.

The clock put up in the Guild-Hall this year.

1591.   On the 16th, 17th, and 18th days of September, was a large assize here, when above sixty prisoners were tried, of which number twenty were condemned, ten of them were reprieved, and one (a woman) begged off by the ladies in the town, eight were hanged at the Old-Heath, and one, whose name was Edward Ixson, who had murdered a young man, apprentice to Matthew Stinton, of Wellington, was hung in chains there.

1592.   Tuesday, 13th day of June, being the Town Court Day, according to the new Composition, one of the Bailiffs, Mr. Ireland, being out of town, the other, Mr. Powell, being sick, was carried in a chair down to the

Booth-Hall, where the Court was called, and then he was in the same manner carried back again to his own house.

"On the 24th day of August this Yeare beinge Thursdaye, the Bayliffes "of Salop made a feaste to the Aldermene, common Counsell, and to a num-"ber of the commons of the sayd towne, in the guylde hall in Shrewsburie, "beinge at 4 tables, above a hundred persons, where they hadd plentie of "venyson, wyne, and other good cheere, the which venyson was gyven by "Mr. Richard Corbett unto the Towne, for to meete and assemble in fryndly "manner and to make myrry, the which was done accordingly." ✳

1594. The Bailiffs ordered a Fast to be observed in Shrewsbury, on Sunday the 11th day of August, when most of the inhabitants went to St. Mary's Church, and continued there, praying and hearing sermons, also bewailing their sins, from eight o'clock in the morning, to four o'clock in the evening.

1596. Wheat sold for 20s. rye for 16s. per bushel.

1599. Mr. Thomas Edwards, one of the Bailiffs, refused to wear scarlet, and to use the accustomed feasting at Christmas.

This year, the Assizes were removed from Shrewsbury to Bridgnorth.

1603. On Sunday, March 27th, in the afternoon, King James was proclaimed, by the Bailiffs and Aldermen in their gowns, together with the worshipful the rest of the Commoners, with trumpets and drums, the people huzzaing and crying God save the King.

1606. Cotton Hill burnt, the houses were set on fire by John Tench's wife.

1607. Mardol Quay built by Mr. Rowland Jenks. To him and to his heirs was granted in fee-farm for ever, so much ground on the south-east side of the Welsh Bridge, viz. from the postern gate along the town wall towards the bridge twenty-seven yards, into the womb of Severn twenty yards, the length along the river side forty-four yards, at the yearly rent of 12d. on condition that he should build the said Quay, pull down one house which stood on the gate, surrender his fee-farm thereof to the Corporation, and never erect again the said house, or any other building upon the Quay, and to permit all manner of barges, of all persons, to load at the said Quay, taking for every barge load of wood or coal 12d. for a ton of other goods off a Burgess, 2d. and off a Foreigner 4d. †

1608. Frankwell Quay built.

1614. One Coles rode from London to Shrewsbury in one day, between the hours of three in the morning and five in the evening. 156 miles.

---

* Dr. Taylor's M. S.   † Exchequer Book, C. 6, p. 205.

1615. Lord Eure, Lord President of the Marches, came here, and was nobly entertained.

1622. Viscount Mansfield came to Shrewsbury, and was entertained here, he gave the soldiers belonging to the garrison £10.

1629. Coleham Wall and Bridge repaired.

1634. A great frost and snow. When the ice went away it took down Coleham Wall, part of the Stone Bridge, and all the Wears upon the River Severn.

1647. August 29. The fish-board was removed to St. John's Hill.

December 23. A woman was burnt in the Dingle in the Quarry, for poisoning her husband.

1669. The Stone Conduit in the Green Market built.

1670. Roushill enclosed, and the Quarry railed.

1683. An earthquake felt here. February 7th, a dreadful fire in the Castle Foregate.

1703. The stone conduit on the Wyle-Cop taken down.

1704. The stone conduit in Mardol taken down.

1708. Wheat sold for 9s. Muncorn, 8s. Rye, 7s. per bushel.

1709. Dr. Sacheveral came to Shrewsbury: Above a thousand horsemen went out to meet him, and brought him into town with great shoutings, &c. He staid only one night, at the Raven-Inn.

1715. Henry Lord Newport, Sir Charles Lloyd, Bart. William Kynaston, Thomas Gardner, and John Fownes, Esqrs. entered into an association, raised both horse and foot, and kept guard here, it being the time of the rebellion; new gates were made about the walls, several passages stopt up, and the trained bands called together. Brigadier Dormer's regiment, at that time in this town, was ordered to march to Preston.

1718. A great meeting of the Quakers here, from all parts of England; they had the Wool-Hall four days to speak in.

The Mayor's Feast held in the Town-Hall; Sir Charles Lloyd, Bart. Mayor.

1719. Roushill leased to Mr. John Thornton, for 99 years: He levelled it and sowed it with rye-grass and clover.

1722. A regiment of foot, commanded by Brigadier Stanwix, encamped on Kingsland, during the summer.

1726. Lamps were put up in several parts of the town, at the expence of the several parishes.

1727. An earthquake felt here, but no great damage done.

In April, a meeting of the Quakers from all parts of England.

NN

The Judges of assize were refused the usual compliments by the Mayor, upon which account, the next assize was held at Bridgnorth. Thomas Jenkins, Esq. High Sheriff.

1729. The summer assizes held at Bridgnorth; a gallows was erected, and criminals executed there.

1730. The assizes were again removed to Shrewsbury.

1732. The assizes again removed to Bridgnorth.

1739. A great frost began on Christmas Eve, and continued till March, the River Severn was frozen up, and a tent was erected thereon, a sheep roasted, a printing press set to work,* &c.

1740. December 29th, part of the cover of the Market-House fell down, and killed two millers horses that stood under it.

1743. One Cadman, a shearman, returning from Bishop's-Castle, with the excise-money, from the collector there to the drapers in Shrewsbury, was robbed and murdered, near Norbury, by Woollaston, and his son Edmund, both of Bishop's-Castle. They were both taken; the father hung himself in Goal, and the son was hung in chains, near Norbury. The murder was committed on the 12th day of May.

1744. In October, a great fire at the Gullet, upon a Friday. Great damage done in the warehouses of Mr. Benion, grocer, and Mr. Morgan, ironmonger.

The conduit reservoir on Clarimond-Hill built.

1745. A regiment of foot, raised by Lord Powis, rendezvoused at Shrewsbury, and several gentlemen in the neighbourhood entered as volunteers. In December, the town was in great confusion, by false alarms of the Scotch rebels being on their march to this place. Many inhabitants left the town, and the regiment before-mentioned, being undisciplined, they marched out, with all their baggage, but soon returned, an express bringing advice that the rebels were gone to Derby.

1752. On Christmas-Day, two houses on the Stone Bridge, which were supported by beams crossing the navigation arch, through a decay of the ends of the beams, fell into the River underneath, with every thing belonging to them. The people who occupied the houses, being at church, happily escaped.

1756. Thirty-seven colliers were brought to Goal, for rioting, and committing outrages in the county, it being a time of scarcity for all kinds of provisions. Four died in Goal, ten were condemned,† whereof two were executed, and the rest pardoned.

---

* A rude engraving of the scene is now in the possession of Mr. Lawrence, of St. Alkmonds Churchyard.
EDITOR.

† Some circumstances attending this affair reflect so much credit upon the courage and humanity of the under-sheriff, that they deserve to be recorded in a note:

1758. The country butchers were again admitted to sell meat in town, and shambles were erected for them near St. Alkmond's Church.————The Fish-Board was removed to the Green-Market.

1759. A regiment of foot was raised and rendezvoused here; they were called the Royal Volunteers; Colonel Crawford had the command.—Upon St. Thomas's Day, December 21st, the colours were received by the regiment, with great pomp, they being carried in procession to St. Chad's Church, where a sermon was preached on the occasion, by the Rev. Rowland Chambre, A. M. from Ephes. vi. ver. 10.

1762. A great fire, in New-Street, Frankwell, on the 23d of February.

1763. The Fish-Board removed to New Fish-Street.

1764. At Lent Assize in March, sixty prisoners were arraigned and tried.

The trial took place at the Spring Assizes 1757; St. John Charlton, Esq. of Apley Castle being high sheriff, and Mr. Leeke of the Vineyard his deputy. Ten of the rioters were left for execution; but the judge sent his report by express to the Attorney-General, with an intimation of the day affixed for the execution, and the individuals, four in number, who, as he deemed it expedient, should suffer the sentence of the law; which report had been transmitted to the office of Mr. Pitt, then Secretary of State; where it lay untouched, and was never laid before the King. The day of execution arrived, without any reprieve or respite: and Mr. Leeke was advised, and even pressed by several of the principal gentlemen in his neighbourhood, whom he consulted in this emergency, to leave all the prisoners to their fate. But he was so much shocked at the thought of executing so large a number, and was so much convinced that this could not be the intention of the judge, that he ventured to postpone the execution, and sent off an express to London, on the return of which he had the satisfaction of finding that his conduct was most highly approved of, and still more, the consciousness that he had saved eight lives. The following is part of a letter written to him on the occasion by Lord Chief Justice Willes, then one of the Commissioners of the Great Seal

    Sir,

Till I saw your letter yesterday I was under the greatest uneasiness; for I took it for granted that all the ten rioters had been executed on Saturday last, as that was the day appointed for their execution; and upon my return from the Home Circuit on Thursday last, I found that by a shameful neglect in one of the Secretary of State's offices, (*I do not mean Lord Holdernesse's*) no reprieve had been sent down; and as it was then too late to send one down, I saw no reason to hope that their execution would be deferred to a longer time. But though, to be sure, you have acted contrary to your duty, you have acted a wise, prudent, and most humane part; and you have not only my thanks, but the thanks of some of the greatest men of the kingdom, for the part you have acted on this occasion. I once more thank you for what you have done, and am, &c.

We add part of a letter from Mr. Leeke's agent in town to him:

" My Lord Commissioner Willes was so afflicted....that it really made him ill; and he did not, for two days, go into the king's closet, so much he feared the effect it might have upon the king's mind, if the affair was communicated to his Majesty while it was under that state of uncertainty.

....Thank God, your prudent and well-judged respite has prevented all the uneasiness and mischiefs that might have happened; and I have the pleasure to assure you, that no step was ever taken that has given more satisfaction, or gained more applause than this of yours has done. My Lord Commissioner Willis this day waited on the King with your letter, and has directed me to acquaint you, by his Majesty's order, that his Majesty entirely approves what you have done; and so does his lordship and all the judges who are in town, to whom it has been communicated."

Ancient Rome would have decreed her crown, OB CIVEIS SERVATOS, to an act of such *civil courage.—Owen and Blakeway's History of Shrewsbury.*

NN2

Dannely and Newcombe, were condemned and executed for robbing the house of Samuel Griffiths, of Dinthill, Esq ; of a large quantity of plate, &c.

1766. Upon the 12th, 13th, and 14th of February, there fell a great snow in Shrewsbury, and lay on the ground for several days, 18 inches deep. Provisions of all kinds were very dear in the market while it lasted, butter sold for 15d. per pound.

Some buildings projecting into the street, at the bottom of Dogpole, very much incommoded the passage. They were this year purchased by the Corporation, in the names of Edward Elisha, and John Ashby, Esqrs. of Mr. Thomas Fox, skinner, and taken down, whereby the street was laid open, and made more convenient. The purchase-money paid was £115, and was raised by subscription.

1768. A snow fell, near two feet deep upon the level, it being a very hard frost when it fell, and went away gradually, without a flood.

June 7th. About three o'clock in the afternoon, there fell a great hail-storm, accompanied with terrible thunder and lightning, which lasted half an hour. The hailstones appeared to be irregular pieces of ice, congealed together, and glutinized with dust and gravel, weighing from half an ounce to an ounce; several were two inches and more in circumference.

1772. On Monday night, February 17th, about five minutes before twelve o'clock, a smart shock of an earthquake was felt here, which continued about twelve seconds, and occasioned a general terror and consternation.

1773. On Friday, May 14th, came on in the Court of Common Pleas, a motion made by Mr. Serjeant Burland, and Mr. Serjeant Glynn, to set aside a verdict of the last Salop assizes, establishing a right to the tolls of corn and grain, claimed by the Corporation. On hearing Mr. Serjeant Walker, Council for the Corporation, the Judges unanimously expressed their approbation of the verdict, and refused to set it aside.

1774. On Good-Friday, April 1, between two and three o'clock in the afternoon, a dreadful fire broke out in the Abbey-Foregate, and raged with great fury till seven o'clock in the evening, in which time forty-seven houses were burnt down, and five more much damaged, also sixteen barns, fifteen stables, four shops, and several stacks of hay were burnt. The next day, April 2nd, the gentlemen of the town and neighbourhood met at the Town-Hall, and a subscription being opened for the relief of the sufferers, the following sums were collected, and as far as necessary, applied to that purpose, viz.

	£.	s.	d.
Received by Contributions - - - -	794	18	9

DISBURSEMENTS.

	£.	s.	d.
For the immediate relief of the poorer sufferers -	3	3	9
To the men who assisted in extinguishing the fire -	37	1	9

	£.	s.	d.
· Lost by light money received - - - -	0	16	0
Paid for printing - - - - - -	0	10	6
Disbursed to the sufferers - - - - -	326	8	0
Returned overplus to the contributors 10s. 9d. per £ -	426	7	4
Balance given to the man who returned it - -	0	11	5
	794	18	9

Towards the above collection, the Worshipful Company of Drapers gave £50. The managers of this charity, immediately afterwards entered into another subscription for purchasing a large fire engine, a quantity of buckets, and fire hooks, and for making fire plugs, for the use of the town; towards which the following sums were subscribed, viz.

	£.	s.	d.		£.	s.	d.
The Drapers Company	26	17	6	Brought on	108	9	6
Right Hon. Lord Clive	26	17	0	John Corbet, Esq. -	11	11	0
Noel Hill, Esq. - -	21	10	0	Charlton Leighton, Esq.	5	5	0
William Pulteney, Esq.	21	10	0	The Company of Mercers,			
Mrs. Lyster - -	11	15	0	Ironmongers, &c. -	5	5	0
	108	9	6	Total	130	10	6

An engine was procured, which cost upwards of £100. and presented to the Managers of the Sun-Fire-Office, for the benefit of the town, to be by them kept in constant repair.

August 26th this year, General Paoli came to this town, and staid two days. During his stay, he visited several of the first families here.

1775. On Friday night, September 8th, at ten o'clock, the town was much alarmed with a shock of an earthquake. In the midst of a calm, a rumbling noise, much like that of a strong wind was heard; this was soon followed by two tremulous motions of the earth, succeeding each other instantaneously. The doors and windows of houses shook, tables, chairs, &c. were moved, but no considerable damage done.

1776. An association was entered into by the inhabitants of Shrewsbury, for bringing offenders to justice. It was named "The Shrewsbury General Association," and was made and ratified at the Town-Hall, January 29th, in the Mayoralty of William Owen, Esq.

April 9th. A petition from the inhabitants of this town, was presented to the House of Commons, by John Corbet, Esq. (elected member for this Borough on the death of Lord Clive) against a bill then depending in Parliament, for building a bridge across the Severn, at Gloucester, and for taxing all vessels passing under the said bridge. The petition was heard, and the taxation clause left out.

1778. Thursday, May 7th, The Shropshire Militia marched from Shrewsbury to Bridgnorth, where they were reviewed, and remained till June 12th, when they marched from thence to encamp on Cox-Heath, near Maidstone, in Kent, and on their route were reviewed by his Majesty in Hyde-Park, June 26th.

THE EDITOR'S CONTINUATION OF "CHRONOLOGICAL ACCOUNTS."

SELECTED EITHER FROM ORIGINAL MANUSCRIPTS AND PUBLISHED AUTHORITIES, OR RECORDED FROM PERSONAL KNOWLEDGE.

1779. A great fire broke out in a large malthouse, near the Quarry, occupied by Mr. Gronna, the whole of which was in a short time burnt down, together with a large quantity of malt therein; and the dwelling house adjoining very much damaged. The above fire was occasioned by a servant carelessly carrying a candle into the malthouse, which by accident, he let fall amongst some straw. Neither the building, stock, or furniture were insured. All the adjoining buildings would have fallen victims to the devouring flames, had not the night been very calm, and the greatest activity used by the firemen, and the Shropshire Volunteers, who nobly displayed themselves on this very alarming occasion.—The whole loss to the sufferers was computed at £1500.

1780. A Stage Coach was established by way of Oswestry, Corwen, &c. to Holyhead, by the Indefatigable Mr. Robert Lawrence, of the Lion Inn, Shrewsbury.

1782. Baron Hotham laid a fine of £2000 upon the county, at the Summer assize, till they should build a new shire-hall. The new hall was used for the first time March 17, 1786.

1783. Aug. 23 The Shrewsbury Chronicle contains an extraordinary account of an immense globe of fire which appeared in the atmosphere about nine o'clock at night; seeming in magnitude about twenty times larger than the apparent face of the moon, with a tail like a comet, and moving with great velocity from S. W. to N. E., and apparently about one hundred yards above the tops of the houses.

1786. May 31. One Spoonly, a shoe-maker, of Shrewsbury, jumped off the top of the Tower at the Welsh-Bridge, into the Severn, by way of exploit, to collect money from the spectators; having laid out a plank from the top of the Tower, and taking a smart run along, in order to spring off at the end of it, one of his feet slipped, and he fell on his breast into the water. He appeared quite dead for some time, and had not a boat (which was in waiting) taken him up, he would have lost his life by this presumptuous act.

1788. July 23. being the day appointed for a public thanksgiving to Almighty God, for the wonderful interposition of Divine Providence, in the falling down of St. Chad's Church at a time when the congregation was not assembled, the same was observed by the parishioners in the most solemn manner. The shops were kept shut during the whole day. In the morning public worship was held at St. Mary's Church, which was very much crowded. The psalms and lessons were admirably well adapted, and the sermon was preached by the Rev. Mr. Stedman. The whole of the service was attended with great solemnity.

1789. T. Phipps, Esq. and his son, of Lwyney Mapsis, were executed at the Old Heath, for forging and uttering a note of hand for £20, purporting to be the note of Mr. Richard Coleman, of Oswestry, knowing the same to have been forged. It was proved on the trial of these unfortunate men, that Mr. Coleman never had any transactions with Mr. Phipps that required the signing of any note whatever. That about Christmas last Mr. Coleman was served with a writ, by order of Mr. Phipps at his own suit, which action Mr. C. defended; that Mr. Phipps not supporting it, a *non pros.* was signed in the action, with £2. 3s. costs; whereupon Mr. Phipps and his son, with William Thomas their clerk, made an affidavit, stating that the note was for a trespass in carrying away some hay from off the land of one of Mr. Phipps's tenants, which Mr. Coleman had taken.

Upon this affidavit the Court of Exchequer granted a rule to shew cause why the *non pros.* should not be set aside. Mr. Coleman insisting that the note was a forgery, the matter rested in suspense till the event of this prosecution. After a full hearing of the evidence on both sides, and the Judge's charge to the Jury, the two Phipps's were pronounced Guilty of uttering and publishing the note, knowing the same to be forged. The Judge immediately passed sentence of death upon them, and recommended the Jury to acquit William Thomas, who was accordingly found not guilty.

Mr. Phipps and his son, from the time of their condemnation till the morning of their execution persisted in their innocence. However, before they left gaol, young Phipps confessed that he committed the forgery, avowed his father's innocence of it, and ignorance of its being forged when published. They were taken in a mourning coach to the place of execution, accompanied by a clergyman, and another pious person* who had visited them daily since their condemnation. On their way to the fatal tree, the father said to the son, "Tommy, thou hast brought me to this shameful end, but I freely forgive thee." To which the son made no reply. It being remarkably wet weather, their devotions were chiefly performed in the coach.

Mr. Phipps was in his 47th year, and his son just twenty years of age two days before his execution.

---

* The late Mr. Brocas.

Their fate was not so much lamented, on account of several similar matters appearing against them, and not a little aggravated, when it is considered Mr. Phipps was possessed of about £300 a year landed property, besides his practice.

August 20th. New St. Chads Church was consecrated.

1793. Jan. 11. The Shrewsbury Chronicle records, that the large luminous body of fire which had been seen in the air at a distance from Shrewsbury, a few nights previous, had surprised the inhabitants of the farther part of Montgomeryshire; it was observed to move swiftly from west to east, with a rumbling noise like distant thunder, and fell about ten miles from Machynlleth, appearpearing in its descent like a pyramid many miles in height from the earth upwards; in a very short time it disappeared, scattering by degrees like small sparks from the top downwards.

May 13. The First stone of the New Welsh Bridge was laid by the Rev. John Rocke, Mayor, in the presence of a vast number of respectable inhabitants of the town. The following inscription was engraved on a plate, and inserted in the stone:

"In the Month of November, 1791, the Corporation of Salop, on the Motion of John Bishop, Esq. Mayor, seconded by Joseph Loxdale, Esq. Steward, consented to join the inhabitants of the County and Town in a Petition to Parliament for an Act to abolish the Tolls due to the Burgesses, on the payment of £6000 into the Chamber, and to give £4000 towards a fund for erecting this Bridge. In February 1792, in the Mayoralty of Thos. Eyton, Esq. the subscriptions commenced, and in a few months upwards of £8000 was paid into the hands of a Committee, who paid £2000 to the Corporation, and retained the remaining £4000, with the other subscriptions towards the Bridge Fund. In February 1792, in the Mayoralty of John Rocke, Clerk, the Fund being £7000 and upwards, it was agreed to begin the Bridge, and the first stone was accordingly laid by the Mayor, on the 13th day of May following."

Carline and Tilley, Architects and Builders.

1794. April 28. Died in Frankwell, in the 101st year of his age, John Pritchard, *linen-draper*, formerly of Cophall, near Clun, in this county. He had ten children by his first wife, and twenty-two by the second.

1795. Feb. 7. One of the greatest floods ever remembered in the Severn; on Wednesday the 11th it was at the highest; to the reflecting beholder the scene was awfully grand; wrecks of houses, &c. at times, almost covered the surface of the rapid stream, and unfortunately Mr. Johnson, of the Can Office, and his man, in a boat, endeavouring to recover a large barrel, were both drowned. This flood exceded the great flood of November 18, 1770, six inches and a half.

1796. The Prince and Princess of Orange visited Shrewsbury.

1798. August 4. Bust of Mr. Howard,* by Bacon, placed over the gate-way of the New Gaol.

1800. September 29th. The School opened, founded by John Allatt, Esq. The Founder died in 1796.

1802. Sept. 12. A Sturgeon 8 feet 6 inches long, 3 feet 4 in girth, and weighing 192lb. caught in the wear below the Castle.

1803. July 30. Prince William of Gloucester, now Duke, visited this place, on his road to Liverpool, where he was about to take the command of the north west military district. His Highness having been asked at what hour he would permit the corporation to have the honour of waiting upon him, was pleased to appoint the following morning at half-past ten o'clock, at the Lion Inn, when, after an appropriate address pronounced by the high steward, Joseph Loxdale, Esq. to which the prince made a suitable return, extremely well expressed and pretty much at length, on the existing circumstances of the country, a circle being formed, he paid his compliments to each individual of the body. He then, accompanied by the mayor and other officers, proceeded to divine service in St. Chad's church, and left a very pleasing impression on the minds of the inhabitants, who witnessed the propriety of his demeanour. He was the first prince of the blood that had visited Shrewsbury since the Revolution.

1804. Oct. 9th. His Royal Highness, the Duke of Gloucester passed through this town, on returning from a visit to his son at Liverpool.

1806. Sept. 9th. His Royal Highness, George, Prince of Wales, our late King, (accompanied by the Duke of Clarence, his present Majesty,) passed through Shrewsbury, on his way to Rossall and Loton, the seats of Cecil Forester, Esq. (afterwards Lord Forester) and Sir Robert Leighton, Bart. His Royal Highness made no stay in the town, but having changed horses in the Abbey Foregate, passed under the walls of St. Chad's church and down Barker Street to Rossall, where, on the following morning he was, according to his Royal Highness's pleasure, signified to that effect, attended by a select deputation, consisting of the mayor, senior alderman, and high steward,† which last gentleman delivered a loyal address and received a gracious answer. On this occasion the freedom of the Borough was conferred on the royal visitors.

---

* Mr. Howard was the son of a wealthy tradesman in London. In 1773 he served the office of Sheriff of the County of Bedford, and this brought the distress of prisoners more immediately under his notice, and led him to the humane design of visiting the gaols of England; he afterwards travelled on the Continent with the same benevolent zeal. His efforts in the cause of humanity proved at last fatal to him; while at Cherson, a town of European Russia, he visited a patient under a malignant epidemic fever, and taking the disorder he fell a victim to his compassion, January 20th, 1790, and was buried at the Villa of M. Dauphine, about eight miles from Cherson, where a monument is erected over his grave.—EDITOR.

† William Wilson, William Smith, and Joseph Loxdale, Esquires.

1808. Mr. John Lawrence, brother and successor of Mr. Robert Lawrence, of the Lion Inn, first contracted with government for working the mail coach to Holyhead. To this gentleman the town is in no small degree indebted, for the noble spirit of enterprise he manifested in the establishment and working of stage coaches to and from Shrewsbury, during the time he was a proprietor. It is gratifying to record the same spirit has been kept alive by his successor, Mr. Tomkins, and by Mr. Jobson of the Talbot Hotel.

1809. Feb. 7. The Suburbs of the Town were deeply inundated by the rise of the Severn ; providentially no lives were lost. The benevolence of the town was nobly exerted on the occasion, and sums of money, coals, victuals, &c. were distributed to the sufferers.

October 25th. The 50th Anniversary of the accession of George the Third to the throne of these dominions was commemorated in Shrewsbury, in a manner that must ever reflect the highest credit on the benevolence and good sense of the town. A very liberal subscription was raised, and placed under the management of a General Committee of Subscribers, who elected a committee for general distribution. After various sums had been voted for the relief of poor debtors, the sick, &c. every subscriber of one guinea and upwards had the privilege of recommending two persons for every guinea subscribed ; and in order that such distribution might be divested of the appearance of a public charity, seven shillings were sent to the subscribers for every person recommended ; by which means the subscribers (not the Committee) had the pleasure of presenting their own gratuity : on this plan 479 families were made joyful on the jubilee day. A surplus still remaining, on the Monday following about 300 families received two shillings and sixpence each ; and nearly 200 families (recommended by subscribers of small sums, and other respectable inhabitants) were on this occasion visited at their own houses, by several members of the committee,* and presented with two shillings each. Upwards of 3000 individuals partook of the loyal benevolence of Salopians.

1811. The most extraordinary inundation we have to record, happened this year, on the night of Monday, May 27th. On the afternoon of that day, a violent storm of hail, thunder and lightning was widely felt, particularly S. W. of this town. The air was sultry, the lightning very vivid, and the thunder is described by persons near Minsterly, to have been similar to the report of many cannon immediately over their heads ; near the White Grit, hailstones two inches in circumference, lay almost a foot deep. About five o'clock in the afternoon, a cloud burst upon the ridge of hills called the Stiperstones, and a torrent of water, with irresistible force, and thundering sound, rushing down the hill side, swept away several cottages belonging to the White Grit miners. Part of the vast body of water took a direction through

---

* Of this Committee the Editor of this work had the honour to be a member, and he can truly say that no appointment ever afforded him greater delight.

Habberley, but the greatest quantity pursued its course along the valley through which runs Minsterly Brook.

Between five and six o'clock the deluge reached Minsterly, flooding almost every house in the village. Mr. Vaughan, a farmer, was swept away from his fold, and carried several hundred yards through the bridge, where the current threw him upon a pigstie, from whence he climbed to the roof of a house and was saved; his sister was carried a great distance and left in the branches of a tree. Not a trace was left of his thrashing machine, or stabling; but five horses escaped. Thirteen persons were miraculously saved in the Angel public house; on the first alarm they ran up stairs, and when the water had reached the second story, they clung to the rafters. The stabling, with all other contiguous buildings were swept away. In the stables were seventeen horses, and they swam out. The stables of the Rev. Mr. Williams, and part of the church wall were both carried away. The persons who perished in this village were, Mr. Hoggins, a farmer; Holmes, a labourer, and another person.

The next scene of desolation was Pontesford, where it is enough to mention its ravages only at one spot. At Mr. Heighway's it burst into the house through the windows, till at length the walls gave way, and Mr. H's venerable grandmother, aged 83, with two female servants and a labourer, were hurried into the abyss. Meanwhile Mr. Heighway's wife and another lady climbed upon the roof of the house, from whence they beheld Mr. H. clinging to a pole, and was lifted by two men upon the bridge about thirty yards distant. Mr. Bennett, an overseer of Pontesbury coal works, and two others, got into a hay-loft, where deeming themselves secure, they were in the act of petitioning the Almighty to deliver the persons upon the bridge, part of which had just fallen in; when instantly the building was swept away, and the unfortunate men were all lost. At this place the water was at least twenty feet deep.

At Minsterley, the water was from six to eight feet deep in some houses; the house and mill at Plott's Green were carried away.

The torrent following the course of Meole Brook, reached Coleham, one of the suburbs of this town, about half-past ten o'clock at night, with a tremendous roaring noise. The cellars and lower rooms belonging to the Seven Stars public house, and all the houses adjoining were deluged; the street in front of the Cotton Factory was inundated to the depth of nearly three feet by an instantaneous gush. At this time the noise of the current was inconceivably dreadful, and the cries, "Help!—Help!"—"Drowning," &c, contributed to the horror of the sound. The force of this great body of water rushing into the Severn from Meole Brook, actually turned the current of the river Severn, which rose near the English Bridge, four feet perpendicular in less than ten minutes.

The number of lives lost amounted to 9 at Pontesford, and 3 at Minsterly.

In this instance, the benevolence of Salopians was almost unbounded; the sum of £1,862 was subscribed, leaving £514 14s. over and above the liberal aid afforded to such sufferers as were known to require it, or who applied for relief.

oo2

Aug. 24. John Taylor, James Baker, Isaac Hickman, William Turner, and Abraham Whitehouse, were executed at the New Drop for a burglary and robbery in the dwelling house of W. C. Norcup, Esq. of Betton, near Drayton. The scene was one of the most awful and affecting nature. The wretched men when on the scaffold and in view of death, joined in loud and piercing cries to the God of Mercy, to pardon their multiplied crimes. It is humbly hoped their prayers were not in vain.

1812. The Royal Lancasterian School established. On this occasion, at the suggestion of the Editor of this work, the late William Smith, Esq. senior alderman of Shrewsbury, generously bestowed the land on which the building is erected.

1813 June. The following paragraph appeared in the Shrewsbury Chronicle.—"The arrival of Mr. Webb in Shrewsbury was mentioned in our last Chronicle; and although it was not his intention to distribute any sums (for what private fortune can be commensurate with such bounty?) yet the applications were so numerous and importunate, that, to his benevolent mind, they were irresistible. Six orphan boys, and others, from Knighton and Leominster, for whom he had not provided masters in Ludlow, followed him hither, and they have been clothed and apprenticed to respectable masters. Mr. Williamson, of this town, who had long known Mr. Webb, assisted him in clothing them and procuring masters; and Dr. Johnson, in compliance with Mr. Webb's request, devoted his time to the examination of cases of real distress, and became the distributor of his alms. The doors of the Lion Inn were besieged by the ragged, the wretched, and the unfortunate; and it was in vain they were told that Mr. Webb wished to confine his gifts to widows, orphans, the diseased, the lame, the dumb, and the blind. On Friday, he visited the Infirmary, the House of Industry, the Royal Free Grammar School, and those founded by Bowdler and Allatt, those on the system of Dr. Bell and Mr. Lancaster, and also St. Chad's School of Industry. He expressed his approbation at the regularity, order, and comfort, visible among the inmates at the Infirmary, the Prison, and the House of Industry, and was pleased at the girls in Dr. Bell's and Mr. Lancaster's Schools being instructed in sewing and knitting, which, with reference to the situations they would hereafter fill, he thought more serviceable to them than being taught writing.

Among numerous cases of distress, Mr. Webb relieved the following: A family, where there had been four children, two of which were living—one lame, the other diseased; a blind man, his lame wife, and diseased daughter; a journeyman shoemaker who had reared eleven children, and paid taxes seventeen years without parochial relief; to two orphan girls, £20; a bankrupt's son, £10; a distressed clergyman's family £25; a widow and six children £20; a haulier who had lost three horses £30; to the Public Charities, viz. the Infirmary £21; Prison Charities £21; Dr. Bell's School £5; Mr. Lancaster's £5; St. Chad's School of Industry £5; General Sunday School £5; Union Sunday School 5£; Swan Hill School £5; the Sick Man's Friend £5.

For the purpose of apprenticing 29 boys he gave premiums, from £15 to £30 each, and in one case £35) amounting in the whole to about £700. He appointed a Committee, consisting of the Rev. W. Rowland, Dr. Johnson, and the Rev. E. P. Owen, to select cases, from the applications which he himself did not attend to, and left in their hands, £60, besides £50 to clothe and educate boys; he also left £10 with the Rev. Mr. Weaver, to relieve cases of distress; and a like sum with the Rev. Mr. Palmer."

1814. June 30. On Lord Hill's first visit to Shrewsbury, after the peace of Paris, thousands went out to meet him; in many places the trees were adorned with flowers, and even the road was strewed with emblems of gratitude and esteem. This was a day of general festivity; the landlord regaled his tenants, and the master his workmen; at the same time the poor were made partakers of the bounty of their richer fellow-townsmen. Sheep were roasted at the different inns. Shortly after thousands partook of tea in the Quarry; the scholars of the different Charity and Sunday Schools amounting to nearly 1300, were particularly attended to.—The crowds assembled on the occasion from every part of the county, formed one of the most lively and agreeable scenes ever witnessed in Shrewsbury.

Dec. 17. First stone laid of the column in Honour of Lord Hill. The capstone was laid June 18th, 1816.

1818. The New Butter Market erected.

1821. June 3rd. The Shrewsbury Chronicle records an awful catastrophe in this town, which suddenly snatched into another world three individuals of one family, and had nearly overwhelmed *five* families, comprising upwards of twenty persons. " Between the hours of twelve and one on Monday night, a dreadful crash awakened several persons in the vicinity of the Theatre, on St. John's Hill. The crash was followed by a deep and confused rumbling which continued for a minute——and then all was still. One or two neighbours hastened to the spot. The interior of the house which adjoins the Theatre was found in ruins—part of the roof, with two chimnies, having fallen through three rooms down to the kitchen floor, and two beds from the garret were lying *upon* the rubbish. At this moment some of the inmates were escaping through the window of the second story: one young woman was carried out wounded and bloody; and four children, with other persons, were rushing from the fallen edifice, all of them unclothed, and every countenance distorted with terror, and so much blackened with soot and dust as scarcely to be recognized. The house contained so many inhabitants that it was not instantly known whether any were missing. After several hazardous attempts to enter the premises, by the front door and through various parts of the Theatre, a young man named Wilde, whose courage and humanity are truly honourable, commenced, with the assistance of one or two others, the removal of the rubbish, rafters, and stones, and soon a small cry was heard beneath. Presently the bodies of

Edward Davies, his wife, and a son (aged 8 years), were taken out : the two former quite dead, and the latter opened his eyes for an instant only.

Beneath the entire mass was an infant of the deceased (aged 8 months,) safely protected, by a piece of timber and some heavy stones—the very implements which had destroyed its parents—after it had fallen from the garret through 3 floors, and was covered by several tons of stone and ruins. This wonderful preservation can be explained only by supposing that the child was held, or clung, in its mother's arms while falling downwards, and slipped from the foot of the bed into the receptacle which Providence allotted it. In this same small garret slept 4 other children, but, happily, under a part of the roof, which was not broken. In the room below were 2 beds; Mr. Jones and his wife in one, which also escaped the falling mass; but the bedstead on which their neice slept was shattered, and she was bruised, not dangerously. On the floor still lower were Mr. Hunt and his wife, who also escaped unhurt. In the rooms adjoining all these were other persons; and had one piece of framework been broken (which lay exposed) the entire roof must unavoidably have buried all in its ruins.

The deceased man had been 15 years employed by Mr. Williams, gardener of this town, and also distributed the Shrewsbury Chronicle in the districts of Pool and Llanfyllin, Montgomeryshire. Six orphans survive the calamity, all girls, except the eldest, aged seventen or eighteen, who is in service."

A very handsome subscription was raised for the benefit of the orphans, which has been most judiciously applied.

July 19. The Coronation of George IV. celebrated with great solemnity in Shrewsbury. The Corporation and incorporated companies, the teachers and children belonging to the Charity Schools and Sunday Schools walked in procession, and afterwards partook of liberal entertainments, &c.

1827. July 19. First stone of the new Infirmary laid by General Lord Hill. Opened for the reception of patients, September 1830.

1828. Aug. 4, was executed on the new Drop, in front of the county gaol, John Steventon, for the murder of John Horton, at Hales Owen, Joseph Pugh and John Cox, junior, for the murder of James Harrison, at Drayton. The following particulars relative to the latter diabolical affair, and the extraordinary conduct of the parties connected may not be undeserving of record.

At eight o'clock on Saturday morning, August 2nd, 1821, the trial of John Cox. the elder, John Cox, the younger, Robert Cox, Joseph Pugh and Ann Harris, charged with the wilful murder of James Harrison commenced.

Mr. Richards, in opening the case for the prosecution, thought he should best discharge his duty by briefly laying before the Jury the evidence he possessed to support this charge, without launching forth into any great length of observation. " In the spring of last year, said the learned counsel, " depredations to a considerable extent, on the sheep of the farmers, prevailed in the neighbourhood of Drayton. In consequence of information given by the deceased James

Harrison, a person named Ellson was apprehended and sent to gaol for this offence. The apprehension of this man, who was related to four of the prisoners at the bar, would it was supposed, from the evidence of the deceased, in reference to his case, have involved the safety of the rest of the family. As Harrison was the principal witness against him, it became necessary, therefore, in order to prevent discovery, that he should be put out of the way. When the trial of Ellson came on, Harrison was not to be found ; but as he was known to have been an associate of the prisoner Ellson, his absence was not considered very extraordinary ; but when it was protracted to a considerable length of time, rumours began to arise that he had not been fairly dealt with. It was not, however, until Ellson was again apprehended, for another felony, that any clue was afforded ; but in consequence of information which would appear in evidence, the prisoners Joseph Pugh and Ann Harris were apprehended. Search was made for the body before this time, but to no purpose. On Pugh, however, being taken, he immediately gave such information as led to the discovery of the body, in a place called Hocknell's Field, and disclosed such facts as led to the apprehension of the other prisoners."

The case was altogether of a most revolting description. Pugh, the father, was called to convict his son ; Ellson to convict his own mother, and father-in-law, and brothers-in-law ; his wife corroborated his evidence against her father and brothers ; and the evidence of Mary Blakeman, the daughter of Ann Harris tended to confirm the testimony which fixed the guilt on her mother.

The cool deliberation with which the murder was planned and executed could only be equalled by the calmness of these witnesses whilst giving their testimony. When Ellson was brought from the cell in court to give his evidence, he hurried past the prisoners in the dock with an apprehensive look, as if he were afraid to be within their reach. His Mother held her head away till he reached the witness-box, when she took one look at him, to which he returned a careless stare, and proceeded with his evidence. His father and brothers-in-law looked at him stedfastly—the old man with an expression of mirth in his countenance. When he avowed that he knew what he was saying would hang his mother, she raised her hands to her face, and wrung them bitterly, exclaiming, " Oh ! Christ !" On his return to the cell, he hurried past the dock as he did on his entry. His evidence was delivered without embarrasment, and he seemed to soften none of the horrible facts which told against his relatives.

A verdict of Guilty was pronounced against all the prisoners, and all were condemned. Joseph Cox, John Cox the younger, and Robert Cox, were ordered to be executed on the Monday following. Early on the morning of execution, a reprieve for Robert Cox was received by Mr. Griffiths, Governor of the County Prison. The execution of Ann Harris took place on Saturday, August 22nd, The nature of her crime precluded the hope of that mercy which had been extended to two of her associates ; and she was domed to satisfy the offended laws of God and her country, by an ignominious death on the scaffold.

Of her son Ellson, who convicted her, she spoke in the most forgiving terms, hoping that her fate, and his own narrow escape would teach him to forsake his guilty courses, and to try if possible to amend his life. She seemed wrapt up in him, notwithstanding his behaviour to her ; and did not appear to think the crime she had committed as particularly heinous, because it had saved his life. On Mrs. Kitson, the matron, expressing her horror at the crime of mur-der, the old woman did not appear to comprehend the guilt of an act " which saved," (as she expressed it) " the life of her dear lad." In fact, her guilt, as well as that of her companions, seemed to arise in a great measure from ignorance ; she never had heard of Jesus Christ till she came to gaol, and the plainest doc-trines of christianity were to her unknown before she entered within its walls!

1830. Aug 24. St. Michael's Church in the Castle Foregate consecrated.

1831. Feb. 10. In consequence of the sudden melting of the snow, the river Severn rose to a most alarming and destructive height. The suburbs of the town were deeply inundated, and in low situations, but for very great exer-tions, many lives must have been lost. In some cottages in Roushill, the water covered the first floor, even to the ceiling. The cellars of many trades-men were filled, and their property destroyed ; the stables belonging to the Sun and Ball Inn, Castle Foregate were washed down, and in the new Bap-tist Chapel, the water covered the tops of the pews. From eight to ten o'clock on the 9th, the river rose very rapidly, and at that time a bargeman in a fishing coracle sailed for a wager over the Town walls at Roushill, and under an arch of the Welsh Bridge.

Though this was considered a very high flood, according to the evidence of brass plates, affixed to the inside the window jambs in the house of Mrs. Davies, Malster, in Frankwell, the Severn in that end of the town was lower by $23\frac{1}{2}$ inches than in 1672, and $25\frac{1}{2}$ inches lower than the flood of 1770, and $31\frac{1}{2}$ inches than the great flood in 1795. The lowest plate bears the following inscription.

" This is to let you know
The Severn up to me did flow.
December 21, Anno. 1672."

A second plate, 2 inches above the preceding, records,

" To this line flowed Severn,
Nov. 8, 1770."

On the third plate, six inches higher than the second, is inscribed :

" This plate is fixed to let you know
That Severn to this line did flow.
Feb. 11, 1795." EDITOR.

ADDENDA.

1832. September. Shrewsbury Races were first held on the present ground near Underdale, and in the vicinity of the Abbey Foregate.

1832. The Cholera Morbus, in its destructive career through the kingdom, visited Shrewsbury.—The humanity and kindness of the higher classes of the inhabitants with the parish officers, and the skill and attention of the medical gentlemen of the town, were manifested on the occasion, in a most exemplary degree; every thing was done to alleviate the sufferings of the afflicted, and to stay the march of the direful malady,—in consequence of which exertions, not more than 100 persons, it is supposed, fell victims to its fury, including the town and its vicinity.

A circumstance may also be adverted to, as being more favourable to the adoption of measures of precaution and cure in Shrewsbury, than was found in many other towns, otherwise similarly situated;—the working classes of our town are in general better educated, and have learned to place more confidence in their superiors, than do the poor of some other towns and districts; hence they readily conformed to the regulations recommended for their benefit: while in some places, the introduction and continuance of the disease was ascribed to the surgeons, who were believed to be in league with government to destroy the poor, and that the cause of the speedy interment of the dead, was to avoid detection;—these opinions existed both in England and Wales, but to the greatest extent in the Sister Kingdom of Ireland.

Same year, in the month of October, Shrewsbury and its vicinity had the honour of receiving most DELIGHTFUL and WELCOME visitors,—their Royal Highnesses the Duchess of Kent and the Princess Victoria, honoured Pitchford Hall, the hospitable seat of the Earl of Liverpool, with a visit, and also the loyal town of Salop. The joy of all ranks, on the occasion, was most lively and sincere.

The royal party had previously visited some interesting parts of North Wales, particularly Caernarvon, the Lake and Pass of Llanberis, and the Ruins of the Hall of Prince Llewellyn, near to the place where, tradition says, King Edward the First embarked to attack the Cambrians, when they made their memorable stand for liberty and independence.

1833. Oct. 5. Intelligence arrived in Shrewsbury of the death of Richard Heber, Esq. of Hodnet Hall; Sheriff of the County in 1821, M.P. for the University of Oxford.—He was the distinguished friend of literature; collected, with great avidity, the manuscripts, as well as printed works, of the early English Poets, and was well acquainted with their contents. His Libraries at Hodnet and London, were of almost unequalled rarity and value. *(Vide page* 113, *vol.* 2.)

1835. In consequence of the passing of the Municipal Reform Bill, the ancient chartered Trading Companies of the town, sixteen in number, were dissolved. The Annual Show was considered also at an end, and much of the festival, grandeur, &c. of the Shrewsbury Corporation, fell into disuse.— The last Chief Magistrate of the town, under the ancient charter, was ROBERT BURTON, Esq.—the first Mayor, under the new law, was WM. HAZLEDINE, Esq. *(See Appendix, page 28.)*

1836. August 1st. At the County Assizes, came on the trial of Patrick M'Daniel, alias Patrick Donelly; John Mulholland, alias John Holland; Edward M'Daniel, alias Edward Donelly; Lawrence Curtis, alias James Macguire; and Owen M'Daniel, alias John Rooney,—charged with having, on the 23rd of March last, at the parish of Loppington, in this county, assaulted and nearly killed Mr. Thomas Woodward and Mr. Thomas Urwick, both of Shrewsbury, and stealing from the person of the said Mr. Woodward, £25 in notes, £9 19s. in gold and silver, and a silk handkerchief; and a silver watch, four half crowns, a shilling, and a sixpence, from the person of the said Mr. Urwick, his Nephew. They were all found guilty, and received sentence of death.—After condemnation, they made many extraordinary disclosures of robberies they had committed in Yorkshire, Lancashire, and Cheshire: their confessions were corroborated by the discovery of portions of the stolen property, through the indefatigable exertions of Mr. Sadler Thomas, a native of Shrewsbury, now at the head of the Manchester Police, and formerly of Covent Garden, London.

Owen M'Daniel and John Mulholland had their sentence commuted to transportation for life. On the 13th of August, Edward Donelly, Patrick Donelly, and Lawrence Curtis, suffered the extreme penalty of the law; on which occasion, it is said, 10,000 persons visited Shrewsbury, to witness their execution.

1836. The New Town Hall, erected on the site of the former one, was nearly completed.

Same year. The New Church in Coleham, was also in course of erection.

END OF VOLUME THE FIRST,

To which the APPENDIX may or may not be subjoined.

PRINTED BY C. HULBERT, PROVIDENCE GROVE, NEAR SHREWSBURY.

APPENDIX.

PREFATORY INFORMATION.

SO great a number, of the Subscribers and Patrons of this Publication residing in different parts of the Kingdom, particularly in Counties adjacent to Shropshire, I have been induced, throughout the whole of the volume, to pay some attention to circumstances, events, and places which may appear to many readers, not exactly relevant in a Shropshire History; but this I have done without abridging or witholding a single line originally designed as a portion of the Work,—so that numbers will be gainers, and not one will be a loser.—Of this character will appear the following List of principal English Monasteries; the Catalogue of *all* I could collect, which existed in counties adjoining our own, and in North and South Wales, with the value of each, as stated at the time of their Suppression; but which Bishop Burnet, in his History of the Reformation, considers far below their real annual value.—For says he, "*An abuse had run over Europe of keeping the rents of the Church at their first rates, and instead of raising them, the Incumbents exacted great fines when the Tenant's Leases were renewed, so that some houses valued at £200 per annum, were in reality worth many thousands.*"

Of this immense wealth, a small portion only was retained for the support of the future clergy: More than one half the tithes, nearly all the splendid mansions and great estates, jewels, gold and silver utensils and ornaments belonging to the Church, were seized and sold, by order of the King and Parliament, to Laymen, and some at very low prices.

The whole value is estimated, by the Right Reverend author above cited, at £132,607 6s. 4d, but which he believes was not one tenth their true value; now, if we multiply that sum by ten, we have £1,426,073 3s. 4d.—The value of money at that period was more than ten times its value in the present day, we may therefore fairly conclude that the revenue of the Church was more, by a considerable sum, than half the revenue of the Nation.

Among the principal Monasteries suppressed by the King and his Parliament, were :—*

Abingdon, in Berkshire, an abbey of benedictines, valued at 2042*l.* 2*s.* 8*d.*

St. Alban's, in Hertfordshire, an abbey of the order of St. Benedict, valued at 2510*l.* 6*s.* 1½*d.*

Barking, in Essex, the first nunnery in England of the order of St. Benedict, valued at 1084*l.* 6*s.* 2½*d.*

Battle, in Sussex, a benedictine abbey, valued at 987*l.* 11*s.* 0½*d.*

Canterbury, in Kent. Here was an abbey of Benedictines, valued at 2489*l.* 4*s.* 9*d.*

Ditto, in ditto, another monastery, afterwards called St. Austin's abbey, valued at 1413*l.* 4*s.* 11½*d.*

Cirencester, in Gloucestershire, an abbey of black canons, valued at 1051*l.* 7*s.* 1½*d.*

Durham, in Durham, an abbey, and afterwards a bishopric, valued at 1615*l.* 14*s.* 10½*d.*

St. Edmunds-bury, in Suffolk, a Benedictine abbey, valued at 2336*l.* 16*s.*

Ely, in Cambridgeshire. It was first a nunnery, then a convent of Benedictine monks, then a bishopric; its revenues at the dissolution were 1301*l.* 8*s.* 2*d.*

Malmsbury, in Wilts, a Benedictine abbey, valued at 803*l.* 17*s.* 7*d.*

Peterborough, or Medeshamstede, in Northamptonshire, a Benedictine abbey, converted afterwards to a Bishopric, valued at 1972*l.* 7*s.* 0½*d.*

---

*It is but just to observe, that the entire suppression of Religious Houses was contemplated by the Commons of England, one hundred years before Henry the Eighth's time, The Parliament of Henry the Fourth, more than once advised the King to seize all the conventual revenues, and to leave the cure of the parishes to the *secular clergy*, with a stipend of 7 Marks a piece yearly; and to create out of the Property, income for 15 new Earls, 1500 Knights, and 6000 Esquires, to endow 100 Hospitals, and to leave the King an annual revenue of 20,000 Marks; but this the King rejected. It may also be observed, that out of the 10,041 Religious Houses Suppressed, only 653 have a valuation attached at the present day.

Appendix.　　　A

Ramsey, in Huntingdonshire, a Benedictine abbey, valued at 1983*l.* 15*s.* 3¼*d.*
Shaftesbury, in Dorsetshire, a Benedictine nunnery, valued at 1329*l.* 1*s.* 3*d.*
Westminster, in Middlesex, a Benedictine abbey, now a college church for a dean and canon, valued at 3977*l.* 6s. 4*d.*

Ditto, in ditto. Here was likewise a college begun by king Stephen, but finished by Edward III. for a dean, twelve secular canons, thirteen viears, four clerks, six choristers, dedicated to St. Stephen, valued at 1085*l.* 10*s.* 5*d.*

The sixteen religious houses above named, possessed a revenue, *unitedly*, of £28,683 9*s.* 6*d.* which multiplying by ten according to Bishop Burnet's supposition of their real value, and we have £286,834 15*s.*; which, according to our former rule, again multiplying by ten, the supposed reduction in the value of money, or advance in price of land whichever we may call it, and we have £2,868,347 10*s.*—A sum, exceeding by £600,000, the whole revenue, taken in 1825, of all the Episcopal and Clerical Livings now pertaining to the English Church: comprising, two Archbishoprics, 24 Bishoprics, and 11593 Livings: engaging, probably, 8000 Rectors, Vicars, &c. and nearly 5000 Curates.

Religious Houses suppressed in English Counties adjoining to Shropshire, and in North and South Wales :—

CHESHIRE.

Bunbury, a college for a dean & 6 regular canons.
Chester, a Benedictine abbey, valued at 1073*l.* 17*s.* 7½*d.*
Ditto, a Benedictine nunnery, valued at 99*l.* 16*s.* 2*d.*
Cumbermere, an abbey of Cistercian monks, valued at 225*l.* 9*s.* 7*d.*
Dernhalle, an abbey for one hundred monks of the Cistercian order.
Ilbre, a cell of black monks to Chester.
Macclesfield, a college of secular canons.
Mobberley, a priory of black canons.
Norton, an Austin priory of canons regular, valued at 259*l.* 11*s.* 8*d.*
Pulton, a Cistercian abbey.
Stanlaw, a Cistercian abbey.
Vale Royal, a monastery, valued at 540*l.* 6*s.* 2*d.*

HEREFORDSHIRE.

Acornebury, a nunnery of the order of St. Austin, valued at 75*l.* 7*s.* 5½*d.*
Clifford, a priory of Cluniac monks, valued at 65*l.* 11*s.* 11*d.*
Creswell, an alien priory.
Ewias, a Benedictine priory.
Hereford, the church of St. Peter. Here was a cell to the abbey of St. Peter, at Gloucester.
Here was also a Benedictine nunnery, valued at 121*l.* 3*s.* 3*d.*

Kilpeke, a cell to the abbey of St. Peter, at Gloucester.
Lemster. It was first a nunnery, then a college, and last a cell of Benedictine monks.
Limbroke, a Benedictine nunnery, valued at 23*l.* 17*s.* 8*d.*
Monkenlane, an alien priory, given to Windsor college.
Rowney, olim Munde, a Benedictine nunnery, valued at 13*l.* 10*s.* 9*d.*
Scobbedon, a priory of black canons.
Titley, an alien priory.
Wigmore, was first a college for secular canons, then a priory for black canons, valued at 302*l.* 12*s.* 3*d.*
Wormesley, olim Pyonia, a priory of black canons, valued at 83*l.* 10*s.* 2*d.*

STAFFORDSHIRE.

Blithbury, a Benedictine nunnery.
Brivern. Here were two priories, one of black monks, and the other of white nuns.
Burton, an abbey of Benedictines, valued at 356*l.* 16*s.* 3¼*d.*
Calwich, a cell of black canons.
Canwell, a monastery for Benedictine monks, valued at 25*l.* 10*s.* 3*d,*
Delacres, a Cistercian abbey, valued at 234*l.* 3*s.* 6*d.*
Dudley, a priory of Cluniac monks.
Fairweld, a Benedictine nunnery.

Hulton, a Cistercian abbey, valued at 76*l*. 14*s*. 10*d*.

Lappele, an alien priory of black monks.

Litchfield, a cathedral church.

Penkridge, a collegiate church.

Radmore, a Cistercian abbey.

Raunton, a priory of black canons, valued at ·90*l*. 2*s*. 10*d*.

Roucester, a priory of black canons, valued at 111*l*. 13*s*. 7*d*.

Sandwell, a Cluniac monastery, valued at 38*l*. 8*s*. 4*d*.

Stafford, a priory of black canons, valued at 141*l*. 13*s*. 2*d*.

Ditto, a college of a dean and canons.

Stone, a college of secular canons, then a priory of black canons, valued at 119*l*. 14*s*. 11*d*.

Tamworth, a Benedictine nunnery, then a priory of secular canons.

Tetnall, a collegiate church.

Trentham, a priory of black canons, valued at 106*l*. 3*s*. 10*d*.

Tutbury, a Cluniac priory, valued at 244*l*. 16*s*. 8*d*.

Wolverhampton, a college of secular canons, annexed to the dean and chapter of Windsor.

WORCESTERSHIRE.

Astley, an alien priory.

Bordesley, a Cistercian abbey, valued at 392*l*. 8*s*. 6*d*.

Clive, a monastery.

Evesham, a Benedictine abbey, valued at 1268*l*. 9*s*. 9*d*.

Fladbury, or Fledanbirig, an ancient monastery.

Kemsey, a cell to Worcester abbey.

Malvern Major, a Benedictine abbey, valued at 375*l*. 0*s*. 6½*d*.

Malvern Minor, a Benedictine priory, valued at 102*l*. 10*s*. 9½*d*.

Pershore, a college for secular canons, afterwards Benedictine monks, valued at 666*l*. 13*s*.

Westwood, a cell of black nuns, valued at 78*l*. 8*s*.

Whiston, a nunnery, valued at 56*l*. 3*s*. 7*d*.

Worcester, an abbey for secular canons, then for Benedictine monks, valued at 1386*l*. 12*s*. 10½*d*.

Wudiandun, a nunnery, made a cell to Worcester.

NORTH AND SOUTH WALES.

Aberconway, in Caernarvonshire, a Cistercian abbey, valued at 179*l*. 10*s*. 10*d*..

Aberguilly, in Caermarthenshire, a collegiate church for twenty-two prebendaries, valued at 42*l*.

St. Asaph, in Flintshire, first a monastery, then a bishopric.

Bardsey, in Caernarvonshire, an abbey, valued at 58*l*. 6*s*. 2*d*.

Basing Werke, in Flintshire, an abbey of white canons, valued at 157*l*. 15*s*. 2*d*.

Bethkelert, in Caernarvonshire, a priory of black canons, valued at 69*l*.

Brecknock, in Brecknockshire, a priory of benedictines, valued at 134*l*. 11*s*. 4*d*.

Ditto, in ditto, here was a college of fourteen prebendaries, translated from Caermarthenshire.

Caermarden, in Caermarthenshire, a priory of black canons, valued at 164*l*. 0*s*. 4*d*.

Cardigan, in Cardiganshire, a priory of black monks, valued at 13*l*. 4*s*. 9*d*.

St. Clare, in Caermarthenshire, an alien priory, but given to All-Souls college, in Oxford.

Clunoch Vaur, in Caernarvonshire, a Cistercian abbey.

Combe Hire, in Radnorshire, a Cistercian priory, valued at 24*l*. 19*s*. 4*d*.

St. David's, in Pembrokeshire, a bishopric.

Haverford, in Ditto, a priory of black canons, valued at 135*l*. 6*s*. 1*d*.

Hawston, in Flintshire, a preceptory, valued at 160*l*. 14*s*. 10*d*.

Holyhead, or Caer Guby, in the isle of Anglesea, a college of prebendaries, valued at 24*l*.

Kimmer, in Merionethshire, a Cistercian abbey, valued at 58*l*. 15*s*. 4*d*.

Kydwelly, in Caermarthenshire, a priory of Benedictines, valued at 29*l*. 10*s*.

Lancadane, in Ditto, a college church, consisting of a præceptor and 21 canons.

Llandaff, in Glamorganshire, a cathedral church.

Llandewibrevy, in Cardiganshire, a college of a dean and twelve prebendaries.

Llangenith, in Glamorganshire, an alien priory, given to All Souls college, in Oxon.

Llanlier, or Llanclere, in Cardiganshire, a Cistercian nunnery, valued at 57*l*. 5*s*. 4*d*.

Llan Lugan, in Montgomeryshire, a nunnery, valued at 22*l*. 14*s*. 8*d*.

Llanrustyt, in Cardiganshire, a nunnery.

Llansanfride, in ditto, a nunnery.

Margan, in Glamorganshire, a Benedictine priory, valued at 188*l*. 14*s*.

Mounton, in the suburbs of Pembroke, in Pembrokeshire, a priory of black monks.

Neath, in Glamorganshire, a Cistercian abbey, valued at 150*l*. 4*s*. 6*d*.

Pulla, or Pilla, in Pembrokeshire, an alien priory, valued at 52l. 2s. 5d.

Ruthin, in Denbighshire, a cell of Bonhommes.

Siriolis, in Caernarvonshire, a priory, valued at 47l. 14s. 3d.

Stratflour, in Cardiganshire, a Cistercian abbey, valued at 122l. 6s. 8d.

Stratmargel, in Montgomeryshire, a Cistercian abbey, valued at 73l. 7s. 3d.

De Valle Crucis, in Denbighshire, a Cistercian abbey, valued at 214l. 3s. 5d.

Wrexham, in ditto, a collegiate church.

Prior to concluding these particulars, it may not be improper to give some account of Monastic Orders and Distinctions, the names of which are of so frequent occurrence in the Appendix, and other portions of the work.

Wherever a society of religious persons existed, whether male or female, and were under the direction of an Abbot or Abbess, the building in which such society resided was called an *Abbey*.

When the chief person in the Monastery bore the title of Prior, it was called a *Priory*.— When the Priory belonged to some Convent abroad, it was called an *Alien Priory*.

When the society of religious persons consisted of Males, it was called a *Monastery*; when of females, a *Nunnery*.

When any Monastery or Nunnery was subject to another it was called a *Cell*.

When a certain number of secular canons were governed by a Warden, Dean, Provost, or Master, they were called a *College*, and the Church *Collegiate*; as the Old Church at Manchester, and some others remain to this day.

Chantries were a sort of Chapels, erected and endowed for the purpose of singing Masses for the Souls of the deceased.

Societies of men living together as monks, but belonging to no particular society or order, were called *Guilds*.

Preceptories were a kind of Religious Schools.

CHARLES HULBERT.

Providence Grove,
January, 1836.

A General ACCOUNT of the Dissolution of MONASTERIES, &c.

By Statutes of Henry VIII,

As given by Mr. PHILLIPS, in conclusion of his History of Shrewsbury, 1778.

IN the 27th year of Henry VIII. 370 of the lesser Monasteries under £200 per annum, were dissolved, and the revenues thereof given by the Parliament to the King. The annual rents of these were £32,000, the moveable goods £1000, and 1000 religious persons were put out of them.

In the 31st year of the same King, 645 of the greater Abbies suffered the same fate; he quarrelling with the Pope, Clement VII. for not divorcing him from Queen Catherine of Arragon.

In the 37th year of the same King, 90 Colleges, 110 Hospitals, and 2374 Chantries and free Chapels were granted to free the King's necessities, besides the houses, lands, and goods of the Knights of St. John of Jerusalem.

On the 28th April, 1539, the Parliament confirmed these acts of the King and their own, divided the wealth and revenues among the most active nobility and gentry in the suppression of them, and in this year they pulled down and destroyed most of the buildings of the aforesaid Abbies, &c. lest any domestic stirs or alterations should arise, or the kingdom be invaded by the French King, or Emperor of Germany, who then threatened it, as these levellers politically pretended. The yearly value of all which were £16,110, besides plate, cattle, corn, lead, bells, &c.

It may be said in favour of the suppressed religious houses, that while they stood, no act was ever passed for the relief of the poor, so amply did these houses succour those who were in want. And Sir William Dugdale says, upon their dissolution ensued a great decay of learning. Bale says, the loss of ancient historians was irreparable, for these Mansions contained some of the greatest libraries the English nation ever produced, and which were destroyed without consideration or esteem; two noble libraries being then purchased for only 40s. by a merchant, who took them over sea, though they were the more valuable as being all manuscripts.

In every Abbey there was a large room called the *Scriptorium*, wherein it was the business of several writers to transcribe books of all subjects for the use of the publick library of such Abbey, where they remained in manuscript, until William Caxton, of London, Mercer, brought the art of printing into England, in 1471. And Henry VIII. at the time of the dissolution appointed John Leland to search for, and save such books and records as were most valuable amongst them.

In the Danish wars many Abbies, Priories, &c. suffered much in their immunities and buildings, but when these were ended they were soon repaired again, inhabited, and continued so, till the above mentioned time of dissolution: The first estimates of their rents and riches were taken by Visitor Cromwell, and between the 31st and 37th of Henry VIII. they were gradually seized upon and divided as aforesaid, and many of them converted into Bishopricks, Deaneries, &c. This period of time was called the reformation. The Abbots of 645 Mitred Abbies were supreme, claiming episcopal power alone, and had seats in Parliament. They were stiled Barons, and were of the King's Council. The Priors of the lesser Convents, with the Monks, Sub-Priors, Secretaries, Treasurers, Cellerers, Porters, and other Officers, were all obedient to the Abbots, (except Canterbury and Coventry.) In each Abbey was a great Hall for the Monks to dine in. The Oriel for the infirm. The Locutory, or Parlour for the Monks to discourse in. The Dormitory, or Sleeping Place. The Laundry. The Library. A Church and Sanctuarium for criminals and debtors to fly to. A Gaol for incorrigible Monks. And an Oratory, or place for prayer.

Appendix.   B

The Abbot of St. Alban's, was first and principal Abbot; and the Prior of St. John's of Jerusalem, in Middlesex, first and chief Baron in England. Their foundations were rated at £2385 19s. 8d. per annum.

In 1200, Pope Innocent the Third enjoined, that every man should pay general parochial tythes throughout England, and set up Ecclesiastical Courts to recover them; before this, every man paid them to what Abbey or Monastery he pleased. The Monasteries had also many rich Rectories appropriated to them, till Henry VIII. sold them to lay persons, who have retained them ever since. They had, not only above the third part of the Vicarages and best impropriations, but had likewise got most of the best lands in England into their possession, it is said seven tenths of it. The yearly reserved rents, herriots, deodands, renewals, &c. of all the Monastic Houses and Church Tenures in England, before the Dissolution, amounted to about £13,655,345 4s. 7d. per annum, which the Monks had upon lives; and the demense lands which they were lords of, came to about £14,101,558 11s. 2d. per annum.

Whoever fled to these Monasteries and Churches, and registered themselves therein for sanctuary men, they were afterwards secure, and none could touch them, even for murder.

The degrees of church officers, or ecclesiastical persons in Monasteries were divided into three orders.

First Order.—Pope, Patriarch, Primate, Arch Primate, Bishop, Arch Presbyter, Arch Deacon, Provost, Dean, Sub-Dean, Precentor, Succentor, Treasurer, Organist, and Choristers.

Second Order.—Deacon, Sub-Deacon, and Priest.

Third Order.—Door-Keeper, Readers, Taper-Bearers.

Their habits were the same as the Canons of the Reformed Church, a black gown and surplice to the feet, wide sleeves, and ruff bands about their necks, and had their distinct maintenance in prebendaries, vicarages, &c. as those in collegiate churches now have. Every Abbot of each Monastery, kept a Monastery Register (which they called a Ledger Book) of all the material things belonging to the estate of their Abbey, and likewise another transcript, or true copy of the same, and deposited it in the hands of some neighbour Abbot, thereby to prevent fraudulent dealing in erasing, or altering it, or the loss of it, by fire, or other accidents. As thus, the Ledger Book of Lilleshul Abbey, was kept in Haughmon Abbey, as well as at Lilleshul.

An exact CATALOGUE of the RELIGIOUS HOUSES, in SHROPSHIRE, as delivered to King Henry VIII. in the 26th year of his reign, with the yearly Value of each of them, certain persons having been sent to take an Account thereof; this Account was afterwards inserted in the Book of First-Fruits and Tenths. Taken from an ancient manuscript in the Cotton Library.

	£	s.	d.
St. Cedde Coll. Church,	14	14	4
Shrewsbury. { St. Mary Collegiate,	13	1	8
Benedictine Abbey,	132	4	10
Haghmond Ab. Can. St. Aug.	259	13	7¼
Buyldewas Ab. Cist.	110	19	3¼
Brewood Ab.	17	10	8
Wombridge Pr. Can. St. Aug.	65	7	4
Battlefield College,	54	1	10
Tong College,	22	8	1
Lylleshul Ab. Can. St. Aug.	229	3	1¼
Bridgnorth Hospital,	4	0	0
Ludlow St. John's Hospital,	17	3	3
Wygmore Ab. Can. St. Aug.	267	2	10¼
Halysewen Ab. Prem.	280	13	2¼
Wenlock Pr. Cluniac,	401	0	7¼
	£1889	4	8¼

Bromfield Benedict.
St. Mary, near Dublin, a Cell to Buyldewas Cist.

A Catalogue of the Religious Houses and Colleges in Shropshire.
BY JOHN SPEED.

Places.	Dedications.		Founders—Benefactors.	Order.	Value.		
					£	s.	d.
Shrewsbury.	St. Peter, St. Paul, St. Milb.	M.	Roger Earl of Montgomery, 1081, 16th of William the Conqueror.	Black Monks.	615	4	3¼
	St. Chad,	C.	———————		14	4	4
	St. Mary,	C.	———————		13	1	8
Shrewsbury.	St. August.	F.	—— Lord Stafford. —	Augustine Fryars.			
	St. Mary.	F.	—— De Jenneville. —	Carmelite Fryars.			
	St. Francis.	F.	Geffrey Lord Powis. —	Francisc. Fryars.			
	St. Dominic.	F.	—— De Charlton. —				
Alberbury given to All Souls Col. Oxf. by Hen. VI.	—Alien.	P.	The King's ancestors. —				
Battlefield.	St. Mary Mag.	C.	King Henry IV. —		54	1	1
Bildewas.	St· Mary.	M.	Roger Bishop of Chester.	Bernard Monks.	129	6	10
*Brewood.	———————	M.			31	1	4
Bridgnorth.	St. Francis.	F.	John Talbot, Earl of Shrewsbury, cousin and heir to Lord Strange.	Grey Fryars.	4	0	0
Brumfield.	———————	M.	———————	Black Monks.			
Chirbury.	———————	P.	———————		87	7	4
Hales Owen.	———————	M.	Peter De la Roche, Bishop of Winchester, in time of King John.—King John a benefactor.		337	15	6¼
Haughmond.	St. Mary. St. John Ev.	M.	William Fitz Allen.—Edm. Earl of Arundel, a benefactor. 18th Edward III.	Black Canons, (Lel.) alias White Canons.	294	12	9
Ludlow.	St. Mary.	F.	Sir Lawrence Ludlow, Knt. 1349, 24th Edward III.	White Fryars.			
	St. August.	F.	Edmund de Pontibusive.— Bridgman, a benefactor.	Augustine Fryars.			
	St. John.	H.	———————		17	3	0
Lyleshul.	———————	M.	—— De Beauveis.—Lord Zouch, a benefactor.	Black Canons.	327	10	0
*Stone.	St. Michael.	P.		Black Monks.			
Tonge.	St Barthol.	C.	Isabel, wife of Sir Fulk Pembridge, Knt.—Sir Richd. Vernon, Knt. repair'd it.		22	8	1
Wenlock.	St. Milburgh.	P.	Leofrick Earl of Mercia, per Holin. Roger E. of Mont. and Salop, 108, 16th of Will. Conq. per Fabian.	Black Monks.	434	0	1
Wombridge.	———————	P.			72	15	8
*Wigmore.	———————	M.	Hugo de Mortuamary, 1172.	Black Canons.	302	12	3¼
					£2757	14	6¼

Note.—M. Monastery.   P. Priory.   F. Friary.   C. College.   H. Hospital.

* Brewood, Stone, and Wigmore are not within the County of Salop, as supposed by Speed; the two former are in Staffordshire and the latter in Herefordshire.—C. H.

MONASTERIES of the annual value of £200, or upwards, in Shropshire.

Dissolved by Stat. 31st Henry VIII. and by that means capable of being discharged of tythes.

			£	s.	d.
Haughmond Abbey.	Canons of St. Austin.	Anno 1100	259	13	7
Lilleshul Abbey.	Canons of St. Austin.	Per A. d'Elfleda R. Merc.	229	3	1
Wigmore Abbey.	Canons of St. Austin.	Anno 1172, per Speed,	267	2	10
Wenlock Priory.	Cluniacs.	Anno 1181.	401	0	7
Salop Abbey.	Canons of St. Austin.	Anno 1081, per Speed	615	4	3
Halesowen Abbey.	Præmonstratensis.	T. K. John.	537	15	6

All religious Monks, or Canons, were obliged to join themselves either to the order of St. Bennet, St. Basil, or St. Austin; these were the principal orders. Some, instead of St. Basil, who wrote his rule for Monks, anno 350, reckon St. Francis.

The Benedictines, were of the order of St. Bennet, who wrote his rule at Mount Cassin, about the year 651, which was approved of by the whole Church.—Of this order have been four Emperors, twelve Empresses, forty-six Kings, and fifty-one Queens.

The Cluniacs, are a reform of St. Bennet's order, the first institutor of which was Abbot Berno, to whom William, then Duke of Aquitain, gave the place called Clugny, in Burgundy, for their first habitation, anno 890.

HAGHMON ABBEY.—*No.* 1.

NEAR Shrewsbury; a Monastery of the Order of St. Augustine. Was founded in the year 1100, being the last of King William Rufus, by William Fitz Allen, as appears by Bulls of Pope Alexander III. and he conferred on it the land on which it stood, with all its appurtenances.

All grants made to these Canons are recited and confirmed in the charter of the 13th of King Edward II. William Zouch also, by deed confirmed to them the grant of the mill of Rocheford, made by his ancestors.

King Henry II. at the request of Alured, Abbot of St. John's of Haghmon, granted to William Fitz Allen, or his heirs, for ever, the keeping of the said Abbey, and all its possessions, in times of vacation; so that neither the said Henry, nor any of his successors, Kings of England, should ever intermeddle in the affairs of the said Abbey, upon the death of any Abbot.

Ralph the Abbot, and the Monks of Haghmon, in the 3rd year of the reign of Henry V. at the request of the most excellent, and most reverend Lord Thomas, Earl of Arundel and Surrey, granted to Robert Lee of Uffington. a corrody for life, to be a 'Squire to the Abbot, with one servant and two horses, taking sufficient meat and drink for himself, like others the said Abbot's 'Squires, and for his servant as the servants of the Abbot and his 'Squires have, and to take hay and corn for his horses, like the Abbot's other 'Squires, whensoever the said Robert shall be in the Monastery, and that he have the habit of the said 'Squires, of as many ells, and such like cloth, when the Abbot shall give the same to the other Esquires.

King Henry VI. granted license to Thomas Holden, Esq. and his wife Elizabeth, to give a messuage and garden in the parish of St. Peter, near North-gate, in Oxford, to the Prior of the church of the Holy Trinity in the city of London, and the convent there, for them, there to erect a College, for the entertainment of the students of the order of St. Augustine; and the said Prior and Convent, obliged themselves to the Abbot of Haghmon, and his Monastery, under the forfeiture of forty pounds, if ever the said messuage and garden, or any part thereof was alienated, or put to any other use, than that of the said College, to remain there for ever.

It was found by inquisition, anno 37th of King Henry II. that upon the death or resignation of the Abbot of Haghmon, the predecessors of John Fitz Allan, used to have the keeping of that Abbey, and that the Prior, religious men, were wont to ask leave of them to proceed to an election, and that the King never had the same.

Richard, Bishop of Coventry, authorised this Monastery to appoint a Sacrist under the Abbot, who might baptize as well Jews as infants in the said Monastery, and exercise parochial jurisdiction upon their friends and servants.

Nicholas, Abbot of this Monastery, ordered a new kitchen to be built, assigning certain revenues for defraying the expence of fish and flesh, and twenty hogs to be kept for bacon, with several other regulations not material in this place.

Richard Burnell, another Abbot, prescribed several rules for the Prior and Sub-Prior of the said Monastery, as their walking in processions, sitting in the choir, saying mass, receiving of revenues, and other particulars of no great curiosity.

Pope Alexander III. in the year 1172, granted to this Abbot many privileges. (1.) That the order of St. Augustine should continue there for ever. (2.) That they should enjoy all the possessions, as also all immunities granted them. (3.) That they should not pay tithes. (4.) That they might bury such as desired it. (5.) That none should receive or entertain any that had professed among them, without their leave. (6.) That none should disturb them with unjust exactions. (7.) That no one should be made Abbot, but by election, by the religious men. (8.) That none should presume to invade any of their possessions; excommunicating any that should infringe any of the said liberties. (9.) That they might relieve and entertain any persons designing to quit the world. (10.) That they might present Priests to the Bishop, for any of the churches belonging to them. (11.) That when there should happen to be a general interdict, that they might perform the divine office in a low voice, and their doors shut. (12.) That their church and all belonging to it, should be under the immediate protection of the Pope. (13.) That they should not pay tithes for their mills and meadows. (14.) That they might receive the right of patronage of any churches which should be offered them. (15.) That none should build any church or oratory within their parishes without the Bishop's consent, or theirs. (16.) That none should presume to set fire, commit rapine, or take, or kill a man within their lands. (17.) That none should exact any thing of them for the blessing or enthroning of their Abbot.*

All this was confirmed by Pope Honorius III. Pope Nicholas III. Pope Boniface IX. and Pope Martin IV.

Leland says,† "there was an hermitage and a chapel on this spot before the Abbey was "built. William Fitz Allen and his wife, with Robert Fitz Allen, and others, are there buried, "also Richard Fitz Allen, a child, who fell out of his nurses arms from the battlements of "Shrawardig Castle."

Its yearly revenues at the dissolution were £259 13s. 7½d. as per Dugdale, £294 12s. 9d. as per Speed. This abbey is registered as in the custody of one William Barker, in the year 1653, who with his family (it is said) are buried under an old tomb stone in the vestry of St. Mary's Church, Shrewsbury. The ruins are fine and picturesque.

BATTLEFIELD CHURCH.—*No.* 2.

A Collegiate Church of secular Canons, three miles north of Shrewsbury. King Henry IV. in the 4th year of his reign, 1403, gave and granted to Roger Yoe, of Leaton, Rector of the Chapel of St. John Baptist at Adbrighton Husee, in the county of Salop, a piece of ground with all the buildings in it, within the lordship of Adbrighton Husee, near Shrewsbury, in the field called Battlefield, where a battle had been lately fought between the said King, and Henry Piercy, whose adherents he calls rebels; which piece of ground was ditched in, and contained in length and breadth two acres of land, together with two inlets and outlets, along the lands of Richard Husee, one twenty feet wide, and the other fifteen feet wide. This piece of ground had been before granted to the aforesaid Roger, by the said Richard Husee (who held the same of the King), for him to build thereon a chapel, in honour of St. Mary Magdalen; of which the said Roger, and his successors, were for ever to be called Masters, and for five other Chaplains to

* Monasticon.   † Itinerary, vol. VIII. p. 129.

Appendix.   C

pray for the King, benefactors, &c. The King therefore granted that the said chapel, built as aforesaid, should be a chantry of six Chaplains, and that the chapel of St. John Baptist, should for ever be annexed to it, and that Richard Husee, and his heirs aforesaid, should be perpetual patrons of the same, as also that the said Roger, and his successors, might appropriate to themselves the parish church of St. Michael Eskirke, in Lancashire, and the parish church of St. Andrew, at Idesale, with the free Royal Chapel of St. Michael, in the Castle of Shrewsbury, and that of St. Juliana in the said town. The said Master and Chaplains to be for ever exempt from tenths, fifteenths, subsidies, tallages, contributions, or any other impositions from the Crown, and they to have a fair there yearly at the festival of St. Mary Magdalen.

The aforesaid founder, Roger Yoe, by his last will and testament, dated 1444, ordered his body to be buried near the high altar of this Church; he gave and bequeathed to the five Chaplains in his college, 3 silver gilt chalices, one paxbrede of silver, gilt, 2 silver cruets, 3 brass bells, hanging in the belfrey, 2 cases, after the manner of Sarum, otherwise called lyggers, 3 gilt copper crosses, 2 new missals, 2 new graduals, 3 old missals, covered with red leather, 1 old case, 1 processional, 1 executor of the office, 1 book of collects, 4 placebo, and dirage, 1 pair of vestments of red velvet, 1 red velvet cope, with 2 velvet dalmaticks, 1 pair of vestments of white silk, 1 white silk cope, with 2 dalmaticks, 4 pair of other vestments, and a yearly manual.

ITEM. He left and bequeathed to them, a Mansion for themselves, with proper Offices, and the following Utensils, viz. A long table, with 2 benches, 3 towels, a bason and ewer; 3 brass pots in the kitchen, 2 spits, and 2 iron racks, 1 cupboard, a jack, with iron wheels and weights to turn the meat, a laton chafer, 20 pewter dishes and plates, &c.

ITEM. All the profits and emoluments of the parish church of St. Michael, at Wyre, in the diocese of York, and they to repair the chancel of the said church of Idesale, the chapel of Dadale, and the town of Aston, with the Grange of Astone; and the profits of the church of St. Juliana, in Shrewsbury.

ITEM. That the alms gathered on pretence of indulgences, and the offerings, be spent in building the belfrey, and when that is finished, in maintaining the poor in the said College, and repairs of their house.

ITEM. That the five Chaplains of the College live in community, and none of them be absent by day, or by night, without the master's leave, under forfeiture of three shillings for every offence, and each of them at his admittance, to swear obedience to the said master.

Every Chaplain to have for his allowance ten marks yearly, besides four-pence a week for their good performance of the divine office, as here particularly enjoyned.

All remaining over and above this, to go to the works of the College, and the maintenance of the poor belonging to it, &c. as in others.* The chancel is used for Divine Worship.

BILDEWAS ABBEY.—*No. 3.*

OR Buldewas Abbey, lies about two miles south-east of the foot of the Wrekin, and close to the River Severn, over which there is a bridge, said by the inhabitants to have belonged to, or to have been built for, the convenience of this abbey, but its appearance does not bespeak that of antiquity.

This abbey was founded in the year 1135, by Roger, Bishop of Chester, (which Tanner says was the same with that now called Litchfield and Coventry) for monks of the order of Savigny, united afterwards to the Cistercians. It was dedicated to St. Mary and St. Chad. The foundation was confirmed by King Stephen, in the year 1139. It had afterwards many noble benefactions, and donations, several of them were confirmed by charter of King Richard I. anno 1189, being the first year of his reign; and Henry II. by his charter to Randolph, Abbot of this place, subjected St. Mary's, Dublin, to the government of the Abbots of Bildewas.

Leland, in his Itinerary, says, " Matilda de Bohun, wife to Sir Robert Burnel, was founder " of Bildewas Abbey, though some, for only the gift of the scite of the house, take the Byshope " of Chester, for founder." Camden, seems likewise of the same opinion, as he mentions Bildewas,

* Monasticon.

as the burial place of the family of the Burnels, patrons thereof, but among all the charters of the Monasticon, there is no mention of this Matilda, or Sir Robert, but the foundation is in two or three places expressly ascribed to Roger, Bishop of Chester.

About the time of the suppression, here were twelve Monks, who were endowed with one hundred and ten pounds, nineteen shillings, and three-pence per annum, according to Dugdale; but Speed estimates the value at £129 6s. 10d. The scite, with all the lands belonging to this Monastery in Shropshire, Staffordshire, and Derbyshire, were granted to Lord Powis, in the 29th year of the reign of Henry VIII.

Great part of the walls of the church are now standing, which shew it was once a magnificent building : the arches of the aisles, are supported by columns of a remarkable thickness.*

BRIDGNORTH CASTLE.—*No.* 4.

BURGH, Brugge, or Bridgnorth, was built by Queen Ethelfleda, in the time of the Saxon Heptarchy ; it consists of an Upper and a Lower Town, which are divided by the River Severn, over which there is a stone bridge with a gate-house.

The Castle stands on the south end of a lofty rock, which forms the Upper Town. When or by whom built, is not certain. It is mentioned as early as the 3rd of Henry I. anno 1102; when, according to Stowe and others, both that, and the town, were strengthened by Robert de Belesme, Earl of Shrewsbury, eldest son of Roger de Montgomery, and held against the King, who after a short resistance made himself master of it, and permitted Belesme to retire to Normandy, but seized his estates here. Robert finished within the walls of the Castle, a chapel, which was afterwards made a collegiate church for a Dean and six Prebendaries, and dedicated to St. Mary Magdalen. This chapel, Tanner says, was begun by his father, and till the general Dissolution, was accounted a royal free chapel. The 21st Elizabeth, it was granted to Sir Christopher Hatton.

In the seige above-mentioned, Sir Ralph de Pitchford, one of the King's commanders, behaved himself so gallantly, that Henry granted him an estate in the neighbourhood, called The Little Brugge, to hold by the service of finding dry wood for the King's great chamber in the Castle, as often as he should come there.

This Town and Castle being thus in the possession of the Crown, it continued there for some time. But in the reign of Henry II. anno 1165, was held by Hugh de Mortimer, against that Monarch, who beseiging it in person, gave occasion to one of the most romantic acts of loyalty ever recorded : Hubert de St. Clare, constable of Colchester Castle, seeing one of the enemy taking aim at his Sovereign, stepped before him and received the arrow in his own breast, thereby saving the King's life at the expence of his own. He died justly lamented by his Royal Master, who took his only daughter into his immediate protection, and when of a proper age, provided very advantageously for her in marriage.

Nothing more occurs concerning this fortress, till the 18th of King John, when it was entrusted to the keeping of Philip D'Aubigney.

In the 10th Henry III. Henry de Alditheley, or Audley, was constable ; and it appears from Maddox's History of the Exchequer, that in the 40th year of the same King, it was committed to Hugh de Akor, together with the castles of Shrewsbury, and counties of Salop and Stafford, during the King's pleasure. Hugh was to render £126 yearly, for the *proficiium* of the counties, and was to keep the said castles at his own cost.

In the 10th Richard II. Hugh Lord Badlesmere, was constituted governor of this castle, and had certain lands in the town ; but the manors remained in the Crown, till John Sutton, Lord Dudley, in the 1st Richard III. obtained a grant of it, for himself and heirs male. The succession, it is said, did not long continue in this family : His son being a weak and extravagant man, was tricked out of the estate by usurers.

In the last civil wars, a garrison being placed here by the King, who marched here from Shrewsbury to meet the Parliament army, an engagement happened near St. Leonard's church, wherein the Royalists were defeated, the castle totally demolished, and the collegiate church so injured, that it was taken down and rebuilt.

* Grose's Antiquities.

The following Account of this Castle, is given by LELAND, in his Itinerary.

" The Castle standeth on the South part of the Towne, and is fortified by East, with the
" profound valley instead of a Ditch : the Walls of it be of great height, there were two or
" three strong wards in the Castle that now go totally to ruine. I count the Castle to be more
" in compasse than the third part of the Towne.
" There is one mighty Gate by North in it now stopped up, and a little posterne made of
" force thereby through the Wall to enter into the Castle. The Castle Ground, and especially
" the base Court, hath now many dwelling Houses of tymbre in it, newly erected.
" There is a college Church of St. Mary Magdalen, of a Deane, and six Prebendaries,
" within the Castle ; the Church itself now a rude thing. It was first made by Robert de
" Belasmo, for a Chappell only for the Castle, and he endowed it with landes, and afore that
" this Chappell was established in the Castle, there was a like foundation made at Qualeford,
" a Chappell of St. Mary Magdalen, by Robert de Belesmo, Earl of Scrobbesbury, at the desyre
" of his wyfe, that made vow thereof in the tempest of the Sea."
At present there is nothing left standing, but what seems to have been a part of the tower,
which by undermining was made to incline so much, that it appears to threaten destruction to
such as approach it. It makes nearly an angle of 73 degrees with the horizon, or 17 from the
perpendicular.*

LUDLOW CASTLE.—*No.* 5.

WAS built by Roger de Montgomery, soon after the Conquest, all the country here-
abouts having been given him by the Conqueror. Its walls by some are said to have formerly
been a mile in compass, but Leland in this measure includes those of the town.
The Castle was seized by Henry I. its owner, Robert de Belesme, son of Roger de Montgomery, having joined the part of Robert de Courthose, against the King. It remained in
possession of the Crown at the accession of King Stephen, but was nevertheless; garrisoned and
held out against him by Gervase Pagnal, during the contest with the Empress Maud. Stephen
besieged, and as some write took it, anno 1139, but others assert he was obliged to raise the
seige. In one of the attacks Prince Henry, son of David, King of Scots, newly created Earl
of Northumberland, rashly approaching too near the walls, was snatched from his horse by
a kind of grappling iron, perhaps something similar to the Corvus, one of the machines
invented by Archimedes, for the defence of Syracuse, and mentioned by Tacitus, as used by the
Romans against Civilis. From this danger Henry was delivered by the King, who himself
with great risque and difficulty, disengaged him.
It remained in the Crown, till the succeeding reign, when Henry II. bestowed it on Fulk
Fitz Warine, called de Dinan, together with the vale below it, which lies in the banks of the
River Corve, called Corve-Dale. It was again in the Crown, in the 8th of King John, who
granted it to Philip de Albani, from whose family it came to the Lacies, of Ireland, the last of
that house, Walter de Lacy, dying without issue male, left the Castle to his grand-daughter
Maud, the daughter of his deceased son Edward, and wife of Peter de Geneva, or Jeneville,
a Poictevan, and as some say, of the house of the Duke of Lorrain ; from whose posterity it
again descended by a daughter to the Mortimers, from whom it passed hereditarily to the
Crown. But one moiety of the manor of Ludlow, upon the division of the estate of Walter
de Lacy, fell to Margery, another daughter to the before named Edward, who married John
de Verdon ; by whose daughter Isabel, it passed by marriage to William de Ferrers, of Okham.
During the troubles between Henry II. and his Barons, anno 1264, this Castle was taken by
Simon Montford, Earl of Leicester.
In the 30th year of King Henry VI. 1451, it belonged to Richard, Duke of York, who there
drew up the declaration of his allegiance to the King, pretending the army of 10,000 men he
had assembled in the Marches of Wales, " was for the public wealth of the realme." This
declaration, Stowe says, he subscribed as follows : " In witness whereof I have signed this

* Grose's Antiquities.

9

" Schedule, with my sign manuall, and set thereunto my signet of arms, written in my Castle
" of Ludlow, the 9th of January, the 30th yeere of the raigne of my Sowveraigne Lord
" Henry the sixt." Another apology, much to the same effect, was likewise dated from this
Castle by the same Duke, eight years afterwards, when Lord Audley had been defeated at
Blore Heath in Staffordshire, by the Earl of Salisbury, and Andrew Trollop, and John Blunt
had withdrawn from his party. Notwithstanding which he, with divers others, were attainted
of treason, at a Parliament then held at Coventry, where (says the last recited authority) " their
" goods and possessions were escheated, and their heirs (were) disinherited unto the ninth de-
" gree, their tenants spoiled of their goods, bemaimed and slain, the towne of Ludlowe, belong-
" ing to the Duke of Yorke, was robbed to its bare walls, and Dutchess of Yorke spoiled of
" her goods." Hall says the Castle was likewise spoiled, and that the King sent the Dutchess
of Yorke with her two younger sons " to be kept in Ward with the Dutchess of Buckynham,
" her suster, where she continued a certain space."

It came again to the crown in the reign of Edward IV. whose eldest son, Edward, for a
while held his court here, under the tuition of Lord Anthony Woodvile, and the Lord Scales,
being sent by his father, as Hall says, " for Justice to be doen in the Marshes of Wales, to
" the ende that by the authoritie of hys presence, the wilde Welshemenne, and evil disposed
" personnes should refrain from their accustomed murthers and outrages." It was here the two
sons of Edward IV. resided. when their uncle Richard III. sent for them to London.

In the reign of Henry VII. this Castle was inhabited by Prince Arthur, that King's eldest
son, who died here, anno 1502, aged only sixteen years. His bowels are buried in the church
of this town, and it is said his heart, contained in a leaden box, was taken up some time ago.
The particulars of his funeral are printed in the last edition of Leland's Collectanea, where
a very remarkable circumstance occurs : "All things thus finished, (says this account) there was
" ordeyned a great dinner ; and in the morne a proclamation was made openly in the citie,
" that if any man could shew any victuals unpaid in that country, that had been taken by any
" of that noble Prince's servants, before that daye, they should come and shewe it to the late
" Steward. Comptroller, and Cofferer, and they should be contented." This proclamation does
great honour to Henry VII. especially considering the avaricious temper ascribed to him.

From the reign of Henry VIII. when the Court of the Marches of Wales was instituted, it
seems to have remained in the Crown, the Court being held in the Castle, and the Lord President of the Marches residing here.

It was in repair in the reign of Charles I. and inhabited anno 1634, by the Earl of Bridgwater, at that time Lord President; when Milton's Masque of Comus was represented, the
principal parts being performed by his Lordship's son and daughter; in which Masque the
Castle was represented in one of the scenes.

During the civil war of that reign, Ludlow was, for a while, kept as a garrison for the
King, but on the 9th of June 1646, was delivered up to the Parliament.

At present (1778) it belongs to the Crown, and a sort of Governor is appointed to it,
but the buildings are suffered to fall to ruin.

A very just and accurate account of this Castle is given in the Tour through Great Britain,
in these words, " The Castle of Ludlow shews plainly in its decay, what it was once in its
" flourishing estate. It is the Palace of the Prince of Wales, in right of his Principality ;
" its situation is indeed most beautiful ; there is a most spacious plain, or lawn in its front,
" which formerly continued near two miles, but much of it is now enclosed ; the country
" round it is exceeding pleasant, fertile, and populous, and the soil rich, nothing can be added
" to it by nature to make it a place fit for a Royal Palace. It is built in the north-west
" angle of the town, upon a rock, commanding a delightful prospect northward, and on the
" west is shaded by a hill, and washed by the river. The battlements are of great height
" and thickness, with towers at convenient distances; the half which is within the walls of
" the town, is secured with a deep ditch, the other is founded on a solid rock. A chapel here
" has abundance of coats of arms on the pannels, as has the hall, together with lances, spears,
" firelocks, and old armour.

" This noble Castle is in the very perfection of decay.—All the fine courts, the royal
" apartments, halls, and rooms of state, lie open and abandoned, and some of them falling
" down, for since the Courts of the Presidents of the Marches are taken away, here is nothing

Appendix.   D

" that requires the attendance of any public persons, so that time, the great devourer of the
" works of men, begins to eat into the stone walls, and spread the face of ruin upon the whole
" fabric. Over several of the stable doors are the arms of Queen Elizabeth, the Earls of
" Pembroke, &c. The sword of state, carried before the Prince of Wales, was remaining
" there till very lately.

" The town of Ludlow, was called by the Welsh, Dinian & Lhystwasoe, _i. e._ The Prince's
" Palace, probably from the Castle. It stands at the confluence of the Temd and Corve, and
" had a wall and towers, seven gates, and a handsome church, with curious painted glass, it
" is a Corporation, governed by Bailiffs and Burgesses, sends two members to Parliament, and
" has a market on Monday. Its chief note was from its being the place where the Court for
" the Marches of Wales was kept, first instituted by Henry VIII. for the convenience of the
" Welsh and neighbouring inhabitants. It consisted of a Lord President, several counsellors,
" a secretary, an attorney, solicitor, and four justices of the counties of Wales, and was held
" in the Castle, but this Court becoming a great grievance to the subject, was dissolved by an
" Act of Parliament, passed in the first year of King William and Queen Mary.*

WENLOCK MONASTERY.—_No._ 6.

THIS Monastery took its denomination from the town of Wenlock, near which it stands,
and which is situate about twelve miles south-east of Shrewsbury, and gives name to the
Hundred.

This House was, as it is said, founded about the year 680, by Milburga, daughter of King
Merwald, and niece to Wolphere, King of Mercia; she presided as Abbess over it, and at her
death was buried here. According to Matthew of Westminster, her grave was long after discovered by accident, when many miracles were performed. This Monastery was destroyed by
the Danes, but restored by Leofrick, Earl of Chester, in the time of Edward the Confessor; but
again falling to decay, and being forsaken, it was in the 14th of William the Conqueror rebuilt,
and endowed by Roger de Montgomery, Earl of Arundel, Chichester, and Shrewsbury, a person
of vast possessions in these parts.—So says William of Malmsbury; but both Brompton and
Leland, attribute its restoration to Warine, Earl of Shrewsbury.

This last re-founder, (whoever he was) placed therein a Prior and Convent of Cluniac
Monks,† who were looked upon as a Cell to the House de Caritate, in France, and suffered the
same fate with other Alien Priories, till the 18th of Richard II. when it was made indigenous,
or naturalized. In Rymer, this is called the Second House of the Order; but Prynne mentions
it as a Cell to the Abbey of Cluny. It was dedicated to St. Milburga, and in the 26th of Henry
VIII. had revenues to the yearly value of £401 0_s._ 7_d._ q. Clear, as Dugdale, and £434 1_s._ 2_d._
ob. in the whole. It was granted 36th of Henry VIII. to Augustino de Augustini. This
Monastery was at first called Wimnicas; but in after times, its legal stile was Wenlock Magna,
or Moche Wenlock.

In the Monasticon is the patent of King Edward III. reciting and confirming the charter of
Isabella de Say, Lady of Clun, whereby she granted these Monks the Chapel of St. George, at

* Grose's Antiquities.

---

† From Clugny in Burgundy, where a Monastery was founded in 910, governed by the rules of St. Benedict;
but in addition to his rules, the Monks adopted a more rigid discipline, and numbers were reformed in France
and England, and consequently denominated CLUNIAC MONKS.

Monks of the present day are of the same orders as formerly, viz. the Chartreux, Benedictines, Benardines,
&c. The Mendicants are those that beg, as the Capuchins and Franciscans, are more generally called Friars. Both
Monks and Friars are distinguished by the colour of their habits, into Black, White, Grey, &c. Anciently the
Monks were all laymen, and only distinguished from the people by their dress and greater devotion.

Nuns derived their name from Nonnus, an Egyptian term, or from the Saxon Nunne. The Sisterhood have
their peculiar dresses, one part of which is a kind of veil called _Sacrum Velamen_, another a kind of mitre or coronet
worn upon the head.—At the time of consecration, or taking the veil, the Nun receives a ring, by which she is
married to Christ, and crowned with the Crown of Virginity, after which an Anathema is denounced against all
who shall attempt to make her break her vows.—C. H.

Clun, with seven Chapels depending on it, namely, the Chapel of St. Thomas, at Clun, of St. Mary, at Waterdune, St. Swithin, at Clumbierie, St. Mary, at Clintune, St. Mary, at Appitune, with those of Eggedune and Subbledune. There is likewise an inquisition, taken the 29th Edward I. determining the right of presentations to the Cell of Ferne, to be in the Monks of Wenlock. In Stephen's Supplement, *vol. ii, page* 14, seven deeds are translated in English, from Latin originals, then in the hands of Francis Canning, Esq. of Foxcote, in the county of Warwick, *viz.* The deed of Goeffrey de Say, for the manor of Dointon, a confirmation of that deed, by Henry II. Another deed of the same King, granting that these Monks might always enjoy the said manor, unless he or his heirs gave them eleven pounds per annum in churches, or other things in lieu of it. The charter of Henry III. to them for the said manor, Anno Regni 46. *Page* 15, The deeds of William Mitleton, and Adam Fitz William, about a yard land in Middleton. A composition between Simon Dean, of Brug, and the Prior and Convent of Wenlock, about the chapel of Dudinton."

A LIST of the PRIORS of WENLOCK ABBEY, from Browne Willis's List of Abbies. *viz.*

Imbertus, about the year 1145	Henry, - - - - 1325	Thomas Sutbury, - - 1482
Peter de Leja, - - - 1176	Henry de Myons, - - 1363	Richard Wenlock, - - 1485
Joybertus, - - - - 1198	Roger Wyvel, - - - 1395	Richard Singar, - - -
Richard, - - - - 1221	John Stafford, - - - 1422	Rowland Gracewell, - 1521
Guycardes, - - - - 1265	William Brugge, - - 1437	John Cressage, surren-
Aymo de Montibus, - - 1270	Roger Barry, - - - 1437	dered with a pension
John de Tyeford, - - 1272	William Walwyn, - - 1462	of £80 per annum, in
John Tubbe, - - - 1277	John Stratton, - - - 1468	the year - - - - 1539
Henry de Bonville, - - 1291	John Shrewsbury, - - 1479	

Anno 1553, here remained in charge £7 13s. 4d. in fees, and £75 10s. 6d. in annuities and corrodies ; and these pensions, *viz·* To Richard Fennymore and William Benge, £6 each; William Morphew, John Leighe, Thomas Balle, and John Hopkins, £5 6s. 8d. each. The arms of this Monastery were Azure, 3 Gorbs Or, in pale a Croysier Argent.

This Monastery is situated in a small bottom, having the town on the west, and is surrounded on all sides, by gently ascending grounds. At the present it has no body of water near it, but from some neighbouring dams, it seems as if here had been formerly some ponds, or pools.— Indeed, all religious houses distant from the sea, must have had these conveniencies, in order to supply the Monks with fish, which made a very considerable part of their diet.

Of the buildings there now (1772) remain what is made a good dwelling house, with proper offices for a farm ; adjoining to this house, is a range of cloisters. The church was built in form of a cross, part of its walls are standing, those particularly of the southern, and of the transept, are pretty entire. At the extremity of it are seen the remains of a chapel, into which the entrance lies under three circular arches, adorned with undulating zigzags, the pillars are so far buried, that the architraves appear but just above the ground. On the inside of the walls are razed figures of pointed and circular arches, mutually intersecting ; the other broken and detached parts of the body of the church remain, and the bottom of the south aisle is converted into stabling.

About half a century ago, a considerable part of the ruins were taken down by an agent of the manor, to rebuild some houses, of which he had a lease; but the late Sir Watkin Williams Wynne, Bart. put a stop to any further demolition. The walls that encompassed the Monastery, and part of the gateway remain. Here are neither any remarkable monuments, nor inscriptions, neither have any such been digged up, although it is said, (I think by Leland) that the body of King Merwald, was found in a wall of the church.

The common people have an absurd tradition of a subterraneous communication between this house and Buildwas Abbey, which has not the least foundation in truth, the nature of the ground rendering such an attempt impracticable, but indeed there is scarce an old Monastery in England, but has some such story told of it, especially if it was a convent of Men, and had a Nunnery in its neighbourhood. These reports were probably invented and propagated in order to exaggerate the dissolute lives of the Monks and Nuns, and thereby to reconcile the multitude to the suppression of religious houses.

This Monastery and Manor, soon after the dissolution, came into the possession of Thomsa Lawley, Esq. who lived in the house; by a marriage with a Lawley, it devolved to Robert

Bertie, Esq. of the Ancaster family; and from him it passed into the family of Gage. Sir John Wynne, of Wynnstay, in the county of Denbigh, bought it off Lord Viscount Gage, and devised it with his other estates to his kinsman, the late Sir Watkin Williams Wynn, Bart. whose son of the same name is the present proprietor.*

Cause Castle.—*No.* 7.

NEAR Westbury. Caus or Caos was one of those twenty-four lordships, which Roger de Corbet held of Roger de Montgomery, and which Robert his brother, who held divers other lordships in this county of the same Earl, inherited after his brother Roger's death.

He left his whole estate to his son Robert, who 1st of John, obtained that King's charter for a market every week upon Wednesdays, at this his manor of Caus, where he had a Castle, but because his son Thomas took part with the rebellious barons at the latter end of King John's reign, it was seized into the King's hands, as it remained all the rest of that reign. But when King Henry III. came to the Crown, Thomas having made his peace, and doing his homage, had restitution of the Castle, but dying soon after, left it to his son and heir Thomas. In his time there was an inquisition made about the bounds of the Forest de Hayes, and it was found that this manor of Caus, with the appurtenances, Worthin, Horton, Minsterleigh, Yokehull, and Wentenour, were out of the bounds of it. He died the 2nd of King Edward I. being then seized of this manor of Caus, and the above-mentioned appurtenances, and left it to his son Peter, as he also did to his son of the same name, 8th of Edward II.—But Beatrix, the wife of this last Peter, having been jointly infeoffeed with him in the manor of Caus, and its appurtenances, held them all for life, and for want of heirs of their bodies, the whole passed by the marriage of Alice, the sister of the said Peter, to Robert de Stafford and his issue, but there happening a long interval between the death of the last Peter de Corbet, and the possession obtained by Ralph de Stafford, viz. about thirty years, it appears that Sir John de Leybourne was by some way entituled to them, for in the 7th of Edward III. he obtained a charter for free warren in all his demense lands, throughout his lordships of Caus, Worthin, &c. but died without issue, so they came to the right heirs.

This Robert de Stafford being thus intituled to this manor of Caus, with the appurtenances, which was held by Barony, by the service of five Knights' fees, his grandson Ralph came into possession of them about the 21st of Edward III. but not without opposition from the husband and heirs of the younger sisters of Alice, which controversy being soon ended, Ralph had the quiet possession of all, which he died seized of, 46th of Edward III. and left them to his son and heir Hugh de Stafford, from whom they all descended to his heirs in a lineal succession, down to the Reign of Charles I. when Henry Lord Stafford, leaving only one daughter and heir Mary, Sir William Howard, Knight of the Bath, marrying her, inherited her estate, and in her right and title was created Viscount Stafford by the said King.

Not far from Caus Castle, lies Newton, (a township within itself) where formerly there was a castle (called Brow Castle) surrounded by a deep moat; which was given by Peter Lord Corbet, Baron of Caus, to Sir Robert Corbet, Knt. the son of Robert Corbet his uncle, for his valour and service in war.

This township of Newton has been in the Corbets family ever since the Norman conquest, and is now the property of Mr. Vincent Corbet.

Ellesmere Castle.— *No.* 8.

THIS Castle stood on an artificial mount on a rising ground. At present no vestige of it is to be seen, the top of the mount being formed into a Bowling-green, from whence is an extensive prospect.

It is uncertain by whom built, but settled by King John, A. D. 1204, upon Lewellyn ap Jorweth, Prince of North Wales, when he made up the match between that Prince and his

* Grose's Antiquities.

natural daughter Joan, which he had by Agatha, the daughter of Robert Ferrers, Earl of Derby. Being thus placed in the Marches of North Wales, she had an opportunity of seeing and observing the treasonable motions and conspiracies the English and Welsh were carrying on against her father, which she carefully gave him secret intelligence of, and much prevented their ill effects. This Castle King John took out of the hands of Llewellyn, in the 10th year of his reign, A. D. 1209, he having turned his arms against the English. In the 4th of Henry III. Roger L'Estrange held this Castle for life, after him, 21st of the same King, Anno 1236, it was in the hands of John Le Strange, of Knockin, and was continued to his successors, as long as the heirs male of the Knockin family lasted; but it seems that afterwards the manor of this place was in the Crown; for Hamond Le Strange, a collateral branch of the same family, continuing steadily loyal, when Montfort Earl Leicester, with many other Barons, revolted from King Henry III. Anno 1267, the King to reward his fidelity, gave him this manor of Ellesmere, and Stretton, until he could otherwise bestow on him elsewhere lands of an hundred pounds a year. It is probable that was afterwards done, and the castle and manor of this place returned to the Crown, for it appears that Oliver de Ingham, who was a person of great note in his time, for many special services, was made Governor of the Castle here by King Edward in the year 1320. We observe nothing more in this place till we find Thomas Egerton, the great lawyer, created Baron Ellesmere. He was the natural son of Sir Richard Egerton, of Ridley in Cheshire, Knt. and having studied the law in Lincolns Inn, became so famous for his knowledge therein, that Queen Elizabeth, in the 23rd year of her reign, made him her Solicitor General, and afterwards in her 34th year, raised him to be her Attorney General, from which advancements he was soon after, for his merits, promoted by the same Queen to the Mastership of the Rolls, and the office of Keeper of the Great Seal, which he held till that Queen's death. King James I. found him in that office, and was so highly pleased with his gravity (for he was hardly ever seen so much as to smile) and wise management of his place, that in the 1st year of his reign, he raised him to the degree of a Baron of this realm, by the title of Lord Ellesmere, and then, or soon after made him Lord High Chancellor of England; and fourteen years after he was further dignified with the honour of Viscount Brackley, which he enjoyed but two years, and then died at York-house in the Strand, Anno 1617, 15th of James I. Etat 70. It is now (1778), together with great property about the town, in possession of the Duke of Bridgewater.

HALES-OWEN ABBEY.—No. 9.

HALES, or Hales-Owen, a Monastery of the Order of Præmonstratenses, was founded after this manner. The manor and adowson of the church of Hales, was given by King John, 1215, to Peter de Rupibus, Bishop of Winchester, for the erecting of a religious house upon it, which was accordingly performed by the Bishop, and the manor settled upon it. King Henry III. confirmed the whole; and Roger, Bishop of Coventry and Litchfield, in the year 1248, appropriated the church of Waleshale to this abbey, after the death of one Vincent, then Rector of that church, saving out of the same a vicarage of thirteen marks, to be assigned to a vicar, with all obventions.

In the year 1270, Godfrey, Bishop of Worcester, made a settlement between the Abbot of Hales, and the perpetual Vicar of the parish church there, viz. That the said Vicar shall have and receive from the Abbot ten marks yearly, an house, with out-houses, orchard, garden, and vesture of the church-yard; and that the canons should find another Priest (*Presbyterum secundarum*) to be under the Vicar, and to bear all ordinary and extraordinary charges.

Joan de Botetourt, widow of Thomas Botetourt, and one of the sisters and coheirs of John de Someri, Baron Dudley, gave the manor of Werveley, or Wely, in the county of Worcester, to the Canons of this house, to found certain chantries, and perform some alms-deeds, according to the tenure of an indenture made between her and the Abbot of this house. She died soon after; but her son and heir. John de Botetourt, as if he inherited her pious disposition as well as her estates, gave the advowsons of the churches of Clent and Rowley, with the chapels thereto belonging, unto the said Canons of Hales; John de Hampton also gave some lands to this house. Wolston, Bishop of Worcester, appropriated to this abbey the above-mentioned church or chapel of Rowley, reserving to the perpetual Vicar, who shall have the cure of souls there, a revenue of

Appendix.   E

ten pounds per ann. *viz.* a messuage and curtelage on the south side of the church-yard, with the tithes of calves and lambs, and all small tithes, (except of the lands belonging to the monastery) mortuaries, the herbage and trees of the church-yard, and all the allterage.

Sir Hugh Burnell, Governor of the Castle of Bridgnorth, and one of the favorites of King Richard II. by his testament, dated October 2, 1417, 5th of Henry V. bequeathed his body to be buried in the choir of this Abbey of Hales, under a fair tomb of alabaster (which he had before prepared) near the body of Joyce his wife, appointing his funeral to be honorably solemnized, his debts paid, his servants rewarded, &c. This monastery at the dissolution was valued at £280 13*s.* 2¼*d.* per ann. Dugdale. £337 15*s.* 6¼*d.* per ann. Speed ex Leland.

CLUN CASTLE.—No. 10.

WILLIAM FITZ-ALAN being in possession of the manor of Clun, built a castle on it, called Clun Castle, which probably took its name from the town, and not from the river, as Mr. Cambden thinks; for the town was built long before the castle. He inhabited the castle; for we observe that after his death, Guy L'Estrange, then Sheriff of Shropshire, accounted to the King for the profits of his land, and for money paid in wages to the servants of his castle of Clun.

Isabel survived this her second husband Fitz-alan, and for the health of his soul, in her pure widowhood, gave the Monks of Wenlock the church of St. George, at Clun, with all the chapels thereunto belonging.

William Fitz-alan, the son of the aforesaid William and Isabel, succeeded them upon this manor, and other their estates, which were very great; for in the 12th Hen. II. upon levying an aid for the marriage of the King's daughter, he certified his Knight's fees to be in number thirty-five and a half, whereof nineteen were *de Veteri feofmento,* and sixteen and a half *de novo.* He nobly entertained Baldwin, Archbishop of Canterbury, at his castle of Oswestry, in his journey into Wales, and was Sheriff of this shire eleven years. He obtained a charter for a fair at this town, died the 16th of John, and left this manor to his posterity, who long inherited it, but with some special distinctions from their other estates.

This family, after they became Earls of Arundel, were Lords Marchers, and much annoyed the Welshmen by their inroads.

Near Clun is a hill called Caer Caradock, on which are the remains of an ancient fortification, supposed to have been raised by the British Prince Caractacus, about the year 53. The occasion of which was, the Silures, or inhabitants of South Wales, could not be brought to bear the Romish yoke of subjection, and relying much upon the courage and bravery of their Prince Caractacus, maintained the opposition against them; Caractacus knowing his own strength was not a match for the enemy, by policy thought to supply that deficiency, and having advantage of the country, removed the war into the Ordovices, or North Wales, where numbers joined him, who either feared or disdained to hold peace with the Romans; Caractacus chose this place (Caer Caradock) to encamp upon, as being naturally defended, and where it appeared accessible, he stopt up the passage with heaps of stone; near the foot ran a river, to the ford of which he sent a troop of his best soldiers, to receive the enemy. Caractacus and the other leaders went about among the soldiers, animating them with all inducements, and endeavouring to remove all fear, Their resolution much distracted the Romans, especially the captains and leaders, who saw before them the river and the guard placed there, on both sides them high hills projecting a considerable way, and the fort strong and commodious for their enemy. Ostorius, the Roman general passed the ford with some difficulty, and leading his army up to the rampart, was met with such a shower of darts, that many were killed and wounded; yet at length having made a breach with their rams horns, they came afront the enemy, and had a close engagement; but the Britons having better courage than armour, (for they had neither helmet, nor coat of mail) were sorely gauled with the javelins and the two-handed swords, and thrown into such disorder, that they immediately fled; Caractacus's wife and daughter were taken prisoners, and he fled to Cartesmunda, Queen of the Brigantines, who treacherously delivered him up to Ostorius, and he carried him in chains to Rome.

When he was to appear before Cæsar, the Emperor's guard in arms, were placed in the field before the camp, before whom passed in order, first the vassals of Caractacus, who going forward bowed to the people as they passed, and seemed by their countenances to discover their calamity; after them were carried the caparisons, chains,. and.other spoils taken from the enemy; then Caractacus's wife, daughter, and brethren followed, and last of all himself; his body was mostly naked, and painted with figures of beasts, he wore a chain of iron about his neck, and another about his middle; the hair of his head hanging down, in curled locks, covered his back and shoulders, and the hair of his upper lip parting to both sides, lay upon his breast. He neither hung down his head as daunted, nor did he beg mercy, but with a confident spirit and bold countenance held on, till he came before the Imperial Seat, where making a stand, and for a while beholding Cæsar, at last he broke out in the following speech:—

"Had my moderation in prosperity been adequate to my family and fortune, then had I en-
"tered your city rather as a friend than as a captive, nor would you, Sir, have disdained an alli-
"ance with a Prince descended from illustrious ancestors, and the Chief of many nations. My
"present condition, to me is dishonourable, to you is glorious! I was master of horses, men,
"arms, and riches.. No wonder then I was unwilling to lose them: for though your ambition is
"universal, does it follow that all mankind are obliged to submit to the yoke? Had I been sooner
"betrayed, I had neither been distinguished by misfortune, nor you by glory. And had I fallen,
"oblivion had been the immediate consequence of my fate. But if you now save my life, I shall
"be an eternal monument of your clemency."

The Emperor generously granted the Hero his request, and he remained long after, in the highest esteem, at Rome. The remains of the camp shew it to have been a place of great strength, surrounded by a deep ditch; but it was not sufficient to oppose the regularity of the Roman discipline.

There are the remains of some other camps in the neighbourhood, which plainly appear to have been Roman works, and doubtless were thrown up by Ostorius, from which we are led to believe these ambitious adventurers did not find Briton so easy a conquest, as Tacitus, Suetonius, and some other writers would make us believe; but some allowance must be made for that flattery, which the learned at all times are ready to bestow on the great.

WHITTINGTON CASTLE.—*No. 11.*

WHITTINGTON, near Oswestry, was the Estate of William de Peverell, and descended from him to Pain Peverell, whose son William having only two daughters, and being a valiant Knight himself, resolved to marry his eldest daughter Mellet, to none but a Knight of great valor, and to that end appointed that some noble young men should meet at Peverell's Place, in the Peak of Derby, and he that performed best, should have his daughter Mellet, with the Castle of Whittington. When Guarine de Meez, or Mets, then Lord of Alberbury, a branch of the House of Lorraine, Sheriff of this Shire, and one of the chief Counsellors of Roger de Montgomery, Earl of Shrewsbury, heard it, he went there, and fighting with a son of the King of Scotland, and a Baron of Burgoine, vanquished them both; having a silver shield and a peacock for his crest. Whereupon, Mellet was given him by her father to wife, and he scated himself at Whittington. Residing here, he often engaged in the war with the Welsh (who under their Prince, Joreward, often made inroads into his territories), and at length worsted them. His posterity after this, enjoyed their patrimony quietly, for some successions, but Fulke, who lived in the reign of King Richard I. was forced to give a fine of 40 marks to the King for livery of the Castle here; but after the death of King Richard, Maurice the son of Roger, who had this Castle given him by the Prince of Wales, was made Warden of the Marches, by King John, and obtained a confirmation of it under the Great Seal, having sent a present to the King, then at Montgomery Castle.

Fulke and his brethren, being thus deprived of their inheritance, desired Justice of the King to restore it to them; but not prevailing, they quitted their fidelity, fled to Winchester, and afterward to Brittany. The King sent men twice to apprehend them, but they encountering them, were killed, which much incensed the King; but upon the death of Maurice, the Prince of Wales restored Whittington to him, which when King John had notice of, he privately sent to Llewellyn, then Prince of Wales, to fall upon him and his brethren by surprize, and cut off their heads. Hugh got information of it by Llewellyn's wife, and first fled into France, and then into Barbary, to save himself; but being weary of banishment, he returned into England, and at length, through the mediation of Ranulph, Earl of Chester, with some others of the nobility, and Hubert, Archbishop of Canterbury, he obtained restitution of his Castle of Whittington, (upon his giving two hundred marks, and two coursers, to the king) as his hereditary right; and the King gave command to the Sheriff of Shropshire to give him possession of it accordingly. This was that famous Fulk Fitzwarine, whose strange and various fortune in war was so much admired by our ancestors, and on whom the poets of that time bestowed such large encomiums. He was slain* at the battle of Lewis in Sussex, leaving Fulke, his son and heir, and a daughter named Eve, who was married to Llewellyn, Prince of Wales. She was his second wife.

This Fulke, having made proof of his age, 1st Edward I. 1272, obtained his inheritance, and attending the King in the expedition he made into Wales, merited so well by his service, that the King forgave him a debt of two hundred pounds, which he owed to the Exchequer, and granted him a charter for free warren in all his demesne lands in this place. He died in the reign of Edward II. His son was at that time engaged in divers expeditions into Gascoigne, Flanders, Scotland and France, where, because he abode some time, Eleanor his wife, was permitted to have livery of this manor of Whittington, till his return into England to perform his homage. Upon his coming back from France, Edmund Earl of Kent, (who was convicted of endeavouring to restore King Edward II. to his throne, giving out that he was alive,) charged him that he had promised him his assistance in so doing; whereupon the King seized upon this Castle of Whittington; but being satisfied the next year, that he was falsely accused, he was restored to the possession of it, and died seized of it and the manor, 23d Edward III. A. D. 1850.

His son and heir, Fulke, was but seven years old at his death, but arriving at full age, had livery of his lands, and became an active and warlike man; for he attended the Black Prince into Gascoigne, and Thomas, Earl of Warwick, into Flanders; and being one of the Barons Marchers, was with others, appointed to restrain the incursions of Llewellyn, Prince of Wales, but died that year, being the 47th of Edward III. and was then seized of this Castle and Lordship.

He left Fulke, his son and heir, who dying soon after he came to his inheritance, left it to his son Fulke, who being under age, the custody of this Castle was committed to James Alditheley till he came to age; which having attained, and livery of his lands, he soon after died, having bequeathed his body to be buried in the chancel of the church of Whittington, and ordered a tomb to be set upon his grave. He left Fulke his son and heir, then but three years old, who arrived at full age, and having no heirs, he gave all his lands and tenements to his sister Elizabeth, to be disposed of for the health of his, and his parents souls. She married Richard Haukford, Esq. who died in 1430, and left a daughter, who married to Sir William Bourchier, created on account of that marriage, Lord Fitz Warine. John, Earl of Bath, his descendant, exchanged this manor with Henry VIII. for other lands. Edward VI. gave it to Henry, Duke of Suffolk, and Mary, when the Duke was attainted, bestowed it on Henry, Earl of Arundel. The Earl mortgaged it to William Albany, and several other citizens of London. They released their title to Albany; and his heiress married Thomas Lloyd, of Aston, Esq.

This castle stands on a low ground, some parts of the towers, &c. yet remain.

KNOCKIN CASTLE—*No* 12.

KNOCKIN, or Cnuckin, in the hundred of Oswestry, the lordship of the family of the L'Estrange, or Extranei, who built the town, and fixed their seat there, taking from it the name of L'Estrange, of Knockin. Guy L'Estrange was the founder of this family, which hath flourished ever since King Henry the Second's reign, and spread into divers countries, being many of them eminent in their generations; for Guido Extraneus, or L'Estrange, was High-Sheriff fourteen years together, in the reign of King Henry II., and John Extraneus, was High-Sheriff, in the 2d of King Edward II., and another John Extraneus, of Erkelau, was Knight of the Shire, the 1st and 2d of the same King. Guy L'Estrange, Lord of Knockin, was succeeded by Ralph his son, who leaving no issue, this manor passed to John L'Strange, his father's younger brother, who obtained the King's Precept to the High-Sheriff of Shropshire,

* Dugdale says he was drowned in a river during the battle.

for aid to rebuild part of his Castle of Knockin, in 3d Henry III., which had been ruined by the civil wars, in the preceding reign of King John, and repair all the rest. This John was one of the Baron Marchers. His posterity, Lords of Knockin, enjoyed the Castle and Manor of this place, to the reign of King Edward IV. when John L'Estrange, Lord of Knockin, leaving no male issue, his estate passed with his sole daughter and heir Joan, by marriage, to George Stanley, son and heir apparent to Thomas Stanley, the first Earl of Derby. Thus the Knockin family ended; but divers collateral branches sprang up and settled in other places, in this and other counties, as at Alvethely, Ellesmere, Blackmere, Lutheham, and Hunstanton, in Norfolk; yet is the title of the Stranges of Knockin kept up in the Derby family, the eldest son being called Lord Strange. Of this family, in the last century, Hamon L'Estrange, and Sir Roger L'Estrange, were accounted men of wit, and much engaged in the political controversies of their times.

Mr. Gough, in his manuscript account of Middle, and its neighbourhood, (without date,) mentions the following affair, which happened in Knockin.

One Thomas Elkes, being guardian to his eldest brother's child, who was young, and stood in his way to a considerable estate; to remove the child, he hired a poor boy to entice him into a corn-field to get flowers. Elkes met the two children in the field, sent the poor boy home, took his nephew in his arms to the further end of the field, where he had placed a tub of water, into which putting the child's head, left it there. The child being missed, and enquiry made after him, the poor boy told how he was hired, and where he had left him, where, upon search, he was found dead. Elkes fled, and took the road to London: the neighbours sent two horsemen in pursuit, who, riding along the road near South Mims, in Hertfordshire, saw two ravens sitting on a cock of hay, making an unusual noise, and pulling the hay about with their beaks, upon which they alighted, and found Elkes asleep under the hay. He confessed that these two ravens had followed him from the time he did the fact.* He was brought to Shrewsbury, tried, condemned, and hung in chains on Knockin Heath.

No. 13.—Tong Castle,

NEAR Shiffnal, was formerly the seat of Hengist, the Saxon, whom Vortigern, the British King, called in to his assistance; and he proving fortunate in his attempts, afterwards begged of Vortigern as much land as an ox hide would compass; which request being granted, he cut an ox hide into small thongs, and got this Castle and Manor, from thence called Thong Castle; and after this, invited over some others of his countrymen, the Saxons, who soon conquered the Britons. Before the Conquest, we find that this Castle belonged to Morkar, Earl of Northumberland, in the reign of Edward the Confessor; but after the Conquest, we may reasonably suppose it was given to Hugh de Montgomery, who had the greatest part of this county.

The present building is a magnificent structure, built on the ruins of the above-mentioned Castle; was long the residence of the noble Veres, Earls of Oxford; and afterwards came into the possession of the Duke of Kingston. It is now the residence of George Durant, Esq. member in the last parliament (says Mr. Phillips, in 1778) for Evesham, in Worcestershire.

This Castle was rated at £22 8s. per Annum.

No. 14.—Alberbury Priory,

FOR Monks of the Order of St. Benedict, founded by Guarine de Meez, one of the Chief Counsellors of Roger de Montgomery, and having been endowed by him and his successors, was given by Fuldo Fitz Warine, to the Monks of Grandmont, in Normandy, with divers lands, and so it became a cell to that Abbey. King Henry II. confirms these grants, Reg. 17, as did also Thomas Corbeth, in 1262. This House being alien, was given to King Henry V. to carry on his war with France; and remaining in the crown in King Henry the 6th's reign, that Prince gave it to All-Soul's College, in Oxford, with some other small Priories, which King Edward IV., upon his first accession to the crown, is said to have confiscated and detained in his hands, till the society submitted themselves to his dominion, and acknowledged their fault, in adhering to King Henry VI.

---

* The truth of this circumstance, extraordinary as it is, has not, I believe, ever yet been questioned.—C. H.

Appendix.   F

Bromfield Monastery.—*No.* 15.

OF the Benedictine Order, of which we find, that Anno. 1155, the Canons of it, by the authority, and with the concurrence of Theobold, Archbishop of Canterbury, gave their Church to the Abbey of St. Peter, at Gloucester; and that King Henry II. much about the same time, confirmed all the estates belonging to it (under the title of the Church of St. Mary, of Bromfield,) to the Priors and Monks there serving God, to hold of him and his heirs in perpetual alms. King Henry III. made the like confirmation to it. The revenues, at the suppression, were valued at £87 7*s.* 4*d.* per Annum.—Speed ex Lel.

Chirbury Priory.—*No.* 16.

THIS Priory was of the Order of St. Bennet, and founded in King John's time, but when is uncertain. 11th Henry III. the Church of Chirbury was given to the Prior, with the lands all along the road side, *usque Mesebroc.* By a composition entered into between Philip, Prior of this House, the Parson of Montgomery, and the Parson of Chirbury, the right of burials and christenings was reserved to the Church of Chirbury. The same year the Canons of this Monastery had a grant of the tythes of Montgomery Wood, and of the Mill there. Hubert de Burgh was a benefactor to this Priory; but 9th Edward I. the Prior and Convent removed to Snede, the place of their first institution and abode; for Chirbury it seems, was represented as a situation not so convenient for celebrating divine mysteries.

It was agreed, that the removal was to be no prejudice to the souls of those that were buried at Chirbury; but that the Prior and Convent were to perform the same good offices for them at Snede, as by custom at the other places. Also, the religious were to lose nothing of their rights at Chirbury, no more than if the said translation had not been. However, 20th Edward I. at the assizes, the Prior at the King's suit was to shew by what title he claimed and held the Manor of Sneth, or Snede. For plea he said, that King John gave the Manor to the Church of St. Michael, at Chirbury. 7th Edward II. this Monastery obtained the King's confirmation, in which no notice is taken of the removal of the Convent to Sneth, but as if it had still remained at Chirbury; and two years after the impropriation of the Chapel at Hysington was given to the Prior of Chirbury. We meet with no other benefaction to this House, nor any thing memorable till the time of its dissolution, when 37th Henry VIII. the King granted to Edward Hopton and Elizabeth, his wife, the house and land on which it stood, for their lives, the remainder to the heirs of the said Edward for ever. 13th Elizabeth, the rectory and parsonage of Chirbury to the late Priory belonging, was given to augment the income of the grammar school of Shrewsbury, where it remains at present.—See account of the Free Schools.

Watlesburg Castle.—*No.* 17.

THE name at first view directs us to Watling Street, to which famous road it joins: but a quere may be made, whether the denomination of the place might not as well be derived from some garrison of the Vandals who came into Britain by the orders of the Emperor Probus; and as Mr. Cambden, out of Gervasius Tilburiensis, conjectures, those soldiers had a station in Cambridgeshire, as there is an ancient rampire in that county called Vandelesburg; so that with a small variation of letters, Watlesburg resolves itself into Vandelesburg, and the rather, that its situation is upon a military road, which gives some colour to the etymology. But the reader is left to judge as he pleases. In Domesday it is called Wetesburg, and being part of the possessions of Roger Corbet, it was afterwards given to a younger son of the house of Caux. 56th Henry III. Roger Corbet de Watlesburg had a grant of a market on a Tuesday, at his manor of Watlesburg, and to hold a fair on the eve, day, and day after, the feast of St. James the Apostle. 12th Edward 1st, Robert Corbet had a grant of free warren at Moreton Corbet, and at Watlesburg, and died seized of this manor, 29th Edward I. Thomas Corbet, his son, was the father of Sir Robert Corbet, who, 30th Edward III., had a grant of view of frankpledge at the manors of Watlesburg, Morton Corbet, Rowton, and Besford. He was father to Sir Foulk Corbet. 2nd of Henry V. Fulk Mowthe died seized of this manor, and 9th of Henry VI. Hugh Burgh, Esq. and Elizabeth, his wife, had seizen here of Sir John Burgh, their son and heir, who died 9th Edward IV. And 14th Edward IV. Sir John Lyngien, Knt., William Newport, John Leghton, Thomas Mytton, Esqrs. and others, released and confirmed to Johanna, relict of Sir John Burgh, the manor of Watlesburgh, Heye, Loughton, Cardeston, Yoketton, Stretton, and two acres of pasture in Brodeshull, for term of her life. This manor now (1836) belongs to Sir Baldwin Leighton, Bart.

OSWESTRY CASTLE.—No. 18.

THIS Castle is built on an artificial mount, (as it should seem) with a deep ditch extending to the Beatrice Gate on the one side, and Willow Gate on the other. Anno 1148, or 13th Stephen, Madoc, Prince of Powis, son of Meredith ap Bleddyn, built this Castle, according to Cradoc of Lancarvan; but the English records shew that the Fitz Alans had then possession of the place. 6th Henry II. Guy Le Strange, Sheriff of Shropshire, accounted in the Exchequer for salaries paid out of the King's revenues, to the Wardens in the Castle of Blancminster, the inheritance of William Fitz Alan, then lately deceased. 15th John, John, nephew of William Mareshall, Earl of Pembroke, being Guardian of the Marches of Wales, was at the same time constituted Governor of the Castles of Blancminster and Shrawarden, in com. Salop. Llewellyn, son of Griffin, son of Maddoc, made his complaint to the Archbishop of Canterbury, against the Constable of Oswestry, for disturbing him in the possession of the third part of the Ville of Ledrot, and had compelled him to send two young noblemen to be put to death, after an ignominious manner, in derogation of their birth and extraction; which disgrace their parents would not have undergone for £300 sterling: also that the Constable had twice imprisoned sixty of his men, for which they were found to pay 10s. each man for their liberty; also, that when the Welsh came to Oswestry fair, the Constable would seize their cattle by driving them into his Castle, and refusing to pay for the same.

Upon the death of John Fitz, Lord Allan, 24th Henry III. John Le Strange had a grant of the custody of the lands of John Fitz Allan, his son, then in his minority, with an allowance of 300 marks per annum, for guarding Blancminster, Scrawarthin, and Clun. John de Oxinden, 1st Edward I. had the custody of the Castle of Blancminster, upon the death of John, Earl of Arundel. 2nd Edward I. Bogo de Knovil was Sheriff of the county and of the Castle of Blancminster. 6th Edward I. the King granted a murage for the space of six years, for the walling of the town of Oswaldstrey, the Burgesses of Salop being exempted from the said toll.

The walls were about a mile in compass, with a deep ditch on the outside, that had rivulets of water running to fill it. There were no towers on the walls but the four gates, the inlets into the town. 8th Edward I. Isabel, mother of Richard, Earl of Arundel, had the custody of the Castle of Blancminster, and of the Hundred of Oswaldster, during her son's minority; but two years after, Edmund de Mortimer, her brother, supplanted her, and got the grant to himself. 18th Edward I. Adam de Montgomery, died, Governor of this Castle. 27th Edward I. Peter Meuvesine de Berewicke, juxta Akinton, died in the same office, after the attainder of Edmund, Earl of Arundel. In Edward II.'s time, the Lord Mortimer, of Wigmore, had a grant of this Castle. By an inquisition, 21st Richard II. after the death of Richard, Earl of Arundel, it appears, that there was a free Chapel,[*] dedicated to St. Nicholas, *infra Castrum*

---

* Besides the Chapel of St. Nicholas, there was the CONVENT of ST. OSWALD, or WHITE MONASTERY.— This religious house, of which no vestige at present remains, was, it is generally believed, situate near the parish church, as traces of foundations in digging graves, have been discovered: some very judicious antiquaries believe the Monastery stood on the place where Oswald was slain by Penda.—The battle is supposed to have commenced about 400 yards west of the church, and that Oswald compelled Penda to fall back to a field called Cae Nef, on the left of the turnpike road leading to the Free School:—here the pious Oswald fell, and the conqueror, with savage barbarity, caused his body to be cut in pieces, and exhibited on poles, or in trees, as trophies of his victory. According to a Manuscript Account of Oswestry, cited by its history, written in 1635—" There was an old oak lately standing in this time, within the Parish of Oswestry, whereon one of King Oswald's arms hung, say the neighbours, by tradition." At the time Leland visited the English Monasteries, in the reign of Henry VIII. little of the Monastery remained: in some of the predatory wars of the Welsh, or by the destructive hand of King John, who burned the town, it had no doubt been greatly delapidated. Leland however, relates, that within the memory of persons then living, the cloister was standing. Glynn, a Welsh Poet, who flourished about the middle of the fifteenth century, says—" I know not of any Convent of Monks, superior to White Minster." In the reign of Henry II. it is related, that Regner, Bishop of St. Asaph, resided at Oswestry, at which time he bestowed all the tithes of hay and

de Oswaldestre; and that the advowson belonged to the Earls of Arundel. A tower here, went by the name of Madoc's tower, (says Leland), which seems to confirm the History of Lancarvan, concerning the founder of the Castle; but I should rather think that that tower was the King's lodging when he came to this place, than that it was designed for the use above mentioned.

Besides the tenants of the manor and hundred of Oswestry, there were several in the hundreds of Bradford and Pimhill, whose tenure was to do service as this Castle, as may be seen in the *Feodarium in App.*

LILLESHULL ABBEY.—*No.* 19.

LILLESHELE was held by Godebaldus, Presbyter of the church of St. Alkmond, in Shrewsbury. Philip de Beumeys, gave all that tract of land between Watling Street and Merdiche, to build a religious house in honour of the Virgin Mary, and for the use of the Canons Regular of St. Peter, of Dorchester, who were afterwards stiled the Regular Canons of Doninton. Rich. de Beumeys, Dean of the church of St. Alkmond, translated his secular Canons from Salop, to the new foundation in *Bosco de Lilleshull.* The principal benefactors were Alanta Zouche, and John Le 'Strange, who gave the church of Hulme; and Hillaria de Trussebut, the first wife of Robert de Budlers, who gave several parcels of land, and here she devoted her corpse to be interred. A charter, 1st John, recites the possessions of this House at that time; but the largest account of the revenues of this Monastery, is expressed in the confirmation of Richard II. Some particulars may be mentioned, that are not in those charters; as 34th Henry III. the Abbot had leave to assart, or grub up twenty-three acres in the woods of Lilleshull; and 7th Edward I. to make an assart of the wood near Watling Street, in the Forest of Wombridge. 2nd Edward I. the Abbot had leave to make a park. A *Quo Warranto* being brought against the Abbot, 20th Edward I. for usurping several liberties in the manors, he pleaded a right by prescription, and the charter of King John; to which plea the King's council took exception; and as to the manor of Cold-Attone, the King recovered the seizen, and the arrearages of rents which were taxed to ten shillings.

Alan la Zouche, who died 7th Edward II. left Elen, the wife of Nicholas St. Maur, Maud, the wife of Robert de Holland, and Elizabeth, a Nun at Brewode, his daughters and co-heirs; Maud, the wife of Robert de Holland, had for her purpartie, the advowson of this Abbey. Robert, the son of the said Lord Holland, died 46th Edward III. leaving one sole daughter and heir, Maud, who was married to Sir John Lovell, Knt. and had livery of her lands.—47th Edward III. the church of Badminton was given to this Monastery. 14th Edward III. Roger de Norborough, Bishop of Coventry and Litchfield, granted to these Canons the appropriation of the church of Farnborough, which was purchased off Sir William Shareshull, Knt. 13th Richard 2nd, the Abbot had a grant of a view of frankpledge, in Lilleshull and Mockleston. 16th Richard 2nd, John Knode, a benefactor. 11th Edward 4th, the Hospital of St. John, at Bridgnorth, was put under the direction of this Abbot. 17th Henry 6th, a commission was granted to Humphrey, Earl of Strafford, and others, to enquire what inclosures had been made

---

corn, belonging to White Minster, on the Abbey of Shrewsbury, and by the Pope's authority, expelled twelve secular priests. There was formerly a Chapel upon or near St. Oswald's Well, situated in a field to the west of the Free School. Tradition says, that when Oswald was slain, an eagle tore from the body one of his arms, or rather seized upon one already separated by the cruel, victorious Penda?[*] but Divine judgement seized the eagle, it fell down, and perished upon the spot, and immediately a torrent of water gushed out of the earth, and has continued to flow ever since. 'Tis possible the pious of that period, who were also superstitious, surveying the field of battle and its vicinity, discovered the spring, and immediately ascribed its existence to a miracle. The well is enclosed with a stone wall, arched over, and an iron grate in front. Several trees were standing on or near it a few years ago; one an ancient yew tree, on my last visit, had disappeared,—borne away by some authority, not sanctioned by taste or due regard to the venerable character of the place.—C. H.

[*] Of the ferocious Penda, we have, in King's Vale Royal of England, the following compendious particulars:—"This King was a notable warriour, as these memorable passages do amply testifie. Anno. Dom. 629, he warred against Kinigilsus, K. of West-Saxons, at Cirencester in Gloucestershire, and compelled him to composition. Anno. Dom. 633, Oct. 12, he slew the famous Edwin, King of Northumberland, at Hethfield, or Hatfield-chace, in strasforth Wapentake, in the West Riding of Yorkshire. Anno. Dom. 635, he besieged and burnt the City of Bebbanburg, now the ruinated Castle of Bamburgh in Northumberland. The same year he received a notable overthrow by Oswald, King of Northumberland, at Heavenfield, now Halydon, or Holydown, in the same County. Anno. 636, he slew Erpenwald, alias Carpwald, alias Eorpwald, King of the East-Angles. Anno. 633, he slew Sigebert, King of the same province. Anno. Dom.642, he slew Oswald, the most Christian King of Northumberland, August 5, at Maserfield, now Oswald-street, or Oswestre, (from that fatal accident) in Shropshire. The same year also he slew Egrick, King of East-Angles; as by computation of the years of his reign may appear out of Malmsbury and Florence. Anno 644, he invaded Kenwalch, King of West-Saxons, and deprived him of his Kingdome for some years. Anno. 654, he slew Anna, King of East-Angles, in a sore battel; but was at last, for all his cruel wars, slain himself by Oswy, King of Northumberland. An. 655, Nov. 15."

out of the lands of St. Mary, of Lilleshull. 33rd Henry 8th, the Earl of Rutland obtained a grant of the manor of Braunston, in the County of Northampton, that belonged to this Abbey. 35th Henry 8th, the King granted to James Leveson the manor of Lilleshull.

Lady Katharine Leveson left rent of £120 per annum, issuing out of Foxley, for the maintenance of twelve poor widows, whereof three were to be chosen by the Minister, Church Warden, and Overseers of the poor of Lilleshull ; and to each of them a gown of grey cloth, with these letters, K. L. in blue cloth, affixed thereto; as likewise for the placing of ten poor boys apprentices, whereof two were to be of this parish.—The revenues of this Abbey, at the dissolution, were valued at £229 3s. per annum. This house lying near the Chester road, the Abbots sometime were known to complain that their income was too scanty for the entertainment of the passengers that troubled that road.*

No. 20.—MORETON-CORBET CASTLE,

NEAR Shrewsbury.—The remains shew that this has been a magnificent building ; it is situate upon a plain, the outside walls are for the most part standing, but the roof is fallen in. Several dates are upon different parts of the building, but the time of its erection uncertain ; the windows are large, and unlike those in most castles, and prove it a modern structure. A garrison was here in 1644, when a part of them were drawn out against Shrewsbury, together with a part of the garrisons of Wem and Stoke ; this and Nantwich being at that time Parliament garrisons : Oswestry, High Ercal, Shrawardine, and Shrewsbury being garrisoned for the King. Great care has been taken to prevent the ruins from going to further decay, by the present proprietor, (1778), Andrew Corbet of the Park, Esq.†

ACTON-BURNELL CASTLE.—No. 21.

THE lordship belonging to the Burnells, a very honourable family in this county, was so called, because they had their seat here, and to distinguish it from another Acton in this county, called Acton-Pigot. Sir Robert Burnell lived in the Conqueror's reign, and his posterity long flourished here.

Robert Burnell, 54th Henry III. obtained that King's charter for a market weekly on Tuesday, and two fairs yearly ; one upon the eve, day, and morrow of the feast of the Annunciation of the Virgin Mary ; and the other on the eve, day, and morrow of St. Michael the Arch-Angel. How long they continued we know not, but at present there is no market, and the fair yearly is now (1778) kept on Good-Friday. The manor continued in the family of Burnells, till 9th Edward II., when Edward Lord Burnell dying without issue male, left this and his other estates to Maud his sister and heir, who marrying to John de Handlou, transferred her estate into his family, in which it continued till 8th Henry V., when Edward Lord Burnell dying without heirs male, left this manor and his other estates to his grand-daughters Joyce, Catharine, and Margery. Mr. Cambden tells us, that Maud above-mentioned, the heir of Edward Lord Burnell, married for her first husband, John Lord Lovel, and so brought this manor into his family, but how it doth not appear ; yet, in the reign of King Henry VI., the Lovells are found in possession of it, and Francis Lord Lovell, by adhering to King Richard III. forfeited his whole estate ; and King Henry VII. being settled on the throne, seized it, and gave to Jasper, Earl of Bedford, a grant in special tail of this and

* This proves travellers were *freely* entertained.—C. H.

† When King Charles I. came to Shrewsbury, in the year 1642, one William Prees, alias Scoggan, a serjeant in the trained bands, enlisted as a soldier in the King's service, and after some time, was promoted to be a serjeant. Being some time afterwards taken prisoner by the Parliament's forces, he was brought to Wem and imprisoned there. The first night of his confinement he broke the prison, and the next night came to Shrewsbury. At that time the soldiers from Wem garrison greatly distressed the country thereabout, and frequently came in parties almost to the walls of Shrewsbury. To prevent their insolence, the Governor of Shrewsbury placed a garrison at Abright Hussey, near Battlefield, and made Scoggan the Governor of it. A party of horse, in the interest of Parliament, came one Sunday afternoon and sat down before this small garrison. Scoggan at that time had only eight men in the house with him, but in order to intimidate the horsemen, he placed himself near a window in an upper room, and cried aloud that they might hear, " Let ten go to such a place, ten to such a place, and twenty come along with me, and *we'll* drive the rascals." Upon which he came to the window, and with a fowling-piece shot one Phillip Bunny, a taylor, of Hadnall, who was with the enemy : the shot went through his leg and killed his horse. The Parliament's soldiers being frightened, took up Bunny and retreated. This garrison was soon after recalled, at the request of Pelham Corbet, Esq. ; he being apprehensive the Parliament's soldiers would return and destroy his buildings. Scoggan continued in the King's service, till his Majesty was apprehended and beheaded, January 30, 1649, when he married, and settled at Whixall near Wem, and there died.

Appendix.　G

certain other manors in the county, which he held for life; but dying without any legitimate issue, they all reverted to the Crown, and King Henry VIII. gave them almost all to Thomas Howard, Earl of Surry, whom he also created Duke of Norfolk at the same time, as a reward for his valour and conduct in conquering the Scots, in Flodden-field. He left it with his other estates, to his son, who obtained the fee of it, and left it to his posterity.

This place is famous for a Parliament that sat here in the 11th year of Edward I. and for a Statute enacted there; of which see further in Chap. III.

MIDDLE CASTLE.—*No.* 22.

CAMBDEN says, Lord Strange built Knockin Castle, and it is not improbable that he built this, it being alternately with Knockin, the place of his residence. The stone of which the Castle was built, was got on the end of Harmaer-Heath nearest to Middle. Some part of the walls of this Castle were remaining about the year 1640. It was built four-square, within a square moat, and had a square court inside. There was a piece of ground, near half an acre, on the east side of the Castle, which piece was moated round; the entrance to this piece was through a gate-house which stood near the north-east corner of the Castle moat. In the gate-house were four chambers. Adjoining this gate-house was a slaughter-house for the use of the Castle, and near it a draw-bridge over the Castle moat. The passage from the end of the bridge went into the middle of the Castle Court, on the south side of which was a large room, supposed to have been used as a kitchen, having a large chimney in it, and other conveniences necessary; on the same side was the parlour, and opposite the passage a large hall. The Castle was only two stories high, with a flat roof, part of it fell down by an earthquake in the year 1688, and the rest is now entirely demolished.

After the death of Lord Strange, who resided part of the year in this Castle, it descended to the Derby family, when a Constable or Keeper was appointed; the first mentioned is William Dod, and after him Sir Roger Kynaston of Hordley, was by commission appointed Keeper of Middle and Knockin Castles. Upon the decease of Sir Roger, his son Humphrey, (who for his dissolute and riotous living was called Wild Humphrey) was tenant here; he had two wives, con-tracted many debts, and being for divers reasons outlawed, he left Middle Castle, which he had suffered to go ruinous and out of repair, and went and sheltered himself in a Cave near Nescliff, which is to this day called Kynaston's Cave. During Kynaston's residence here, several attempts were made to take him, without success: one time, when he was got over Montford's Bridge, on the side next Shrewsbury, and must return to his Cave over that Bridge, the Under Sheriff came with a considerable company of men, and the Bridge being then composed of stone pillars, and planks laid from pillar to pillar, they took up several planks, left such an open as they thought no horse could leap over, and laid themselves in ambush for his return. When Humphrey came, and was about to enter the Bridge, they rose up to apprehend him, which he perceiving, put spurs to his horse, and riding full speed, leapt over the space, and escaped. The measure of this leap was afterwards marked out upon a green plat on Knockin Heath, in the road between Knockin and Nescliffe, with an H. and K. cut in the ground at the end of the leap. The letters were about an ell long, and were usually repaired yearly, by Mr. Kynaston of Ryton, but are not now to be found.—After this Humphrey's time, Middle Castle was never inhabited, but went to ruin.

RELIGIOUS HOUSES IN SHROPSHIRE,

Of which no account is given by Mr. Phillips; chiefly from Cox's "Magna Britannia et Hibernia." Various others, and Castles, are described or mentioned in my Salopian History.—C. H.

BRIDGNORTH CONVENT and other RELIGIOUS HOUSES.

THERE was, adjoining to the church-yard of St. Leonard's (which was a Chantry), a large edifice, called a COLLEGE, supposed to be an habitation for such Priests and Monks as were to pray for departed souls, by performing the Popish Obits and Dirges, &c. It was destroyed by fire, when the town was burnt, together with the church of St. Leonard.

Upon the west bank of the river Severn, in a rich soil, is an old building, called the FRIARS, being, in the times of Popery, a Convent of Franciscans, or Minor Friars, and was doubtless much larger than now it appears, there being some plain marks of its ancient magnificence yet visible; for in the court or yard thereof are vaults under ground, which run parallel to the house, for some space, and extend themselves several ways, but how far in some places, is not known. The end of one of these subterraneous passages was lately (1720) discovered.—It resembled the hearth of a chimney, with seats on each side of it, without any appearance of a funnel: in it were found jars, and other earthen vessels. The height of this cavity was such, that a man of an ordinary stature might walk in it almost upright. It was walled on both sides, and arched with stone on the top, and paved at the bottom. What was the intent, design, and use of them, is not yet discovered.

There was also here another Religious House, dedicated to the Blessed Virgin Mary, situate in the Middle Street, in the High Town: and another, dedicated to St. John Baptist, standing in the Lower Town, in the Street that is still denominated from it. There is a stately new House lately erected in the place where the Monastery stood, and yet bears the title of St. John's.

There is also another ancient structure at the south end of the Lower Town, called St. James's, because it was dedicated to that Saint. It is said, that before the Act of Dissolution, this House was a Lazaret, or Hospital for Lepers.

An Hospital, of which it was found by inquisition, taken the 14th Edward IV. that Radulfe le Strange founded, and endowed it in honour of the Blessed Trinity, the Virgin Mary, and St. John Baptist. Ankaret, the daughter and heir of John le Strange of Blackmere, marrying to Richard Lord Talbot, brought the patronage of this Hospital into that family; and John Talbot, the first Earl of Shrewsbury, being lineally descended from the family of the Le Stranges, was a considerable benefactor to it. It was at the same time further found, that the name of the Custos of this Hospital had been in process of time changed into that of Prior. At the dissolution, it was valued at £4 per Ann. *Dug. Speed.*

LUDLOW PRIORY,

DEDICATED to the Virgin Mary, founded by Sir Lawrence Ludlow, Knt. Anno. 1349, 24th Edward III.; and another of Augustine Friars, dedicated to St. Augustine, to which Edmund de Pontibus or Bridgman, was a benefactor; but we have no other account of them, nor any other Religious Houses in this town, except an Hospital, dedicated to St. John Baptist, situate near the Bridge, founded by Peter Undergod, and by him endowed with divers lands, &c. for the maintenance of certain religious brethren, and for the sustenance of poor and infirm people. He also granted to the brothers, that after his decease, they might freely choose one of themselves to be their Master or Custos; and as often as occasion should be, the Master or Custos to admit the brothers, and both of them the poor, &c.; which lands, &c. so given as is above said, were confirmed by Walter de Lacy, the chief Lord of the Fee, and by King Henry III. Reg. 5. This Hospital, at the dissolution, was valued at £17 3s. 3d. per Annum.— *Dugd. Speed ex Lel.*

NEWPORT COLLEGE,

ERECTED by Thomas Draper in that town, after this manner:—King Henry VI. in the 20th year of his reign, licensed the said Thomas Draper to purchase and receive from the Abbot and Convent of St. Peter at Shrewsbury, the parish church of Newport, and therein to found and erect a College for one Custos, a Priest, and four Chaplains, whom, by the name of the Custos and Chaplains of St. Mary College of Newport, be incorporated, with a licence to endow the same with lands, &c. of the value of ten pounds per annum, and appropriate the parish church to the same, provided that the Custos for the time being, take upon him the cure of souls, and minister all and singular the sacraments to the parishioners, &c.

TONG COLLEGIATE CHURCH,

THUS founded:—King Henry IV. Reg. 12, for the sum of forty pounds paid into the Hanaper, granted his license to Isabel, the widow of Fulke de Penbrugge Chivalier, and others, to purchase of the Abbot and Convent of the Abbey of Shrewsbury, the Advowson of the church of St. Bartholomew at Tonge, and to erect and change the same into a College of five Chaplains, of which one should be the Custos; and to endow the same with lands and churches, for the maintenance of the said Custos and Chaplains, and thirteen poor people, more or less, whom he incorporated, &c., settling the patronage of the said College on Richard de Penbrugge, in special tail, with divers remainders over. The revenues, at the dissolution, were valued at £29 8s. 1d. per Ann. *Dugd. Speed ex Lel.*

SHERIFFS OF SHROPSHIRE.

SHERIFFS or Shire-Reeves, it is probable, were first appointed by King Alfred, who divided England into Shires. He began his reign Anno 872.

From the reign of the Conqueror to Edward III. the Kings received neither silver nor gold, but a certain quantity of victuals were provided by the different counties, for the use of the household and army. Officers were appointed in each county, to collect the provisions, &c. But when this country became more engaged in foreign wars, these duties were changed into pecuniary payments.

" 10th Edward I. Anno. 1282. The Sheriffs of Stafford and Salop, were obliged to provide " two hundred wood-cutters, in the presence of William de Percy, who was commissioned for "that purpose. The business of these wood-cutters was, to cut down timber, and other ob-" structions, to make passages for the King's army to enter into Wales. The wages of every " wood-man was 3d. per day.

" 12th Edward II. 1284. The Sheriff of Lincoln was to provide salt and bacon, for the use " of the King's army.—The Sheriff of Yorkshire, pease and beans.—And the Sheriffs of Stafford "and Salop, to find horse-shoes, nails, and saddles.

" 15th Edward II. 1287. The county of Salop raised five hundred foot soldiers, with arms " and ammunition, for the Scotch wars.

" 36th Edward III. 1363. When Lionel, Earl of Clarence, the King's son, was sent Lieu-" tenant into Ireland, he had one hundred archers on horseback in his retinue, at 6d. per day, " of which number, Shropshire furnished six."*

SHERIFFS.

WILLIAM THE CONQUEROR.
1066 Warin.†
    Reginald, or Rainald.
    Hugh.

WILLIAM RUFUS.
1098 Fulco.

HENRY I.
1102 Richard de Belmeis.
    Pagan, or Payne Fitz John.
1121 Fulco.
    Alan.

STEPHEN
Began his reign 1st August, 1135.

N. B.—The preceding are from " The Sheriffs of Shropshire," by Mr. Blakeway, who expresses his belief that Mr. Phillips's List was furnished by the late Dr. Hart, of Shrewsbury: it is here given without any deviation.—C. H.

HENRY II.
1154 William Fitz Allan.
1160 Guy Strange.
  65 Godfrey de Vere.
1170 Guy Strange.
  79 Hugh Pantulf.

RICHARD I.
1189 William Fitz Allan.
1190 Reginald Hesden.
  91 William Fitz Allan.
  92 William de Hadley.
  96 William Fitz Allan.
  97 Reginald de Sodinge.
  98 William Fitz Roberts.

JOHN.
  99 William Fitz Allan.
1200 Warner de Willely.
   1 Rainer de Lea.
   2 Richard de Amberaley.
   6 Thomas de Erdington.

HENRY III.
1216 Radulph, Earl of Chester.
  17 Henry de Aldithelcy.
  19 Philip Kinton.
  23 John Bovel.
  25 Henry de Aldithcley.
  27 William de Bromley.
  31 Peter de Russel.
  35 John Strange.
  36 Robert de Aston‡ and John Strange.
1247 Thomas Corbet.
1251 Robert de Grandon.
  59 William de Bagod.
1262 Jacob Audley.
  69 Walter de Hopton.

EDWARD I.
1272 Roger Mortimer.
  78 Roger Sprenghouse.
1287 Henry de Romethey.
  89 Robert Corbett.
1290 William de Thickley.
  97 Radulph de Harley.
1300 Thomas Corbett.

1302 Richard de Harley.
   4 Walter de Burton.
   5 John de Aston.
   6 John de Deane.

EDWARD II.
1307 Roger Scumtoyne.
   8 John Scumtoyne.
   9 Hugh de Croft.
  11 Hugh de Audley.
  14 William de Mere.
  15 Roger de Cheney.
  16 Roger de Scumtoyne.
  18 Robert de Grendon.
  21 John de Swinnerton.
  23 Henry de Bishbury.

EDWARD III.
1327 John de Linsell, by the King.
    Henry de Bishbury, by the People.
  28 Henry de Bishbury.
  33 Richard Peshall.
  35 John de Linsell.
  36 Simon de Bagley.
  37 Richard de Peshall.
  41 Adam de Peshall.
  42 Thomas de Swinnerton.
  44 John de Aston.
  45 Richard, Earl of Arundel.
  75 Richard de Peshall.
  76 Robert de Cornwall.

* M. S. Cotton Library.
† Where the dates are omitted, the preceding Sheriffs served until the year next mentioned.
‡ Aston was chosen by the People, and Strange by the King.

RICHARD II.

1377 Brian de Cornwall, of Birford,
78 J. de Ludlow, of Hodnet,
79 J. Drayton, of Drayton,
1380 Roger Hoord,
81 John Sharry,
82 Edward de Acton, of Aldenham,
83 John de Stepleton,
84 Edward de Acton, of Aldenham,
85 N. Sandford, of Sandford,
86 Robert Lea, of Lea Hall,
87 John Mowethe,
88 Bt. de Ludlow, Hodnet,
89 Edward de Acton, of Aldenham,
1390 John de Stepleton,
91 William de Hungerford,
92 Henry de Winsbury,
93 John Eyton, of Eyton,
94 Thomas Lea, of Lea Hall,
95 William de Worthen,
96 William Hungerford,
97 } Ad. de Peshall, Esquires.
98 }

HENRY IV.

1399 Sir John Cornwall, of Burford, Knt.
1400 William Hungerford,
1 John Dacras,
2 Wm. Bannaster, of Wem,
3 Thomas Newport, of Ercal, Esquires.
4 J. Cornwall, of Burford, Chevalier.
5 Thomas Whitton, of Whitton,
6 William Bromshall,
7 John Borely, of Bramcroft Castle, Esquires.
8 Roger Acton, of Aldenham, Chevalier.
9 Edward Sprengaux,
1410 Robert Tiptoft, alias Tipton, Esquires.
12 Robert Corbett, of Moreton, Chevalier.

HENRY V.

1413 Robert Corbett, of Moreton, Chevalier.
14 Ditto, ditto.
15 Rich. Lacon, Chevalier.
16 George Hawkeston,
17 William Ludlow, of Hodnet, Esquires.
18 Sir Adam Peshall, Knt.
19 Robert Corbett, of Moreton,
1420 John Brayne, Esquires.
21 Ditto.

HENRY VI.

1422 John Brayne,
23 Hugh Harnage, of Cund,
24 Thomas le Strange,
25 Wm. Boreley, of Bramcroft Castle,
26 Thomas Corbett, of Moreton,
27 William Lichfield,

1428 John Winnesbury,
29 H. Burgh and T. Hopton,
1430 Richard Archer,
31 John Brayne,
32 William Ludlow, of Hodnet,
33 Thomas Corbett, of Lee,
34 Hugh Cresset, of Upton-Cresset,
35 Robert Inglefield,
36 William Ludlow, of Hodnet, Esquires.
37 William Lichfield, Chevalier.
38 Humphrey Lowe,
39 Nich. Eyton, of Eyton,
1440 Ditto.
41 John Burgh,
42 William Ludlow, of Hodnet,
43 Thomas Corbett, of Moreton Corbett,
44 Nich. Eyton, of Eyton,
45 Hugh Cressett, of Upton-Cressett,
46 Fulco Sprengeaux,
47 William Ludlow, of Hodnet, Esquires.
48 Sir John Burgh, Knight.
49 Roger Eyton, of Eyton,
1450 Thomas Herbert, of Chirbury,
51 William Lacon, Esquires.
52 Sir John Burgh,
53 Sir Robert Corbett, of Moreton Corbet, Knts.
54 Nich. Eyton, of Eyton,
55 Gabriel Mytton, of Shipton,
56 Thomas Hoord,
57 Fulco Sprengeaux,
58 Thomas Cornwall, of Burford, Esquires.
59 Sir Robert Corbett, of Moreton, Knight.
1460 Humph. Blunt, of Kinlet, Esq.

EDWARD IV.

1461 Roger Kynaston, of Hordley, Esquire.
62 Ditto.
63 Ditto.
64 Sir John Burgh, Knight.
65 Radulph Lea, of Lea Hall,
66 Roger Eyton, of Eyton,
67 Humph. Blunt, of Kinlet,
68 John Leighton, of Wattlesbury,
69 Robert Cresset, of Upton Cresset,
1470 R. Kynaston, of Hordley,
71 Ditto,
72 Robert Charlton,
73 William Newport, of Ercall,
74 John Leighton, of Wattlesbury,
75 Humph. Blunt, of Kinlet,
76 John Hewin,
77 Richard Lacon, Esquires.
78 Sir Richard Ludlow, of Hodnet, Knight.
79 Richard Lea, of Lea Hall,
1480 Tho. Blunt, of Kinlet, Esquires.
81 Sir John Harley, Knt.
82 John Leighton, of Wattlesbury, Esquire.

RICHARD III.

1483 John Mytton, of Shipton,
84 Thomas Hoord,
85 Robert Cressett, of Upton Cresset, Esquires.

HENRY VII. August 22.

Sir Gilbert Talbot, Knt.
1486 Richard Laken,
87 Thomas Hoord,
88 Edward Blunt, of Kinlet, Esqs.
89 Sir Richard Ludlow, of Hodnet, Knt.
1490 John Newport, of Ercall, Esq.
91 Sir William Young, of Kenlop, Knt.
92 Edward Blunt, of Kinlet, Esq.
93 Sir Thomas Blunt,
94 Sir Thomas Leighton, of Wattlesbury, Knights.
95 Richard Lea, of Lea Hall,
96 Thomas Scryven, of Frodgley, Esquires.
97 Sir Richard Laken,
98 Sir John Harley, Knts.
99 William Ottley, of Pitchford,
1500 John Newport, of Ercall, Esqs.
1 Sir Tho. Blunt, of Kinlet, Knt.
2 } P. Newton, of Heytley,
3 }
4 George Mainwaring, of Chester, Esquires.
5 Sir Thos. Cornwall, of Burford,
6 Sir Robert Corbett, of Moreton, Knights.
7 } Thomas Kinnaston, of Hordley, Esquire.
8 }

HENRY VIII.

1509 Thomas Laken,
10 John Newport, of Ercall,
11 Thos. Scryven, of Frodgley,
12 Peter Newton, of Heytley,
13 Wm. Ottley, of Pitchford,
14 Thomas Laken, Esquires.
15 Sir Thomas Cornwall, of Burford, Knight.
16 Robert Pigott, of Chetwynd,
17 Peter Newton, of Heytley, Esqs.
18 Sir Thomas Blunt, of Kinlet,
19 Sir Thomas Cornwall, of Burford, Knights.
1520 John Salter, of Oswestry,
21 George Bromley, of Bromley,
22 Peter Newton, of Heytley,
23 Tho. Vernon, of Hodnet, Esqs.
24 Sir Thomas Cornwall, of Burford, Knight.
25 John Corbet de Lee,
26 Thomas Scryven, of Frodgley, Esquires.
27 Sir John Talbot, of Albrighton, Knight.
28 R. Needham, of Shinton,
29 R. Corbett, of Moreton, Esqs.
1530 Sir Thomas Cornwall, of Burford, Knight.

Appendix. H

1531 Thomas Mainwaring, of Chester,
32 Thomas Laken, Esquires.
33 Sir John Talbot, of Albrighton, Knight.
34 Tho. Vernon, of Hodnet, Esq.
35 Sir Robert Needham, of Shinton, Knight.
36 John Corbett, of Moreton, Esq.
37 Sir John Talbot, of Albrighton,
38 Sir Richard Mainwaring, of Chester,
39 Sir Robert Needham, of Shinton, Knights.
40 Richard Laken, Esquire.
41 Sir John Talbot, of Albrighton, Knight.
42 Thomas Newport, of Ercall,
43 Rich. Mytton, of Shipton, Esqs.
44 Sir Richard Mainwaring, of Chester, Knight.
45 Thomas Vernon, of Hodnet,
46 Tho. Lea, of Lea Hall, Esquires.

EDWARD VI.

1547 Wm. Young, of Kenlop,
48 Rich. Cornwall, of Burford,
49 Tho. Newport, of Ercall, Esqs.
1550 Sir Andrew Corbett, of Moreton, Knight.
51 Rich. Newport, of Ercall, Esq.
52 Sir Richard Mainwaring, of Chester, Knight.

PHILIP & MARY.

1553 Sir Adam Mytton,
54 Sir Rich. Cornwall, of Burford,
55 Sir Andrew Corbett, of Moreton,
56 Sir Rich. Levison, of Lilleshull, Knights.
57 Rich. Newport, of Ercall,
58 Thomas Hanmer, Esquires.

ELIZABETH.

1559 Richard Mytton,
1560 Richard Corbett, Moreton,
61 Richard Cornwall, Burford,
62 Arthur Mainwaring, Esquires.
63 Sir Geo. Blunt, of Kinlet, Knt.
64 Robert Needham, of Shinton,
65 Hum. Onslowe, of Onslowe,
66 Thomas Eyton, of Eyton,
67 Edward Leighton, of Wattlesbury, Esquires.
68 Sir Richard Newport, of Ercall,
69 Sir Andrew Corbett, of Moreton, Knights.
1570 Richard Laken,
71 William Gratewood.
72 Thomas Powell, of Wortden,
73 Robert Pigott, of Chetwynd,
74 John Hopton, of Hopton,
75 Walter Levison, of Lilleshull, Esquires.
76 Sir Arthur Mainwaring, Knight.
77 Fra. Lawley, of Spoonhill,
78 William Young, of Kenlop,
79 Richard Cornwall, of Burford,
1580 Thos. Williams, of Woolaston.

1581 William Gratewood,
82 Charles Fox, of Chainham,
83 Rich. Cresset, of Upton-Cresset,
84 Rowland Barker, of Haghmond,
85 Francis Newport, of Ercall,
86 Robert Needham, of Shinton,
87 Ed. Leighton, of Wattlesbury,
88 Thomas Cornwall, of Burford,
89 Andrew Charlton,
1590 William Hopton, of Hopton,
91 Robert Eyton, of Eyton,
92 Richard Corbett, of Moreton,
93 Robert Powell, of Worthen,
94 Francis Albany, of Ternhill,
95 Robert Needham, of Shinton,
96 Edward Scryven, Frodgley,
97 Chas. Fox, of Chainham, Esqrs.
98 Sir Edward Kynaston, of Hordley, Knight.
99 Humphrey Lea, of Lea Hall,
1600 Francis Newport, of Ercall,
1 Francis Newton, of Heytley,
2 Roger Kynaston, Esquires.

JAMES I.

1603 Sir Roger Owen, of Condover, Knight.
4 Humph. Briggs, of Houghton, Esquire.
5 Sir Henry Wallop, of Red-Cresset,
6 Sir Robert Needham, of Shinton, Knights.
7 Edward Fox, of Chainham,
8 Robert Purslow,
9 Richard Thornes,
1610 Richard Mytton,
11 Bonam Norton, of Shinton, Esquires.
12 Sir Francis Lacon, of Kinlet,
13 Sir Thomas Jervise, Knights.
14 John Coates, of Woodcont,
15 Tho. Pigott, of Chetwynd, Esqrs.
16 Sir Thos. Cornwall, of Burford,
17 Sir Rowland Cotton, of Belaporte, Esquires.
18 Robert Owen, of Condover,
19 Thomas Harries, of Boreatton, Esquires.
1620 Sir William Whitmore, of Apley, Knight.
21 Walter Barker, of Haghmond,
22 Thos. Edwards, of Creete, Esqrs.
23 Sir William Owen, of Condover, Knight.
24 Walter Pigott, of Chetwynd, Esquire.

CHARLES I.

1625 Thomas Jones,
26 Fra. Charlton, of Apley, Esqrs.
27 Sir Richard Newport, of Ercall,
28 Sir Rich. Prynce, of Salop, Knts.
29 Sir John Corbet, of Stoke, Bart.
1630 Walter Acton, Aldenham,
31 Humphrey Walcott, of Walcott.
32 Thomas Ireland, of Albrighton, Esquires.

1633 Sir Philip Eyton, of Eyton,
34 Sir Thomas Thynne, of Cause Castle, Knights.
35 John Newton, of Heytley,
36 Robert Corbett, of Stanwardine, Esquires.
37 Sir Paul Harries, of Boreatton, Knight.
38 William Pierepont, of Tong Castle, Esq.
39 Sir Rich. Lea, of Lea Hall, Bart.
1640 Roger Kynaston, Hordley,
41 Thomas Nichols, of Salop,
42 John Wilde, of Willey,
43 Henry Bromley, of Wear,
44 Thomas Edwards, Esquires.
45 { Sir Fr. Ottley, of Ottley, Knt. By the King.
{ Thomas Mytton, Esq. By the Parliament.
46 Robert Powell, of the Park,
47 Wm. Cotton, of Bellaport, Esqrs.
48 Ditto.

OLIVER THE PROTECTOR.

1649 Thomas Baker, of Swinney,
1650 William Fowler, Esquires.
51 Sir Edward Corbett, Bart.
52 Francis Forrester,
53 George Norton,
54 Thomas Kinnersley, of Badger,
55 Matthew Herbert,
56 Thomas Hunt, Esquires.

RICHARD THE PROTECTOR.

1657 { Edmund Waring, of Humphrison, Esq.
58
59

CHARLES II.

1660 William Oakley,
61 John Walcott, of Walcott,
62 John Cotes, of Woodcott, Esqrs.
63 Sir Samuel Jones, Bart.
64 Charles Mainwaring,
65 Francis Charleton, Esquires.
66 Sir Humphrey Briggs, of Houghton, Bart.
67 Francis Levison Fowler,
68 Robert Owen,
69 Thomas Mackworth, Sutton,
1670 Richard Creswell, Esquires.
71 Sir Phil. Prynce, of Salop, Knt.
72 Rowland Hunt,
73 Robert Ireland, Albrighton,
74 Robert Clive, of Styche,
75 Rowland Nichols, Esquires.
76 Sir John Corbett, of Adderley, Bart.
77 Roger Evans, of Oswestry,
78 Thomas Cotton, of Pulley,
79 Lingham Topp, Whitton,
1680 Edward Kynaston, of Ottley,
81 Thomas Hill, of Soulton,
82 Edward Kinnaston, of Albright Lee,
83 Richard Lyster, of Rowton, Esquires.

1684 Sir Edward Acton, of Aldenham, Bart.

JAMES II.

1685 Henry Davenport, of Horn,
86 Richard Mytton, of Halston.
87 Ralph Browne, Benthall,
88 Robert Leighton, of Wattlesbury, Esquires.

WILLIAM & MARY.

1689 Jonathan Langley, Salop,
1690 John Kynaston, of Acton,
91 John Tayleur, of Roddington.
92 Thomas Wingfield, of Preston, Esquires.
93 Sir Ed. Leighton, of Loton, Bt.
94 Francis Prynce, of Salop,
95 Rich. Leighton, of Leighton,
96 Francis Herbert, of Bromfield,
97 Robert Pigott, Chetwynd,
98 John Powell, of Worthen, Esqrs.
99 Sir Francis Charlton, of Ludford, Bart.
1700 Thomas Jones, of Salop, Esq.
1 Sir Robert Corbett, of Adderley, Bart.

ANNE.

1702 Edward Cresset, of Cound,
3 Henry Biggs, of Benthall, Esqrs.
4 Sir William Williams, of Stanwardine, Bart.
5 Thomas Child, of Kinlet,
6 Barth. Lutley, Loughton,
7 Robert Stanley, of Hatton,
8 Roger Owen, of Condover,
9 Robert Burton, of Longnor.
1710 Charles Walcott, of Walcott,
11 Richard Creswell, of Sidbury, Esquires.
12 Sir Wm. Fowler, of Harnage, Bart.
13 William Taylenr, Rodington,
14 Buckley Mackworth, of Betton, Esquires.

GEORGE I.

1715 Wm. Church, of Tunstall, Esq.
16 Sir John Woolriche, of Dudmaston, Bart.
17 Thomas Powell, of Park,
18 Thomas Hunt, of Boreatton,
19 Edward Browne, Caughley,
1720 Edward Jorden, Priors Lee,
21 John Kinnersley, Badger,
22 Bromwich Pope, of Woosaston,
23 William Cludde, of Orleton,
24 Richard Oakley, of Oakley,
25 Francis Walker, of Ferny Hall,
26 Richard Leighton, of Leighton, Esqu'res.

GEORGE II.

1727 Edward Lloyd, of Leaton Shelf, Esquire.
28 Sir Whitmore Acton, of Aldenham, Bart.
29 Thomas Jenkins, of Salop,
1730 John Harries, of Cruckton,
31 Grey James Grove, Pool Hall, Esquires.

1732 Sir Rowland Hill, of Hawkstone, Bart.
33 Charles Jones, of Salop,
34 Thomas Beale, of Heath,
35 Sherrington Davenport, of Horn;
36 Thomas Lloyd, of Heytley,
37 John Powell, of Worthen,
38 Adam Ottley, of Pitchford,
39 Thomas Smith, of Stoke,
1740 Richard Stainer, of Bridgnorth,
41 Thomas Eyton, of Eyton,
42 Revel Moreton, Shiffnal,
43 Thomas Langley, of Golden,
44 William Tayleur, of Salop,
45 Thomas Jones, of Salop,
46 George Weld, of Willey, Esqrs.
47 Sir H. Briggs, of Haughton, Bt.
48 Job Charlton, of the Park, Esq.
49 Sir Charlton Leighton, of Loton, Bart.
1750 William Lutwiche, of Lutwiche, Esquire.
51 Sir Richard Acton, of Aldenham, Bart.
52 Thomas Sandford, of Sandford,
53 Rowland Wingfield, of Preston Brockhurst,
54 Edward Pemberton, of Wrockardine,
55 Fr. Turner Blithe, of Whitley,
56 Anthony Kinnersley, of Leighton,
57 Saint John Charlton, of Apley,
58 John Amler, of Ford,
59 Sam. Griffiths, of Dinthill, Esq.
1760 Sir Thomas Jones, Knight.

GEORGE III.

1761 John Smytheman, of Little Wenlock,
62 Thomas Powys, of Berwick,
63 Robert Burton, of Longner,
64 Edward Rogers, of Eaton,
65 John Topp, of Whitton,
66 Charles Pigott, of Peplow,
67 Thomas Ottley, of Pitchford,
68 Edward Botterell, of the Heath,
69 John Owen, of Woodhouse,
1770 Rich. Morhall, jun., of Onslow,
71 Joseph Griffiths, of Dinthill,
72 Nich. Smyth, of Condover,
73 Robert Dodd, of Whitchurch,
74 Robert Pigott, of Chetwynd,
75 John Charlton Kinchant, of Park,
76 Thos. Jelfe Powys, of Berwick,
77 Dudley Ackland, of Salop,
78 Robert Corbett, of Longnor,
79 Thos. Eyton, of Eyton, Esqrs.
Continuation by C. H.
1780 Edward Horne, of Hales Owen,
81 Edward Charles Windsor, of Harnage,
82 Charles Walcot, of Bitterley,
83 Isaac Hawkins Browne, of Badger,
84 William Childe, of Kinlet,
85 Robert More, of Linley, Esqrs.
86 Sir Rt. Leighton, of Loton, Bt.
87 Humphrey Sandford, of the Isle,
88 Joseph Muckleston, of Prescot,
89 Jos. Oldham, of Cainham, Esqrs.

1790 St. John Charlton, of Apley Castle,
91 Thomas Pardoe, of Faintree,
92 Thomas Compson, of Hopton Wafers,
93 John Corbet, of Sundorn,
94 William Yelverton Davenport, of Davenport House,
95 Henry Bevan, of Shrewsbury,
96 Ralph Leeke, of Longford,
97 Wm. Tayleur, of Buntingsdale,
98 Andrew Corbet, of Shawbury Park,
99 Thomas Dickin, of Wem,
1800 William Challnor, of Dudliston,
1 Thomas Clarke, of Peplow,
2 Thomas Harries, of Cruckton,
3 Thomas Kynnersley, of Leighton,
4 Robert Burton, of Longner,
5 Thomas Whitmore, of Apley,
6 William Botfield, of Malinslee,
7 Wm. Charlton, of Apley Castle,
8 Ralph Browne Wylde Browne, of Caughley,
9 William Sparling, of Petton,
1810 William Lloyd, of Aston,
11 George Brooke, of Haughton,
12 Richard Lyster, of Rowton,
13 William Church Norcop, of Betton,
14 William Cludde, of Orleton,
15 F. Taylor, of Chicknell, Esqrs.
16 Sir Thos. John Tyrwhitt Jones, of Stanley, Bart.
17 William. Ormsby Gore, of Porkington,
18 Thomas Botfield, of Hopton Court,
19 Edward William Smythe Owen, of Condover Park,

GEORGE IV.

1820 Thos. Taylor, of Ellerton Grange,
21 Richard Heber, of Hodnet,
22 Robert Bridgman More, of Linley,
23 John Mytton, of Halston,
24 John Wingfield, of Onslow,
25 John Whitehall Dod, of Cloverley,
26 John Cotes, of Woodcote,
27 Wm. Tayleur, of Buntingsdale,
28 Wm. Lacon Childe, of Kinlet,
29 Charles Kynaston Mainwaring, of Oteley Park,
1830 Row. Hunt, of Boreatton, Esqrs.

WILLIAM IV.

1831 Sir Edward J. Smithe, Bart. of Acton Burnel.
32 William Oakley, Esq. of Oakley House,
33 Walter Moseley, Esq. West Coppice, Esqrs.
34 Hon. Henry Wentworth Powis, Berwick House.
35 Sir Baldwin Leighton, Bart. Loton Park.
36 Sir Wm. Ed. Rouse Boughton, Bart. of Downton Hall, Stanton Lacey.

KNIGHTS of the SHIRE for the County of SALOP, since 1660.

1660 Sir Wm. Whitmore, Esq.	1734 Sir John Astley, Bart.	1819 Sir J. K. Powell, Bt. (late Esq.)
Henry Vernon, Esq.	Corbet Kynaston, Esq.	John Cotes, Esq.
1661 Sir Francis Lawley, Bart.	1741 Sir John Astley, Bart.	1820 Ditto.
Sir Richard Oakeley, Bart.	Richard Lyster, Esq.	Ditto.
1678 Sir Vincent Corbett, Bart.	1747 Ditto.	Mr. Cotes died August 24th, 1821,
Richard Newport, Esq.	Ditto.	when Rowland Hill, Esq. was
1681 William Gower, Esq.	1754 Ditto.	elected without opposition.
Richard Newport, Esq.	Ditto.	Sir John Powell dying Oct. 25th, 1825,
1685 John Walcot, Esq.	1761 Sir John Astley, Bart.	J. C. Pelham, Esq. succeeded, after
Edward Kynaston, Esq.	Richard Lyster, Esq.—died 1760	a spirited opposition from W.
1688 Richard Newport, Esq.	Chas. Baldwyn, Esq. elected.	Lacon Childe, Esq. of Kinlet.
Edward Kynaston, Esq.	1768 Sir John Astley, Bt.—died 1772	1826 Sir Rowland Hill, Bt. (late Esq.)
1690 Ditto.	Sir W. Williams Wynn, Bart.	J. C. Pelham, Esq.
Ditto.	elected.	1830 Sir Rowland Hill, Bart.
1695 Ditto.	Charles Baldwyn, Esq.	J. C. Pelham, Esq.
Ditto.	1774 Charles Baldwyn, Esq.	1832 The Reform Act gave the County
1698 Sir Edward Leighton, Bart.	Noel Hill, Esq.	of Salop two additional Represen-
Edward Kynaston, Esq.	*Continuation by C. H.*	tatives, when was elected, for the
1701 Robert Lloyd, Esq.	1780 Noel Hill, Esq.	Northern Division,
Richard Corbett, Esq.	Richard Hill, Esq.	Sir R. Hill, Bart.
1702 Roger Owen, Esq.	1784 Sir Richard Hill, Bart.	John Cotes, Esq.
Richard Corbett, Esq.	John Kynaston, Esq.	Southern Division,
1705 Robert Lloyd, Esq.	1790 Ditto.	Earl of Darlington.
Sir Robert Corbett, Bart.	Ditto.	Hon. R. H. Clive.
1709 Lord Newport.	1796 Ditto.	1835 The same, with the exception of
Sir Robert Corbett, Bart.	Ditto.	J. Cotes, Esq. who declined a con-
1710 Robert Lloyd, Esq.	1802 Ditto.	test.—Wm. Ormsby Gore, of Por-
John Kynaston, Esq.	Ditto.	kington Hall, Esq. was elected.
1713 Lord Newport,	1806 John Kynaston Powell, Esq.	
John Kynaston, Esq.	John Cotes, Esq.	
1714 Lord Newport.	Sir Richard Hill declining to offer	REPRESENTATIVES FOR THE
Sir Robert Corbett, Bart.	himself again, on account of ill	TOWN, since 1832.
1721 Robert Lloyd, Esq.	health, Mr. Cotes was elected.—	1832 Sir John Hanmer, Bart.
John Kynaston, Esq.	Sir Richard died Nov. 28th, 1809.	R. A. Slaney, Esq.
1727 John Walcot, Esq.	1812 John Kynaston Powell, Esq.	1835 Sir John Hanmer, Bart.
Wm. Lacon Child, Esq.	John Cotes, Esq.	J. C. Pelham, Esq.

The following Gentlemen have filled the MUNICIPAL CHAIR of the Borough of Shrewsbury, since the conclusion of the List in our edition of Phillips's History, vide page 186 of that volume. The date of the year in which they were *elected* is given.

1829 Robert Gray, Esq.	The Colonel dying suddenly,	Some years succeeded
1830 Joseph Loxdale, Esq. Jun.	during his Mayoralty, was	William H. ....caine, Esq., the
1831 Thomas Farmer Jukes, Esq.	succeeded by	first Mayor under the New
1832 Thomas Tomlins, Esq.	Richard Drinkwater, Esq.	Municipal Law.
1833 Col. John Wingfield.	1835 R. Burton, Esq.—The *last Chief*	1836 John Bickerton Williams, Esq.,
1834 Col. Francis Knyvett Leighton.	*Magistrate* of the ancientCorporation.	a *Dissenter.* *

The present ALDERMEN of the Borough are

William Clement, J. Bickerton Williams, C. B. Teece, Richard Ford, J. W. Watson, Jeremiah Marshall, Edward Locke, John Tomkies, Thomas Ward ; Esquires.

RECORDER, John Bather. TOWN CLERK and REGISTRAR, Wm. Cooper. CLERK of the PEACE for the BOROUGH, John W. Bythell. CORONER, Robert Jones. TREASURER, John Gregory Brayne ; Esquires. The Common Council are Thirty in number.

* On Mr. W.'s election, after an unanimous vote of thanks, by the Council, to his predecessor, he delivered a brief but candid address, of which the following is a portion:—"That although, in some respects, I shall not be able to emulate my renowned predecessor, you will find me your willing helper in all that pertains to good government ; to moderation in spirit and conduct ; to the conservation of our unrivalled constitution ; to the upholding, in short, of all that is dear to us as Protestants and Englishmen.—And cherishing, as I do, the strongest possible conviction, that, while the MIXTURE of MONARCHY and NOBILITY is necessary to give ORDER and STABILITY to POPULAR FREEDOM, the amalgamation of CHRISTIANITY with CIVIL AFFAIRS is essential to our well-being, I cannot but take the earliest opportunity to express my hope, that, having elected me Mayor, you will ACCOMPANY me NEXT SUNDAY to CHURCH." C. H.

A LIST OF SOME OF THE MOST INTERESTING OF THE FLOWERING PLANTS,

GROWING IN THE VICINITY OF MUCH WENLOCK, WITH THEIR RESPECTIVE LOCALITIES.

Obligingly communicated by W. P. BROOKES, Esq. Surgeon, WENLOCK.

Pinguicula vulgaris, common Butterwort. At Rowley, near Much Wenlock, on a farm in the occupation of Mr. Pinkney. *Orchis bifolia*, butterfly orchis. Wenlock Edge, and in fields and coppices round Wenlock, frequent. *Orchis pyramidalis*, pyramidal orchis. Shadwell, a part of the Standhill coppice, near Much Wenlock. *Orchis morio*, meadow orchis. In fields on Kenley common. *Orchis mascula*, early spotted orchis. On hedge-banks and in fields round Wenlock, frequent. *Orchis maculata*, spotted hand orchis. Ditto, ditto. *Orchis conopsea*, aromatic orchis. Shadwell coppice. *Satyrium viride*, green satyrium. Field at Rowley. *Ophrys nidus-avis*, birds'-nest twayblade. Ash coppice, near Wenlock. *Ophrys spiralis*, triple twayblade. In a field at the springs, near Harley. *Ophrys muscifera*, fly orchis. Field at Rowley, and on lime rocks at Fairley. *Ophrys apifera*, bee orchis. Field at Rowley, and near some lime-kilns at the Hill-top, on the right of the road from Wenlock to Lutwyche. *Serapias latifolia*, broad-leaved helleborine. Mog forest, near Lutwyche, and in Buildwas Park, seat of Walter Moseley, Esq. *Serapias palustris*, marsh helleborine. In a field at Rowley. *Pulmonaria officinalis*, Jerusalem cowslip. In Fairley coppice. *Echium vulgare*, viper's bugloss. Wilmore hill, near Wenlock. *Menyanthes trifoliata*, trefoil buck-bean. Marsh pool, near Wenlock. *Anagallis tenella*, bog pimpernel. In a field at Rowley. *Campanula patula*, spreading bell flower. On the road side near Larden Hall. *Campanula latifolia*, broad-leaved bell flower. Near Muckley Cross, in a lane leading from the Bridgnorth road to Wheaton Aston. *Campanula trachelium*, Canterbury bell. Hedges about Harley. *Campanula hybrida*, corn bell flower. Corn fields round Wenlock. *Campanula glomerata*, clustered bell flower. In a lane leading from the Hill-top to Easthope. *Verbascum nigrum*, black mullein. Near the Church-yard, Shineton. *Hyoscyamus niger*, common henbane. On lime-rocks, at Presthope, near Wenlock. *Euonymus Europæus*, spindle tree. In a coppice between Harley and Wenlock. *Viola hirta*, hairy violet. Shadwell coppice. *Hydrocotyle vulgaris*, marsh pennywort. In a field at Rowley. *Parnassia palustris*, grass of parnassus. Field at Rowley. *Narcissus pseudo-narcissus*, common daffodil. Near Larden Hall. *Triglochin palustre*, marsh arrow-grass. Shadwell coppice. *Colchicum autumnale*, meadow saffron. Meadows round Wenlock, abundantly. *Chlora perfoliata*, yellow centaury. Gleeton Hill, near Wenlock, and on the road from Wenlock to Harley. *Vaccinium Myrtillus*. Woods in Willey park. *Daphne laureola*, spurge laurel. Wenlock Edge. *Butomus umbellatus*, flowering rush. By the river side, Cressage. *Cotyledon umbilicus*, navel-wort. On old walls at Church Preen. *Sedum telephium*, live-long. Near the summit of the Wrekin. *Sedum rupestre*, rock stonecrop. On walls at Callaughton, near Wenlock. *Spiræa filipendula*, dropwort. Coppices at Fairley. *Nymphæa alba*, white water lily. In a pool on a farm, in the occupation of Mr. Partridge, Preen Common. *Aquilegia vulgaris*, columbine. Standhill coppice. *Clematis vitalba*, travellers' joy. Harley church. *Helleborus fœtidus*, fœtid hellebore. In a coppice at Fairley. *Verbena officinalis*, simplers' joy. Harley. *Lathræa squamaria*, greater tooth-wort. In a wood on Wenlock Edge, near the road from Presthope to Hughley. *Digitalis purpurea*, purple fox-glove. On road sides round Wenlock, common. *Orobanche major*, common broom-rape. In woods in Willey park. *Althæa officinalis*, marsh mallow. Near Lutwyche Hall. *Fumaria claviculata*, white climbing fumitory. On the lodge hill near Frodesley. *Anthyllis vulneraria*, ladies finger. In a field close to Standhill coppice. *Vicra sylvatica*, wood vetch. Near the lodge, Buildwas park. *Carduus eriophorus*, friar's crown. Shadwell coppice, near Wenlock. *Erigeron acre*, blue flea-bane. Walls round Wenlock Abbey. *Inula helenium*, elecampane. In a hedge close to a cottage garden near Mr. Davies's barn, on the road from Harley to Wenlock.

Among others of the FERN TRIBE, Mr. B. found the following:—

Ophioglossum vulgatum, adder's tongue. In the first field on the right side of the road from Wenlock to Shrewsbury. *Osmunda lunaria*, moonwort. Homer common, near Wenlock. *Polypodium oreopteris*, heath polypody. Mog forest, near Lutwyche. *Polypodium dilatatum*, scaly stemmed polypody. On the decaying stumps of old trees in Shinewood, near Wenlock. *Polypodium dryopteris*, three-branched polypody. On a bank near a brook which crosses a bye-road leading from Hughley common through Easthope wood to Easthope.

For a general List of Plants and Flowers in Shropshire, see page 25 to 29, this vol.

Appendix   I

BIRDS, WILD ANIMALS, AND REPTILES OF SHROPSHIRE.

THE Birds, *Aves*, peculiar to our County, are in no way distinguished from those found in the adjoining Counties.—The Author of this work, always an admirer of the feathered families, has not observed one exclusive peculiarity in any of them. In the following desultory observations, the common ENGLISH NAMES* only are given.

Of this interesting part of the creation, some individuals have taken up their abode at or near Providence Grove, several to the annoyance, but more to the amusement and gratification of its proprietor. Crows, Rooks, and Magpies, *unwelcome visitors*; Jack-daws, occasionally; Jays, ditto; Starlings build and rear their young, as do Martins and Swallows; the Missel Thrush, the Common Throstle, and the Blackbird (Ouzle) build in the Orchard and Fruit Garden: the Chaffinch, Bullfinch, Yellow Hammer, the Redbreast, Redstart, the Common Wren, the White Throat, the Hedge Sparrow, the Skylark, Titlark, and probably the Woodlark (for we often hear his song), the Greenfinch, the Common Flycatcher, each build their nests, and give life and interest to the little domain. The whole of the tribe of Tomtits are constantly flitting about among the trees in the garden; and not unfrequently the Goldfinch or Red Linnet, the Grey Linnet, and the Brown Linnet, in spring delight us with their melody. We often see the elegant Green Woodpecker, *or Rain Fowl*, sometimes the richly plumed Kingsfisher, and frequently the Yellow, the Pied, and the Grey Wagtails.

We have also Wood Pidgeons, Pheasants,† Partridges, and Lapwings; the Reed Sparrow, the Land-rail, the Golden-crested Wren, the Willow Wren, and the Whinchat. The Common Owl and the Sparrow-hawk may be frequently seen about Providence Grove; a young one of the latter kind, is now an undaunted domestic ranger in my garden; another, of some years of age, inhabits the garden of Mr. Blantern, of Haston. The Swift and the Sand Martin, are not seen in our immediate vicinity. We have Field-fares and Red-wings in winter, and in due season, the Cuckoo, the never-failing harbinger of delightful May.

Not being in the vicinity of lakes, marshes, or running streams, we never see the Coot, the Gallinule or Water Hen, the Brook Ouzel, the Grebe, nor any of the web-footed tribe, though many of these are common in the upper division of the Parish of Middle, and in the Parishes of Baschurch and Ellesmere.

The Heron, the Curlew, the Bittern, though seen in other parts of the County, are seldom, if ever, seen in our neighbourhood; equally rarely are seen the Raven, the Kite, the Judcock, the Hen-harrier, the Yellow Owl, the Long-eared ditto, the Buzzard, the Ring, and Turtle Doves, the Ring Ouzle, the Ash-coloured Shrike, Red-backed Shrike, the Grosbeaks or Buntings: Red-poles, sometimes; Snipes and Woodcocks, occasionally; Nightingales, never. Last winter, a flock of the beautiful little Aberdevine alighted near Providence Grove; I have seen them frequently near Worsley, in Lancashire. The Eagle, the Vulture, and the birds of the mountains, the Gulls and other marine wanderers, are seldom seen in any part of the County.

WILD ANIMALS OF SHROPSHIRE.—Of these, we have Squirrels, Foxes, Hares, Rabbits, Weasels, Pole Cats, the Stoat, and the Hedge-hog: the Badger, and Otter, rarely;—old Isaak Walton calls the latter "villainous Otters." Rats and Mice, of course. The interesting little Dormouse I have not seen in Shropshire, though no doubt it exists in the County.

REPTILES, INSECTS, and FLIES, same here as adjoining Counties, except that I have never seen a Viper in our vicinity. We have the little Blind Worm, and the Common Adder; common Lizards and Newts.—Happening to be present when one of my workmen discovered a Newt four feet deep in the ground, closely imbedded in solid unbroken clay, I endeavoured to keep it alive,—it lived several days without sustenance, but finally perished. Some years ago, a live Toad was found imbedded in a solid block of stone, in the quarry at Grinshill.

---

* For the Latin names of British Birds, their habits and peculiarities, the reader is referred to White's History of Selborne, by Captain Brown. A copious List of Birds, seen in the neighbourhood of Shrewsbury, from the pen of J. F. M. Dovaston, Esq., is attached to the new Shrewsbury Guide.—C. H.

† Of this most elegant of British Birds, Lord Clive, it is said, lately shot one, a Hen, of a beautiful cream colour, near Powis Castle. An equally rare specimen has been also recently killed by Mr. Philip Hill, at Hawkstone; and a fine Cock Golden Pheasant, by a sportsman, in our vicinity: all are intended for preservation.—C. H.

Lightning Source UK Ltd.
Milton Keynes UK
UKHW03f0644181018
330753UK00006B/735/P